Australian Climate Law in Global Context

Australian Climate Law in Global Context is a comprehensive guide to the nature and scope of current climate change law in Australia and internationally. It includes discussion of:

- emissions trading schemes and carbon pricing laws
- laws on renewable energy, biosequestration, carbon capture and storage, and energy efficiency
- the trading of emission offsets between developed and developing countries
- the new international scheme for the protection of forests (REDD) and the transfer of green finance and technology from developed to developing countries
- the facilitation of adaptation to climate change through legal frameworks.

The book assesses the international climate change regime from a legal perspective, focusing on Australia's unique circumstances and measures, and its domestic implementation of climate-related treaties. It also considers how the challenge of climate change should be integrated into broader environmental law and management.

Australian Climate Law in Global Context is an engaging text that provides a clear, well-structured and up-to-date analysis of climate change law. It is a valuable resource for students in law and environmental science, for current and future legal practitioners working in climate law and related fields, and for policy-makers and those in the commercial sector seeking information on the expanding range of climate change measures. It is accompanied by a companion website at www.cambridge.edu.au/academic/climate, which contains updates to the law.

ALEXANDER ZAHAR is Senior Lecturer at Macquarie Law School and Co-Director, Education, at Climate Futures at Macquarie University. His research interests are in the areas of state compliance with climate treaty obligations and the operation of the Clean Development Mechanism.

JACQUELINE PEEL is Associate Professor at Melbourne Law School, University of Melbourne. Her research interests include international and domestic environmental law, risk regulation and the precautionary principle, and climate change law.

LEE GODDEN is Professor and Director of the Centre for Resources, Energy and Environmental Law at Melbourne Law School, University of Melbourne. Her research interests include climate change law and environmental governance, natural resources law and indigenous peoples' rights.

Australian Climate Law in Global Context

Alexander Zahar
Jacqueline Peel
Lee Godden

CAMBRIDGE
UNIVERSITY PRESS

University Printing House, Cambridge CB2 8BS, United Kingdom

One Liberty Plaza, 20th Floor, New York, NY 10006, USA

477 Williamstown Road, Port Melbourne, VIC 3207, Australia

314-321, 3rd Floor, Plot 3, Splendor Forum, Jasola District Centre, New Delhi - 110025, India

79 Anson Road, #06-04/06, Singapore 079906

Cambridge University Press is part of the University of Cambridge.

It furthers the University's mission by disseminating knowledge in the pursuit of education, learning and research at the highest international levels of excellence.

www.cambridge.org
Information on this title: www.cambridge.org/9780521142106

© Alexander Zahar, Jacqueline Peel, Lee Godden 2013

This publication is in copyright. Subject to statutory exception and to the provisions of relevant collective licensing agreements, no reproduction of any part may take place without the written permission of Cambridge University Press.

First published 2013

Edited by L. Elaine Miller, Otmar Miller Consultancy Pty Ltd, Melbourne
Cover design by Kerry Cooke at Eggplant Communication
Typeset by Integra Software Services Pvt. Ltd

A catalogue record for this publication is available from the British Library

National Library of Australia Cataloguing in Publication data
Zahar, Alexander.
Australian climate law in global context/Alexander Zahar,
Jacqueline Peel, Lee Godden.
9780521142106 (pbk.)
Includes index.
Environmental law – Australia.
Environmental policy – Australia.
Environmental law.
Australia – Environmental conditions.
Peel, Jacqueline.
Godden, Lee.
344.94046

ISBN 978-0-521-14210-6 Paperback

Additional resources for this publication at www.cambridge.edu.au/academic/climate

Reproduction and communication for educational purposes

The Australian *Copyright Act 1968* (the Act) allows a maximum of one chapter or 10% of the pages of this work, whichever is the greater, to be reproduced and/or communicated by any educational institution for its educational purposes provided that the educational institution (or the body that administers it) has given a remuneration notice to Copyright Agency Limited (CAL) under the Act.

For details of the CAL licence for educational institutions contact:

Copyright Agency Limited
Level 15, 233 Castlereagh Street
Sydney NSW 2000
Telephone: (02) 9394 7600
Facsimile: (02) 9394 7601
E-mail: info@copyright.com.au

Cambridge University Press has no responsibility for the persistence or accuracy of URLs for external or third-party internet websites referred to in this publication, and does not guarantee that any content on such websites is, or will remain, accurate or appropriate.

Contents

Acknowledgments page ix
Abbreviations and definitions xi
Figures, tables and boxes xx
Table of cases xxii
Table of statutes xxiv
Table of treaties and other international instruments xxx

     Introduction: Arguments, themes and overview   1
     Introduction   1
     Arguments and themes   2
     Chapter overview   8

1   **Climate law: Meaning and context**   12
     Introduction   12
     A 'global–global' problem   12
     First-mover constraints   14
     The context of Australian climate law   16
     Discovering climate law   18
     Is there a foundational principle of climate law?   22
     Climate law is both 'top-down' and 'bottom-up'   24
     Interdisciplinarity   30
     Human values and competing interests   33
     Environmental values in developing countries: The case of Africa   35
     Is popular apathy a result of misinformation?   38
     Our continuing dependence on fossil fuels   39
     A very brief introduction to the science of climate change   44

2   **Legal elements and ongoing development of the international climate change regime**   52
     Introduction   52
     Background to the UNFCCC   52
     Legal principles and rules of the UNFCCC   54
     Legal principles and rules of the Kyoto Protocol   83
     Outlook for the international climate change regime   90

3 Measurement and verification of state emissions and legacy of the Kyoto Protocol's compliance system 92
   Introduction 92
   Treaty provisions on reporting and compliance 93
   Direct measurement versus state reporting 96
   Reliability of state emission reports 97
   State regulation of inventory compilation 100
   Verification (review) procedures 102
   Role of Expert Review Teams 103
   The Kyoto Protocol's compliance system 106
   Determining a 'question of implementation' 106
   The Kyoto Protocol's Compliance Committee 109
   Procedure before the Enforcement Branch 111
   Historical workload of the Compliance Committee 113
   Assessment of the Kyoto Protocol's compliance system 116
   Limitations of the Kyoto Protocol's review function 118
   Could international reporting of greenhouse gas emissions be improved? 120
   The future: Transparent reporting by all states 125

4 Development of climate law in Australia 127
   Introduction 127
   Factors in the genesis of Australian climate law 128
   Development of Australian climate law and policy 139
   Australian climate change regulation: The international context 139
   Early national policy measures: Climate change and ESD 145
   'No regrets' climate policy 147
   Mandatory Renewable Energy Target 150
   Action by states and territories 151
   Proposals for national emissions trading 155
   Carbon pricing 160
   Conclusion 163

5 Putting a price on carbon: Regulatory models and emissions trading schemes 164
   Introduction 164
   Regulatory models for climate change mitigation 165
   The 'global' carbon market: ETS around the world 177
   Carbon pricing in Australia 187
   Conclusion 197

6 The regulatory network of the Clean Development Mechanism 199
   Introduction: Offsets under the Kyoto Protocol 199

A case study in CDM practice and principle   203
Persisting concerns about the CDM's environmental integrity   220
The CDM's performance on sustainable development   222
CDM project distribution and equity of access   224
Administrative review of CDM Executive Board decisions   225
What future for the CDM?   227

7   **The emerging scheme for the protection of forests in developing countries (REDD)**   229
Introduction: REDD's place in the international climate regime   229
Deforestation: Some facts and figures   233
Rescaling the deforestation problem   237
Causes of deforestation and REDD's fractious social context   238
Steps towards the international regulation of REDD   242
REDD funding for the preparatory stage   246
Monitoring, reporting and verification of REDD projects   248
Australia's involvement with REDD   250
Conclusion: Will REDD be effective?   253

8   **Climate finance, technology transfer and capacity-building for sustainable development**   255
Introduction   255
Green finance and technology for countries in need   256
The existing international regime on finance and technology transfer   259
Role of the Global Environment Facility   263
Breathing life into neglected treaty provisions   268
The new institutions of the Cancun COP   271
Roles and responsibilities of the Cancun institutions   274
Australia's contributions to finance and technology transfer for developing countries   282
The lurking issue of intellectual property rights   284
Intellectual property law and politics in the climate change arena   288
Conclusion   291

9   **Legal and regulatory frameworks for transition to a low-carbon economy**   293
Introduction   293
Transition to a 'low-carbon' economy   295
Improving energy efficiency: 'Picking the low-hanging fruit'   301
Promoting renewable energy   312
Carbon capture and storage   320
Nuclear power   332
Integration of regulatory measures for technology innovation   335
Conclusion   338

10 Biosequestration and emission reduction regulation in the Australian land sector 339
    Introduction 339
    Land sector abatement: Concepts and technical requirements 341
    Legal issues in biosequestration rights 347
    Federal regulation of biosequestration and offsets: The Carbon Farming Initiative 350
    State-based regulation of biosequestration and offsets 361
    Ensuring integration 370
    Conclusion 372

11 Adaptation to climate change through legal frameworks 373
    Introduction 373
    Nature of climate change adaptation 374
    Coastal adaptation: Sea-level rise 384
    Adapting to climatic variability: Water scarcity and increased flood risk 390
    Natural disasters: Bushfire risk and adaptive responses 396
    The effectiveness of legal frameworks in Australia 401
    Regional adaptation: Climate change displacement 401
    Conclusion 406

    Postscript 410

Bibliography 413
Index 449

Acknowledgments

Alexander Zahar would like to thank the past and present students in Macquarie University's Climate Change Law class for helpful discussions. The contributions of the following students were particularly valuable: Jack Crittenden, Tasmin Dilworth, Guy Dwyer, Elizabeth Makin, Lucy McQuillan, Jessica Millington, Elissa Playford, and John Zorzetto.

Jacqueline Peel and Lee Godden would like to extend particular gratitude to our fantastic research assistants involved in this project: Anita Foerster, Emma Cocks, Lisa Caripis, Carly Godden, and Marina Lou. Lisa Caripis deserves particular recognition for her diligent research, contributions to the text of several of their chapters (particularly Chapter 9), preparation of tables of cases and legislation, and careful following up of footnote references. Anita also made contributions to earlier drafts of Chapters 10 and 11. Peel and Godden also wish to acknowledge the funding support provided for the research and writing of Chapters 4–5 and 9–11 under ARC Discovery Project Grant DP0987850, 'Responding to Climate Change: Australia's Environmental Law and Regulatory Framework'. They are grateful to their grant partner, Professor Rod Keenan of the School of Land and Environment, University of Melbourne, for the feedback and insights he provided for several chapters, particularly Chapter 10, dealing with biosequestration and offsets. They too have benefited from exploring issues with their climate change law students and co-teachers.

The authors collectively wish to thank the manuscript's editor, L. Elaine Miller, for her thoughtful, painstaking, yet patient approach to the task. They also wish to thank the proof reader, Sarah Shrubb.

All references to online sources were current as of March 2012.

We are grateful to the following individuals and organisations for permission to use their material in *Australian Climate Law in Global Context*.

Figure 1.3: Timothy M. Lenton et al. (2008) 'Tipping Elements in the Earth's Climate System', 105(6) *Proceedings of the National Academy of Sciences of the United States of America* 1786; **7.1**, **7.2**: Reproduced with permission from the Food and Agriculture Organization and ITTO; **8.1**: **K.** Caldeira and S. J. Davis (2011) 'Accounting for Carbon Dioxide Emissions: A Matter of Time' 108(21) *Proceedings of the National Academy of Sciences of the United States of America* 8533. Copyright (2011) National Academy of Sciences, USA; **Table 11.1**: IPCC,

Climate Change 2001: Impacts, Adaptation and Vulnerability. Contribution of Working Group II to the Third Assessment Report of the Intergovernmental Panel on Climate Change, Glossary of Terms, Cambridge University Press.

Every effort has been made to trace and acknowledge copyright. The publisher apologises for any accidental infringement and welcomes information that would redress this situation.

Abbreviations and definitions

2°C limit	The upper limit of politically acceptable global mean temperature rise according to the 2009 Copenhagen Accord.
1.5°C limit	A safer limit than the 2°C limit. It is referred to in the Copenhagen Accord as a possible alternative to the 2°C limit, if the evolving science were to find that the higher limit is more dangerous than previously thought.
350/450/550 etc. ppm targets	These commonly cited figures refer to the stabilisation of CO_2 concentration in the atmosphere at an upper limit of 350, 450, etc. parts per million (ppm) by 2100. The concentrations are associated with different degrees of warming.
AAU	Assigned Amount Unit. An emission allowance issued pursuant to the provisions of Kyoto Protocol *Decision 13/CMP.1*. It is equal to one metric tonne of CO_2 eq.
ACCU	Australian Carbon Credit Unit. The tradable offset credit under the Carbon Farming Initiative (Australia).
adaptation	Measures taken to manage the consequences of climate change by reducing the vulnerability of human communities and ecosystems.
Adaptation Committee	Established by the UNFCCC COP as part of the Cancun Adaptation Framework. The Adaptation Committee's task is to promote the implementation of adaptation measures.
afforestation (under the Kyoto Protocol)	The conversion of land that has not been forested for a period of at least 50 years to forested land, by direct human intervention in the form of planting, seeding, or promotion of natural seed sources. Cf. reforestation.
AGO	Australian Greenhouse Office (now superseded)
Annex B	List of emission reduction obligations by Annex I parties for the first commitment period under the Kyoto Protocol (2008–12).

Annex I parties	The parties listed in Annex I to the UNFCCC, consisting of industrialised countries and countries in transition to a market economy. All Annex I parties except the United States are also parties to the Kyoto Protocol, and in this context they are referred to as *Annex I parties to the Kyoto Protocol*.
APP or AP6	Asia–Pacific Partnership on Clean Development and Climate, established in 2006.
ARENA	Australian Renewable Energy Association. A body set up under the Clean Energy Future Package to administer Australian government funding for renewable energy technologies.
atmospheric lifetime (of a GHG)	The average lifetime of a GHG in the atmosphere before it is broken down or removed through natural processes. For example, the atmospheric lifetime of methane is 12.2 years, that of nitrous oxide is 120 years, and that of CO_2 is variable, which is to say uncertain overall.[1]
Australia Clause	Article 3.7 of the Kyoto Protocol, included (primarily for Australia's benefit) to allow parties 'for whom land-use change and forestry constituted a net source of greenhouse gas emissions in 1990' to include those emissions when calculating their 1990 emission levels, which form the baseline for emission cuts over the first commitment period.
Australian Carbon Unit	The main trading unit (emission allowance) under the Australian CPM.
AWG-KP	Ad Hoc Working Group on Further Commitments for Annex I Parties under the Kyoto Protocol. It was established in 2005 at CMP 1 on the basis of Protocol Article 3.9, which mandates consideration of the further commitments (emission reductions, etc.) by Annex I parties at least seven years prior to the end of the first commitment period (i.e. 2012).
AWG-LCA	Ad Hoc Working Group on Long-term Cooperative Action under the Convention. At COP 13 in 2007, the UNFCCC parties established the AWG-LCA with a mandate to focus on key elements of long-term action

---

[1] Intergovernmental Panel on Climate Change, *Climate Change 1995: The Science of Climate Change: Contribution of Working Group I to the Second Assessment Report of the IPCC* (Cambridge University Press, 1996), p. 22, Table 4; and D. Archer and V. Brovkin, 'The Millennial Atmospheric Lifetime of Anthropogenic CO_2', 90 *Climatic Change* 283 (2008).

ABBREVIATIONS AND DEFINITIONS xiii

	(mitigation, adaptation, finance, technology, and a 'shared vision') in order to improve and strengthen the UNFCCC.
Bali Action Plan	Adopted at COP 13 in 2007. The Plan has guided the work of the AWG-LCA.
baseline, or business as usual	That which would have been observed – for example in terms of GHG emissions or another variable – in the absence of some form of intervention, such as a government policy or a CDM project; a historical trend that is to continue into the future if left undisturbed.
baseline-and-credit	A type of emissions trading scheme in which regulated entities earn tradable credits for reducing their emissions below a certain baseline.
BCA	Building Code of Australia
bilateral finance	The term applies to grant-based assistance provided directly through multi-regional, regional and bilateral programs rather than as contributions to multilateral funds or organisations. Cf. multilateral finance.
biosequestration	The removal of carbon from the atmosphere and its subsequent storage in carbon sinks, such as vegetation, soils or oceans.
Cancun Adaptation Framework	The UNFCCC COP adopted the Cancun Adaptation Framework in 2010. In this instrument, the UNFCCC parties affirmed that adaptation must be addressed with the same level of priority as mitigation.
cap-and-trade	A type of emissions trading scheme in which regulated entities must hold and surrender sufficient emission permits to cover the volume of GHG emissions they produce. The government sets a cap on the total number of emission permits made available in any period under the scheme.
capacity-building	A process that seeks to build legal, scientific and technical skills and institutions in developing countries to enable them to pursue environmentally sustainable pathways.
carbon pricing	The range of economic instruments for GHG emission reduction through pricing of emissions, including carbon taxes and emission trading.
CCA	Climate Change Authority (Australia). An independent expert body tasked with the conduct of reviews and the recommendation of scheme caps under the CPM.
CCS	Carbon capture and storage, an emerging technology for capturing CO_2 through an

	industrial separation process. The gas is then liquefied and sealed in underground reservoirs.
CDM	Clean Development Mechanism. One of the three market (flexibility) mechanisms of the Kyoto Protocol.
CEFC	Clean Energy Finance Corporation (Australia). An entity established under the Clean Energy Future package to stimulate private investment in clean energy.
CER	Certified Emission Reduction. An emission allowance issued pursuant to Article 12 of the Kyoto Protocol (Clean Development Mechanism) and the provisions of Kyoto Protocol Decision 3/CMP.1. It is equal to one metric tonne of CO_2 eq.
CFI	Carbon Farming Initiative (Australia). The policy behind the *Carbon Credits (Carbon Farming Initiative) Act 2011* (Cth).
CH_4	Methane, a greenhouse gas controlled by the Kyoto Protocol.
Clean Energy Future Package	The Australian government's package of climate change policies released in July 2011.
CMP (or COP/MOP)	The *Conference* of the Parties Serving as the *Meeting* of the *Parties* to the Kyoto Protocol. Occasionally referred to as 'MOP' (Meeting of the Parties to the Protocol). The CMP is held in November–December each year and runs in parallel with the Conference of the Parties (COP) to the UNFCCC. Decisions made at CMP meetings are referred to as CMP decisions.
CO_2	Carbon dioxide, a greenhouse gas controlled by the Kyoto Protocol.
CO_2 equivalent (CO_2 eq.)	A unit normally following a quantity in tons, indicating that the global warming potential of a non-CO_2 greenhouse gas, or a mix of them, is being expressed in terms of the quantity of CO_2 that would have the same warming impact. See also 'global warming potential'.
COAG	Council of Australian Governments
COP	Conference of the Parties to the UNFCCC. The COP is held in November–December each year and runs in parallel with the Conference of the Parties Serving as the Meeting of the Parties to the Kyoto Protocol (CMP). Decisions made at the annual COP meetings are referred to as COP decisions.
commitment period	Under the Kyoto Protocol, Annex I parties to the UNFCCC that are also parties to the Kyoto Protocol agreed to reduce their overall emissions of scheduled (Annex B) greenhouse

	gases by an average of 5.2 per cent below 1990 levels over a five-year commitment period, 2008–12. A second commitment period (2013–17 or possibly 2013–20) was agreed to at the Durban CMP in 2011.
Compliance Committee	Created by the Kyoto Protocol, it makes determinations about state-party compliance with mandatory obligations on reporting and accounting for emissions and for meeting emission targets. It is divided into a Facilitative Branch and an Enforcement Branch.
Copenhagen Accord	At COP 15 in 2009, informal negotiations in a group consisting of major economies and representatives of regional and other negotiating groups resulted in a political agreement known as the Copenhagen Accord. Over objections from a minority of states, the COP 'took note' of the Accord without adopting it.
CPM	Carbon Pricing Mechanism (Australia)
CPRS	Carbon Pollution Reduction Scheme (Australia) (never implemented)
CTCN	Climate Technology Centre and Network (UNFCCC)
DNA	Designated National Authority (CDM)
DOE	Designated Operational Entity (CDM)
EEO Program	Energy Efficiency Opportunities Program (Australia).
EIA	Environmental Impact Assessment
EITE activities	Emission-Intensive Trade-Exposed activities
EPBC Act	*Environment Protection and Biodiversity Conservation Act 1999* (Australian federal legislation)
ERU	Emission Reduction Unit: an emission allowance issued pursuant to the provisions of Kyoto Protocol Decision 13/CMP.1 (Joint Implementation). It is equal to one ton of CO_2 eq.
ESD	Environmentally Sustainable Development.
ETS	Emissions Trading Scheme
EU ETS	European Union Emission Trading System
FAO	Food and Agriculture Organization of the United Nations
'fast-start' and long-term climate finance	As part of the Copenhagen Accord, developed countries agreed to provide US$30 billion of fast-start finance in 2010–12 for adaptation and mitigation in developing countries, as well as to jointly mobilise US$100 billion per year by 2020 for the same purpose.
financial mechanism (of the UNFCCC)	The totality of legal, institutional and procedural arrangements that facilitate and regulate the flow of financial resources mainly

from developed to developing countries (as mandated by the UNFCCC).

fugitive emissions — Emissions that do not come from combustion, but are released unintentionally during industrial processes such as coal mining and gas extraction.

Garnaut Review — The Garnaut Climate Change Review, established in 2007 by the then Leader of the Opposition in Australia, Kevin Rudd, to examine the impacts of climate change on the Australian economy and recommend policies in response. The Review published its report in 2008, with an updated report published in 2011.

GCF — Green Climate Fund, an operating entity of the UNFCCC's financial mechanism, created in 2010 by Decision 1/CP.16.

GEF — Global Environment Facility. The first operating entity of the UNFCCC's financial mechanism, it pre-existed the UNFCCC.

geosequestration — Separation of CO_2 from other gases in the course of an industrial process, capture and transport of the CO_2 to a geological storage site, and injection of the CO_2 into the site, following which the site is sealed.

GGAS — Greenhouse Gas Reduction Scheme (New South Wales, Australia)

GHG — Greenhouse gas. The Kyoto Protocol controls the GHGs listed in its Annex B. The list was extended in 2011 with the addition of nitrogen trifluoride (NF_3). The set of known GHGs is larger than that controlled by the Kyoto Protocol. Some GHGs are controlled by the Montreal Protocol (1987) to the Vienna Convention for the Protection of the Ozone Layer (1985).

global warming potential (GWP) — The Kyoto Protocol provides that the GWP for a time horizon of 100 years is to be used to convert the Annex B gases to the common unit of 'CO_2 equivalent'. Under this convention, the GWP_{100} of CO_2 is set at 1. The GWP_{100} of methane works out to 21 times that of CO_2. Nitrous oxide has a GWP_{100} of 310, and so forth.[2]

GNI — Gross national income

Gt — Gigatonne (also gigaton)

---

[2] Intergovernmental Panel on Climate Change, *Climate Change 1995: The Science of Climate Change* (1996), p. 22, Table 4. The table also presents the values for GWP_{20} and GWP_{500}. The 1995 figures have been slightly revised (Intergovernmental Panel on Climate Change, *Climate Change 2007: The Physical Science Basis: Contribution of Working Group I to the Fourth Assessment Report of the IPCC* (Cambridge University Press, 2007), pp. 212–13, Table 2.14, as corrected at <http://www.ipcc.ch/publications_and_data/ar4/wg1/en/ch2s2-10-2.html#table-2-14>), but they continue to apply for the purposes of the Kyoto Protocol.

GtC/y	Gigatonnes of carbon per year
IAR	International Assessment and Review (UNFCCC)
ICA	International Consultation and Analysis (UNFCCC)
IEA	International Energy Agency
IGAE	Intergovernmental Agreement on the Environment (Australia)
INC	Intergovernmental Negotiating Committee (pre-UNFCCC)
IP (IPR)	intellectual property (rights)
IPCC	Intergovernmental Panel on Climate Change.
JI	Joint Implementation, one of the three market (flexibility) mechanisms of the Kyoto Protocol.
Kyoto Protocol	Kyoto Protocol to the UNFCCC. Opened for signature in 1997, entered into force on 16 February 2005.
leakage (or carbon leakage)	Leakage occurs where GHG emission reduction measures implemented in one jurisdiction result, normally unintentionally, in an increase in such emissions in another jurisdiction. Leakage can occur at any jurisdictional level, including at the project level. For example, it occurs where the implementation of a CDM project causes emissions to rise outside the project boundary.
leakage, specifically in forestry projects	The situation where the protection of forest carbon causes carbon-emitting activities to shift to a location outside the project boundary. For example, forest protection measures may constrain the supply of agricultural products or timber, causing market prices to rise, thereby encouraging producers outside the boundary to increase their activities, which in turn causes damage to forests in other areas.
LDC	Least Developed Countries
LULUCF	Land use, land-use change, and forestry.
MEPS	Minimum Energy Performance Standards (Australia)
mitigation measures	Measures taken to decrease emissions of greenhouse gases, for the purpose of reducing climate change and its effects.
MPCCC	Multi-Party Climate Change Committee (Australia)
MRET/RET	(Mandatory) Renewable Energy Target (Australia)
MRV	Measurement, reporting, verification
Mt	Megatonne (or megaton)
multilateral finance	Finance that promotes institutional structures governed jointly by developed and developing

	countries. These are structures that are needed for a coordinated global response to climate change. Such multilateral assistance works across a wide range of countries. Cf. 'bilateral finance'.
MWh	Megawatt hour
NAMA	Nationally Appropriate Mitigation Action (UNFCCC)
NAPA	National Adaptation Programme of Action (UNFCCC)
NEL	National Electricity Law (Australia)
NEM	National Electricity Market (Australia)
NGER Act	*National Greenhouse and Energy Reporting Act 2007* (Australian federal legislation)
NGO	non-governmental organisation
non-Annex I party	A UNFCCC party not listed in Annex I to the convention. Often used as equivalent to 'developing country'.
NSESD	National Strategy for Ecologically Sustainable Development (Australia)
NSWLEC	New South Wales Land and Environment Court (Australia)
OECD	Organization of Economic Cooperation and Development
offset credit	A tradable unit (emission allowance) representing an amount in CO_2 eq. of carbon sequestered or GHG emissions avoided.
operating entity (of the UNFCCC's financial mechanism)	A fund, such as the GEF or GCF, designated by the COP as a component of the UNFCCC's financial mechanism.
Pacific Islands Forum	The key regional political organisation in the Pacific region, of which Australia and New Zealand are members.
ppm	Parts per million
REDD (UNFCCC)	Reducing Emissions from Deforestation and forest Degradation in developing countries. An extended version of REDD, incorporating forest conservation, sustainable management of forests, and enhancement of forest carbon stocks in developing countries is known as REDD+.
reforestation (under the Kyoto Protocol)	The conversion of non-forested land to forested land, by direct human intervention in the form of planting, seeding, or promotion of natural seed sources on land that once was forested but that has been converted to non-forested land. Cf. 'afforestation'.
RGGI	Regional Greenhouse Gas Initiative (United States). It covers the New England states of the north-east, as well as some of those in the mid-Atlantic region, including New York.

RMU	Removal Unit: an emission allowance issued pursuant to the provisions of Kyoto Protocol Decision 13/CMP.1 (emission reductions attributed to the land sector in Annex I parties). It is equal to one ton of CO_2 eq. Net emission removals from LULUCF activities carried out by an Annex I party to the Protocol will result in the issue of RMUs, which the party may add to its assigned amount for the commitment period.
SBI (UNFCCC)	Subsidiary Body for Implementation
SBSTA (UNFCCC)	Subsidiary Body for Scientific and Technological Advice
Secretariat (UNFCCC and Kyoto Protocol)	Administrative body of international public servants common to the UNFCCC and the Kyoto Protocol.
sequestration	Removal or absorption and subsequent storage of GHGs (mainly carbon dioxide) from the atmosphere.
sinks	Sites that sequester carbon, such as trees, biomass and oceans.
Technology Mechanism	Consists of the Technology Executive Committee and the Climate Technology Centre and Network.
tipping point (tipping element)	A critical state of a system component, beyond which the system enters a qualitatively different mode of operation. Tipping points may be crossed as a result of natural variability or human activity and may imply large-scale effects on human and ecological systems. Components with tipping points are called tipping elements.
tonne (also ton)	A unit measure equal to 1000 kilograms. In climate science, 'ton' and 'tonne' are used interchangeably to refer to this metric measurement.
UNFCCC	United Nations Framework Convention on Climate Change. Opened for signature in 1992, entered into force on 21 March 1994.
VCAT	Victorian Civil and Administrative Tribunal (Australia)
WCI	Western Climate Initiative (North America). A cap-and-trade scheme covering seven western US states and four Canadian provinces.
white certificate scheme	A trading scheme designed to achieve energy efficiency targets.
WMO	World Meteorological Organization (United Nations).

Figures, tables and boxes

Figures

Figure 1.1	Fill in the gaps: Who is not invested in the status quo?	page 40
Figure 1.2	Extent of monthly Arctic sea ice, 1979–2012	47
Figure 1.3	Potential policy-relevant tipping elements in the climate system	50
Figure 2.1	Per capita emissions and wealth	55
Figure 2.2	Australia: Projected population	56
Figure 3.1	Procedure before the Kyoto Protocol's Compliance Committee	107
Figure 3.2	Enforcement Branch procedures with time limits	112
Figure 5.1	Cap-and-trade ETS	175
Figure 7.1	Forest area as percentage of total land area by country in the world's three tropical forest regions, 2010	233
Figure 7.2	Trends in wood removals, 1970–2009	236
Figure 8.1	Indicators of sustainable growth in developed and developing countries	257
Figure 9.1	Stabilisation wedges	297

Tables

Table 1.1	Important dates in the global response to climate change	page 25
Table 2.1	Greenhouse gas emissions of the UNFCCC's Annex II states 1990–2009	78
Table 3.1	Reporting of Annex I and non-Annex I GHG emission inventories under the UNFCCC	94
Table 3.2	Questions of implementation before the Enforcement Branch of the Compliance Committee, 2006–12	114
Table 4.1	Climate change and energy efficiency legislation in Australian states and territories	153
Table 4.2	Elements of Australia's 'Clean Energy' policy package	161
Table 5.1	Regulatory options for climate change mitigation	166
Table 5.2	Carbon taxes versus ETS	172
Table 5.3	ETS and carbon taxes around the world	175
Table 7.1	Main forestry projects funded by Australia in developing countries under the informal preparatory framework for REDD	251
Table 8.1	Examples of projects funded by the GEF under the UNFCCC umbrella	267
Table 9.1	Australian state energy efficiency schemes	311
Table 9.2	Australian state feed-in-tariff laws	316
Table 9.3	Australian state onshore CCS legislation	328
Table 9.4	Australian Commonwealth nuclear legislation	334
Table 10.1	Key provisions of Australian state biosequestration legislation	366

Table 11.1 Types of adaptation   377
Table 11.2 Australian national adaptation policy initiatives   381
Table 11.3 Key Australian state adaptation policies   381

Boxes

Box 1.1   The greenhouse effect   *page* 14
Box 1.2   Tipping elements   29
Box 1.3   Degrees of agreement about climate change   32
Box 2.1   Imagining society in the future   72
Box 2.2   The main state obligations and rights in Article 4 of the UNFCCC   73
Box 4.1   The Energy Efficiency Opportunities Act   149
Box 5.1   A carbon tax case study   173
Box 5.2   Design issues for ETS   178
Box 5.3   Institutional infrastructure: The Climate Change Authority   192
Box 6.1   Simplified CDM project approval procedure   203
Box 7.1   Governance conditions and challenges for an international REDD credit mechanism   245
Box 8.1   Overview of key international financial institutions relating to climate change   261
Box 8.2   Australia's main commitments to international finance and technology transfer since 2008   283
Box 8.3   Two case studies in technology transfer projects funded by Australia   285
Box 9.1   Smart grids   307
Box 9.2   Large-scale and small-scale renewable energy schemes   313
Box 9.3   Australian Commonwealth legislative framework for CCS   326
Box 9.4   Queensland legislative framework for CCS   329
Box 10.1 Federal biosequestration approaches prior to the CFI   351
Box 10.2 Core elements of the CFI   353
Box 10.3 CFI methodologies: A case study   355
Box 10.4 Overview of Australian state biosequestration laws   363
Box 10.5 Achieving greater integration with the CFI: The Queensland biosequestration regime   369
Box 11.1 Adaptation imperatives in Australia and the Pacific region   375
Box 11.2 Potential local government liability   383
Box 11.3 Case study: Victorian coastal policy   389
Box 11.4 Case study: Queensland flood risk response   393

Table of cases

Australia

Aldous v Greater Taree City Council [2009] NSWLEC 17   387
Anvil Hill Project Watch Association v Minister for the Environment and Water Resources (2007) 159 LGERA 8   138
Anvil Hill Project Watch Association v Minister for the Environment and Water Resources (2008) 166 FCR 54   138
Australian Conservation Foundation v LaTrobe City Council (2004) 140 LGERA 100   133, 135–6
Gippsland Coastal Board v South Gippsland Shire Council (No. 2) [2008] VCAT 1545   387–9
Graham Barclay Oysters Pty Ltd v Ryan (2002) 211 CLR 540   394
Gray v Minister for Planning (2006) 152 LGERA 258   132, 136–7, 138
Greenpeace Australia Ltd v Redbank Power Company Pty Ltd and Singleton Council (1994) 86 LGERA 143   30, 135
Hunter Environment Lobby Inc v Minister for Planning [2011] NSWLEC 221   137
ICM Agriculture Pty Ltd v Commonwealth (2009) 84 ALJR 87   349
Matthews v SPI Electricity – SPI Electricity Pty Ltd v Utility Services Corporation Ltd (No. 2) [2011] VSC 168   400
Matthews v SPI Electricity – SPI Electricity Pty Ltd v Utility Services Corporation Ltd (No. 5) [2012] VSC 66   400
Minister for Planning v Walker (2008) 161 LGERA 423   386
Myers v South Gippsland Shire Council [2009] VCAT 1022   390
Myers v South Gippsland Shire Council (No. 2) [2009] VCAT 2414   390
Northcape Properties Pty Ltd v District Council of Yorke Peninsula [2007] SAERDC 50   385
Northcape Properties Pty Ltd v District Council of Yorke Peninsula [2008] SASC 57   385
Powercor Australia Ltd v Thomas [2012] VSCA 87   397
Queensland Conservation Council Inc. v Xstrata Coal Queensland Pty Ltd (2007) 155 LGERA 322   132
Re Xstrata Coal Queensland Pty Ltd [2007] QLRT 33   132
Taralga Landscape Guardians Inc v Minister for Planning (2007) 161 LGERA 1   4
Thomas v Powercor Australia Ltd (No. 1) [2010] VSC 489   397
Thomas v Powercor Australia Ltd [2011] VSC 614   397
Walker v Minister for Planning (2007) 157 LGERA 124   132, 386, 387
Wildlife Preservation Society of Queensland Proserpine/Whitsunday Branch Inc. v Minister for the Environment and Heritage (2006) 232 ALR 510   138

European Union

Case C-366/10 Air Transport Association of America and Others v Secretary of State for Energy and Climate Change   88, 179

United States of America

American Electric Power Company v Connecticut 131 S Ct 2527 (2011)   134
Association of Irritated Residents, et al. v California Air Resources Board, et al., San Francisco Superior Court, Case Number CPF-09–509562, 20 May 2011   184
Association of Irritated Residents, et al. v California Air Resources Board, et al., San Francisco Superior Court, Case Number CPF-09–509562, 6 December 2011   185
Massachusetts v Environmental Protection Agency 549 US 497 (2007)   132, 133–5, 137, 162, 170

Table of statutes

AUSTRALIAN COMMONWEALTH

Australian Climate Change Regulatory
    Authority Bill 2009   159
Australian Constitution   362
   s 51   362
   s 51(xxix)   362
   s 52   362
   s 90   362
   s 109   146, 362
   s 122   362
Australian Radiation Protection and
    Safety Act 1998   333
   s 10   333
Australian Renewable Energy Agency Act
    2011   314
   s 3   314
   s 8   314
Building Energy Efficiency Disclosure Act
    2010   308
Carbon Credits (Carbon Farming
    Initiative) Act 2011   141, 350, 352
   Pt 2 Div 3   356
   Pt 3 Div 5   360
   Pt 4   357
   Pt 6 Div 2   356
   Pt 7   360
   Pt 8 Div 2   360
   Pt 8 Div 3   360
   Pt 9   354
   Pt 9.1   355
   Pt 9.2   355
   Pt 9.3   355
   Pt 11, Div 3   350
   Pt 11.1   355
   Pt 11.2   355
   Pt 12 Div 5   358
   Pt 21   360
   s 5   353, 363, 368
   s 16(2)   361
   ss 16–17   360
   s 17(2)   361
   s 22   364
   s 23(1)(g)   358, 370
   s 24(4)(b)   354
   s 27(4)(c)   354
   s 27(4)(d)   356
   s 27(4)(f)   357
   s 27(4)(h)   357, 369
   s 27(4)(i)   357
   s 27(4)(j)   358
   s 27(4)(k)   357
   s 27(4)(m)   358
   s 27(5)   357
   s 28   358
   s 41   356
   s 41(2)   356
   s 41(3)   356
   s 43   359, 363
   s 44   357
   s 44(4)   353
   s 45   357
   s 45A   357
   s 46   353
   s 53   352
   s 54   352
   s 55   353
   s 56   358
   s 60   353
   s 64(3)(a)   357
   s 64(3)(d)   357
   s 76   356
   s 83   358, 370
   s 90   360
   s 91   360, 361
   s 97(6)   360
   s 97(9)   360
   s 97(10)   360

ss 106(1)–(3)   354
s 106(4)(b)   354
ss 106–7   354
s 112   354
s 133(1)(b)   355
s 133(1)(d)   355
s 133(1)(f)(i)   369
s 133(1)(h)   355
s 150   349, 359
s 150A(1)   359
s 150A(2)   359
ss 151–3   359
ss 154–7   359
s 158   359
s 294   362
Carbon Credits (Carbon Farming Initiative) Regulations 2011   356
reg 3.28   356
Carbon Pollution Reduction Scheme Bill 2009   159
Pt 10   351
Carbon Pollution Reduction Scheme Bill (No. 2) 2009   159
Carbon Pollution Reduction Scheme Bill 2010   160
Carbon Pollution Reduction Scheme Bill 2011   190
cl 15   190
Carbon Pollution Reduction Scheme Amendment (Household Assistance) Bill 2009   159
Carbon Pollution Reduction Scheme Amendment (Household Assistance) Bill (No. 2) 2009   159
Carbon Pollution Reduction Scheme Amendment (Household Assistance) Bill 2010   160
Carbon Pollution Reduction Scheme (Charges – Customs) Bill 2009   159
Carbon Pollution Reduction Scheme (Charges – Customs) Bill (No. 2) 2009   159
Carbon Pollution Reduction Scheme (Charges – Customs) Bill 2010   160
Carbon Pollution Reduction Scheme (Charges – Excise) Bill 2009   159
Carbon Pollution Reduction Scheme (Charges – Excise) Bill (No. 2) 2009   159
Carbon Pollution Reduction Scheme (Charges – Excise) Bill 2010   160
Carbon Pollution Reduction Scheme (Charges – General) Bill 2009   159
Carbon Pollution Reduction Scheme (Charges – General) Bill (No. 2) 2009   159
Carbon Pollution Reduction Scheme (Charges – General) Bill 2010   160
Carbon Pollution Reduction Scheme (Consequential Amendments) Bill 2009   159
Carbon Pollution Reduction Scheme (Consequential Amendments) Bill (No. 2) 2009   159
Carbon Pollution Reduction Scheme (Consequential Amendments) Bill 2010   160
Carbon Pollution Reduction Scheme (CPRS Fuel Credits) Bill 2009   159
Carbon Pollution Reduction Scheme (CPRS Fuel Credits) Bill (No. 2) 2009   159
Carbon Pollution Reduction Scheme (CPRS Fuel Credits) Bill 2010   160
Carbon Pollution Reduction Scheme (CPRS Fuel Credits) (Consequential Amendments) Bill 2009   159
Carbon Pollution Reduction Scheme (CPRS Fuel Credits) (Consequential Amendments) Bill (No. 2) 2009   159
Carbon Pollution Reduction Scheme (CPRS Fuel Credits) (Consequential Amendments) Bill 2010   160
Clean Energy Act 2011   16, 19, 159, 162, 163, 187, 188, 189, 191, 197, 331
Pt 6 Div. 2   353
Pt 7   196
Pt 7 Div. 5   196
Pt 8   196
s 3   193
s 3(c)   191
s 3(c)(i)   134
s 5   188, 191, 353
s 14   191
s 16(1)   193

Clean Energy Act 2011 (cont.)
  ss 17–18   193
  s 20(4)   188
  s 30   188, 189
  s 30(1)   191
  s 30(2)   191
  ss 30(2)–30(12)   188
  s 30(4)   191
  s 30(6)   191
  s 100   194
  s 103   193
  s 111   194
  s 116   194
  s 123   195
  s 125(7)   195
  ss 128(7)–(9)   195
  s 133(6)(b)   194
  s 133(7)   195
  s 156(2)(e)   196
  s 156(4)   196
  ss 177–180   196
  s 289   193
  s 292(2)   193
Clean Energy (Consequential Amendments) Act 2011   188
  s 2   188
  s 282   188
  s 308   188
  s 334   188
  s 340   188
  s 352   189
  s 353   189
  s 367   189
Clean Energy Regulations 2011   196
  cl 907(4)   196
Clean Energy Regulator Act 2011   189, 354
Climate Change Authority Act 2011   354
  Pt 4   354
  Pt 4 Div. 2   354
  Pt 4 Div. 4   354
  s 62   354
Conveyancing Act 1919   363
  Pt 6 Div. 4   363
Energy Efficiency Opportunities Act 2006   151, 163, 302
Energy Efficiency Opportunities Amendment Regulations (No. 1) 2011   149
  reg 3   149

Environment Protection and Biodiversity Conservation Act 1999   155, 311, 312, 348, 362
  s 3A(b)   69
  ss 12–15C   362
Greenhouse Gas Benchmark Rule (Carbon Sequestration) 2003   361
  cl 5   361
National Electricity Law   318
  s 7   318
National Greenhouse and Energy Reporting Act 2007   30, 127, 157, 187, 189, 350, 355
  Pt 3A   189
  s 5   146
  s 7   191
  s 9   188
  s 10(1)   188
  s 13(1)(d)   157
  s 15A   189
  s 19(1)   189
  s 19(2)   157
National Greenhouse and Energy Reporting Regulations 2008   188
  regs 2.14–2.23   188
  reg 2.23   188
Offshore Petroleum Amendment (Greenhouse Gas Storage) Act 2008   325
Offshore Petroleum and Greenhouse Gas Storage Act 2006   325–6
  s 364   327
  s 372(c)   327
  s 388   327
  s 399   327
Offshore Petroleum and Greenhouse Gas Storage (Environment) Regulations 2009   325
Offshore Petroleum and Greenhouse Gas Storage (Greenhouse Gas Injection and Storage) Regulations 201   325
Offshore Petroleum and Greenhouse Gas Storage (Resource Management and Administration) Regulations 2011   325
Offshore Petroleum and Greenhouse Gas Storage (Safety) Regulations 2009   325

Ozone Protection and Synthetic Greenhouse Gas (Import Levy) Act 2011 192
Ozone Protection and Synthetic Greenhouse Gas (Manufacture Levy) Act 2011 192
Ozone Protection and Synthetic Greenhouse Gas Management Act 1989 192
Renewable Energy (Electricity) Act 2000 312
   Pt 4 313
   s 17 312
   s 17(1) 150
   s 17(2) 313
   s 31 150, 313
   s 32 150, 313
   s 33 150, 313
Renewable Energy (Electricity) Amendment Act 2009 151, 313
Renewable Energy (Electricity) Amendment Act 2010 151, 313
Renewable Energy (Electricity) Amendment Regulations 2011 313
Renewable Energy (Electricity) (Large-scale Generation Shortfall Charge) Act 2000 313
Water Act 2007 391

STATES AND TERRITORIES
Australian Capital Territory

Civil Law (Sale of Residential Property) Act 2003 308
   Pt 3 308
Climate Change and Greenhouse Gas Reduction Act 2010 151
   s 7 151
Emergencies Act 2004 399
Water Resources Act 2007 393

New South Wales

Carbon Rights Legislation Amendment Act 1998 363
Clean Coal Administration Act 2008 328
Conveyancing Act 1919 363
   Pt 6 Div 4 363
   s 87A 363, 364
   s 88AB(2) 363
   s 88B 363
   s 88EA 363
   s 88F 363
Electricity Supply Act 1995 152, 311
Electricity Supply (General) Regulation 2001 152
Energy and Utilities Administration Act 1987 310
Energy and Utilities Administration Regulation 2006 310
   reg 4 310
   reg 16 310
Environmental Planning and Assessment Act 1979 386
   Pt 3A 319, 386, 387
   Pt 4 319
   Pt 5 319
   s 4 386
   s 5(1) 386
Greenhouse Gas Benchmark Rule (Carbon Sequestration) No. 5 of 2003 361
   cl 8.3 361
Greenhouse Gas Storage Bill 2010 328
Local Government Act 1993 395
   s 733(1) 395
Protection of the Environment Administration Act 1991 386
   s 6(2) 386
Real Property Act 1900 368
   s 47 368
State Environmental Planning Policy (Major Projects) 2005 319
Water Management Act 2000 393

Queensland

Building Act 1975 308
Electricity Regulation 2006 310
   regs 139–140 310
   reg 152 310
   s 266 310
Forestry Act 1959 363
   s 32AA 369
   s 61J(1) 364
   s 61J(1A) 369
   s 61J(3) 364
   s 61J(3)(c) 364
   s 61J(5) 364
   s 61M 369
   s 61N 369
Forestry Act 1969 364
   sch 3 364

Forestry and Land Title Amendment Act 2001   363
Greenhouse Gas Storage Act 2009   327
   s 270   327
Land Act 1994   368
   Part 8C   369
   s 373R   368
   s 373SS   368
Land Title Act 1994   364
   s 97N   369
   s 521ZC   364
Sustainable Planning Act 2009   393
   s 41   393
Waste Reduction and Recycling Act 2011   367, 369
Water Act 2000   393

Tasmania

Climate Change (State Action) Act 2008   151
   s 5   151
Forestry Rights Registration Act 1990   363
   s 5   364
   s 5(2)   368
   s 6   364
Water Management Act 1999   393

South Australia

Climate Change and Greenhouse Emissions Reduction Act 2007   151
   s 3   151
Development Act 1993   385
Electrical Products Act 2000   310
Electrical Products Regulations 2001   310
Forest Property Act 2000   363
   s 3A   363
   s 3A(1)   364
   s 3A(2)   364
   s 7(1)   368
   s 9   364, 368
Forest Property (Carbon Rights) Amendment Act 2006   364
National Electricity (South Australia) (Smart Meters) Amendment Act 2009   306
Natural Resources Management Act 2004   393

Victoria

Bushfires Royal Commission Implementation Monitor Act 2011   397
Climate Change Act 2010   34, 155, 170, 188, 191, 335, 365
   Pt 5   365
   s 5   151
   s 19   163
   ss 21–24   363
   s 22   365, 368
   s 23   365
   s 24   365
   s 26(6)   368
   ss 26(6)–(7)   365
   s 27   365
   s 28   365
   s 29   365
   s 32   365
   s 33   365
   s 34   365
Coastal Management Act 1995   388
Electricity Industry Act 2000   306
   Div 6A   306
Electricity Safety Act 1998   310
Electricity Safety (Equipment Efficiency) Regulations 1999   310
Emergency Management Act 1986   399, 400
Environment Protection Act 1970   170
   s 4   170
   s 13(1)(ga)   170
Environment Protection Act 1994   327
Forestry Rights Act 1996   363, 365
Greenhouse Gas Geological Sequestration Act 2008   327
   s 56   329
   s 112   327
   s 224   327
Offshore Petroleum and Greenhouse Gas Storage Act 2010   325
   s 426   327
   s 433   327
   s 694   327
Planning and Environment Act 1987   310, 389
   s 60   388

s 60(1)(e) 389
s 60(e) 388
s 173 359
Supreme Court Act 1986 399
  Pt 4A 399
Victorian Renewable Energy Amendment Act 2009 315
Water Act 1989 393

Western Australia

Barrow Island Act 2003 328
Carbon Rights Act 2003 363
  s 5 364
  s 6 364, 368
  s 6(1) 364
Transfer of Land Act 1893 364
  Pt 4 Div 2A 364

OTHER COUNTRIES
New Zealand

Climate Change (Agriculture Sector) Regulations 2010 351
Climate Change Response Act 2002 185, 351
  Sch 3 185
  s 18CB 185
Climate Change Response (Moderated Emissions Trading) Amendment Act 2009 185

United States

17 CCR §§ 95800 – 96022
California Global Warming Solutions Act 2006 183
Clean Air Act 1963 133, 134
Environmental Quality Act 1970 184

Table of treaties and other international instruments

United Nations

Convention against Torture and Other Cruel, Inhuman or Degrading Treatment or Punishment   404
Convention on Biological Diversity   18, 145, 264
Convention on the Rights of the Child   404
   Art. 30   404
Convention Relating to the Status of Refugees   402, 406
Copenhagen Accord   5, 7, 26–7, 43, 143, 274, 404
International Covenant on Civil and Political Rights   403
   Art. 1(1)   404
   Art. 6   404
   Art. 27   404
International Covenant on Economic, Social and Cultural Rights   403
   Art. 1(1)   404
   Art. 11   404
   Art. 12   404
International Tropical Timber Agreement   237
Kyoto Protocol   3, 4, 6, 16, 17, 21, 23, 28, 30, 46, 62, 71, 83–9, 106, 116–20, 121, 125, 132, 139, 140–1, 168, 177, 178, 186, 187, 200, 206, 231, 235, 256, 259, 271, 301, 345, 352, 353, 362
   Annex B   26, 46, 85, 102
   Art. 2   83, 230
   Art. 2.1(a)   139
   Art. 2(2)   88
   Art. 3   84, 86, 117
   Art. 3(1)   83–4, 86
   Art. 3(7)   85
   Art. 3(8)   85
   Art. 3(9)   86
   Art. 3(13)   86
   Art. 3.3   141, 339
   Art. 3.4   141, 339
   Art. 3.7   140
   Art. 5   87, 95, 117
   Art. 5(1)   95, 102
   Art. 5(2)   95, 102, 104
   Art. 6   89
   Art. 7   87, 95, 116, 117, 141
   Art. 7(3)   95, 102
   Art. 8   87, 95, 108, 141
   Art. 8(1)   102
   Art. 8(3)   102, 103
   Art. 10(b)   28
   Art. 10(c)   263
   Art. 11(2)(b)   263
   Art. 12   89, 193–200, 203
   Art. 12(2)   193, 222, 227, 259
   Art. 12(5)   203
   Art. 12(7)   201
   Art. 12(8)   379
   Art. 12(9)   200
   Art. 18   87, 102, 112
Marrakech Accords   95
Rio Declaration on Environment and Development   403
   Annex 1   145
   Principle 15   69, 403
Stockholm Convention on Persistent Organic Pollutants   264
Stockholm Declaration on the Human Environment   59
   Art. 1A(2)   402
   Principle 21   59, 403
United Nations Convention to Combat Desertification   264
United Nations Declaration on the Rights of Indigenous Peoples   404
United Nations Framework Convention on Climate Change   3, 4, 19, 23, 30, 42, 43, 54–74, 86, 87–8, 94, 102, 103, 119, 125, 139, 140, 142, 145, 201, 230, 263, 270, 273, 301, 403, 411
   Annex I   13, 64
   Annex II   13, 64
   Art. 2   64
   Art. 3   64, 67–71, 79
   Art. 3(4)   23
   Art. 4   64, 74–82, 263

Art. 4(1)(a) 74, 75
Art. 4(1)(b) 28
Art. 4(1)(d) 231
Art. 4(1)(e) 378
Art. 4(1)(h) 262
Art. 4(2)(a) 77, 140
Art. 4(3) 259–60
Art. 4(4) 260
Art. 4(5) 260, 261
Art. 4(7) 260, 378
Art. 7 64
Art. 8 64
Art. 9 64
Art. 9(2)(c) 262
Art. 10 64
Art. 11 64, 260, 276
Art. 12 64, 80, 87
Art. 12(5) 74
Art. 12(9) 98
Art. 13 95
Arts 15–17 64
Art. 17 83
Art. 21 64
Art. 21(3) 260
Preamble 54–64
Vienna Convention on the Law of Treaties 54

Art. 2 83
Art. 31(2) 54

European Union

Directive 2002/91/EC 308
Directive 2003/87/EC 178
  Art. 9 180
  Art. 9a 180
  Art. 10 180
  Art. 10a 180
  Art. 11b(8) 180
  Art. 11b(9) 180
Directive 2009/28/EC 180
Directive 2009/29/EC 180
Directive 2009/31/EC 321
European Convention for the Protection of Human Rights and Fundamental Freedoms 404

World Trade Organization

World Trade Organization Agreement on Trade Related Aspects of Intellectual Property Rights 291

Introduction
Arguments, themes and overview

Introduction   *page* 1
Arguments and themes   2
Chapter overview   8

Introduction

Climate change is a global problem touching all nations, yet one that manifests itself in innumerable local forms that have their own immediacy in the domestic context. Any legal analysis of the response to climate change must, therefore, encompass multiple dimensions. Accordingly, this book is addressed to an Australian as well as an international audience. We have attempted to explain and contextualise Australia's regulatory responses to the problem of climate change within the global regulatory currents, analysing its domestic response as a case study in the international one. It is a premise of this book that in order to understand Australia's actions, it is necessary to highlight the salient international pressures and governance models affecting its decisions. In the course of doing so, the book also refines our understanding of the international climate change regime.

The regulation of climate change is an international responsibility. As we argue in Chapter 1, it is *necessarily* international. Nevertheless, we recognise that 'top-down' international rule-making is complemented by 'bottom-up' national and regional contributions to the shaping of legal concepts in the field. The steps that Australia is taking to introduce a framework for climate change regulation may have broader significance, as a model for legal developments elsewhere. The country responds to international regulation, but its own measures may also reverberate outwards and upwards. This dynamic makes the book a contribution to international climate law studies, with Australia serving as a recurrent illustration from the sphere of practical application.

Given this emphasis on international and Australian interactions in climate change law, the predominant focus of the book is on law in its 'public' dimensions. While private law issues such as tort liability are examined, typically these matters arise in the context of public regulation, such as the liability of statutory authorities. The book does not attempt to provide a comprehensive analysis of the private law pertaining to climate change law regulation in Australia; rather, it

1

focuses on the themes of climate governance at the international, transnational, and national levels. It explores concepts and arguments arising from the authors' research interests, which are also, we hope, of value to the general reader. While some chapters, especially in the earlier part of the book, are primarily concerned with international regulatory approaches to climate change, all chapters contain material on Australia's situation, with Chapters 4–5 and 9–11 analysing Australia's laws and institutions in considerable detail.

Arguments and themes

Before proceeding to an overview of the book's chapters, we provide a summary of the main contextual issues and themes that run through the book.

A global-scale problem

Climate change is a truly global problem caused by human activity around the world. It is gradually changing the whole of our natural and cultural environment. As such, it may be thought of as more than just another environmental problem, but instead as one that envelops and affects all others. It demonstrates as does no other phenomenon the impact that humans have on the natural world, and it challenges the systems humans have or are able to devise to limit their impact on the environment as no environmental problem has done before. From a legal point of view, climate law does not fit a pre-existing category. It does not slot easily into any developed branch of environmental law, for example, nor does it share all of environmental law's basic principles. As a global phenomenon, climate change establishes an entirely new framework within which our relationships with nature and with each other play out, but it also draws on existing law. Because it is such an influential framework, it has the potential to overwhelm smaller-scale environmental issues. The only other environmental problem with a claim to universality is anthropogenic ozone depletion. By comparison with climate change, though, it has been minuscule in its causes and impacts.

Fragmentation of the problem

The climate change problem could be solved by reducing anthropogenic greenhouse gas (GHG) emissions to a sustainable level. As with ozone-depleting substances, we know what the physical cause of the problem is and we know that if the cause is withdrawn, the problem will largely go away. At least causally, the situation is a straightforward one. Unfortunately, though, it is impossible in practice to approach the problem in simple terms. Social interests (including legal frameworks) carve up the climate change problem into many subordinate ones. In this way, additional concepts (poverty eradication, North–South inequity, nationalistic visions of economic expansion and dominance, differing philosophies about the limits of government, the ascendancy of materialistic values, etc.) are added to the mix. A problem with a clear solution fragments, not into simpler components, but into other complex problems whose solutions are less visible, as well as dependent on conflicting sets of preferences and values. (Nuclear power is climate-friendly: should we therefore tolerate more of it? If China's one-child policy is climate-friendly, should we tolerate more of *that*?) One consequence of the broadening of the nature of the inquiry into the several social causes of climate change is a broadening of the concept of 'climate law'.

Interdisciplinary character of a developing legal field

As a truly global problem, climate change makes immense new demands on lawyers, from students of the law to practising lawyers and academics. A basic understanding must be acquired of the contributions of other disciplines (science, economics, etc.) to framing and finding solutions to the problem of climate change. A new language heavy with scientific notions must be understood, and one must know how to operate on local, national, regional, and international levels of analysis even when dealing with a single concrete case (such as the extension of a coal mine). Legal precedent, which has been built around smaller-scale environmental issues, is helpful in some respects but not in others.

International climate law: Weak and non-directive

The UN Framework Convention on Climate Change (UNFCCC) and the Kyoto Protocol to the Convention affirmed pre-existing principles of international law. They established a framework of objectives and institutions with ongoing responsibility for bringing climate change under control. They also established reporting and compliance systems that have helped to harmonise the measurement of GHG emissions in developed states (but not yet in developing ones). Especially in procedural matters, the international regime has in many ways been effective. International rules with an impact on domestic systems have overwhelmingly pertained to reporting on country-level climate policies and measures, accounting for national GHG emissions, trading of international carbon credits and sovereign emission allowances, and compliance checks on national institutions charged with carrying out these functions. The procedural rules are more strictly applied to developed than to developing countries, but to some extent they apply to countries in both categories, and together with the fundamental principles set down in the UNFCCC (the precautionary principle, common but differentiated state responsibility, the interests of future generations, etc.), they may be said to constitute a rudimentary international (procedural) climate law. Substantively, however, there is less on which to report. Under the Kyoto Protocol, developed states have agreed to specific emission reduction commitments, with measurable outcomes, over a period of several years. The transfer of finance and technology from North to South for emission reduction projects in developing countries has been occurring at a modest rate under the Protocol's Clean Development Mechanism, but other assistance to date (such as the project grants awarded by the Global Environment Facility) has been ad hoc.

While these are important first steps, the legal regime remains weak. The UNFCCC's fundamental principles include national sovereignty and the right to exploit natural resources and to create wealth. These have a strained relationship with measures to control climate change. The United States' rejection of the Kyoto Protocol, the unambitious mitigation targets of the Protocol's commitment periods, and the economic recession that struck developed countries in 2009 (early in the Protocol's first commitment period) have not merely failed to substantially strengthen the climate regime over the years; they have moderated its demands.

A principle of 'globally sustainable development'?

The pre-existing general legal principles affirmed in the UNFCCC and the Kyoto Protocol include that of 'sustainable development', but climate law requires a more powerful principle to respond to the larger environmental threat. That principle, which we call *globally sustainable development*, has yet to evolve – and there is no guarantee that it ever will. The existing principle of sustainable development *simpliciter* has a limited scope that does not necessarily extend beyond that of national interest. Globally sustainable development, by contrast, is the kind of legal principle that would fit the logic of the climate change problem. A public authority or government bound by the principle would be obliged to weigh global sustainability in decisions that have an environmental impact, even if no negative impact is expected within its own jurisdiction. The principle would oblige the authority to consider undesirable impacts, such as drought and sea-level rise, in other parts of the world. Courts in Australia have, on occasion, evinced moves in this direction, interpreting the domestic principle of 'ecologically sustainable development' as requiring attention to the global aspects of climate change, for example by balancing 'geographically narrower concerns' with 'the broader public good of increasing the supply of renewable energy' (*Taralga* case).

Entrenched climate politics in a fast-changing world

The UNFCCC and the Kyoto Protocol partitioned the world into groupings of responsibility and action/inaction based on a North–South divide (developed and developing countries). Twenty years later, the dichotomy no longer seems useful. For example, depending on how emissions are calculated, the countries of the South have overtaken those of the North in aggregate GHG emissions, and this presents a new difficulty in regard to the apportionment of responsibility and action on climate change. Related to this, economic growth in many countries of the North has slowed considerably. (Australia and countries with a similar resource base, such as Canada, are notable exceptions in this regard.) Fossil-fuel-intensive production has shifted to developing countries such as China and India, where economic growth has been strong but where income per capita is still relatively low. Among the poorest and least developed of the developing country group are some that are likely to suffer the harshest impacts of climate change. The global population is predicted to grow from seven to nine or even ten billion people by mid-century, with most of this growth occurring in developing countries. Energy supply will have to meet both the increasing demands of individuals and the increasing number of them. (The extent to which access to energy will grow equitably and sustainably is largely unknown.) Australia's own population is likely to grow to 35 million or more by mid-century, and the country's economy is likely to remain highly dependent on the mining of fossil fuels and close political ties with emerging (and GHG-polluting) economies. The United States and a handful of other countries would like to see an end to the North–South politics. They say that environmental goals cannot be met without broad-based obligatory reductions in GHG emissions, and that every country must make a contribution. Yet the United States government has never itself been a model contributor. Developing countries, defending the benefits bestowed on them twenty years ago by the UNFCCC and later by the Protocol, are surrendering their ground very reluctantly, citing requirements of equity. The world politics on climate change is not keeping up with the changing realities on the ground.

A weak climate law into the future

International climate change law is likely to remain weak and non-directive until at least 2020. Regulation in the period 2013–20 will be essentially an extension of that enacted between 2008 and 2012, which is to say unambitious and risky from a scientific point of view, as the window of opportunity to avoid dangerous climate change closes. In 2020, a new international legal regime is promised to come into effect. The new regime is expected to impose binding mitigation targets on states currently classified as 'developing'. The burden will of course be proportional to their capacities, but it is a notable break with the past in that this group of countries has so far been exempted from compulsory mitigation measures. The weakness of the existing legal framework does not imply a lack of progress. Every year there is some advancement. The Copenhagen Accord for the first time set a global limit for rising temperatures (2°C above the pre-industrial average). This limit is a significant top-down feature that the Kyoto Protocol lacks (the Protocol limits aggregate emissions, not global warming). On the other hand, the Copenhagen Accord traded ambitious goals for non-binding commitments by the largest polluters (countries including the United States, China and India), who had indicated that they would opt out of a stricter regime. Their participation in the Accord and the United States' agreement to consider participation in a post-2020 regime are a kind of progress.

The effect on Australia of a weak international climate regime is that the country has considerable discretion to decide on its own action – or inaction. Change in the country came about only very gradually in the 1992–2007 period, with targeted interventions in the renewable energy sector (mainly through the Mandatory Renewable Energy Target scheme to support growth in renewable energy sources). Since 2007, Australia has been middle-of-the-road in its reforms: doing neither too much nor too little, with a political stalemate contributing to the inertia. Obligatory reporting of GHG emissions by corporations in Australia went into effect in 2008, and a national emissions trading scheme was legislated in 2011.[1] In terms of its international obligations, Australia went from a negotiated emission limit under the Kyoto Protocol of 8 per cent above the 1990 level in 2008–12 to a self-selected unconditional target in the post-2012 period (5 per cent below 2000 emissions by 2020). Australia's target will in due course be quantified and inscribed into the Kyoto Protocol's second commitment period, and will become binding on the country, but apart from meeting this modest mitigation target, Australia is free to do as much or as little as it likes in response to climate change, for example in its ongoing financial and technical assistance to developing countries for adaptation and mitigation.

Little appetite for strong domestic regulation

Strong and coordinated domestic laws enforced in all major economies before 2020 would give our societies a chance to 'bridge the emissions gap' and keep warming below 2°C. But such laws are possible only if climate change and its effects on current and future generations are seen by a majority of people and states as a serious threat that is of the greatest policy priority. The evidence suggests that, at least since the Global Financial Crisis, this is not the case. This could be because the predicted impacts of climate change are long-term and very gradual, becoming apparent only over the course of decades, and thus lie mostly in the future. Moreover, problems facing future generations are hardly likely to be experienced in the present as substantial relative to the problems of the present. This phenomenon is manifest in the debates over the discount rates for future climate change impacts. Many people are in any case used to having to 'adapt' to changing circumstances, and by comparison with other issues presently occupying them – international terrorism and war, instability in employment and economic outlook, increasing urbanisation, globalisation of language and culture, rapid development and spread of technological innovations, changing constellations of economic and industrial power, the persistence of conventional, tangible environmental problems, and so on – people's adaptation to an almost

---

[1] The text of the Kyoto Protocol refers to 'emissions trading' (instead of 'emission trading'), and we have adopted that usage in this book. In other such constructs ('emission reduction', 'emission limitation', etc.) the usual grammatical form is employed, as indeed it is in the text of the international conventions.

imperceptibly changing global climate may seem comparatively manageable or secondary.

Slow pace of domestic climate law

Initiatives at the country level are varied in their methods and are not always implemented through legislation. Change comes slowly through conceptual shifts (for example, greenhouse gases have been redefined as pollutants in some jurisdictions, including in the state of Victoria in Australia), technical interventions (carbon taxes and emissions trading schemes), support for a more varied energy mix, and changes in popular values. The problem with this alternative approach is that it only incidentally addresses climate change: the motivating force is not reduction of carbon emissions, as such, but the need to modernise the economy through efficiency gains (including greater efficiency in the ongoing combustion of fossil fuels), maintain competitiveness in the technology sector, and hedge against commercial risks in a low-carbon economic future. From a climatic perspective, the modest emission reductions that this soft form of intervention has delivered in Australia and elsewhere lack coordination, as they are not part of a planned and comprehensive contribution to an agreed global atmospheric stabilisation. The Copenhagen Accord's 2°C warming limit has not yet been translated into obligatory concrete actions. Still, steps towards greater sustainability make sense in economic terms, even if they do little to halt climate change. There is also the possibility that incremental actions taken now in a number of countries may produce a snowball effect, accelerating ambitious action.

Integration and regulatory coordination

Within domestic climate change regulation, the emerging trend of making use of a range of measures – for example an emissions trading scheme coupled with complementary measures addressing such matters as energy efficiency, renewable energy, and offsets – raises complex questions about how the different regulatory regimes will interact, without conflicting, to ensure a coordinated response to problems of emission reduction and adaptation. These questions are only now beginning to receive substantial attention in the literature on law and policy. Less attention has been paid to regulatory coordination between measures for GHG mitigation and those relating to adaptation to climate change, even though there is often an intimate connection between the two. Another looming challenge concerns the issue of integration: that is, how regulatory measures to address climate change will affect broader areas of environmental management, such as water allocation or biodiversity conservation. Questions of integration are particularly pertinent where – as in the case of the Australian carbon farming legislation – there is an attempt to achieve other benefits in addition to climate change regulation.

Chapter overview

The book commences in Chapter 1 ('Climate law: Meaning and context') with an examination of law's role within the international climate change regime: its sources, the new concepts it introduces or demands, and its relationship with other disciplines that contribute to our understanding of, and response to, climate change. An important preliminary point discussed in this chapter is the unique character of the climate change problem: it is a singular problem, one experienced globally, with global causes and effects. As such, the nature of the problem supports universal action against the causes of climate change, but by the same token, it creates a disincentive for corrective action that is not widespread and coordinated. Other sections of the chapter show that human wealth-related needs and aspirations, as well as social and infrastructural momentum in the use of fossil fuels, make it difficult to establish the conditions for widespread and coordinated action to control climate change. We conclude the chapter with an overview of the basic scientific argument for the existence of climate change and its impacts. Chapter 1 thus introduces several concepts, relationships and themes that are relevant to the book as a whole.

The international climate change regime is reviewed in Chapter 2. Here, we focus primarily on the UNFCCC's conceptual foundations. We inquire into the success of the Convention in tackling global emissions. The essential elements of the Kyoto Protocol are also introduced in this chapter. Subsequent chapters return to the most important of these elements of the international regime to develop them further. The UNFCCC, for all the generality of its text, has been extensively developed in party decisions – and its development continues apace. Considering that the United States, and as of 2011, Canada, have rejected the Kyoto Protocol, the UNFCCC remains the one and only global climate change treaty. It is no exaggeration to say that the very possibility of avoiding dangerous climate change hangs on the thread of the UNFCCC's negotiation process.

The activities of measuring, reporting and verifying state greenhouse gas emissions are foundational to our response to climate change. The international climate change regime, which parcels out responsibility for action to states, needs a way to know whether states are responding in line with their treaty obligations; if they are not, it must be able to bring them into line. Chapter 3 ('Measurement and verification of state emissions and legacy of the Kyoto Protocol's compliance system') focuses on the Kyoto Protocol's demanding system of checks and penalties for the reporting of emissions by Annex I parties. The Protocol's system of integrity in reporting is overseen by a Compliance Committee, unprecedented on the international stage, which operates rather like a court of law. There have been relatively few instances of reporting-related non-compliance to date, possibly due to the very existence of a Compliance Committee. In addition to keeping states compliant with their reporting obligations under the Protocol, the Committee is empowered to deal with the situation where an Annex I country fails to meet its quantified emission cap for a commitment period. The Kyoto Protocol's first commitment period expires in December 2012. Because emissions from the 2012 calendar year will not be verified until several months after they are submitted to the UNFCCC's Secretariat in 2013, the Compliance Committee's power to deal with non-compliance with emission caps will not be tested before mid-2014. The prospect of non-compliance with GHG caps was enough to drive Canada out of the Kyoto Protocol in December 2011.

Chapter 4 ('Development of climate law in Australia') departs from the international focus of the preceding chapters to delve more deeply into the development of climate law at the domestic level, focusing on the situation in Australia. The chapter identifies various drivers for the emergence of a body of Australian climate law – now much more substantial with the addition of federal legislation on carbon pricing and carbon farming – including the role that courts have played in bringing the climate change issue to the public's attention and highlighting the part that general environmental law frameworks and principles may play in climate change regulation. The remainder of the chapter traces the main stages in the evolution of Australian climate law and policy, from the 'no regrets' measures favoured by the Howard government to current efforts to introduce an emissions trading scheme that will 'price' greenhouse emissions.

'Putting a price on carbon' has become a dominant response to climate change, both at the international level and in the climate law of many countries. As discussed in Chapter 5 ('Putting a price on carbon: Regulatory models and emissions trading schemes'), this approach responds to a conception of climate change as a problem of 'market failure' requiring regulatory correction. We consider the different regulatory models that have been introduced to deal with climate change at the domestic level, focusing particularly on carbon taxes and the most common measure: emissions trading schemes. The chapter outlines emissions trading schemes operating around the world, including the influential EU scheme, before turning to discuss the Australian carbon-pricing mechanism and its supporting infrastructure.

The Clean Development Mechanism of the Kyoto Protocol, examined in Chapter 6, is a remarkably original and successful contribution of the climate change regime to the relationship between developed and developing countries. It is fascinating also from a legal point of view, for it creates myriad new legal relationships that transcend national jurisdictions and are delicately balanced by new institutions at the international level. The CDM is designed to smooth the transition of both developed and developing countries to greener economies by facilitating the creation of emission reduction projects in developing countries. The projects generate attractively priced credits that developed countries purchase to write off, or counterbalance (offset), some of their emissions at home. In the process, finance, technology and know-how flow into developing countries to accelerate environmentally sustainable development. Chapter 6 illustrates the workings of the CDM through a detailed case study and explains why Australia is likely to be dependent on the CDM's continuation long into the future. Many NGOs campaign against offsetting emissions, and to date there have been several proven scams to supply them with ammunition. Thus, while CDM offsets are counted upon by states to assist their transition to a low-carbon economy and to transfer funds and technology to developing countries, the environmental integrity of an international system heavily reliant on offsetting will remain open to serious doubt.

Forests store vast amounts of carbon. Deforestation and forest degradation add carbon to the atmosphere, thus contributing to climate change. An expanding forest, by contrast, takes carbon out of the atmosphere. Forested regions in developing countries, which include almost all remaining tropical forest, are at risk of anthropogenic deforestation and degradation. Their preservation and enhancement are critical to any strategy to avoid dangerous climate change. Yet the international climate change regime has been slow to prove itself in this area. The CDM has had a small capacity to protect forests, but its drawback is that it is project-based and does not operate at the country-wide level required for a holistic approach to forests. In substance, the world's vulnerable forests remain unregulated under the international legal climate regime. Chapter 7 considers the still early stages of the emerging scheme under the UNFCCC, called REDD or REDD+, to protect forests in developing countries by setting reference levels for existing forest-carbon stocks (or for GHG emissions from forests) and rewarding countries for maintaining their stocks or expanding them (or reducing their forestry emissions). The UNFCCC's REDD scheme is far more complex than the Kyoto Protocol's CDM, laying down an unprecedented multilevel legal as well as political challenge. Australia has already invested millions of dollars in the establishment of REDD+.

Chapters 6 and 7 therefore deal with aspects of finance and technology transfer from North to South, channelled through the two distinct programs of the CDM and (in the future) REDD. However, climate-related finance and technology transfer to developing countries covers an area much larger than that occupied by those two special-purpose mitigation programs. A principle of international law that is very nearly settled is that the wealthier countries to an international agreement must assist those with lesser capacity to meet their obligations under the treaty. Financial assistance to developing parties was a fundamental demand since the earliest days of climate negotiations, but no general, permanent solution to the challenge was settled upon before late 2010, when the UNFCCC parties agreed to the establishment of the Green Climate Fund. A Technology Mechanism was agreed to in the same year. Chapter 8 ('Climate finance, technology transfer, and capacity-building for sustainable development') reviews these developments from a legal perspective, as well as Australia's contributions to the distribution of finance and technology under the international climate change regime.

Chapter 9 ('Legal and regulatory frameworks for transition to a low-carbon economy') examines the legal frameworks for climate change mitigation technologies: energy efficiency, renewable energy, nuclear power, and carbon capture and storage. These options primarily target emissions in the power-generation sector, but we also consider technological improvements to reduce emissions in building, construction and transport. A core question is whether such technologies can stabilise emissions and enable a transition to a low-carbon economy. At least from a technical perspective, climate change mitigation is feasible, working in concert with energy efficiency. A potentially more difficult hurdle is the adequacy of legal and regulatory frameworks to allow rapid deployment of green technologies, and impediments posed by those frameworks. Another key issue is whether a single regulatory model or a range of mechanisms will best drive technological change.

Chapter 10 ('Regulation of biosequestration and emission reductions in the land sector in Australia') explores the role of biosequestration (carbon sinks) and the contribution of the land-use sector more generally to reducing emissions in Australia. Biosequestration may lower the cost of achieving overall emission reductions, and it may provide other benefits as well. Abatement in the land sector may be achieved more rapidly than transformation elsewhere. Nevertheless, complex practical and legal issues arise in this area in terms of ensuring the integrity of schemes and genuine long-term abatement. Australia now has a federal legislative regime that provides for biosequestration as well as for emission reductions from activities based on changes in land use (the Carbon Farming Initiative); it coexists with an array of state-based schemes. Chapter 10 explores these laws in some depth.

Chapter 11 ('Adaptation to climate change through legal frameworks') provides a snapshot of key adaptation challenges for Australia and its region. Until recently, adaptation – action taken to manage or reduce the consequences of a changed climate – did not figure as prominently as mitigation in legal analyses. Policy attention has now emphatically turned to ways of addressing the consequences of climate change, and a range of legal and planning measures are developing. In contrast to mitigation, though, no specific, purpose-built legal instruments are available for adaptation. Much adaptation law derives from the development or modification of existing legal frameworks, such as planning laws. The chapter highlights case studies involving sea-level rise, water allocation, natural disasters, and displacement of communities in the Pacific Island nations. These case studies remind us of the urgent need to effect robust legal responses to the challenges of avoiding dangerous climate change.

1

Climate law
Meaning and context

Introduction   *page* 12
A 'global–global' problem   12
First-mover constraints   14
The context of Australian climate law   16
Discovering climate law   18
Is there a foundational principle of climate law?   22
Climate law is both 'top-down' and 'bottom-up'   24
Interdisciplinarity   30
Human values and competing interests   33
Environmental values in developing countries: The case of Africa   35
Is popular apathy a result of misinformation?   38
Our continuing dependence on fossil fuels   39
A very brief introduction to the science of climate change   44

Introduction

In this chapter we discuss the unprecedented nature of the climate change challenge, legal principles relevant to solving it, and the interdisciplinary demands placed on those working in this area of law, science, and policy.

A 'global–global' problem

Our response to climate change has been unlike our response to any other global problem, whether physical or social. There has been an expectation from the start that the world's wealthiest countries (in particular, the OECD countries)[1] would move in lock step to solve it. Even developing countries are expected to

---

[1] The Organisation for Economic Cooperation and Development was established in 1961. Today it has 34 member countries, all of them democratic, committed to a market economy, and relatively rich (see <http://www.oecd.org>).

march in unison, albeit at some distance behind the wealthier states.² Our response to climate change has assumed that all states will work together and there will be no laggards. Thus international law and regulation have always been considered critical to solving the problem.

Other global problems – for example, older environmental harms such as water pollution, deforestation, species loss or overfishing – are 'global' in the narrow sense that they occur everywhere where large concentrations of people live. Human populations have similar environmental impacts throughout the world. Or, to take another type of global problem, abuse of human rights occurs in all locations where there are people, concentrated or not.

In all such cases we are actually referring to global–*local* problems (the same kind of problem repeated all around the world). A global–local problem can be solved as local problems are solved, that is, without necessarily being concerned about whether the same type of problem is being tackled simultaneously (or instead ignored) in other parts of the same country or in other parts of the world. At most, environmental harm of the non-climate variety presents a global–regional challenge that can be solved through cooperation of the affected adjacent states: for example, the protection of wetlands. On the human rights side (to keep that comparison going), a human rights treaty can define rights at the highest threshold and still be considered an effective instrument, even though half the world ignores it in practice.

Global–local problems thus have *causes* that are purely local, or at most cross-border. They are local problems that are similarly experienced everywhere, but because they have local causes, are amenable to local solutions.

Anthropogenic climate change is of a different order because it is an indivisible problem with global causes and effects. Its causes are everywhere. Every human being contributes to the problem simply by being alive (exhaling carbon dioxide, for example) and drawing on traditional energy sources or methods of agriculture. The globally dispersed human contributions to the 'greenhouse effect' (see Box 1.1) produce the singular phenomenon of climate change with observable physical effects everywhere in the world.

The only other global–global type of problem we can claim to have had experience with is the problem of damage to the ozone layer caused by ozone-depleting substances (ODS) that people and industries have released into the atmosphere.³ The challenge of phasing out ODS production is still a live one,⁴ although it is a much smaller problem than that of climate change. However,

---

2 OECD membership was used as the main criterion for distinguishing 'developed' from 'developing' countries in the UN Framework Convention on Climate Change. Annex II of the Convention is in essence a list of OECD countries, as the membership stood at the time. Annex I consists of OECD countries as well as some former Soviet republics and other Eastern Bloc states (called 'economies in transition'), some of which have since become OECD members. 'Non-Annex I parties' are mostly developing countries.
3 For more information, see the Ozone Secretariat, created under the Vienna Convention for the Protection of the Ozone Layer (1985), at <http://ozone.unep.org/>.
4 See <http://ozone.unep.org/Data_Reporting/Data_Access/> for the latest quantities of ODS still being produced in certain countries. Indonesia, for example, is responsible for the release of large quantities of ODS. Chlorine compounds persist for decades in the upper atmosphere, meaning that it will probably not be before

> **BOX 1.1 The greenhouse effect**
>
> Human beings everywhere contribute to the greenhouse effect, mainly through the combustion of fossil fuels. Over the past century, with strong population growth and ever increasing demand for energy, the human contribution to the greenhouse effect has been enormous, as detailed throughout this book. In simple terms, 30 per cent of the sun's energy that reaches the earth is reflected back to space by clouds, gases and small particles in the atmosphere, and by the earth's surface. The remainder is absorbed by the atmosphere and the earth's surface. To balance the absorption of the sun's energy, the earth's surface and atmosphere must emit the same amount of energy into space. They do so as infrared radiation.
>
> On average, the earth's surface emits significantly more energy than it receives from the sun, but the net effect of absorption and emission of infrared radiation by atmospheric gases and clouds has been to reduce the amount reaching space until it approximately balances the incoming energy from the sun. The surface is thus kept warmer than it otherwise would be, because in addition to the energy it receives from the sun, it also receives infrared energy emitted by the atmosphere. The warming that results from this infrared energy is known as the *greenhouse effect*. The effect is welcome, up to a point! But an intensification of the greenhouse effect could change environmental conditions that have prevailed for millennia.
>
> The two gases making the largest contribution to the greenhouse effect are water vapour followed by carbon dioxide (CO_2). There are smaller contributions from many other gases, including ozone, methane, nitrous oxide, and human-made gases such as chlorofluorocarbons (CFCs). In this book, by 'anthropogenic greenhouse gases' (GHGs) we generally mean the greenhouse gases controlled by the Kyoto Protocol (listed in Annex A of the treaty), which, it is important to note, are only a subset of the GHGs responsible for the greenhouse effect.

Source: Adapted from The Royal Society, *Climate Change: A Summary of the Science* (2010), p. 2.

ODS comprise a few artificial chemicals produced in a small number of countries, and for which alternatives are readily available. The logic is similar, but the ODS problem is not only smaller in scale than the problem of climate change; it also concerns substances whose manufacturing sources can be phased out without our having to rebuild our economies and ways of life.

First-mover constraints

A local campaign to address a genuinely global problem like climate change is both possible and sensible: emissions of greenhouse gases can be eased locally, and measures can be taken at the smallest scale (house by house even) to defend against the impacts of climate change. However, in the context of dealing with climate change, we cannot say that local action is ever independent of measures taken elsewhere in the world. This is because what occurs elsewhere in the world may simply cancel out the local effort, rendering it pointless. In the response to climate change, there is no logical equivalent of a determined, environmentally activist society with extensive national parks and clean rivers, which, having eliminated the local causes of environmental harms, waits for other countries to

---

2050 that the ozone layer will have been restored to its pre-industrial health. In fact, in 2011, ozone loss over the Arctic was so severe that for the first time it could be called an 'ozone hole' like the hole above the Antarctic: see G. L. Manney et al., 'Unprecedented Arctic Ozone Loss in 2011', 478 *Nature* 469 (27 October 2011).

follow its model and clean up, restore and protect. 'First movers' in the response to climate change do exist, but unless they belong to a radical fringe, they never move very far ahead on their own and are always demanding that everybody else catch up quickly. There is widespread distrust of potential free riders.[5]

A country in the first-mover category is Norway. It is an exceptionally wealthy country, which can afford to move ahead of the pack in domestic emission reduction reforms (it intends to become 'carbon neutral' by 2030)[6] while also spending generously on climate-related programs such as, for instance, forest protection in developing countries.[7] At the same time, though, Norway pushes hard at international negotiations for universal action to stem climate change, and there is no suggestion that it sees its unilateral initiatives as anything but stopgap measures or demonstration projects.[8] Its expenditures on carbon capture and storage demonstration technology (the underground storage of CO_2 captured during the extraction or combustion of fossil fuels)[9] are in its national interest as a country that wishes to maintain its dominance of the market for natural gas.[10] It seems unlikely that its decision to edge ahead of other countries and invest in climate-friendly technologies is driven only by altruism.

The European Union (which does not include Norway) is also able to stay one step ahead of other wealthy economies, partly due to a strong underlying environmental movement and partly because its large size reduces economic competitiveness concerns about the cost of unilateral action. In addition, the European Union applies its might to pressure non-EU states to take action themselves.[11] Yet, because the EU is already significantly financially extended relative to other economies, many EU member states are resisting further changes to the common EU emissions trading scheme (EU ETS). In particular, they are resisting a lowering of the emissions ceiling for the EU (to 30 per cent below 1990-level emissions by 2020), which would make the EU ETS's operation even more burdensome to its economies.[12] At the international

---

[5] W. Shobe and D. Burtraw, 'Rethinking Environmental Federalism in a Warming World', 3 *Climate Change Economics* (forthcoming 2012): '[L]ocal investments will raise costs and prices relative to jurisdictions that do not reduce emissions and will not have a measurable benefit to the local jurisdiction, placing the low-emissions jurisdiction at a competitive disadvantage.'
[6] International Institute for Sustainable Development, 12(506) *Earth Negotiations Bulletin* (10 June 2011), p. 3.
[7] See for example Norwegian Agency for Development Cooperation, *Real-Time Evaluation of Norway's International Climate and Forest Initiative: Contributions to a Global REDD+ Regime 2007–2010* (Norad, March 2011).
[8] On Norway's insistence that all major emitters should move ahead together as one, see, for example, International Institute for Sustainable Development, 'SB 34 and AWG Highlights: Monday, 13 June 2011', 12(509) *Earth Negotiations Bulletin* (2011), p. 4.
[9] Fossil fuels are oil, natural gas and coal. A fossil fuel is formed over millions of years from the remains of plants. For a basic introduction to natural gas, see OECD, International Energy Agency, and Eurostat, *Energy Statistics Manual*, <http://www.iea.org/stats/docs/statistics_manual.pdf> (2005), pp. 55–68; on oil, see ibid., pp. 69–91; and on coal and other solid fossil fuels, see ibid., pp. 93–114.
[10] Norway is the world's fifth-largest producer of natural gas and the second-largest exporter: International Energy Agency, *Key World Energy Statistics* (2010), p. 13; Q. Schiermeier, 'The Great Arctic Oil Race Begins', 482 *Nature* 13 (2 February 2012), p. 13.
[11] See for example K. Kulovesi, '"Make Your Own Special Song, Even If Nobody Else Sings Along": International Aviation Emissions and the EU Emissions Trading Scheme', 2(4) *Climate Law* 535 (2011).
[12] J. de Cendra de Larragán, 'Case Note: Republic of Poland v Commission (Case T-183/07, 23 September 2009)', 1(1) *Climate Law* 199 (2010).

climate change conference in Durban in December 2011, the European Union made clear that it had done quite enough already about climate change and that it would withdraw from the Kyoto Protocol unless all the countries of the world committed to a process leading to an agreement on action binding upon all.[13]

The nearly universal current practice is that wealthy countries, as well as some countries with large, fast-growing economies, 'pledge' reductions in their future emissions, conditioned on comparable pledges being made and implemented by others in the same state groupings.[14] For example, the Australian government's pledge is for an emission reduction target of 5 to 15 per cent below 2000 emission levels by 2020, where the higher figure of 15 per cent is conditional upon a global agreement in which all major economies substantially cut their emissions or reduce emission growth. The Australian government has said that it would even consider a 25 per cent reduction target in the context of a global agreement of comparable ambition.[15] This tiered, conditional approach to climate policy avoids the first-mover problem while also avoiding the appearance of inaction.

The context of Australian climate law

A truly global problem requires everyone to act together to stamp out its causes. This means that discussion of an Australian 'climate law' must be carried out in parallel with a consideration of international agreements and ongoing negotiations about the global way forward, and must be informed by a comparison with policies and actions implemented or planned in other countries, especially other OECD countries and Australia's emerging trading partners in the developing world, such as China and India. Australia's own measures, in turn, inform those of other countries. For example, Australia went to great lengths at the Durban conference at the end of 2011 to publicise the scheme created by its *Clean Energy Act 2011* (Cth).

Australia's choice of policy instruments that respond to climate change, and its progress with implementing them, are thus only partially matters of domestic decision-making. The policy instruments have often already been trialled in other countries.[16] Moreover, the underlying character of the climate change problem leads to a reciprocal and symbiotic process of regulation, in which international consensus (when it is achieved) supports domestic reform agendas and actual domestic reforms keep a check on international ambition, while country-to-country peer pressure and the desire of some states to stand out as

---

13 See Chapter 2. In Durban, the European Union supported a multilateral system with broad state participation; in the process, it strenuously denounced inaction by other states and said that it would sign up to a second commitment period of the Kyoto Protocol only as part of a transition to a wider legally binding framework. See International Institute for Sustainable Development, 'Durban Highlights: Monday, 28 November 2011', 12(524) *Earth Negotiations Bulletin* (2011), p. 2.
14 See for example 'Summary of the Bangkok Climate Talks: 3–8 April 2011', 12(499) *Earth Negotiations Bulletin* (2011), pp. 3–4. Australia is typical in this respect; see Department of Climate Change and Energy Efficiency, *Securing a Clean Energy Future: The Australian Government's Climate Change Plan* (2011), p. xi.
15 Ibid., p. xi.
16 See Australian Productivity Commission, *Carbon Emission Policies in Key Economies: Research Report* (2011).

model international citizens – or to take bets on where future profits lie – also have a role in determining the overall pace of change. Australia is entangled as much as other states are in the logic of the problem, which dictates that it must neither advance too far ahead of other similarly situated countries nor allow itself to fall too far behind.[17]

Australia has never, in fact, cared to advance too far ahead of other countries, not even after December 2007, when it ratified the Kyoto Protocol – one of the last states to do so. Its responses to climate change, like the emissions trading scheme it intends to begin in 2015, are generally adaptations of ideas that have been implemented elsewhere first.[18] While Australia's strategic alliances, natural resources, and geographical advantages have meant that its international clout is greater than the size of its population would suggest, its political influence is nevertheless modest. It must be seen to be changing its ways domestically if it is to avoid having its voice ignored in international negotiations. Its reluctance to do so is deeply rooted. Australia is the world's largest exporter of coal.[19] This most polluting of the greenhouse-enhancing fuels earns the country a huge income.[20] As for emissions produced domestically, its per capita emissions of greenhouse gases are the highest in the world,[21] suggesting an underlying way of life that is resistant to change. Weighed down by its dependence on fossil fuels, there is as yet no particularly 'Australian model' of climate change regulation.

In law and policy related to climate change, too, the country's pace of reform is heavily determined by external forces. Too advanced and climatically vulnerable to stay on the sidelines, but too small and fossil-dependent to lead, the country is carried along by the international current. It must improve the energy efficiency of its economy and find new money to invest in research and development for clean energy technology and in clean energy infrastructure. The climate change legislation passed by the country in 2011 responds to the external pressures while raising some of the money needed to pave the way to a less emission-

---

17 That attitude is exemplified in reported comments by Australian Prime Minister Julia Gillard: 'In an address to the annual Minerals Industry Parliamentary Dinner tonight, the Prime Minister said she favoured a scheme applied as widely as possible to the economy, rejecting calls to include exemptions similar to those in Europe ... She dismissed suggestions that Australia was acting in front of the rest of the world. "The government's approach is not that Australia should lead the world in environmental policy – it is that Australia should not be left behind in economic transition"' (Sid Maher, 'Carbon Tax Necessary, Julia Gillard Tells Miners', *The Australian* (online edition), 1 June 2011). Similarly, Australia's Deputy Prime Minister and Treasurer Wayne Swan said, approvingly, that '*Australia was in the middle of the pack* in terms of efforts to reduce carbon pollution' (Sid Maher, 'Carbon Tax on Coal Is "Ahead of World"', *The Australian* (online edition), 8 June 2011, emphasis added).
18 Such as the EU ETS: see A. Petherick, 'Duty Down Under', 2 *Nature Climate Change* 20 (January 2012), p. 21.
19 International Energy Agency, *Key World Energy Statistics* (2010), p. 15.
20 In the 2008–09 financial year, Australia exported 263.4 million tonnes of coal (metallurgical and thermal), valued at A$58.4 billion: Australian Coal Association, 'The Australian Coal Industry – Coal Exports', <http://www.australiancoal.com.au/the-australian-coal-industry_coal-exports_coal-export-details.aspx>. The combustion of that coal overseas would release more than 500 million tonnes of CO_2 into the atmosphere. (For this calculation, see EECA Business, 'CO_2 Emission Calculator', <http://www.eecabusiness.govt.nz/wood-energy-resources/co2-emission-calculator>, or another web-based calculator.) This is of the same order as Australia's annual domestic GHG emissions.
21 Department of Climate Change and Energy Efficiency, *Securing a Clean Energy Future* (2011), p. xi. See also Chapter 2, Figure 2.1.

intense economy. The lesson that emerges is that the state of Australian climate law cannot be understood but in a global context.

Discovering climate law

In recent years, the reaction to the reality of climate change among politicians, academics, non-government organisations and others has ranged from seeing it, with an almost religious fervour, as a singular, coherent issue (in 2007, Kevin Rudd, then Australia's prime minister, referred to it as 'the great moral and environmental challenge of our generation')[22] to using it as a term of convenience laid atop a range of disparate issues. The latter tendency goes with the fragmentation of the subject alluded to earlier. Focal issues include the environmental harm of oil drilling and transportation; the landscape spoliation and fatalities associated with coal mining; popular resistance to the expansion of nuclear power; overdependence on Middle East oil; energy security and price stability; funding for the development and commercialisation of cleaner and safer sources of energy; biodiversity loss and its potential impact on the emerging field of biotechnology; deforestation in the tropics; degradation of coral reefs through ocean acidification; the North–South developmental divide and methods of transferring finance and technology to support economic development and eradication of poverty in the South; the threat of displacement of human populations from low-lying areas because of sea-level rise; civil war in water-depleted and famine-prone regions such as the Sudan; the increasing intensity of extreme weather events and associated insurance costs – and so on. While scientists continue their elaboration of a unified *science* of climate change, the policy and legal perspectives on the problem can be quite diverse.[23]

In recent years, the political mood around the world, including Australia's, has swung away from addressing climate change as a singular issue in a comprehensive universal treaty, and towards enshrining ad hoc solutions to social, environmental, economic, and energy problems. Solutions presently considered include the creation of monetary incentives in developing countries for the protection of forests; establishing an administration to distribute funds to countries for adaptation and mitigation projects; achieving a steady stream of adequate funding from multiple sources, including private investment, for adaptation and sustainable development in the poorest economies; strengthening action under relatively narrowly focused agreements such as the Convention on Biological Diversity; encouraging countries to reduce greenhouse gas emissions voluntarily; supporting home insulation schemes, feed-in tariffs, and more efficient building design; and trialling safer technologies for nuclear-power production. The list could be extended indefinitely. If the way forward is along several such separate paths,

---

22 As quoted by the ABC, 'The 7.30 Report'; transcripts available at <http://www.abc.net.au/7.30/content/2010/s2884108.htm> and <http://www.abc.net.au/7.30/content/2011/s3159735.htm>.
23 R. Meyer, 'Finding the True Value of US Climate Science', 482 *Nature* 133 (9 February 2012).

with no legal instrument at the international level to unify all the initiatives under a coherent aim, we might conclude that a 'settled' climate law as a distinct field of law is unlikely to emerge at any level of governance.

In fact, climate law's centre of gravity has for almost twenty years been the UN Framework Convention on Climate Change. Ideas about an emerging legal discipline under the climate change umbrella generally treat the UNFCCC as foundational. At least on its face, the UNFCCC does articulate a core set of obligations that could be taken to state the essence of an international climate law (Chapter 2). The open-ended and relatively mild Convention has so far been able to withstand swings in political majorities quite well. The Kyoto Protocol that supplements it has not been so fortunate. As the pendulum has swung away from holistic, long-term thinking about the environment, the Protocol has been found too demanding. If the politics that determines our response to climate change continues to treat the subject as disparate and fragmented, the unifying effect which the UNFCCC has exerted on the emerging strands of climate law may well be lost.

What, then, is the 'climate law' covered in this book? Where do we find it and how do we recognise it? One way to discover the law is to look to traditional sources of law (domestic statutes, regulations, and court decisions, as well as international conventions, customary law, and general principles of law derived from national laws) for content that has been developed in response to the problem of climate change or has been made applicable to it by extension. Such content having been identified, it can be subdivided into topics (for example, emission-reporting obligations, mandatory renewable energy targets, biosequestration property rights, trading markets for emission allowances, domestic and international compliance) under which the detail of each separate source of law or legal scheme would be presented and interpreted. The basic method may be difficult to apply in cases where, for example, small amendments are buried in pre-existing statutes with general titles, as where a government has responded to climate change in an ad hoc fashion, making minor adjustments within existing legal categories (for example by providing for legal title to biosequestered carbon within a pre-existing Forestry Act). Nevertheless, the method is likely to yield a significant amount of information about the applicable law. Whether such an exercise, in the absence of a flagship national law such as Australia's *Clean Energy Act 2011*, would leave us with a 'climate law' or merely an assemblage of laws relating to climate change is a question we return to below.

Another way to go about the task of discovering climate law is to focus on a measure intended to slow down climate change, or adapt to it, and work back from that implemented measure to the factors that facilitated it, highlighting those that have a distinctly legal content. For example, a small community that has managed to obtain all of its energy needs from renewable sources,[24] and has

---

[24] In the category of 'renewable resources' is energy from hydropower, wind, tide, wave, ocean, solar photovoltaic, and solar-thermal generation technologies. For a basic introduction to renewables, see OECD, International Energy Agency, and Eurostat, *Energy Statistics Manual* (2005), pp. 115–33 ('renewable energy is energy that is derived from natural processes that are replenished constantly').

an amount left over to sell to the regional electricity company, might have started down this path by winning a government-sponsored competition for a renewable energy project. Let us imagine that this bestowed on the community a prestigious award, public attention, and some seed funding. Company law (enabling shareholder ownership of expensive wind turbines, for example) and the regional utility's policy (or statutory obligation) to buy the community's self-generated energy at a fixed price for a period of years (taking some of the risk out of the community's investment in wind farming by passing on the cost to society at large) are two factors, we might suppose, in addition to the prize, that made the experiment possible. This analysis reverse-engineers a project aimed at mitigating greenhouse gas emissions to discover its enabling regulatory framework.[25]

Of the two methodologies just described, the more straightforward one – that of seeking law in traditional sources – would not have inevitably led us to all three of the enabling elements of the imaginary community's small-scale venture into renewables. Is a government-sponsored competition 'climate law'? We may think not, even as we acknowledge that the environmental governance of today employs a range of innovative instruments that are deliberate alternatives to the command-and-control choices of the past.[26] From that perspective, one might be prepared to say that the government competition, had it been instituted in line with what the governmental authorities saw as their obligation to reduce greenhouse gas emissions in the country, is positively a form of climate law: law by other means.

A more complex example of the reverse-engineering method of discovering climate law is to inquire about the regulation that has gone into realising a project under a complex international arrangement, such as the Clean Development Mechanism. (See Chapter 6 for a detailed account of the CDM.) A CDM project is intended to produce a reduction in GHG emissions (when measured against a predicted domestic business-as-usual emission trajectory, namely the emission trajectory that would have eventuated in the absence of the project) in one part of the world (developing country) in order to offset (neutralise) an excess of emissions in another (developed country). The industry that causes the excess in the wealthier country purchases the CDM project's offsets produced in the poorer country, with the combined pollution released into the atmosphere being, in theory, nil.

Much domestic and international regulation is needed to make the Clean Development Mechanism possible, as well as a multitude of purpose-built institutions with validation or oversight responsibility for the CDM.[27] When considering this example, we would perhaps not hesitate to say that the Mechanism in all its

---

[25] The example is based on an actual case described by Elizabeth Kolbert, 'The Island in the Wind', *The New Yorker*, 7 July 2008, p. 68.
[26] For a definition of 'environmental governance', see L. Godden and J. Peel, *Environmental Law: Scientific, Policy and Regulatory Dimensions* (Oxford University Press, 2010), p. 61.
[27] The CDM has been described as densely regulated, with a complex set of methodological rules (see P. Newell and M. Paterson, *Climate Capitalism: Global Warming and the Transformation of the Global Economy* (Cambridge University Press, 2010), p. 149); it has also been described as a 'highly dynamic body of legal text':

complexity is an expansion of, and a positive contribution to, climate law, even though in fact the CDM is built out of a motley of decisions under the Kyoto Protocol, national and international project development and approval processes, transnational contracts and financial transfers, and the market mechanisms that give value to CDM credits – but of very little statutory law, case law of the courts, or any such traditional building block of law. The CDM example intersects with the earlier point about Australian climate law being dependent for its full meaning and sense on the global context. Australia, as a Kyoto Protocol party, is entitled to buy and use a CDM unit (a CER) to offset an amount of the country's emissions equivalent to one tonne of CO_2, and is likely to need a considerable quantity of such units to meet its Kyoto Protocol emission caps for the first and second commitment periods (these concepts are explained in later chapters). However, almost all of the 'law' that facilitates the creation of the offset does not subsist in the Australian jurisdiction, but in decisions by a collective of states, treaty-derived international bodies such as the CDM Executive Board, and the domestic law of the developing country in which the CDM project supplying the offset purchased by the Australian government is based.

In conclusion, our response to climate change has produced certain patterns of regulated action that do not draw on traditional legal sources and do not occur within traditionally delineated legal jurisdictions. In this book we rely on the methods described above to determine the content of climate law. We draw on traditional sources of law as well as on arrangements that facilitate or encourage conduct directed to mitigation of, or adaptation to, climate change. We define 'climate law' broadly, so as to enable a fuller view (a non-legalistic view) of the elements that go towards the governance of this extraordinarily complex problem.[28] Climate law under our definition encompasses the concept of 'sustainable development', which is a central principle of national as well as international environmental law. The principle of sustainable development indeed imbues the CDM with one of its legal aspects. The CDM could be described as the world's largest single program supporting sustainable development, for in the process of creating emission credits it transfers money and technology from developed to developing countries in support of climate-friendly development in the latter.[29] It implements environmental law for a climate-related purpose, which is one way to think about 'climate law'.

In the notion of 'climate law' one may even wish to include the features of our socio-legal system that make the problem of climate change more *difficult* to bring under control. These include fossil fuel subsidies, rebates and tax breaks, each of which makes fossil energy more affordable or profitable, while pricing

---

M. Krey and H. Santen, 'Trying to Catch up with the CDM Executive Board: Regulatory Decision-Making and Its Impact on CDM Performance', in *Legal Aspects of Carbon Trading*, eds D. Freestone and C. Streck (Oxford University Press, 2009), p. 232.
28 A similar approach is taken to environmental law, in general, in Godden and Peel, *Environmental Law* (2010), p. 72 and passim.
29 However, as we discuss in Chapter 6, on the CDM, sustainability has not always been a demonstrable outcome of CDM projects.

out clean energy alternatives;[30] zoning laws supporting sprawling suburbs and exurbs, leading to energy inefficiencies and automobile dependence; and environmental impact assessments that give no weight to the aspects of a project directed to adaptation or mitigation of climate change.

Is there a foundational principle of climate law?

The reader may wish for more. After all, the test for the existence of a discipline is that it builds upon a principle that is unique to it. This is analytically true if one aims to distinguish the discipline from others on conceptual grounds. Put differently, a field of law is usually held together not only by the particular problem it addresses (e.g. crime and punishment) but by the substantive, evidentiary and procedural rules and principles that have come to characterise it. In criminal law, for example, the principle of legality, the recognition of the rights of the accused and so on define a largely settled landscape. Other familiar fields of law have the same quality. Is there anything settled about climate law? Does it have a foundational principle that belongs to it alone?

The short answer is that it does not, but that an obvious candidate for such a principle does exist and its acceptance as a general legal principle may not be that far off. The principle we have in mind is intimately connected with the kind of problem climate change is.

Climate change is an environmental problem. Whatever its social causes, and whatever problems we come up against when we attempt to solve it, climate change *changes* the natural environment as we know it, and from our point of view it mostly changes it for the worse. The next question is whether climate change is an environmental problem of a different *kind*, with novel normative consequences. The first part of this question has already been answered in the affirmative, by characterising climate change as the pre-eminent global–*global* problem. The essence of this kind of problem is that any contribution to it (a ferry idling in Sydney Harbour) exacerbates the problem *globally*, and only globally. The emissions dissipate. The event has no relevant environmental effect limited to the local, national, or other non-global arena.[31]

As an environmental problem, the principles of environmental law should apply to climate change, unless the peculiar nature of the problem renders the ordinary principles of environmental law inapplicable. A key principle of environmental law, as mentioned above, is that of sustainable development. The scope of that principle has mirrored the scope of traditional environmental law problems. These days, it is almost universally applied within the levels of governance of

---

30 World fossil-fuel subsidies totalled $312 billion in 2009: International Energy Agency, *World Energy Outlook* 2010: Executive Summary (2010), pp. 4 and 13–14. The US oil industry receives $4 billion a year in tax incentives: John M. Broder, 'Obama Shifts to Speed Oil and Gas Drilling in US', *The New York Times (Online Global Edition)*, 14 May 2011.
31 P. Singer, 'One Atmosphere', in *Climate Ethics: Essential Readings*, eds S. M. Gardiner et al. (Oxford University Press, 2010), pp. 181–99.

domestic jurisdictions. In Australia, it is widely inscribed in statutory law. It has become so enriched through subordinate concepts as to be fairly described as a foundational principle of environmental law.

However, sustainable development that safeguards local environments does not necessarily safeguard the global one. We could imagine a case where all countries are developing sustainably from a national perspective and yet are causing climate change globally. We now know, of course, that no country is shielded from the deleterious effects of climate change in the long run. Therefore, a localised conception of sustainable development is an illusion if it is severed from considerations of global climatic sustainability. It also follows that a country like Australia, which is very vulnerable to climatic change, cannot implement domestic sustainable development (for example protect its World Heritage sites) when global greenhouse gas emissions are at unsustainable levels.

Globally sustainable development, the legal principle we believe is necessary to address climate change, has yet to crystallise in domestic or international law. Thus there is no law that requires the Australian government, or any other government, to take global climatic effects into account when going about its business. Australia has emission reduction commitments under the Kyoto Protocol, and voluntary emission reduction targets through to 2020 and beyond, and must adjust its policies in recognition of these constraints. It must also defend itself against the impacts of climate change. But these are essentially domestic matters. If it wishes to expand its coal exports, it may do so without giving any weight to a principle of global sustainability. It may import products without regard to their carbon footprint. It may negotiate bilateral and multilateral treaties, including climate treaties, adopting positions focused exclusively on its own economic advantage. And so on.

Neither the UNFCCC nor the Kyoto Protocol articulates a principle of 'globally sustainable development'. In the Convention, 'sustainable development' is used to affirm an interest of developing countries in economic development that is free from, rather than constrained by, imperative global mitigation. Thus:

> The Parties have a right to, and should, promote sustainable development. Policies and measures to protect the climate system against human-induced change should be appropriate for the specific conditions of each Party and should be integrated with national development programmes, taking into account that economic development is essential for adopting measures to address climate change.[32]

In the Kyoto Protocol, too, references to sustainable development never rise above the notion of *national* sustainability – they are never about global sustainability, and never unambiguously about national sustainability conditioned on global sustainability. Once it becomes clear that no principle of global sustainability has emerged in law, and that climate law therefore lacks a core, the sense

---

32 UNFCCC, Art. 3(4).

we get (see Chapter 2) that the Convention and the Protocol do not add up to a conceptually consistent whole is easier to explain.[33]

Climate law is both 'top-down' and 'bottom-up'

Even if there is little to be said about climate law's core, much has been said about the levels from which the climate change problem may be regulated. There are those who believe that climate change should be regulated from the top down, others who believe that bottom-up measures can also be effective, and there are also views that one direction should be preferred to the other.[34] Our own position on the meaning of these terms and the significance of the distinction is set out below.

As already explained, the peculiar nature of the climate change problem comes down to the fact that all greenhouse gas emissions from human activity are poured into a global, well-mixed atmospheric pool, and thus have global consequences. The emissions are the by-product of economic activity powered from sources – mainly fossil fuels – that have no straightforward substitute. Any attempt at substitution will therefore be costly. A community that decides at some cost or inconvenience to itself to cut back its emissions cannot be unaware that it is having little or no beneficial effect on the global problem of climate change if people elsewhere do not also change their ways. Indeed, there is a risk that people elsewhere will deliberately take advantage of the reductions achieved by the trailblazing community by staying with the cheaper route of pouring more and more greenhouse gases into the global pool in a quest for economic advantage.[35]

The continuing exponential growth of the human population,[36] with its associated upward pressure on GHG emissions, is another factor discouraging grassroots action. Traditional legal intervention (including treaties and national laws) seems an obvious and even necessary method to ensure that everyone moves ahead in a coordinated manner. To date, we have seen some 'top-down' action (the two international climate treaties being the prime example: see Table 1.1) as well as some grassroots or 'bottom-up' efforts, especially in polities where the national government has been slow to react to the global warming problem.

---

[33] A 'diagnosis' of the structural opposition to globally sustainable development has been offered in a brilliant review by Joel Cohen, 'What Will it Take to Save the Earth?', 59(7) *New York Review of Books* 47 (26 April 2012), p. 49 (describing the debilitating collision of, on the one hand, 'national democracies and other forms of government, with their own parochial perspectives in space and time', and on the other hand, 'the global reach and short-term incentives of economic globalization').

[34] For example S. Rayner, 'How to Eat an Elephant: A Bottom-up Approach to Climate Policy', 10(6) *Climate Policy* 615 (2010).

[35] The logic is exploited in a comment by Australian Liberal Party Senator Nick Minchin: 'Given we are responsible for about one per cent of the world's emissions of CO_2 and when it's clear that China's additional emissions over the next few decades will completely swamp any reductions in our emissions, anything Australia does will be utterly pointless and have no impact whatsoever on the global climate' (J. Kelly and J. Massola, 'Climate Report Reveals Coalition Divisions, as Lib Sceptic Calls It "Offensive"', *The Australian* (online edition), 23 May 2011). The comment succeeds in being misleading. What the senator ought to have said, had he wished to be accurate, is that, for Australia's emission reductions to be meaningful, they need to be made within the framework of a capped global emission budget.

[36] K. Smith, 'We Are Seven Billion', 1 *Nature Climate Change* 331 (October 2011).

Table 1.1 Important dates in the global response to climate change

	World	Australia
1988	Intergovernmental Panel on Climate Change (IPCC) jointly established by World Meteorological Organization and UNEP	
1990	IPCC First Assessment Report of the causes and impacts of climate change	
1992	UN Framework Convention on Climate Change (UNFCCC) adopted (9 May)	Australia ratifies UNFCCC (30 December)
1994	UNFCCC enters into force (21 March)	
1995	IPCC Second Assessment Report 1st UNFCCC Conference of Parties (COP), Berlin (decision made to work towards a protocol)	
1997	Kyoto Protocol adopted (11 December)	
2001	In the US, the Bush Administration withdraws from Kyoto Protocol (March) IPCC Third Assessment Report 7th COP, Marrakech (many rules agreed to for the implementation of the Kyoto Protocol)	**2003** New South Wales Greenhouse Gas Reduction Scheme (GGAS) commences (1 January)
2005	Kyoto Protocol enters into force (16 February) European Union Emissions Trading Scheme (EU ETS) goes into operation	
2006	Al Gore's book and film, *An Inconvenient Truth*, gain a wide audience	Asia–Pacific Partnership on Clean Development and Climate launched in Sydney
2007	IPCC Fourth Assessment Report 13th COP, Bali (adoption of Bali Road Map, aimed at reaching a new global and comprehensive agreement on climate change mitigation by 2009) IPCC and Al Gore awarded Nobel Peace Prize	South Australia passes *Climate Change and Greenhouse Emissions Reduction Act* Newly elected Labor Government ratifies Kyoto Protocol (3 December)
2008	Start of Kyoto Protocol's first commitment period (2008–12) Britain passes *Climate Change Act*, which requires the country to cut GHG emissions to 80% of 1990 levels by 2050	Federal government *White Paper* on Carbon Pollution Reduction Scheme (CPRS)
2009	15th COP, 'Copenhagen Accord' of non-binding pledges patched together at last minute	CPRS defeated in Senate
2010	16th COP, Cancun: Copenhagen Accord elements adopted as COP decisions	Gillard replaces Rudd as prime minister
2011	Debt and growth crises in Europe and US dominate headlines throughout year At Durban COP, the EU and most other developed countries (not including the US, Canada, Japan and Russia) agree to a second commitment period under the Kyoto Protocol (2013 to 2017 or 2020) Canada completely withdraws from Kyoto Protocol, effective December 2012	*Clean Energy Act* (Cth) and associated legislation pass both houses of parliament
2012	December: end of first Kyoto Protocol commitment period; verified GHG emissions for period 2008–12 not available until 2013; any penalties for excess emissions not decided until 2014	New national climate laws commence (April) Introduction of fixed carbon price for three years (1 July)

California is famous for its grassroots efforts at both the community and state levels, and Australia also has a well-established history of bottom-up climate action in the face of a sceptical federal government.[37]

Thus Diringer is led to ask: 'Is the best approach [to dealing with the climate change problem] a binding top-down treaty with sanctions for non-compliance, a loose bottom-up arrangement with countries free to define their own voluntary commitments, or something in between?'[38]

The top-down/bottom-up distinction has not always been employed clearly in the literature.[39] In this book, when we refer to a framework as 'top-down' we mean that it is guided by a quantified multinational target set by an international agreement. An example of a top-down approach to climate change mitigation is the scheme agreed to by the Annex I parties to the Kyoto Protocol (developed countries), whereby they are to reduce their emissions by an average of 5.2 per cent below their 1990 levels over the 2008–12 period by implementing the state-level reductions listed in Annex B of the Protocol. The targets in Annex B, taken together, are consistent with the quantified obligation in Article 3(1) of the Kyoto Protocol, that 'Parties included in Annex I shall ... reduc[e] their overall emissions of such gases by at least 5 per cent below 1990 levels in the commitment period 2008 to 2012.'

Australia's target for the 2008–12 period is, in fact, 8 per cent *above* its 1990 emissions, which still amounts to a reduction from its business-as-usual trajectory. According to our definition, any measures taken by Australia at the national, state/territory, or local government level pursuant to its quantified Annex B obligation count as top-down measures, because they are part of a coordinated effort to achieve an international mitigation target.

The Kyoto Protocol's Annex B obligation is treaty-based,[40] but not all top-down action needs to flow from an obligation inscribed in a legally binding treaty ratified by national parliaments. States have several ways of committing themselves to future conduct. There are 'many shades of grey associated with the "binding" concept'.[41] For example, most of the rules that guide the conduct of the Kyoto Protocol parties (including highly invasive ones, like those relating to the Compliance Committee – see Chapter 3) are in the form of CMP[42] (i.e. plenary) decisions rather than schedules to a treaty. The 2009 Copenhagen Accord is another example of obligations not inscribed in a ratified treaty. The Accord

---

37 The poverty of Australian federal climate law gave rise to private court actions, largely levelled against the accelerating extraction of coal in Australia for export or local combustion. The achievements of bottom-up action in Australia prior to the point when the Commonwealth government started taking climate change seriously, that is, prior to 2007, should not be exaggerated. A book of essays published in 2007, entitled *Climate Law in Australia*, reviews the most important court cases in which climate change was fought 'from below'. See T. Bonyhady and P. Christoff, *Climate Law in Australia* (Federation Press, 2007). Private actions can have symbolic value but can quickly be rendered irrelevant.
38 E. Diringer, 'Letting Go of Kyoto', 479 *Nature* 291 (17 November 2011), p. 292.
39 See for example Rayner, 'How to Eat an Elephant' (2010).
40 As discussed in Chapter 2, the UNFCCC itself may be characterised as top-down on the strength of its Article 4 (2)(a), which in effect calls on developed country parties to return to 1990-level emissions by the year 2000.
41 Diringer, 'Letting Go of Kyoto' (2011), p. 292.
42 For the meaning of this and other abbreviations, see the table at the front of this book.

commits the signatory states to such emission reductions as are necessary to keep global mean surface temperature from rising more than 2°C from pre-industrial levels.[43] The Accord's achievement was to make the two-degree limit the multinational target for the post-2012 period. In our use of the term 'top-down', any measure flowing from a coordinated multilateral effort to comply with this new agreed global target of maximum acceptable warming is 'top-down'.

Since 2010, developed countries, as well as some developing countries, have pledged emission reductions for the 2013–20 period that, in aggregate, are insufficient to achieve the long-term goal of a two-degree limit for global warming.[44] Negotiations aimed at raising the ambition of the pledges are continuing.[45] The shortfall in aspiration does not change the top-down character of the process, according to our definition, so long as state negotiations are genuinely aimed at making good the shortfall.

In contrast to the top-down approach to the climate problem, bottom-up action does not implement a quantified multinational target set by an international agreement. Like the top-down method, the bottom-up method can manifest itself at any level of governance. For example, the Asia–Pacific Partnership (APP) on Clean Development and Climate – a regional agreement entered into in 2006 by Australia, the United States, and some other Pacific Rim countries – has emission reductions as one of its objectives,[46] but the reductions do not represent a share of a global target, however defined. The APP is an example of a bottom-up approach at the international level. Other examples are the Californian model (unconnected with US federal policy and thus unrelated to any global target);[47] Australia's MRET scheme discussed in Chapter 4 (in the 2000–07 period, that is, prior to Australia's ratification of the Kyoto Protocol, the scheme was achieving emission reductions through the accelerated construction of renewable energy sources, but not pursuant to any quantified international obligation – there was no such obligation then); Abu Dhabi's project to create a 'carbon-neutral' city in the desert (and other such city-level projects undertaken in countries with no national emission caps),[48] and the dozens of court actions initiated by individuals and environmental groups in industrialised countries, including Australia, with the aim of blocking the expansion of coal-fired electricity generators, coal-mining operations, etc.[49]

---

[43] UNFCCC, *Decision 2/CP.15, Copenhagen Accord* (2009), FCCC/CP/2009/11/Add.1, para. 1.
[44] See UN Environment Programme, *Bridging the Emissions Gap: A UNEP Synthesis Report* (November 2011). There is considerable scientific evidence that an increase in temperature of more than 2°C is 'dangerous' by most definitions, but this evidence also shows that there are significant risks of serious impacts in various sectors and locations with temperature increases of less than 2°C: W. Steffen, *The Critical Decade: Climate Science, Risks and Responses* (Australian Climate Commission, 2011), p. 16. Nevertheless, the 2°C guardrail has been a widely accepted and quoted political goal.
[45] UNFCCC, *Decision 2/CP.17, Outcome of the Work of the Ad Hoc Working Group on Long-Term Cooperative Action under the Convention* (2011), Part II.
[46] Asia–Pacific Partnership on Clean Development and Climate, 'Purposes of the Partnership', <http://www.asiapacificpartnership.org/english/about.aspx>.
[47] See California Environmental Protection Agency, Air Resources Board, 'Assembly Bill 32: Global Warming Solutions Act', <http://www.arb.ca.gov/cc/ab32/ab32.htm>.
[48] Masdar City, 'The Global Centre of Future Energy', <http://www.masdarcity.ae/en/>.
[49] Examples are discussed in Chapter 4.

On the basis of these definitions, we can now attempt to answer Diringer's question. Bottom-up mitigation action generally occurs where top-down measures are lacking, or as a way of *spurring* a government to make a top-down commitment to mitigation, such as by ratifying the Kyoto Protocol. Yet even where bottom-up action is occurring, because of the nature of the climate problem, top-down mitigation should never be abandoned as an objective.[50] Conceivably, a bottom-up approach to a global environmental problem could be sufficient on its own where the problem is linear. A linear environmental problem is one that gradually becomes worse as the harmful cause persists, or gradually improves as the harmful cause is withdrawn. Climate change, though, is not a linear environmental problem. There is a physical threshold in it, which we do not want to cross. If we cross that threshold, or 'tipping point', climate management will be taken out of our hands as climate change takes on a momentum of its own, unaided by us. The existence of one or more tipping elements (Box 1.2) that could allow global warming to spiral out of control makes a top-down approach to the climate problem highly advisable. Bottom-up action may therefore be regarded as an interim placeholder for top-down action,[51] for in an ideally governed world all bottom-up initiatives would be integrated into a top-down plan that imposes a ceiling on global emissions from human activities. Jacobs writes that:

> Since ... Copenhagen, it has become fashionable in some circles to discount the possibility of progress under the United Nations, and to argue that the focus should now be entirely on domestic policy in the high-emitting countries. But this is to misunderstand the interdependence of these processes ... it is implausible [to suppose] that, through solely domestic political and economic processes, every major country will simultaneously increase its targets by enough to close the gap. Only international pressure will do that.[52]

Given our definitions of 'top-down' and 'bottom-up', almost all measures under the heading of *adaptation* to climate change would be 'bottom-up'. This is because adaptation has no minimum threshold or upper limit. It is unrelated to any natural tipping point. Adaptation can be neglected, done poorly or passably, or done very well. Under the UNFCCC and the Kyoto Protocol there is a general obligation to implement and provide for adaptation.[53] But there is no quantified multinational target for adaptation, nor could there be such a thing.[54]

---

50 Shobe and Burtraw, in 'Rethinking Environmental Federalism', 3 *Climate Change Economics* (forthcoming 2012) evaluate the argument that the governmental authority for addressing an environmental problem should match as closely as possible the geographic extent of the problem itself.
51 Some proponents of a bottom-up approach see it as an interim strategy for achieving a top-down arrangement through incremental steps. Thus Diringer writes: 'In the long term, Kyoto's adherents are right: emissions commitments should be binding. Strong, sustained action to preserve a global good requires confidence that all are indeed contributing their fair share. But we need to be more realistic about how and when we get there': Diringer, 'Letting Go of Kyoto' (2011), p. 292.
52 M. Jacobs, 'Deadline 2015', 481 *Nature* 137 (12 January 2012), p. 138.
53 For example UNFCCC, Article 4(1)(b); Kyoto Protocol, Article 10(b).
54 Nevertheless, states can take a top-down approach to matters incidental to adaptation itself, such as the issue of international finance for adaptation in developing countries. The Copenhagen Accord set a fundraising

> **BOX 1.2 Tipping elements**
>
> Four examples are presented from Lenton et al.'s shortlist of ten most likely scenarios that could tip global warming past the point of human intervention.
>
> Arctic sea ice — Sea ice reflects more radiation back into space than the dark ocean surface that is exposed when the sea ice melts. As the Arctic has warmed, the sea ice has undergone thinning and shrinkage since 1988. Half the climate models predict that an ice-free Arctic during the month of September will be observed in this century. Lenton et al. conclude that 'a summer ice-loss threshold, if not already passed, may be very close and a transition could occur well within this century'.[55]
>
> Greenland ice — Warming at the periphery of the Greenland ice sheet GIS is already lowering the altitude of the ice, increasing surface temperature and causing positive feedback. Lenton et al. write that the tipping point for the GIS resides at approximately 3°C of local warming above the pre-industrial average (3°C of warming in Greenland would be reached under 1–2°C of global warming, as 'global mean temperature rise' does not manifest itself in the same way everywhere[56]). This warming would constitute 'a critical threshold beyond which there is ongoing net mass loss and the GIS shrinks radically or eventually disappears' over a period of 300 years.[57] Consequent sea-level rise would be 2–7 metres.
>
> Antarctic ice — The West Antarctic ice sheet (WAIS) could begin to collapse, triggered by the intrusion of warming ocean water beneath its ice shelves or by surface melting. It would require approximately 5°C of local warming (3+°C of global average warming) for surface atmospheric temperatures to exceed the melting point in summer on the major WAIS ice shelves. 'Although the timescale is highly uncertain, a qualitative WAIS change could occur within this millennium, with collapse within 300 years being a worst-case scenario. Rapid sea-level rise (>1 m per century) is more likely to come from the WAIS than from the GIS.'[58]
>
> Amazon forest — Deforestation in the Amazon affects the amount of precipitation in the region (a large fraction of the precipitation is recycled locally), and thus deforestation causes drying, increased summer temperatures, and increased frequency or intensity of fire, leading to forest dieback. Forest re-establishment becomes difficult under these circumstances. Global average warming of 3–4°C could itself cause drying and dieback. 'Thus, the fate of the Amazon may be determined by a complex interplay between direct land-use change and the response of regional precipitation and ENSO [El Niño–Southern Oscillation] to global forcing.'[59] The tipping point's transition timescale would be about 50 years.

target for 2010–12 (US$30 billion) and for the period starting in 2020 (at least US$100 billion per year from that time onward). Subsequent efforts to raise these funds (see Chapter 8) would be described in our terms as a top-down approach to climate adaptation finance.

[55] T. M. Lenton et al., 'Tipping Elements in the Earth's Climate System', 105(6) *Proceedings of the National Academy of Sciences of the United States of America* 1786 (2008), p. 1789.
[56] For example, warming of the Arctic region is proceeding at three times the global average: C. M. Duarte et al., 'Abrupt Climate Change in the Arctic', 2 *Nature Climate Change* 60 (February 2012), p. 60.
[57] Lenton et al., 'Tipping Elements' (2008), p. 1789.   [58] Ibid., p. 1789.   [59] Ibid., p. 1790.

Interdisciplinarity

The role of the law in the study of climate change is, we suggest, a modest one. The body of climate law has been growing, but there is still not much of it. The small amount of climate law that does exist at the international level is mostly unenforceable. In the UNFCCC itself we find only the most abstract legal principles. The Kyoto Protocol is more detailed and prescriptive, but even though this treaty has permitted the emergence of an 'Enforcement Branch' (see Chapter 3), it is a weak enforcement of insubstantial targets, and failure to achieve them would not necessarily have any consequences. (On 15 December 2011, Canada commenced its withdrawal from the Kyoto Protocol, partly to avoid penalties for not meeting its targets.[60]) An insubstantial climate law regime is the norm for the overwhelming number of national jurisdictions.[61]

In Australia, the slow pace of legal development is palpable (Chapter 4). In the same year as the coming into force of the UNFCCC, a suit to limit the human causes of climate change first made it into an Australian courtroom in the case of *Greenpeace v Redbank*,[62] but it was not until 2003 that the New South Wales government commenced its Greenhouse Gas Reduction Scheme (GGAS),[63] not until 2007 that the Australian federal government passed the first important piece of national climate change legislation (the *National Greenhouse and Energy Reporting Act*), and not until late 2011 that a minority federal Labor government, which needed the support of the Greens and independent MPs, passed legislation for a national emissions trading scheme to commence in 2015.[64]

Following on from our reflections on the notion of climate law is the related question about where to draw the line between climate law, such as it is, and other, non-legal, subject matter that it would be appropriate to include in a book on climate law. This may be understood as the second main axis that determines the scope of this book. As with the first question (on the scope of climate law), how far one moves along the axis of coverage of non-legal disciplines depends on how much *explanation* of the climate problem in its physical and social aspects one hopes to provide.

Some basic terminology concerning physical and social phenomena (such as the greenhouse effect (Box 1.1), how the primary energy supply contributes to

---

[60] UN Secretary-General, *Kyoto Protocol to the United Nations Framework Convention on Climate Change; Canada: Withdrawal* (United Nations, 16 December 2001), C.N.796.2011.TREATIES-1 (Depositary Notification).
[61] The main exception is the EU, where there is a wealth of statutory law and even case law of the European Court of Justice pertaining to the EU ETS. See, for example, M. Peeters, 'The EU ETS and the Role of the Courts: Emerging Contours in the Case of *Arcelor*', 2(1) *Climate Law* 19 (2011).
[62] *Greenpeace Australia Ltd v Redbank Power Company Pty Ltd and Singleton Council* (1994) 86 LGERA 143.
[63] See <http://www.greenhousegas.nsw.gov.au/>.
[64] Until the 2011 reform, statutes in the Australian jurisdictions consisted of a smattering of Acts in the larger states and the Commonwealth, mainly concerned with sourcing electricity from renewables, geological storage of carbon dioxide, and property rights to carbon in forest-based sequestration, as well as some 'framework' statutes that were to prepare the stage for future action by states and territories.

it, trading in emission allowances, etc.) needs to be introduced for the benefit of readers new to the subject. Other ideas, equally unavoidable, require more extensive discussion. The conceptualisation of a person's or product's 'carbon footprint' as an economic externality – here meaning the uncosted use of a natural resource, where the 'resource' is the capacity of the atmosphere to absorb additional greenhouse gases without noticeable climatic change – is clearly an economic insight into our pricing practices and their environmental blind spots. Enlightened by this insight from another discipline, the law is called upon to implement mechanisms that would internalise the cost of the carbon footprint. Taxation is one such mechanism; pricing externalities by making them scarce is another. The rationale for preferring one mechanism over the other, and the choice of a concrete design from among a range of possible designs, are largely non-legal matters: they are for an economist to find explanations for. Any choice of economic mechanism will be open to criticism on the ground of justice and fairness (for example, will the chosen measure create greater poverty?), which is closer to the neighbourhood of traditional legal concerns. In order to engage with the dilemma outlined above (tax or cap-and-trade?), some amount of economic theory has to be laid out. Thus, as we await the development of a mature climate law, we must depend heavily on other disciplines, in particular climate science and economics, to frame the problem of climate change.

There are other reasons for lawyers to be keenly interested in the climate-related findings of the non-legal disciplines. For example, scientific predictions are characterised by different levels of uncertainty. Thus sea-level rise is 'very likely' to continue to happen and is straightforwardly measurable, whereas the effect of sea-level rise on human populations (e.g. on their farming techniques or migration choices) is 'highly uncertain' and not straightforwardly observable (Box 1.3). This is obviously an important distinction for anyone working in the field, including lawyers. Lawyers also need an appreciation of the *urgency* of the climate problem. Is the climate 'destabilising' dangerously and irreversibly through human-induced warming? Are we at a tipping point, following which positive feedback loops will quickly accelerate warming, placing it beyond our control? If so, immediate and strong action is required. If destabilisation is instead only a future possibility, then a gradual pace of reform may be more appropriate. If we believe that the climate *may* be crossing a tipping point now or in the near future, but we are unsure about what the evidence is telling us, then yet another set of considerations is engaged (many lawyers would argue for a 'precautionary' approach in such a situation).

Leaving tipping points aside, if a 2°C global mean temperature rise is the most we are prepared to tolerate, how decisively must we act and by when? If action is needed urgently, national economies may need to be constrained by strong carbon-emission caps, paired with a mechanism to trade emission allowances. By contrast, a longer horizon for action might allow us to continue with business as usual while directing large sums of money towards research and development of new technologies that would become commercially

> **BOX 1.3 Degrees of agreement about climate change**
>
> The following are examples of elements of anthropogenic climate change known with different degrees of confidence. Information of this kind from non-legal disciplines is important for a climate lawyer.
>
> **The Earth's surface has warmed since 1850** *Wide agreement*
> Measurements show that, with temperatures averaged over the globe, Earth's surface has warmed by about 0.8°C (±0.2°C) since 1850. This warming has not been gradual, but has been largely concentrated in two periods, from around 1910 to around 1940 and from around 1975 to around 2000.[65]
>
> **Warming has steadily increased since the 1970s** *Wide agreement*
> When surface temperatures are averaged over ten-year periods to remove some of the year-to-year variability, each decade since the 1970s has been clearly warmer (given known uncertainties) than the one immediately preceding it. The decade 2000–09 was, globally, around 0.15°C warmer than the decade 1990–99.[66]
>
> **Sea-level rise will continue as a result of global warming** *Consensus and debate*
> Because of the thermal expansion of the ocean, it is very likely that for many centuries the rate of global sea-level rise will be at least as large as the rate of 20 cm per century that has been observed over the past century.[67]
>
> **Melting ice sheets will accelerate sea-level rise** *Not well understood*
> There is currently insufficient understanding of the enhanced melting and retreat of the ice sheets on Greenland and West Antarctica to predict exactly how much the rate of sea-level rise will increase above that observed in the past century for a given temperature increase.[68]
>
> **Tropical storm intensity will increase with sea-level rise** *Not well understood*
> Increases in the extreme high-water marks due to rises in mean sea level or changes in storm characteristics are of widespread concern. Models suggest that both tropical and extra-tropical storm intensity will increase. This implies that coastal areas will be affected to a greater degree than can be attributed to sea-level rise alone, especially for tropical and mid-latitude coastal systems.[69]

available some years or decades hence, and subsequently to phase out fossil fuels quickly. A medium-term strategy might involve gradually placing a price on greenhouse gas emissions through fiscal reform. Both the fiscal and cap-and-trade mechanisms are framework solutions that allow the degree of government intervention in the economy to be ramped up (by raising the tax or lowering the cap), or scaled back, depending on renewed scientific assessments of the severity of climate change. Merely pouring money into R&D, on the other hand, does not allow for the same high degree of control by government, because we do not know when the R&D payoff will eventuate or how beneficial it will be.

The point of this simplistic analysis is that the decision about when and how strongly to apply the brakes to GHG emissions depends on which characterisation

---

65 The Royal Society, *A Summary of the Science* (2010), p. 5.   **66** Ibid.
67 Ibid., p. 10; Editorial, 'Climate Outlook Looking Much the Same, or Even Worse', 334 *Science* 1616 (23 December 2011).
68 The Royal Society, *A Summary of the Science* (2010), p. 11.
69 Intergovernmental Panel on Climate Change, *Climate Change 2007: Impacts, Adaptation and Vulnerability: Contribution of Working Group II to the Fourth Assessment Report of the IPCC* (Cambridge University Press, 2007), p. 324. See also ibid., p. 695.

of the physical problem of climate change we accept as most accurate. For this, we must be informed by climate science. The next decision concerns the form of intervention that is to be chosen, and this depends on an economic evaluation of the competing options, on public policy priorities, and on the government's desire to hold onto or let go of the economy's reins – an ideological matter.

Lawyers resign themselves to the fact that scientists and economists, as well as engineers working at the frontiers of technology, call most of the shots in the field of climate change. In current responses to climate change, we see the law's subordinate and facilitative position in a stark light. In the end, though, agreements must be struck, institutions must be set up and governed, disputes must be resolved – and in these matters and more, lawyers come into their own. As law is mixed in with almost everything important in our society, it is a natural home for interdisciplinarians. Many lawyers are also law *reformers*. An effective reformer must be able to argue at the level of public policy – a necessarily transdisciplinary occupation.

In sum, a climate lawyer must have some understanding of how the evidence on the physical science of climate change and the adaptive responses to it combine with the available economic models, technological possibilities, and public policy concerns to determine the range of options for legal intervention. Understanding the data and framing concepts provided by other disciplines is difficult and risky, but it is achievable if undertaken cautiously. The interdisciplinary demands of studying and practising climate law may ease as the legal infrastructure grows over the years (perhaps one day it will be possible to take a course in black-letter climate law), but irrespective of the development of climate law as a discipline, a lawyer will need to spend *some* time tracking climate science, economics, technology, politics, and so forth – and this is the approach we have taken in this book.

Human values and competing interests

Why should people care about climate change? There are plenty of other problems competing for our species' attention. Even if we accept that climate change is a concern, why should it rank as a problem of highest priority? Why should we heed those who claim that we are not ranking the problem high enough? Why should we assign scarce resources to minimising the intensity of climate change, and not of some other problem?

These seem to be questions of pure value, not law, but value is built into the law, and is yet another area with which the lawyer (and those who write about the law) must be conversant. Values influence public policy and decision-making. If a person believes that global warming is harmful and should be avoided, and that it should be taken more seriously than it currently is, and if this position affects the person's public pronouncements or writings, his or her audience is entitled to know how the position is justified.

Reformist lawyers must struggle with the dominant values. A law that rests on values that most people do not actually espouse is a law whose legitimacy can be questioned. Values have been the main obstacle for pro-environment reforms. Independent polling done in the United States in 2010 (prior to the mid-term elections that year, in which the Democrats were trounced by the Republicans) found that few Americans cared about the state of the natural environment and fewer still cared about global warming.[70] In choosing their 'top priorities' for the US president and Congress, 83 per cent of respondents put strengthening the nation's economy first; improving employment was second (81 per cent) and fighting terrorism third (80 per cent).[71] Protecting the environment was ranked sixteenth in the list (at 44 per cent).[72] Dealing with global warming was ranked *twenty-first*, at the very bottom of the public's list of priorities (only 28 per cent of respondents considered it a top priority for their country).[73]

As for the trend in these opinions through time, the poll, which is taken annually in the United States, asked about climate change for the first time in 2007. The 2010 result represented the lowest ranking for climate change in the history of the poll. Addressing global warming as a top priority had fallen ten percentage points since 2007, when 38 per cent of those polled considered it a top priority (the indifference in 2010 was greatest among Republicans, with just 11 per cent considering it a top priority).[74] Another poll, towards the end of 2010, confirmed the findings of the previous one, both in the absolute level of the US public's concern about climate change and in the downward trend in expressed concern. The later poll revealed, moreover, that a smaller proportion of people believed that there is solid evidence that Earth's mean temperature is rising than believed this four years earlier: 59 per cent in 2010 compared with 79 per cent in 2006. Paradoxically, the increasing scientific certainty about global warming is accompanied by increasing doubt among the US public about the same phenomenon.[75] Doubt affects the public's values and priorities, and these in turn affect public policy in well-functioning democracies, because politicians must set their priorities to reflect those of their voting public.

Following the 1970s, environmentalism in its most modest form sought to avoid further harm to the world, so as to 'pass it down' to the next generation in a state no worse than that in which it was received. However, if most people are not environmentalists in even this modest sense – if they are content to live in a kind of universal shopping centre surrounded by an ersatz nature on the condition that they remain wealthy, healthy and entertained – then those advocating

---

[70] Pew Research Center, *Energy Concerns Fall, Deficit Concerns Rise – Public's Priorities for 2010: Economy, Jobs, Terrorism* (25 January 2010).
[71] Ibid., p. 1. [72] Ibid.
[73] See also L. Saad, 'Water Issues Worry Americans Most, Global Warming Least', <http://www.gallup.com/poll/146810/water-issues-worry-americans-global-warmingleast.aspx>.
[74] Pew Research Center, *Public's Priorities for 2010* (2010), pp. 2 and 4.
[75] Pew Research Center, *Increasing Partisan Divide on Energy Policies: Little Change in Opinions About Global Warming* (27 October 2010), pp. 1–2. The US public's remarkable lack of interest in climate change has been made the subject of a psychological study: E. M. Markowitz and A. F. Shariff, 'Climate Change and Moral Judgement', 2 *Nature Climate Change* 243 (2012).

measures against climate change are in the minority. Humans continue to expand their dominance over nature, and nature is progressively being paved over, while our species is turning in on itself and seeking sustenance in diverse worlds of its own creation. Environmental advocates are reduced to trying to save some of the natural world that remains. The newly discovered phenomenon of climate change has given them a foothold to argue for a global rescue program. The message from the polls, though, is that the need to prevent climate change is too remote a concept to be valued highly.[76]

Another hindrance to efforts against climate change is a strong current of highly elaborated and personalised human rights, first articulated in the 1960s: before the birth of environmentalism. These rights of the person overwhelmingly support the improvement of the individual's condition above competing values, and the emergent environmental values have had little chance to develop to the same extent.[77] A lawyer whose cause is a globally inclusive interest, or the interest of future generations of humans, or an ecological interest encompassing numerous non-human species, has to contend with one of the greatest political advancements in human history, namely the law's recognition of each and every living person's individual self-interest and his or her right to pursue it without interference. Human rights might be a utopian ideal, but it is one that seems to have a stronger grip on people than that of a pristine environment or of a climate in equilibrium, unaffected by mankind.[78]

Environmental values in developing countries: The case of Africa

In developing countries, human societies cocooned by wealth and human rights are relatively rare. But there, too, the fight against climate change does not appear to be a matter of high priority, despite their governments' criticism of the North for not reducing GHG emissions fast enough. The situation in Africa illustrates the point. Many countries of that continent are rich in natural resources that remain underexploited.[79] Africa's population of one billion people in 2010 is forecast to grow to 1.3 billion by 2020 and 1.5 billion by 2030, an increase

---

[76] The updated sceptical position on climate change concerns not whether the phenomenon is real but whether we may simply shrug it off. For example, James Taylor, a fellow at the Heartland Institute, a libertarian think tank in Chicago that opposes the regulation of carbon emissions, said: 'The core issue is not whether global warming is happening, or whether humans are involved, but whether it is a crisis' (J. Tollefson, 'Evolution Advocate Turns to Climate', 481 *Nature* 248 (19 January 2012), p. 248).
[77] This is why some scholars argue that ethical obligations exist at the *state* level in addition to the personal level: see, for example, J. C. Dernbach and D. A. Brown, 'The Ethical Responsibility to Reduce Energy Consumption', 37(985) *Hofstra Law Review* (2009).
[78] See G. Wagner and R. J. Zeckhauser, 'Climate Policy: Hard Problem, Soft Thinking', 110 *Climatic Change* 507 (2012), p. 519 ('[T]he emission of carbon in significant quantity must be treated like the exploitation of children: something not to be done – not because it would not be profitable, but because it would not be ethical or tolerated').
[79] P. Collier, *The Bottom Billion: Why the Poorest Countries Are Failing and What Can Be Done About It* (Oxford University Press, 2008).

of half a billion people in the course of twenty years.[80] These two facts point to a path towards economic development and increased wealth for a growing number of people, which potentially entails significant harmful consequences for the natural environment of the continent and for the global commons. The harm will be proportional to the quantity of the as-yet-untapped natural resources that are successfully exploited. Even if low-impact methods are used, the overall environmental impact on the continent could be enormous. Historical experience with economic growth is that per capita GHG emissions increase with income, even when low-impact technology is factored in.[81]

Presently, the African population is mostly poor (the GNI per capita in sub-Saharan Africa was US$1126, or US$3 per day, in 2009)[82] and living in poorly governed polities (many governments in Africa are corrupt and undemocratic),[83] and there are few public services. As a result, the indicators in all essential areas of life in Africa today are miserable. Child mortality for the continent as a whole during 2005–10 was 82.6 infant deaths per 1000 live births (compared with 4.1 in Western Europe);[84] in sub-Saharan Africa in 2008 life expectancy at birth was only 52 years.[85] In the same region in the same year the completion rate for *primary* school was 64 per cent.[86] Personal security and the rule of law are still a distant dream for most Africans.[87] Official unemployment levels are high compared with the West (in relatively industrialised South Africa the unemployment rate in 2008 was 20 per cent for males and 26 per cent for females),[88] and the development of Africa's agricultural and manufacturing sectors is a 'dismal' twin failure, according to the International Labour Office.[89] Persons holding jobs are mostly not occupied in 'decent work' (a technical term):[90] in 2009, 63.7 per cent of those with jobs in Africa's least developed countries were the working poor

---

[80] United Nations, *World Population Prospects: The 2010 Revision*, online database at <http://esa.un.org/unpd/wpp/index.htm>.
[81] B. Melenberg, H. R. J. Vollebergh and E. Dijkgraaf, *Grazing the Commons: Global Carbon Emissions Forever?* TILEC Discussion Paper No. 2011–020 (Tilburg University, 2011), and G. P. Peters et al., 'Rapid Growth in CO_2 Emissions after the 2008–2009 Global Financial Crisis', 2 *Nature Climate Change* 2 (January 2012), p. 2 ('For recent decades, the growth in global CO_2 emissions can be explained mainly by the growth in economic activity corrected for decreases in the fossil-fuel carbon intensity').
[82] World Bank, <http://data.worldbank.org/region/SSA>.
[83] According to the Ibrahim Index (see below) for 2010, Mauritius was ranked first in governance among Africa's states, with a score of 83/100, whereas Somalia was last with 7.9/100. About half of all African countries scored below 50 on the scale. See <http://www.moibrahimfoundation.org/en/section/the-ibrahim-index>. On corruption in Africa, see also International Labour Office, *Growth, Employment and Decent Work in the Least Developed Countries: Report of the International Labour Office for the Fourth Conference on the Least Developed Countries, Istanbul, 9–13 May 2011* (Geneva, 2011), pp. 45–6.
[84] United Nations, *World Population Prospects: The 2008 Revision*, online database at <http://esa.un.org/unpd/wpp2008/index.htm>.
[85] The World Bank, <http://data.worldbank.org/region/SSA>. [86] Ibid.
[87] See the Safety and Rule of Law scores in the Ibrahim Index for 2010, according to which 21 of the 53 African countries scored below 50 on a scale to 100: <http://www.moibrahimfoundation.org/en/section/the-ibrahim-index>.
[88] World Bank, <http://data.worldbank.org/indicator/SL.UEM.TOTL.MA.ZS>, <http://data.worldbank.org/indicator/SL.UEM.TOTL.FE.ZS>.
[89] International Labour Office, *Growth, Employment and Decent Work* (2011), pp. 30–1. See also N. Gilbert, 'Dirt Poor', 483 *Nature* 525 (29 March 2012).
[90] See <http://www.ilo.org/global/about-the-ilo/decent-work-agenda/lang–en/index.htm>.

(defined by an income not exceeding US$1.25 per day);[91] only 19.1 per cent of 'employed' persons in those countries were classed by the ILO as employers or wage-and-salary workers, with the remainder (80.9 per cent) falling into the categories of own-account workers and unpaid family workers – that is, they were in vulnerable and low-productivity employment.[92]

Under these conditions, even the simplest environmental problems are not likely to be effectively addressed. They will be given low priority, and the know-how and capacity to deal with them will be lacking. Africa's population is understandably focused on securing improvements to basic services, economic opportunities, and human and political rights. They are not likely to be focused on the comparatively distant and abstract problem of climate change. In 2011, in the uprisings that became known as the Arab Spring, the demands of Arabic-speaking populations in northern Africa were loud and clear: in essence, people were demanding jobs and better governance. While Mediterranean Africa is wealthier than the sub-Saharan part (Egypt's GNI per capita in 2009 was US$2070[93] and Tunisia's US$3720),[94] the relative advantage is no cause for contentment in those countries. Their frame of reference is a prosperous and free Europe across the Mediterranean. Africa's potential transformation into a continent of strong economic growth is conditional on a freedom to prosper materially, and this condition tells us something about the likely place of environmental values in the transformation.

For the particulars, there is no better place to look than the Ibrahim Index.[95] The Index was developed by the Mo Ibrahim Foundation, an organisation that encourages better governance in Africa as a catalyst for its economic transformation.[96] The Index is built from the most comprehensive collection of qualitative and quantitative data assessing governance in Africa. As such, it has become a critical reference point for decision-making, both by African governments (angling for a better rank in the Index) and by donor countries and international organisations (concerned to direct investment and aid to where it will produce the best results). The Index ranks countries on about 100 different equally weighted indicators, only *three* of which could be said to be linked in some way with the mitigation of climate change.[97] From this perspective, the values that inform Africa's economic transformation are overwhelmingly *not* about maintaining a stable global mean surface temperature.

---

[91] International Labour Office, *Growth, Employment and Decent Work* (2011), p. 8.   [92] Ibid., pp. 9, 41.
[93] World Bank, <http://data.worldbank.org/country/egypt-arab-republic>.
[94] World Bank, <http://data.worldbank.org/country/tunisia>.
[95] Mo Ibrahim Foundation, 'The Ibrahim Index', <http://www.moibrahimfoundation.org/en/section/the-ibrahim-index>.
[96] Mo Ibrahim Foundation, <http://www.moibrahimfoundation.org/en>.
[97] Namely, Environmental Sustainability, Role of Environment in Policy Formulation, and Land and Water for Agriculture. See <http://www.moibrahimfoundation.org/en/section/the-ibrahim-index>. For another example of this kind, see International Labour Office, *Growth, Employment and Decent Work* (2011), pp. 61–74, where a recommended 'new approach' to 'catching-up growth and productive transformation' in Africa does not linger on any environmental considerations.

Whether we look at the United States or at Africa, then, public values suggest that climate change is of little concern. There is much recent talk of 'sustainable development', especially as a condition of aid to developing countries, but on the current evidence the widespread implementation of this constraint on development remains doubtful.

Is popular apathy a result of misinformation?

How much we care about the effects of climate change is thus as important a precondition for timely and resourceful action as the position we take on the reality and intensity of global warming and the proximity of climate tipping points. We have seen in the results of US polling that there is no guarantee that what scientists portray as a dangerous change to the climatic system will be perceived in the same way by all sections of the voting public. For an optimist, this raises the possibility that a lack of public concern, or a concern lowly ranked, could be the result of misinformation. People who are not concerned about climate change or about preserving the natural environment may believe or assume that their lifestyles will continue to improve despite a changing climate. They may assume that they will be able to adjust to the climatic changes just as they are able to adjust to the many other changes that confront them. On an optimistic analysis, what is lacking is better information.

An optimist's argument to counter the general lack of interest could attempt to show that, with higher global temperatures, the rate of species' loss would increase, extreme weather events would become more intense, and rising seas would cause inundation of low-lying islands and delta regions, leading to the relocation of millions of people. Arguments of this kind are often made and may have some beneficial effect. Made in these terms, however, the argument does not show that human beings would be worse off on the whole. In raising the prospect of some damage to nature and some human suffering, the argument misses a critical point: future generations *might be better off*, even after the effects of global warming have been taken into account, depending on the factors chosen in making the assessment of 'better off' and the weighting given to them. The ill-aimed counterargument also presumes a degree of altruistic sympathy (environmentalism, humanism) towards island-dwelling people and other, non-human species – a sentiment that in fact may not be very widespread.

If it is possible to mount a more direct argument to show that the assumption about increasing human well-being under strong climatic change is erroneous, then should it not be possible, rationally, to change the value-set of the average person? The kind of information presented for this purpose might look at the impact of global warming on food production. A 2011 study of climate trends and global crop yields in the period 1980–2008 concluded that models linking yields of commodity crops to weather 'indicate that global maize and wheat production declined by 3.8% and 5.5%, respectively, compared to a counterfactual without climate trends'.[98] Information about such gradual, almost imperceptible effects of climate change might shock some people into new ways of thinking. Easier to make would be the weaker argument that a responsible evaluation of the assumption about ever-increasing human well-being under strong climatic change should lead people to resile from that assumption, because of the *risk* that it is wrong. But the weaker argument sounds technical and is unlikely to inspire.

In mounting such retorts, we recognise the importance of values in the climate change debate without falling into a helpless relativism. Still, the argument about the misery of human life in the future under 'business-as-usual' GHG emissions, as opposed to its greater desirability under a scenario of mitigation, is difficult to make convincingly, even where the language of certainty is replaced with the language of risk.[99] There are too many factors to consider and too many unknowns. So we may feel that, despite the rapid advances in the scientific understanding of climate change, we are stuck in a kind of de facto relativism because we do not have enough information to overturn the assumptions on which the values favouring inaction are based. Alternatively, we may feel that it is only a matter of time before we have the necessary information to expose the false assumptions and make the case that our civilisation is in danger.

Knock-out argument or not, lawyers will need to engage with the values that underlie the priorities of the day. For this, they will need an understanding of what the scientific consensus is saying about the expected impacts of climate change under any one of several scenarios. They will also need to be aware of the existing economic and technological pathways to avoiding the worst consequences of global warming.

Our continuing dependence on fossil fuels

Human activity releases greenhouse gases into the atmosphere through several processes. One of the most important, as is well known, is the combustion of fossil fuels.[100] A critical question, therefore, is: How committed are we to burning

---

98 D. B. Lobell, W. Schlenker and J. Costa-Roberts, 'Climate Trends and Global Crop Production since 1980', *Sciencexpress* 1 (5 May 2011), p. 1. See also Oxfam, *Growing a Better Future: Food Justice in a Resource-Constrained World* (2011), at <http://www.oxfam.org/en/grow/reports/growing-better-future>; and Justin Gillis, 'A Warming Planet Struggles to Feed Itself', *The New York Times*, 4 June 2011 (based on interviews with more than 50 agricultural experts working in nine countries: 'These experts say that in coming decades, farmers need to withstand whatever climate shocks come their way while roughly doubling the amount of food they produce to meet rising demand. And they need to do it while reducing the considerable environmental damage caused by the business of agriculture').
99 See, for example, the rather weak and hesitant statements in UN Development Programme, *Human Development Report 2010 – The Real Wealth of Nations: Pathways to Human Development* (2010), pp. 102–3.
100 When coal, which is mostly carbon, is burnt, CO_2 is released. The formula is: $C + O_2 \rightarrow CO_2$ + Energy. Natural gas is mostly constituted of methane (CH_4). When methane is combusted, it releases CO_2 and water vapour: $CH_4 + 2O_2 \rightarrow 2H_2O + CO_2$ + Energy. The global warming potential of methane is much higher than that of CO_2, so even though methane combustion leads to CO_2, it is better to burn methane than to allow it to escape.

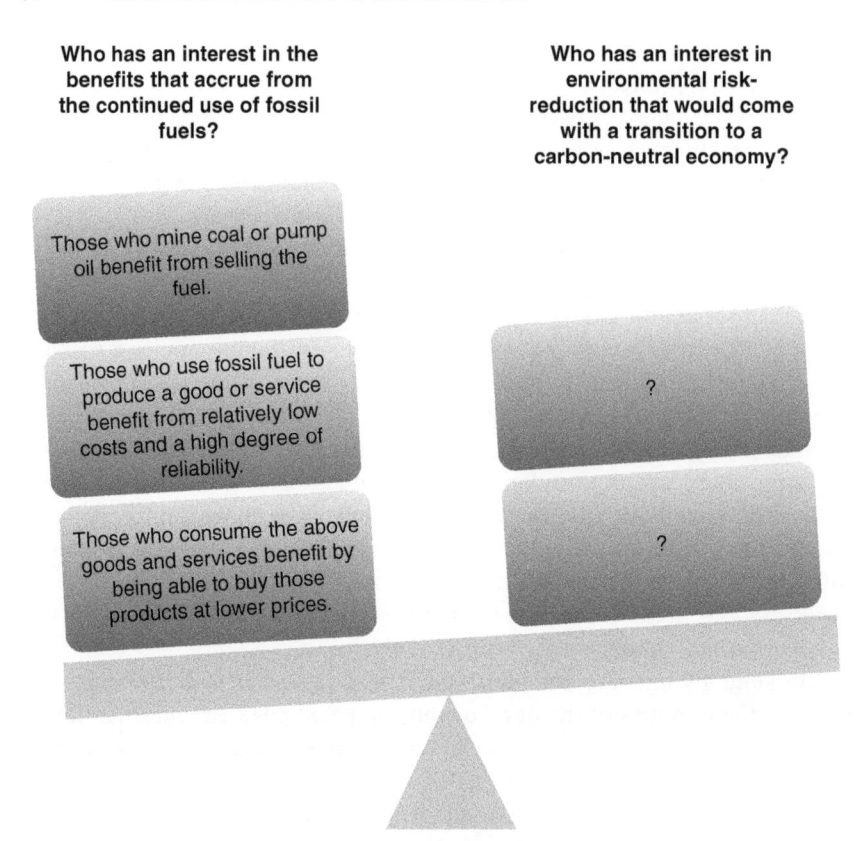

Figure 1.1 Fill in the gaps: Who is not invested in the status quo?
Some candidates for the right-hand column might include inhabitants of low-lying Pacific Island states, future human generations, and coral reefs. The point of the exercise is to see whether enough 'interest' can be found, to be added to the right side of the scale to balance or outweigh the interest in uninterrupted use of fossil fuels for energy in the left side of the scale.
Source: Based on comments by K. Caldeira and S.J. Davis, 'Accounting for Carbon Dioxide Emissions: A Matter of Time' (24 May 2011) 108(21) *Proceedings of the National Academy of Sciences of the United States of America* 8533, p. 8534.

fossil fuels into the future? Or to put it another way: How invested are we in the status quo? (See Figure 1.1.)

Between 1980 and 2007 world primary energy demand,[101] which is mainly met by fossil fuels, grew by 2 per cent per year. Under an optimistic scenario in which states take measures to reduce their dependence on fossil fuels, the International Energy Agency forecasts continued growth in primary energy demand between 2008 and 2035 at a rate of 1.2 per cent per year (to be contrasted with 1.4 per cent for the business-as-usual projection), with fossil fuels accounting for more than

---

101 For the IEA's definition of 'primary energy demand', see International Energy Agency, *World Energy Outlook 2009* (2009), p. 670.

half of the increase.[102] Under all IEA scenarios, even the most optimistic, fossil fuels remain the dominant energy source in 2035 (the outer year of the projection), although their share in the overall primary fuel mix varies depending on the assumptions made.[103] In the most likely case for 2035, oil's share drops to 28 per cent (from 33 per cent in 2008), demand for coal rises through around 2020 and starts to decline closer to 2035, and demand for natural gas, which generally has lower carbon emissions per unit of energy,[104] far surpasses that of other fossil fuels throughout the period.[105] Under this scenario, annual energy-related emissions of GHGs rise from 29 gigatonnes of carbon dioxide equivalent (CO_2 eq.) in 2008 to 35 gigatonnes in 2035: a 17 per cent increase.[106]

While oil's share of the energy mix declines proportionately into the future, there is one sector where oil will dominate as far ahead as we can see: transport. At present, 95 per cent of all transport runs on oil. Under the IEA's most optimistic scenario, oil is expected to fuel over half of all transport in 2050.[107]

The IEA also predicts that 93 per cent of the projected increase in world primary energy demand will be in non-OECD countries, with China accounting for 22 per cent of world demand, up from 17 per cent in 2010.[108] Back in 2000, when the United States was still the world's largest energy user, its energy consumption was twice the size of China's. By 2009, China had overtaken the United States to become the world's largest consumer of energy.[109] China's huge domestic market was, in 2010, underdeveloped, with per capita energy consumption at only one-third of the OECD average.[110] In terms of electricity supply, China is projected to add, in just fifteen years, a generating capacity equivalent to the 2010 installed capacity of the whole of the United States.[111] Most of it will be coal-fired.[112] (The predicted large increase in coal-fired generation in non-OECD countries will be partially offset by a fall in electricity generated from coal in OECD countries.)[113]

A report released in December 2011 by BankTrack, a network of civil society organisations that investigates the banking industry, found that banks' total investments in coal-fired electricity in 2010 were almost twice what they were in 2005 when the Kyoto Protocol came into effect.[114]

In many developing countries, human population growth will continue to outstrip the ability of the governments of those countries to meet the growing

---

102 International Energy Agency, *World Energy Outlook 2010* (2010), pp. 4–5.   103 Ibid., p. 4.
104 However, see Editorial, 'Gas and Air', 482 *Nature* 131 (9 February 2012), p. 132 ('[M]ethane emissions from natural-gas operations could be substantially higher ... than was thought ... [T]he climatic benefits [of natural gas] are murky at best').
105 International Energy Agency, *World Energy Outlook 2010* (2010), p. 5.
106 Ibid., p. 11. This represents the 650 ppm scenario of 3.5+ °C warming. (On the various warming scenarios, see Chapter 2.) For the 450 ppm scenario, emissions must reach a peak of 32 Gt just before 2020, then slide to 22 Gt by 2035 (ibid.).
107 S. van Renssen, 'The Final Carbon Frontier', 2 *Nature Climate Change* 11 (January 2012), p. 11.
108 International Energy Agency, *World Energy Outlook 2010* (2010), p. 5.   109 Ibid.   110 Ibid.
111 Ibid., p. 8.   112 A. Petherick, 'Dirty Money', 2 *Nature Climate Change* 72 (2012), p. 73.
113 International Energy Agency, *World Energy Outlook 2010* (2010), p. 8.
114 Petherick, 'Dirty Money' (2012), p. 72. Elaborate greenwashing, such as JPMorgan Chase's slogan 'helping the world transition to a low-carbon economy' and Citi's 'most innovative bank in climate change', is used to cover up these choices (ibid., p. 73).

demand for energy, thus maintaining a long tail of unmet energy demand. In 2010, 1.4 billion people (over 20 per cent of the world's population) lacked access to electricity.[115] With the population in developing countries expected to grow by many hundreds of millions by 2030, the IEA predicts that even by that date, 1.2 billion people will still have no access to electricity.[116] The tail will remain long for a long time, meaning that for decades into the future there will exist a suppressed demand for energy, which gradual increases in wealth will unleash.

Several developing countries are not only committed to economic development powered by fossil fuels; their economies are propped up by the production of oil and gas. Kazakhstan, Nigeria and Venezuela are examples of states in that situation, as are, of course, the Gulf States, which under the UNFCCC classification are also 'developing'.[117] These countries would require assistance to switch to climatically sustainable economies, but would also have to be compensated for the massive loss of export income resulting from the winding down of their fossil-fuel extraction industry.[118] Australia, as a developed country, is in an even worse position, because while coal exports prop up *its* economy, no one would suggest compensating the country for ceasing those exports. Thus several countries rich in fossil-fuel deposits have a strong incentive to continue mining them, for without them they would risk economic ruin.

According to the IEA, although a transformation of the global energy system is urgently needed, little is being done to ensure that it happens quickly enough.[119] Non-fossil sources are predicted to grow, but too slowly. Global demand for nuclear power is predicted to increase only slightly, with its share rising from 6 per cent in 2008 to 8 per cent in 2035.[120] (This estimate predates the 2011 nuclear disaster in Japan; it thus also predates Germany's consequent decision to scale down its nuclear power program.) The use of renewable energy (hydropower, wind, solar, geothermal, biomass, and marine energy) is forecast to triple in absolute terms by 2035, increasing its share of total primary energy demand from 7 per cent to 14 per cent.[121] Hydropower, whose infrastructure often takes a severe environmental toll, will continue to dominate among renewables.[122] This is in contrast to electricity produced from solar photovoltaics, which despite

---

115 International Energy Agency, *World Energy Outlook 2010* (2010), p. 14. In Kenya and Uganda, for example, only 1 per cent of rural households had access to electricity in 2004: S. Karekezi and J. Kimani, 'Have Power Sector Reforms Increased Access to Electricity among the Poor in East Africa?', 8(4) *Energy for Sustainable Development* 10 (2004), p. 10. Having no access to electricity, poor people use LPG where it is affordable, or else fall back on kerosene and charcoal or other biomass: see, for example, G. Bravo, R. Kozulj and R. Landaveri, 'Energy Access in Urban and Peri-Urban Buenos Aires', 12(4) *Energy for Sustainable Development* 56 (2008); and S. Karekezi, J. Kimani and O. Onguru, 'Energy Access among the Urban Poor in Kenya', 12(4) *Energy for Sustainable Development* 38 (2008).
116 International Energy Agency, *World Energy Outlook 2010* (2010), p. 14.
117 An enormous growth in oil and gas production in Kazakhstan and Turkmenistan is forecast all the way up to 2030. The economic development of these two countries hinges almost entirely on proceeds from their fossil-fuel exports: ibid., p. 10.
118 This issue, under the heading of 'response measures', is being kept alive on the UNFCCC agenda by oil-exporting countries: see UNFCCC, *Decision 8/CP.17, Forum and work programme on the impact of the implementation of response measures* (2011).
119 International Energy Agency, *World Energy Outlook 2010* (2010), p. 3.   120 Ibid., p. 5.
121 Ibid.   122 Ibid., p. 9.

its expected very rapid increase, is likely to have a share of only 2 per cent of global energy generation by 2035.[123]

Fossil fuels are and will remain plentiful, and with no global price on carbon-based greenhouse gas emissions (note that not all GHGs are carbon-based), coal and natural gas will remain relatively cheap sources of energy, to a greater extent than oil. A telling indicator is the staggering investment in infrastructure for the extraction and distribution of natural gas. In 2011 there was a glut of global gas-supply *capacity* of over 200 billion cubic metres (the difference between supply capacity and the volume of gas actually traded), an amount equal to half of all Middle East natural gas in 2010.[124] We have already mentioned the doubling since 2005 of investment in coal. With respect to oil, with the warming of the Arctic 'the race is on' for access to its vast untapped fossil fuel resources. Norway's oil and gas company Statoil hopes to extract hundreds of millions of barrels of oil equivalent a year from new wells in the Arctic.[125] A view of our long-term commitment to fossil fuels is afforded by the vastness of the exploration, extraction and transportation infrastructure.

This evidence also reveals a gulf between the reality of our dependence on fossil fuels and the talk of abatement of climate change at international conferences. The Global Financial Crisis made a small dent in expected emissions, but also turned minds away from climate change and towards economic growth. Meanwhile, we have returned to business-as-usual emissions.[126] In Australia:

> The surreal carbon tax debate is taking place amid the biggest fossil fuel investment boom in Australia's history. Just last week, Queensland Premier Anna Bligh unveiled a $6.2 billion plan to expand Abbot Point into one of the world's biggest coal ports, capable of shipping out close to 300 million tonnes a year. The week before, Julia Gillard was at Gladstone to launch Santos's $16bn project to suck vapour out of Queensland coal seams and chill it into liquefied natural gas. [Australia's Deputy Prime Minister and Treasurer] Wayne Swan predicted 'a very big role for the Australian coal industry'.[127]

As of December 2009, when the Copenhagen Accord was signed at the 15th COP of the UNFCCC,[128] the position of most countries officially became one not of preventing global warming, but, as we noted earlier, of avoiding warming in excess of a global average of 2°C above pre-industrial times.[129] As part of the Accord, all of the world's major economies pledged emission reductions for the

---

123 Ibid.   **124** Ibid., p. 8.
125 Q. Schiermeier, 'The Great Arctic Oil Race Begins', 482 *Nature* 13 (2 February 2012), p. 13. Note: 'We are not running out of oil, but we are running out of oil that can be produced easily and cheaply': J. Murray and D. King, 'Oil's Tipping Point Has Passed', 481 *Nature* 433 (26 January 2012), p. 434.
126 The GFC had only a minimal impact on emission growth in the larger developing economies. Carbon dioxide emissions in developing countries grew 4.4 per cent in 2008, 3.9 per cent in 2009, and 7.6 per cent in 2010. The GFC caused a 40 per cent decrease in these countries' emission *growth* in 2009 (there was still growth in emissions in that year, but less of it) compared with the trend since 2000: Peters et al., 'Rapid Growth in CO_2 Emissions after the 2008–2009 Global Financial Crisis' (2012), p. 2.
127 Michael Stutchbury, 'Carbon Price May Take the Heat Off', *The Australian* (online edition), 7 June 2011.
128 UNFCCC, *Copenhagen Accord* (2009).
129 Ibid., para. 2. The 2°C target was reaffirmed a year later in a decision of the UNFCCC parties: UNFCCC, *Decision 1/CP.16, The Cancun Agreements: Outcome of the Work of the Ad Hoc Working Group on Long-Term Cooperative Action under the Convention* (2010), FCCC/CP/2010/7/Add.1, para. 4.

years following 2012 and up to 2020.[130] As we also noted earlier, countries are still trying to agree to further emission cuts, because studies have shown that even if all the pledged cuts were fully implemented, the 2°C ceiling would still be exceeded. The pledges of the Accord are in fact in line with stabilising the concentration of GHGs at over 650 ppm of CO_2 eq., resulting in a likely temperature rise of more than 3.5°C.[131] (For comparison, a greater than 66 per cent chance of limiting global temperature increase to below 2°C would imply GHG concentrations at equilibrium to be around 415 ppm of CO_2 eq.[132]) The IEA has expressed serious doubt that the necessary economic transformation away from fossil fuels could happen fast enough to achieve the official objective of a 2°C limit.[133]

A very brief introduction to the science of climate change

The science of climate change is vast and complex. It deals with the biophysical causes and impacts of human-induced warming on a global scale, in the past and in the present. On this information, it builds forecasts about the future. The extent of the subject may be gleaned from the IPCC's report on *The Physical Science Basis* of climate change, the first volume in the IPCC's most recent (fourth) assessment report: it runs close to a thousand dense pages.[134] The 'impacts' on Earth's physical systems and organisms are discussed in a second volume of the same size.[135] (A third large volume covers the costs and benefits of different approaches to the mitigation and avoidance of climate change.[136])

Even climate scientists must find it difficult, we might imagine, to stay abreast of all the discoveries and advances occurring in the various fields contributing to our understanding of climate change. The IPCC, itself a vast organisation, regularly surveys and synthesises the thousands of independent studies conducted each year into the increasingly abstruse questions of climate change.[137] This help is at least as valuable to scientists as to policy-makers.

---

130 UNFCCC, *Copenhagen Accord* (2009), para. 4. For a compilation of the pledges, see <http://unfccc.int/meetings/cop_15/copenhagen_accord/items/5264.php>, and pursuant to UNFCCC, *Decision 1/CP.16* (2010), para. 36, the revised compilation: Secretariat (UNFCCC), *Compilation of Economy-Wide Emission Reduction Targets to Be Implemented by Parties Included in Annex I to the Convention* (7 June 2011), FCCC/SB/2011/INF.1/Rev.1.
131 UN Environment Programme, *Bridging the Emissions Gap* (November 2011), p. 12.
132 Ibid., p. 17.
133 International Energy Agency, *World Energy Outlook 2010* (2010), p. 3. See also International Energy Agency, 'Prospect of Limiting the Global Increase in Temperature to 2°C Is Getting Bleaker', <http://www.iea.org/index_info.asp?id=1959>.
134 Intergovernmental Panel on Climate Change, *Climate Change 2007: The Physical Science Basis: Contribution of Working Group I to the Fourth Assessment Report of the IPCC* (Cambridge University Press, 2007).
135 Intergovernmental Panel on Climate Change, *4AR: Working Group II* (2007).
136 Intergovernmental Panel on Climate Change, *Climate Change 2007: Mitigation of Climate Change: Contribution of Working Group III to the Fourth Assessment Report of the IPCC* (Cambridge University Press, 2007).
137 The IPCC has so far undertaken four assessments of climate change: the First Assessment Report was completed in 1990; the Second Assessment Report in 1995; the Third Assessment Report in 2001; and the Fourth Assessment Report in 2007. See also Table 1.1. A Fifth Assessment Report will be completed in 2014.

How then is the non-scientist to get a purchase on the material? Fortunately, high-quality outlines of the science of climate change that are more accessible than the IPCC's have been produced at regular intervals, for policy-makers specifically[138] and for non-scientists in general (both policy-makers and the general public).[139] Considering the accessibility and currency of such overviews, there is little reason to attempt to produce another one here. We have thus limited our discussion to some introductory points on the science of climate change, with the aim of facilitating further exploration by the reader.

Proof of anthropogenic climate change and all that it entails for life on Earth is an argument in several steps. Each step is associated with a body of evidence. The argument may be represented in ten simplified steps:

1. Certain natural and industrial gases in the atmosphere have the effect of trapping energy close to the earth's surface: the greenhouse effect.

Solar radiation is absorbed by the earth's surface, then emitted back into space as infrared radiation. The greenhouse gases in the atmosphere absorb the infrared radiation leaving the earth and reflect some of it back to the earth's surface (radiative forcing). See also Box 1.1.

Greenhouse gases have atmospheric lifetimes that differ greatly in length. Their potential to reflect heat also differs greatly.[140] For example, methane (CH_4) has a shorter atmospheric lifetime than CO_2, but a higher warming potential. One tonne of CH_4 released now has 25 times the impact over the next 100 years as 1 tonne of CO_2 released now. If the assessment were made over 20 years, a CH_4 release would have 72 times the warming impact as the same amount of a CO_2 release. Conversely, avoiding 1 tonne of CH_4 emissions now would, over a 100-year time frame, be as climate-friendly as avoiding 25 tonnes of CO_2 emissions now (or avoiding 72 tonnes, if the time frame is 20 years). The industrial gas sulphur hexafluoride(SF_6) has 22 800 times the warming power of CO_2 (over a period of 100 years) and remains in the atmosphere for around 3200 years.[141] Like the gaseous equivalent of modern-era trash, all the SF_6 ever emitted by humans is still floating in the atmosphere.

At the Durban CMP, the Kyoto Protocol parties decided to extend the list of Annex B gases for the Protocol's second commitment period by adding nitrogen

---

138 For example Intergovernmental Panel on Climate Change, *Climate Change 2007: Synthesis Report* (WMO, UNEP, 2007); N. Stern, *The Economics of Climate Change: The Stern Review* (Cambridge University Press, 2007); The Royal Society, *Summary of the Science* (2010); R. Garnaut, *The Garnaut Review 2011: Australia in the Global Response to Climate Change* (Cambridge University Press, 2011), pp. 1–18; and Steffen, *The Critical Decade* (2011).
139 For example T. F. Flannery, *The Weather Makers: How Man Is Changing the Climate and What It Means for Life on Earth* (Atlantic Monthly Press, 2005); E. Kolbert, *Field Notes from a Catastrophe: A Frontline Report on Climate Change* (Bloomsbury, 2007); A. Gore, *An Inconvenient Truth: The Planetary Emergency of Global Warming and What We Can Do About It* (Bloomsbury, 2006); L. D. D. Harvey, 'An Overview of Climate Change Science in 1977 Marking the Publication of Volume 100 of *Climatic Change*', 100 *Climatic Change* 15 (2010); B. McKibben, *Eaarth: Making a Life on a Tough New Planet* (Henry Holt, 2010); and Steffen, *The Critical Decade* (2011).
140 For a list of all known greenhouse gases, which also shows their lifetimes and global warming potentials, see Intergovernmental Panel on Climate Change, *4AR: Working Group I* (2007), pp. 212–13, Table 2.14 (as corrected at <http://www.ipcc.ch/publications_and_data/ar4/wg1/en/ch2s2-10-2.html#table-2-14>).
141 See ibid.

trifluoride (NF_3).[142] They noted that other new GHGs with high global warming potentials listed in the IPCC Fourth Assessment Report 'are not yet produced in significant quantities but ... should be further monitored to identify whether it is necessary to address them as part of mitigation commitments'.[143]

2. The concentration of these greenhouse gases in the atmosphere has markedly increased in recent decades.

The Keeling Curve, summarising daily measurements of atmospheric CO_2 at Mauna Loa Observatory since 1958, is a famous representation of the increasing concentration of the most plentiful of the GHGs.[144] The scientist Charles Keeling found that at the end of each annual carbon cycle[145] there was more CO_2 in the air than the year before.

3. The observed increase in the concentration of GHGs is attributable to human activity.

In particular, it is attributable to the intense mining and combustion of fossil fuels over the last century. Methane and nitrous oxide, which are the two most important anthropogenic GHGs after CO_2, are released in vast quantities from agriculture and landfills, among other sources. There is no other known source of the otherwise naturally occurring GHGs (CO_2, CH_4, and nitrous oxide) to explain the anomaly.

4. Earth's average surface temperature has increased over the past century, and its rise has accelerated in recent decades.

According to the World Meteorological Organization, global temperatures in 2011 were the tenth highest on record, with thirteen of the warmest years on record occurring after 1997. The global average surface temperature over 1991–2011 was 0.4°C higher than the 1961–90 average.[146]

Evidence of the changing state of snow, ice and frozen ground is consistent with the warming of the earth's surface.[147] In 2011, the extent of Arctic sea ice was the second lowest on record (Figure 1.2); its minimum was 35 per cent below the 1979–2000 average minimum.[148] Near complete loss of the summer sea ice is forecast for the middle of this century, if not before.[149] Most glaciers and mountain ice-caps around the world are in retreat.[150]

---

[142] Kyoto Protocol, *Decision 4/CMP.7, Greenhouse Gases, Sectors and Source Categories, Common Metrics to Calculate the Carbon Dioxide Equivalence of Anthropogenic Emissions by Sources and Removals by Sinks, and Other Methodological Issues* (2011), para. 1.
[143] Ibid., para. 2.
[144] The Keeling Curve has been widely reproduced. A version of it was published in C. D. Keeling, 'Rewards and Penalties of Monitoring the Earth', 23 *Annual Review of Energy and the Environment* 25 (1998), p. 53.
[145] Annual carbon cycle: Leaf growth in spring and summer takes CO_2 out of the air; in autumn and winter, as the leaves fall and decompose, CO_2 is given off again. Because there is more vegetation in the northern hemisphere, the atmospheric impact of that cycle predominates.
[146] World Meteorological Organization, Press Release No. 935, <http://www.wmo.int/pages/mediacentre/press_releases/pr_935_en.html> (29 November 2011); see also UN Environment Programme, *Bridging the Emissions Gap* (November 2011), p. 16.
[147] Steffen, *The Critical Decade* (2011), p. 8.
[148] World Meteorological Organization, Press Release No. 935; Duarte et al., 'Abrupt Climate Change in the Arctic' (2012), p. 61.
[149] Duarte et al., 'Abrupt Climate Change in the Arctic' (2012), p. 61.
[150] Steffen, *The Critical Decade* (2011), p. 11. See also Intergovernmental Panel on Climate Change, *4AR: Working Group II* (2007), Table 6.3, p. 323, and p. 694.

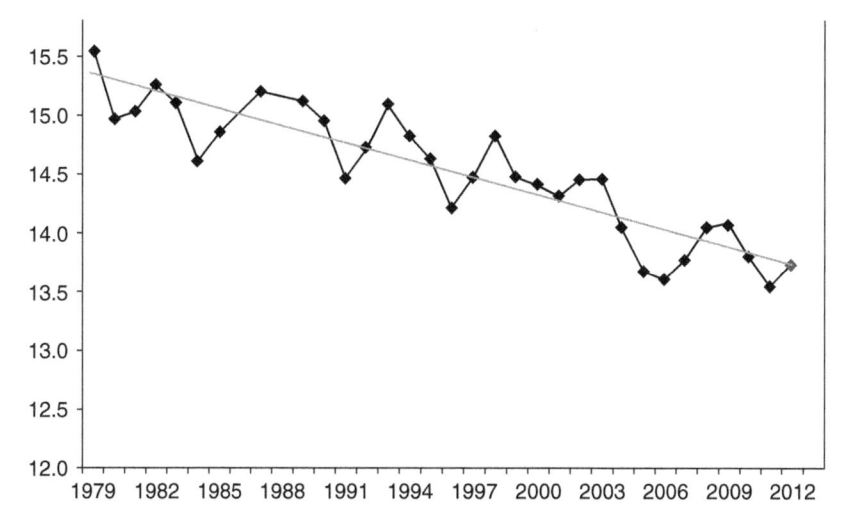

Figure 1.2 Extent of monthly Arctic sea ice, 1979–2012, in millions of square kilometres.
The nodes in the irregular curve represent the extent of sea ice in the month of April; the straight line that cuts through it shows the linear rate of decline.
Source: US National Snow and Ice Data Center, <http://nsidc.org/arcticseaicenews/>.

5. The steady increase in atmospheric greenhouse gases from human activity is the main cause of the observed increase in surface temperature.

We know from the ice-core record that the concentration of GHGs in the atmosphere has fluctuated over time, and that these fluctuations have occurred roughly in tandem with changes in the climate.[151] This suggests a causal relationship. Computerised climate models that exclude the anthropogenic gases (and their effect of increased heat retention) do not produce the post-1960s temperature rise.[152] Natural climate variability, for example variations in the intensity of solar radiation, cannot alone explain the rise.[153]

6. Natural feedbacks amplify the effect of the increasing concentration of GHGs in the atmosphere, and thus accelerate anthropogenic temperature rise.

An example of a positive feedback loop is melting sea ice. The highly reflective ice melts away into a darker (lower-albedo) ocean surface, which absorbs more solar radiation, heats up, and accelerates the demise of the remaining ice.[154] Another feedback loop is caused by water vapour and cloud, whose atmospheric presence increases as temperatures rise, trapping more heat. The combined greenhouse effect of increasing vapour and cloud exceeds the greenhouse effect of the anthropogenic atmospheric CO_2 operating alone: that is, without the feedback.[155]

---

[151] J. D. Shakun et al., 'Global Warming Preceded by Increasing Carbon Dioxide Concentrations During the Last Deglaciation', 484 *Nature* 49 (5 April 2012).
[152] Intergovernmental Panel on Climate Change, *Synthesis Report* (2007), p. 40.
[153] Steffen, *The Critical Decade* (2011), pp. 13–14.
[154] M. C. Serreze, 'Climate Change: Rethinking the Sea-Ice Tipping Point', 471 *Nature* 47 (2 March 2011), p. 47.
[155] Steffen, *The Critical Decade* (2011), p. 16.

The burning of coal triggers natural feedbacks not just by adding CO_2 to the atmosphere but also by depositing black carbon (soot) on Arctic snow and ice. This decreases the reflective capacity of the surface, making a significant contribution to warming and ice melt.[156]

7. The effects of anthropogenic climate change on physical and biological systems (sea-level rise, change in species' ranges, etc.) are already observable and are expected to be felt even more strongly in the future. However, the sensitivities of the various systems are not all equally well understood.

Climate change is affecting the sea in several ways. As sea water warms, it expands and rises. Melting land-based ice adds to the sea-level rise. Abundant atmospheric CO_2 mixes with the sea water, making it more acidic (ocean acidification).[157] Satellite altimeter data for 1993–2009 show that the global sea level is rising about 3.2 mm per year.[158] The best estimate for sea-level rise by 2100 relative to the average level for 1980–99 is between 28 centimetres (under the moderate B1 scenario)[159] and 43 centimetres (under the fuel-intensive A1FI scenario).[160] Steffen writes that for coastal areas around Sydney and Melbourne, 'a rise of 0.5 m leads to very large increases in the incidence of extreme events, by factors of 1000 or 10 000 for some locations. A multiplying factor of 100 means that an extreme event with a current probability of occurrence of 1-in-100 ... would occur every year'.[161] In other words, bad weather, when it happens, will be more extreme in its intensity.

Biological systems are demonstrably being affected by recent climate change. Across species groups, increasing temperatures have been associated with shifts in seasonal timing and shifts in the distribution of species from lower to higher altitudes or closer to the poles.[162] Parmesan and Yohe report 'very high confidence' that climate change is affecting living systems: analyses of more than 1700 species document significant range shifts, averaging 6.1 kilometres per decade towards the poles (or 6.1 metres per decade upward in altitude), and significant mean advancement of spring events by 2.3 days per decade.[163] In the northern hemisphere, birds and butterflies have shifted an average of 37 kilometres and 114 kilometres northward, respectively.[164] Some Arctic species, with nowhere to go, have experienced a contraction in the size of their range.[165] Change in human land use is still the factor having the

---

[156] UN Environment Programme, *Near-Term Climate Protection and Clean Air Benefits: Actions for Controlling Short-Lived Climate Forcers* (2011); and O. L. Hadley and T. W. Kirchstetter, 'Black-Carbon Reduction of Snow Albedo', 2 *Nature Climate Change* 437 (June 2012).
[157] On acidification in the Pacific Ocean, see Australian Bureau of Meteorology and CSIRO, *Climate Change in the Pacific: Scientific Assessment and New Research. Volume 1. Regional Overview* (Commonwealth of Australia, 2011), pp. 176–7.
[158] Steffen, *The Critical Decade* (2011), p. 11.   [159] On the IPCC scenarios, see Chapter 2.
[160] Intergovernmental Panel on Climate Change, *4AR: Working Group II* (2007), Table 6.3, p. 323. See also ibid., p. 694.
[161] Steffen, *The Critical Decade* (2011), p. 26.
[162] M. E. Visser, 'Birds and Butterflies in Climatic Debt', 2 *Nature Climate Change* 77 (February 2012), p. 77.
[163] C. Parmesan and G. Yohe, 'A Globally Coherent Fingerprint of Climate Change Impacts across Natural Systems', 421 *Nature* 37 (2 January 2003), p. 37.
[164] Visser, 'Birds and Butterflies in Climatic Debt' (2012), p. 77.
[165] Parmesan and Yohe, 'A Globally Coherent Fingerprint' (2003), p. 39.

strongest impact on wild plants and animals,[166] but a 'significant climate signal' can now be detected, with a potential to 'alter species interactions, de-stabilize communities and drive major biome shifts'.[167]

There is much climate change science that is now confidently understood and for which there is strong evidence. Yet, however well any complex system is known, it is known with some degree of uncertainty, and the uncertainty with which complex facts are known is a central notion in the science of climate change (Box 1.3).[168] Causal attribution of recent trends at a local level to climate change will always be characterised by complexity and significant uncertainty because non-climatic influences dominate local, short-term changes.[169] In this area, non-scientists must take great care. An example of a remarkably localised attribution is a study of the butterfly *Heteronympha merope*'s response to warming in the region of Melbourne. The authors of the study were able to link the observed air temperature rise of 0.148°C per decade around Melbourne to anthropogenic emissions, and they were able to link the shift in the mean emergence date of *H. merope* of minus 1.6 days per decade over a 65-year period to the observed temperature rise.[170]

8. *Because of the long atmospheric lifetime of GHGs like CO_2 and the inability of the natural carbon cycle to remove anthropogenic emissions over short time frames, Earth will continue to warm for decades and perhaps centuries into the future from the gases already present in the atmosphere and still being released.*[171]

9. *It follows from the last point that the rate of future climate change depends to an extent on policy choices made now about the level of future anthropogenic emissions. We still retain some control over the climate, but climatic tipping points may soon render the problem unmanageable.*

The existence of tipping points in the climate system introduces a dramatic note.[172] Lenton et al. compiled a list of potential tipping elements relevant to the making of policy, and ranked a subset of them according to their sensitivity to global warming and the associated uncertainty.[173] (Four of their tipping elements were described in Box 1.2.) The list of elements relevant to policy

---

166 T. P. Dawson et al., 'Beyond Predictions: Biodiversity Conservation in a Changing Climate', 332 *Science* 53 (1 April 2011), p. 53.
167 Parmesan and Yohe, 'A Globally Coherent Fingerprint' (2003), p. 41.
168 See also, for example, Steffen, *The Critical Decade* (2011), p. 21 (Warming: virtually certain; human causation: virtually certain; sea-level rise: certain, but extent of rise uncertain; response of Greenland and Antarctic ice sheets: not well known; changing patterns of precipitation: not well known; risks that climate change poses for human societies: even greater uncertainty).
169 Parmesan and Yohe, 'A Globally Coherent Fingerprint' (2003), p. 37.
170 M. R. Kearney et al., 'Early Emergence in a Butterfly Causally Linked to Anthropogenic Warming', 6(5) *Biology Letters* 674 (23 October 2010).
171 D. Archer and V. Brovkin, 'The Millennial Atmospheric Lifetime of Anthropogenic CO_2', 90 *Climatic Change* 283 (2008); S. Solomon et al., 'Irreversible Climate Change Due to Carbon Dioxide Emissions', 106(6) *PNAS* 1704 (10 February 2009).
172 Intergovernmental Panel on Climate Change, *4AR: Working Group I* (2007), pp. 775 ff. and pp. 818 ff.; Lenton et al., 'Tipping Elements' (2008), p. 1786; M. Molina et al., 'Reducing Abrupt Climate Change Risk Using the Montreal Protocol and Other Regulatory Actions to Complement Cuts in CO_2 Emissions', 106(49) *PNAS* 20616 (8 December 2009), p. 20616; Duarte et al., 'Abrupt Climate Change in the Arctic' (2012); A. Levermann et al., 'Potential Climatic Transitions with Profound Impact on Europe: Review of the Current State of Six "Tipping Elements of the Climate System"', 110 *Climatic Change* 845 (2012).
173 Lenton et al., 'Tipping Elements' (2008).

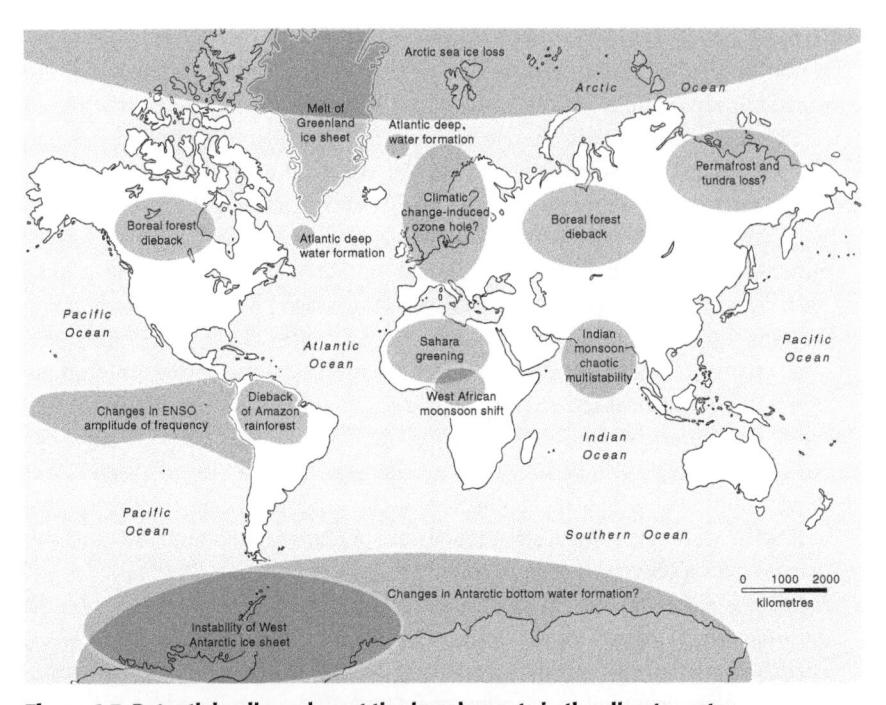

Figure 1.3 Potential policy-relevant tipping elements in the climate system
The highlighted events could be triggered this century and the relevant climate subsystems could undergo a qualitative change within this millennium. Question marks indicate events whose status as tipping elements is the most uncertain.
Source: T. M. Lenton et al., 'Tipping Elements in the Earth's Climate System' 105(6) *PNAS* 1786 (2008), Fig. 1.

was kept short by imposing a 'political time horizon'. This meant that the authors limited their consideration to those tipping events that could be triggered by human decisions within a time frame that they set at 100 years, 'based on the human life span and our (limited) ability to consider the world we are leaving for our grandchildren'.[174] They also limited their list by an 'ethical time horizon' (1000 years), which 'recognizes that events too far away in the future may not have the power of influencing today's decisions'.[175] Finally, they limited policy-relevant tipping elements to those that a significant number of people would care about, because of the impact of the changed physical state on human welfare or on a unique and valued feature of the biosphere.[176] See Figure 1.3 for the results.

Melting of permafrost soils could trigger a feedback cycle with an impact so vast and irreversible as to count as a tipping element. As permafrost defrosts, microbes decompose the ancient carbon and release CH_4 (methane) and CO_2.

---

174 Ibid., p. 1787.   **175** Ibid.
176 As might be expected, scientific discussion of policy-relevant tipping points is imbued with normative judgments, which are necessary to distinguish between tipping points we care about and the rest. See the discussion earlier in this chapter on human values and climate change.

Schuur and Abbott estimate that permafrost thaw could release 'the same order of magnitude of carbon as deforestation if current rates of deforestation continue. But because these emissions include significant quantities of methane, the overall effect on climate could be 2.5 times larger.'[177] Under a high-warming scenario, the release from permafrost degradation would equal 30 billion to 63 billion tonnes of CO_2 eq. by 2040, reaching 232 billion to 380 billion tonnes by 2100 and 549 billion to 865 billion tonnes by 2300.[178] (For comparison, global anthropogenic emissions from all sources in 2009 totalled 49.5 billion tonnes.[179]) Permafrost is widely dispersed across remote landscapes. We do not have the option of trapping CH_4 emissions from the thawing soil, as we do, for example, at landfill sites close to cities. It should be emphasised, though, that gaps in our knowledge mean that the effect of a melting permafrost on global warming is still highly uncertain.[180]

While the transitions discussed by Lenton et al. imply massive impacts in amplified warming, drought, biodiversity loss, etc., perhaps the greatest long-term concern for humans is the permanent loss to our species of large tracts of habitable land.

10. Because the impacts of climate change are already being felt, and more are inevitable, adaptation measures are required to help human beings (and possibly other species) to adjust to the impacts.

Adaptation measures, for example in agriculture,[181] are different from and additional to policies for the mitigation of emissions mentioned in step 9.[182]

The ten-step skeleton argument is a handy tool for the non-specialist, for it helps to, among other things, categorise factual evidence for climate change, including its causes and effects. It is worth reiterating that the IPCC assessment reports and synthesis report contain a wealth of information on the full range of climate change topics, including law and policy, with much of the synthesis report, at least, written in language understandable to the non-specialist. It is also worth recalling that while the science of climate change describes causes and impacts and underscores the severity of the warming problem, it does not determine the solution to the problem. A pure scientific body of facts cannot deliver policy conclusions. Instead, socioeconomic considerations must be factored in with the scientific knowledge to determine the desirable future pathways.

---

[177] E. A. G. Schuur and B. Abbott, 'High Risk of Permafrost Thaw', 480 *Nature* 32 (1 December 2011), p. 32. Most of the released carbon will be in the form of CO_2, with only about 2.7 per cent in the form of methane. However, methane has a much higher global warming potential than CO_2 (ibid., p. 33).
[178] Ibid. [179] UN Environment Programme, *Bridging the Emissions Gap* (November 2011), p. 15.
[180] Schuur and Abbott, 'High Risk of Permafrost Thaw' (2011), p. 32; see also E. Kriegler et al., 'Imprecise Probability Assessment of Tipping Points in the Climate System', 106(13) *PNAS* 5041 (31 March 2009), p. 5041.
[181] Lobell, Schlenker and Costa-Roberts, 'Global Crop Production' (2011).
[182] For a discussion of human adaptation needs in a (quite likely) world of 4°C above the pre-industrial average, see K. Anderson and A. Bows, 'Beyond "Dangerous" Climate Change: Emission Scenarios for a New World', 369 *Philosophical Transactions of the Royal Society A* 20 (2011), and the other papers in that special issue of the *Transactions*.

2

Legal elements and ongoing development of the international climate change regime

Introduction *page* 52
Background to the UNFCCC   52
Legal principles and rules of the UNFCCC   54
Legal principles and rules of the Kyoto Protocol   83
Outlook for the international climate change regime   90

Introduction

This chapter undertakes a close examination of the key provisions of the UN Framework Convention on Climate Change and the Kyoto Protocol, reflecting on the significance of these provisions and their links with broader climate change issues. For twenty years the UNFCCC has defined the international climate change regime. It will probably retain this role for many years to come. While it lacks the specificity of the Kyoto Protocol in the critical area of emission reductions, its ongoing role as a 'framework' for international cooperation is generally accepted. A careful study of the Convention is still a requirement for understanding the present state of the international negotiations and the international law on climate change. As the Kyoto Protocol's fortunes have diminished, the UNFCCC has reasserted itself as the treaty of greatest consequence. While the Convention will certainly outlast the Protocol as an operative treaty, the Protocol also repays close study, both for the governance model it represents and for the institutions it has created.

Background to the UNFCCC

Work on an international climate change convention began in 1988 with the creation of the Intergovernmental Panel on Climate Change by the World

Meteorological Organization and the UN Environment Programme.[1] The work of the IPCC underpins not only the science but also the law of climate change. In December 1988, the UN General Assembly endorsed the IPCC as an institution 'to provide internationally co-ordinated scientific assessments of the magnitude, timing and potential environmental and socio-economic impact of climate change and realistic response strategies'.[2]

The IPCC's First Assessment Report was published in 1990.[3] The third volume of the report contains a chapter on legal and institutional mechanisms needed for the regulation of climate change.[4] The objective of the chapter was to compile the elements for a future 'framework' convention on climate change. In the IPCC's view, such a convention was to be modelled on the Vienna Convention for the Protection of the Ozone Layer.[5] In order for the new convention to gain broad support quickly, the IPCC suggested that the framework be limited to broad principles and obligations and that it make provision for the creation of protocols to deal with specific issues in the context of separate negotiations.[6]

In a further resolution on climate change, in December 1990, the UN General Assembly decided to establish an intergovernmental negotiating process, under UN auspices and supported by the WMO and UNEP, for the preparation of a framework convention on climate change. The convention would be drafted by an Intergovernmental Negotiating Committee (INC).[7] The resolution directed the INC to take into account the IPCC's First Assessment Report, including the discussion therein of a convention's desired elements.[8]

The first meeting of the INC, in February 1991, was attended by representatives of more than 100 states, a range of UN agencies and intergovernmental organisations, and a large number of NGOs.[9] At the meeting, the states clarified the future role and status of the IPCC: it was not to be a negotiating forum but an independent scientific body that was entitled to provide technical and scientific assistance to the INC.[10]

The history of the Convention's development from early 1991 until its opening for signature on 4 June 1992 at the Earth Summit in Rio has been well described

---

[1] Intergovernmental Panel on Climate Change, 'History', <http://www.ipcc.ch/organization/organization_history.shtml#.T1LWi8wnpFo>.
[2] UN General Assembly, *Protection of Global Climate for Present and Future Generations of Mankind (Resolution Adopted by the General Assembly)* (6 December 1988), A/RES/43/53, para. 5.
[3] Intergovernmental Panel on Climate Change, *Working Group I: Scientific Assessment of Climate Change* (World Meteorological Organization, 1990); Intergovernmental Panel on Climate Change, *Working Group II: Potential Impacts of Climate Change* (World Meteorological Organization, 1990); Intergovernmental Panel on Climate Change, *Working, Group III: Formulation of Response Strategies* (World Meteorological Organization, 1990).
[4] Intergovernmental Panel on Climate Change, *Climate Change 1990: The IPCC Response Strategies. Report Prepared for Intergovernmental Panel on Climate Change by Working Group III* (1990).
[5] Ibid., p. 261.   [6] Ibid.
[7] UN General Assembly, *Protection of Global Climate for Present and Future Generations of Mankind*, Resolution Adopted by the General Assembly (21 December 1990), A/RES/45/212, para. 1.
[8] Ibid., para. 15.
[9] Intergovernmental Negotiating Committee, *Report of the Intergovernmental Negotiating Committee for a Framework Convention on Climate Change on the Work of Its First Session, Held at Washington, DC, from 4 to 14 February 1991* (United Nations, 8 March 1991), A/AC.237/6, paras. 14–18.
[10] Ibid., para. 61(b).

elsewhere.[11] As it turned out, the UNFCCC's drafters would adhere closely to the IPCC's early advice on the form and substance of a climate change convention.

Legal principles and rules of the UNFCCC

What obligations does the Convention create? How well-defined are they and what is their force? How have Australia and other states performed in relation to each of those obligations? These are some of the questions we will consider in the sections that follow. We have limited our discussion to the Convention's most consequential provisions.

Preamble

The Convention is prefaced by a relatively long preamble. A preamble to a treaty provides part of the 'context' in which the treaty may be interpreted.[12] It does not contain binding obligations. It often tells us about the motives that led parties to develop and sign up to the agreement, or contains aspirations and general principles that play the role of background assumptions.

The third paragraph in the UNFCCC preamble is a compound statement that merits analysis. It makes three observations, as we see from the original passage:

> ... that the largest share of historical and current global emissions of greenhouse gases has originated in developed countries; that per capita emissions in developing countries are still relatively low; and that the share of global emissions originating in developing countries will grow to meet their social and development needs ...

As statements of fact, the paragraph's three elements are true. Some evidence for the assertions they make was presented in Chapter 1. On the question of per capita emissions, those of some developing countries have grown strongly since 1992, although it is still true that, overall, they are 'still relatively low' (see Figure 2.1). The three elements of the quoted passage from the UNFCCC's preamble also state or imply entitlements. The first implies that wealthy countries have exceeded their entitlement to emit greenhouse gases into the atmosphere; the second, that people in poorer countries are entitled to increase their per capita emissions (absolute increase); and the third, that developing countries are entitled to increase their share of atmospheric pollution (relative increase) in order to achieve economic growth.

---

11 See for example J. Barrett, 'The Negotiation and Drafting of the Climate Change Convention', in *International Law and Global Climate Change*, eds R. Churchill and D. Freestone (Graham and Trotman/Martinus Nijhoff, 1991), pp. 183–200; F. Yamin and J. Depledge, *The International Climate Change Regime: A Guide to Rules, Institutions and Procedures* (Cambridge University Press, 2004), pp. 22–5; E. Louka, *International Environmental Law: Fairness, Effectiveness, and World Order* (Cambridge University Press, 2006), pp. 357–9; P. W. Birnie, A. E. Boyle and C. Redgwell, *International Law and the Environment*, 3rd edn (Oxford University Press, 2009), pp. 356–8.
12 Article 31(2) of the 1969 Vienna Convention on the Law of Treaties.

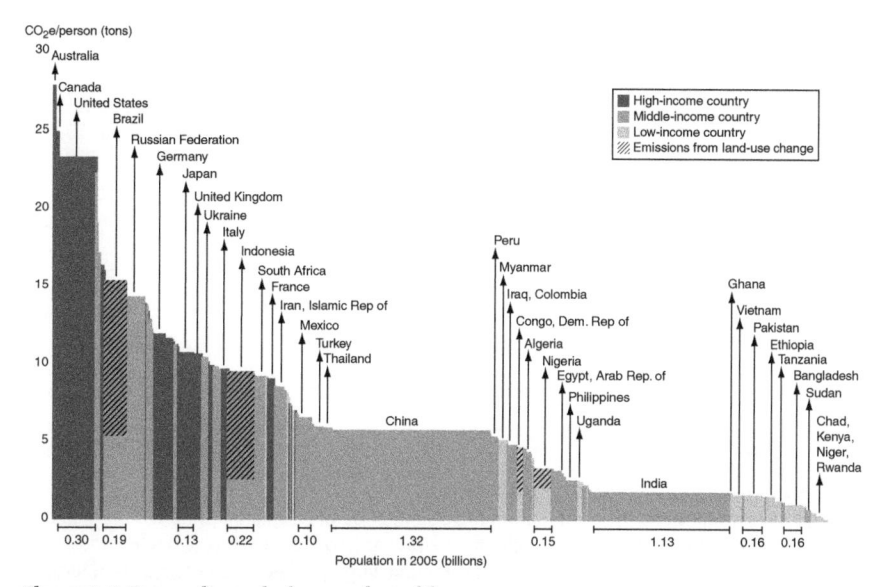

Figure 2.1 Per capita emissions and wealth
Per capita emissions in high-income countries far exceed those in developing countries. In the figure, the width of each column represents population and the height represents per capita emissions. The area of the column therefore represents total emissions for the country in question. Australia's absolute emissions are relatively small, but its per capita emissions are the highest in the world. Among larger countries, Brazil, Indonesia, the Democratic Republic of Congo, and Nigeria have low energy-related emissions but significant emissions from land-use change. For these four special cases the share from land-use change is indicated by hatching in the columns.
Source: World Bank, *World Development Report 2010: Development and Climate Change* (2010), p. 39.

A statement about an entitlement could be an assertion of a legal right. Yet, because no international legal right to emit GHGs (as well as no obligation to limit their emissions) existed prior to the Convention, the above statements of entitlement cannot be asserting legal rights. They must amount to moral positions. That is, they must be understood as statements about responsibility and equal opportunity – about fair play and about taking one's rightful turn on the world stage after a period of exclusion.[13] Thus, at the very beginning of the Convention's text, we are confronted with a distinction between developed and developing countries, which are said to have different entitlements to emit GHG pollution based on an unstated moral principle.

---

13 Now, twenty years after the UNFCCC was signed, when the urgency of the climate change problem is better understood and GHG emissions have accelerated, the same commitment to further growth in emissions in developing countries has been reiterated in a COP decision: '*Reaffirming* that social and economic development and poverty eradication are the first and overriding priorities of developing country Parties, and that the share of global emissions originating in developing countries will grow to meet their social and development needs': UNFCCC, *Decision 1/CP.16, The Cancun Agreements: Outcome of the Work of the Ad Hoc Working Group on Long-Term Cooperative Action under the Convention* (2010), FCCC/CP/2010/7/Add.1, III.B.

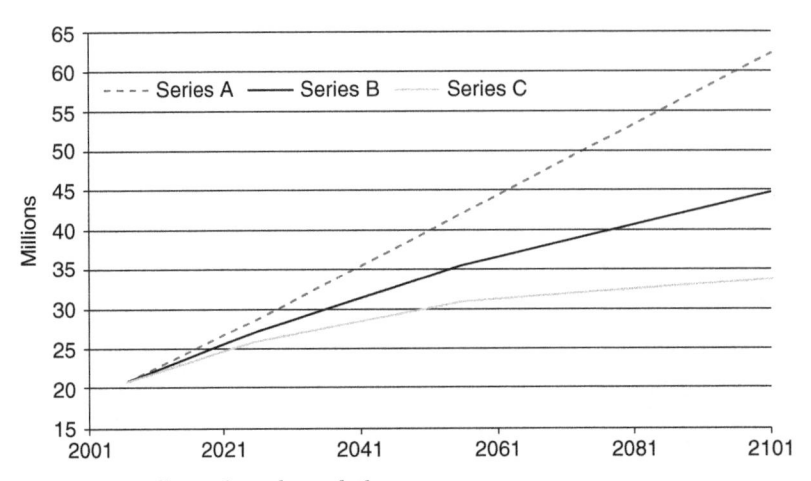

Figure 2.2 Australia: Projected population
Australia's estimated resident population at 30 June 2007 of 21 million people is projected to increase to between 30.9 and 42.5 million by 2056, and to increase further to between 33.7 and 62.2 million by 2101. The figure's Series B curve largely reflects current trends in fertility, life expectancy at birth, and net overseas migration, whereas the Series A and C curves are based on high and low assumptions for each of these variables, respectively. It should be noted that all projections involving human behaviour are very uncertain.
Source: Australian Bureau of Statistics, 'Population Projections, Australia, 2006 to 2101', <http://www.abs.gov.au/ausstats/abs@.nsf/mf/3222.0>.

We also notice that while the apparent focus of this preambular passage is on states, there is at least a suggestion, in the expression 'per capita emissions', that this treaty is about the rights and responsibilities of individual people everywhere. In an international agreement regulating state relations, 'per capita' causes us to stop and reflect. Because changes in a state's 'share of global emissions' can be driven as much by a growth in population[14] as by a larger personal average 'carbon footprint', the absolute emissions of each state have to be considered at the level of the individual person (total emissions divided by total population) for an interstate comparison to begin to be meaningful.

It seems just possible that the moral principle implicit in the section of the preamble we are considering is along the lines that people have equal rights to the atmosphere. Precisely what this would mean, though, how it might be justified and qualified, and how it is to be reconciled with bringing global warming under control are matters that require further exploration.

Another distinction of interest raised in the preambular passage is that between 'historical and current' emissions. 'Historical' connotes GHG emissions from the period following 1750, when the industrial revolution in Western Europe

---

14 In Australia's case, the population grew by over one million people between 2001 and 2006, from 18 769 249 to 19 855 288 (Australian Bureau of Statistics, '2006 Census Quickstats', <http://www.censusdata.abs.gov.au>) and is projected to continue to do so: see Figure 2.2.

and America began to gather pace, until around 1950, by which time industrialisation had spread and had become the developmental goal, if not reality, everywhere. The revolution was powered by steam from coal, internal combustion engines running on liquid fossil fuels, and fuel wood from forests, with further deforestation undertaken to open up new farmland to feed a growing population. All of this led to the West's modernisation and widespread prosperity, while industrialisation in other parts of the world lagged.

Did the unilateral appropriation of the atmospheric space during the industrial revolution create a moral debt that the West now owes to the rest of the world, as some authors seem to imply?[15] Is the preamble's implied aspersion well grounded? No one during the industrial revolution knew that the practices were changing the climate for the worse (as lawyers would say, they had no guilty mind).[16] Considering this, along with the fact that the finished machinery of Western industrialisation eventually[17] spread around the world in successive waves of development – meaning that the emissions from the 'historical' period underpinned economic progress that was not, finally, to the exclusive enjoyment of the West – we might question the moral relevance of historical emissions.[18] Still, they have been written into the Convention.

The point to remember is that these few preambular lines conceal assumptions about past, present and future that mix historical fact with values and politics, perhaps including a dissatisfaction with our highly inequitable world. They are written into an international legal instrument, but they state no law.

The next preambular paragraph of interest informs us that 'there are many uncertainties in predictions of climate change, particularly with regard to the timing, magnitude and regional patterns thereof'. This claim is very generally formulated, and as a result continues to be true today, and perhaps will always be true. As a factual statement, therefore, it risks being rather empty. The UNFCCC's drafters took it almost word for word from the IPCC's First Assessment Report, dating from 1990:[19] that is, from the early days of climate science, when the uncertainties were indeed high compared with the state of our knowledge twenty years later. For example, in 1990 the IPCC expressed 'certainty' on only two points about the physical science of climate change: it is certain, it said, that a natural

---

15 For example H. Shue, 'Global Environment and International Inequality', 75 *International Affairs* 531 (1999); E. Neumayer, 'In Defence of Historical Accountability for Greenhouse Gas Emissions', 33 *Ecological Economics* 185 (2000); S. M. Gardiner, 'Ethics and Global Climate Change', 114 *Ethics* 555 (2004); and M. Grasso, 'An Ethics-Based Climate Agreement for the South Pacific Region', 6 *International Environmental Agreements* 249 (2006).
16 For example S. Caney, 'Cosmpolitan Justice, Responsibility, and Global Climate Change', in *Climate Ethics: Essential Readings*, eds S. M. Gardiner et al. (Oxford University Press, 2010), pp. 130–2.
17 See for example A. Read and D. Fisher, *The Proudest Day: India's Long Road to Independence* (Norton, 1997), p. 34 ('The export of textile machinery [from the United Kingdom] was prohibited by law until 1843, though the East India Company continued to ban all imports of machinery [into India] until the very end of its existence').
18 However, there is no overt questioning of it by the UNFCCC parties. The idea is reiterated unchanged in decisions right up to the present, as, for example, UNFCCC, *Decision 1/CP.16* (2010), s. III.A ('the largest share of historical global emissions of greenhouse gases originated in developed countries and ... owing to this historical responsibility, developed country Parties must take the lead in combating climate change').
19 Intergovernmental Panel on Climate Change, *First Assessment Report, Vol. 1: Overview and Policymaker Summaries* (World Meteorological Organization, 1990), p. 53.

greenhouse effect keeps Earth warmer than it would otherwise be; and it is certain that emissions resulting from human activities are substantially increasing the atmospheric concentration of CO_2 and other GHGs, with the result that the greenhouse effect could be expected to be enhanced.[20] There was no 'certainty' at the time that the climate had recently warmed or that the warming effect had been caused by human activity. However, by 2007, when the IPCC's Fourth Assessment Report was released, the IPCC could state 'unequivocally' that the climate is warming; and it could state with 'very high confidence' that the warming is caused by anthropogenic emissions.[21] The IPCC could also state with very high confidence that the warming is having a strong impact upon terrestrial biological systems.[22]

This point reminds us that, as the science of climate change evolves, the text of the UNFCCC remains the same. In relation to the particular lines we are considering, no real inaccuracy results. The Convention is, of course, a product of its time. If the UNFCCC manages to remain current, it is because the state parties to the Convention rely on other processes, such as their annual Conference of the Parties and the decisions taken in that forum, to stay abreast of developments in the field. The Convention, perhaps because it is perceived only as a framework for concrete action, has never so far had its text amended.

The Convention's preamble continues with the following acknowledgment, implicit in which is the notion of a 'framework':

> [T]he global nature of climate change calls for the widest possible cooperation by all countries and their participation in an effective and appropriate international response, in accordance with their common but differentiated responsibilities and respective capabilities and their social and economic conditions.

As explained in Chapter 1, the truly global nature of the climate change problem has a peculiar logic: mitigation action in willing countries is hindered where other countries with substantial greenhouse emissions favour a business-as-usual approach or only trivial departures from it. That same logic, when conjoined with a warming problem that is portrayed as urgent, strongly determines the kind of treaty that comes into being. The nature of the situation requires an agreement that will be signed *by all states*, and the urgency of the situation requires the initial agreement to be little more than an unobjectionable shell, creating no more than a *process* for agreeing to concrete actions.[23] Hence the preamble's emphasis on 'the widest possible cooperation', as opposed to, say, the deepest possible cuts in emissions. An objective of the latter type is muted in the Convention; if it is implicit in the Convention's text at all, it has been put on hold for a separate agreement further down the road. We have already seen that

---

20 Ibid.
21 Intergovernmental Panel on Climate Change, *Climate Change 2007: Synthesis Report* (WMO, UNEP, 2007), pp. 30 and 37.
22 Ibid., p. 33.
23 Barrett, 'The Negotiation and Drafting of the Climate Change Convention' (1991), p. 184 ('There was broad agreement ... that [the UNFCCC] should be framed in such a way as to gain the adherence of the largest possible number ... [and] that it should contain provisions for separate annexes and protocols to deal with specific obligations').

the Convention concedes the inevitability of an *increase* in per capita emissions in developing countries, on the basis of a vaguely formed notion of entitlement. It follows that the only thing left to ask of all countries in order to kick-start the international process is 'cooperation' in a framework agreement.

Do states have a legal obligation (outside of any treaty) to cooperate to solve a serious global problem? This is a question of public international law. The answer is undoubtedly 'No'.[24] In fact, the legal status quo is even weaker than that. States do not even have an obligation to cooperate in accordance with their aforementioned 'common but differentiated responsibilities and respective capabilities'. States do generally cooperate as a matter of fact, but not out of any legal obligation in the absence of a treaty. Only after deciding to cooperate by signing an agreement obliging them to do so does a state incur legal obligations. When a state throws in its lot with the rest in a joint legal venture, it may condition its treaty cooperation on the degree of its 'responsibility' for the problem addressed by the treaty, as well as on its 'capability' to act and on its 'social and economic conditions'. As the Convention's preamble acknowledges all of this, the first statement of 'law' we encounter in the Convention concerns the right of each signatory state to limit its cooperation in accordance with those three criteria. A law qualified by conditionalities is necessarily a weak law. The UNFCCC's preamble consistently talks down the treaty's legal force.

There follows directly in the preamble another statement of law, this one emphasising the sovereign right of states 'to exploit their own resources pursuant to their own environmental and developmental policies'. The only limitation on this right seems to be the obligation, also reiterated in the preamble, to ensure that activities within a state's jurisdiction or control 'do not cause damage to the environment of other States or of areas beyond the limits of national jurisdiction'. The prohibition of transboundary harm is a well-established principle of public international law,[25] reproducing almost verbatim Principle 21 of the Stockholm Declaration of 1972.[26] It so obviously predates the discovery of climate change attributable to human activity that it may seem irrelevant to, or even irreconcilable with, the concerns of the Convention. Indeed, to those who claim that public international law already contains the rules to deal with responsibility for climate change,[27] this fundamental principle is a thorn in the side. Why so? As discussed in Chapter 1, GHG emissions from human activity are conceptualised as

---

[24] A case could be made for a customary state duty to cooperate with other states in matters of marine or cross-border pollution, based on, for example, the ITLOS case of *Ireland v United Kingdom (MOX Plant Case)*, Provisional Measures, Order of 3 December 2001, 41 ILM 405 (2002). Yet the existence of even this narrow kind of duty has been called into question, for example by D. Bodansky, *The Art and Craft of International Environmental Law* (Harvard University Press, 2010), p. 199.
[25] Discussed in, for example, G. Handl, 'Transboundary Impacts', in *The Oxford Handbook of International Environmental Law*, eds D. Bodansky, J. Brunneé and E. Hey (Oxford University Press, 2007), pp. 531–49. Bodansky argues that the duty to prevent transboundary pollution is a principle that reflects an 'attitudinal regularity' among states, rather than a behavioural regularity (that is, it is not the kind of international law that is grounded in consistent practice): Bodansky, *Art and Craft* (2010), p. 200.
[26] Declaration of the United Nations Conference on the Human Environment, 11 ILM 1416 (1972).
[27] For example M. Wewerinke and C. F. J. Doebbler, 'Exploring the Legal Basis of a Human Rights Approach to Climate Change', 10 *Chinese Journal of International Law* 1 (2010).

becoming instantly part of a well-mixed atmospheric pool that has global climatic consequences.[28] One extra tonne of CO_2 emitted in Angola has exactly the same physical effect as one extra tonne emitted in Australia – we are to think of it as joining an indistinguishable atmospheric whole. This differs from our notion of a non-greenhouse gas, like sulphur dioxide. In the case of SO_2, either this gas has local effects (or limited cross-border effects) in the form of acid rain, or it has no effects worth being concerned about at all. The situation is different with GHGs because we know that global GHG emissions are currently above a sustainable level (that is, we know that they are progressively changing our climate), and we know that emissions are on the rise in almost every country. It follows that states are, to use the language of the preamble, causing 'damage to the environment of areas beyond the limits of their jurisdiction', and therefore are in violation of the aforementioned principle of international law.

The difficulty with saying that in the case of climate change most states are already breaching the transboundary harm principle is that a principle that is deliberately and universally not adhered to either is not a legal principle at all (for example because it has been abandoned, in the way that head-of-state immunity from prosecution for genocide has been abandoned) or is a principle whose scope of application has in the given circumstances been exceeded. In the climate change context, the first possibility can be excluded simply on the ground that the UNFCCC state parties went to the trouble of reasserting the principle in the Convention's preamble.

Are we not faced, then, with a case of misapplication of a principle of international law? If so, are we not obliged to play down its role in the Convention? The preamble's statement that states' right to exploit resources is unlimited except as to transboundary harm is a principle developed in a different age and for a different purpose and does not sit well in the Convention. Any other reading implies that states have been in violation of international law from the moment they came to realise that their exploitation of their natural resources is harming the global environment. The point to remember from this discussion is that the UNFCCC is built out of some primitive elements that do not make a whole lot of sense in the climate change case.

We continue with our analysis of the preamble. A country that distinguishes itself by taking rapid strides towards a 'green economy'[29] might in theory decide to limit its barrier-free trade to similarly progressive countries, penalising those whose carbon footprint (or that of their exports) is relatively high by some measure. Because countries in the former category are likely to be rich, and those in the latter poor, developing countries are often heard to express anxiety that the new veneration of the green economy could leave them even further behind unless

---

28 This is a simplifying assumption. It does not deny the differential concentration of GHGs – over industrial parks, cities, or countries – at any moment in time.
29 On the idea of a 'green economy' as the new rallying call for the future, see UN Environment Programme, *Towards a Green Economy: Pathways to Sustainable Development and Poverty Eradication* (2011).

clear rules are agreed to at an international forum.[30] In fact, several such rules already exist (for example, under the World Trade Organization[31]). In the preamble to the UNFCCC we find a rather abstractly phrased statement which belongs, in part, to the same category of rules:

> [E]nvironmental standards, management objectives and priorities should reflect the environmental and developmental context to which they apply, and ... standards applied by some countries may be inappropriate and of unwarranted economic and social cost to other countries, in particular developing countries.

The latter half of this passage implies disapproval of using trade measures to influence environmental policy in countries of the global South. We witness again the emphasis in the Convention's text on state self-determination, as well as the principled contrast between developmentally advanced and developmentally lagging states.

We are less than halfway through the preamble, and already a definite tone has been set – and political choices made. Twenty years after the signing of the Convention, these early choices, especially that of distinguishing between developed and developing countries, still weigh heavily in the international negotiations.[32] The preamble returns repeatedly to make the same set of points: 'immediate action' on GHGs is to be taken by the industrialised countries, albeit in a 'flexible manner' and 'with due consideration of their relative contributions to the enhancement of the greenhouse effect'; by contrast, developing countries have other priorities: 'the achievement of sustained economic growth' and 'the eradication of poverty'. The difference in priorities is to be taken into 'full account' when elaborating a paradigm for action on the part of developing countries, and it is not to be used to justify measures by wealthy countries that have 'adverse impacts' on the less developed group of states.

The preamble foresees that the paradigm for participation of developing countries in the response to climate change must contain mechanisms for the

---

30 For example, at a recent international gathering, Nicaragua said that a 'green economy' should not be used to justify trade barriers to developing countries' products, nor as a condition for cooperation, loans or debt relief: 'Summary of the Second Session of the Preparatory Committee for the UN Conference on Sustainable Development: 7–8 March 2011' (11 March 2011) 27(3) *Earth Negotiations Bulletin*, p. 4. Also, at a joint SBI/SBSTA forum on response measures, India made submissions on protectionist unilateral trade measures, saying that carbon footprint standards, as well as aviation emissions in the EU ETS and the proposed American Clean Energy and Security Act, restrict market access by developing countries: International Institute for Sustainable Development, 'SB 34 and AWG Highlights: Monday, 13 June 2011', 12(509) *Earth Negotiations Bulletin* 1 (2011), p. 4. The concern, in other words, is that a rich country that is making an effort to reduce its emissions might try to protect its own more expensive products (which have a built-in price for carbon) from competition from products from countries that do not internalise carbon costs. In another example, the WTO's Committee on Trade and Environment considered the consistency of carbon footprint schemes with international trade rules: 'Regarding carbon border adjustment (CBA) measures members discussed a proposal by Singapore to request the Secretariat to prepare a compilation of existing studies on the role that CBAs can play in addressing competitiveness and leakage concerns with as minimal economic and trade impacts as possible; how CBAs can be applied in a WTO consistent manner; and the usefulness of developing a set of multilaterally agreed guidelines to pre-empt the abuse of CBAs. This proposal was not adopted as, reportedly, some members considered there is no room for CBAs under the WTO'; IISD News, 'WTO CTE Considers Carbon Border Adjustments and Carbon Footprint Schemes', <http://climate-l.iisd.org/news/wto-cte-consideres-carbon-border-adjustments-and-carbon-footprint-schemes/>. See also N. S. Ghaleigh and D. Rossati, 'The Spectre of Carbon Border-Adjustment Measures', 2(1) *Climate Law* 63 (2011).
31 See GATT Articles I, III, and XI.   32 See below.

transfer of finance and technology from the front line of action to the rear. The need for additional aid and technology transfer has been on the agenda of developing countries since the very beginning of the climate negotiations.[33] Developing countries, accordingly, 'need access to resources required to achieve sustainable social and economic development'. In order for development of this kind to occur, their energy consumption will have to become more efficient and their GHG emissions will have to be constrained, 'including through the application of new technologies on terms which make such an application economically and socially beneficial'.

Is the Convention's text here suggesting that developed countries have a legal obligation to provide monetary aid and transfer of technology, or is it merely engaging in a non-legal reflection on the shape of a fairer world? In other words, will wealthier countries be *obliged* under the Convention to help poorer countries, or is it merely an aspiration that they do so? An argument for such an obligation could be constructed as follows: (1) The Convention places an obligation on all states to act. (2) If the wealthier group of states has a greater obligation to cut back on greenhouse pollution while allowing the developing world to give greater priority to the elimination of poverty, and if the development to which the latter states are entitled must be accomplished 'cleanly', and if that means at a cost they cannot afford (considering that developing countries can hardly afford to exploit the older technologies, let alone the new ones[34]), then (3) it seems to follow that rich countries are indeed obliged, under UNFCCC law, to transfer wealth to the South.

However, one must remain suspicious of such conclusions based solely on formal readings of the Convention's text. It is plainly evident from the annual negotiations of the UNFCCC parties that states do not feel legally bound to anything that is not explicit, concrete, preferably quantified, and in proper legal form. Climate lawyers must look both to the text and to practice to understand the law, perhaps especially in the case of a framework convention.

Whether or not the Convention's text and the subsequent practice of states bear out the existence of an obligation of wealth transfer, we can see why the UNFCCC and the Kyoto Protocol have enjoyed the unflagging support of developing countries even as their OECD counterparts have begun to resile from the two treaties: most principles in the Convention's preamble do suggest, on a literal reading, that the Convention could be pressed into the decades-old struggle to collapse the North–South economic divide through an acceleration of supported economic development in the South.[35] If, from this perspective, the Convention is more about wealth redistribution than climate change, it is a perspective

---

[33] Barrett, 'The Negotiation and Drafting of the Climate Change Convention' (1991), pp. 186, 196–9.
[34] As noted in Chapter 1, China is projected to add a generating capacity for electricity equivalent to the 2010 installed capacity of the whole of the United States. Most of it will be coal-fired. International Energy Agency, *World Energy Outlook* 2010: *Executive Summary* (IEA, 2010), p. 8.
[35] Shue, 'Global Environment and International Inequality' (1999), pp. 101–11.

which, like targeted domestic taxation of the well-off, is guaranteed to win it strong enemies as well as strong friends.

The preamble makes two brief references to 'future generations'. Neither of these references adopts a legal or moral position in relation to future generations, and it would be too much to read an 'interest' or 'right' of future generations into them. They merely assert a determination 'to protect the climate system for present and future generations'. The notion of 'intergenerational equity', which is a very difficult concept philosophically, let alone legally, has been kept at bay in the UNFCCC preamble. Had it been allowed in at this point, in relation to present generations (*intra*generational equity) as much as future ones, the Convention would have been imbued with a much stronger human rights flavour than it has acquired through its mention of 'per capita' emission entitlements. Legally, future generations are non-state entities; if they are anything at all (for they do not yet exist except as an idea), they are *people*. We may presume, in the absence of clear contrary evidence, that states signing up to a framework agreement were intent on defining state rights and obligations and did not mean to create new climate-related human rights.

We note, finally, the parts of the preamble focusing on science and economics. The work of several international and intergovernmental bodies is acknowledged here, for their coordination of scientific research and analysis of the results of that research. In a statement encapsulating the interdisciplinary nature of climate change regulation, the preamble emphasises that policy addressing climate change is to be based on 'scientific, technical and economic considerations and continually re-evaluated in the light of new findings in these areas'. This could be taken to imply that state climate policy is to be increasingly refined with the passage of time, as the science of climate change advances, economic modelling and technology become more sophisticated, and so on.

In fact, climate policy has not evolved through a process of re-evaluation and fine-tuning. In both Australia (until 2011)[36] and the United States,[37] for example, government policy has been fragmented and ad hoc, and has swung from one direction to another without making any significant break with the past. Conflicting human interests of the kind discussed in Chapter 1 have made its trajectory very difficult to predict. At the international level, climate policy has effectively been put on hold since 2009 despite the steady flow of dire scientific reports. The most we can say about a legal obligation subsisting in this segment of the Convention is that the makers of public policy (governments) are obliged to take account of scientific, technical and economic developments as 'relevant considerations' in the making of public policy decisions, but those developments

---

36 See Chapter 4.
37 For example, in May 2011, President Barack Obama announced several steps aimed at speeding oil and gas drilling on public lands and waters: John M. Broder, 'Obama shifts to speed oil and gas drilling in the US', *The New York Times*, 14 May 2011 (online).

do not *determine* policy. This weak obligation undoubtedly is met in practice: governments do take climate science 'into account'.

We mentioned in the introduction to this chapter that the IPCC, in its First Assessment Report, put forth suggestions for possible elements of an international framework convention on climate change.[38] Many of its suggestions concerning a preamble for a future convention found their way into the UNFCCC's actual preambular text. Suggestions that did *not* make it included:

- a statement recognising 'the need for an environment of a quality that permits a life of dignity and well-being for present and future generations', and
- a state 'duty to protect and conserve [the] climate for the benefit of mankind'.[39]

It is possible that these two elements were left out of the UNFCCC text because of the strong human rights tone of their language. The IPCC did observe, for the benefit of those who would be drafting the convention, that certain preliminary questions suggesting a human rights bent could not be avoided: 'Should mankind's interest in a viable environment be characterized as a fundamental right?' 'Is there an entitlement not to be subjected, directly or indirectly, to the adverse effects of climate change?'[40]

It will have been clear from our discussion of the actual preamble that these two questions were avoided, or perhaps implicitly answered in the negative.[41]

Objective and principles

We now turn to the body of the Convention. It is headed by a substantive part, made up of the Convention's objective (Article 2), its principles (Article 3), and the state parties' commitments (Article 4). The substantive part, on which the rest of this chapter primarily focuses, is followed by several process-oriented and institution-building sections. They include provision for regular decision-making conferences for the state parties (Article 7); establishment of a Secretariat for coordination and other support (Article 8); reporting requirements for states (Article 12); formation of two subsidiary technical bodies (the SBSTA and SBI, in Articles 9 and 10, respectively); a financial mechanism (Articles 11 and 21); and procedures for the amendment of the Convention and the adoption of protocols (Articles 15–17).

The Convention's two annexes serve to create three groups of states, approximately in these terms: *Annex I* stands for OECD countries (as the membership stood in 1992) and economies making a transition to a market economy (economies in transition);[42] *Annex II* is a subset of Annex I, consisting of OECD countries only.[43] The third group is an implied one, consisting of all the states not listed in

---

38 Intergovernmental Panel on Climate Change, *IPCC Response Strategies* (1990).   **39** Ibid., p. 263.
40 Ibid., p. 264.   **41** However, they continue to be useful as essay topics!
42 'Economies in transition' are countries of the former Soviet bloc.
43 The UNFCCC Secretariat defines 'Annex I Party', 'Annex II Party' and 'non-Annex I Party' on its website: <http://www.unfccc.int/parties_and_observers/items/2704.php>.

the annexes: the *non-Annex* states. The differentiation of states effected by the annexes provides the centrepiece of 'differentiated responsibilities' among states, as discussed below.[44]

The UNFCCC's *objective* is:

> stabilization of greenhouse gas concentrations in the atmosphere at a level that would prevent dangerous anthropogenic interference with the climate system. Such a level should be achieved within a time frame sufficient to allow ecosystems to adapt naturally to climate change, to ensure that food production is not threatened and to enable economic development to proceed in a sustainable manner.

The objective is thus made up of three elements:
(i) stabilisation of GHG concentrations;
(ii) at a level below 'dangerous interference';
(iii) over a time frame bounded by three general conditions (adaptation of ecosystems, security of food production, and sustainable economic development).

'Stabilisation' in (i) means the return to a relatively unvarying concentration of CO_2 in the atmosphere (measured in parts per million). The concentration of CO_2 in the pre-industrial era (up until the end of the 18th century) was relatively unvarying, ranging from 275 to 285 ppm. Following industrialisation, the 10 ppm margin of variation was shattered. In 2005, the CO_2 concentration measured 379 ppm and had been rising by about 2 ppm per year.[45] When the effect of all GHGs in the atmosphere is taken into account, the CO_2 eq. concentration in 2005 was around 455 ppm.[46] Greenhouse gases have thus built up so significantly over the last century as to have almost doubled their pre-industrial period concentration.

'Stabilisation' is a difficult concept. First, stabilising the CO_2 (or CO_2 eq.) concentration in the atmosphere in order to stabilise global mean surface temperature is not achieved by 'stabilising' our GHG emissions at current levels, for example. To keep anthropogenic emissions at current levels and never to emit any more than we do at present would not work to stabilise concentrations, because CO_2 and most of the other GHGs have long atmospheric lifetimes.[47] They accumulate; they do not flow away. Given that we are currently adding more CO_2 to the atmosphere than the land and oceans can absorb, if we were to hold emissions constant at current levels, the build-up in the atmosphere and the consequent global warming would only continue. Stabilising the concentration

---

44 There have been some shifts of states across the Annexes over time. For example, Annex I of the Convention was amended in 2011 to include Cyprus: UNFCCC, *Decision 10/CP.17, Amendment to Annex I to the Convention* (2011).
45 Intergovernmental Panel on Climate Change, *Climate Change 2007: The Physical Science Basis: Contribution of Working Group I to the Fourth Assessment Report of the IPCC* (Cambridge University Press, 2007), p. 137.
46 Intergovernmental Panel on Climate Change, *Climate Change 2007: Mitigation of Climate Change: Contribution of Working Group III to the Fourth Assessment Report of the IPCC* (Cambridge University Press, 2007), p. 97.
47 Intergovernmental Panel on Climate Change, *4AR: Working Group I* (2007), pp. 137–46.

therefore means *reducing* collective emissions. Second, reducing collective emissions would not result in an immediate stabilisation of the global mean temperature. The accumulated excess GHGs will continue to warm the climate for some time to come.[48]

The Convention's objective, by calling for 'stabilization of greenhouse gas concentrations in the atmosphere', thus entails an eventual overall cut in anthropogenic GHG emissions, even if it does not say so in so many words.

When all three elements of the UNFCCC's objective are considered together, they may be understood to impose an upper limit on future GHG emissions. While they do not quantify the limit, they logically imply one. To set an upper limit of CO_2 eq. concentration in the atmosphere is a first step towards determining the extent of climate change still ahead of us, as well as the speed with which we must cut emissions in order to stay within the limit. For stabilisation at no more than 490 ppm CO_2 eq., the decline in collective emissions would need to start before 2015 (about now!) and continue through to 2050, by which time emissions would have to be at about half the level they are at today.[49] For a higher stabilisation level, at 590 ppm CO_2 eq., global emissions would need to peak before 2030 and return to 2000 levels by 2040.[50] The likely amount of warming associated with the 490 target is 2 to 2.4°C above the pre-industrial average; the 590 target would likely keep the increase in the range of 2.8 to 3.2°C.[51] These are two pathways that are often discussed. There are infinitely many others, of course. How do we choose from among them?

The Convention provides little practical assistance to answer this question. The only guidance found in the Convention's objective is the imperative to prevent 'dangerous' interference with the climate system. It is a vague test: for example, dangerous for whom? As the IPCC has observed, defining 'dangerous' and the limits to be set for policy purposes 'are complex tasks that can only be partially based on science, as such definitions inherently involve normative judgments'.[52] Nevertheless, the IPCC lists five main concerns related to dangerous climate change:

- risks to unique and threatened systems (risk of losing unique ecological and social systems);
- risk of extreme weather events (extreme events with substantial consequences for societies and natural systems);
- distribution of impacts (spatial scale of impacts);

---

[48] P. Wu et al., 'Temporary Acceleration of the Hydrological Cycle in Response to a CO_2 Rampdown', 37 *Geophysical Research Letters* L12705 1 (June 2010) ('The drying trend under global warming over the Amazon, Australia and western Africa may intensify for decades after CO_2 reductions. The inertia due to accumulated heat in the ocean implies a commitment to hydrological cycle changes long after stabilisation or reduction of atmospheric CO_2 concentration').
[49] Intergovernmental Panel on Climate Change, *4AR: Working Group III* (2007), p. 172.   [50] Ibid.
[51] Ibid., p. 173.
[52] Ibid., p. 97. The term 'dangerous climate change' is still in common use today, and it is now generally associated (by scientists as well as politicians) with a global mean surface temperature rise greater than 2°C from pre-industrial levels. See, for example, W. Steffen, *The Critical Decade: Climate Science, Risks and Responses* (Australian Climate Commission, 2011), p. 18.

- aggregate damages (monetary damages or monetary losses, and lives affected or lives lost);
- risks of 'large-scale discontinuities' (likelihood of reaching tipping points).[53]

We may conclude from the above discussion that while the UNFCCC's objective does begin to articulate a legal obligation upon state parties (namely the obligation to reduce collective emissions), it is an ill-defined one, both because 'stabilisation' entails a global obligation as opposed to one at the state level where international law traditionally applies, and because the term 'dangerous' is so open-ended in the treaty text that it might as well be replaced by the term 'unwanted'. Should it not be the task of the Convention to tell us what is unwanted? The answer probably is this: Not if it is only a framework convention. Do legal obligations that are too vague to be pinned down bind states at all? Here too the answer is probably in the negative. While there is relatively greater specificity in certain other provisions of the UNFCCC, its indeterminacy is the main reason why the state parties sped into negotiations for a protocol.

Article 3 of the Convention is called 'Principles'. This is both promising, as it entitles us to think of the constituent elements of this provision as 'legal' principles, and challenging, for the general reason that the directive force of principles laid down in an international treaty is less certain than the force of principles implemented in domestic legislation, where their proper interpretation and application generally become clear when matters are taken to court. (The application of international law by courts of any kind is still a relatively rare event, and almost nonexistent for environmental law or climate change law.) The opening paragraph of Article 3 states that the parties are to be 'guided, inter alia' by the principles listed within it. To be 'guided' is not the same as to be 'bound', and 'inter alia' opens the door to other, unspecified guiding principles, whose content according to standard rules of interpretation is limited only by the implicit requirement that they are consistent with the Convention's objective, which, as we have seen, is itself quite broadly phrased. Five principles make up Article 3:

(i) the parties 'should protect the climate system for the benefit of *present and future generations* of humankind, on the basis of equity';
(ii) they should do so 'in accordance with their *common but differentiated responsibilities* and respective capabilities. Accordingly, the developed country Parties should take the lead in combating climate change and the adverse effects thereof';
(iii) the parties 'should take *precautionary measures* to anticipate, prevent or minimize the causes of climate change and mitigate its adverse effects. Where there are threats of serious or irreversible damage, lack of full scientific certainty should not be used as a reason for postponing such measures, taking into account that policies and measures to deal with

---

53 See C. M. Duarte et al., 'Abrupt Climate Change in the Arctic', 2 *Nature Climate Change* 60 (February 2012), Table 1, p. 60.

climate change should be cost-effective so as to ensure global benefits at the lowest possible cost';
(iv) the parties 'have a right to, and should, promote *sustainable development*; [moreover,] economic development is essential for adopting measures to address climate change';
(v) the parties should 'promote a supportive and *open international economic system* ... Measures taken to combat climate change, including unilateral ones, should not constitute a means of arbitrary or unjustifiable discrimination or a disguised restriction on international trade'.[54]

We have commented on some of these notions already, as they were anticipated by the preamble. The first in the list refers to 'equity'. In this context, 'equity' most likely means 'fairness' in a straightforward moral sense. First of all, it is fairness towards future generations, who do not yet exist. Secondly, it is a judgment to be made by the *current* generation. These two elements reveal the strangeness of the intergenerational principle as an ethical principle and as a principle in an international law instrument. What are we to make of a state signing up to an obligation towards a 'future generation'? The principle can seem very exotic from a traditional legal perspective, since states' obligations relate to other states or to other legal entities, but a future generation is neither of these.

The imperative of fairness must also inform decisions about *present* generations (this follows from a plain reading of the quoted passage in (i) above). The first principle in the Convention's Article 3 thus seems to oblige states to respond to the climate change problem while keeping an eye on two sets of scales: one scale balances future interests against those of the present; the other balances the differing interests of people living in the present. The *inter*generational balancing exercise is conceptually challenging for the reasons given already, but also because it involves a significant conflict of interest. Are we not likely to prioritise present needs and discount those of people in the future?

Perhaps, though, all that this amounts to is that state parties to the UNFCCC are legally obliged to apply the principle of intergenerational equity as best they can in their decision-making about climate change. Its prominent position in the Convention means that it would be a factor that states *must* consider, alongside other factors. But it remains a very ill-defined consideration. One could easily read intergenerational equity down, reducing it to the following threadbare principle: 'Protecting the climate system for the benefit of future generations is not the demanding moral requirement that we be *custodians* of the climate for future generations. We are not custodians but exploiters of our environment. Keeping the climate *liveable* is sufficient to comply with the principle.' Indeed, the principle must be joined with other beliefs and values about what a good life requires before it could make a difference in present-day decision-making.

---

54 Italics added. The numbering of the principles is that of the authors and does not correspond to the numbering of Article 3 of the Convention's text.

The second balancing exercise, aimed at an *intra*generational balance, is elaborated by the second principle in Article 3 – principle (ii) in the list above. Unlike principle (i), which concerns decision-making procedure, principle (ii) is both a procedural and a *substantive* principle. It may be understood as saying that, in fairness to present generations, beginning here and now, rich countries should sacrifice proportionately more than poor countries should have to sacrifice in order to solve the climate problem. If we accept this as a legal principle, then under Convention law there will always be a class of states (developed states) that are obliged to do proportionately more than another class (developing states) to combat climate change. It is not a controversial principle when stated in these general terms. But a legal imperative, as we have noted more than once already, must not be so general as to be non-directive. Financial aid will not flow in a steady stream, for example, unless the Convention establishes who will contribute and how much. The expression 'take the lead' in principle (ii) is open to several interpretations, from doing just a fraction more than other states, to doing one kind of thing (for example capping fossil-fuel emissions) while poorer states are doing a different kind of thing (unrestricted economic expansion). 'Proportionately more' must be defined. It must be written into a treaty, or no state will be clear about what it is required to do. The concrete interpretation of the legal force of principle (ii) is still a matter of great controversy. It is fleshed out to some extent in the Convention's Article 4 on 'Commitments', which is discussed below.

The precautionary principle, which is the third principle in Article 3, is formulated in a way similar to Principle 15 of the Rio Declaration. The latter dates from the same year as the UNFCCC and includes the statement: 'Where there are threats of serious or irreversible damage, lack of full scientific certainty shall not be used as a reason for postponing cost-effective measures to prevent environmental degradation.'[55] Both versions of the principle use the threshold of 'serious or irreversible damage', and both call for action on the condition that the action is 'cost-effective'. There is thus a double conditionality built into the 1992 version of the precautionary principle. (The second condition has not always been carried into domestic formulations.[56]) Besides the two conditions limiting its application, the principle is stated negatively, as an instruction about what should *not* be done in deciding a course of action. The sense of the principle might be easier to grasp when reformulated positively in this way:

> If a proposed or ongoing human action creates a risk of serious or irreversible environmental damage, and if the action could be avoided (or the risk of damage reduced) at a reasonable cost, then the avoidance of the action (or reduction of the risk) should be afforded significant weight by decision-makers with influence over the action.

---

55 Rio Declaration on Environment and Development, 31 *International Legal Materials* 874 (1992).
56 See, for example, Australia's *Environment Protection and Biodiversity Conservation Act 1999* (Cth) s 3A(b).

This is pure procedure. It leaves states with great leeway about what to do. While it could be considered a general principle of law,[57] it could also be thought of as a standard (*how to decide* how to act) rather than a rule (how to act).[58] The same is true of the intergenerational principle: it is a standard that applies to decision-making that affects the environment.

The fourth principle under UNFCCC Article 3 – that the parties 'have a right to, and should, promote sustainable development' – could easily be misread as providing for a *right* to sustainable development, when in fact it provides only for a right to the *promotion* of sustainable development. The difference may seem a fine one, but if, as we presume, the state parties to the Convention were intent to avoid the creation of new human rights, the placement of the second comma (after 'should' instead of after 'promote') is critical. That parties have a right *to promote* sustainable development does not seem like a legal principle at all, actually. The fact that the meaning of 'sustainable development' has always been difficult to pin down adds to the challenge of appreciating the force of this principle.

The more interesting part of the fourth principle is the idea that 'economic development is essential for adopting measures to address climate change'. This could be a restatement of the principle that (poor) countries have a right to develop economically before accepting burdens under the international climate change regime (burdens ranging from having to keep an inventory of their GHG emissions, at one end, to having to reduce their emissions in absolute terms, at the other). Or it could be the proposition that the only way to transform a 'brown' economy into a 'green' one is to maintain its strong growth, breaking from its old ways gradually by using income from that growth to undertake structural reform. Is this a plausible proposition? Probably not, given that growth is presently associated with increased, not decreased, GHG emissions. What we can be sure about is that the fourth principle of Article 3 is 'pro-development'. Whether it creates any new legal obligation is less clear. It would have been useful, legally, for the Convention to declare that all economic development must be sustainable (in a national or, better still, global sense), but the Convention imposes no such general condition.

Lastly, appearing as (v) in our list, is the principle of the 'open international economic system'. The state parties to the Convention are obliged to 'cooperate to promote' such a system, with the aim that it should lead 'to sustainable economic growth and development in all Parties'.

An 'open international economic system' is a vision of global organisation in an ideal future. A remarkable element of climate change studies, which is relevant also to climate law, is the preoccupation with forecasting the future, frequently decades ahead of the present. We see this in public policy, where countries pledge that, say, by 2020 they will have reduced their emissions by a certain amount; in economics, where the energy share of renewable sources is predicted

---

[57] Bodansky, *Art and Craft* (2010), p. 201.   [58] Ibid., pp. 201–2.

decades into the future; in population projections; and, of course, in climate science, for example in relation to changing precipitation patterns, degradation of coral reefs, and sea-level rise, sometimes drawn out to 2100. We do not just periodically come across such references; they are at the centre of the climate change discourse. It is a discourse whose orientation contrasts with the backward-looking stance that dominates in law.

These forecasts, which are the lifeblood of climate change studies, rest on assumptions about the characteristics of human society in the future. The assumptions are openly debated because different forms of social organisation lead to different intensities of GHG emissions. Do we know the direction our society is taking? Probably not with any confidence. Even population growth forecasts are quite uncertain. We commonly experience reversals in predictions about even relatively simple policy outcomes, such as whether Australia will institute an emissions trading scheme or whether there will be a second commitment period under the Kyoto Protocol. (Both seemed certain prior to the 2009 Copenhagen COP. Both eventually materialised, but not before they went through successive stages of looking certain, expiring, and being resurrected.)

Against this background, the fifth principle in the Convention's Article 3, encouraging open economies, implicitly recognises that global economic openness is not a future certainty. As the IPCC has put it, 'By 2100 the world will have changed in ways that are difficult to imagine, as difficult as it was at the end of the 19th century to imagine the changes of the 20th century.'[59] This remark was made in the context of the IPCC's development of 'emission scenarios' (see Box 2.1), which have come to assume a central place in research-based and scholarly accounts of the future. The IPCC's emission scenarios treat as uncertain the extent to which economic globalisation and increased social and cultural interactions will continue over the course of the twenty-first century. Because of this, and as summarised in Box 2.1, the so-called A1 and B1 'storylines' emphasise global economic convergence as well as intensive social and cultural interaction, whereas the storylines known as A2 and B2 focus on possible regional developmental pathways that take our societies in diverging and traditionalist directions. These two dimensions are strongly correlated with the intensity of anthropogenic GHG emissions. The scenario method enables the IPCC to adopt a relatively neutral stance about the future of human civilisation by computer-based modelling of several storylines in parallel. In the process, a new discourse emerges, one about life on Earth under the designated scenarios.

The role of the 'open economy' principle in UNFCCC Article 3 might therefore be understood as a preference of state parties for the A1 and B1 storylines, which are constructed around global economic integration. Does that mean party support for the least harmful emission scenarios? As noted in Box 2.1, A1

---

59 Intergovernmental Panel on Climate Change, 'Special Report on Emission Scenarios', <http://www.ipcc.ch/ipccreports/sres/emission/index.php?idp=91#4.2.1.>.

> **BOX 2.1 Imagining society in the future**
>
> The IPCC developed the following four 'families' of scenarios to help it model potential trends in GHG emissions. The selected development pathways derive from and build on a range of demographic, economic and technological driving forces. The emission projections based on these scenarios are widely used in the assessment of future climate change.[60]
>
> The **A1** storyline and scenario family describe a future world of very rapid economic growth, low population growth, and the rapid introduction of new and more efficient technologies. Major underlying themes are convergence among regions, widespread capacity-building, and increased cultural and social interactions, with a substantial reduction in regional differences in per capita income. The A1 scenario family branches out into four groups that describe alternative directions of technological change in the energy system. *GHG emissions under the A1 scenario (and all subordinate groups) are relatively high.*
>
> The **A2** storyline and scenario family describe a very heterogeneous world. The underlying theme is self-reliance and preservation of local identities. Human fertility tends to maintain regional patterns and to converge very slowly, and population growth is high. Economic development is primarily regionally oriented, and per capita economic growth and technological change are more fragmented and slower than in other storylines. *Emissions under A2 are mostly lower than A1, but higher than in other scenarios.*
>
> The **B1** storyline and scenario family describe a convergent world with the same low population growth as in the A1 storyline, but with rapid changes in economic structures toward a service and information economy, with reductions in material intensity (that is, less material needed to produce goods) and the introduction of clean and resource-efficient technologies. The emphasis is on global solutions to economic, social and environmental sustainability, including improved equity, but without additional climate action initiatives. It is a world that many readers of this book would consider ideal. *B1 emissions are at the low end of the scale.*
>
> The **B2** storyline and scenario family describe a world in which the emphasis is on local solutions to economic, social and environmental sustainability. It is a world with moderate population growth, intermediate levels of economic development, and less rapid and more diverse technological change than in the B1 and A1 storylines. While the scenario is also oriented toward environmental protection and social equity, it focuses on the local and regional levels.[61] *GHG emissions under this scenario are also relatively mild, but higher than in B1.*

is relatively emission-intensive, and one of its varieties (known as A1FI) is the most intensive of all IPCC scenarios.[62] The point to note is that economically 'open' arrangements are not necessarily better for climate change mitigation than their opposites. The principle of economic 'openness' therefore expresses a political ideology and is another element of the Convention that is not fully consistent with the Convention's objective. Moreover, the principle of economic openness may have had the effect of delaying domestic action on emission abatement, due to a concern that a carbon price would raise the price of products of the domestic jurisdiction that imposed it, thereby making those products less competitive than like products imported from countries without laws pricing GHG emissions.

---

60 L. Bernstein et al., *Climate Change 2007: Synthesis Report* (IPCC, 2007), p. 44.
61 From IPCC, *Special Report on Emission Scenarios* (2000), <http://www.ipcc.ch/ipccreports/sres/emission/index.php?idp=91#4.2.1.>.
62 L. Bernstein et al., *4AR Synthesis* (2007), Table 3.1 (p. 45) and Fig. 3.2 (p. 46).

BOX 2.2 The main state obligations and rights in Article 4 of the UNFCCC

Article 4 of the UNFCCC, titled 'Commitments', contains certain state obligations and rights, summarised below. These have been extended and elaborated in COP decisions in ways that are not reflected here.

Obligations

All parties	Annex I parties	Annex II parties (OECD)
→→→→→→→→→→→→→increasing burden→→→→→→→→→→→→→→		

- **All parties**
  - Prepare GHG inventory – but in the case of developing parties, only if capacity permits.
  - Implement, publish, and regularly update national measures to mitigate climate change, as well as measures to facilitate adaptation to climate change, including integrated plans for the management of water resources and agriculture.
  - Promote sustainable management of GHG sinks/reservoirs including forests and oceans.
  - Ensure that Environmental Impact Assessments take climate change into account.
  - Cooperate in scientific research and systematic observation with the aim of reducing the remaining uncertainties about climate change.

- **Annex I parties**
  - Implement national mitigation policies and measures limiting anthropogenic GHG emissions and aimed at returning emissions to 1990 levels by 2000.
  - Provide periodic detailed reports to COP on above policies and measures, specifying estimated impact on state's GHG emissions.
  - The calculation of reported emissions and removals must be scientifically sound and based on agreed methodologies.

- **Annex II parties (OECD)**
  - Provide new and additional financial resources to meet costs incurred by developing country parties in complying with their reporting obligations under the treaty.
  - The above applies also to transfer of technology, etc., needed by developing country parties to meet the implementation costs (of the measures in the far left column).
  - Assist developing country parties that are particularly vulnerable to the adverse effects of climate change to meet adaptation costs.
  - Take all steps to facilitate and finance other parties' access to environmentally sound technologies and know-how so as to enable implementation of the Convention's provisions.

Developing country party *rights*

A developing country party may request technical and financial support in compiling and communicating information required under the Convention.

It may propose mitigation or adaptation projects for financing by Annex II parties, including specific technologies needed, along with an explanation of the resulting benefits.

The extent to which developing country parties implement their commitments will depend on financial resources and transfer of technology from Annex II parties.

Developing country parties with economies that are highly dependent on income from the production of fossil fuels must be given special consideration.

What are we to make of the cluster of principles in Article 3 of the Convention? Do they impose any new obligations on an Annex I country such as Australia? Certainly Australia, together with other wealthy states, is called upon to take the lead in combating climate change, which is not a responsibility it had prior to ratifying the Convention. However, there is little else in Article 3 that makes a difference to how a state should run its affairs, in concrete terms.

Commitments

The UNFCCC's Article 4, on 'Commitments', has a long and complex structure, summarised in Box 2.2. The article is divided into obligations common to all parties, obligations pertaining only to Annex I parties (OECD states and states with economies in transition), and obligations exclusive to Annex II parties (OECD states). Consistently with the Convention's provisions up to this point in the treaty text, even the general commitments relating to all parties do not impose equal obligations on all states or demand uniform adherence. They are, instead, subject to the parties' 'common but differentiated responsibilities and their specific national and regional development priorities, objectives and circumstances'.[63]

The first of the Article 4 commitments is of great conceptual and practical importance. The Convention requires all states to '[d]evelop, periodically update, [and] publish ... national inventories of anthropogenic emissions by sources and removals by sinks of all greenhouse gases ... using comparable methodologies'.[64] This is the foundation of a complex web of international regulation whose influence can be traced from the top level of the UNFCCC down to the organisational minutiae of state parties' bureaucracies. It can be reduced to the question: What quantity of GHGs from human activity does each state emit? Twenty years ago we had no ready or accurate answer to this question. Without an answer, we cannot compare pollution levels (absolute or per capita) across jurisdictions, assign emission limits to states, determine mitigation progress from one year to the next, or enforce compliance with emission caps. The answer is far from easily obtained – which is unsurprising when one considers the enormity of the task.

In Chapter 3 we take a detailed look at the processes through which the national GHG inventories of Annex I parties are compiled, reported and checked. (The extent of international regulation of these processes justifies a separate chapter.) The Convention does not specify the required frequency of production of the emission inventories, but instead refers the matter to the COP for determination.[65] The treaty text acknowledges the need for 'comparable methodologies', which are necessary to ensure that national inventories are prepared in such a way as to be as complete and accurate as possible and comparable across states. Such methodologies have since been developed by the IPCC[66] and approved by the parties to the Convention.[67] The methodologies

---

[63] UNFCCC, Art. 4.   [64] UNFCCC, Art. 4(1)(a).   [65] UNFCCC, Art. 12(5).
[66] Intergovernmental Panel on Climate Change, *Revised 1996 IPCC Guidelines for National Greenhouse Gas Inventories* (1996) (replacing the *1995 IPCC Guidelines for National Greenhouse Inventories*). The 1996 Guidelines were further elaborated in Intergovernmental Panel on Climate Change, *Good Practice Guidance and Uncertainty Management in National Greenhouse Gas Inventories* (2000).
[67] The *1995 IPCC Guidelines* (see previous footnote) were approved in November 1994. The UNFCCC Conference of the Parties adopted them at its first meeting: UNFCCC, *Decision 4/CP.1, Methodological Issues* (1995), FCCC/CP/1995/7/Add.1. The *Revised 1996 IPCC Guidelines* (also cited in previous footnote) were

are periodically revised and supplemented, and they have found extensive application, especially among Annex I parties.

To what extent have *developing* countries complied with their (heavily qualified) obligation to produce national GHG inventories? At the time of writing, the last compilation of non-Annex I inventory information prepared by the UNFCCC Secretariat was from 2005.[68] By that date, 122 of the 148 non-Annex I parties had submitted a 'national communication' with inventory information.[69] All submissions followed, to one degree or another, the standard IPCC methodologies for making inventory estimates. Almost all the reporting developing parties provided an estimate for at least one year (generally 1994) of their emissions of the three main GHGs: carbon dioxide, methane, and nitrous oxide.[70] About half of the reporting parties conceded that some important 'activity data' (information about human activity leading to the release or absorption of a GHG) were either lacking or were not accessible due to inadequate data collection or management systems within their national jurisdiction.[71] There was little uniformity in presentation of the emission data in these national communications or in explaining the underlying calculations.[72] For these reasons, and considering that the non-Annex I inventory information is not reviewed by Expert Review Teams (on the ERT system, see Chapter 3), the emission data derived from the relatively loose reporting system for developing countries lacks the indicators of reliability needed for accurate mitigation planning at the global level.[73]

The two-track system of states created by the Convention has thus led to a bifurcation of, among other things, the global emission inventory. Nevertheless, on the positive side, many non-Annex I states have recognised and followed up on their inventory-reporting commitment in Article 4(1)(a) of the Convention by submitting at least one inventory in the past twenty or so years since the Convention came into effect.

In the 'all parties' section of Article 4, the remaining 'commitments' cover other areas of state housekeeping:

---

adopted at the Convention's fifth COP: UNFCCC, *Decision 3/CP.5, Guidelines for the Preparation of National Communications by Parties Included in Annex I to the Convention, Part I: UNFCCC Reporting Guidelines on Annual Inventories* (1999), FCCC/CP/1999/6/Add.1.

68 Secretariat (UNFCCC), *Sixth Compilation and Synthesis of Initial National Communications from Parties Not Included in Annex I to the Convention; Addendum: Inventories of Anthropogenic Emissions by Sources and Removals by Sinks of Greenhouse Gases* (25 October 2005), FCCC/SBI/2005/18/Add.2.
69 Ibid., p. 3. By 2005, almost all developing country parties had submitted an initial national communication to the UNFCCC, and a handful had also submitted a second. In the period 2008–11 (which is outside the scope of the Secretariat's compilation), 50 non-Annex I countries submitted a second national communication, and two countries (Mexico and Uruguay) even managed to submit a third. See UNFCCC, 'Non-Annex I National Communications', <http://www.unfccc.int/national_reports/non-annex_i_natcom/items/2979.php>.
70 Secretariat (UNFCCC), *Compilation and Synthesis Addendum* (2005). Only 18 parties provided estimates of hydrofluorocarbons (HFCs), perfluorocarbons (PFCs), or sulphur hexafluoride (SF_6).
71 Ibid., p. 4. **72** Ibid., p. 5.
73 Aggregating the reported GHG emissions (excluding the LULUCF sector), the Secretariat concluded that the 122 non-Annex I parties that had submitted national communications by 2005 were responsible for a total of 11.7 billion tonnes of CO_2 eq. emissions per year, as at around 1994: ibid., p. 7. This compares with about 13 billion tonnes of emissions from Annex I countries in the same year: see Table 2.1 later in this chapter.

(i) All states must have policies to mitigate climate change and facilitate adaptation.
(ii) They must all cooperate in the development and distribution of climate-friendly technologies and expand the 'sustainable management' of their natural resources, including their forests.
(iii) Their economic growth and environmental planning should incorporate thinking about adaptation to the likely impacts of climate change, and the relevant branches of government, which often operate separately, should now become 'integrated'.
(iv) All states are to promote scientific, socioeconomic, and other research into topics related to climate change, improve education and public awareness about the subject, and encourage the widest participation of the public and NGOs in the general discussion and policy formation process.

It is a sensible, if anodyne, list. As with all regulation, the critical question is: How do we know whether these obligations are being fulfilled or not?

In relation to (iv) in the list, we should note that, in a democratic society, scientific research generally has a life of its own. So at the very least, what we would be looking for as evidence of the fulfilment of that promise is an injection of new government funding for scientific research related to climate change, or an adjustment to the criteria used to allocate research grants, so that, in one way or another, more publicly funded research happens in the area of climate change.[74] As for the commitment in (iv) to raise public awareness about climate change, encourage participation and involve NGOs, by 2006 the concern about climate change seemed to be on everybody's lips, largely due to the efforts of a former politician, Al Gore, and NGOs such as WWF and Greenpeace, rather than the efforts of any particular government. The non-government sector, as it turned out, did not have to wait to be 'encouraged' – it took the lead. In Australia, it was not until 2011 that the government created a body, the Climate Commission, with a responsibility to 'educate' the public on climate-related topics.[75] It is easy in retrospect to appreciate that, in the case of climate change, government inaction risked not a dearth of information but a plethora of misinformation. Gore's influence as a source of clear and reliable information was complemented by that of environmental NGOs and UN agencies, but much distortion and scepticism was peddled at the same time. In Australia's case, misinformation has variously frustrated or sunk the government's reforms.

The commitment in Article 4 of the UNFCCC that most directly tackles climate change is one made by Annex I parties. It is to the effect that they must 'limit'

---

[74] In Australia, for example, the federal government considers research in the broad area of 'Responding to climate change and variability' to be a national research priority within the framework of its grant-giving body, the Australian Research Council. See <http://www.arc.gov.au/>.

[75] See <http://www.climatecommission.govspace.gov.au/>. The Commission's tasks are 'to provide information and expert advice to explain the science of climate change and the impacts on Australia; report on the progress of international action dealing with climate change; [and] explain the purpose and operation of a carbon price and how it may interact with the Australian economy and communities'. The Commission's first report (Steffen, *The Critical Decade* (2011)) provided an updated summary of the science in relatively accessible terms.

their anthropogenic GHG emissions. To limit is not the same as to cut (for example where the limit is set above current emission levels), and a limitation that caps not overall emissions but *the rate of emissions growth* is compatible with uninterrupted growth in emissions, albeit at a slower rate. After referring, ambiguously, to a 'limit', the language of Article 4 becomes diluted to such an extent that the limitation commitment is reduced to a mere aim or aspiration:

> [P]olicies and measures will demonstrate that developed countries are taking the lead in modifying longer-term trends in anthropogenic emissions consistent with the objective of the Convention, recognizing that the *return by the end of the present decade* [i.e. by 2000] *to earlier levels* of anthropogenic emissions of carbon dioxide and other greenhouse gases not controlled by the Montreal Protocol would contribute to such modification, and taking into account the differences in these Parties' starting points and approaches, economic structures and resource bases, the need to maintain strong and sustainable economic growth, available technologies and other individual circumstances, as well as the need for equitable and appropriate contributions by each of these Parties to the global effort regarding that objective.[76]

In the next paragraph of Article 4 we learn that the phrase 'earlier levels' of emissions means Annex I emissions as they stood in 1990.

Thus the quoted text succeeds in carving out a temporal period in which to test the parties' commitment to 'modify longer-term trends' in their emissions: by the year 2000, the article implies, Annex I parties should have returned collectively to their 1990 emission levels. (This syntax – by year X there shall be reduction Y with reference to year Z – has become commonplace since 1992 in shorthand descriptions of state commitments. The year 1990 has remained the standard reference year, or *base* year for the purposes of the UN.) The implication we have drawn out here is in fact so heavily qualified by the text of Article 4, as quoted above, that it could be read, if necessary, as one option among others. That is to say: *One* way to modify long-term trends is to return to 1990 emission levels by 2000.

In the event, only seven out of the twenty-three Annex II states were able to do so (Table 2.1). The economic slowdown resulting from the restructuring and technological renewal of the former Soviet Bloc countries in the 1990s caused a corresponding (unplanned) fall in GHG emissions in those countries.[77] Thus Table 2.1 does not list all Annex I states, tracking the performance only of the Annex II (OECD) subset. In the table, moreover, the emission quantities exclude emissions and removals from LULUCF.[78] The shaded rows highlight the countries that could be said to have complied with the implied commitment in Article 4 of the UNFCCC to return their GHG emissions to 1990 levels by the year 2000. (Most

---

76 UNFCCC, Art. 4(2)(a), emphasis added.
77 Secretariat (UNFCCC), *Compilation and Synthesis of Fourth National Communications: Executive Summary* (2007), FCCC/SBI/2007/INF.6, pp. 3–4.
78 LULUCF stands for land use, land-use change and forestry. The estimation of GHG emissions and removals in this sector is relatively uncertain. Moreover, human control over LULUCF emissions and removals is not as pronounced as in other economic sectors (for instance, people cannot entirely prevent fires from natural causes from occurring in forests under state management). Hence state emissions are conventionally reported using two sets of numbers, one including the LULUCF contribution and the other excluding it.

Table 2.1 Greenhouse gas emissions of the UNFCCC's Annex II states 1990–2009, in megatonnes (Mt) of CO_2 eq.

Annex II state	1990	2000	2008	2009	2009 change over 1990 (%)
Australia	418.5	496.3	550.9	545.9	30.4
Austria	78.2	80.5	87.0	80.1	2.4
Belgium	143.3	145.4	135.1	124.4	−13.2
Canada	591.3	717.6	733.7	691.8	17.0
Denmark	69.4	69.3	65.2	62.3	−10.2
Finland	70.4	69.2	70.4	66.3	−5.7
France	565.0	571.0	544.3	522.4	−7.7
Germany	1248.0	1042.1	981.1	920.0	−26.3
Greece	104.6	126.2	128.7	122.7	17.4
Iceland	3.4	3.8	4.9	4.6	35.1
Ireland	54.8	67.9	67.8	62.4	13.8
Italy	519.2	551.6	541.7	491.1	−5.4
Japan	1266.6	1341.8	1280.6	1209.2	−4.5
Luxembourg	12.8	9.8	12.2	11.7	−8.9
Netherlands	212.0	213.2	204.6	199.0	−6.1
New Zealand	59.1	68.4	72.8	70.6	19.4
Norway	49.8	53.4	53.7	51.3	3.1
Portugal	59.4	81.3	78.0	74.7	25.6
Spain	283.2	379.6	404.8	367.5	29.8
Sweden	72.5	69.0	63.6	60.1	−17.2
Switzerland	53.1	52.0	53.4	51.9	−2.2
United Kingdom	779.4	673.5	624.1	570.1	−26.9
United States	6166.8	7076.3	7027.9	6608.2	7.2
Total	12880.8	13959.2	13786.5	12968.3	0.7

Source: Adapted from Secretariat (UNFCCC), *National Greenhouse Gas Inventory Data for the Period 1990–2009* (16 November 2011), FCCC/SBI/2011/9, Table 5.

likely, the treaty commitment actually refers to aggregate rather than country-level reductions.) The years 2008–09 are the first two years of the Kyoto Protocol's first commitment period.

A few countries shown in Table 2.1, including the United Kingdom, could boast a consistent downward trend at least partially attributable to government policy. (In the UK's case there was a major shift from coal to less polluting gas-based power generation in the 1990s.[79]) Three of the seven shaded countries (Finland, Luxembourg and Switzerland) were unable to maintain their downward trend past 2000, their emissions rising again by 2008. Most OECD countries, though, seem to have paid scant regard to the trajectory urged upon them by Article 4 of the Convention. Australia, Canada and the United States, among others, decisively increased their emissions in the 1990–2000 period, with Australia also reporting higher annual emissions in 2008–09 than in 2000.

---

[79] Secretariat (UNFCCC), *Compilation and Synthesis Executive Summary* (2007), p. 3.

A critical factor in understanding the 2008–09 figures is the Global Financial Crisis.[80] The GFC certainly helped the Annex I countries shown above to meet their emission reduction commitments in 2008–09. With the easing of the financial crisis, emissions seem to be picking up again. According to draft emission data for 2010, CO_2 emissions in developed countries increased 3.4 per cent.[81] In interpreting the country emission trajectories in Table 2.1, we should also keep in mind that some easing in the level of Annex II emissions is attributable to the 'outsourcing' of GHG-intensive industry to industrialising nations like China or Vietnam (from where the manufactured products are imported ready-made into the OECD zone) – which means that any improvement in the Annex II trend apparent from the above information is partly accounted for by a migration of emissions out of the zone.[82] In Australia's case, outsourcing of emissions embedded in domestic consumption is paralleled by a growth in coal exports to South Korea, Taiwan, China and India, among other developing countries, to power industrialisation there.[83] Because the coal is not burnt in Australia, it has no effect on Australia's national GHG inventory.

Finally, it is relevant to a correct understanding of the above figures that Australia's population was growing strongly over the period covered by the table,[84] and therefore the growth in *per capita* emissions is less steep than the growth in *total* emissions. Population growth in European countries, by contrast, was flat during that period,[85] putting less pressure on their total emissions.

As summarised in Box 2.2 (p. 73), Annex I parties are on a stricter reporting schedule than the other parties to the Convention. Article 4 requires them to report 'in detail' about their policies and measures aimed at returning them to 1990 emission levels by 2000. The first submitted set of such reports containing the required information – called national communications – was to be 'reviewed', according to Article 4, at the first COP, which in fact did not take place until March 1995. It was therefore not until about halfway through the 1990–2000 decade that Annex I parties to the Convention came to know the 'policies and measures' through which other Annex I parties were planning to meet their quasi-commitment in Article 3 to alter their emission trajectory so as to end the decade at the same level at which they started it. The delay in

---

80 UN Environment Programme, *Bridging the Emissions Gap: A UNEP Synthesis Report* (November 2011), p. 16.
81 G. P. Peters et al., 'Rapid Growth in CO_2 Emissions after the 2008–2009 Global Financial Crisis', 2 *Nature Climate Change* 2 (January 2012), p. 2.
82 Taking into account the carbon embodied in international trade, Caldeira and Davis write that '[i]n 1990, 0.4 Gt CO_2 were emitted in developing countries to subsidize consumption in developed countries. By 2008, this subsidy increased to 1.6 Gt CO_2. ... Thus, consideration of international trade reverses the decreasing trend in emissions in developed countries, turning a 2% decrease into a 7% increase': K. Caldeira and S. J. Davis, 'Accounting for Carbon Dioxide Emissions: A Matter of Time', 108(21) *PNAS* 8533 (24 May 2011), p. 8534. The identified increase exceeds the Kyoto Protocol emission reductions. The underlying data are from G. P. Peters et al., 'Growth in Emission Transfers Via International Trade from 1990 to 2008', 108(21) *PNAS* 8903 (24 May 2011).
83 See <http://www.australiancoal.com.au/the-australian-coal-industry_coal-exports_coal-export-details.aspx>.
84 See Figure 2.2 earlier in this chapter.
85 Department of Economic and Social Affairs Population Division, *World Population Prospects: The 2010 Revision, Volume II: Demographic Profiles* (United Nations, 2011), ST/ESA/SER.A/317, p. 167.

'discovery' did not leave much time for coordination, of course; nor did it leave much time to develop the mechanisms needed to minimise implementation costs. It is perhaps no surprise, then, that the majority of Annex I states failed to meet the modest target contained in the Convention.

Annex I parties continued to submit national communications every few years, pursuant to Article 4 (and Article 12) of the Convention, as elaborated by the decisions of the COP. The fifth round of submissions was completed in 2010. By that point, the process of using national communications had been developed and systematised to such an extent that it had become a universe of legal obligation in its own right. Regulation of communication about national measures and outcomes might not sound like a very ambitious or exciting area of international law, yet it is a precondition of international collaboration at every higher level of policy. It is also an area that is relatively uncontroversial. All states can agree on the need to share basic information about their emissions and about their mitigation and adaptation policies.[86] By the fifth COP, in 1999, the Convention parties had agreed to detailed guidelines on reporting.[87]

In a synthesis report from 2007 based on the fourth national communications of 39 Annex I countries, the UNFCCC Secretariat noted that the parties had generally developed and implemented varied portfolios of policies and measures to mitigate GHG emissions. These included emission pricing mechanisms (for example carbon taxes, and, especially in the energy industries, tradable emission allowances); barrier reduction policies aimed at overcoming financial and market barriers to the deployment of existing climate-friendly technologies (for example feed-in tariffs and green certificates for energy from renewables); measures directed towards energy and performance efficiency (including regulatory measures and voluntary industry sector-based commitments for fuel economy in cars); regulations affecting product and building standards in the commercial and residential sectors; policies aimed at long-term research and development in new technologies; and information and awareness programs (for example product labels).[88]

The Secretariat also found that Annex I parties were increasingly preferring harder (economic and regulatory) instruments over softer (voluntary) instruments to effect emission reductions. Exceptions included Australia and the United States, which relied heavily on voluntary enterprise challenges and partnerships.[89] Carbon taxes had played a role in some countries for some time, but innovative forms of regulation, in particular tradable certificate systems, were growing more quickly and were more widely in use by 2007 than in

---

[86] However, the issue of where to draw the line and how to share the reporting burden can become vexed, as we shall see in Chapter 3.
[87] See UNFCCC, *Decision 4/CP.5, Guidelines for the Preparation of National Communications by Parties Included in Annex I to the Convention, Part II: UNFCCC Reporting Guidelines on National Communications* (1999), FCCC/CP/1999/6/Add.1.
[88] Secretariat (UNFCCC), *Compilation and Synthesis of Fourth National Communications: Executive Summary* (2007), p. 6.
[89] Ibid., p. 7.

earlier years, with the EU ETS standing out in terms of its scale.[90] Parties were increasing their use of 'multilevel governance' for climate change issues – that is, coordinated action by multiple scales of government (local to national) and across governmental departments and NGOs.[91] The majority of the OECD (Annex II) states reported an increase in their contribution to the Global Environment Facility (on the GEF, see Chapter 8) in the 2001–04 period compared to the 1997–2000 period.[92] On technology transfer, the majority of the activities took place in the energy sector, in particular in the area of energy efficiency and renewable energy.[93]

The Secretariat noted certain shortcomings in the submitted national communications. There was little reported information on how entities covered by cap-and-trade schemes such as the EU ETS balanced their emissions and carbon allowances, whether it was through improving and better implementing existing technologies – developing new technologies, purchasing carbon allowances from domestic or foreign entities, or shifting high-emission operations to other countries.[94] Annex I countries were not reporting on all of the elements of their response to climate change, and not all parties tried to estimate the actual effects of their policies and measures on the mitigation of emissions or on financial assistance and technology transfer.[95] By any measure, though, barely a decade into the UNFCCC's life, a sophisticated system of reporting had emerged among Annex I states, at a high level of compliance. Moreover, Article 4's demand for periodic national communications on the matters discussed is no doubt of significant value to the complying Annex I party itself. Producing a national communication is an exercise that requires the country to get its house in order, so to speak – to articulate and streamline its response to the climate change problem, identify gaps in its actions, and compare its performance to that of other countries.

What goes into an economy in the form of policies and measures is not as important, of course, as what comes out in the form of GHG emissions. Thus national communications on policies and measures must be read in conjunction with the accompanying inventory of actual national emissions, as we have sought to do by introducing the information in Table 2.1. The GHG inventory is both the first layer of regulation and the final test of regulatory success. The inventory is quantitative rather than qualitative and is reported in a standard, unvarying format, which enables interstate comparisons. Most Annex I parties now have inventories for every year since 1990, providing a picture of emission trends.

Yet how does one compare the *efforts* that countries are making? Do interstate comparisons based on reported per capita emissions in each country (as seen in Figure 2.1) and other information in national communications enable fair conclusions about each country's effort to comply with its UNFCCC obligations? Is Europe, for example, doing more to cut its emissions and help developing countries achieve sustainable economic growth than Australia is? This is an important question for climate lawyers because if regulation is to be *fair*, it must distribute

[90] Ibid., p. 7.   [91] Ibid., p. 8.   [92] Ibid., p. 10.   [93] Ibid.   [94] Ibid., p. 7.   [95] Ibid., p. 12.

burdens equitably according to some criterion. Has the international climate change regime managed to resolve the issue of comparability of effort?

The short answer is 'No'. It remains an area of considerable disagreement.[96] It is easy to see why. Each country has different needs, depending on factors such as weather, population density, type of economic activity, natural resources and so on. Differences in heating needs are an example. Even if we were to make corrections for latitude, the problem of deciding on a per capita allowance for heating-related emissions does not go away. Iceland is a very cold country, so one might expect its per capita emissions in the energy sector to be relatively high. In fact, they are negligible, because geothermal energy in Iceland is plentifully available. Heat bubbling up from below literally envelops Icelanders in perpetual warmth.[97] Australia's own unique situation provides another illustration of the difficulty of defining compliance effort. Australia's transportation-related emissions are high compared, for example, with the European Union's.[98] Is this because Australia is a vast and thinly populated country? Or is it because Australian governments have failed to invest enough in urban public transport? If it is the former, per capita comparisons with the transportation-related emissions of other countries would need to take account of differences in geography. If it is the latter, how could one impose a comparatively appropriate level of per capita emissions in Australia today without punishing today's population for bad decisions about infrastructure made decades ago?[99] While the national communications submitted under the Convention are important sources of information and play an important regulatory function, they do not necessarily help us with the trickier judgments, such as those about comparability of effort. Throughout the twenty years of the international climate change regime, states have made one pledge after another, informed by complex factors, but not by any common measure to ensure comparability.

Extending the Convention

We have seen that the UNFCCC imposes different types of obligation on states, from procedural obligations (state reporting to the COP) to outcome obligations (caps and long-term emission trends). Some obligations have a direct environmental impact, others do not; some are measurable, others are not. Consequences for breach are never referred to, though, and a prescriptive international regulation of domestic emissions was never effected through the Convention. For this, a new legal model was necessary.

---

96 The idea of a universally applicable formula (based on Gross Domestic Product, population, energy intensity, etc.) was floated more than twenty years ago in the Intergovernmental Negotiating Committee, but has never gained a foothold: Barrett, 'The Negotiation and Drafting of the Climate Change Convention' (1991), p. 194.
97 Expert Review Team (Kyoto Protocol), *Report of the Individual Review of the Annual Submission of Iceland Submitted in 2010* (UNFCCC, 2011), FCCC/ARR/2010/ISL, para. 36.
98 H. Turton, *Greenhouse Gas Emissions in Industrialised Countries: Where Does Australia Stand?* Discussion Paper Number 66, (The Australia Institute, June 2004), Figure 3, p. 11.
99 In fact, the evidence suggests that urban car travel is particularly high in Australia, implying that the country's higher levels of vehicle ownership and use cannot be attributed to geographic features alone: see ibid., p. 14.

In Article 17, the UNFCCC provides for the addition of protocols. A protocol, like the parent convention, is an international treaty in its own right.[100] It has to be agreed to separately, and not all states that are party to the parent convention necessarily sign up to it. This leads to considerable complexity, nowhere more evident than in the climate change regime, with its parent Convention and offspring Protocol.

Legal principles and rules of the Kyoto Protocol

The Kyoto Protocol went into force on 16 February 2005. It has been ratified by all the parties to the UNFCCC except the United States.[101] Canada announced its withdrawal from the Protocol at the end of 2011.[102]

The UNFCCC's negotiation may have been difficult,[103] but the negotiation of the Kyoto Protocol was even more contentious, at times coming close to failure.[104]

Introduction

As the Protocol's short preamble does little more than adopt the Convention's objective and principles, we proceed directly to the treaty's substantive part.

The Kyoto Protocol will be remembered primarily for its imposition of quantified emission caps on Annex I parties, yet its substantive opening article (Article 2) is a catalogue of obligations of a rather general kind. It calls on parties to implement measures to enhance energy efficiency, increase their use of renewable energy and CO_2-sequestration technology, and trap methane emissions from waste management. Other duties are even broader, such as state cooperation and coordination, avoidance of adverse effects from response measures, and so on. In their generality, the Protocol's provisions are reminiscent of the language of the UNFCCC. The formulations do not lend themselves to reporting on demonstrable progress, for they do not set benchmarks.

Capping Annex I emissions

The Protocol's imposition of quantified emission caps occurs in Article 3(1):

> The Parties included in Annex I shall, individually or jointly, ensure that their aggregate anthropogenic carbon dioxide equivalent emissions of the greenhouse gases listed in Annex A do not exceed their assigned amounts, calculated pursuant to their quantified

---

[100] See the definition of 'treaty' under Article 2 of the 1969 Vienna Convention on the Law of Treaties.
[101] See <http://www.unfccc.int/kyoto_protocol/status_of_ratification/items/2613.php>.
[102] UN Secretary-General, *Kyoto Protocol to the United Nations Framework Convention on Climate Change; Canada: Withdrawal* (United Nations, 16 December 2001), C.N.796.2011.TREATIES-1 (Depositary Notification).
[103] Barrett, 'The Negotiation and Drafting of the Climate Change Convention' (1991), p. 186.
[104] M. Grubb and F. Yamin, 'Climatic Collapse at The Hague: What Happened, Why, and Where Do We Go from Here?', 77(2) *International Affairs* 261 (2001).

emission limitation and reduction commitments inscribed in Annex B and in accordance with the provisions of this Article, with a view to reducing their overall emissions of such gases by at least 5 per cent below 1990 levels in the commitment period 2008 to 2012.

This passage has become the most divisive of all provisions in the Kyoto Protocol. In fact, little else in the Protocol has been called into question. The ongoing defence of the Protocol has boiled down to the defence of the idea behind the quoted passage; and the increasingly vocal opposition to the Protocol is simply the rejection of this idea. The idea in question is that those UNFCCC parties that are wealthy and have historically high emissions accept a legally binding obligation to reduce their emissions over a certain period (in this case 2008–12) by a certain amount ('at least 5 per cent') below a historical benchmark (1990 emissions); by contrast, the remainder of the UNFCCC parties are to have no such obligation, only generally worded sustainability aims. Article 3(1) of the Kyoto Protocol, more than any other passage in the two climate treaties, emphasises the divided world on which the international climate change regime is based. The main reason for the opposition is that the actual and projected growth in emissions in the unbound group of countries exceeds that of the bound group and renders the effort in the bound group ineffective. And the main reason for the support for the Protocol is that without internationally agreed binding emission caps – without compliance mandated by law – each country's emission-control policy will vary unpredictably.

Each of the opposing sides emphasises the 'environmental integrity' of its position. We could also frame the conflict as one of differing moral visions or economic interests. However it is framed, the forces opposed to the Protocol, and in particular to the legal model implied by the passage quoted above, are not able to show conclusively that it is misguided or doomed to failure. In dealing with a global problem that is weighed down by thresholds (tipping points) that we do not want to cross, legally binding emission reductions by an ever-growing group of countries is a governance model with clear advantages. Critics of the Protocol are eager for an alternative because they want to break through the entrenched negotiating positions that have stalled progress.[105] But if the Protocol were allowed to evolve over time, incrementally enlarging the group of countries with emission caps, it could tackle climate change as well as could any other arrangement. Instead, the UNFCCC parties agreed at the Durban COP in 2011 to create a new agreement for the post-2020 period outside the framework of the Kyoto Protocol (see further below).[106]

Article 3 of the Protocol devotes considerable space to specifying the emissions and removals from the land use, land-use change and forestry (LULUCF) sector that will be allowed to count towards an Annex I party's assigned amount for a

---

105 See for example E. Diringer, 'Letting Go of Kyoto', 479 *Nature* 291 (17 November 2011), p. 292.
106 UNFCCC, *Decision 2/CP.17, Outcome of the Work of the Ad Hoc Working Group on Long-Term Cooperative Action under the Convention* (2011).

commitment period. LULUCF emissions are both highly uncertain and highly variable from year to year, and thus are treated as a sector apart from the rest (see for example Table 2.1). In accordance with Article 3(3), the only LULUCF activities that count towards the 2008–12 calculations are (i) emissions from deforestation and (ii) carbon sequestration from afforestation and reforestation. If (i) is larger than (ii), a positive amount will be added to a country's emissions from the non-LULUCF sectors; if forestry sequestration exceeds emissions from deforestation, a negative amount will be added, thus lowering emissions overall. In Australia's case, for example, the verified accounts for 2008 (the first year of the commitment period) show that 16.9 Mt CO_2 eq. was sequestered through afforestation and reforestation activities in that year, while 49.7 Mt CO_2 eq. was released through deforestation, bringing net forestry-related emissions to 32.8 Mt CO_2 eq.[107] This amount, added to emissions from other sectors (549.6 Mt CO_2 eq.), results in Australia's total emissions for 2008 (582.4 Mt CO_2 eq.).[108]

The LULUCF rule also applies to 1990, the Protocol's base year for all the main gases.[109] Because a country's assigned amount for the first commitment period is a proportion of its base year emissions multiplied by five, the higher the base year emissions are set, the greater is the country's assigned amount. We therefore expect countries to try to have their base year emissions set as high as possible, for this is in their economic interest. Australia is a case in point. Article 3(7) of the Kyoto Protocol is often referred to as the 'Australia clause' because Australia fought the hardest to have it inserted.[110] It says that Annex I parties for whom land-use change and forestry constituted a net source of GHG emissions in 1990 'shall include in their 1990 emissions base year or period the aggregate anthropogenic carbon dioxide equivalent emissions by sources minus removals by sinks in 1990 from land-use change for the purposes of calculating their assigned amount'.[111] Australia's net forestry emissions in 1990 were very high by any measure: 131.5 Mt CO_2 eq.[112] were added to Australia's 1990 emissions from other sectors, that is, to 416.2 Mt CO_2 eq. The total was then increased by 8 per cent (for Australia was allowed to increase its emissions from base year emissions, unlike most other countries)[113] and multiplied by five, to produce Australia's assigned amount for the commitment period: 2957.6 Mt CO_2 eq.[114] Deforestation emissions in Australia fell dramatically after 1990 (recall that they stood at 49.7 Mt CO_2 eq. in

---

107 Expert Review Team (Kyoto Protocol), *Report of the Individual Review of the Annual Submission of Australia Submitted in 2010* (UNFCCC, 2010), FCCC/IRR/2007/AUS, p. 5, Table 2. Forestry-related removals only count where the afforestation/reforestation activity began after 1990 and where the carbon stocks can be verified.
108 Ibid.
109 See Kyoto Protocol, Art. 3(8): Annex I parties may use 1995 as their base year for hydrofluorocarbons, perfluorocarbons and sulphur hexafluoride.
110 C. Hamilton and L. Vellen, 'Land-Use Change in Australia and the Kyoto Protocol', 2 *Environmental Science and Policy* 145 (1999).
111 Kyoto Protocol, Art. 3(7).
112 Expert Review Team (Kyoto Protocol), *Report of the Review of the Initial Report of Australia* (UNFCCC, 2009), FCCC/IRR/2007/AUS, p. 6, Table 3.
113 Kyoto Protocol, Annex B.
114 Expert Review Team (Kyoto Protocol), *Review of the Initial Report of Australia* (2009), para. 152.

2008), leaving the country with plenty of room to increase its emissions from energy production and industrial processes before any real mitigation measures would have had to be taken to avoid exceeding the assigned amount.[115]

Commitment periods fuel the Kyoto Protocol

Article 3 of the Protocol outlines a procedure for the creation of commitment periods additional to the first.[116] According to the treaty text, party negotiations on a subsequent commitment period are to be initiated by the CMP at least seven years before the end of the existing period. As the Kyoto Protocol went into force in 2005, negotiations on a second commitment period had to be initiated almost immediately.[117]

By aim and by internal design, the Kyoto Protocol needs rolling commitment periods. It is amorphous without them. Without contiguity of periods of capped emissions, several provisions cease to make sense. For example, Article 3 introduces one of the Protocol's several incentives for a country to do better than merely not exceeding its cap: if the country emits less than its assigned amount, it can add the difference to its assigned amount for a subsequent commitment period.[118] Indeed, as other Protocol articles provide, it could profit by *selling* the difference. Flexibility and market mechanisms go hand in hand. But the Protocol becomes vapid as soon as there is doubt about a subsequent commitment period being in the offing.

A second commitment period was agreed to at the Durban CMP in 2011.[119] The European Union, through its EU ETS, has invested heavily in the Kyoto Protocol, with the result that it was the Protocol's main champion at Durban. The agreement was reached very late in the negotiations: in the second day of extra time. Thirty-five Annex I countries agreed to a second commitment, three fewer than the first time around (Japan and Russia, in addition to Canada, did not join). They also agreed to transform their Copenhagen/Cancun pledges into quantified emission caps and submit them to the CMP for review by May 2012.[120] This time there will be no aggregate global mitigation target – no equivalent to the 'at least 5 per cent below' of Article 3(1) – although the preamble to the new agreement reiterates the desirability of aggregate Annex I emissions to be reduced by 'at least 25–40 per cent below 1990 levels by 2020'. There is little chance of achieving such an ambitious target without the participation of four of the world's top economies (the three mentioned plus the United States). The last-minute Durban

---

115 For a compilation of the base year emissions and assigned amounts for the first commitment period of all Annex I parties to the Kyoto Protocol, see Secretariat (UNFCCC), *Annual Compilation and Accounting Report for Annex B Parties under the Kyoto Protocol for 2011* (16 November 2011), FCCC/KP/CMP/2011/8, Table 2.
116 Kyoto Protocol, Art. 3(9).
117 See Kyoto Protocol, 'Ad Hoc Working Group on Further Commitments for Annex I Parties under the Kyoto Protocol (AWG-KP)', <http://www.unfccc.int/bodies/body/6409.php>.
118 Kyoto Protocol, Art. 3(13).
119 Kyoto Protocol, *Decision 1/CMP.7, Outcome of the Work of the Ad Hoc Working Group on Further Commitments for Annex I Parties under the Kyoto Protocol at Its Sixteenth Session* (2011).
120 Ibid., paras. 4–5.

outcome meant that many other details have not been worked out, including the length of the second commitment period. It is to begin on 1 January 2013 and end either on 31 December 2017 or on 31 December 2020.

Reporting, review and compliance obligations

Regulation of state reporting, review and compliance under the international climate change regime is discussed in detail in Chapter 3. In the present chapter, we have made reference to the reporting requirements of the UNFCCC in Box 2.2 and the text following it. Here, we provide only a brief reference to the applicable Convention and Protocol rules. Most of the rules are to be found in COP and CMP decisions rather than in the treaties themselves. Reporting and review obligations under the two treaties overlap heavily and are best considered together.

All state parties have reporting obligations under Article 12 of the UNFCCC; however, in the case of a non-Annex I party, only 'to the extent its capacities permit'. Several decisions and guidance documents elaborate this obligation.[121] The Kyoto Protocol intensifies the reporting demands on Annex I parties. According to Article 5 of the Protocol, parties are required to establish 'national systems' that facilitate, among other things, estimation of anthropogenic emissions using standard IPCC methodologies,[122] and they must regularly report their emissions pursuant to Article 7 of the Protocol.[123]

Annex I state reports are to be independently reviewed both under the UNFCCC[124] and under the Kyoto Protocol (Article 8).[125] However, the *compliance* system, adumbrated in Article 18 of the Protocol and fleshed out by CMP decisions, applies only to Kyoto Protocol Annex I parties.[126] (The compliance

---

[121] Intergovernmental Panel on Climate Change, *Good Practice Guidance* (2000); Intergovernmental Panel on Climate Change, *Revised Guidelines* (1996); Intergovernmental Panel on Climate Change, *Good Practice Guidance for Land Use, Land-Use Change and Forestry* (IPCC, 2003); UNFCCC, *Decision 17/CP.8, Guidelines for the Preparation of National Communications from Parties Not Included in Annex I to the Convention* (2003), FCCC/CP/2002/7/Add.2; UNFCCC, *Decision 18/CP.8, Guidelines for the Preparation of National Communications by Parties Included in Annex I to the Convention, Part I: UNFCCC Reporting Guidelines on Annual Inventories* (2002), FCCC/CP/2002/7/Add.2; UNFCCC, *Decision 19/CP.8, UNFCCC Guidelines for the Technical Review of Greenhouse Gas Inventories from Parties Included in Annex I to the Convention* (2002), FCCC/CP/2002/7/Add.2; Subsidiary Body for Scientific and Technical Advice (UNFCCC), *Guidelines for the Preparation of National Communications by Parties Included in Annex I to the Convention, Part I: UNFCCC Reporting Guidelines on Annual Inventories (Following Incorporation of the Provisions of Decision 13/CP.9)* (2004), FCCC/SBSTA/2004/8; Intergovernmental Panel on Climate Change, *IPCC Guidelines for National Greenhouse Gas Inventories* (2006); and Subsidiary Body for Scientific and Technical Advice (UNFCCC), *Updated UNFCCC Reporting Guidelines on Annual Inventories Following Incorporation of the Provisions of Decision 14/CP.11* (2006), FCCC/SBSTA/2006/9.
[122] Kyoto Protocol, *Decision 19/CMP.1, Guidelines for National Systems under Article 5, Paragraph 1 of the Kyoto Protocol* (30 March 2006), FCCC/KP/CMP/2005/8/Add.3.
[123] Kyoto Protocol, *Decision 15/CMP.1, Guidelines for the Preparation of the Information Required under Article 7 of the Kyoto Protocol* (30 March 2006), FCCC/KP/CMP/2005/8/Add.2.
[124] UNFCCC, *Decision 19/CP.8* (2002); and Secretariat (UNFCCC), *Handbook for Review of National GHG Inventories* (undated).
[125] Kyoto Protocol, *Decision 20/CMP.1, Good Practice Guidance and Adjustments under Article 5, Paragraph 2 of the Kyoto Protocol* (30 March 2006), FCCC/KP/CMP/2005/8/Add.3; and Kyoto Protocol, *Decision 22/CMP.1, Guidelines for Review under Article 8 of the Kyoto Protocol* (30 March 2006), FCCC/KP/CMP/2005/8/Add.3.
[126] Kyoto Protocol, *Decision 27/CMP.1, Procedures and Mechanisms Relating to Compliance under the Kyoto Protocol* (30 March 2006), FCCC/KP/CMP/2005/8/Add.3.

system is discussed in detail in Chapter 3.) The presence of a compliance system in the Protocol is unusual for an international environmental treaty; it is a measure of the strong 'legal force' that the contracting parties wished the instrument to carry.

Emissions from the aviation and shipping sectors are a special case because a large fraction of global civil aviation and shipping emissions are 'international' and not fully attributable to a particular country. These emissions – the so-called emissions from bunker fuels – are not reported by Annex I states. The issue of bunker fuels is meant to be resolved in a negotiation process involving the CMP, the International Civil Aviation Organization (ICAO), and the International Maritime Organization (IMO).[127] However, regulation of bunker fuels was not achieved by the time the Kyoto Protocol went into force. Almost a decade later, progress remains slight.

The European Union brought the issue to a head in 2009. It decided to include aviation emissions in the EU ETS from 2012 onwards.[128] Foreign airlines would be affected to the extent that they operated flights to EU airports. They would be charged for their GHG emissions in international airspace. In 2009, American Airlines, Continental Airlines, United Airlines, and the Air Transport Association of America launched a legal challenge against the UK Minister of Energy and Climate Change concerning the EU's trading scheme for aviation emissions.[129] In May 2010, the High Court of England and Wales referred the case to the Court of Justice of the European Union (CJEU) for a ruling.[130] The applicants' contention was that Kyoto Protocol parties are committed through Article 2(2) to resolve the issue of bunker fuels collectively, in cooperation with the ICAO and IMO, not unilaterally, as the EU had done. This contention was rejected by the CJEU's Advocate-General,[131] as well as by the Court itself.[132]

Emission allowances and market mechanisms

The Kyoto Protocol creates a variety of emission allowances linked to its three market (flexibility) mechanisms.[133] Each emission allowance has the same value:

---

[127] Kyoto Protocol, Art. 2(2).
[128] See European Union, 'Directive 2008/101/EC of the European Parliament and of the Council of 19 November 2008 Amending Directive 2003/87/EC So as to Include Aviation Activities in the Scheme of Greenhouse Gas Emissions Allowance Trading within the Community', *Official Journal of the European Union* [L 8] 3 (13 January 2009).
[129] See generally K. Kulovesi, '"Make Your Own Special Song, Even If Nobody Else Sings Along": International Aviation Emissions and the EU Emissions Trading Scheme', 2(4) *Climate Law* 535 (2011).
[130] European Union, 'Case C-366/10: Reference for a Preliminary Ruling from High Court of Justice Queen's Bench Division (Administrative Court) (United Kingdom) Made on 22 July 2010 – The Air Transport Association of America, American Airlines, Inc., Continental Airlines, Inc., United Airlines, Inc. v The Secretary of State for Energy and Climate Change', 53 *Official Journal of the European Union* [C 260] 9 (25 September 2010).
[131] Court of Justice of the European Union, *Case C 366/10: The Air Transport Association of America and Others: Opinion of Advocate General, Juliane Kokott* (6 October 2011), paras. 174–87.
[132] Court of Justice of the European Union, *Case C 366/10: The Air Transport Association of America and Others: Judgment of the Court (Grand Chamber)* (21 December 2011).
[133] For a general introduction, see E. Haites and F. Yamin, 'Overview of the Kyoto Mechanisms', 5(1) *International Review for Environmental Strategies* 199 (2004).

1 tonne of CO_2 eq. The types of emission allowance are distinguished by the rules that govern their creation, use and lifespan. They are also distinguished by their denominations: AAUs, ERUs, RMUs and CERs. The CER category includes t-CERs and l-CERs, two special-purpose denominations limited to forestry projects. These denominations are the currency of the Kyoto Protocol's economy.

An AAU is the unit that denotes an Annex I party's assigned amount for a commitment period. Australia's assigned amount of 2957.6 Mt CO_2 eq. for 2008–12 equates to almost 3 billion AAUs. The Joint Implementation (JI) scheme outlined in Article 6 of the Protocol creates ERUs.[134] These, of all the units, are most closely related to AAUs, because an Annex I state hosting a JI project will convert a portion of its AAUs (corresponding to the emission reductions achieved by the JI project) into ERUs and transfer them to the partner Annex I country. The LULUCF sector of an Annex I country, by sequestering carbon, can generate RMUs.[135] Lastly, CERs are offsets produced under the Clean Development Mechanism (Article 12 of the Protocol). They bear a similarity to ERUs, because they are created through a transnational arrangement, but in other respects the JI and the CDM are very different institutions. The CDM is covered in detail in Chapter 6.[136]

In essence, despite their formal differences, the Kyoto Protocol's emission allowances are the same: an AAU, ERU, RMU or CER is a permit to emit 1 tonne of CO_2 eq. into the atmosphere. In a jurisdiction where all GHG emissions are accounted for and controlled, any emission must be backed by a permit. Where a country has excess permits – 'excess' is defined relative to a country's commitment-period ceiling – it may sell them. Where it has excess emissions, it must buy permits. The Kyoto Protocol and the subordinate decisions issued by the CMP regulate this scheme in all its complexity.

By creating the emission permits described above, the Protocol has thereby created international arrangements designed to help states to meet their domestic emission reduction obligations more easily. The facility of trading sovereign emission allowances (AAUs) together with the institutions of the JI and CDM are commonly referred to as the Kyoto Protocol's flexibility mechanisms. While participation in them is not obligatory, the legal structures put in place to facilitate their operation are some of the most complex of the international regime.

---

[134] C. Streck, 'Joint Implementation: History, Requirements, and Challenges', in *Legal Aspects of Implementing the Kyoto Protocol Mechanisms: Making Kyoto Work*, eds D. Freestone and C. Streck (Oxford University Press, 2005), pp. 107–26.
[135] Secretariat (UNFCCC), *Accounting Report for Annex B Parties, 2011* (2011), para. 23.
[136] The CDM is to be contrasted with the Joint Implementation scheme. JI is not an offset scheme. It does not lead to excess emissions within the zone of states with emission caps. By contrast, the CDM does lead to such an excess (the excess is 'offset' by emission reductions outside the zone). Moreover, in JI, the host state (an Annex I party) has an important stake in accurately estimating the emission reduction potential of the project in its territory, because what it is transferring to the partner/investor state (which is also an Annex I party) is a parcel of its own AAUs (converted into ERUs), that is, a part of its sovereign allowance, which reduces its assigned amount for the applicable commitment period.

Outlook for the international climate change regime

Over the course of the Kyoto Protocol's 2008–12 commitment period, Annex I states that are also parties to the Protocol must reduce their emissions of GHGs by an average of about 5 per cent per year below 1990 emissions. With the help of offsets purchased through the CDM, and indeed the Global Financial Crisis, most states are on track to meet their emission caps for the first commitment period.[137] The full details of the second commitment period remain to be worked out. Huge challenges remain. The greatest of all is how to proceed after the expiry of the second commitment period in 2017 or 2020.

At the Durban COP, the UNFCCC states decided to *commence a process* that would lead to the adoption of a universal legal agreement on climate change not later than 2015.[138] A new group was formed – the Ad Hoc Working Group on the Durban Platform for Enhanced Action – to oversee work towards that objective. The COP/CMP, which has extended the life of its other two Ad Hoc Working Groups three times already,[139] is acquiring a reputation for commencing processes that do not end. Moreover, the universal legal agreement that would in theory be struck in 2015 would not go into force until after 2020. It is precisely the period between now and 2020 that is crucial to 'bridging the emissions gap'.[140] A 'review' of progress under the Convention has also been promised for 2015.[141] The terms of the review remain to be decided.

There is therefore much ahead in the way of process. Those who instead look to science to measure success have been dismissive of the Copenhagen/Cancun/Durban promises. Tollefson wrote in *Nature* that the Durban Platform 'represents an exercise in legalese that does little or nothing to reduce emissions, and defers action for almost a decade'.[142] *Nature*'s editors put it this way: 'It takes a certain kind of optimism – or an outbreak of collective Stockholm syndrome – to see the Durban outcome as a significant breakthrough on global warming . . . It is clear that the science of climate change and the politics of climate change, which claims to represent it, now inhabit parallel worlds.'[143] *Nature Climate Change*

---

137 For example: 'Germany described its current emissions as 26.5% below 1990 levels, with a future target of 40% emission reductions below 1990 levels by 2020': International Institute for Sustainable Development, 'Summary of the Bangkok Climate Talks: 3–8 April 2011', 12(499) *Earth Negotiations Bulletin* (2011), p. 3. 'France highlighted that his country had exceeded the national target under the Kyoto Protocol and that France has almost entirely de-carbonized electricity generation due to the use of nuclear, hydroelectricity and other technologies': ibid. 'Hungary . . . confirmed that its Kyoto Protocol target had been met while growing gross domestic product (GDP) in the period 1990–2009': ibid., p. 2.
138 UNFCCC, *Decision 1/CP.17, Establishment of an Ad Hoc Working Group on the Durban Platform for Enhanced Action* (2011), paras. 2, 4.
139 Latest extensions for the AWG-KP and AWG-LCA, respectively: Kyoto Protocol, *Decision 1/CMP.7* (2011), para. 1; and UNFCCC, *Decision 1/CP.17* (2011), para. 1.
140 UN Environment Programme, *Bridging the Emissions Gap* (November 2011).
141 UNFCCC, *Decision 2/CP.17* (2011), para. 158. For an account of the Durban outcome that provides one of the clearest explanations of the 2011 conference's contribution to the evolution of the two-track international negotiating process, see C. Carpenter, *Taking Stock of Durban: Review of Key Outcomes and the Road Ahead* (UN Development Programme, 2012), especially pp. 7–10.
142 J. Tollefson, 'Durban Maps Path to Climate Treaty', 480 *Nature* 299 (2011), pp. 299–300.
143 Editorial, 'The Mask Slips', 480 *Nature* 292 (15 December 2011), p. 292.

warned of 'a dangerous hiatus between the end of the first Kyoto commitment period later in 2012 and the full implementation of a new global climate agreement, assuming that such a thing materializes by 2020 as intended'. It concluded: 'One way or another, the protocol will limp on ... but the likelihood of avoiding global warming in excess of 2°C seems increasingly remote.'[144] *Science* took the same view.[145]

The weak international climate change regime that will govern us to the decade's end will almost certainly fail to bridge the emissions gap. On the evidence of what has been acted upon rather than what is possible, we must conclude that the outlook is grim.

---

[144] Editorial, 'Cool Response to Durban Compromise', 2 *Nature Climate Change* 59 (February 2012), p. 59.
[145] Editorial, 'Climate Outlook Looking Much the Same, or Even Worse', 334 *Science* 1616 (23 December 2011).

3

Measurement and verification of state emissions and legacy of the Kyoto Protocol's compliance system

Introduction   *page* 92
Treaty provisions on reporting and compliance   93
Direct measurement versus state reporting   96
Reliability of state emission reports   97
State regulation of inventory compilation   100
Verification (review) procedures   102
Role of Expert Review Teams   103
The Kyoto Protocol's compliance system   106
Determining a 'question of implementation'   106
The Kyoto Protocol's Compliance Committee   109
Procedure before the Enforcement Branch   111
Historical workload of the Compliance Committee   113
Assessment of the Kyoto Protocol's compliance system   116
Limitations of the Kyoto Protocol's review function   118
Could international reporting of greenhouse gas emissions be improved?   120
The future: Transparent reporting by all states   125

Introduction

From the preceding chapters it may be concluded that the regulation of climate change at the international level is clustered around a small number of institutions or programs. One of them is the IPCC – the grand enterprise that synthesises empirical data and supplies information on the climate system in a digestible form for policy-makers. Other elements of the international regime fall under the UNFCCC and the Kyoto Protocol. The Convention's meeting schedule and procedural rules, its Secretariat and general administration, may be treated as a distinct program. While this facilitative regulation is not a main focus of this book, its importance to the operation of the climate change regime

should not be underestimated. When the administrative institution is put to one side, we are left with three important and distinct clusters of regulation:
- The Clean Development Mechanism of the Kyoto Protocol (discussed in Chapter 6);
- The financial mechanism of the Convention and the Kyoto Protocol, including the Global Environment Facility. The GEF, created in 1990, pre-existed the UNFCCC, but was co-opted by it, and is administered by the UNFCCC in conjunction with the World Bank (more about the GEF and the new Green Climate Fund in Chapter 8);
- The monitoring, reporting, and verification system (sometimes labelled MRV) under the Convention, which under the Kyoto Protocol has been extended by a unique compliance system for Annex I (developed) states.

Other regulatory clusters, such as the emerging scheme under the Convention to protect forests (REDD, Chapter 7) and the technology transfer mechanism under both treaties (covered in Chapter 8), are still being constructed and therefore have few well-established, binding aspects.

This chapter examines the climate change regime's MRV program and the Kyoto Protocol's compliance system. Around them has coalesced a distinct and vitally important body of rules within the broader international climate regime.

Treaty provisions on reporting and compliance

Reporting and review under the Convention revolve around the following two elements, which are compulsory for Annex I parties:

(i) *National communications*, produced by each state party to the Convention. A national communication (as noted in Chapter 2) contains information on national GHG emissions, climate-related policies and measures, GHG emission projections, financial assistance and technology transfer to non-Annex I states (if applicable), and actions on raising public awareness about climate change.

(ii) *National GHG inventories*, detailing activity data, emission factors, and the methodologies used to estimate national GHG emissions. (Activity data and emission factors are technical terms referring to the extent and intensity, respectively, of a polluting activity.)

National communications are submitted by Annex I parties to the UNFCCC Secretariat every four to five years. (Different rules apply to non-Annex I parties.) They are prepared based on agreed reporting guidelines.[1] They are reviewed, within two years from their submission date, by Expert Review Teams

---

1 UNFCCC, *Decision 4/CP.5, Guidelines for the Preparation of National Communications by Parties Included in Annex I to the Convention, Part II: UNFCCC Reporting Guidelines on National Communications* (1999), FCCC/CP/1999/6/Add.1.

(ERTs are discussed in detail later in this chapter) in accordance with general procedures for review.[2]

Under the Convention, national GHG inventories – numerical tables quantifying the GHG emissions from each sector of a state's economy – are reported annually by Annex I parties (and by non-Annex I parties occasionally or at their discretion: see Table 3.1), in accordance with reporting guidelines agreed to by the COP and on the basis of IPCC methodologies.[3] The inventories of Annex I parties are reviewed annually by ERTs.[4]

This whole process of national communications and inventories had to be more or less duplicated when the international climate regime's second treaty, the Kyoto Protocol, came into effect. To minimise repetition, this chapter focuses on MRV under the Protocol, which is more thorough than MRV under the Convention. Moreover, MRV under the Protocol includes the additional layer of a compliance system. The more thorough provisions that constitute the Protocol's MRV system are necessary because, under the Protocol, state parties are bound by a commitment period.

Articles 5, 7 and 8 of the Kyoto Protocol establish the basic MRV framework. Article 5 commits Annex I countries to develop 'national systems' for estimating

Table 3.1 Reporting of Annex I and non-Annex I GHG emission inventories under the UNFCCC[5]

	Annex I	Non-Annex I
Frequency	Annual submission of national inventory	National inventory is submitted in conjunction with the national communication, at an interval agreed to by the COP. Least Developed Countries[6] complete inventories at their discretion.
QC/QA	Annex I parties must have a quality control/quality assurance plan for their GHG inventory and implement general inventory QC procedures in accordance with the IPCC's guidance[7]	Not applicable. Some advanced developing countries (e.g. South Africa) voluntarily apply QC/QA procedures.
Review process	Annual individual review conducted by an Expert Review Team to assess conformity of methodologies and data sources used with IPCC guidelines	UNFCCC Secretariat produces a compilation and synthesis of the information submitted, identifying gaps in national communications and inventories as well as problems and capacity-building needs.

---

2 UNFCCC, *Decision 2/CP.1, Review of First Communications from the Parties Included in Annex I to the Convention* (1995), FCCC/CP/1995/7/Add.1.
3 UNFCCC, *Decision 18/CP.8, Guidelines for the Preparation of National Communications by Parties Included in Annex I to the Convention, Part I: UNFCCC Reporting Guidelines on Annual Inventories* (2002), FCCC/CP/2002/7/Add.2.
4 UNFCCC, *Decision 19/CP.8, UNFCCC Guidelines for the Technical Review of Greenhouse Gas Inventories from Parties Included in Annex I to the Convention* (2002), FCCC/CP/2002/7/Add.2.
5 For a thorough comparison, see T. Fransen, 'Enhancing Today's MRV Framework to Meet Tomorrow's Needs: The Role of National Communications and Inventories' (World Resources Institute Working Paper, 2009), <http://wri.org> p. 9.
6 For a list of Least Developed Countries, see <http://www.unctad.org/Templates/Page.asp?intItemID=3641&lang=1>.
7 Intergovernmental Panel on Climate Change, *Good Practice Guidance and Uncertainty Management in National Greenhouse Gas Inventories* (2000).

anthropogenic emissions and removals, and provides specifications related to quantification methodologies and global warming potentials.[8] Article 7 requires Annex I parties to submit national communications and inventories on a regular basis, and to include supplementary information demonstrating compliance with the Protocol. Article 8 deals with the ERT process for Annex I communications and inventories.

The Marrakech Accords, adopted in 2005 under the Kyoto Protocol, contain detailed provisions on accounting, reporting and review. The Accords are decisions of the CMP made to flesh out the bare bones of the Kyoto treaty. The Marrakech Accords require Annex I parties to the Kyoto Protocol to establish a national system (in accordance with Article 5 of the Protocol) and a registry to track transactions of Protocol tradable-allowance units.[9] The Accords also contain provisions on the expert review of Annex I inventories, and charge ERTs with making recommendations about adjustments to inventories and raising 'problems of implementation' with the Kyoto Protocol's Compliance Committee.[10]

To summarise, state parties to the UNFCCC have reporting obligations under the Convention,[11] and state parties to the Kyoto Protocol have additional reporting obligations.[12] The Protocol parties retain all of the Convention's reporting obligations and take on additional ones flowing from the Protocol's special features, in particular its imposition of emission caps and provision of flexibility mechanisms (emission-trading privileges) for the parties to more easily comply with their caps.[13] Due to the country-specific emission limits imposed on Annex I states by the Protocol, the breach of which could lead to

---

[8] Kyoto Protocol, Article 5.1 commits Annex I Parties to have established, no later than 2007, national systems for the estimation of GHG emissions by sources and removals by sinks. See Kyoto Protocol, *Decision 19/CMP.1, Guidelines for National Systems under Article 5, Paragraph 1 of the Kyoto Protocol* (30 March 2006), FCCC/KP/CMP/2005/8/Add.3. A national system includes the institutional, legal and procedural arrangements for estimating emissions and removals of GHGs covered by the Protocol, and for reporting and archiving this information. Absorption of CO_2 by vegetation is a kind of 'removal'.

[9] These units (AAUs, ERUs, etc.) were introduced in Chapter 2. Kyoto Protocol, *Decision 19/CMP.1* (30 March 2006); and Kyoto Protocol, *Decision 12/CMP.1, Guidance Relating to Registry Systems under Article 7, Paragraph 4, of the Kyoto Protocol* (30 March 2006), FCCC/KP/CMP/2005/8/Add.2.

[10] Kyoto Protocol, *Decision 22/CMP.1, Guidelines for Review under Article 8 of the Kyoto Protocol* (30 March 2006), FCCC/KP/CMP/2005/8/Add.3; Kyoto Protocol, *Decision 20/CMP.1, Good Practice Guidance and Adjustments under Article 5, Paragraph 2 of the Kyoto Protocol* (30 March 2006), FCCC/KP/CMP/2005/8/Add.3; and Kyoto Protocol, *Decision 27/CMP.1, Procedures and Mechanisms Relating to Compliance under the Kyoto Protocol* (30 March 2006), FCCC/KP/CMP/2005/8/Add.3.

[11] Article 13 of the UNFCCC requires the preparation of country inventories.

[12] The relevant provisions of the Kyoto Protocol are in Articles 5(1) (mandating a national system), 5(2) (requiring application of IPCC methodologies), and 7(3) (mandating annual submission by states of itemised information starting with the first year of the commitment period).

[13] The review mechanism for reporting under the Kyoto Protocol is spread over several documents, all December 2005 decisions published in 2006. The most important are: Kyoto Protocol, *Decision 15/CMP.1, Guidelines for the Preparation of the Information Required under Article 7 of the Kyoto Protocol* (30 March 2006), FCCC/KP/CMP/2005/8/Add.2 (specifically about Kyoto 'units' and the national registry); Kyoto Protocol, *Decision 19/CMP.1* (30 March 2006) (specifically about national systems); Kyoto Protocol, *Decision 20/CMP.1* (30 March 2006) (specifically about 'adjustments'); and Kyoto Protocol, *Decision 22/CMP.1* (30 March 2006) (setting out the procedure for the 'Annual Review', alongside institutional arrangements, including the requirements of prior qualification, state nomination, training, rostering, and appointment to individual teams of expert reviewers; the last three actions are included in the responsibilities of the Secretariat).

penalties (or 'consequences' as they are called), there is a greater emphasis on systematic 'accounting', as opposed to the less demanding type of 'reporting', in the Kyoto Protocol's regime.

Direct measurement versus state reporting

Measuring and reporting of state emissions may seem like a mundane task, but it is, upon reflection, the foundation on which the rest of the international climate regime is built. If we are to manage the climate by managing state emissions, we need to know how much each state emits. To put it another way, if we are to price GHGs so that 'the polluter pays', we must be able to track GHGs, just as we track other regulated pollutants, and if for the purposes of economic efficiency we set up a market in which greenhouse pollution allowances are traded, we will have to ensure a correspondence between the certificates and the physical GHG emissions. One way or another, much regulation gravitates down to the level of measuring and reporting. Considering the subject's foundational status, academically it is a rather neglected area.

When we refer to a state's GHG emissions in quantified terms (see, for example, Table 2.1 in Chapter 2), we must rely on:

- *estimates* of those emissions, which are
- generated by the state itself.

In other words, we must rely on self-reported approximations at the country level.

There is an obvious distinction to be made between our knowledge of GHG emissions gleaned from state reports to the UNFCCC and our direct knowledge of GHG levels in the atmosphere derived from scientific instruments. The political side of the climate change regime is built around state reports, whereas scientists (such as Charles Keeling[14]) have measured gases directly. The political approach can lead to 'legal compliance' – meeting obligations on paper – which is not the same as 'scientific compliance' in the sense of reducing emissions in fact, to keep global warming below a certain threshold.[15] In an ideal world, emissions as reported by states would correspond to GHG concentrations as measured by scientists. But we are not at that point yet. For decades we have known about the build-up of atmospheric CO_2 and other GHGs, as we have been able to measure them directly.[16] But we have never had, and still do not have, quantified greenhouse accounts resolved at the state level that tally with the atmospheric readings. We want the

---

[14] C. D. Keeling, 'Rewards and Penalties of Monitoring the Earth', 23 *Annual Review of Energy and the Environment* 25 (1998).
[15] This point was first made by T. Berntsen, J. Fuglestvedt and F. Stordal, 'Reporting and Verification of Emissions and Removals of Greenhouse Gases', in *Implementing the Climate Regime: International Compliance*, eds J. Hovi, O. Stokke and G. Ulfstein (Earthscan, 2005), pp. 85–6.
[16] A. C. Manning et al., 'Greenhouse Gases in the Earth System: Setting the Agenda to 2030', 369 *Philosophical Transactions of the Royal Society A* 1885 (2011), p. 1885.

polluter to be accountable, but the only official accounts we have are those of the small number of Annex I countries.

From the regulatory point of view, the critical information is not the measured total atmospheric concentration of the various gases, but the amount of such gases that each *state* puts into the atmosphere over a given accounting period. Regulation presupposes the attribution of responsibility, and under international law the main subject of responsibility is the state. For political and legal reasons, the attribution of state responsibility under the international climate change regime is based on the reports of some states (Annex I), not yet on the reports of all states, and certainly not on the direct measurement of anthropogenic emissions in the atmosphere.

Reliability of state emission reports

Given that under the international regime emission information is constructed and reported by the states themselves (Annex I annually, non-Annex I less frequently or not at all), we must ask: How complete are state emission reports, in particular the Annex I inventories?

It is common for states to consider certain emissions as 'negligible' and not to report them for that reason. For example, how much barbecue charcoal (a biomass fuel) is produced in and combusted by the citizens of a given country in the course of a year? The state authorities may consider that they have no practical way of knowing the answer. In fact, a state has several options when considering a domestic source whose GHG emissions are not known. Let us take the case of emissions from the production of barbecue coal, an energy-intensive process that releases its own particular mix of GHGs into the atmosphere. The state might commission a study to collect the activity data and emission factors needed to calculate total domestic emissions; it might rely on a pre-existing study, carried out in another country, as a basis for making an estimation about emissions in its own territory; it might do nothing about the gap in its accounts and not think it necessary to inform the UNFCCC that there is such a gap; or it might do nothing about collecting the data and inform the UNFCCC that, while the information is incomplete, the amount involved is negligible.

Other varieties of under-reporting have their origin in malfunctions in an Annex I state's national system set up to manage UNFCCC and Kyoto Protocol reporting. For example, a budget cut affecting the state's statistics bureau might cause the bureau to cease collecting information on, say, training flights in the civil aviation subsector. Again, this is a 'negligible' amount of emissions, and the state may or may not report the problem to the UNFCCC. Another cause of gaps in reporting is the fact that the IPCC has not developed a methodology for the calculation of every source of domestic emissions,[17] and where no such

---

[17] Berntsen, Fuglestvedt and Stordal, 'Reporting and Verification of Emissions' (2005), p. 86.

methodology exists the state need not report emissions from that source.[18] In addition, a state may choose not to report emission information it considers confidential for commercial or national security reasons.[19]

Thus there are several reasons for incompleteness of the inventory besides the powerful financial incentive an Annex I state has not to exceed its Kyoto Protocol cap during a commitment period. (If it does exceed its cap, the state will have to buy sufficient emission allowances to offset the excess.)

Even in those Annex I states possessing sophisticated systems for generating inventories, the uncertainties built into their GHG estimates are considerable. The uncertainty that is a feature of these inventories has several components. They are summarised below. Two components are well described in the literature:[20]

- First, there is what is called *activity data* uncertainty. 'Activity data', as we have noted, refers to the *extent* of a human activity causing the release of GHGs. For example, the total area of a country's landfills (landfills release methane) constitutes the country's activity data for landfills.
- Second, there is *emission factor* uncertainty. Different types of activity are associated with different emission profiles. Even within a single human activity, such as the use of landfills, the intensity of emissions can differ from one landfill to another, depending on the composition of the waste, climatic conditions, and other circumstances.

The use of landfills is a component of what the IPCC calls the waste sector. If we knew the combined size of a country's landfills and the average methane emissions from sample areas of such landfills, we could estimate the methane emissions from the country's waste sector originating in landfills. The answer will only ever be a better or worse approximation.

Uncertainty levels vary greatly within the standard IPCC sectors. Within the energy sector, emissions from transport can be estimated with much greater certainty than fugitive emissions from gas production and distribution. (This is because we know the amount of transport fuel sold, the number and type and age

---

[18] Secretariat (UNFCCC), *Handbook for Review of National GHG Inventories* (undated), Chapter 2, p. 13, leaves any follow-up to the ERT's discretion: 'The UNFCC reporting guidelines encourage Parties to estimate all existing (anthropogenic) source and sink categories, including sources/sinks for which there are no agreed IPCC methodologies. However, it may be inappropriate to expect a particular Party to provide an estimate of a country-specific source/sink when estimating such a source/sink would divert resources from key categories, unless that source/sink is likely to be significant. The ERT should therefore consider the likely significance of an unreported country-specific source, as well as the overall key categories of the Party, in evaluating whether to encourage the Party to investigate the significance of the source.'

[19] UNFCCC, Article 12(9), broadly provides for confidentiality where requested by a party, subject to criteria to be developed by the COP.

[20] The presence of uncertainty has been extensively discussed by the IPCC and in the scholarly literature. For the IPCC's work on uncertainty, see Intergovernmental Panel on Climate Change, *Revised 1996 IPCC Guidelines for National Greenhouse Gas Inventories* (1996), vol. 1, Annex 1; Intergovernmental Panel on Climate Change, *Good Practice Guidance and Uncertainty Management* (2000), Chapter 6; Intergovernmental Panel on Climate Change, *Climate Change 2007: The Physical Science Basis: Contribution of Working Group I to the Fourth Assessment Report of the IPCC* (Cambridge University Press, 2007), pp. 81–91, 921–5; and Intergovernmental Panel on Climate Change, *Climate Change 2007: Mitigation of Climate Change: Contribution of Working Group III to the Fourth Assessment Report of the IPCC* (Cambridge University Press, 2007), pp. 131–4. In other literature, see M. Jonas et al., 'Benefits of Dealing with Uncertainty in Greenhouse Gas Inventories: Introduction', 103 *Climatic Change* 3 (2010), and other articles in the same special issue of that journal; and US National Research Council, *Verifying Greenhouse Gas Emissions: Methods to Support International Climate Agreements* (NRC, 2010), pp. 18–20, 29–31.

of cars on the road, etc., whereas the activity data and emission factors for gases escaping the fossil-fuel production and distribution system through leaks or deliberate releases are less well known.) Uncertainty levels also vary across the sectors. For example, overall emissions from the energy sector are known with much greater confidence than overall emissions from land use, land-use change, and forestry (LULUCF). Some other examples:

- Uncertainty about estimates of CO_2 emissions from energy consumption and from some industrial processes is 5 to 10 per cent.[21]
- Uncertainty about estimates of emissions is higher for agriculture (5 to 52 per cent) and LULUCF (10 to 93 per cent), primarily because of uncertainty pertaining to nitrous oxide (N_2O) emissions from agricultural soils and uncertainty about changes in carbon stocks in living biomass and soils. Further complicating matters, the LULUCF sector serves as both a source of and a sink for GHGs.[22]
- Within the agricultural sector, uncertainty about methane (CH_4) emissions from animal husbandry is between 20 and 30 per cent,[23] and for emissions from rice production it is greater than 50 per cent.[24]
- Uncertainties about N_2O emissions from synthetic fertilizer use are 50 to 100 per cent.[25]
- A medium band of uncertainty applies to estimates of fugitive emissions,[26] emissions from most industrial processes, and emissions of non-CO_2 gases in the energy sector.[27]
- Synthetic gases have an uncertainty of about 27 per cent.[28]

To take a representative case of an Annex I country, emission uncertainty in the Czech Republic's energy sector ranges from just over 5 per cent for CO_2 from stationary combustion to over 70 per cent for all energy-related emissions of N_2O.[29] The country's *overall* uncertainty for anthropogenic GHG emissions, including those from the LULUCF sector, is 9.8 per cent for the

---

[21] Intergovernmental Panel on Climate Change, *Revised 1996 Guidelines* (1996), vol. 1, Annex 1, Table A1–1; and US National Research Council, *Verifying Greenhouse Gas Emissions* (2010), p. 29.
[22] US National Research Council, *Verifying Greenhouse Gas Emissions* (2010), p. 31.
[23] Intergovernmental Panel on Climate Change, *Revised 1996 Guidelines* (1996), vol. 1, Annex 1, Table A1–1; and US National Research Council, *Verifying Greenhouse Gas Emissions* (2010), p. 31.
[24] Intergovernmental Panel on Climate Change, *Revised 1996 Guidelines* (1996), vol. 1, Annex 1, Table A1–1; and US National Research Council, *Verifying Greenhouse Gas Emissions* (2010), p. 31.
[25] US National Research Council, *Verifying Greenhouse Gas Emissions* (2010), p. 3. In relation to the above-quoted figures from the agriculture sector, see also A. Leip, 'Quantitative Quality Assessment of the Greenhouse Gas Inventory for Agriculture in Europe', 103 *Climatic Change* 245 (2010), Table 4.
[26] See, for example, Netherlands Environmental Assessment Agency, *National Inventory Report 2010* (2010), p. 67 ('The uncertainty in CO_2 emissions from gas flaring and venting is estimated to be about 50%, while the uncertainty in methane emissions from oil and gas production (venting) and gas transport and distribution (leakage) is estimated to be 25% and 25% in annual emissions, respectively').
[27] For example, Department of Climate Change, *National Inventory Report 2007* (Commonwealth of Australia, 2009), vol. 1, p. 18, and vol. 2, pp. 237–8.
[28] US National Research Council, *Verifying Greenhouse Gas Emissions* (2010), p. 30.
[29] Czech Republic, *National Greenhouse Gas Inventory Report 2010* (Czech Hydrometeorological Institute, 2010), p. 70.

absolute level (annual value) and 2.9 per cent for the post-1990 trend (relative value).[30]

In its 2010 submission to the UNFCCC, as is common for Annex I submissions, the Czech Republic did not report on certain categories. Among emissions it did not report on were N_2O emissions from liquefied petroleum gas and biomass combustion in road transport; CO_2 from coal mining and handling; CO_2 and N_2O from refining and storage; and CO_2 and CH_4 from distribution of oil products.[31] The reason it did not report on these categories is not that it had no emissions from them but because default IPCC methodologies for reporting such activities were not available. Fuel use for international navigation in the Czech Republic's rivers was, for the third year in a row, not reported because the state authorities considered it 'negligible'.[32] It is fair to say that these details illustrate the complexity of country inventories as much as their lacunae.

In neighbouring Austria, the uncertainty in the GHG inventory was similar to that of the Czech Republic: 5.2 per cent for the absolute level and 2.4 per cent for the trend. The most important factor contributing to the former was uncertainty about N_2O emissions from agricultural soils.[33] The uncertainties we have described are relatively large, considering that the Kyoto Protocol's target during the first commitment period is to reduce Annex I emissions to an average of 5.2 per cent below 1990 levels. As Berntsen and his colleagues have noted, 'where obligations are met with a margin less than the uncertainty, compliance may be questioned from a scientific point of view'.[34]

State regulation of inventory compilation

The accuracy of a state's inventory is in part dependent on how much we understand about the physical processes that produce GHG emissions, such as activity data and emission factors. In addition, the preparation of an inventory is a regulatory/administrative matter, and this will also affect accuracy. As we have seen, preparation of a state inventory is a state-governed activity undertaken within a framework of international regulation. Within a state, the different layers of emission-data collection are organised according to different rules. For example, direct measurement of methane emissions from a coal mine, which is a measurement that some

---

30 Ibid., p. 36. The reason why uncertainty in the *trend* over time is lower than for the *absolute level* for a given reporting year is that systematic errors that increase uncertainty in the absolute level for a given year are likely to affect the estimates throughout the period over which the trend is manifested – and thus the trend itself will be free of those systematic errors.
31 Czech Republic, *Common Reporting Format Tables 2008* (2008), Tables 1A–1C.
32 See ibid., Table 1C. See also Expert Review Team (Kyoto Protocol), *Report of the Individual Review of the Greenhouse Gas Inventories of the Czech Republic Submitted in 2007 and 2008* (2009), FCCC/ARR/2008/CZE, para. 27; and Expert Review Team (Kyoto Protocol), *Report of the Individual Review of the Annual Submission of the Czech Republic Submitted in 2009* (2010), FCCC/ARR/2009/CZE, para. 50.
33 These figures are from the 2005 reporting year: see W. Winiwarter and B. Muik, 'Statistical Dependence in Input Data of National Greenhouse Gas Inventories: Effects on the Overall Inventory Uncertainty', 103 *Climatic Change* 19 (2010); and Berntsen, Fuglestvedt and Stordal, 'Reporting and Verification of Emissions' (2005), pp. 94–5.
34 Berntsen, Fuglestvedt and Stordal, 'Reporting and Verification of Emissions' (2005), p. 95.

countries with sophisticated national systems will undertake to identify the coal mine's emission factor, is several layers of abstraction removed, and subject to different rules, from the methodology followed by the state's authorities to assemble countrywide information on GHG emissions, including the emissions from that particular mine. Inaccuracies in one layer are conceptually different from, and independent of, inaccuracies in another.

For simplicity, we could think of inventory compilation as consisting of two main layers, with inaccuracies falling into two corresponding categories.[35] The first category, which may be called 'physical–technological uncertainty', comprises inaccuracies resulting from 'hard' uncertainties (concerning activity data and emission factors) in the calculation of the production and release of any given GHG from any given source.[36] Physical–technological uncertainty arises from the limitations of our measuring instruments and knowledge of physical processes, and from the complexity in modelling highly variable sources of emissions over space and time, particularly for some biological sources. As indicated earlier, these uncertainties differ from gas to gas and from one IPCC sector to another. Put simply, some kinds of emissions are more difficult to measure than others.

The source of inaccuracy at the higher layer, which we refer to as 'regulatory–administrative uncertainty', is the product of regulatory or administrative systems instituted at the state level to gather and report data about emissions inside the jurisdiction of each state.[37] Faulty or incomplete or biased reporting systems, or dishonestly implemented systems, will tend to capture fewer data on GHG emissions than are actually available (or are straightforwardly available) at the physical–technological level, and thus will tend to under-report emissions even of gases that are relatively easy to measure. Two cases of incompleteness mentioned earlier – non-reporting of emissions from the production of barbeque charcoal and from training flights in civil aviation – are examples of regulatory–administrative shortcomings.

To summarise our observations up to this point, our knowledge of the GHG emissions of each state is actually limited to Annex I states, and is for the most part obtained from the GHG inventories that Annex I countries must submit to the UNFCCC Secretariat in their annual reports under the Convention and (with the exception of the United States) their annual reports under the Kyoto Protocol.[38] Presently there is no other representation of the information on emissions required in order to plan our response to climate change. Simple direct

---

[35] For a more complex 'typology of uncertainty', see H. H. J. Vreuls, 'Uncertainty Analysis of Dutch Greenhouse Gas Emission Data: A First Qualitative and Quantitative (Tier 2) Analysis', GHG Uncertainty Workshop, Warsaw (24–25 September 2004), p. 35.
[36] The same is true of absorption of GHGs by sinks.
[37] An Annex I party's legislative and administrative arrangements relating to the compilation of its national GHG accounts are usually summarised in its National Inventory Report.
[38] In accordance with Article 12 of the UNFCCC and Article 7 of the Kyoto Protocol. For a summary of the reporting-and-review requirements under these two treaties, see UNFCCC, 'Existing Requirements for Reporting and Review for Annex I Parties under the Convention and the Kyoto Protocol', <http://unfccc.int/national_reports/reporting_and_review_for_annex_i_parties/items/5689.php>. In brief, 'Reporting comprises a National Inventory Report (NIR) and Common Reporting Format (CRF) tables. The NIR includes qualitative and

measurement of GHGs in the atmosphere does not resolve *responsibility* for their presence there; for that, we must rely on state reports. Thus the completeness and reliability of state-reported emissions is a critical issue. The UNFCCC's website acknowledges this point: 'The ability of the international community to achieve this objective [of stabilising GHG concentrations in the atmosphere at a level that would prevent dangerous human-induced climate change] is dependent on an accurate knowledge of GHG emissions trends, and on our collective ability to alter these trends.'[39] Elsewhere on the website, it is said: 'The Kyoto Protocol's effectiveness will depend upon ... whether the emissions data used to assess compliance is reliable.'[40]

We have seen in the course of this brief survey that the margins of uncertainty in state emission reports remain high relative to the reduction targets.

Verification (review) procedures

In response to the challenges of accurate accounting of GHG emissions and state compliance with UNFCCC and Kyoto Protocol obligations, a state-driven verification system has been implemented to keep a check on the completeness and reliability of state-generated emission inventories.[41] In what follows, we will present an overview of the international review system.[42]

Formally, two review procedures for states have been set up, one concerned with reviews under the Convention[43] and the other with reviews under the Kyoto Protocol.[44] The reason, again, is that the two climate treaties have somewhat different objectives and create two different sets of obligations. Notable differences are that the Kyoto Protocol has emission reduction obligations specified in its Annex B and entitles parties to trade in emission allowances. The Protocol's

---

qualitative information, such as a description of methodologies used, emission factors, activity data and emission trends and analysis thereof, uncertainties, quality assurance and quality control. The CRF tables include data and results from inventory estimates.' (Ibid.)

39 UNFCCC, 'Annex I Greenhouse Gas Inventories', <http://unfccc.int/national_reports/annex_i_ghg_inventories/items/2715.php>.

40 UNFCCC, 'Guidelines under Articles 5, 7 and 8: Methodological Issues, Reporting and Review under the Kyoto Protocol', <http://unfccc.int/national_reports/
accounting_reporting_and_review_under_the_kyoto_protocol/items/1029.php>.

41 The treaty basis for this is Article 18 of the Kyoto Protocol.

42 For more detailed accounts, see C. Breidenich and D. Bodansky, *Measurement, Reporting and Verification in a Post-2012 Climate Agreement* (Pew Center on Global Climate Change, 2009); and Fransen, 'Enhancing Today's MRV Framework to Meet Tomorrow's Needs' (2009).

43 Article 13 of the UNFCCC requires national inventories to be prepared, but does not include an ERT procedure. Nevertheless, an ERT procedure has since been adopted by the parties. Key documents in the UNFCCC review process include UNFCCC, *Decision 6/CP.5, Guidelines for the Technical Review of Greenhouse Gas Inventories from Parties Included in Annex I to the Convention* (1999), FCCC/CP/1999/6/Add.1 (adopting the guidelines in document FCCC/CP/1999/7). Annual review became mandatory for Annex I parties in 2003. Revised review guidelines were brought into force by UNFCCC, *Decision 19/CP.8* (2002) (adopting the guidelines in document FCCC/CP/2002/8).

44 The relevant provisions of the Kyoto Protocol are in Articles 5(1) (mandating a national system), 5(2) (requiring application of IPCC methodologies; also authorising the application of 'adjustments' by ERTs), 7(3) (mandating annual submission by states of itemised information starting with the first year of the commitment period), 8(1) (making compulsory the review of the aforementioned information by ERTs), and 8(3) (specifying that the review is to be *a thorough and comprehensive technical assessment of all aspects* of the party's implementation of the Protocol's requirements).

emission accounting requirements are therefore necessarily more elaborate, and this detail is reflected in the corresponding review procedures.

Reviewing is compulsory for Annex I parties under the Convention as well as under the Kyoto Protocol. The Protocol, at Article 8(3), calls for 'a thorough and comprehensive technical assessment of all aspects' of a state's national system, including its emission inventory. Inventories are to be reviewed against the standard of being 'transparent, documented, consistent over time, complete, comparable, assessed for uncertainties, [and] subject to quality control and quality assurance'.[45] Under the Convention, reviewing of state reports continues year after year, for as long as the Convention is in existence. By contrast, under the Kyoto Protocol, the verification/review of national systems and emission inventories is limited to the commitment periods. The first five-year commitment period (2008–12) will be followed by a second commitment period (2013–17 or 2013–20), which means that the Protocol's review system will be with us for some years to come.[46]

Role of Expert Review Teams

For each year of a commitment period, each party to the Protocol with Annex B emission caps must undergo an 'Annual Review'.[47] The review of the parties' annual reports, including their GHG inventories, is conducted mostly in the form of a 'centralised' review, at the Bonn headquarters of the UNFCCC, by ERTs.[48] The balance of the reviews (about a fifth) is conducted by ERTs in the course of in-country visits.

An ERT is international in composition and has about six members. ERT members serve in their personal capacity: as experts rather than as representatives of their states. For obvious reasons having to do with conflict of interest, an ERT never includes a citizen of the country under review. The ERT reviewers have expertise in one or more IPCC sectors (for example emissions from energy industries or emissions from waste).

---

45 Preface to Intergovernmental Panel on Climate Change, *Good Practice Guidance and Uncertainty Management* (2000).
46 Kyoto Protocol, *Decision 1/CMP.7, Outcome of the Work of the Ad Hoc Working Group on Further Commitments for Annex I Parties under the Kyoto Protocol at Its Sixteenth Session* (2011).
47 Prior to the first Annual Review, an Annex I party must undergo a review of its base-year inventory, known as an 'Initial Review'. The controlling instrument here is Kyoto Protocol, *Decision 13/CMP.1, Modalities for the Accounting of Assigned Amounts under Article 7, Paragraph 4 of the Kyoto Protocol* (30 March 2006), FCCC/KP/CMP/2005/8/Add.2, in particular paras. 6–8 of the annex to that decision. Because of the direct mathematical link between base-year and commitment period emissions, the base-year inventory must be checked with the same rigour as any inventory of the commitment period. An Initial Review is centred on the 'Initial Report' of an Annex B party. For the review reports of the ERTs, as well as the Initial Reports of the states, see UNFCCC, 'Initial Reports under Article 7, Paragraph 4, of the Kyoto Protocol and Initial Review Reports', <http://unfccc.int/national_reports/initial_reports_under_the_kyoto_protocol/items/3765.php>.
48 For some of the detail concerning reviews under the ERT system, see A. Zahar, 'Does Self-Interest Skew State Reporting of Greenhouse Gas Emissions? A Preliminary Analysis Based on the First Verified Emissions Estimates under the Kyoto Protocol', 1(2) *Climate Law* 313 (2010). The constitutive instrument for ERTs is Kyoto Protocol, *Decision 22/CMP.1* (30 March 2006), especially paras. 20–45.

The work of ERTs is facilitated by the UNFCCC Secretariat. The Secretariat's many organisational responsibilities include assembling teams from the UNFCCC-administered international Roster of Experts[49] with an eye to geographical spread and North–South balance.

In a centralised review, an ERT will be assigned an average of four state inventories, which it must review in the course of six days on the basis of written submissions from the states under review. In an in-country review, a team of about five inventory experts focuses on the operations of a single state during a week-long visit to the country.[50] During that time, the team members read written submissions and other documentation and conduct interviews with government personnel involved in the local system's administration.[51]

An ERT has the power to 'adjust'[52] a state's reported inventory if it does not agree with the state's accounting of its emissions. This would happen if, for example, the ERT becomes aware of a significant lack in completeness that the state is refusing to acknowledge or act upon. The ERT would here be placing itself above the state under review: assuming the authority to correct the quantity of emissions the state is reporting. In the field of environmental treaties, this is one of the most striking features of the Kyoto Protocol's regulatory system, for it is rare for a state to concede such powers to an external body. In practice, however, there is a considerable give and take between the ERT conducting the review and the subject state. The state is entitled to receive guidance from, and to respond to, the preliminary findings of the ERT.[53] In fact, the state retains much of its sovereign power and the UNFCCC Secretariat carefully manages the ERTs to ensure that their attitude is facilitative and respectful of the age-old customs of international law. To date, adjustments to a state's emission inventory have been rare.[54] Nevertheless, from a legal point of view, we are now in a very interesting situation: an international team of GHG experts has been given power over the inventory of an Annex I state. How does the situation develop from here?

---

49 UNFCCC, 'UNFCCC Roster of Experts', <http://maindb.unfccc.int/public/roe/>.
50 UNFCCC, 'Existing Requirements for Reporting and Review for Annex I Parties under the Convention and the Kyoto Protocol', <http://unfccc.int/national_reports/reporting_and_review_for_annex_i_parties/items/5689.php>.
51 While the days taken for the centralised review or the time spent in a country for the in-country review represent the core of an ERT's review work, this is not the end of the matter; typically there is a period of written correspondence with the state both before and after the review, in which the ERT queries elements of the state's submission, seeks additional information from the state, or solicits the state's response to the ERT's preliminary conclusions.
52 Article 5.2 of the Kyoto Protocol states that, where agreed methodologies are not used to estimate emissions and removals, appropriate 'adjustments' should be applied; see also Kyoto Protocol, *Decision 20/CMP.1* (30 March 2006).
53 This period of dialogue provides the state with, in effect, an opportunity to voluntarily revise its initial emission accounts before any adjustment is applied by the ERT. If the ERT agrees with the revisions, the revised total becomes the state's conclusive and formally approved quantity of emissions for the year. If the ERT does not agree with the state's final revised amount, it may apply an adjustment, but only if that would have the effect of pushing down the state's estimate for the base year or increasing it for a commitment year. See Kyoto Protocol, *Decision 20/CMP.1* (30 March 2006), at paras. 51–57 of the annex to the decision. In other words, an ERT's adjustment may only be 'conservative'.
54 Zahar, 'Does Self-Interest Skew State Reporting?' (2010), pp. 319–21.

An ERT has at its disposal some modest tools with which to test the accuracy of a state's accounting of its GHG emissions:
  (i) The ERT is provided with the state's inventories from earlier years, in most cases going back all the way to 1990. A significant trend disruption from one year to the next will call for an explanation. If the state does not explain the anomaly of its own accord, the ERT may demand an explanation.[55]
 (ii) States must use standard IPCC methodologies[56] to calculate their GHG emissions from each of the IPCC emission sectors and subsectors.[57] An ERT will check that the standard methodologies have been followed.
(iii) Another indicator that ERTs routinely rely on[58] is country-level statistics on fuel production and the import and export of fuel, available from the International Energy Agency. The IEA data serve as a reference line against which to plot the reviewed state's own 'bottom-up' (sectoral) estimates of emissions from its energy sector.[59] The Food and Agriculture Organization is another source of country-level data (for example on the size of animal populations, fertilizer use, agricultural production, land use (forested areas), and human food intake) relied on by an ERT for the purpose of cross-checking state-reported emission estimates submitted to the UNFCCC.
 (iv) Yet another possibility is for an ERT to compare the average per capita GHG emissions of one state (in, say, the waste sector) with those of one or more other states in comparable circumstances, and to query any significant variations. (This method can be very inaccurate and thus is rarely used.)

---

55 As implied by Kyoto Protocol, *Decision 22/CMP.1* (30 March 2006), para. 65: 'The expert review team shall, inter alia ... (d) Compare emission or removal estimates, activity data, implied emission factors and any recalculations with data from previous submissions of the Party included in Annex I to identify any irregularities or inconsistencies.'
56 These are found in the following three key documents: Intergovernmental Panel on Climate Change, *Revised 1996 Guidelines* (1996); Intergovernmental Panel on Climate Change, *Good Practice Guidance and Uncertainty Management* (2000); and Intergovernmental Panel on Climate Change, *Good Practice Guidance for Land Use, Land-Use Change and Forestry* (2003).
57 This obligation is implied by Kyoto Protocol, *Decision 22/CMP.1* (30 March 2006), para. 65: 'The expert review team shall, inter alia: (a) Examine application of the requirements of the IPCC Guidelines as elaborated by any IPCC good practice guidance adopted by the COP/MOP and the reporting guidelines on annual inventories and relevant decisions of the COP/MOP, and identify any departure from these requirements ... (c) Examine whether the IPCC good practice guidance and any other good practice guidance adopted by the COP/MOP was applied and documented, in particular noting the identification of key source categories, selection and use of methodologies and assumptions, development and selection of emission factors, collection and selection of activity data, reporting of consistent time-series, reporting of uncertainties relating to inventory estimates and methodologies used for estimating those uncertainties and identify any inconsistencies.'
58 As underpinned by ibid., para. 65: 'The expert review team shall, inter alia ... (e) Compare the activity data of the Party included in Annex I with relevant external authoritative sources, if feasible, and identify sources where there are significant differences.'
59 The IEA provides the UNFCCC Secretariat annually with data sets, reported by country, that include energy balances and net calorific values. The reference and sectoral approaches and their differences are discussed in, for example, International Energy Agency, *CO_2 Emissions from Fuel Combustion: Highlights* (IEA, 2010), pp. 27–30.

(v) More generally, the very fact that every Annex I state must go through the procedure of giving a detailed annual account of its GHG emissions makes it difficult, in the long run, for any state to perpetuate or conceal systemic deficiencies in its data collection systems. Here, an ERT's higher-level view of the field gives it a natural advantage: even though the ERT scrutinises only about four reports at a time, differences in national systems' transparency, completeness, and capacity to learn and improve inevitably emerge from the comparative aspect of the exercise.[60]

The Kyoto Protocol's compliance system

The capping of state emissions by the Kyoto Protocol elevated 'compliance' in the Protocol's framework to a position of central importance. Compliance implies that a line exists between compliance and non-compliance, and that it can be objectively determined. In contrast to the Protocol, compliance has never been closely supervised under the Convention, at least partly because the Convention creates only general obligations that are not quantified or particularised in a way that would support a clear threshold between compliance and non-compliance (see Chapter 2). The Convention is not the kind of treaty for which a strict compliance regime would make sense.

The situation is different under the Kyoto Protocol: reporting on state obligations to meet emission caps calls for verification, verification calls for determination of compliance and enforcement in cases of non-compliance, and the decisions of an enforcement body call for an 'appeal' mechanism where disputes arise between the decision-maker and the subject state. The Protocol's system of checks and balances operates to some extent on all four of these levels (Figure 3.1). The next section focuses on the designated compliance function and the way in which it is triggered.

Determining a 'question of implementation'

The ERT process can be thought of as the second rung in the Kyoto Protocol's MRV/compliance ladder: the first rung is occupied by the reporting state; then comes the ERT; a rung above the review teams is the Kyoto Protocol's Compliance Committee; at the fourth and final level is the Protocol's plenary of states (the CMP), which is ultimately responsible for the whole process and which decides appeals.

---

60 To assist with the comparative overview, the UNFCCC Secretariat produces an annual Synthesis and Assessment Report based on the Annex I state submissions; for the most recent such report, see Secretariat (UNFCCC), *Synthesis and Assessment Report on the Greenhouse Gas Inventories Submitted in 2010* (15 July 2010), FCCC/WEB/SAI/2010.

Expert Review Team annual review report

An Annex I state's inventory for any year of a commitment period must be reviewed by an Expert Review Team. The ERT may raise one or more 'questions of implementation' in its review report.

If the ERT report raises a question of implementation

The UNFCCC Secretariat refers the report to the Bureau of the Compliance Committee.

Compliance Committee Bureau

The Bureau is made up of the chairperson and vice-chairperson of each of the Compliance Committee's two branches. The Bureau decides whether the referred question is a matter for the Facilitative Branch or the Enforcement Branch. The two branches have different mandates. The Facilitative Branch is set up to provide advice and assistance to parties in order to promote compliance. The Enforcement Branch is responsible for deciding whether parties are meeting their commitments, and if not, what 'consequences' to apply.

Referral to Facilitative Branch or Enforcement Branch

No referrals have yet been made to the Facilitative Branch. We therefore consider the procedure's progress through to the Enforcement Branch.

Enforcement Branch may apply 'consequences'

For each recognised type of non-compliance there is a set and non-discretionary course of action. For example, if a defect is found in the state's national system, the Enforcement Branch may suspend the state's eligibility to participate in the Protocol's flexibility (market) mechanisms. In certain circumstances, the Enforcement Branch may determine whether to adjust a state's GHG inventory or correct the central database for the accounting of states' 'assigned amounts'.

State appeal to CMP against Enforcement Branch decision

A country found to be in non-compliance may appeal to the CMP against a decision of the Enforcement Branch, but only on an issue relating to the country's assigned amount, and then only on the ground that it was denied procedural fairness by the Compliance Committee.

CMP decides appeal

No case has been decided at this level to date. Croatia, the only state to have appealed a decision of the Enforcement Branch, withdrew its appeal before it was decided.

Figure 3.1 Procedure before the Kyoto Protocol's Compliance Committee

The Compliance Committee receives questions of implementation from the ERT level below it.[61] Questions of implementation are essentially non-compliance issues detected by an ERT. Before considering the role of the Compliance Committee itself, the nature of questions of implementation and the ERTs' role in their production need to be examined.

An ERT is given a broad remit on what it may list as a question of implementation.[62] As we have noted, Article 8 of the Kyoto Protocol refers to expert reviews in bare outline. It is supplemented by review guidelines contained in a 2005 decision of the CMP. These guidelines set out a procedure for listing questions of implementation. In the passage below, which is from the review guidelines, the phrase 'pertaining to language of a mandatory nature in these guidelines influencing the fulfillment of commitments' is key:

> If the expert review team identifies potential problems during the review, it shall put questions to the Party included in Annex I regarding these potential problems and offer advice to the Party on how to correct them . . . Only if an unresolved problem pertaining to language of a mandatory nature in these guidelines influencing the fulfilment of commitments still exists after the Party included in Annex I has been provided with opportunities to correct the problem within the time frames established under the relevant review procedures, shall that problem be listed as a question of implementation in the final review reports. An unresolved problem pertaining to language of a non-mandatory nature in these guidelines shall be noted in the final review report, but shall not be listed as a question of implementation.[63]

The plain meaning of this text is that (1) an ERT must ('shall') list non-compliance with a mandatory requirement of the Kyoto Protocol as a question of implementation; and (2) a shortcoming in state conduct that does not breach a mandatory rule *must not* be listed as a question of implementation. In actual practice, the passage quoted above has been interpreted as vesting in ERTs a discretion about whether or not to list a question of implementation for action by the Compliance Committee. The UNFCCC's website itself suggests that the process involves a discretionary assessment; among other things, the 'shall' of the review guidelines has, in the online rendering, given way to a discretionary 'has the authority to'.[64]

---

[61] See S. Oberthür and R. Lefeber, 'Holding Countries to Account: The Kyoto Protocol's Compliance System Revisited after Four Years of Experience', 1(1) *Climate Law* 133 (2010); and M. Doelle, 'Early Experience with the Kyoto Compliance System: Possible Lessons for MEA Compliance System Design', 1(2) *Climate Law* 237 (2010).
[62] A question of implementation originates with an ERT. The Compliance Committee must wait for such a question to reach it from an ERT before it may act in any of the ways it is empowered to act. The system includes non-ERT triggers (see Annex to Kyoto Protocol, *Decision 27/CMP.1* (30 March 2006), Part VI: Submissions), but a conviction has already set in that these will be utilised rarely, if at all (Oberthür and Lefeber, 'Compliance System Revisited' (2010), pp. 143 and 153). The Committee's docket is, in practice, ERT-dependent.
[63] Kyoto Protocol, *Decision 22/CMP.1* (30 March 2006), paras. 7 and 8.
[64] 'If the ERT identifies a problem with a Party's implementation of a particular commitment that is not resolved by the Party during the review, the ERT has the authority to list the problem as a 'question of implementation' in its final review report. An ERT can raise questions of implementation only when there is an unresolved problem regarding implementation by a Party of a mandatory commitment . . . If an ERT is of the opinion that a Party's inventory is incomplete, or has been prepared in a manner which is not consistent with the IPCC methodologies: UNFCCC, 'Existing Requirements for Reporting and Review for Annex I Parties

In practice, the introduction of a discretionary element means that the Kyoto Protocol review system, in the manner in which it has been implemented, forbids an ERT to pass up to the Compliance Committee an issue of completeness or reliability of an inventory that does not offend against a mandatory rule, and it *entitles* (but no more than entitles) the ERT to pass up an issue involving a breach of a mandatory rule. This arrangement leaves the ERT with the freedom not to pass up the issue at all if it feels that the Compliance Committee's involvement is not necessary. In the next section we consider what happens to a question of implementation that an ERT does pass up to the Compliance Committee. Later in the chapter we discuss the tendency of ERTs to hold back most implementation issues, as well as the effect this has had on the operation of the Kyoto Protocol's compliance system.

The Kyoto Protocol's Compliance Committee

The Kyoto Protocol's Compliance Committee became operational in 2006[65] following the CMP's adoption of the procedures relating to compliance.[66] The Committee's members and alternates are chosen by the CMP so as to achieve a balance of developed and developing country representation. All members take an oath, which includes a commitment to be impartial and conscientious in decision-making.[67] Like ERT members, they serve in their personal expert capacity, not as representatives of their governments.[68]

Of the Compliance Committee's two branches, the mandate of the Facilitative Branch is to provide advice and assistance to states implementing the Protocol, and to 'promote' compliance by parties with Annex B emission caps. This branch of the Compliance Committee could in theory provide 'early warning' of potential non-compliance with emission caps or with reporting or methodological obligations relating to GHG inventories. To remedy implementation problems, the branch is empowered to provide advice and financial and technical assistance to a state, including technology transfer and capacity-building.[69]

---

under the Convention and the Kyoto Protocol', <http://unfccc.int/national_reports/reporting_and_review_for_annex_i_parties/items/5689.php>. And see Oberthür and Lefeber, 'Compliance System Revisited' (2010), p. 153, whose interpretation leaves the ERT with broad discretion: 'Only if serious implementation problems remain unresolved during the ERT process will a question of implementation be indicated in the ERT report submitted to the Committee.'

[65] Compliance Committee (Kyoto Protocol), *Report on the First Meeting* (29 May 2006), CC/1/2006/4.
[66] Kyoto Protocol, *Decision 27/CMP.1* (30 March 2006).
[67] The Kyoto compliance system has been analysed from many angles in J. Brunnée, M. Doelle and L. Rajamani, eds, *Promoting Compliance in an Evolving Climate Regime* (Cambridge University Press, 2011).
[68] To be contrasted with the Montreal Protocol's Implementation Committee, which consists of parties rather than independent experts and is therefore a political body. J. Barrett, 'The Negotiation and Drafting of the Climate Change Convention', in *International Law and Global Climate Change*, eds R. Churchill and D. Freestone (Graham and Trotman/Martinus Nijhoff, 1991), p. 200.
[69] Kyoto Protocol, 'An Introduction to the Kyoto Protocol Compliance Mechanism', <http://unfccc.int/kyoto_protocol/compliance/items/3024.php>.

The Enforcement Branch of the Compliance Committee is very different from the Facilitative Branch. It is made up of legal experts. Questions that the Enforcement Branch is limited to dealing with are laid down in the CMP decision containing the Compliance Committee's procedures and mechanisms:

> The enforcement branch shall be responsible for determining whether a Party included in Annex I is not in compliance with:
> (a) Its quantified emission limitation or reduction commitment under Article 3, paragraph 1, of the Protocol; [i.e. emission caps]
> (b) The methodological and reporting requirements under Article 5, paragraphs 1 and 2, and Article 7, paragraphs 1 and 4, of the Protocol; and
> (c) The eligibility requirements under [the three flexibility mechanisms, namely] Articles 6 [Joint Implementation], 12 [Clean Development Mechanism] and 17 [international emission trading] of the Protocol.[70]

The functions of the Enforcement Branch are thus specifically and exclusively defined. In the case of a finding of non-compliance, the branch must apply 'consequences'. The regulations leave the branch with no discretion about the application of the consequences at its disposal. In line with its mandate, it must apply the consequences corresponding to the three possible kinds of non-compliance listed in the text quoted above.[71] In particular:

(a) In case of non-compliance with the state party's emission target (Annex B of the Protocol), the Enforcement Branch must deduct 1.3 times the excess tonnes from the party's assigned amount for the *next* commitment period, request the submission of a 'compliance action plan', and suspend the party's eligibility to trade in emission allowances. The main penalty here is, in effect, the shrinking of the country's emission allowance for the subsequent commitment period by the amount of the overrun inflated by a 30 per cent penalty.

(b) Where the non-compliance relates to methodological and reporting requirements, the branch must declare the state concerned non-compliant and request it to submit a 'plan' for returning to compliance.

(c) Where the non-compliance concerns the eligibility requirements for participation in the Protocol's flexibility (market) mechanisms, the branch must suspend the party's eligibility to trade in emission allowances. This works as a penalty because it increases a country's compliance costs: emission reductions that could have been achieved by purchasing emission allowances from other jurisdictions must now be achieved as reductions in territorial emissions, however high the cost might be.[72]

Non-compliance with emission targets – possibility (a), above – is not an issue that can come before the Enforcement Branch before the end of the first commitment period, in 2012. This is because an Annex I party's 'assigned amount' for the

---

70 Kyoto Protocol, *Decision 27/CMP.1* (30 March 2006), Part V(4).   **71** Ibid., section XV.
72 An exception applies to ERUs generated from Joint Implementation projects hosted by the country, as well as to CERs forwarded by a developing country hosting a CDM project for the developed country in question.

commitment period is an amount for the whole commitment period: it is not broken down into years. A country whose emissions have exceeded its 2008–12 assigned amount has 100 days after the ERT's review of its final emission inventory to make up the shortfall (that is, to buy international credits in the form of AAUs, ERUs, etc.). If a country still misses its target (for example because it cannot afford to buy enough credits or has been excluded due to some breach of the rules from accessing the flexibility mechanisms), it must make up the difference, plus 30 per cent, in the new commitment period that follows 2012.

The Bureau of the Compliance Committee decides whether to assign a question of implementation to the Facilitative Branch or the Enforcement Branch. The Facilitative Branch is essentially responsible for addressing any question of implementation that does not fall under the authority of the Enforcement Branch. However, the Facilitative Branch's powers have so far remained somewhat theoretical, as the Bureau has never received a question of implementation that it has deemed appropriate for the Facilitative Branch.[73] To date, all questions of implementation have been directed to the Enforcement Branch.

Procedure before the Enforcement Branch

In the international climate change regime, the Enforcement Branch of the Kyoto Protocol's Compliance Committee is most like a court, in that it hears evidence, follows rules of procedure, is sensitive to due process, and speaks through written decisions.[74] The initiating action, as we have seen, is a question of implementation raised by an ERT and referred to the Enforcement Branch by the Compliance Committee's Bureau. As part of the procedure before the Enforcement Branch, the country concerned may make written submissions to the branch, and request a hearing to present its views. The branch has the power to call upon expert advice to supplement the evidence it has received from the ERT and the state party.[75] Because the branch members are mostly lawyers, expert advice on the technical side of measuring and reporting GHGs is usually sought, sometimes in great detail.[76] Intergovernmental and non-governmental organisations may submit factual and technical information for the branch's consideration.

Where non-compliance is found, the Enforcement Branch must make a public declaration of the state's non-compliance and the consequences it has applied. A country found to be in non-compliance must in every case submit a compliance

---

[73] The CMP is considering ways to improve the usefulness of the Facilitative Branch; see Compliance Committee (Kyoto Protocol), *Annual Report of the Compliance Committee to the Conference of the Parties Serving as the Meeting of the Parties to the Kyoto Protocol* (3 November 2011), FCCC/KP/CMP/2011/5, para. 48f.
[74] On the procedures of the Enforcement Branch, see Oberthür and Lefeber, 'Compliance System Revisited' (2010), pp. 146–8.
[75] Ibid., p. 144.
[76] See for example Compliance Committee (Kyoto Protocol), *Enforcement Branch Request for Expert Advice: Lithuania* (11 October 2011), CC-2011–3–3/Lithuania/EB.

action plan, which is subject to assessment (and acceptance or rejection) by the Enforcement Branch. If a party's eligibility to participate in the Protocol's flexibility mechanisms is suspended, the party may apply to have its eligibility restored as soon as it believes that it has rectified the original problem. Questions of implementation are meant to be resolved within 35 weeks of their receipt by the Enforcement Branch (Figure 3.2).

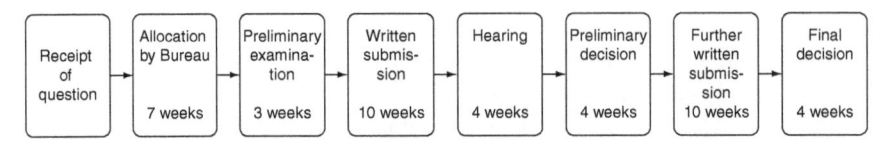

Receipt of question	Allocation by Bureau	Preliminary examination	Written submission	Hearing	Preliminary decision	Further written submission	Final decision
	7 weeks	3 weeks	10 weeks	4 weeks	4 weeks	10 weeks	4 weeks

Figure 3.2 Enforcement Branch procedures with time limits
Source: Based on Oberthür and Lefeber, 'Compliance System Revisited' (2010), p. 142

The CMP can receive appeals from state parties dissatisfied with decisions of the Compliance Committee.[77] The appellate process is highly constrained (as indicated earlier, it is limited to a decision of the Enforcement Branch that affects a party's assigned amount and in relation to which the party claims to have been denied due process).[78] The party's disagreement with the substance of the decision of the Enforcement Branch is insufficient for an appeal. Moreover, the bar for a successful appeal to the CMP is set quite high: a CMP decision overriding the Enforcement Branch's decision requires a three-fourths majority of the parties present and voting. In a case where the CMP upholds an appeal, it does not have the authority to decide the question of implementation itself but must refer it back to the Enforcement Branch.[79] Oberthür and Lefeber write that this unusual limitation on the power of states – along with the fact that the CMP is not required to confirm the decisions of either branch of the Compliance Committee on questions of implementation – 'shield[s] the quasi-judicial decision-making of the Committee from political interference'.[80]

Would it be unlawful for a state not to abide by the 'consequences' applied by the Enforcement Branch? In other words, are decisions of the Compliance Committee legally binding on the parties to the Kyoto Protocol? Article 18 of the Protocol provides that procedures and mechanisms to address cases of non-compliance 'entailing binding consequences' must be adopted by means of an amendment to the Protocol. No such amendment has been made. The compliance system has instead been adopted by the CMP in the form of a decision that is not legally binding on states. So far, states have gone along with this arrangement, demonstrating that a formal commitment to a process through a CMP

[77] See, generally, Oberthür and Lefeber, 'Compliance System Revisited' (2010), pp. 150–1.
[78] Kyoto Protocol, *Decision 27/CMP.1* (30 March 2006), section XI. The applicable law has been discussed in a paper by the Secretariat: Secretariat (UNFCCC), *Procedural Requirements and the Scope and Content of Applicable Law for the Consideration of Appeals under Decision 27/CMP.1 and Other Relevant Decisions of the Conference of the Parties Serving as the Meeting of the Parties to the Kyoto Protocol, as Well as the Approach Taken by Other Relevant International Bodies Relating to Denial of Due Process* (15 September 2011), FCCC/TP/2011/6.
[79] Kyoto Protocol, *Decision 27/CMP.1* (30 March 2006), sections XI.3 and XI.4.
[80] Oberthür and Lefeber, 'Compliance System Revisited' (2010), p. 140.

decision can be *effective*, even if it is non-binding. The compliance system was established by a CMP decision, and no country would lightly disobey a valid decision by a body it had itself agreed to establish and support.[81]

Another reason why the Protocol's legally non-binding compliance system has been effective to date is that the consequences that have been applied have not been severe. We recall that the most severe consequence in the Enforcement Branch's armoury (the 30 per cent penalty for emissions in excess of a country's assigned amount that have not been cancelled through emission allowance purchases) cannot be applied until after the end of the first commitment period.[82] Partly in order to avoid this penalty, Canada announced its withdrawal from the Kyoto Protocol on 15 December 2011.[83]

Historical workload of the Compliance Committee

The Compliance Committee's workload to date has been light. Since 2006, when the compliance system went into operation, just seven cases of non-compliance have come before the Enforcement Branch (Table 3.2).[84] (The Facilitative Branch, as we noted, has not received a single case.[85])

Of the Enforcement Branch's seven cases, those involving Greece and Canada have already been resolved. They involved process infractions or faults in system design that were quickly dealt with.[86] The case of Croatia was about a disagreement over the interpretation and legal effect of a decision of the COP under the Convention regarding the country's assigned amount for the first commitment period. The case went on appeal to the CMP,[87] but Croatia eventually withdrew its appeal without giving reasons.[88] The other four cases arose from ERT concerns about the non-cohesiveness of the national systems of those states. None of these cases has involved an inventory issue as such, but an issue of inaccurate or incomplete reporting. Issues of that type have been resolved by the ERT.

---

81 Moreover, at a technical level, when a country has been suspended from the Protocol's flexibility mechanisms, the order to suspend goes from the Enforcement Branch to a centralised transaction log held by the UNFCCC Secretariat. The effect is to mechanically discontinue trading by that country. There is little the country can do to get around the fact that the computerised log will no longer cooperate. For an extended discussion on this point, see ibid., pp. 151–2. See also Secretariat (UNFCCC), *Applicable Law for the Consideration of Appeals under Decision 27/CMP.1* (15 September 2011).
82 Oberthür and Lefeber, 'Compliance System Revisited' (2010), p. 149.
83 UN Secretary-General, *Kyoto Protocol to the United Nations Framework Convention on Climate Change; Canada: Withdrawal* (United Nations, 16 December 2001), C.N.796.2011.TREATIES-1 (Depositary Notification) ('The action will become effective for Canada on 15 December 2012 in accordance with article 27(2) [of the Kyoto Protocol]').
84 For the current status of non-compliance cases, see Kyoto Protocol, 'Compliance under the Kyoto Protocol', <http://unfccc.int/kyoto_protocol/compliance/items/2875.php>.
85 UNFCCC, 'Facilitative Branch', <http://unfccc.int/kyoto_protocol/compliance/facilitative_branch/items/3786.php>.
86 The facts of these cases are usefully summarised in Doelle, 'Early Experience with the Kyoto Compliance System' (2010), pp. 242 and 243.
87 Ibid., pp. 252–4.
88 Kyoto Protocol, *Decision 14/CMP.7, Appeal by Croatia against a Final Decision of the Enforcement Branch of the Compliance Committee in Relation to the Implementation of Decision 7/CP.12* (2011).

Table 3.2 Questions of implementation before the Enforcement Branch of the Compliance Committee, 2006–12

Party	Issue	Result
Greece	Greece submitted its initial report in December 2006. The ERT's initial review report was published in December 2007. It contained a question of implementation about the country's national system. A national system enables a country to account for its emissions and demonstrate compliance. In April 2008, the Enforcement Branch found Greece to be in non-compliance with the requirements for national systems. The 'consequence' it applied was to exclude Greece from participation in the Protocol's market mechanisms (Clean Development Mechanism, Joint Implementation, and trading in sovereign emission allowances).	On 13 November 2008, after consideration of a further ERT report on Greece, the Enforcement Branch decided that there was no longer any question of implementation with respect to Greece's national system. The branch reinstated the party's eligibility to participate in the flexibility mechanisms.[89]
Canada	Canada submitted its initial report in March 2007. The ERT's initial review report was released in April 2008. It contained a question about Canada's implementation of the Protocol's national registry requirements. A national registry is a computerised state-level system used to track holdings of GHG credits. In May 2008, on the basis of a preliminary examination, the Enforcement Branch decided to proceed with the question of implementation against Canada.	On 15 June 2008, after a hearing with Canada, the Enforcement Branch decided to discontinue the case. No non-compliance finding was made and no 'consequence' was applied.
Croatia	Croatia submitted its initial report in August 2008. The ERT's initial review report was published in August 2009. The report contained two questions of implementation. They related to Croatia's assigned amount and its commitment period reserve. The commitment period reserve limits the percentage of sovereign emission credits (AAUs) that a party may sell to other states. At issue in this case was whether a certain decision taken under the UNFCCC (rather than the Kyoto Protocol) would entitle Croatia to a larger allocation of sovereign emission credits under the rules of the Protocol. In November 2009, the Enforcement Branch issued a non-compliance decision. The 'consequence' applied was to exclude Croatia from participation in the flexibility mechanisms. In January 2010, Croatia appealed to the CMP against the decision. In August 2011, Croatia notified the CMP that it wished to withdraw its appeal against the decision of the Enforcement Branch. No reasons were given.[90] The CMP at its Durban meeting in December 2011 acknowledged that the matter was closed. In the same month, Croatia submitted a plan to address its non-compliance.	In February 2012, the Enforcement Branch decided that there was no longer any question of implementation for Croatia, and the country became fully eligible to participate in the flexibility mechanisms.

---

89 For an extensive analysis of this case, see Doelle, 'Early Experience with the Kyoto Compliance System' (2010), pp. 242–51.
90 Kyoto Protocol, *Withdrawal by Croatia of Its Appeal against a Final Decision of the Enforcement Branch of the Compliance Committee* (16 August 2011), FCCC/KP/CMP/2011/2.

Table 3.2 (cont.)

Party	Issue	Result
Bulgaria	Bulgaria submitted its 2009 annual inventory in April 2009. The ERT's review report was released in March 2010. It contained a question of implementation about Bulgaria's national system. At the country's request, the Enforcement Branch held a hearing in May 2010. After considering a further written submission by Bulgaria, the branch, in June 2010, found the country's national system to be non-compliant. The consequence applied was to exclude Bulgaria from further participation in the flexibility mechanisms. On 12 August 2010, Bulgaria submitted a plan to address the non-compliance issue. This was rejected by the branch as inadequate. In October 2010, Bulgaria submitted a second plan.	On 4 February 2011, after consideration of the most recent ERT report with respect to Bulgaria, as well as the revised plan submitted by the Bulgarian government, the Enforcement Branch decided that there was no longer any question of implementation, and that Bulgaria was thenceforth eligible to participate in the flexibility mechanisms.
Romania	Romania submitted an annual GHG inventory in April 2010. The ERT's review report was published in May 2011. It contained a question of implementation about Romania's national system. The question was allocated to the Enforcement Branch in May 2011. A written submission was made by Romania in June 2011. At Romania's request, a hearing was held in July 2011. The Enforcement Branch made a finding of non-compliance in August 2011. The consequence applied was exclusion of Romania from the flexibility mechanisms. In November 2011, Romania submitted a plan to address its non-compliance, including a progress report on the implementation of the plan. In the same month, the Enforcement Branch sought independent expert advice on Romania's plan. It assessed the plan and concluded that it met the relevant requirements.	The case was ongoing at the time of writing. Romania was expected to submit a second progress report on the implementation of its plan.
Ukraine	Ukraine submitted an annual inventory in April 2010. The ERT's review report was published in June 2011. The ERT found that Ukraine's national system did not fully comply with the Kyoto Protocol's guidelines on national systems, raising a question of implementation. After considering several submissions from Ukraine, the Enforcement Branch, in October 2011, decided that the country was not compliant. The consequence it applied was exclusion of Ukraine from the flexibility mechanisms. In December 2011, Ukraine submitted a plan to address its non-compliance. The branch approved the plan in the same month. In January 2012, on the basis of conclusions contained in another ERT report – this one on the country's 2011 annual submission – Ukraine submitted a request for reinstatement of its eligibility to participate in the flexibility mechanisms.	The case was ongoing at the time of writing. In February 2012, the Enforcement Branch decided to defer a decision on Ukraine's request for reinstatement, pending the receipt of expert advice.

Table 3.2 (cont.)

Party	Issue	Result
Lithuania	Lithuania submitted an annual inventory in April 2010. In September 2011, the ERT published its report on the inventory. The question of implementation relates to Lithuania's national system, especially its reporting of the LULUCF sector. The Enforcement Branch sought expert advice to help it interpret the technicalities behind the ERT's report. In November 2011, the branch adopted a preliminary finding of non-compliance. The consequence applied was exclusion of Lithuania from the flexibility mechanisms.	At the time of writing, Lithuania was expected to submit a plan to address its non-compliance.

If one were to look only to the Compliance Committee for a verdict on state non-compliance, one would perhaps be left with the impression that full compliance is the norm, that states have little difficulty meeting their Kyoto Protocol obligations during the 2008–12 commitment period, and that what we see in Annex I inventories is a representation of the actual amounts of GHGs that these states have been putting into the atmosphere. The true picture, as we explain below, is less rosy.

Assessment of the Kyoto Protocol's compliance system

In fact, the inactivity of the Facilitative Branch and the modest workload of the Enforcement Branch are poor indicators of state compliance with Kyoto Protocol commitments. For one, Canada declared early in the first commitment period that it would not meet its 94 per cent Annex B target.[91] This is a highly visible case of non-compliance foretold, but as illustrated at the start of this chapter, non-compliance also manifests itself less visibly in a multitude of completeness issues, buried in state emission reports or the review reports of ERTs. The history of the Kyoto Protocol review system demonstrates that only very rarely will an issue be listed by an ERT as a question of implementation. Without that trigger, the Compliance Committee is kept at bay.[92] (It is a little like the police trying to deal with all matters themselves without passing anything up to the prosecutors or the courts.)

The facilitative spirit that guides the work of the ERTs is written into the rules of the Protocol's system of reporting and review. It is built into the system's objectives ('[t]o promote consistency and transparency in the review of information submitted by Parties included in Annex I under Article 7 of the Kyoto Protocol' and '[t]o assist Parties included in Annex I in improving their reporting

---

[91] See Oberthür and Lefeber, 'Compliance System Revisited' (2010), pp. 155–6.
[92] On triggering, see ibid., pp. 141–3.

of information under Article 7 and the implementation of their commitments under the Kyoto Protocol'[93]); and it is reflected in the ERTs' official advisory role ('The expert review team should offer advice to Parties included in Annex I on how to correct problems that they identify, taking into account the national circumstances of the Party'[94]). In this context, if a state can demonstrate that its emission accounts are improving year by year, an ERT might be content to think of reported gaps as improvement targets for later reporting years rather than as matters to be immediately corrected. The ERTs, operating under a formally facilitative regime, and in practice viewing their function as primarily facilitative, may allow regulatory–administrative shortcomings (as defined earlier in the chapter) to persist for years.

In addition to the presence of discretion at the ERT level, there is the problem of defining a 'question of implementation'. We have seen that it is defined by the CMP rather unhelpfully as an 'unresolved problem pertaining to language [in the guidelines] of a mandatory nature ... influencing the fulfilment of commitments'. The phrases '*a problem pertaining to language*' and '*influencing the fulfilment*' do not seem to have been chosen for narrow effect. As for '*language of a mandatory nature*', salient instances of it in the review guidelines themselves (utilising, say, the word 'mandatory' or an equivalent device) are not to be found; the closest we come to some sort of specification is in the following paragraph:

> Problems should be identified as a failure to follow agreed guidelines under [Kyoto Protocol] Article 5, paragraph 2, in preparing greenhouse gas inventories, as a failure to follow section I of the guidelines for the preparation of the information required under Article 7, and as a failure to follow agreed methodologies for estimating and reporting activities under Article 3, paragraphs 3 and 4, as adopted by the COP/MOP.[95]

This is all quite general and leaves plenty of room for interpretation.

While the guidelines do provide some focus,[96] in the context of an ERT's facilitative role they do not help an ERT decide *when* to consider whether to exercise its discretion to refer a problem up the ladder to the Compliance Committee. In practice, implementation issues that countries face are probably perceived by ERTs as lying along a continuum, with discretion to decide how much weight to give to each issue resting with the ERT – including whether to label an issue a question of implementation and thus trigger an intervention by the Compliance Committee. In this way, not only do ERTs assume a discretion about whether a question of implementation is to be referred to the Compliance Committee; they also assume discretion about what might qualify as a question of implementation in the first place.

---

[93] Kyoto Protocol, *Decision 22/CMP.1* (30 March 2006), paras. 2(b) and 2(c).
[94] Ibid., para. 5; see also ibid., paras. 106 and 117.   [95] Ibid., para. 69.
[96] See further A. Zahar, 'Verifying Greenhouse Gas Emissions of Annex I Parties: Methods We Have and Methods We Want', 1(3) *Climate Law* 409 (2010), p. 421.

Having surveyed the broad discretion available at the ERT level, it becomes easier to understand why the Kyoto Protocol's compliance system has generated so few cases for the Compliance Committee's Enforcement Branch and none for the Facilitative Branch. It is because the ERTs have been assiduously pursuing facilitation efforts themselves, passing 'problems' down to the first rung (the states) rather than up to the third.[97] Tact and diplomacy play a role here. An ERT listing an issue as a question of implementation, automatically triggering action by the Compliance Committee, is not only a sign that the ERT and the state under review have failed to see eye to eye on a particular point, it elevates a behind-the-scenes factual dispute into an open *quasi-legal* dispute, with the question of implementation seen by everyone as a kind of indictment. On the strength of this quasi-indictment, the state is hauled before the quasi-judicial Enforcement Branch to defend itself. Greece and Canada, the first two countries to be put in this situation, reacted with indignation.[98] Whatever the rules may say, there is a marked desire by all involved in the Kyoto Protocol's process of monitoring and review to avoid questions of implementation.

This sensitivity about applying the full weight of the Kyoto Protocol's compliance system to states will perhaps dissipate with time. But it is an element worth tracking as the climate regime matures. We have spent some time on it to illustrate the fact that international regulation of state action can look different in practice from how it appears on paper. The more important point is that the global causes of climate change demand global commitments and global enforcement. By design, the Kyoto Protocol takes us about half the way, by imposing commitments and enforcement on Annex I state parties. Whatever its shortcomings, the Protocol's compliance system is an outstanding example of a legal framework used to respond to climate change on a global scale.

Limitations of the Kyoto Protocol's review function

In the previous section we discussed the tendency of ERTs to block the passage of implementation of questions to higher levels of the Protocol's compliance system. For a complete evaluation of the international regime's checks on state emission reports, we must now return to consider the actual investigative powers of ERTs.

---

97 This has been noted by Doelle, 'Early Experience with the Kyoto Compliance System' (2010), p. 259 ('The ERT process [is] not consistently bringing issues of implementation before the compliance committee ... Whether the review by ERTs, in particular through in-country reviews, is sufficiently detailed and frequent for the credibility and integrity of the reporting system is unclear based on the experience to date').

98 Canada, which at the relevant time had already declared that it did not intend to meet its emission reduction target (Oberthür and Lefeber, 'Compliance System Revisited' (2010), pp. 155–6), reacted indignantly when it was brought before the Enforcement Branch, and even sought to have the record reflect that there had been no need, in its view, to activate the non-compliance procedure, because very early in the process it had put right the identified problem. (See Compliance Committee (Kyoto Protocol), *Annual Report of the Compliance Committee to the Conference of the Parties Serving as the Meeting of the Parties to the Kyoto Protocol* (31 October 2008), FCCC/KP/CMP/2008/5, para. 30 and Annex V.) Greece's responses were also terse: see the documentation at Kyoto Protocol, 'Question of Implementation – Greece', <http://unfccc.int/kyoto_protocol/compliance/enforcement_branch/items/5455.php>.

Notwithstanding the various validity checks available to an ERT during a review of a state's GHG inventory (a sample of which was provided earlier), the ERT does not have access to independent information that would allow it to check the inventory's completeness and reliability. The tests either involve checking compliance with procedural (mainly IPCC) guidelines,[99] or they are consistency checks. An example of the latter is the IEA's fuel data. This information is provided to the IEA by the states themselves. The same is true of all 'activity' statistics that an ERT obtains from an international organisation like the IEA or FAO to conduct its cross-checks: the state authorities are the ultimate source of this information. ERTs are prohibited from using data from a non-state source if the data were not formally supplied to that source by the government of the state under review.[100] Therefore, this type of check reveals little more about the state inventory than whether the state has made the same (or essentially the same) representations to the UNFCCC/Kyoto Protocol as it has made to other treaty bodies or intergovernmental organisations from which the ERT has drawn the reference data. This can be a useful check, but it is not an independent one.

As for conformity to IPCC methodological and good-practice guidelines, this is neither a necessary nor a sufficient condition for accuracy in emission estimates. Because the guidelines are skeletal, and because in their practical application much discretion is left to the states, the best that can be said about conformity to guidelines is that it signifies a functioning national system for reporting GHG emissions to the treaty body. While this is an important precondition for accounting completeness and reliability, it is not a guarantee of an accurate GHG inventory.

A related issue is that ERTs are not as independent as one might expect. Almost all reviewers work in their regular jobs for their national governments and have some role in the preparation of their countries' inventories. They serve on two rungs of the reporting/verification ladder: for the most part, they are engaged in compiling their own country's inventory, but once a year or so they help to verify those of other countries. 'Conflict of interest' is too strong a term to characterise this arrangement. Nevertheless, some objectivity is sacrificed. The likely reason for the phenomenon of double service is that the pool of persons qualified to serve as ERT experts is small, and most of them already work in generating their own countries' inventories.

To summarise, the Kyoto Protocol's MRV process, like that of the UNFCCC, focuses on formal and procedural matters. The review process, embodied by the ERTs, does not have access to data that would provide an independent verification of self-reported national GHG emission estimates. This means that a state may underestimate (or, for that matter, overestimate[101]) its emissions in any number of ways, and an ERT, operating within currently approved methods, could not detect that in the short time frame allowed for its review, or at all.

---

99 See Intergovernmental Panel on Climate Change, *Revised 1996 Guidelines* (1996); Intergovernmental Panel on Climate Change, *Good Practice Guidance and Uncertainty Management* (2000); and Intergovernmental Panel on Climate Change, *Good Practice Guidance for LULUCF* (2003).
100 Secretariat (UNFCCC), *Handbook for Review of National GHG Inventories* (undated), Chapter 2, pp. 11–12.
101 See Zahar, 'Does Self-Interest Skew State Reporting?' (2010), Table 2.

While the ERTs enjoy a broad mandate, the Kyoto Protocol parties do not, in fact, use them to scrutinise GHG inventories or their underlying national systems at the level of detail and independence required to allay concerns about the accuracy of national emission estimates.[102] The review system established by the two treaties is rather soft on states.

Little is to be found about these shortcomings in the literature, no doubt because they are not evident from the system's design alone. They become apparent in the system's practical implementation. As we have explained, the ERTs in practice see their role as facilitative, and an ERT would sooner encourage the state under review to fix faults discovered in its GHG reports than pass the issue up to the Compliance Committee. Certainly, ERTs will question states where there is evidence of significant underestimation of emissions. But other problems will not be aggressively pursued. They will be listed as recommendations for improvement for the next time around. If the improvements are not implemented in the course of the following year, the next (differently constituted) ERT assigned to review the state might re-list the desired improvements for another year.[103] Or it might relinquish them, as a different set of issues catches its eye. Because the ERTs, the UNFCCC Secretariat, and the parties are anxious to avoid questions of implementation, functions that by design are assigned to the third rung of the accountability ladder (the Compliance Committee) are currently being held back in an ad hoc manner at the second rung. This weakness in the system of international review further contributes to our uncertainty about the accuracy with which Annex I states report their GHG emissions.

Could international reporting of greenhouse gas emissions be improved?

In most Annex I countries, physical–technological uncertainty concerning national CO_2 emissions from fossil fuel use is reported to be at around 5 per cent for the level (with less for the trend).[104] This may seem like a workable margin of

---

102 See for example UNFCCC, *Conclusions and Recommendations: Sixth Meeting of Inventory Lead Reviewers* (16–17 March 2009); Fransen, 'Enhancing Today's MRV Framework to Meet Tomorrow's Needs' (2009), pp. 8 and 12; and Compliance Committee (Kyoto Protocol), *Annual Report of the Compliance Committee to the Conference of the Parties Serving as the Meeting of the Parties to the Kyoto Protocol* (2 November 2009), FCCC/KP/CMP/2009/17, para. 23. The assessment of Breidenich and Bodansky that '[b]ecause of the intense focus on Annex I inventories over the past several years, current reporting and review requirements are sufficiently rigorous to provide a reliable basis to assess implementation of parties' quantitative emission targets' (Breidenich and Bodansky, *Measurement, Reporting and Verification* (2009), p. 12) is presented without evidentiary support. Their statement that '[t]he success of the Annex I review process, particularly for GHG inventories, has demonstrated that expert review teams can provide objective, critical, and credible assessments' (ibid., p. 19) suffers from the same shortcoming. One hopes that they are right. But how is it to be demonstrated?
103 Kyoto Protocol, *Decision 22/CMP.1* (30 March 2006), para. 48: 'All final review reports prepared by the expert review team, except for status reports, shall include the following elements ... (b) ... (iii) An assessment of any efforts by the Party included in Annex I to address any potential problems identified by the expert review team during the current review or during previous reviews that have not been corrected.'
104 Intergovernmental Panel on Climate Change, *Revised 1996 Guidelines* (1996), vol. 1, Annex 1, Table A1–1; and US National Research Council, *Verifying Greenhouse Gas Emissions* (2010), p. 29.

uncertainty for the purposes of managing Annex I emissions: plus or minus 5 per cent sounds like a small error margin. Yet it is only part of the picture. Uncertainties in emissions from deforestation, reforestation, and forest degradation are much higher, ranging from 25 to 100 per cent. Uncertainty about agricultural emissions is of the same order, as earlier noted. When all physical–technological emission uncertainties are combined, the overall uncertainty is about the same as the expected emission reductions over the Kyoto Protocol's first commitment period (5.2 per cent below 1990 levels).[105] Our confidence in Annex I emission estimates is further affected by the regulatory–administrative uncertainties that are the consequence of imperfectly operating national systems of data collection and compilation. We have seen that the ability of the Kyoto Protocol's MRV system to reduce regulatory–administrative uncertainty through the ERT–Compliance Committee process is limited, and that the uncertainty subsists in the finalised state accounts, alongside that of the physical–technological kind.

The climate change regime's current reporting coverage is not universal but is limited to a minority group of wealthy countries containing most, though not all, major economies. Only Annex I states prepare inventories annually, and only Annex I inventories are independently checked. In the meantime, shifting economic trends have led to the situation where, since 2005, most GHG emissions originate in non-Annex I countries.[106] Thus the largest and growing proportion of global anthropogenic emissions is either not regularly reported at all or not independently reviewed, making state responsibility for this class of emissions difficult to quantify with any confidence.[107] We have no official 'snapshot' of global GHG emissions, and it remains difficult to construct a global picture from the information submitted by states. Overall, then, our knowledge of individual state responsibility for anthropogenic emissions since 1990 is significantly uncertain, and will remain so for the foreseeable future.

Improvements to the international MRV system for GHG emissions could come through extending the reporting-and-review system to more countries and through encouraging countries that already are under the system to use the IPCC's higher methodological tiers in their reporting (that is, methodologies that forgo default values and use, for example, country-specific emission factors, which are of course more difficult and expensive to obtain). The Kyoto Protocol's compliance system is demonstrably underutilised, so this too could be improved.[108]

---

[105] W. Winiwarter, 'National Greenhouse Gas Inventories: Understanding Uncertainties vs. Potential for Improving Reliability', paper presented at GHG Uncertainty Workshop, Warsaw (24–25 September 2004), p. 17 ('With trend uncertainties of several percentage points being typical of industrialized countries, reduction targets of 6–8% as formulated in the Kyoto Protocol can not be monitored unambiguously'); and, for comments to the same effect, US National Research Council, *Verifying Greenhouse Gas Emissions* (2010), pp. 4, 28.
[106] Using fuel production and import data and other general indicators, we are able to estimate that non-Annex I countries accounted for over 50 per cent of global GHG emissions in 2005, and are expected to account for an increasing proportion in the future: J. Ellis, S. Moarif and G. Briner, *Core Elements of National Reports* (OECD/IEA, 2 June 2010), COM/ENV/EPOC/IEA/SLT (2010)1, p. 10. See also G. P. Peters et al., 'Rapid Growth in CO$_2$ Emissions after the 2008–2009 Global Financial Crisis', 2 *Nature Climate Change* 2 (January 2012), p. 3.
[107] US National Research Council, *Verifying Greenhouse Gas Emissions* (2010), p. 29.
[108] Doelle, 'Early Experience with the Kyoto Compliance System' (2010), p. 260.

Constant improvement is certainly necessary to avoid loss of confidence in the system. Some improvement will be effected by the IPCC's ongoing work on expanding the stock of methodologies available for emission reporting, but for the most part reliance must be placed on the willingness of states themselves to keep the MRV system under review. No doubt, improvements in transparency and reliability will continue for as long as the Kyoto Protocol's compliance system (or an equivalent regime) is extended. Still, we might ask: Are we limited to making improvements to the current system? Is there no alternative?

A nascent community of scientists has come forth with proposals for a systematic improvement in our knowledge of GHG attribution. The group hopes to see state reporting under the Convention and the Protocol checked by direct atmospheric measurements from ground stations and satellites. The advantage of direct verification is that it is independent of the subjective judgments about sources that are an unavoidable element of the preparation of a state's inventory. Moreover, 'the atmosphere does not misrepresent data or make mistakes; nor does it bend to ideology or political will'.[109] The goal of reconciling state-reported emissions (bottom-up estimates) with those calculated from atmospheric measurements (top-down) is an important one, for it would give us greater certainty about the amount of atmospheric pollution that humans are responsible for. How might this work?

The number of scientists who specialise in measuring GHGs in the atmosphere is still relatively small (around 200 worldwide, by one estimate).[110] They have constructed a global network of almost 120 CO_2-monitoring stations, many of which also measure the concentration of methane and other GHGs.[111] The network is small compared with, for example, the thousands of surface temperature monitoring stations in existence. The network's small size means that there are large gaps in places like Africa, Asia, and South America – places distant from the main research centres of atmospheric scientists.[112] Readings at the CO_2-monitoring stations are being supplemented by satellite remote sensing. A satellite provides a more general view than a ground station, and its data can be checked against the highly accurate measurements on the ground.[113] A dedicated GHG-monitoring satellite (called OCO-2) is due to be put into orbit by NASA in July 2014.[114] (The first OCO satellite was destroyed during launch.[115]) The third element in the developing field of knowledge consists of modelling tools (trajectory models) that combine

---

[109] Editorial, 'Gas and Air', 482 *Nature* 131 (9 February 2012), p. 132.
[110] Manning et al., 'Greenhouse Gases in the Earth System' (2011), p. 1885.
[111] Ibid., p. 1885. Data from the individual monitoring stations may be obtained from the World Meteorological Organization, 'World Data Centre for Greenhouse Gases', <http://gaw.kishou.go.jp/wdcgg/>.
[112] Manning et al., 'Greenhouse Gases in the Earth System' (2011) p. 1886.   [113] Ibid., pp. 1886–7.
[114] NASA Jet Propulsion Laboratory, 'OCO-2: Orbiting Carbon Observatory', <http://oco.jpl.nasa.gov/>; NASA, 'Orbiting Carbon Observatory 2 (OCO-2)', <http://eospso.gsfc.nasa.gov/eos_homepage/mission_profiles/show_mission.php?id=99&mission_cat_id=19>.
[115] US National Research Council, *Verifying Greenhouse Gas Emissions* (2010), pp. 63–4. The National Research Council authors write of OCO that it has the high precision (1–2 ppm) and small sampling area (1.29 x 2.25 km) needed to monitor 'large local sources and to attribute their CO_2 emissions to individual countries. No other satellite has its critical combination of high precision, small footprint, readiness, density of cloud-free measurements, and ability to sense CO_2 near the Earth's surface' (ibid., p. 6.).

information about airborne GHGs, measured at monitoring stations or from satellites, with data on wind flows. The models allow scientists to work backwards from measured emissions to the sources of emissions, and thus locate emission sources in the territory of a state.[116] This is vital, as explained earlier, because emissions must be attributable to states to give rise to legal responsibility. Another method for working backwards to GHG sources is to combine information from multiple ground stations through mathematical-inversion modelling.[117]

The growing scientific interest in top-down estimates of state emissions has received some high-level institutional support, although none yet from state governments. As an example of institutional support, in 2010, the National Research Council of the United States, through its Committee on Methods for Estimating Greenhouse Gas Emissions, released a report looking at the quality of state GHG inventories and asking what could be done to lower the uncertainty in the estimates and provide for their independent verification. The short-term potential of top-down scientific initiatives was described in the report as follows:

> Strategic investments would, within 5 years, improve reporting of emissions by countries and yield a useful capability for independent verification of greenhouse gas emissions reported by countries ... [F]ossil-fuel CO_2 emissions could be estimated by each country and checked using independent information with less than 10 percent uncertainty. The same is true for satellite-based estimates of deforestation, which is the largest source of CO_2 emissions next to fossil-fuel use, and for afforestation, which is an important sink for CO_2. However, self-reported estimates of N_2O, CH_4, CFC, HFC, PFC, and SF_6 emissions will continue to be relatively uncertain and we will have only a limited ability to check them with independent information.[118]

The 'strategic investments' referred to at the start of this passage would be for the purpose of putting in place more equipment for atmospheric monitoring in ground-based stations and in satellites, and while such a program would be expensive,[119] it could save governments money in the long run.[120] New measurement stations would need to be established near cities and other large local GHG sources,[121] and eventually also in developing countries, where, as we noted, few exist at present. More satellites that sense CO_2 and read forest cover would need to be launched to strengthen current capacity for space-based measurement of GHG emissions. Improvements in the measurement of radiocarbon would be necessary to distinguish fossil fuel CO_2 emissions from CO_2 from other sources.[122] The first generation of tracer-transport inversion models (the trajectory models mentioned above) currently in use would need to be further

---

116 Manning et al., 'Greenhouse Gases in the Earth System' (2011)   **117** Ibid.
118 US National Research Council, *Verifying Greenhouse Gas Emissions* (2010), p. 1.
119 Establishing five to ten new ground measurement stations per year in the United States would require a budget of US$15–20 million per year. The replacement mission for OCO, with a two-year lifetime, would cost around US$278 million: ibid., pp. 63–4.
120 A. J. Durant et al., 'Economic Value of Improved Quantification in Global Sources and Sinks of Carbon Dioxide', 369 *Philosophical Transactions of the Royal Society A* 1967 (2011).
121 US National Research Council, *Verifying Greenhouse Gas Emissions* (2010), pp. 5–6.
122 Ibid., pp. 6–7, 61f.

developed and tested to improve their predictive capacity.[123] Finally, the bottom-up inventories produced by states would need to be rendered at sub-national territorial divisions and reported more frequently than annually (which is to say that the bottom-up information must be more finely resolved spatially and temporally) to assist with independent verification using the top-down method.[124] In addition to systematic and long-term state funding, the idea of strategic investment calls for international research partnerships to develop and harmonise the various scientific techniques, scientific coordination with the COP and CMP (for the greater integration of law and science), and eventual amendment of the UNFCCC/ Kyoto Protocol state reporting and review rules.

The proposed expansion of the current rudimentary scientific network would enhance our understanding of, and ability to monitor, GHG emissions. Specifically in connection with inventory improvements, useful data for verification of CO_2 fossil fuel emissions could be achieved within a few years, at an uncertainty level of less than 10 per cent and perhaps as low as 5 per cent. The new technique is being tested in Europe, where ground stations are relatively plentiful, to verify national emissions of methane.[125] New applications are being reported with greater frequency. For example, in 2011, scientists from the US National Oceanic and Atmospheric Administration and the University of Colorado in Boulder studied methane emissions from a Denver natural gas operation where 'fracking' methods were being used. The scientists estimated cumulative emissions from the gas field using concentrations of pollutants in air samples. They found that the industry's own reports underestimated the methane emissions by about 50 per cent.[126] Some researchers are already demonstrating the added value of linking bottom-up and top-down carbon accounting.[127]

The scientific developments and potentials summarised in this section suggest that one day we may have at our disposal an independent, top-down check on the emissions reported by states. Under this enhanced regime, procedural verification by an international body, namely the ERTs, would be supplemented by independent scientific checks, probably starting with emissions from fossil fuel combustion. It would take years for the two mechanisms to mesh legally and in practice, and in the meantime the top-down, science-driven mechanism would have a chance to grow in infrastructure and sophistication, and consequently in verification value. What remains to be seen is whether the international legal regime, which is of course controlled by states, is open to independent verification by scientists.

---

[123] Ibid., pp. 53f. See also P. Ciais et al., 'Atmospheric Inversions for Estimating CO_2 Fluxes: Methods and Perspectives', 103 *Climatic Change* 69 (2010); and L. Rivier et al., 'European CO_2 Fluxes from Atmospheric Inversions Using Regional and Global Transport Models', 103 *Climatic Change* 93 (2010).
[124] US National Research Council, *Verifying Greenhouse Gas Emissions* (2010), pp. 34–5.
[125] Manning et al., 'Greenhouse Gases in the Earth System' (2011), p. 1888.
[126] Editorial, 'Gas and Air', 482 *Nature* 131 (9 February 2012), p. 132.
[127] M. Gusti and M. Jonas, 'Terrestrial Full Carbon Account for Russia: Revised Uncertainty Estimates and Their Role in a Bottom-Up/Top-Down Accounting Exercise', 103 *Climatic Change* 159 (2010).

The future: Transparent reporting by all states

The need for national reporting of GHG emissions is generally accepted, but the distribution of the reporting *burden* has been a contentious issue. Non-Annex I countries want developed countries to report more thoroughly and more frequently, while Annex I countries want developing countries to close the reporting gap.[128] The 2013–20 country pledges, first made in Copenhagen in 2009 and officially adopted in Cancun the following year,[129] have been made under the Convention, not the Kyoto Protocol. The Convention has no reporting and review system to deal with the pledged measures, the way the Protocol has for the commitment period caps. Moreover, the Protocol's system is limited to Annex I countries, whereas the 2013–20 pledges include those of a large number of non-Annex I countries. Hence the parties are currently negotiating the terms of International Assessment and Review (IAR) and International Consultation and Analysis (ICA), two different MRV processes with which to monitor Annex I and non-Annex I pledges, respectively, under the Convention.

In Durban, the UNFCCC parties agreed to biennial reporting by Annex I states on their pledges, with the first set of reports due on 1 January 2014.[130] They also agreed to an IAR process of technical reviews to commence two months after the submission of the first round of Annex I biennial reports.[131] This will be in addition to the annual reviews of Annex I national GHG inventories and the quadrennial review of national communications under the Convention.[132] Non-Annex I states are to submit biennial 'update reports' in accordance with their capabilities and level of GEF funding provided for reporting; these reports are due in December 2014.[133] Least Developed Countries and small-island developing states are not required to submit update reports, but may do so at their discretion.[134] The ICA process for non-Annex I update reports is to commence within six months of the submission of the first round of such reports; the cost of ICA is to be met from additional financial contributions by Annex I states.[135]

The UNFCCC's website states: 'A strong and effective compliance mechanism is key to the success of the implementation of the Protocol.'[136] One could hardly

---

128 For example: 'The US [along with Australia] called for biennial reporting from non-Annex I countries on their mitigation actions ... Bolivia expressed disappointment that developed countries wish to submit their next national communications after a four-year period despite the availability of resources to do so sooner ... China, for the G-77/CHINA, lamented that non-Annex I countries are being "pushed" to increase the frequency of their national communications, while Annex I countries are refusing to do likewise ... Spain, for the EU, expressed disappointment at the lack of agreement': International Institute for Sustainable Development, 'SB 32 and AWG Highlights: Wednesday, 9 June 2010', 12(470) *Earth Negotiations Bulletin* 1 (2010), p. 2.
129 UNFCCC, *Decision 1/CP.16, The Cancún Agreements: Outcome of the Work of the Ad Hoc Working Group on Long-Term Cooperative Action under the Convention* (2010), FCCC/CP/2010/7/Add.1, para. 36.
130 UNFCCC, *Decision 2/CP.17, Outcome of the Work of the Ad Hoc Working Group on Long-Term Cooperative Action under the Convention* (2011), paras. 12–13.
131 Ibid., paras. 23, 25; and Annex II of the same decision for the modalities and procedures for International Assessment and Review.
132 Ibid., para. 27.   **133** Ibid., paras. 39, 41.   **134** Ibid., para. 41.
135 Ibid., paras. 58–9; and Annex IV of the same decision for the modalities and guidelines for International Consultation and Analysis.
136 Kyoto Protocol, 'An Introduction to the Kyoto Protocol Compliance Mechanism', <http://unfccc.int/kyoto_protocol/compliance/items/3024.php>.

disagree. However, states cannot be relied upon to report their emissions accurately, and for an international regime to be effective, it must be possible to verify that reductions have actually taken place according to the commitments made by the states.[137] From one point of view, the Kyoto Protocol's compliance system forms an integral part of the treaty's governance system and provides for an unprecedented administrative review of state action by independent international bodies (the ERTs and the Compliance Committee). Certainly, the system is unique among multilateral environmental agreements, especially because it has the objectives not only of facilitating and promoting compliance, but of enforcing it. As states continue to engage in discussions on an international climate regime for the future, the compliance system of the Kyoto Protocol provides an important benchmark for their efforts to promote the fulfilment of treaty commitments. At the same time, the shortcomings of the international climate change regime's MRV system – and the emerging pathways for improvement outlined in this chapter – should also be kept in mind.

137 Berntsen, Fuglestvedt and Stordal, 'Reporting and Verification of Emissions' (2005), p. 85.

4

Development of climate law in Australia

Introduction *page* 127
Factors in the genesis of Australian climate law   128
Development of Australian climate law and policy   139
Australian climate change regulation: The international context   139
Early national policy measures: Climate change and ESD   145
'No regrets' climate policy   147
Mandatory Renewable Energy Target   150
Action by states and territories   151
Proposals for national emissions trading   155
Carbon pricing   160
Conclusion   163

Introduction

Climate change, as we have seen, is the quintessential global environmental issue in the sense of being an indivisible problem with global causes and effects. Its global dimensions support the logic of the development of an international climate law framework, as described in the previous chapters. However, climate change also has important implications for domestic legal frameworks. This is partly because international climate change treaties, like other international environmental laws, depend heavily upon the national implementation of measures such as reliable reporting systems for their effectiveness.[1] It is also because the complex environmental and economic consequences of climate change include local effects (in the area of biodiversity, for example), as well as regional and national effects (for example, shifts in patterns of energy use).[2]

With continuing uncertainty at the international level over the shape of future legal arrangements,[3] climate law at the national level has taken on a new

---

[1] See Chapter 3. Australia's implementing legislation in this regard is the *National Greenhouse and Energy Reporting Act 2007* (Cth). See further Chapter 5.
[2] R. Garnaut, *Garnaut Climate Change Review* (Cambridge University Press, 2008), pp. 121–52.
[3] At COP17 in Durban in December 2011 the parties to the United Framework Convention on Climate Change agreed to a process for negotiating a new, international climate change arrangement of 'legal

prominence. This is not to say that domestic climate law has been completely freed from the bonds imposed by international agreements, nor from the imperatives created by the need for a collective effort to respond to the global problem. However, as we highlighted in Chapter 1, an increasing refrain in climate law scholarship and policy discussion is debate over whether regulation should be 'top-down' or 'bottom-up'.[4] This has seen greater attention paid to legal developments taking place at the sub-national, national and regional levels, in addition to top-down regulation at the international level establishing emission reduction obligations for states.

This chapter considers the course of development of climate law in a specific national jurisdiction – namely Australia – in response to both global and domestic factors. Subsequent chapters explore, in greater depth, the specific Australian legal arrangements relevant to different areas of climate change concern such as emission trading, renewable energy technologies, energy efficiency, carbon capture and storage, biosequestration and adaptation.[5] In this chapter, our aim is to provide context for this discussion by highlighting the factors driving Australian climate law and policy development, as well as the main trends and milestones. Depending on the perspective taken, this history of Australian climate law may be seen as one of discontinuity, with sharp divergences in law and policy in response to political changes, or as an incremental evolution from early measures addressed to 'low-hanging fruit' towards mandatory carbon pricing measures. As bottom-up approaches have gained prominence, questions are also being raised as to whether national climate change regulation should be based primarily in a single or centralised measure (such as a carbon price designed to implement internationally agreed emission reduction commitments) or should embrace a multifaceted, multilevel approach.

Factors in the genesis of Australian climate law

As Bonyhady and Christoff note in their 2007 book, *Climate Law in Australia*, the problem of climate change and legal responses to it have an extensive history.[6] Indeed, the first scientific article discussing possible global warming as a result of CO_2 emissions was published in 1896,[7] although as we have seen, a dedicated international scientific and legal framework for dealing with climate change did

---

force' by 2015, to come into effect by 2020: UNFCCC, *Decision 1/CP.17, Establishment of an Ad Hoc Working Group on the Durban Platform for Enhanced Action* (11 December 2011), FCCC/CP/2011/L.10, para. 2.
4 See Chapter 1. See also S. Rayner, 'How to Eat an Elephant: A Bottom-Up Approach to Climate Policy', 10(6) *Climate Policy* 615 (2010); R. Eckersley, 'Kyoto or Copenhagen: From Legally Binding Treaty to DIY Climate Policy', Presentation at *Beyond a Carbon Price: A Framework for Climate Change Regulation in Australia*, Melbourne Law School, 11–12 August 2011.
5 See particularly Chapter 5 and Chapters 9–11.
6 T. Bonyhady and P. Christoff, 'Introduction', in *Climate Law in Australia*, eds T. Bonyhady and P. Christoff (Federation Press, 2007), pp. 1–2.
7 S. Arrhenius, 'On the Influence of Carbonic Acid in the Air Upon the Temperature of the Ground', 41 *Philosophical Magazine* 237 (1896). See also R. Revelle and H. Suess, 'Carbon Dioxide Exchange between Atmosphere and Ocean and the Question of an Increase of Atmospheric CO_2 during the Past Decades', 9 *Tellus* 18 (1957); and R. Revelle, 'Carbon Dioxide and World Climate', 247(2) *Scientific American* 35 (1982).

not develop until a century later.[8] In recent years, scientific and sociopolitical debates over climate change have intensified, with a growing sense of urgency about the need to address the problem. In Australia, Bonyhady and Christoff identify 2006 as the year that climate change matured into an issue of significant public, and inevitably political, concern.[9] Since that time we have seen the emergence of dedicated climate change legislation at both federal and state levels, which has coalesced with developments in other areas (particularly environmental and planning law) to form a body of law dubbed 'climate law'.[10]

A number of factors have been important in bringing about a renewed focus on climate change issues and paving the way for the emergence of climate law in Australia. Many of these influences have their origins outside the Australian context, reflecting the extent to which Australian regulatory development in the area is affected and informed by a broader global context.

Developments in climate change science

A major driver of legal and policy development has been the firming of scientific data on the danger that GHG emissions pose to the climate system – data that have marginalised (though certainly not silenced) climate change sceptics. In this regard, a significant milestone was the release of the Intergovernmental Panel on Climate Change (IPCC) Fourth Assessment Report in 2007, declaring warming of the earth's climate system to be 'unequivocal'.[11] The IPCC also warned that the effects of global warming over 2°C above pre-industrial levels will be severe. These include increases in human mortality, widespread loss of biodiversity, mass coral reef mortality, deglaciation, greater frequency of extreme weather events, decreasing global agricultural productivity and food shortages.[12]

Since the IPCC's 2007 report, other scientific reports have been released that suggest the IPCC's findings are quite conservative in their predictions. For instance, sea-level rise is already tracking above the IPCC's projections, and sea levels may rise at least twice as much as predicted in the 2007 IPCC report.[13] A greater frequency and intensity of extreme weather in Australia in recent years,

---

8 The IPCC (providing scientific assessments of climate change risk and impacts) was established in 1988, followed by the international framework treaty, the *United Nations Framework Convention on Climate Change*, opened for signature 9 May 1992, 1771 UNTS 164 (entered into force 24 March 1994) (UNFCCC).
9 Bonyhady and Christoff, *Climate Law in Australia* (2007), p. 2.
10 J. Peel, 'Climate Change Law: The Emergence of a New Legal Discipline', 32 *Melbourne University Law Review* 922 (2008). See also D. Hodgkinson and R. Garner, *Global Climate Change: Australian Law and Policy* (LexisNexis Butterworths, 2008); W. Gumley and T. Daya-Winterbottom, *Climate Change Law: Comparative, Contractual and Regulatory Considerations* (Lawbook Company, 2008); and N. Durrant, *Legal Responses to Climate Change* (Federation Press, 2010).
11 IPCC, *Climate Change 2007 Synthesis Report: Summary for Policymakers* (2007), p. 2.
12 IPCC Working Group II, *Climate Change 2007: Impacts, Adaptation and Vulnerability* (2007), pp. 781 and 792.
13 I. Allison et al., *The Copenhagen Diagnosis, 2009: Updating the World on the Latest Climate Science*, Executive Summary (UNSW Climate Change Research Centre, 2009).

such as the 2010–11 floods in Queensland, has also highlighted what a world of climate change might bring, in accord with scientific predictions.[14]

In the face of such scientific consensus and concern, even the most reluctant governments began to acknowledge the reality of climate change and the importance of taking action to address the problem. The Coalition federal government led by John Howard had announced in 2002 that it would not ratify the Kyoto Protocol, although it would undertake to meet Australia's emission reduction target under the treaty.[15] However, in 2007 the Howard government put aside its reservations about national action on climate change, with the Prime Minister announcing several measures in July of that year, including a proposal to introduce an emissions trading scheme (ETS).[16] This change of heart ultimately failed to secure the Howard government's re-election in the 2007 federal election. The new Labor government under Kevin Rudd came into power on a platform that included promised climate change action.

Economic costs of inaction on climate change

Another factor instrumental in altering governmental and public attitudes was the release of major economic analyses predicting the high cost, over the long term, of a failure to address anthropogenic climate change. For instance, the Stern Review on the Economics of Climate Change, released in 2006, had an enormous impact worldwide.[17] The Review, commissioned by the British Treasury, stressed that the benefits of strong and early action to address climate change far outweigh the economic costs of not acting and warned of very serious effects on economic growth and development if climate change went unmitigated.

In Australia, the findings of the Stern Review were echoed in the various reports prepared by the Rudd Labor government's climate change advisor, economist Ross Garnaut.[18] In the Final Report of the first Garnaut Climate Change Review, issued in 2008, Garnaut stressed that despite the potential disadvantages of being a 'first mover' on climate regulation, Australia has a greater stake in a strong mitigation strategy than do other developed countries:

> We are already a hot and dry country; small variations in climate are more damaging to us than to other developed countries. We live in a region of developing countries, which are in weaker positions to adapt to climate change than wealthy countries with robust political and economic institutions. The problems of our neighbours would inevitably

---

14 K. Braganza, D. Jones and N. Plummer, *Annual Australian Climate Statement 2010* (Bureau of Meteorology, 2011), <http://www.bom.gov.au/announcements/media_releases/climate/change/20110105.shtml>.
However, Will Steffen states: 'The floods across eastern Australia in 2010 and early 2011 were the consequence of a very strong La Niña event, and not the result of climate change ... There is no evidence that the strength of La Niña events is increasing due to climate change': W. Steffen, *The Critical Decade: Climate Science, Risks and Responses* (Australian Climate Commission Secretariat, 2011), p. 42. See also Chapters 1 and 2.
15 G. Pearse, *High and Dry: John Howard, Climate Change and the Selling of Australia's Future* (Penguin Books Australia, 2007), p. 77.
16 K. Murphy, 'PM to Unveil Details of Carbon Trading Plan', *The Age* (Melbourne), 17 July 2007, p. 3.
17 N. Stern, *The Economics of Climate Change: The Stern Review* (Cambridge University Press, 2007).
18 For copies of all these reports and background information on the review see <http://www.garnautreview.org.au/2008-review.html>.

become our problems. And the structure of our economy means that our terms of trade would be damaged more by the effects of climate change than would those of any other developed country.[19]

Garnaut's 2008 recommendations, including his proposals for the development of an ETS to implement targets for emission reduction in Australia, ultimately were not implemented by the Rudd government, as is discussed further below. However, Garnaut has remained an influential figure in the national climate policy debate.

In 2010, following the narrow re-election of the Gillard Labor government, Garnaut was commissioned once more by the federal government to provide an update of his earlier Review. The conclusions and recommendations of the Garnaut Climate Change Review of 2011 departed little from those issued in 2008, although the Review stressed that the science now establishes anthropogenic climate change 'beyond reasonable doubt' and that Australian emissions are growing at a rate far exceeding that of other developed countries, largely as a result of increased fugitive emissions from coal and gas exports.[20] Overall, the Review still concluded that it is in Australia's national interest to do 'its fair share in a strong global effort to mitigate climate change' and that the best way to achieve emission reduction goals domestically was by reliance on a market-based approach, either a carbon tax or an ETS.[21]

Public opinion on climate change

For the Australian general public, scientific and economic analyses of global warming may have been less salient than media reporting of probable dire impacts, coupled with weather patterns that suggest warming is already occurring. Many also point to the influence of Al Gore's 2006 film, *An Inconvenient Truth*, in bringing the looming 'climate crisis' to worldwide public attention.

In Australia, public concern was excited by reports of 2005 being the 'hottest year on record',[22] and by conditions of severe drought in many areas of the country up until the summer of 2010.[23] Heatwave conditions occurred in Victoria in February 2009, leading to the 'Black Saturday' bushfires.[24] More recently there have been devastating floods in New South Wales, Victoria and Queensland,[25]

---

19 Garnaut, *Garnaut Climate Change Review* (2008), p. xix.
20 R. Garnaut, *The Garnaut Review 2011: Australia in the Global Response to Climate Change* (2011), pp. 26–7.
21 The differences between these regulatory instruments are discussed in Chapter 5.
22 Bureau of Meteorology, *Annual Australian Climate Statement 2005* Media Release, (4 January 2006), <http://www.bom.gov.au/announcements/media_releases/climate/change/20060104.shtml>.
23 Bureau of Meteorology National Climate Centre, *Drought Statement*, (3 July 2008), <http://www.bom.gov.au/climate/drought/drought.shtml>.
24 2009 Victorian Bushfires Royal Commission, *Final Report Summary* (2010), <http://www.royalcommission.vic.gov.au/finaldocuments/summary/PF/VBRC_Summary_PF.pdf>.
25 Queensland Government, *Queensland Floods* (2011), <http://www.qld.gov.au/floods>; and State Government of Victoria, *Recovering from Floods: 2011 Victorian Floods* (2011), <http://www.dhs.vic.gov.au/floods/recovery-status>.

with the last-mentioned state also hit in the north by tropical cyclone Yasi.[26] While the extent to which these events are linked to climate change is not clear, they have nonetheless presented a vivid image to the public of possible weather patterns if warming continues. Even so, public opinion on climate change is a fickle thing, as the varying attitudes recorded in public opinion polling on climate change in the United States demonstrate.[27]

In Australia, public (and political) interest in climate change waned with rising concern over the Global Financial Crisis and climate change was a peripheral issue in the 2010 federal election campaign.[28] Climate change, and how to regulate it, only re-emerged on the federal political agenda when it became apparent that the Gillard Labor government would need the support of the Greens party and independent members in the lower house of parliament in order to form government. This resulted in the establishment of the Multi-Party Climate Change Committee (MPCCC) as a negotiating forum for reaching agreement on a carbon pricing mechanism (see further below).

Public views regarding climate change were thus at their high-water mark during the November 2007 election campaign, when the Labor party argued for a new approach and for the urgency of policy development in the area of climate change. The first major act of the Rudd government following its election was to ratify the Kyoto Protocol.[29] As a party to the Protocol, Australia became subject to the treaty's binding emission reduction requirements and compliance regime.[30] In turn, this gave renewed vigour to debates over the regulatory framework Australia might put in place to meet its Kyoto Protocol commitments and respond to the problem of climate change.

Judicial rulings in climate change cases

As the science and the economic impacts of climate change have become clearer, other state institutions, such as the courts, have followed the lead of governments in recognising, with some exceptions,[31] the reality and importance of climate change.[32] However, judicial rulings in Australian cases related to climate change have played more than a supplementary role. Instead, the courts have often provided an alternative avenue for concerned groups and individuals to pursue policy and legal reform in the face of a lack of national regulatory action. In the United States, a parallel course of litigation has taken place as a response to the lack

26 Queensland Government; *Cyclone Yasi* (2011), <http://www.qld.gov.au/cyclone>.
27 See Chapter 1.
28 ABC Television, 'Climate Change drops off the radar in 2010 election', *The 7.30 Report*, 29 July 2010, <http://www.abc.net.au/7.30/content/2010/s2968227.htm>.
29 T. Hill and L. Moore, 'Australia Ratifies the Kyoto Protocol', 23(1) *Australian Environment Review* 10 (2008). The Kyoto Protocol is discussed in Chapter 2.
30 The Protocol's compliance regime is discussed in Chapter 3.
31 See *Re Xstrata Coal Queensland Pty Ltd* [2007] QLRT 33, [16]–[18], per Koppenol P (overturned on appeal: *Queensland Conservation Council Inc v Xstrata Coal Queensland Pty Ltd* (2007) 155 LGERA 322).
32 For example: *Gray v Minister for Planning and Ors* (2006) 152 LGERA 258, 287; *Walker v Minister for Planning and Ors* (2007) 157 LGERA 124, 192; see also *Massachusetts v Environmental Protection Agency* 549 US 497, 504–5, 521–2 (2007).

of national policy and legal development on climate change issues (particularly in the area of emissions trading) under successive federal administrations.

Seminal decisions in both Australia and the United States, such as the *Hazelwood*, *Anvil Hill* and *Massachusetts* cases, summarised below, have demonstrated alternative avenues for action on climate change based on general environmental law frameworks.[33] Navraj Ghaleigh has classified litigation of this kind as 'promotive', where 'applicants are seeking to deploy more general legal norms which have no necessary climate-change characteristics in ways that can promote positive environmental outcomes by way of regulatory intervention sanctioned or even required by courts'.[34] In this sense, climate litigation may be viewed as a bottom-up driver of legal change seeking to create requirements for regulatory action on climate change where none previously existed.

Massachusetts v EPA

A leading example of this type of case is the *Massachusetts v EPA* decision of the US Supreme Court. The case has been seen as a model for bottom-up action on climate change around the world, including in Australia. Its foundation was a 'rulemaking petition' submitted by a group of environmental and other organisations to the US Environmental Protection Agency (EPA), requesting the EPA to regulate the emission of GHGs from motor vehicles under section 202(a)(1) of the *Clean Air Act*.[35] Section 202(a)(1) provides that the EPA must prescribe by regulation 'standards applicable to the emission of any air pollutant from any class or classes of new motor vehicles or new motor vehicle engines, which in [the EPA's] judgment cause, or contribute to, air pollution which may reasonably be anticipated to endanger public health or welfare'. An appeal of the EPA's rejection of the petition eventually reached the Supreme Court, where the Court faced questions concerning the standing of the State of Massachusetts to bring the claim and the legal correctness of the EPA's decision that regulation of GHG emissions from motor vehicles was not authorised under the *Clean Air Act*.

In terms of the broader significance of the case, it was the judgment of the Supreme Court on matters of standing that was most relevant.[36] The majority concluded that Massachusetts did face a risk of harm that was both actual and imminent.[37] The Court accepted evidence suggesting that various climate-change-related risks would confront Massachusetts if GHG emissions continued unabated, including rising sea levels, severe and irreversible changes to natural

---

[33] These cases form a small subset of the burgeoning area of climate litigation. For full details of the US and Australian case law see the blogs maintained by Michael Gerrard (Columbia University),<http://www.law.columbia.edu/centers/climatechange> and Jacqueline Peel (Melbourne University), *Climate Change Law: Australian and Overseas Developments* <http://blogs.unimelb.edu.au/peel_climatechange/author/jpeel/>.
[34] N. Ghaleigh, '"Six Honest Serving Men": Climate Change Litigation as Legal Mobilization and the Utility of Typologies', 1 *Climate Law* 31 (2010), p. 45.
[35] *Massachusetts v Environmental Protection Agency*, 549 US 497 (2007).
[36] Note that a relaxed standard of standing applied, given that the case was being brought as a judicial review of agency action: 549 US 497, 516–18 (2007).
[37] 549 US 497 (2007).

ecosystems, and a significant reduction in water storage, all of which would have 'direct and important economic consequences'.[38] Moreover, the majority held that the fact that climate change risks were widely shared did not deprive Massachusetts of its right to be heard.[39]

Also of critical importance were the majority's findings on the questions of causation and whether the injury suffered could be redressed. Contrary to the EPA's argument that its decision not to regulate GHG emissions from new motor vehicles made an insignificant contribution to the petitioners' injuries, the majority accepted that a sufficient causal link existed between GHGs from cars in the United States and global climate change to warrant regulation of those emissions by the EPA. In the view of the majority, the US transportation sector's 6 per cent contribution to CO_2 emissions worldwide was 'a meaningful contribution to greenhouse gas concentrations and hence ... to global warming'.[40] Accordingly, while regulating vehicle emissions alone would not reverse global warming, it 'would slow the pace of global emission increases, no matter what happens elsewhere'.[41] The Court also commented that it was uncommon that regulatory action solved complex problems in one fell swoop; a small and incremental step might still assist in addressing the broader issue.[42] These findings help to counter common arguments that regulation or responsibility is not justified because the contribution of a particular action to overall emission levels on a global scale is 'insignificant', or is dwarfed by the emissions from other contributors.[43] They also bolster government efforts to tackle other 'significant' sources of GHG emissions even if individual initiatives will not 'solve' the overall climate change problem.

On the issue of the correct interpretation of the provisions of the *Clean Air Act*, the Supreme Court's findings lend credence to arguments that general environmental protection laws can be used to deal with emerging threats such as climate change.[44] The majority held that GHGs such as CO_2 are air pollutants within the meaning of the legislation, with the consequence that the EPA could avoid prescribing regulatory standards only if 'it determines that greenhouse gases do not contribute to climate change or if it provides some reasonable explanation as to why it cannot or will not exercise its discretion to

---

38 549 US 497, 521–2 (2007). In its more recent decision of *American Electric Power Company v Connecticut* 131 S Ct 2527 (20 June 2011) the Court was more circumspect about climate change science. However, despite closing the door to federal common law nuisance actions involving climate change, the Court's judgment did so in a manner that gave additional emphasis to the federal regulatory approach endorsed in *Massachusetts v EPA*.
39 Ibid.   **40** 549 US 497, 524–5 (2007).   **41** 549 US 497, 500 (2007).
42 549 US 497, 524 (2007).
43 Of course this raises questions as to what is a 'significant' or 'meaningful' contribution of GHG emissions. This question has long occupied environmental law in the field of environmental impact assessment, and ultimately judgments about significance depend heavily upon subjective factors: see J. Peel and L. Godden, 'The *Environment Protection and Biodiversity Conservation Act 1999* (Cth): Dark Sides of Virtue', 31 *Melbourne University Law Review* 106 (2007).
44 For discussion of how the existing environmental law framework – such as pollution control laws administered by state governments – may provide an avenue for climate regulation, see D. E. Fisher, 'The Statutory Relevance of Greenhouse Gas Emissions in Environmental Regulation', 24 *Environmental and Planning Law Journal* 210 (2007).

determine whether they do'.[45] Since the EPA had not made such a judgment, nor, in the opinion of the majority, offered any reasonable explanation why it could not do so, the agency's action was judged 'arbitrary, capricious, or otherwise not in accordance with law'.[46] In an interesting *obiter* comment, the majority of the Court suggested that one explanation that may have been acceptable for the EPA to have offered was that the scientific uncertainty surrounding climate change was so profound that the EPA was unable to reach a judgment on the contribution of GHGs to the problem. The majority clearly did not think that situation obtained in the case, adding that 'residual uncertainty' was not enough.[47]

Hazelwood case

The *Hazelwood* decision[48] of the Victorian Civil and Administrative Tribunal (VCAT) preceded the *Massachusetts v EPA* case by some three years and was the first major Australian case to consider the relevance of climate change to decision-making under general environmental and planning laws.[49]

The case was brought by the Australian Conservation Foundation, which was concerned about the long-term climate change effects of a proposal to extend the life of the Hazelwood power station, Australia's most emission-intensive coal-fired electricity generator. The Victorian government had excluded greenhouse issues from the scope of the environmental assessment required for the project, meaning that the Foundation's concerns about the proposal had to be framed as an objection to a planning scheme amendment that was also necessary for the project. VCAT was therefore required to rule as to whether the environmental impacts of GHG emissions that would be generated by the continuation of the power plant were relevant to the decision on the planning scheme amendment, even though this was a minor part of the approval process for the project.

In finding that such matters were relevant, President Morris of VCAT held that approval of the planning scheme amendment would 'make it more probable that the Hazelwood Power Station will continue to operate beyond 2009; which, in turn, may make it more likely that the atmosphere will receive greater greenhouse gas emissions than would otherwise be the case; which may be an environmental effect of significance'.[50] An essential plank of President Morris' reasoning was that a submission raising possible climate change impacts would still be relevant to consider 'even if it relates to an *indirect* effect of the [planning scheme] amendment'.[51]

The most important contribution of this judgment (which did not ultimately prevent the Victorian government from approving the extension of the Hazelwood plant) lay in the impetus it provided to arguments that 'indirect'

---

[45] 549 US 497, 533 (2007). [46] 549 US 497, 534 (2007). [47] 549 US 497, 534 (2007).
[48] *Australian Conservation Foundation v Latrobe City Council* (2004) 140 LGERA 100.
[49] The earlier decision of *Greenpeace Australia Ltd v Redbank Power Company Pty Ltd and Singleton Council* (1994) 86 LGERA 143 raised climate change claims in similar factual circumstances but is principally known for its rulings on the interpretation of the precautionary principle.
[50] (2004) 140 LGERA 100, 110. [51] (2004) 140 LGERA 100, 109.

climate change effects were relevant to planning and environmental approval processes. This approach was affirmed and extended in the case of *Gray v Minister for Planning and Ors*,[52] more commonly known as the *Anvil Hill* case.

Anvil Hill case

The *Anvil Hill* case, decided in 2006 by Justice Pain of the New South Wales Land and Environment Court (NSWLEC), still stands as the most important of the Australian climate law cases to date. The decision is particularly significant for embracing the idea that the environmental assessment of coal mining projects may require consideration of the environmental impacts of their 'indirect' or offshore GHG emissions.[53] Less remarked upon, but equally noteworthy, is the detailed consideration the judgment gave to principles of ecologically sustainable development (ESD), such as the intergenerational equity and precautionary principles.[54] The intergenerational equity principle, as discussed in Chapter 1, represents the idea that the present generation should pass on to future generations a healthy, diverse and productive natural environment. The precautionary principle provides that where there are threats of serious or irreversible damage, scientific uncertainty should not be used as a basis for postponing measures to prevent environmental degradation (see Chapter 1).

The case was brought by a local environmental activist, Peter Gray, in relation to a proposed coal mine at Anvil Hill in the Hunter Valley in New South Wales. The Anvil Hill mine was to be one of the largest in Australia, capable of producing up to 10.5 million tonnes of coal annually, with GHG emissions averaging 12 414 387 tonnes of CO_2 eq. per annum. Gray challenged the environmental impact assessment (EIA) produced for the mine proposal on the basis that the initial documentation exhibited publicly did not contain an assessment of indirect GHG emissions associated with the burning of the coal that would be harvested from the mine. This omission came despite a requirement in the terms of reference for the EIA for a 'detailed greenhouse gas assessment'.

Justice Pain analysed whether a causal link could be drawn between the mine and climate change impacts on the New South Wales environment. Despite its apparently minimal contribution to GHG emissions in global terms (the Anvil Hill mine was estimated to contribute per annum the equivalent of 0.04 per cent of the world's greenhouse emissions),[55] her Honour accepted the applicant's argument that GHG emissions from the burning of coal to be extracted from the new mine should have been considered in the proponent's environmental

---

[52] (2006) 152 LGERA 258.
[53] L. McAllister, 'Litigating Climate Change at the Coal Mine', in *Adjudicating Climate Change: State, National, and International Approaches,* eds W. Burns and H. Osofsky (Cambridge University Press, 2009).
[54] In Australia, the concept of ESD and its underlying principles are given effect by the National Strategy for Ecologically Sustainable Development (NSESD) and the Intergovernmental Agreement on the Environment (IGAE). ESD principles have been adopted in numerous federal, state and territory environmental laws: J. Peel, 'Ecologically Sustainable Development: More than Mere Lip Service?', 12(1) *Australasian Journal of Natural Resources Law and Policy* 1 (2008).
[55] D. Farrier, 'The Limits of Judicial Review: Anvil Hill in the Land and Environment Court', in *Climate Law in Australia,* eds T. Bonyhady and P. Christoff (Federation Press, 2007), p. 189.

assessment because of their potential contribution to climate change. In a manner similar to the US Supreme Court in *Massachusetts v EPA*, Justice Pain reasoned that, notwithstanding the global nature of climate change and the many contributing sources, the contribution from a single large source should not be ignored.[56]

Another of the grounds of judicial review raised in the case concerned whether the EIA for the mine should be deemed inadequate on the basis that the decision-maker failed to take ESD principles into account.[57] Justice Pain's starting point in considering this question was the informative function of an EIA process: 'to provide information about the impact of a particular activity on the environment to a decision-maker to enable him or her to make an informed decision based on adequate information about the environmental consequences of a particular development'.[58] According to Justice Pain, when this function was considered in the context of the core ESD requirements of intergenerational equity and precaution, it dictated the provision of certain types of information in the EIA process. For instance, her Honour held that one important factor in an EIA that takes into account the intergenerational equity principle 'must be the assessment of cumulative impacts of proposed activities on the environment'.[59] Likewise, an approach to environmental assessment that takes into account the precautionary principle requires knowledge of impacts that are 'cumulative, on going and long term'.[60] As such information was not provided in the EIA for the Anvil Hill mine, the judge found that there had been a failure to take account of principles of intergenerational equity and precaution.[61]

These aspects of the *Anvil Hill* decision are important in establishing the relevance of a consideration of the climate change impacts of proposals – albeit long-term, cumulative and subject to some level of uncertainty – in general environmental assessment procedures. Moreover, it would seem that this consideration needs to be rigorous and substantive. Justice Pain emphasised, for instance, that '[s]imply raising an issue such as climate change/global warming is unlikely to satisfy a requirement that intergenerational equity or the precautionary principle has been considered in the absence of any analysis of the impact of activities which potentially contribute in the NSW context in a substantial way to climate change/global warming'.[62]

Assessment of the case law
Overall, climate change cases, such as the examples discussed above, have served an important function of raising awareness by bringing climate change into the courtroom and the broader public sphere as a relevant factor to be

---

56 *Gray v Minister for Planning & Ors* (2006) 152 LGERA 258, 287-8.
57 For a further recent decision of Justice Pain developing the jurisprudence in relation to the use of principles of ESD in the climate change context, see *Hunter Environment Lobby Inc v Minister for Planning* [2011] NSWLEC 221.
58 *Gray v Minister for Planning & Ors* (2006) 152 LGERA 258, 293.   **59** (2006) 152 LGERA 258, 293.
60 (2006) 152 LGERA 258, 296.   **61** (2006) 152 LGERA 258, 294.   **62** (2006) 152 LGERA 258, 297.

taken into account in planning decisions. In the *Hazelwood* and *Anvil Hill* cases, court decisions have demonstrated the capacity of the general legal system to generate change, even over a short time frame. Nonetheless, the outcomes of climate change challenges brought in Australian courts have been highly variable,[63] signalling the *ad hoc* nature of legal change achievable through the judicial system, and hence the need for a more coherent regulatory approach.[64] In addition, no case so far has brought about a halt to GHG-intensive development, exposing the limitations of climate litigation as a direct form of mitigation policy.

Some commentators, such as Chief Justice Brian Preston of the NSWLEC, suggest that climate litigation provides a more indirect means for generating policy or regulatory change by pushing climate change issues higher on the agenda of busy legislatures.[65] Also important, but difficult to measure in substantive terms, is the contribution climate cases have made to revitalising ESD principles and developing a legal culture more aware of the need to factor climate change considerations into environmental and planning decision-making.

Further, although Australia now has a national carbon pricing mechanism,[66] which took effect on 1 July 2012, this reform does not address several of the issues that have been the subject of climate litigation. In particular, it is predicted that the domestic carbon pricing mechanism will not have a substantial effect on the local coal industry since offshore emissions (that is, emissions resulting from the burning of coal for power generation in countries such as India) fall outside the regime. In the absence of any workable technological remedy (carbon capture and storage, discussed in Chapter 9, is not that at present), we can expect to see continuing high levels of GHG emissions from the combustion of Australian coal, largely unregulated by the proposed centrepiece of the domestic regulatory regime. In this context, climate litigation that seeks to ensure that offshore emissions are factored into decision-making may complement carbon pricing by mediating between the domestically focused operation of regulatory approaches like the carbon pricing mechanism and the global context of GHG emissions' production and effects.

---

63 See for example: *Wildlife Preservation Society of Queensland Proserpine/Whitsunday Branch Inc v Minister for the Environment and Heritage* (2006) 232 ALR 510; *Anvil Hill Project Watch Association v Minister for the Environment and Water Resources* (2007) 159 LGERA 8; and *Anvil Hill Project Watch Association v Minister for the Environment and Water Resources* (2008) 166 FCR 54.
64 J. Peel, 'The Role of Climate Change Litigation in Australia's Response to Global Warming', 24 *Environmental and Planning Law Journal* 90 (2007); B. Preston, 'Climate Change Litigation (Part 2)', 2/2011 *Carbon and Climate Law Review* 244 (2011).
65 B. Preston, 'The Influence of Climate Litigation on Governments and the Private Sector', 2(4) *Climate Law* 485 (2011). As an example Preston cites a new State Environmental Planning Policy (SEPP) – covering mining activities – introduced in New South Wales following the *Anvil Hill* case. For new mine proposals, the SEPP requires an assessment of GHGs including downstream emissions: State Environmental Planning Policy (Mining, Petroleum and Extractive Industries) 2007 (NSW), reg 14.
66 The Australian carbon pricing mechanism is introduced in this chapter, but the detail of the legislative and institutional arrangements for the scheme is addressed in Chapter 5.

Development of Australian climate law and policy

Factors such as developments in climate change science, economic analyses, public attitudes and court action have played an important role in generating and maintaining political attention to the issue of climate change in Australia. Policy and legislative responses to climate change began to emerge in the early 1990s but gathered pace after the election of the Rudd government in 2007. Over time, the form and ambition of climate change regulation in Australia have been heavily influenced by internal dynamics between the federal and state governments, and by the successive climate policies of different governments at all governance levels.

While a strict chronological account of the development of Australian climate law and policy would be logically attractive, in practice this is a complex explanatory task given the mix of international, national and sub-national actions involved. In the following sections we have instead sought to group different legal and policy initiatives according to their substantive focus. (For a timeline of significant dates, see Table 1.1 in Chapter 1.) This account of Australia's climate law and policy history can be read in different ways. Viewed through a political lens, policy disjunctures become more evident, particularly between the 'no regrets' measures favoured by the Howard federal government (1996–2007) and the pursuit of mandatory emission reduction legislation by recent Labor governments (2007–). Another reader, however, might note the consistent focus of successive Australian federal governments on market-based solutions to the problem of climate change,[67] with a gradual transition from low-cost measures to more costly, legislated emission controls.

Australian climate change regulation: The international context

Much of the early development of climate policy and law in Australia took place in response to the emergence of the international climate change regime consisting of the UNFCCC. As we saw in Chapter 2, the UNFCCC obliges developed country (or Annex I) parties, such as Australia, to 'take the lead' in implementing measures to reduce their contribution to global climate change. The international treaty instruments are not prescriptive as to the form that domestic regulatory measures should take,[68] although the endorsement of market-based measures in the Kyoto Protocol has promoted a focus on emissions trading schemes (ETS) as a principal implementation mechanism in many jurisdictions.[69] In addition, links to the 'global' carbon market (of which schemes like

---

[67] This theme is taken up further in the next chapter.
[68] Art. 2.1(a) of the Kyoto Protocol only provides an indicative list of policies and measures.
[69] The reasons underlying the prominence of ETS as a regulatory tool of choice for climate change mitigation are discussed in Chapter 5.

the European Union's ETS form a substantial part) and the Kyoto Protocol's flexibility mechanisms such as the CDM[70] have been seen as 'important to minimising Australia's costs, as it expands Australian businesses' access to cost-effective mitigation'.[71]

During the negotiations for the UNFCCC, Australia was one of several states, including those of the European Union, that argued for the inclusion of binding emission targets in the treaty. The proposal failed due to the opposition of the United States and oil-producing countries, leading to the compromise text found in Article 4(2)(a). This provision was discussed in detail in Chapter 2. In summary, the provision commits developed country parties to (at most) adopting national mitigation policies and measures limiting anthropogenic GHG emissions with the aim of returning their emissions to 1990 levels by 2000.

Australia's Kyoto 'deal'

Under the Hawke and Keating Labor governments (1983–96), there was significant political support for Australia's participation in the international climate change regime, and Australia was one of the first states to ratify the UNFCCC. By the time negotiations for the Kyoto Protocol concluded in 1997, however, the federal political context had altered dramatically with the election of the conservative Howard government in 1996. Australia's new federal government participated in the Kyoto negotiations, with the Australian delegation led by the then Minister for the Environment, Senator Robert Hill. Senator Hill proved a tough negotiator, holding out during the last, all-night, session of the Kyoto conference until key concessions were granted to Australia.[72] These concessions, reflected in the text of the Kyoto Protocol, included a generous emission target for Australia of 108 per cent of 1990 levels (average per annum) applicable during the first commitment period, 2008–12. Only two other Annex I countries, Iceland and Norway, were permitted emission targets exceeding 100 per cent of 1990 levels.

The other major concession made to Australia in the Kyoto Protocol was the inclusion of the so-called Australia clause in Article 3.7.[73] This provision allows those parties 'for whom land-use change and forestry constituted a net source of greenhouse gas emissions in 1990' to include those emissions when calculating their 1990 emission levels, which form the baseline for emission cuts over the first commitment period. In line with this provision, Australia included net emissions from land clearing, which were very high in 1990, in the calculation of its 1990 baseline. Because these emissions dropped sharply after 1990, the effect of the artificially high baseline was to reduce the emission reductions

---

[70] The regulatory network of the CDM is discussed in Chapter 6.
[71] *Carbon Pollution Reduction Scheme: Australia's Low Pollution Future*, White Paper, Volume One (December 2008), p. 3–3.
[72] See C. Hamilton, *Scorcher: The Dirty Politics of Climate Change* (Black Inc., 2007), p. 74.
[73] For discussion see C. Hamilton and L. Vellen, 'Land-use Change in Australia and the Kyoto Protocol', 2(2) *Environmental Science and Policy* 145 (1999). See also Chapter 2.

necessary in other sectors of the economy to meet Australia's allocated target of 108 per cent of 1990 emission levels (for the precise formulation of this obligation see Chapter 2, pp. 83–4). The reduction of land clearing in Australia since 1990 has been the result of state legislative controls, meaning that the nation is on track to meet its Kyoto Protocol target relatively easily, without substantial reductions in emissions from the energy generation, mining and industrial sectors.[74] However, this will not be the case for any subsequent commitment period accepted by Australia under the Kyoto Protocol, since on a 'business as usual scenario', the nation's emissions from sectors other than land clearing are projected to increase sharply after 2012, to 121 per cent of 2000 levels by 2020 in the absence of abatement measures.[75]

Australia also benefits from a number of other provisions under the Kyoto Protocol regime, such as Articles 3.3 and 3.4. Article 3.3 provides that Annex I parties, in meeting their emission reduction commitments under the Protocol, can use 'the net changes in greenhouse gas emissions by sources *and removals by sinks resulting from direct human-induced land-use change and forestry activities*, limited to afforestation, reforestation and deforestation since 1990, measured as verifiable changes in carbon stocks'.[76] So-called sink activities, such as the reforestation of cleared agricultural land, are an attractive climate change mitigation option for a country with large areas of land territory, such as Australia. While Article 3.3 limits permissible land use, land-use change and forestry activities (LULUCF) to afforestation, reforestation and deforestation,[77] Article 3.4 provides an opening for the inclusion of additional LULUCF activities upon agreement of the COP/MOP. Approved LULUCF activities under the international climate change regime now extend to forest management, grazing land management and crop land management, which provide additional opportunities for Australia to meet emission reduction commitments by undertaking sink activities.[78]

Climate policy outside the Kyoto framework

Returning from the Protocol negotiations in Kyoto, Senator Hill received a standing ovation from the Coalition cabinet in recognition of a job (seen to be) well done. Shortly thereafter, in 1998, the Howard government signed the Kyoto Protocol. However, following the election of George W. Bush as President of the United States in 2000, and the Bush administration's

---

[74] Australia's Fifth National Communication on Climate Change, submitted to the UNFCCC Secretariat in March 2010, indicated that Australia was on track to meet its Kyoto target without relying on the Protocol's flexibility mechanisms, with emissions projected to reach 106 per cent of 1990 levels over the first commitment period.
[75] Department of Climate Change, *Australia's Fifth National Communication on Climate Change* (2010), p. 87.
[76] Emphasis added. The GHG emissions by sources and removals by sinks associated with such activities must be reported in a 'transparent and verifiable manner' and reviewed in accordance with Articles 7 and 8 of the Kyoto Protocol. See Chapter 3.
[77] For relevant definitions see Chapter 10.
[78] See *Carbon Credits (Carbon Farming Initiative) Act 2011* (Cth), discussed in depth in Chapter 10.

rejection of the Kyoto Protocol, the Australian government quickly changed its position. On World Environment Day in 2002, Prime Minister John Howard announced that Australia would strive to meet its Kyoto Protocol target, but would not ratify the treaty, because of its potential to damage the Australian economy.[79]

Rather than ratifying the Kyoto Protocol, the government pursued a regional initiative, in conjunction with the United States, China, India, Japan and South Korea: the Asia–Pacific Partnership on Clean Development and Climate (AP6). Initiated by the United States early in 2005, with the inaugural meeting held in Sydney in January 2006, this voluntary, non-binding framework for cooperation was presented as an agreement both 'complementing' and 'going beyond' the Kyoto Protocol.[80] However, as Christoff and Eckersley have argued, there are good reasons to regard it as inconsistent with the international climate change regime.[81] For instance, the AP6 contains no emission reduction targets or timetables, nor enforcement mechanisms, instead putting its faith in the development and dissemination of new 'clean' technologies through voluntary programs and government subsidies. While the AP6 continues to be supported by the Gillard Labor government, it now appears that the UNFCCC is regarded by Australia as the primary arena for international climate change negotiations.[82]

In view of Australia's small contribution to global GHG emissions (in absolute, rather than per capita, terms), the Howard federal government's refusal to join the Kyoto Protocol was not significant in delaying the entry into force of the Protocol (unlike the refusal of the United States). However, Australia's refusal to ratify, together with its support for the United States' efforts to move away from the Kyoto Protocol as the centrepiece of international climate change law and policy, subsequently bought Australia substantial ill will in various international environmental fora given the important concessions that had been made to the country during the Kyoto negotiation process.[83] It was only when the government of Prime Minister Kevin Rudd was elected in 2007 that Australia finally ratified the Kyoto Protocol, some two and a half years after its entry into force on 16 February 2005.

---

[79] Pearse, *High and Dry* (2007), p. 77. In international law, signature of a treaty connotes an intention to be bound, but binding legal obligations arise only upon a country's ratification of the treaty.
[80] Statement of the US Under Secretary of State for Democracy and Global Affairs, Paula Dobriansky, recorded by P. Christoff and R. Eckersley, 'Kyoto and the Asia–Pacific Partnership on Clean Development and Climate', in *Climate Law in Australia*, eds T. Bonyhady and P. Christoff (Federation Press, 2007), p. 34. Statements issued by the Australian Foreign Minister Alexander Downer and Prime Minister John Howard on the AP6 also revealed contradictory objectives.
[81] See also T. Skodvin, 'The Asia Pacific Partnership on Clean Development and Climate: Supplement or Alternative to the Kyoto Protocol?', paper presented at the 48th Annual Convention of the International Studies Association, Chicago, 28 February–3 March 2007, <http://citation.allacademic.com/meta/p_mla_apa_research_citation/1/7/9/0/1/pages179010/p179010-1.php>.
[82] P. Lawrence, 'Australian Climate Policy and the Asia Pacific Partnership on Clean Development and Climate: From Howard to Rudd, Continuity or Change?', 9 *International Environmental Agreements* 281 (2009).
[83] Ibid., p. 288.

International climate change negotiations

In the ongoing negotiations concerning future international arrangements, Australia has proved to be a rather fickle friend of the Kyoto process. At the Copenhagen conference in December 2009 Australia was one of a number of developed countries to advocate the disbanding of the Kyoto Protocol and its replacement with a new treaty that would impose binding requirements for emission reductions on both developed and developing countries.[84] The failure of the Copenhagen conference to produce such a treaty, or anything approaching it, delivered a heavy blow to the Rudd Labor government, which had tied the fate of its domestic mitigation measures in the form of the Carbon Pollution Reduction Scheme (discussed further below) to the emergence of a comprehensive international agreement on cutting GHG emissions.

Australia was, however, quick to associate itself with the non-binding Copenhagen Accord, submitting self-determined emission reduction targets in January 2010. These nominated an unconditional pledge to reduce emissions by 5 per cent from 2000 levels by 2020, with additional reductions of up to 15 per cent and 25 per cent possible depending upon the level of action taken by other states.[85] The federal government also committed to a long-term emission reduction target of 60 per cent below 2000 levels by 2050, raised in July 2011 to a pledge of an 80 per cent cut from 2000 emission levels.[86] These targets broadly follow the recommendations made in the 2008 Garnaut Review as to what constitutes Australia's 'fair share' of global emission reduction,[87] although the unconditional 5 per cent cut by 2020 does not approach the levels of reductions in collective emissions recommended by climate scientists.[88]

Although the climate change negotiations at Cancun in December 2010 exceeded the (low) expectations of most and revived the multilateral UNFCCC process, they still did not deliver the 'comprehensive' agreement on emission reductions sought by countries such as Australia. Instead, the Cancun Agreements, as they were dubbed by the UNFCCC Secretariat, made some progress in less controversial areas, such as support for development of a REDD scheme (reduction in emissions from deforestation and forest degradation in developing

---

84 See Australian Government, *Legal Architecture for a Post-2012 Outcome: Submission to the AWG-LCA and AWG-KP*, <http://www.climatechange.gov.au/government/international/~/media/submissions/international/Legal-Architecture-Post-2012-Outcome-Australian-submission-MAY-09.pdf>.
85 Australian Government, 'Quantified Economy Wide Emissions Targets for 2020' (2010), <http://unfccc.int/files/meetings/application/pdf/australiacphaccord_app1.pdf>. The 25 per cent reduction will apply if there is 'an ambitious global deal capable of stabilising levels of greenhouse gases in the atmosphere at 450 ppm CO_2 eq. or lower'.
86 Department of Climate Change and Energy Efficiency, *Securing a Clean Energy Future: The Australian Government's Plan* (2011), p. 15. See also *Clean Energy Act 2011* s 3(c)(i).
87 Garnaut, *Garnaut Climate Change Review* (2008), p. 209. Garnaut recommended a 2050 target of a 90 per cent reduction from 2000 levels.
88 In 2007, the IPCC concluded that emissions will need to be reduced by 25–40 per cent from 1990 levels by 2020 to stabilise atmospheric concentrations of CO_2 eq. at 450 ppm: IPCC, *Climate Change 2007: Mitigation of Climate Change: Contribution of Working Group III to the Fourth Assessment Report of the IPCC* (Cambridge University Press, 2007), p. 776, Table 13.7.

countries)[89] – a mechanism in which Australia has displayed a keen interest[90] – and adaptation financing.[91]

More recently, and perhaps in light of the introduction of new domestic carbon pricing measures, Australia has changed tack once again in its international climate policy. In September 2011, in the lead-up to the Durban COP, Australia and Norway issued a joint proposal sketching out a pathway for global climate negotiations to agree, by 2015, on a 'legal agreement with binding mitigation commitments by both developed and developing countries, especially from major economies'.[92] The main elements of the proposal were procedural, focusing on ensuring consistent rules and processes for the formulation, accounting, verification and progressive scaling-up of countries' emission reduction targets and actions. The Durban COP was hailed as a success by the Australian government for delivering on what the government claimed were Australia's key objectives going into the negotiations: namely, building on the emission reduction pledges made at the Cancun COP, moving towards a legal framework to cover all major emitters, and promoting market mechanisms.[93]

As far as a binding international treaty is concerned, the UNFCCC parties agreed at Durban to begin a process to negotiate a new multilateral arrangement that would have legal force and enter into effect by 2020.[94] The new agreement will impose obligations on all parties, not just developed country parties, if it is successfully negotiated and agreed to within the proposed time frame of three years (2012–15). The Kyoto Protocol was extended to a second commitment period commencing 1 January 2013, which will enable carbon markets under the CDM to continue[95] – a favourable decision from Australia's perspective, with the operation of the national carbon pricing mechanism likely to rely heavily on international credits in the future. At the time of writing it is unclear how many Annex I countries apart from the European Union will accept binding emission reduction obligations in the second commitment period (Australia has announced no decision in this respect). Moreover, it was acknowledged at the COP that existing Copenhagen–Cancun pledges are insufficient to avoid a

---

[89] UNFCCC, *Decision 1/CP.16, The Cancún Agreements: Outcome of the Work of the Ad Hoc Working Group on Long-Term Cooperative Action under the Convention* (2010), FCCC/CP2010/7/Add.1, paras. 68–79. See also F. Daviet, *From Copenhagen to Cancún: Forests and REDD+* (23 November 2010), World Resources Institute, <http://www.wri.org/stories/2010/11/copenhagen-cancun-forests-and-redd>. The developing legal arrangements for REDD are discussed in Chapter 7.
[90] L. Godden et al., 'Reducing Emissions from Deforestation and Forest Degradation in Developing Countries (REDD): Implementation Issues', 36(1) *Monash University Law Review* 139 (2010).
[91] See Chapter 8.
[92] Australia and Norway, 'Enhanced Action on Mitigation', Australia–Norway joint submission under the Cancún Agreements (September 2011), AWG-LCA, AWG-KP, included in documents FCCC/SB/2011/INF.1 and FCCC/AWGLCA/2011/INF.1 pursuant to paragraphs 36 and 49 of the Cancún Agreements, p. 2.
[93] G. Combet, Minister for Climate Change and Energy Efficiency, 'Breakthrough at Durban Climate Change Conference' (Media Release, GC 343/11, 11 December 2011), <http://www.climatechange.gov.au/minister/greg-combet/2011/media-releases/December/mr20111211.aspx>.
[94] UNFCCC, *Decision 1/CP.17, Establishment of an Ad Hoc Working Group on the Durban Platform for Enhanced Action* (11 December 2011), FCCC/CP/2011/L.10, para. 2. See also Chapter 2.
[95] Kyoto Protocol, *Decision 1/CMP.7, Outcome of the work of the Ad Hoc Working Group on Further Commitments for Annex I Parties under the Kyoto Protocol at its Sixteenth Session* (2011) FCCC/KP/CMP/2011/10/Add., para. 1.

warming of more than 2°C above pre-industrial levels.[96] Outside the multilateral negotiations, Australia established working groups with New Zealand and the European Union to foster closer ties between the carbon markets in those jurisdictions and Australia's carbon pricing mechanism.[97]

Early national policy measures: Climate change and ESD

Around the same time as the conclusion of the UNFCCC in 1992, a flurry of environmental policy-making was occurring at the national level. This took place in anticipation of and in response to not only the UNFCCC, but also the other instruments concluded at the Rio Earth Summit held in 1992, including the Convention on Biological Diversity (CBD),[98] the Rio Declaration on Environment and Development,[99] and the Agenda 21 blueprint for sustainable development.[100] In 1992, the UNFCCC formed a component of a broader package of international instruments that were created in an effort to give content and legal impetus to the concept of sustainable development.[101] Over time, the UNFCCC has developed along its own path, which has tended to emphasise its substantive focus on climate change, rather than its conceptual origins in sustainable development.

The national policy measures that emerged in 1992 also placed climate change within a broader context of sustainable development. The principal policy instruments of the time – still significant as foundational measures in Australian environmental law today – were the National Strategy for Ecologically Sustainable Development (NSESD) and the Intergovernmental Agreement on the Environment (IGAE). The NSESD sets out objectives with respect to sustainable development (or ESD, as it is known in Australia), guiding principles, and guidelines for achieving sustainable development in different sectors. ESD is defined in the NSESD as 'development that improves the total quality of life, both now and in the future, in a way that maintains the ecological processes on which life depends'.[102] The IGAE establishes the basis for a cooperative approach

---

96 UNFCCC, *Decision 1/CP.17, Establishment of an Ad Hoc Working Group on the Durban Platform for Enhanced Action* (11 December 2011), FCCC/CP/2011/L.10, preamble.
97 G. Combet, Minister for Climate Change and Energy Efficiency, 'Australia and New Zealand advance linking of their emissions trading schemes' (Media Release, GC 333/115, December 2011); and G. Combet, Minister for Climate Change and Energy Efficiency and C. Hedegaard, European Commissioner for Climate Action, 'Australia and Europe strengthen collaboration on carbon market' (Joint media release, GC 334/11, 5 December 2011). On the EU and New Zealand trading schemes see Chapter 5.
98 Convention on Biological Diversity, opened for signature 5 June 1992, 1760 UNTS 142 (entered into force 29 December 1993).
99 Rio Declaration on Environment and Development, Annex 1, UN Doc A/CONF.151/26 (Vol. 1), 31 ILM 874 (1992).
100 *Agenda 21: Programme of Action for Sustainable Development*, UN GAOR, 46th Session, Agenda Item 21, UN Doc A/Conf.151/26 (1992).
101 See Chapter 8 for a discussion of finance, technology transfer and capacity-building for sustainable development.
102 Australian Government, Ecologically Sustainable Development Steering Committee, *National Strategy for Ecologically Sustainable Development* (1992), Part 1.

to environmental management in Australia, committing all levels of government to the implementation of particular principles in policy-making and program implementation.[103] These principles, along with the 'guiding principles' in the NSESD, draw heavily on the principles of sustainable development articulated in the Rio Declaration, including the precautionary principle and the principle of intergenerational equity.

The IGAE also served another important function: as a policy agreement delineating the respective roles of the federal and state governments with respect to environmental regulation. The agreement followed a decade of bruising federal–state conflicts, a number of which reached the High Court, over the constitutionality of federal environmental laws.[104] However, as is now well-settled constitutional law, despite the lack of a specific environmental head of power, other federal legislative powers in the Australian Constitution, such as the trade and commerce, corporations and external affairs powers, provide a broad basis for the enactment of federal legislation on environmental issues.[105] Even so, as a constitutional matter, states are not precluded from enacting their own climate change laws, provided that such legislation does not directly conflict with any federal climate change law.[106] In policy terms, the IGAE attempts to draw a dividing line between the respective environmental legislative competencies of the federal and state governments. States agreed under the IGAE that the federal government should have primary responsibility for ensuring that the practices and policies of one state do not have significant interjurisdictional environmental effects, and for facilitating the cooperative development of national environmental standards and guidelines.[107]

In 1992, the federal, state and territory governments agreed to a further specific policy measure to deal with climate change: the National Greenhouse Response Strategy.[108] This framework included a national emission reduction target of 20 per cent below 1998 levels by 2005. It also sought to facilitate a range of other climate change mitigation measures on a 'no regrets' basis: in other words, measures had to have other benefits apart from reducing GHG emissions, and could not result in net adverse economic consequences. Over time the Strategy came to be seen as inadequate as the science on climate change strengthened, techniques for taking inventory of emissions evolved, and the

---

103 *Intergovernmental Agreement on the Environment* (1 May 1992), <http://www.environment.gov.au/about/esd/publications/igae/index.html>, section 3.
104 B. Boer, 'World Heritage Disputes in Australia', 7 *Journal of Environmental Law and Litigation* 247 (1992).
105 J. Crawford, 'The Constitution and the Environment', 13 *Sydney Law Review* 11 (1991). It is beyond the scope of this chapter to discuss the constitutional aspects of environmental law in depth: see L. Godden and J. Peel, *Environmental Law: Scientific, Policy and Regulatory Dimensions* (Oxford University Press, 2010), pp. 129–33.
106 *Australian Constitution* s 109. For an example of an area where state laws are expressly excluded see *National Greenhouse and Energy Reporting Act* 2007 (Cth) s 5.
107 Intergovernmental Agreement on the Environment, 2.2.1(ii).
108 S. Mascher, 'Australia's National Greenhouse Response: Implications for the Energy Sector', 16(2) *Australia Mining and Petroleum Law Journal* 126 (1997).

international community moved towards agreement on the Kyoto Protocol. Work on a new policy response, the National Greenhouse Strategy, began in 1996 and was finalised in 1998 after Australia signed the Kyoto Protocol.

Like the National Greenhouse Response Strategy before it, the National Greenhouse Strategy was developed through a cooperative process involving the federal, state, territory and local governments.[109] It contained principles, guidelines, goals and measures for reducing net GHG emissions, encouraging education on climate change issues, and providing a basis for adapting to climate change. Particular foci were partnerships with government, industry and the community; energy use and supply; transport and planning; greenhouse sinks and land management; and industrial processes and waste management. The Strategy, however, created no legally binding obligations for states and territories. Instead, its primary emphasis was on research and the deployment of a range of voluntary programs run under the auspices of the newly established Australian Greenhouse Office (AGO).[110] The only area in which stronger measures were envisaged was in the development of renewable energy capacity, with a proposal for a mandatory renewable energy target (MRET) that later came into being (see below).

'No regrets' climate policy

With the notable exception of the MRET, climate policy during the years of the Howard federal government in Australia emphasised 'voluntary',[111] 'no regrets' measures.[112] This approach was consistent with government's view that:

> [t]aking precipitate or costly action to reduce emissions, if not placed within a sensible international and domestic framework, would erode Australian industry's ability to compete internationally and would impose serious and damaging costs on the Australian economy.[113]

The centrepiece of the voluntary approach was the federal Greenhouse Challenge Program, later rebadged and extended as the Greenhouse Challenge

---

109 Australian Government, *The National Greenhouse Strategy: Strategic Framework for Advancing Australia's Greenhouse Response* (1998), p. iii.
110 The AGO was established in 1998 as the world's first government agency dedicated to issues of GHG emission reduction and formed a portfolio within the federal Department of Environment. Following the 2007 federal election the functions of the AGO were split between the Department of Environment and Water Resources and a new Department of Climate Change.
111 The term 'voluntary' in this context refers to measures that provide incentives for businesses to reduce emissions but do not introduce mandatory emission controls. For a discussion and critique of voluntary approaches in the environmental field see R. Sullivan, *Rethinking Voluntary Approaches in Environmental Policy* (Edward Elgar, 2005).
112 In addition to the Greenhouse Challenge Program, other voluntary measures and funding initiatives adopted during this period (administered under the auspices of the AGO) included the Renewable Energy Equity Fund, the Renewable Energy Commercialisation Program, the Greenhouse Gas Abatement Program, the Renewable Remote Power Generation Program, the Photovoltaic Rebate Program and the Alternative Fuels Conversion Program: see R. Lyster and A. Bradbrook, *Energy Law and the Environment* (Cambridge University Press, 2006), pp. 86–7.
113 N. Minchin, 'Responding to Climate Change: Providing a Policy Framework for a Competitive Australia', 7 *UNSW Law Journal Forum* 13 (2001), p. 13.

Plus Program. The Program, which operated until 1 July 2009, provided various incentives for companies to make inventories of their emissions, develop action plans for minimising emissions, and report on their performance.[114] Another associated aspect of the program was the 'Greenhouse Friendly' certification system, under which greenhouse-neutral products or services could be labelled with the 'Greenhouse Friendly' logo if enterprises demonstrated significant emission reductions that were permanent and verifiable.[115]

While the voluntary measures introduced by the Howard government aimed to attract participants through the promise of cost savings from energy-efficient technologies and increased sales from 'green' publicity, the voluntary nature of the programs was seen as limiting their effectiveness. Evaluating the Greenhouse Challenge and Greenhouse Challenge Plus program, Sullivan criticised it as 'essentially a business as usual approach that does not provide ... strong incentives for Australian business to significantly reduce its greenhouse gas emissions'.[116] More important in achieving emission reductions were other initiatives that provided funds for technology-related projects to reduce or abate emissions. These included the Greenhouse Gas Abatement Program, the Low Emissions Technology and Abatement Fund, and the Low Emissions Technology Demonstration Fund. These programs were seen as one of the primary methods of achieving Australia's Kyoto Protocol target of a 108 per cent increase from 1990 emission levels over the 2008–12 period.

Over time the Howard government sought to strengthen some of its voluntary climate change measures, perhaps in acknowledgment of their limited efficacy. For instance, from 1 July 2006 the Greenhouse Challenge Plus scheme became mandatory for Australian companies receiving fuel excise credits of more than $3 million. Greenhouse Challenge Plus also directly targeted fossil fuel power stations through the Generator Efficiency Standards initiative, under which power-generating companies voluntarily entered into five-year, legally binding Deeds of Agreement with the federal government. The Agreements required specific actions towards achieving 'best practice' performance targets for meeting efficiency-related criteria.[117] While entry into the agreements was voluntary, participants signed them under the shadow of threatened federal legislation dealing with power station efficiency, which ultimately did not materialise. Instead, the Commonwealth introduced the *Energy Efficiency Opportunities Act 2006* with the aim of encouraging businesses using large quantities of energy to report on and improve their energy efficiency (see Box 4.1).

---

114 For details, see <http://www.environment.gov.au/archive/settlements/challenge/index.html>.
115 For details, see <http://www.climatechange.gov.au/greenhousefriendly>.
116 R. Sullivan, 'Greenhouse Challenge Plus: A New Departure or More of the Same?', 23 *Environmental and Planning Law Journal* 60 (2006), p. 65.
117 For details, see <http://www.environment.gov.au/archive/settlements/ges/index.html>.

BOX 4.1 The Energy Efficiency Opportunities Act

Although it was a legislative initiative imposing mandatory reporting duties, the *Energy Efficiency Opportunities Act 2006* (Cth) ('EEO Act') was consistent with the Howard government's overall policy preference for 'no regrets' climate change measures. Indeed, improving energy efficiency is often considered to be the classic 'no regrets' climate change measure, since in an electricity market dominated by coal-fired power, it both reduces greenhouse emissions and lowers costs for businesses and households. The EEO Act, which remains in effect, aims to encourage 'large energy-using businesses' in the mining, resource processing, manufacturing, transport and commercial sectors to improve their energy efficiency by identifying, evaluating and publicly reporting on cost-effective opportunities for saving energy. However, the businesses are not obligated to implement the energy-saving measures identified in their reports.

Corporations that meet the legislation's criterion for being 'large energy users' (0.5 petajoules (PJ) of energy per year) are required to register under the EEO Act[118] and to prepare public reports on their energy use.[119] The first round of reporting under the scheme took place in December 2008, followed by additional rounds of reporting in December 2009 and December 2010. As of 1 June 2011, 280 corporations were registered under the EEO Act, with 207 obliged to report at the end of 2010 (representing around 30 per cent of Australia's total energy use).[120] A government assessment of the program, undertaken in 2011, credited it with allowing reporting corporations to identify opportunities to save 141.9 PJ of energy per year (equivalent to 2.5 per cent of Australia's total energy use). The report also records that 53 per cent of the identified energy savings have been or will be adopted by corporations, or are in the process of being adopted.[121] While this result is commendable, it nonetheless relies on reporting corporations voluntarily taking measures to implement any identified energy efficiency opportunities.

Although the Labor federal government has introduced a carbon price, it has elected to continue and expand the Energy Efficiency Opportunities program as a complementary measure. The policy rationale is that the EEO program will provide 'corporations with detailed information, tools and assistance to assess energy use and, through that assessment, to reduce energy consumption and emissions – thereby mitigating the impact of a carbon price on energy costs'.[122]

From 1 July 2011, the EEO Act was extended to a new category of large energy users: electricity generators using more than 0.5 PJ of energy in the 2010–11 financial year. These companies were required to register with the program by 31 March 2012 and carry out assessments to identify cost-effective energy efficiency opportunities over a five-year assessment cycle.[123] Further expansion is planned in the future, to include energy transmission and distribution networks, major greenfield developments (i.e. investment in building a new plant or facility), and expansion projects. The government has also committed to extending the base funding of the program through to 2016–17, as well as to enhancing the program's assessment and verification requirements and establishing a voluntary scheme for 'medium energy use' corporations that use less than 0.5 PJ per annum.[124] It is anticipated that with the inclusion of generators, transmitters, and distributors of power, the EEO program will eventually cover 60 per cent of Australia's primary energy use, including all of Australia's largest corporate energy users.

---

118 Section 9.   119 Section 22.
120 Department of Resources, Energy and Tourism, *Continuing Opportunities: Energy Efficiency Opportunities (EEO) Program – 2010 Report, A look at results for the Energy Efficiency Opportunities Program 2006–2010, Taken from public reports of assessments undertaken during the period July 2006–June 2010* (2011), p. 3.
121 Ibid., p. 4.   122 Ibid., p. 3.
123 *Energy Efficiency Opportunities Amendment Regulations (No. 1) 2011* (Cth), reg 3.
124 MPCCC, *Clean Energy Agreement*, July 2011, p. 55, <http://resources.news.com.au/files/2011/07/10/1226091/661526-hs-news-file-clean-energy-agreement.pdf>.

Mandatory Renewable Energy Target

Another important Howard-era legislative initiative focusing on energy use was the Mandatory Renewable Energy Target or MRET. The MRET was first proposed in the 1998 National Greenhouse Strategy as a means of increasing efficient and sustainable energy supply in Australia.[125] It built on the foundations of the relatively successful state-based green power schemes that seek to increase the use of renewable energy resources in electricity production. In these schemes, customers pay a premium for electricity sourced from renewables.[126] The National Greenhouse Strategy outlined the main elements of MRET, which were later enacted under the *Renewable Energy (Electricity) Act 2000* (Cth).

The essential requirement of the MRET, which has since evolved and is now known simply as the Renewable Energy Target (RET), is for wholesale purchasers of electricity – 'liable entities'[127] – to contribute proportionately towards the generation of additional renewable energy capacity.[128] Renewable energy is defined broadly in the legislation to include wind, solar, hydro, wave, tidal, geothermal and waste sources.[129] The definition does not, however, extend to lower-emission sources, such as natural gas or nuclear power.[130] In effect the RET scheme seeks to provide financial incentives to induce liable entities to increase their use of renewable electricity sources, and hence to decrease their reliance on coal-fired power.[131]

Initially the target for renewable energy capacity set by the RET scheme was an additional 9500 gigawatt hours (GWh) of renewable energy per year by 2010. Based on 1997 figures, the 9500 GWh annual requirement was equivalent to a mere 2 per cent increase in the proportion of total electricity produced renewably. Subsequent assessments of the legislation suggested that with rising energy consumption in Australia the RET would in fact deliver only a 0.3–0.9 per cent increase in renewable energy use.[132] In response to such concerns, a review of the legislation was undertaken in 2003, which recommended a steady increase in the RET from 2010 to 2020 towards a target of 20 000 GWh.[133] In response, the Howard government agreed to extend the RET scheme until 2020 but without increasing the target beyond the existing 2 per cent. By contrast, the Rudd

---

[125] Australian Government, *The National Greenhouse Strategy: Strategic Framework for Advancing Australia's Greenhouse Response* (1998), p. 46, para. 4.7.
[126] For discussion see Lyster and Bradbrook, *Energy Law and the Environment* (2006), pp. 155–63.
[127] Liable entities are those that acquire electricity on a grid with a capacity of 100 MW or more: see *Renewable Energy (Electricity) Act 2000* (Cth) ss 31, 32 and 33.
[128] The Renewable Energy Target is introduced here but is discussed in detail in Chapter 9.
[129] *Renewable Energy (Electricity) Act 2000* (Cth) s 17(1).
[130] On the nuclear power–climate change relationship see J. Healey (ed.), *Nuclear Power* (Spinney Press, 2006); I. Lowe, 'Reaction Time: Climate Change and the Nuclear Option', 27 *Quarterly Essay* 1 (2007).
[131] A. Thompson and R. Campbell-Watt, 'Australia and an Emissions Trading Market – Opportunities, Costs and Legal Frameworks', 24(2) *Australian Resources and Energy Law Journal* 151 (2005), pp. 163–5.
[132] See Lyster and Bradbrook, *Energy Law and the Environment* (2006), p. 98.
[133] See Independent Panel Report (chaired by Hon. Grant Tambling), *Renewable Opportunities: A Review of the Operation of the Renewable Energy (Electricity) Act 2000*, Executive Summary, para. [45].

government coming into power in 2007 pledged to increase the share of renewable energy in Australia to 20 per cent by 2020.

Following its election, the Rudd federal government amended the *Renewable Energy (Electricity) Act* to raise the RET from 9500 GWh to 41 000 GWh in 2020.[134] In 2010, further amendments split the scheme into two separate schemes: the Large-scale Renewable Energy Target, which continues the previous scheme, and the Small-scale Renewable Energy Scheme, which applies to the installation of small-scale renewable energy systems such as rooftop solar panels.[135]

Action by states and territories

Notwithstanding legislation such as the EEO Act and that introducing the RET, federal climate law remained sparse during the tenure of the Howard government. The perceived lack of action on climate change at the national level over this period provided an opportunity for state and territory governments – many of which were Labor governments at this time – to institute their own climate change measures. This was a truly bottom-up regulatory approach: although such sub-national measures were often inspired by the Kyoto Protocol's requirements, they were not taken in order to implement Australia's emission reduction target under the Protocol (a national-level responsibility).

Predictably, state and territory climate change measures have varied considerably from jurisdiction to jurisdiction. Some jurisdictions with a fairly minimal GHG contribution, such as the Northern Territory, have done little to address the issue of climate change mitigation. By contrast, New South Wales, which contributes 28 per cent of national emissions (the largest of any state), set an aspirational target in 2005 to reduce emissions by 60 per cent from 2000 levels by 2050.[136] In 2007 South Australia enacted legislation putting in place an emission reduction target of 40 per cent below 1990 levels by 2050.[137] Subsequently other states have legislated their own emission reduction targets. In Victoria's case, this is a target of 20 per cent below 2000 levels by 2020,[138] whereas over the same period the ACT is seeking a reduction of 40 per cent from 1990 levels and Tasmania a reduction of 60 per cent from 1990 levels.[139]

---

134 *Renewable Energy (Electricity) Amendment Act 2009* (Cth).
135 *Renewable Energy (Electricity) Amendment Act 2010* (Cth). See Chapter 9.
136 Department of Climate Change and Energy Efficiency, *Australia's National Greenhouse Gas Accounts: State and Territory Greenhouse Gas Inventories 2009* (2011).
137 *Climate Change and Greenhouse Emissions Reduction Act 2007* (SA) s 3.
138 A change in government in Victoria has seen the new government back away from this target, describing it as merely 'aspirational' and supporting the recommendations of a legislative review that the target be abolished.
139 *Climate Change Act 2010* (Vic) s 5; *Climate Change and Greenhouse Gas Reduction Act 2010* (ACT) s 7; *Climate Change (State Action) Act 2008* (Tas) s 5.

New South Wales was also an early mover – indeed, the first jurisdiction in the world – to introduce a legislatively based ETS to reduce GHG emissions.[140] The state's Greenhouse Gas Reduction Scheme (GGAS) commenced operation on 1 January 2003, with the objective of reducing GHG emissions associated with the production and use of electricity in New South Wales.[141] Unlike most ETS proposals that employ a cap-and-trade model,[142] GGAS is a 'baseline-and-credit' scheme.[143] Under the scheme, the state GHG benchmark is 7.27 tonnes of CO_2 eq. GHG emissions from electricity per head of state population.[144] Electricity retailers and certain other parties involved in the New South Wales electricity market are required to meet mandatory benchmarks based on the size of their share in the state's electricity market. Each year GGAS participants must surrender a prescribed number of GGAS certificates (or renewable energy certificates under the federal RET scheme) for any emissions above their individually assigned targets. If they fail to do so, they are liable to pay a penalty.[145] GGAS certificates, created through activities that reduce or offset emissions (for instance forest management activities), are transferable, thereby creating a market for their purchase. While the GGAS scheme appears to have had some success in reducing carbon emissions from power generation in New South Wales,[146] it is difficult for any one state, acting alone, to effect a significant reduction in Australia's overall GHG production. In this respect a national ETS is considered the best policy option. With the introduction of the national carbon pricing mechanism from 1 July 2012, it is expected that the GGAS will cease operation.[147]

Another area where states and territories have been active in introducing their own climate change measures is with respect to energy use. Regulation in this sphere has taken the form of renewable or low-emission energy, energy efficiency targets, and measures to promote renewable energy uptake, such as feed-in tariffs. During the later years of the Howard government, many such

---

[140] For an overview of the scheme see T. Kearney, 'Market-based Policies for Demand Side Energy Efficiency: A Comparison of the New South Wales Greenhouse Gas Abatement Scheme and the United Kingdom's Energy Efficiency Commitment', 23 *Environmental and Planning Law Journal* 113 (2006), pp. 118–22.
[141] GGAS was created in 2002 through amendments to the *Electricity Supply Act 1995* (NSW) and the *Electricity Supply (General) Regulation 2001* (NSW).
[142] See Chapter 5.
[143] Such schemes set a baseline level of emissions, improvements upon which generate credits for participating firms: M. Wilder and M. Miller, 'Carbon Trading Markets: Legal Considerations', in *Climate Law in Australia*, eds T. Bonyhady and P. Christoff (Federation Press, 2007), p. 68.
[144] The initial level was set at the commencement of GGAS in 2003 at 8.65 tonnes. The benchmark progressively dropped to 7.27 tonnes in 2007, which represents a reduction of 5 per cent below 1990 levels.
[145] Thompson and Campbell-Watt, 'Australia and an Emissions Trading Market' (2005), pp. 156–7.
[146] Lyster and Bradbrook, *Energy Law and the Environment* (2006), pp. 143–4; Kearney, 'Market-based Policies for Demand Side Energy Efficiency' (2006), p. 119; and R. Passey, I. MacGill and H. Outhred, 'The NSW Greenhouse Gas Reduction Scheme: An Analysis of the NGAC Registry for the 2003, 2004 and 2005 Compliance Periods' (DP_070822, Centre for Energy and Environmental Markets, 2007).
[147] The New South Wales government has advised that it will wind back the GGAS when the carbon pricing mechanism commences. See Chris Hartcher, Minister for Resources and Energy, 'Green Scheme to Close when Carbon Tax Starts' (Media Release 5 April 2012), <http://greenhousegas.nsw.gov.au/Documents/Media-Closure-Apr12.pdf>.

initiatives were introduced in response to federal resistance to raising the RET, accompanied by fears that investment in renewable energy technologies within particular states might decline as a result. As Table 4.1 demonstrates, there has been little coordination between jurisdictions with regard to their energy regulations.

A variety of policy and regulatory approaches have also been evident in state-based frameworks covering carbon sequestration, both in the land management sector (biosequestration) and in respect of underground storage reservoirs for

Table 4.1 Climate change and energy efficiency legislation in Australian states and territories

State or territory	Legislation	Initiatives
New South Wales	*Electricity Supply Act 1995; Electricity Supply (General) Regulation 2001*	Greenhouse Gas Reduction Scheme (GGAS): Mandatory GHG reduction targets for electricity retailers
	Electricity Supply Act 1995 s 15A	Solar Bonus Scheme: Gross feed-in tariff set at $0.60 per kWh for connections prior to 27 October 2010; $0.20 per kWh thereafter. No new applications from 28 April 2011
	Energy and Utilities Administration Regulation 2006 regs 4, 16	Mandatory energy efficiency standards and labelling for electrical equipment
	Electricity Supply Act 1995 Part 9; *Electricity Supply (General) Regulation 2001* Part 9A	Energy Savings Scheme (ESS): Imposes statewide energy efficiency improvement targets on energy retailers
	Energy and Utilities Administration Act 1987 s 34Q	Energy Efficiency Reporting Scheme: Prescribed persons must prepare energy savings action plans
	Energy and Utilities Administration Act 1987 Part 6A, Div 3	Climate Change Fund: $700 million was established in July 2007 to help business, households, schools, communities and government save water, energy and GHG emissions
Victoria	*Climate Change Act 2010*	Emission reduction target: 20 per cent from 2000 levels by 2010 (s 5)
		EPA powers to regulate GHG (Part 7)
	Victorian Energy Efficiency Target Act 2007; Victorian Energy Efficiency Target Scheme Regulations 2008	Energy Efficiency Target and scheme
	Electricity Safety Act 1998 and *Electricity Safety (Equipment Efficiency) Regulations 1999*	Minimum energy performance standards and mandatory labelling for appliances and equipment
	Electricity Industry Act 2000	Feed-in tariffs: Premium (net) feed-in tariff for solar energy of $0.60 per kWh. No new applications from 30 September 2011. Transitional (net) solar feed-in tariff of a minimum $0.25 per kWh available from 1 January 2012
Queensland	*Clean Energy Act 2008*	Smart Energy Savings Program for businesses with medium to high energy consumption

Table 4.1 (cont.)

State or territory	Legislation	Initiatives
Queensland (cont.)	Electricity Act 1994	Feed-in tariffs: Net feed-in tariff for small-scale solar power, set at $0.44 per kWh fed into the grid: s 44A
		Queensland Gas Scheme: Electricity retailers and other liable entities must obtain a prescribed percentage (currently 15 per cent) of their electricity from gas-fired generation: Chapter 5A
		Mandatory labelling and performance standards: s 266; see also *Electricity Regulation 2006* (Qld) regs 139–40, 152
	Electricity Regulation 2006 regs 139–40, 152	Minimum energy performance standards and mandatory labelling for appliances and equipment
Western Australia	*Electricity Industry (Licence Conditions) Regulations 2005*	Residential net feed-in tariff scheme: set at $0.40/kWh for connections prior to 30 June 2011; $0.20/kWh thereafter. No new applications from 1 August 2011
South Australia	*Climate Change and Greenhouse Emissions Reduction Act 2007*	Emission reduction targets: Emission reduction target 40 per cent reduction from 1990 levels by 2050 (s 3)
		Renewable energy generation target 20 per cent by 2014 (s 3)
		Renewable energy consumption target 20 per cent by 2014 (s 3)
	Electricity Act 1996	Residential energy efficiency scheme: Energy retailers must meet energy efficiency improvement targets as a condition of their licences
	Electrical Products Act 2000 and the *Electrical Products Regulations 2001*	Minimum energy performance standards and mandatory labelling for appliances and equipment
	Electricity Act 1996 Division 3AB.	Feed-in tariffs for small-scale solar power: set at $0.44 per kWh fed into the grid, to be reduced to $0.16 per kWh from 1 October 2011
Tasmania	*Climate Change (State Action) Act 2008*	Emission reduction targets: 60 per cent below 1990 levels by 2050 (s 5)
Australian Capital Territory	*Climate Change and Greenhouse Gas Reduction Act 2010*	Emission reduction targets: zero net emissions by 2060 (s 6)
		80 per cent below 1990 levels by 2050 (s 7)
		40 per cent below 1990 levels by 2020 (s 7)
	Electricity (Greenhouse Gas Emissions) Act 2004	ACT Greenhouse Gas Abatement Scheme (GGAS)
	Electricity Feed-In (Renewable Energy Premium) Act 2008	Feed-in tariff: No new applications from 14 July 2011

the purpose of carbon capture and storage (geosequestration, or CCS).[148] The dominance of state law in this area reflects Australia's constitutional framework, under which matters of land use regulation and property rights have remained solely state matters.

---

148 See Chapters 9 and 10.

Overall, the pattern evident in state-based climate regulation, both during the Howard government years and since, is one of a mosaic of different policies and legislation, which while not directly contradictory, generally evince no common approach. Instead, regulations have been designed by each jurisdiction in accordance with its own circumstances and policy priorities. Some of the resulting fragmentation may be overcome with the institution of a national ETS.

Nevertheless, the proliferation of climate change measures at different levels of governance (federal, state and territory) raises important questions about how we should evaluate the effectiveness of Australian climate law. On one view, the legal diversity produced by the treatment of climate change at both federal and state levels may be seen as a basis for useful and innovative policy and regulatory experimentation. As the New South Wales GGAS scheme exemplifies, Australian state governments have often led the way with regulatory initiatives in the climate change field. State governments may also have a broader range of regulatory tools at their disposal to address climate change, including reforms to environmental impact assessment and planning laws,[149] or incorporation of GHG 'pollutants' within the scope of general pollution control laws.[150]

On the other hand, within the regulatory mosaic there is significant potential for overlapping or conflicting requirements and a fragmentation of efforts towards mitigation and adaptation. This problem has led some commentators to favour 'comprehensive national regulation' over a more decentralised approach,[151] which might dictate the removal of state-based emission trading and renewable energy measures once the national carbon pricing mechanism has come into effect.[152] Others are more cautious as to the merits of a centralised approach. Bonyhady, for instance, argues that in a context 'where there is little basis for having faith in any level of government', the best approach may instead be one that uses federal regulation to set a floor for climate change protection, which states or local governments are free to exceed in their own laws.[153] Such an approach has the advantage that it introduces a degree of uniformity by way of national minimum standards or targets, yet prevents those measures from becoming the lowest common denominator for all regulation in the area.

Proposals for national emissions trading

Since the conclusion of the Kyoto Protocol in 1997, with its endorsement of 'flexible mechanisms',[154] there has been broad consensus among policy-makers

---

[149] Cf. Commonwealth approvals process under the *Environment Protection and Biodiversity Conservation Act 1999* (Cth).
[150] Fisher, 'The Statutory Relevance of Greenhouse Gas Emissions in Environmental Regulation' (2007): for example, under Victoria's *Climate Change Act* 2010.
[151] Durrant, *Legal Responses to Climate Change* (2010), p. 3.
[152] Garnaut, *Garnaut Climate Change Review* (2008), pp. 317–18.
[153] T. Bonyhady, 'The New Australian Climate Law', in *Climate Law in Australia,* eds Bonyhady and Christoff (2007), p. 26.
[154] See Chapter 2.

that a national emissions trading scheme should be the 'central pillar' of any Australian effort to reduce GHG emissions.[155] Debate has centred on questions of how any such scheme should be designed, as well as on whether it should be introduced in advance of comparable arrangements operating at the global level.

One of the earliest contributions to the policy discussion of this issue was made by the Australian Greenhouse Office. In 1999 it released a series of discussion papers canvassing the arguments for a national emissions trading scheme and the design issues raised by such a proposal.[156] Soon after their publication, however, the AGO's publications sank into obscurity, overtaken by the Howard government's political decision not to ratify the Kyoto Protocol. By 2004, when the Howard government released its Energy White Paper, the federal policy position was firmly against the introduction of a national ETS. The Energy White Paper stated:

> Australia will not impose significant new economy-wide costs, such as emissions trading, in its greenhouse response at this stage. Such action is premature, in the absence of effective longer-term global action on climate change, and given Australia is on track to meet its Kyoto 108 per cent target. Pursuing this path in advance of an effective global response would harm Australia's competitiveness and growth with no certain global climate change benefits.[157]

Despite (and largely as a result of) the federal government's opposition, state and territory governments during the first few years after 2000 took up advocacy of a national ETS. These governments envisioned an interjurisdictional ETS based on linked schemes operating in participating jurisdictions, similar to the regional emissions trading schemes that have since emerged in some parts of the United States.[158] In 2004, state and territory governments agreed to establish a National Emissions Trading Taskforce to investigate the potential for cost-effective achievement of GHG emission reduction targets. As part of this process, the Garnaut Climate Change Review was commissioned; it was later taken over by the Rudd federal government.

In April 2007, in the face of the Howard government's continuing intransigence regarding national emissions trading, the states and territories agreed to introduce a consistent interjurisdictional ETS by the end of 2010.[159] Consultative discussion papers released by the Taskforce, outlining the possible design of the scheme, proposed initial application to the stationary energy sector with a Kyoto Protocol-based cap on total allowable emissions, and

---

155 National Emissions Trading Taskforce, *Final Report* (2007), p. 6.
156 AGO, *National Emissions Trading: Establishing the Boundaries, Discussion Paper 1* (1999); AGO, *National Emissions Trading: Issuing the Permits, Discussion Paper 2* (1999); AGO, *National Emissions Trading: Crediting the Carbon, Discussion Paper 3* (1999); AGO, *National Emissions Trading: Designing the Market, Discussion Paper 4* (1999).
157 Australian Government, Energy Task Force, *Securing Australia's Energy Future* (2004), p. 19.
158 See Chapter 5.
159 Media Release by then Chairman of the Council for the Australian Federation (CAF) Mike Rann, 'Federation Council agree to emissions trading timeframe' (12 April 2007).

permits allocated via a mix of administrative allocation and auctioning.[160] The proposal was put to one side with the commitment by the incoming Rudd government to introduce a national ETS.

As the 2007 federal election neared, the Howard federal government came under increasing public pressure to demonstrate genuine climate change credentials. In response to such pressures, Prime Minister Howard established in December 2006 a joint government–business Task Group on Emissions Trading. The Task Group released its report in May 2007, which, essentially in accordance with its terms of reference, incorporated a recommendation for the establishment of a national ETS.[161] Prime Minister Howard quickly responded with a pledge to 'move towards . . . a cap and trade system beginning no later than 2012'.[162]

Around the same time, the Howard government also enacted an important precursor for any ETS, the *National Greenhouse and Energy Reporting Act 2007* (Cth), which introduced a national scheme for the reporting of information about corporate GHG emissions, energy production and energy consumption. The NGER Act, which came into force on 1 July 2008, requires companies that exceed specified greenhouse emissions or energy thresholds to register and report annually.[163] In general terms, facilities and corporate groups that emit direct annual GHG emissions of 25 000 tonnes of CO_2 eq. or more, or that consume more than 25 000 megawatts of electricity or 2.5 million litres of fuel in a year, are required to register and report under the NGER scheme.[164] In and of itself, the NGER Act did not institute any requirement for reporting corporations to decrease their GHG emissions, as it is purely a procedural and informative mechanism. The broader significance of the NGER Act stems from its capacity to supply the necessary reporting infrastructure for emissions trading and to define the criteria for determining liable entities in that context. This is the role contemplated for the NGER Act as part of the new national carbon pricing mechanism.[165]

While enactment of the NGER Act, coupled with the Howard government's commitment to introduce a national ETS, represented a sea change in federal climate policy, these initiatives apparently came too late for the Australian electorate, which replaced the Howard government in the November 2007 poll. The election of the Rudd federal government promised the emergence of new dynamic in climate policy, with public expectations heightened by the government's swift ratification of the Kyoto Protocol in December 2007. The Rudd government quickly affirmed its commitment to a long-term emission

---

[160] Council of Australian Governments, Inter-Jurisdictional Emissions Trading Working Group, *A National Emissions Trading Scheme: A Report to First Ministers* (16 December 2004) and National Emissions Trading Taskforce, *Discussion Paper: Possible Design for a National Greenhouse Gas Emissions Trading Scheme* (August 2006).
[161] A copy of the Task Group's report can be found at <http://pandora.nla.gov.au/pan/72614/20070601-0000/www.pmc.gov.au/publications/emissions/index.html>.
[162] Prime Minister John Howard, 'Address to the Liberal Party Federal Council', Sydney, 3 June 2007, <http://pandora.nla.gov.au/pan/10052/20070615?0000/www.pm.gov.au/media/Speech/2007/Speech24350.html>.
[163] Section 19(2).   [164] Section 13(1)(d).
[165] The requirements of the NGER Act and its role in the carbon pricing mechanism are discussed further in Chapter 5.

reduction target of 60 per cent below 2000 levels by 2050 and began to investigate options for the introduction of a national ETS. In 2008 the federal government confirmed that it would participate in the Garnaut Climate Change Review process, adding to the Review's mandate of evaluating the impacts of climate change on the Australian economy the task of considering medium- to long-term policy options for responding to climate change.[166]

Garnaut's Final Report was published on 30 September 2008, following the publication of several other reports and discussion papers containing recommendations on such matters as the design of an ETS and targets for emission reductions.[167] In his Final Report, Garnaut urged that Australia 'express its willingness to reduce its own entitlements to emissions from 2000 levels by 25 per cent by 2020 and by 90 per cent by 2050', although only in the context of a conclusion of an international agreement with an objective of holding GHG concentrations to 450 ppm CO_2 eq.[168] He argued that an important aspect of being a party to an effective global agreement was the development of a domestic mitigation strategy with an ETS as its centrepiece.[169]

With respect to the design of a national emissions trading scheme, Garnaut recommended introduction of a cap-and-trade system with an initial Kyoto-based cap of 108 per cent of 1990 levels to 2012 and subsequent caps of increasing stringency. In addition, Garnaut argued for a broad coverage of sectors in the scheme, including the transport sector.[170] His recommendation was for permits to be regularly auctioned (rather than allocated free of charge to participants), with the resulting revenue going towards compensation for adversely affected sectors, such as trade-exposed, emission-intensive industries[171] and low-income households. However, the Garnaut Review was strongly opposed to compensating coal-fired electricity generators for the reduction in profits they might suffer as a result of the introduction of a carbon price.[172]

The Rudd federal government's initial response to this advice was released on 16 July 2008 in the form of a Green Paper on the design of a national ETS (rebadged as the 'carbon pollution reduction scheme' (CPRS)).[173] Following a period of public submissions, the government released a White Paper presenting its policy decisions on critical design issues such as emission reduction targets, the coverage of the scheme, the method by which emission permits would be

---

166 See Garnaut, *Garnaut Climate Change Review* (2008), terms of reference, p. xvi.
167 These documents included an Interim Report, a Discussion Paper on an ETS, a Draft Report and a Supplementary Report on Targets and Trajectories. All reports are accessible from the Review's website at <http://www.garnautreview.org.au>.
168 Garnaut, *Garnaut Climate Change Review* (2008). In IPCC scenario modelling, a CO_2 eq. concentration of 450 ppm is designed to allow stabilisation of global temperatures at 2°C above pre-industrial levels.
169 Ibid., pp. 307, 321.   170 Ibid., pp. 327–9.
171 These were defined as industries at a competitive disadvantage so long as there is no global, comprehensive (i.e. including all major emitters) ETS.
172 Garnaut, *Garnaut Climate Change Review* (2008), pp. 314–16 and Chapter 20 of the Review.
173 Department of Climate Change, *Carbon Pollution Reduction Scheme,* Green Paper (2008).

issued, and the question of compensation to trade-exposed, emission-intensive industries for the economic effects of a carbon price.[174]

The White Paper formed the basis for the Carbon Pollution Reduction Scheme Bills introduced into federal parliament over the course of 2009.[175] Although the bills themselves were never enacted into law, they provide important guidance as to the legal form that a national ETS might take, and many elements of the CPRS are replicated in the new federal carbon pricing legislation.[176] Notable features of the proposed CPRS included its application to all six GHGs covered by the Kyoto Protocol, and to approximately 75 per cent of Australia's emissions: those coming from stationary energy production, industrial processes, waste, fugitive emissions from oil and gas production, and the transportation sector. Agricultural emissions were exempted and the forestry sector was included on an opt-in basis only.[177]

The original CPRS Bills were rejected by a hostile, Coalition-dominated Senate in August 2009. Over the following months, compromise legislation, with greater provision for industry compensation, was negotiated with the Coalition under the leadership of Malcolm Turnbull.[178] However, with a change in Liberal–Coalition leadership to Tony Abbott, a strong opponent of national emissions trading, the compromise legislative package was voted down once again by the Senate in December 2009. Greens Party members of the Senate also voted against the CPRS on the basis of its low emission-reduction target (5 per cent below 2000 levels by 2020) and its extensive provision for compensation to emission-intensive, trade-exposed industries and electricity generators. As some commentators have pointed out, the *Clean Energy* legislation passed in 2011 – this time with Greens support – retains these compensation features, although it is part of a broader climate policy package that includes significant funding for renewable energy development.

---

174 Australian Government, *Carbon Pollution Reduction Scheme: Australia's Low Pollution Future*, White Paper (2008).
175 The package of Bills was: Carbon Pollution Reduction Scheme Bill 2009 (Cth); Australian Climate Change Regulatory Authority Bill 2009 (Cth); and Carbon Pollution Reduction Scheme Amendment (Household Assistance) Bill 2009 (Cth); Carbon Pollution Reduction Scheme (Charges – Customs) Bill 2009 (Cth); Carbon Pollution Reduction Scheme (Charges – Excise) Bill 2009 (Cth); Carbon Pollution Reduction Scheme (Charges – General) Bill 2009 (Cth); Carbon Pollution Reduction Scheme (Consequential Amendments) Bill 2009 (Cth); Carbon Pollution Reduction Scheme (CPRS Fuel Credits) Bill 2009 (Cth); and Carbon Pollution Reduction Scheme (CPRS Fuel Credits) (Consequential Amendments) Bill 2009 (Cth).
176 R. Briese, 'Climate Change Mitigation Down Under – Legislative Responses in a Federal System', 13 *Asia Pacific Journal of Environmental Law* 75 (2010). The Australian Parliamentary Library has also put together a table comparing the CPRS with the carbon price mechanism: <http://tiny.cc/d1dzdw>.
177 The CPRS is now largely of historical interest with the enactment of the *Clean Energy Act 2011* (Cth). However, the similarities between the CPRS and the clean energy legislation make much of the critical commentary on the former relevant for the latter. See for example M. Power, 'Emissions Trading in Australia: Markets, Law and Justice under the CPRS', 27 *Environmental and Planning Law Journal* 131 (2010).
178 Carbon Pollution Reduction Scheme Bill (No. 2) 2009 (Cth); Carbon Pollution Reduction Scheme Amendment (Household Assistance) Bill (No. 2) 2009 (Cth); Carbon Pollution Reduction Scheme (Charges – Customs) Bill (No. 2) 2009 (Cth); Carbon Pollution Reduction Scheme (Charges – Excise) Bill 2009 [No. 2] (Cth); Carbon Pollution Reduction Scheme (Charges – General) Bill (No. 2) 2009 (Cth); Carbon Pollution Reduction Scheme (Consequential Amendments) Bill (No. 2) 2009 (Cth); Carbon Pollution Reduction Scheme (CPRS Fuel Credits) Bill (No. 2) 2009 (Cth); and Carbon Pollution Reduction Scheme (CPRS Fuel Credits) (Consequential Amendments) Bill (No. 2) 2009 (Cth).

In early 2010, the amended CPRS Bills were introduced to the federal parliament once more and passed the House of Representatives.[179] By April 2010, however, the Rudd government had decided to postpone attempted passage of the CPRS Bills until after 2012. Prime Minister Rudd's explanation for the delay cited the lack of bipartisan support for the CPRS and the slow progress in international climate change negotiations. As Rudd had once declared climate change to be 'the greatest moral challenge of our time', this decision significantly undermined the credibility of his leadership and was one of the factors that led to his eventual replacement by Julia Gillard.

Carbon pricing

In the 2010 federal election campaign, Gillard fatefully promised that if elected she would not introduce a carbon tax.[180] However, the political realities that prevailed in the aftermath of the hung parliament election result effectively put the issue of a national carbon price back on the federal political agenda. As a condition of their support for a Labor government, the Greens insisted that the government reconsider the need for national action on climate change, including a means to 'put a price on carbon'. Accordingly, following the election, the government established the Multi-Party Climate Change Committee (MPCCC), constituted of Labor, Greens and independent representatives, to explore options for the implementation of a national carbon price. In December 2010 the Committee released a communiqué, setting out eleven policy principles to be the basis of deliberations on a carbon price mechanism. These principles were very general in nature, encompassing environmental effectiveness, economic efficiency, budget neutrality, maintaining the competitiveness of Australian industry, energy security, fairness, flexibility, administrative simplicity, clear accountability, and ensuring a fair contribution by Australia to global climate change mitigation efforts.[181]

Throughout 2011, negotiations continued on the actual carbon pricing mechanism, culminating in the release in July of the MPCCC's Clean Energy Agreement and the Australian government's plan for 'Securing a Clean Energy Future'.[182] These documents presented the basis for a new wide-ranging federal climate change policy, which extends significantly beyond simply introducing a

---

[179] Carbon Pollution Reduction Scheme Amendment (Household Assistance) Bill 2010 (Cth); Carbon Pollution Reduction Scheme Bill 2010 (Cth); Carbon Pollution Reduction Scheme (Charges – Customs) Bill 2010 (Cth); Carbon Pollution Reduction Scheme (Charges – Excise) Bill 2010 (Cth); Carbon Pollution Reduction Scheme (Charges – General) Bill 2010 (Cth); Carbon Pollution Reduction Scheme (Consequential Amendments) Bill 2010 (Cth); Carbon Pollution Reduction Scheme (CPRS Fuel Credits) Bill 2010 (Cth); and Carbon Pollution Reduction Scheme (CPRS Fuel Credits) (Consequential Amendments) Bill 2010 (Cth).
[180] ABC Television, 'Climate Change drops off the radar in 2010 election', *The 7.30 Report*, 29 July 2010, <http://www.abc.net.au/7.30/content/2010/s2968227.htm>.
[181] MPCCC, Third Meeting Communiqué, Appendix A, <http://www.climatechange.gov.au/en/government/initiatives/multi-party-committee/meetings/third-meeting/communique.aspx#attachmenta>.
[182] Department of Climate Change and Energy Efficiency, *Securing a Clean Energy Future: The Australian Government's Plan* (2011).

price on carbon to measures for promoting renewable energy development, energy efficiency and biodiversity conservation. The main elements of the policy package that the Gillard Labor government put forward as Australia's 'plan' for a clean energy future are summarised in Table 4.2.

Table 4.2 Elements of Australia's 'Clean Energy' policy package

Measure	Description
National Carbon Pricing Mechanism	• In effect 1 July 2012 • Initially a three-year fixed price period (with a starting carbon price of $23 per tonne of carbon pollution) • From 1 July 2015, transition to a fully flexible, cap-and-trade ETS where the price of carbon is driven by the market and trading of emission permits • Coverage of the carbon pricing mechanism is limited to stationary energy, waste, rail, domestic aviation and shipping, industrial processes and fugitive emissions; there is no general coverage of the transportation sector or of agriculture and land sector emissions • Administered by the Clean Energy Regulator
Climate Change Authority	• An independent authority, which will advise the government on pollution caps and progress towards meeting emission reduction targets • Composed of nine experts with a particular focus on climate science, economics, GHG abatement measures, investment, industry and environmental management: *Climate Change Authority Act 2011* (Cth) ss 17 and 18 • The Authority will also have responsibility for undertaking periodic reviews of the carbon pricing mechanism and other climate change mitigation measures: *Climate Change Authority Act 2011* (Cth) s 11
Offsets	• Provision for the use of international credits (e.g. CDM-certified emission reduction units) generated under the Kyoto Protocol in discharging liabilities during the flexible price period of the scheme, subject to some quantitative and qualitative restrictions • Provision for the use of domestic carbon credits generated under the Carbon Farming Initiative (see Chapter 10)
Industry assistance	• Retention of the compensation arrangements from the CPRS for trade-exposed emission-intensive industries, although with some additional safeguards, such as a requirement that the Productivity Commission review industry assistance in 2014–15 with the goal of winding back assistance in 2018 to levels proposed by the Garnaut Review, if the Productivity Commission agrees • A range of other programs offering assistance to industries particularly affected by carbon pricing, such as the $300 million Steel Transformation Plan, a $1.3 billion Coal Sector Jobs Package, and a $70 million Coal Mining Abatement Technology Support Package • Establishment of an Energy Security Fund, which will provide $5.5 billion in free permits and cash (loans) to the electricity generation sector, as well as helping to pay for the closure of up to 2000 MW of highly emission-intensive generation capacity by 2020[183]
Household compensation	• Directed particularly towards low-income households • This assistance will be delivered via a complex mechanism linked to reform of the income tax system

---

[183] It is thought that this Fund will see the closure of some of the nation's dirtiest coal-fired power stations, such as the Hazelwood Power station in Victoria: A. Savage, 'Carbon Tax Concerns Over Jobs, Power Supply', *ABC News* (online), 11 July 2011, <http://www.abc.net.au/news/2011-07-11/carbon-tax-concerns-over-jobs-power-supply/2789528>.

Table 4.2 (cont.)

Measure	Description
Support for renewable energy	• Establishment of new financing and institutional arrangements to support the development, commercialisation and deployment of renewable energy, including the establishment of a Clean Energy Finance Corporation, the Australian Renewable Energy Agency (ARENA), the Clean Technology Program, and the Clean Energy Skills Program
Energy efficiency	• Proposals for a range of measures to improve energy efficiency • Establishment of mandatory standards regulating the permitted levels of CO_2 emissions from all light-duty and passenger vehicles[184]
Land sector measures	• Carbon Farming Initiative (discussed in Chapter 10) • $946 million Biodiversity Fund to support carbon sequestration on private land by establishing carbon plantings in areas of high conservation value and promoting better biodiversity management practices

A suite of legislation to put in place the carbon pricing element of the clean energy package was introduced into federal Parliament on 13 September 2011 and was passed with the support of independents and Greens party members in November 2011. The detail of the carbon pricing mechanism established by the *Clean Energy Act 2011*, and its supporting institutional infrastructure, are discussed in Chapter 5. Over the course of 2012, the government plans to introduce further draft legislation to implement other elements of the Clean Energy Agreement, including, critically, arrangements for the establishment of the Clean Energy Finance Corporation.

Despite passage of the Clean Energy legislation through the federal parliament, significant uncertainty remains as to its future. At the time of writing, the Gillard Labor government was deeply unpopular in the Australian electorate, an attitude attributable in part to the perception that Prime Minister Gillard broke her 'promise' not to introduce a 'carbon tax'. The leader of the Opposition, Tony Abbott, has vowed to repeal the carbon price legislation, as well as all related policies, should he be elected to office at the next federal election, which is due to take place in 2013.[185] As commentators have noted, such an action would face substantial political and constitutional obstacles, not the least being the constitutional requirement for 'just compensation' to be provided in the event of government acquisition of property rights in the form of emission units under the carbon pricing scheme. An attempt by a future government to overturn the carbon pricing mechanism and render emission units invalid could thus be economically and politically costly.[186] With the Greens continuing to hold the balance of power in the Senate after 2013, there may also be difficulties securing the necessary political support to repeal the legislation.

---

[184] This initiative appears to follow in the footsteps of the US federal government, whose regulatory action was prompted by the Supreme Court decision in *Massachusetts v EPA*, discussed above.
[185] M. Grattan and D. Wroe, 'Abbott's Blood Oath to Repeal Carbon Tax', *The Age*, 13 October 2011, <http://www.theage.com.au/national/abbotts-blood-oath-to-repeal-carbon-tax-20111012-1ll80.html>.
[186] G. Williams, 'Abbott Courts Trouble with Carbon Tax Plans', *Sydney Morning Herald*, 25 October 2011, <http://www.smh.com.au/opinion/politics/abbott-courts-trouble-with-carbon-tax-plans-20111025-1mi0d.html>; and F. Green, 'Abbott's Gory Pledge Would Be a Legal Bloodbath', *Crikey*, 13 October 2011, <http://www.crikey.com.au/2011/10/13/abbotts-gory-pledge-would-be-a-legal-bloodbath>.

In the interim, uncertainty over the future of national carbon pricing may make businesses reluctant to pursue domestic emission reduction strategies for fear that the emission credits generated will be worthless in the future. This problem is likely to be compounded by continuing uncertainty over the nature of international arrangements for future emission reductions. As ever, the global context of climate change policy and action will be critical to the effectiveness of domestic regulatory action in Australia.

Conclusion

This chapter's consideration of the driving factors and evolution of Australian climate law and policy shows that climate change is a multidimensional issue that poses significant challenges for existing forms of governance and regulation. Addressing climate change requires the integrated efforts of governments, ideally working across different economic and environmental sectors. In a federal governance system such as Australia's, achieving a nationally consistent and comprehensive approach to climate change regulation has proved to be a particular challenge. Even so, the last two decades have seen Australian climate law develop from very modest beginnings into a much more detailed and diverse body of law.

With the passage of the Clean Energy legislation, Australian climate law has undoubtedly entered a new era. After years of policy debates over the merits and design of a national ETS, we now enter the phase of legal implementation of this mechanism. Questions remain, however, as to how the national carbon pricing mechanism will affect state climate policy and legislative measures,[187] as well as whether it will operate as part of a diversified regulatory package (for example with separate schemes such as the RET and EEO Act also remaining in place) or will eventually displace other forms of climate regulation to become the dominant measure for reducing Australian GHG emissions.

The next chapter considers the different regulatory options available to governments seeking to reduce GHG emissions and mitigate climate change. The chapter explains the reasons why market-based measures, particularly emissions trading schemes (and to a lesser extent carbon taxes) have emerged as a dominant regulatory choice both in Australia and elsewhere. It also explores the principal design issues raised by a preference for market regulatory models in the climate field and reviews how these issues have been approached in other jurisdictions, including the European Union. As will be seen, these comparative law examples have in turn been an important influence on Australia's efforts to put in place a mechanism to 'price carbon' under the federal *Clean Energy Act 2011*.

---

[187] See, for example, the Review of the Victorian *Climate Change Act 2010* undertaken pursuant to s 19, which requires the Act to be reviewed 'without delay' in the event that a bill providing for a national emissions trading scheme is introduced into federal Parliament.

5

Putting a price on carbon
Regulatory models and emissions trading schemes

Introduction   *page* 164
Regulatory models for climate change mitigation   165
The 'global' carbon market: ETS around the world   177
Carbon pricing in Australia   187
Conclusion   197

Introduction

As the previous chapters have highlighted, climate change presents a complex problem for policy and legal frameworks. The effects of climate change are broadscale and are predicted to manifest over long time frames; they have significant implications for socioeconomic systems and infrastructure as well as the potential to exacerbate a range of other environmental issues, such as water availability, loss of biodiversity, and land degradation. Selecting the optimal regulatory model or range of regulatory tools is thus a key task for policymakers and lawyers in seeking to respond to climate change.

The previous chapter provided insights into the various policy and legal responses to climate change that have occurred in the Australian polity over an extended period of time. This chapter builds on that foundation to provide a more detailed examination of Australian legal and policy developments that have seen the introduction of an emissions trading scheme – to 'put a price on carbon' – as well as associated governance and institutional measures, all of which are designed to mitigate climate change. The chapter also broadens the focus to examine more generally questions about the appropriate regulatory models that might fulfil the complex task of reducing greenhouse gas emissions, and in that context turns to consider emissions trading schemes that are in operation in various jurisdictions.

Regulatory models for climate change mitigation

One of the more intriguing aspects of the evolution of governance measures to address climate change has been the progressive redefinition of GHG emissions within legal and regulatory models.[1] Prior to widespread concerns about the role of GHG emissions in accelerating atmospheric warming, they were not regulated by law – that is, they were not conceived of as a subject matter that required attention within regulatory frameworks.[2] Like many forms of incipient harm, it is only when that harm can be identified as a discrete phenomenon, and its causes linked to entities that have responsibility for its effects, that it is conceivable to apply legal and regulatory measures designed to mitigate those effects and to impose legal sanctions.[3] Thus GHG emissions are now considered a harm to be addressed by law, and the measures that have been adopted are examined in this chapter.

Beyond the specific measures required to respond to climate change, there is a wider question of the patterns of development that result in accelerating GHG emissions. Scientific research has long provided a factual basis for challenging the patterns of industrialisation and consumption that, it is predicted, will lead to dangerous climate change.[4] However, it was the growing scientific evidence of the links between GHG emissions and climate change that precipitated a progressive incorporation of such emissions within legal models from the global to the local, commencing in the early 1990s.[5]

Scientific evidence identifying the link between causes and effect does not, however, mandate a specific regulatory instrument in response; thus there has not been a simple translation of scientific concern into the legal and policy realm.[6] Instead, regulatory choices arise from a complex interaction between the definition and identification of the 'harm', its various causes, and the perceived efficacy and feasibility of regulatory options.[7] As we have seen in many jurisdictions, this milieu can generate vociferous debate about policy and legal choices,[8] which may extend to attacks on the underlying scientific

---

1 L. Stein, 'The Legal and Economic Bases for an Emissions Trading Scheme', 36(1) *Monash Law Review* 192 (2010).
2 Regulation is defined here to include the spectrum from statute to judge-made (common) law and extends to various forms of normative regimes that are grounded in law. In this sense it is much broader than the concept of 'command-and-control' regulation.
3 This is the classic utilitarian explanation of law as a response to social and economic problems. See for example S. Bottomley and S. Bronitt, 'Economics and Government Regulation', in *Law in Context*, 3rd edn (Federation Press, 2006).
4 B. Szerszynski, 'On Knowing What To Do: Environmentalism and the Modern Problematic', in *Risk, Environment and Modernity: Towards a New Ecology*, eds S. Lash, B. Szerszynski and B. Wynne (Sage Publications, 1996).
5 D. Liverman, 'Conventions of Climate Change: Constructions of Danger and the Dispossession of the Atmosphere', 35 *Journal of Historical Geography* 279 (2009). See further Chapters 2 and 4.
6 See for example Symposium: 'Responses To Global Warming: The Law, Economics, and Science of Climate Change', 155 *University of Pennsylvania Law Review* 1795 (2007).
7 C. Abbott, 'Environmental Command Regulation', in *Environmental Law for Sustainability*, eds B. Richardson and S. Wood (Hart Publishing, 2006).
8 K. Neuhoff, *Tackling Carbon: How to Price Carbon for Climate Policy*, Version 1.1 (29 September 2008), University of Cambridge, Electricity Policy Research Group, Faculty of Economics, <http://www.eprg.group.cam.ac.uk/wp-content/uploads/2009/03/tackling-carbon_final_3009082.pdf>.

Table 5.1 Regulatory options for climate change mitigation

Regulatory model	Example
Economic incentives	Carbon tax
	ETS
Voluntary/self-regulation	Greenhouse Challenge program
	Energy Efficiency Opportunities program
Government–industry partnership	Greenhouse Friendly program
Direct regulation	Designation of GHG as a waste under the Victorian *Climate Change Act 2010*
	US federal regulation of motor vehicle emissions under the *Clean Air Act*
Tortious liability	Climate litigation brought against local governments
Carbon capture and sequestration	Carbon capture and storage
	Biosequestration and offsets
Fiscal measures	Subsidies and premium feed-in tariffs for renewable energy
Demand-side measures and energy efficiency	White Certificate scheme for energy retailers

research.[9] Therefore, judgments as to the efficacy of any regulatory model must take account of political and jurisdiction-specific factors.

Potential regulatory models for GHG emission reduction envisage differing degrees of government intervention and reflect contrasting policy perspectives.[10] Examples of different regulatory approaches to climate change mitigation include not just emissions trading schemes and carbon taxes, but also voluntary or self-regulation, partnerships between government and industry or community groups to introduce 'offsets' for energy generation, direct regulation of GHG pollution emanating from fossil fuel generation, imposition of liability for GHG emissions via litigation, mechanisms for carbon capture and sequestration, fiscal measures such as subsidies and taxation relief, demand-side measures to reduce energy consumption, and energy efficiency requirements (see Table 5.1). Several such measures were highlighted in the previous chapter using Australia as a representative jurisdiction. This chapter considers economic instruments more specifically within a wider examination of how regulatory choices are given effect.

Given the range of regulatory options available, how can we evaluate their effectiveness? In this inquiry, we must also consider whether different options fulfil specific requirements as robust legal instruments, as well as being strategic policy choices. Some commentators have provided criteria for assessment of regulatory frameworks for climate change. MacGill et al. proposed that '[d]evelopment of a policy framework for climate change has to be assessed on its (1) "effectiveness" in actually mitigating the dangers of climate change, without damaging progress in other societal objectives; and (2) "efficiency" in doing this at reasonable cost and effort when compared against both the benefits of meeting policy objectives, and the other possible frameworks that might be

---

9 For a discussion, see D. Karoly, 'The Climate Series', <http://www.themonthly.com.au/climate-series-david-karoly-latest-climate-science-1492>.
10 L. Godden and J. Peel, *Environmental Law: Scientific, Policy and Regulatory Dimensions* (Oxford University Press, 2010), p. 125.

used'.[11] Taking a more explicitly legal approach, Durrant argues that an effective legal response to the problem of climate change will require the adoption of a series of cohesive legal instruments and mechanisms, internationally and nationally, that create rights and duties (regulatory responses), penalise non-compliance and other unlawful acts (liability response), and promote innovation to minimise GHG emissions (market response).[12]

The efficiency and effectiveness formula, such as that proposed by MacGill et al., is commonly associated with Coasean economic theory (see further below), and to that extent often favours the use of economic instruments such as carbon taxes and ETS.[13] The efficiency rationale is also an important factor in the political acceptability of any economic instrument.[14] For instance, a regime to address the risks of climate change at least cost has been consistently supported by the United States,[15] as well as by most of the economically powerful nations.[16] However, this serves to highlight that regulatory choices do not operate in a vacuum and that economic measures are not necessarily neutral in terms of their present and future implications for society[17] – nor indeed are other forms of regulation. Arguably, however, any robust regulatory framework should include legal models that are transparent and promote accountability,[18] have practical consequences in terms of changing behaviour to reduce emissions,[19] and produce major structural changes towards a low-carbon economy in as equitable a manner as possible.[20]

Market-based mechanisms

To date, the regulatory approach to mitigating climate change has been dominated by market-based mechanisms, which regard the problem of reducing GHG

---

[11] I. MacGill, H. Outhred and K. Nolles, 'National Emissions Trading for Australia: Key Design Issues and Complementary Policies for Promoting Energy Efficiency, Infrastructure Investment and Innovation', 11(1) *Australasian Journal of Environmental Management* 78 (2004), p. 80.
[12] N. Durrant, *Legal Responses to Climate Change* (Federation Press, 2010), p. 3.
[13] For a critique of the 'least cost' rationale in the renewable energy context, see J. Prest, 'A Dangerous Obsession with Least Cost? Climate Change, Renewable Energy Law and Emissions Trading', in *Climate Change Law: Comparative, Contractual and Regulatory Considerations,* eds W. Gumley and T. Daya-Winterbottom (Lawbook Company, 2009).
[14] See for example Department of Climate Change and Energy Efficiency, *Securing a Clean Energy Future* (2011), pp. 21–2, citing cost-effectiveness as a key feature of the carbon pricing mechanism and endorsing the Productivity Commission's research report, *Carbon Emission Policies in Key Economies* (2011), which concluded that 'market-based solutions ... are the most cost-effective way of reducing carbon pollution'.
[15] C. R. Sunstein, 'On the Divergent American Reactions to Terrorism and Climate Change', 107 *Columbia Law Review* 503 (2007).
[16] J. E. Milne, 'Carbon Taxes in the United States: The Context for the Future', in *The Reality of Carbon Taxes in the 21st Century,* ed. J. E. Milne (Vermont Law School Environmental Tax Policy Institute, 2008), p. 2, <http://www.vermontlaw.edu/Documents/020309-carbonTaxPaper(0).pdf>.
[17] C. Spash, 'The Brave New World of Carbon Trading', 15(2) *New Political Economy* 169 (2010), pp. 170, 177 and 180.
[18] See B. A. Ackerman and R. B. Stewart, 'Reforming Environmental Law: the Democratic Case for Market Incentives', 13 *Columbia Journal of Environmental Law* 171 (1988).
[19] See, by contrast, M. Grubb, who argues that political choices and behavioural considerations have been as influential in climate policy as neoclassical economics: 'Global Perspective: Implementing Carbon Pricing in a World of Political Resistance and Evolving International Participation' (Melbourne, 14 April 2011), <http://www.grattan.edu.au/assets/linked_docs/034_transcript_grubb.pdf>.
[20] Neuhoff, *Tackling Carbon* (2008), pp. 18–19 discusses the distributional effects of introducing economic instruments.

emissions as amenable to economic incentive measures – chiefly an ETS.[21] In part, this emphasis can be seen as a consequence of the adoption of such measures in the Kyoto Protocol and by important economic players, such as the European Union.[22] With its legislation to 'put a price on carbon', the Australian government has definitively aligned itself with this broader international trend.

Economic theories underpinning market mechanisms were given particular practical purchase through the early identification of climate change as a global problem requiring a global (trading) solution.[23] Global warming in these terms was conceptualised as an instance of market failure. In the words of Garnaut:

> The failure to place a price on greenhouse gas emissions has led to over-utilisation of a scarce resource: the atmosphere's capacity to absorb emissions without risks of dangerous climate change. The correction of this market failure is the central task of climate change policy, in Australia and in the world.[24]

Such views of the 'problem' and its 'correction' draw heavily upon environmental economic perspectives, such as Hardin's 'Tragedy of the Commons'.[25] Drawing an analogy with Hardin, the proposition is that the global atmosphere has been treated as a freely available commons, overexploited by the release of emissions into the atmosphere, which has resulted in a market failure. Economists prescribe a price to be placed on emissions (carbon) to 'correct' the market failure, thereby giving an economic value to the environmental resource concerned (the global atmosphere). The price signal is designed to reflect the scarcity of the global atmospheric commons and to alter behaviour across the market (society) to reduce its exploitation. Neuhoff suggests that carbon pricing contributes to emission reductions by shifting production towards using low-carbon and more energy-efficient technologies.[26] In addition, a price signal can lead to consumers choosing less emission-intensive products and services. These changes, it is argued, in turn provide incentives for innovation, and the development and dissemination of low-carbon technologies, products and services.

Typically, any policy approach that seeks to 'put a price on carbon' relies upon another important tenet: Coase's 'social cost' theory for dealing with externalities such as global atmospheric warming. The social costs are those not incorporated into the current price paid for resource utilisation and which are borne by third parties (society). In this instance the resource includes resources used to produce energy, such as fossil fuels. Coasean theory also suggests that reductions in

---

[21] A. Moran, 'Tools of Environmental Policy: Market Instruments versus Command-and-control', in *Markets, the State, and the Environment: Towards Integration,* ed. R. Eckersley (Macmillan Education Australia, 1995), p. 75.
[22] More broadly, the use of market mechanisms has been supported by the progressive redefinition of emissions in line with shifts in the regulatory evolution of environmental law and governance: first as atmospheric pollution, a 'waste' and a threat to life, and then as a 'tradable permission', and ultimately as a 'commodity' in terms of ETS that can be utilised in futures markets: Godden and Peel, *Environmental Law* (2010), p. 7.
[23] Stein, 'The Legal and Economic Bases for an Emissions Trading Scheme' (2010), p. 192.
[24] R. Garnaut, *Garnaut Climate Change Review* (Cambridge University Press, 2008), p. 299.
[25] 162 *Science* 1243 (1967). [26] Neuhoff, *Tackling Carbon* (2008), p. 9.

externalities such as atmospheric pollution can be achieved at 'least cost' in a system where emitters have economic incentives to minimise emissions. Under carbon pricing, for example, emission-intensive industries have a strong incentive to make economically efficient changes to production facilities, as they will otherwise be subject to an additional cost (for example by having to purchase permits under an ETS or being subject to a carbon tax to cover the social cost of their pollution).[27] Adherents of this theory argue that it allows industry flexibility in how they meet their emission reduction obligations (for example through technological innovation, changing production methods or buying permits).[28] Accordingly, businesses and industries that can reduce emissions most cheaply will do so. Others will buy permits from this group so that the overall reduction of pollution is achieved at least cost to society.

The adoption of economic instruments as a policy approach has been criticised for raising the possibility of a 'business almost as usual' approach for some sectors of society but more radical adjustments for others, especially where policy-makers are persuaded that direct regulation is too costly to implement.[29] Importantly, then, economic instruments that are designed to deliver a price signal can be regarded as only one of the 'three pillars' of GHG emission reduction policy; with the other two being technology policy[30] and direct regulation.[31]

Direct regulation

Direct regulation, also referred to as command-and-control,[32] relies upon controlling pollutant levels (in this case GHG emissions) through the application of prescriptive standards set out in statute law that regulate industrial and associated activities that emit pollution. Standards may be performance-based or may require the use of a particular technology. Typically, the prescription of standards or emission levels is backed up by government agency enforcement and the imposition of financial and/or other penalties in the case of breach. The underlying policy rationale of this approach is that the regulated entities (that is, industries, such as the power generation sector) will conform to the legislative standard in order to avoid enforcement measures such as financial penalties. There is an extensive body of literature dealing with industry regulation and pollution control, which developed largely in respect of point source

---

27 R. Coase, 'The Problem of Social Cost', 3 *Journal of Law and Economics* 1 (1960). Coasean theory has been criticised on various grounds; for example, it assumes perfect information and minimum transaction costs. In initial scenarios the theory also held that it did not matter which entity paid for pollution reduction – that is, industry or those suffering the effects – an approach fundamentally in conflict with the polluter pays principle.
28 R. Stewart, 'A New Generation of Environmental Regulation?', 29 *Capital University Law Review* 21 (2001), p. 37.
29 D. Driesen, 'Free lunch or cheap fix?: The Emissions Trading Idea and the Climate Change Convention', *Boston College Environmental Affairs Law Review* 1 (1998), p. 43.
30 See Chapter 9. **31** Neuhoff, *Tackling Carbon* (2008), p. 22.
32 We prefer 'direct regulation', as 'command-and-control' has pejorative connotations: see N. Gunningham, 'Environmental Law, Regulation and Governance: Shifting Architectures', 21 *Journal of Environmental Law* 179 (2009).

pollution.[33] Even though GHG emissions are a more diffuse form of pollution, there is scope for regulation of major emitters and stationary sources, such as power stations.[34]

Conceptually, then, it is feasible to treat GHG emissions within a regulatory framework as one of the group of atmospheric pollutants covered by pollution control laws.[35] This approach has been taken in the state of Victoria, with the *Climate Change Act 2010* amending the *Environment Protection Act 1970* to include GHG emissions within the Act's definition of 'waste'.[36] Consequently the state's Environmental Protection Agency was given a mandate to regulate GHG emissions from industrial sources, including, potentially, power stations in Victoria. While direct regulation is a legally feasible approach for dealing with GHG emissions, it is often argued that such models in a climate change context are not equipped to deal with uncertainty: it is difficult to put into place standards that can be readily adjusted to give effect to progressively lower emission reduction targets.[37] There has also been resistance to prescriptive standards, which can be seen as too inflexible and difficult to monitor. Of course, overcoming these constraints is largely a matter of reallocating available financial resources. Nonetheless, the direct regulation option has not been extensively implemented in Australian jurisdictions, and it has only been adopted in a very small number of jurisdictions worldwide. This trend is in keeping with more general policy choices whereby the prescriptive regulatory approach has been progressively displaced by economic models across many sectors.[38] Given the emphasis on market-based models in climate change regulation, we now turn to examine the two main economic instruments, carbon taxes and emissions trading schemes.

Carbon pricing: Carbon taxes and ETS

Economic instruments, such as carbon taxes or ETS, exemplify the application of economic theory to regulatory models. If GHG emissions are an externality, then the use of economic instruments is a means to 'internalise the costs' of dependence on the use of emission-intensive resources and production. Even so, these economic measures still require the support of governments to enact legislation to implement them and impose penalties for lack of

---

[33] 'Point source pollution' refers to pollution that can be traced back to a particular point of origin, for example to a discharge pipe of an industrial facility. See for example N. Gunningham, R. Kagan and D. Thornton, *Shades of Green: Business, Regulation, and Environment* (Stanford University Press, 2008), p. 159. A detailed examination of this literature is beyond the scope of the current chapter but it provides a useful point of reference for considering industry regulation in a climate change context.
[34] See for example emissions performance standards for new power stations in California under Senate Bill 1368, California Energy Commission, Emissions Performance Standard, <http://www.energy.ca.gov/emission_standards/index.html>.
[35] In this regard see *Massachusetts v EPA* 549 US 497 (2007) discussed in Chapter 4.
[36] *Environment Protection Act 1970* (Vic) ss 4, 13(1)(ga).
[37] Stein, 'The Legal and Economic Bases for an Emissions Trading Scheme' (2010), p. 194.
[38] There are ongoing debates about the extent to which economic models should replace command-and-control regulation. The seminal article here is Ackerman and Stewart, 'Reforming Environmental Law: the Democratic Case for Market Incentives' (1988), but for a more nuanced discussion of the trends see Gunningham, 'Environmental Law, Regulation and Governance' (2009).

compliance.[39] For instance, the setting of caps and associated regulation under an ETS is administratively complex.[40] A carbon taxation regime is also not free of these problems, as even though there may be an existing taxation system in place, it may still be plagued by tax avoidance. In sum, there is a considerable degree of government intervention, monitoring and compliance enforcement required in the establishment and long-term administration of market mechanisms.

'Carbon pricing' generally refers to both taxation measures and ETS. A carbon tax works by sending a price signal: it effectively places a levy on the price of a product that (in an ideal world) should reflect the social cost of the associated GHG pollution.[41] Businesses are then free to decide what quantity of pollution reduction to offer in response. At their core, carbon taxes involve taxing or charging the carbon content of fuels or GHG emissions.[42] The basic theoretical premise is the need to correct for the externalisation of the environmental costs associated with carbon emissions.[43]

While an ETS also involves a price signal, it operates on a different principle by controlling quantity (the number of emission permits available for emission reduction) rather than price.[44] Under an ETS, the number of permits to emit GHG emissions is progressively reduced over time. Table 5.2 summarises some of the core differences between an ETS and carbon taxes and lists the advantages and disadvantages of each instrument.

Even where market-based instruments are the preferred approach to climate change mitigation, there remains debate over the relative merits of specific regulatory instruments.[45] Economic analyses of the relative merits of carbon taxes versus ETS abound.[46] Stern, in his influential review, favoured an approach that would best enable global solutions to climate change and proposed an ETS with both short- and long-term goals. Similar objectives were evident in the Garnaut Review, which has been highly influential in setting policy and regulatory choices in Australia.[47] Like Stern, Garnaut viewed climate change as a market failure of global proportions and favoured emissions trading over a

---

39 Stein, 'The Legal and Economic Bases for an Emissions Trading Scheme' (2010), p. 199.
40 For a discussion of the complexities involved at the various stages of adopting and implementing an ETS in the context of the European Union scheme, see J. B. Skjaerseth and J. Wettestad, *EU Emissions Trading: Initiation, Decision-making and Implementation* (Ashgate Publishing, 2008).
41 In practice, political factors may result in much lower tax rates being applied.
42 Milne, 'Carbon Taxes in the United States: The Context for the Future' (2008), p. 4.
43 N. J. Chalifour, 'A Feminist Perspective on Carbon Taxes', 21(2) *Canadian Journal of Women and the Law* 169 (2010), pp. 177–8.
44 These concepts draw on various economic theories that were analysed in M. L. Weitzman, 'Prices v Quantities', 41(4) *Quantities Review of Economic Studies* 477 (1974), which was in turn relied upon by the Stern Review (pp. 201–4). The Stern Review also influenced the later Australian Garnaut Review.
45 See for example N. O. Keohane, 'Cap-and-Trade is Preferable to a Carbon Tax', in *Climate Finance: Regulatory and Funding Strategies for Climate Change and Global Development,* eds R. B. Stewart, B. Kingsbury and B. Rudyk (New York University Press, 2009).
46 See Neuhoff, *Tackling Carbon* (2008); C. Hepburn, 'Regulation by Prices, Quantities or Both: A Review of Instrument Choice', 22 *Oxford Review of Economic Policy* 226 (2006); N. Stern, *The Economics of Climate Change: The Stern Review* (Cambridge University Press, 2007), Chapter 14; W. Pizer, 'Prices vs Quantities Revisited: The Case of Climate Change' (Discussion Paper 98–02, Resources for the Future, October 1997); and W. Pizer, 'Combining Price and Quantity Controls to Mitigate Climate Change', 85 *Journal of Public Economics* 409 (2002).
47 See Chapter 4.

Table 5.2 Carbon taxes versus ETS

		Advantages	Disadvantages
Cap-and-trade emissions trading • Australian carbon pricing mechanism • European Union Emissions Trading Scheme • New Zealand Emissions Trading Scheme • US regional schemes	The government sets a carbon pollution reduction target (scheme cap) and allocates (administratively or via auction) an equivalent quantity of emission units. These can be traded (subject to any scheme limitations). The price of emission units is determined by the market, according to the balance between demand and supply of units.	Certainty over absolute carbon pollution targets. Low fiscal risk associated with meeting targets. Emission units or revenue from auctioning could be used for assistance measures. Delivers abatement within covered sectors at least cost.	Less certainty about carbon price (although price risk can be managed through derivatives markets). Implementation can have a significant lead time. Completely new market with regulation that needs to be established.
Carbon tax • British Columbia's Carbon Levy; • Switzerland's CO_2 Tax	The government sets the price for each unit of carbon pollution based on the objective of achieving a carbon pollution reduction outcome, and the quantity of abatement emerges from the market. The price is charged on the GHGs *produced* within the country.	Delivers abatement within covered sectors at least cost. Would lend short-term certainty to carbon prices, leading to predictable effects on energy prices and assistance rates. Provides a predictable revenue flow that can be used for assistance measures.	Carbon pollution outcomes are uncertain. Fiscal risks associated with failure to achieve targets – if a carbon tax rate is set too low the government may need to purchase units on the international market, at budgetary cost. There may be reduced certainty for investors if the policy is to adjust the tax rate to meet targets in favour of the government purchasing international emission units. Risk of higher than necessary adjustment costs if the tax is set too high and Australia overshoots its target.

Source: Adapted from 'Comparison of Different Design Options for a Carbon Price', summary table provided for third meeting of the MPCCC on 21 December 2010, <http://www.climatechange.gov.au/government/initiatives/mpccc/meetings/third-meeting.aspx>.

carbon tax as a long-term solution.[48] In addition, Garnaut has consistently advocated adoption of an ETS model as the single regulatory model for climate change mitigation, although transitional measures such as renewable energy targets may be acceptable.[49]

---

[48] Garnaut, *Garnaut Climate Change Review* (2008), pp. 227–9 and 307–11. See also R. Garnaut, *The Garnaut Review 2011: Australia in the Global Response to Climate Change* (Cambridge University Press, 2011), pp. 77–88.
[49] Garnaut, *Garnaut Climate Change Review* (2008), p. 299; R. Garnaut, *Update paper 7: Low Emissions Technology and the Innovation Challenge*, Garnaut Climate Change Review – Update 2011 (2011), p. 14. See Chapter 9.

By contrast, other commentators point to the simplicity and 'known entity' qualities of a carbon tax as distinct advantages. Hsu suggests that carbon taxes are more cost-effective and less likely to attract rent-seeking behaviour (for example, industry lobby groups influencing the allocation of permits), and that there are no guarantees that an ETS will significantly reduce emissions.[50] He identifies psychological resistance to a tax on petrol as a major impediment to the imposition of carbon taxes, especially in North America. By contrast, Chalifour argues for a suite of regulatory instruments:

> While carbon taxes are no panacea, used in combination with regulations and other market mechanisms, such as emissions trading systems, they have the potential to stimulate the fundamental restructuring of the economy that is urgently needed to slow climate change.[51]

Cleetus makes the important point that carbon taxes and an ETS will only be effective if the instruments are 'stringent and designed well'.[52] Similarly, Deane contends that the answer to the question of whether to introduce a carbon tax or ETS is in the 'devil of the detail' – that is, in the specific design and implementation of the respective economic instruments.[53]

In the debate between carbon taxes and ETS, a relevant point is that emissions trading schemes are more amenable to the establishment of transnational links, so long as it is possible to harmonise the emission units that are to be traded or to create equivalent exchange values.[54] In contrast to an ETS, carbon taxation regimes are difficult to harmonise across states.[55] Despite this drawback, carbon taxes do already operate in a range of jurisdictions. In addition, there is a growing movement to institute carbon taxes as a component of the spectrum of regulatory responses to climate change, in a number of national and sub-national policy contexts (see Box 5.1).

BOX 5.1 A carbon tax case study

The carbon tax introduced in British Columbia provides an example in which a regional government introduced a carbon tax in the face of stalled national initiatives on climate mitigation. In April 2007, the Canadian federal government released an Action Plan to Reduce Greenhouse Gases and Air Pollution, which proposed a regulatory framework aimed at reducing Canada's GHG emissions by 20 per cent by 2020. Significantly, there was no ETS or federal carbon tax contemplated under the plan. More recently, commitments at a federal level in Canada have been further weakened by the national government's decision to withdraw from the Kyoto Protocol.

---

50 S. Hsu, 'The Politics and Psychology of Gasoline Taxes: An Empirical Study', 15(2) *Widener Law Review* 363 (2010), p. 365.
51 Chalifour, 'A Feminist Perspective on Carbon Taxes' (2010), p. 171.
52 R. Cleetus, 'Finding Common Ground in the Debate between Carbon Tax and Cap-and-Trade Policies', 67(1) *Bulletin of the Atomic Scientists* 17 (2011), p. 23.
53 F. Deane, 'A New Legal Avenue for Pricing GHG Emissions? To Trade or to Tax?' (2011) 28 *Environmental and Planning Law Journal* 111, pp. 129–30 and 133.
54 Stein, 'The Legal and Economic Bases for an Emissions Trading Scheme' (2010), p. 193.
55 Ibid., p. 204. For an alternative view, see G. Metcalf and D. Weisbach, 'The Design of a Carbon Tax', 33 *Harvard Environmental Law Review* 499 (2009), pp. 501–2.

> **BOX 5.1 (cont.)**
>
> Similarly to the position in Australia, several Canadian provinces implemented their own climate change responses. Quebec was the first province in Canada to introduce a carbon tax, followed by British Columbia, which in February 2008 announced a 'revenue neutral carbon tax' that commenced in July 2008.[56]
>
> The design of a carbon tax involves various policy considerations, including the way in which carbon taxes are delivered, i.e. inside or outside of a tax system. Thus a carbon tax could be implemented as an excise tax on the carbon content of fossil fuels (coal, oil and natural gas). Alternatively, the relevant authority could create a requirement to pay the charge through separate legislation and delegate monitoring and collection to a non-tax agency.
>
> In British Columbia, the tax adopted the former model by setting an excise at a rate of $10 per tonne of CO_2, and then increasing the rate by $5 per tonne annually until 2012.

Ultimately, in Australia, a hybrid economic instrument model has been enacted that has features of both carbon taxes and an ETS. A hybrid approach was also favoured in proposed US legislation to introduce mitigation measures; those bills ultimately were unable to gather sufficient support for enactment.[57]

The rise of cap-and-trade ETS

Although carbon taxes are being introduced in an increasing number of jurisdictions, emissions trading schemes are still the dominant regulatory option worldwide (Table 5.3).

Moreover, a cap-and-trade design model for the ETS predominates over the alternative baseline-and-credit design.[58] Under cap-and-trade, an overall level of GHG emissions is set (the cap) and then entities covered by the scheme are allocated rights to emit (permits or allowances) that usually relate to emissions of 1 tonne of CO_2 eq., compatible with units created under international standards. Scheme participants must have sufficient permits to cover their actual amount of GHG emissions in any set period or face sanctions. Progressive tightening of the cap requires that if businesses are unable to meet their required limits, they must buy additional permits from those businesses that are able to reduce their emissions.[59] The operation of a cap-and-trade model in the domestic setting, incorporating carbon offsets through biosequestration,[60] is represented in Figure 5.1. This system has synergies with the Kyoto Protocol's emission-reduction targets and flexibility mechanisms for facilitating such reductions.[61] Why has the cap-and-trade ETS model achieved such prominence? Emissions trading schemes are, after all, not without their drawbacks.

---

[56] British Columbia Ministry of Finance, *Budget and Fiscal Plan 2008/09–2010/11*, pp. 7–36.
[57] Cleetus, 'Finding Common Ground' (2011), p. 24.
[58] The alternative baseline-and-credit model has been adopted in only a few jurisdictions, such as the GGAS scheme in NSW: see Chapter 4.
[59] S. Dickey, 'Emissions Trading: What Works?', in *Climate Change Law: Comparative, Contractual and Regulatory Considerations*, eds W. Gumley and T. Daya-Winterbottom (Lawbook Company, 2009), p. 64.
[60] See Chapter 10.   [61] Kyoto Protocol, Art. 17. See the discussion in Chapter 2.

Table 5.3 ETS and carbon taxes around the world

Countries and regions with ETS	Countries imposing taxes on carbon fuels
Australia – carbon pricing mechanism	China – under consideration[62]
China – trial ETS in four cities (Beijing, Chongqing, Shanghai and Tianjin) and two provinces (Hubei and Guangdong)	Denmark, Finland, Ireland, Netherlands, Norway, Sweden, UK, Switzerland (companies exempt if they participate in country's voluntary ETS)
European Union ETS (27 Member States), together with Norway, Iceland and Liechtenstein	India – tax on coal produced in and imported to India
Switzerland – voluntary ETS	Canada – carbon taxes imposed by Alberta, British Columbia and Quebec
New Zealand	
USA – RGGI scheme (north-eastern states) ETS in California WCI (US western states and Canadian provinces)	USA – City of Boulder, Colorado
Japan – Tokyo Metropolitan Trading Scheme	
India – energy efficiency trading scheme	
South Korea (proposed start 2015)	

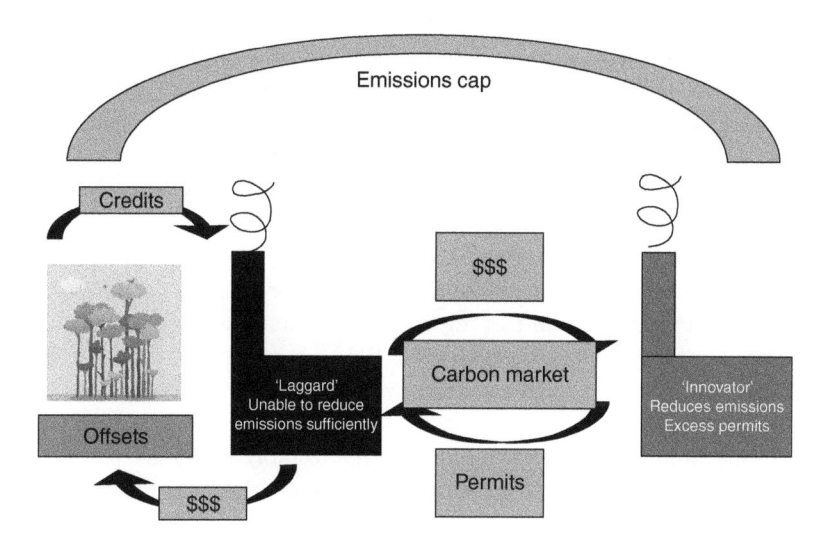

Figure 5.1 Cap-and-trade ETS

As noted above, they are vulnerable to rent-seeking on the part of lobby groups. In addition, the issue of the extent to which trade-exposed industries and the stationary energy sector should be compensated for introduction of a price on carbon has proven highly contentious within Australia. Similarly, there are strong arguments that socially vulnerable groups such as low-income households should be shielded from the full consequences of carbon price increases (although this argument applies equally to a tax). There are also persistent concerns over whether carbon trading will ultimately lead to significant GHG

---

[62] See <http://www.chinadaily.com.cn/bizchina/2012-01/06/content_14391943.htm[0]>.

emission reductions,[63] especially as the effectiveness of a particular ETS is contingent upon the specific design options selected.[64]

One of the most compelling explanations for why cap-and-trade schemes have been the favoured regulatory choice for climate change mitigation points to the importance of global conceptions of climate change. Stein argues, for example, that '… the emission trading scheme is an inevitable consequence of perceiving climate change as requiring a "top down approach" where the problem is a global as opposed to a domestic issue'.[65]

Initially, the European Union and many non-governmental organisations were opposed to the use of emissions trading because it does not incorporate sanctions against polluting entities. Instead, those groups favoured measures involving a tax on carbon as the substantive implementation instrument under the Protocol. Yet the United States successfully argued that cap-and-trade policies associated with carbon markets are more effective.[66] The Umbrella Group (a loose coalition of UNFCCC countries, which includes the United States, Russia, Japan, Australia, New Zealand, Canada, Iceland and Ukraine – many of which are major exporters of fossil fuels) strongly supported carbon trading and other 'flexibility mechanisms',[67] as these would assist Annex I nations (developed countries) in meeting mandatory targets and allow time for industry within those countries to make the transition to low-carbon economies.

A decisive argument in favour of flexibility mechanisms was the success of the national sulphur dioxide trading system that had been trialled in the United States.[68] Closer inspection of the scheme suggests, however, that its touted success requires qualification, as the reductions achieved were not due solely to the market mechanism.[69] In this regard, Hannemann argues that while a cap-and-trade system may be necessary for GHG emission reductions, it is not sufficient, and so must be accompanied by complementary measures, including regulatory requirements.[70]

With the United States' decision in 2001 not to ratify the Protocol, the Kyoto regime teetered on the edge of international legal obscurity in the following years. In the meantime, some Annex I countries, led by the EU, began to introduce specific legislation for ETS and other regulatory tools designed to help them

---

63 D. Campbell, M. Klaes and C. Bignell, 'After Cancun: The Impossibility of Carbon Trading', *University of Queensland Law Journal* 163 (2010), p. 164.
64 A number of commentators have developed criteria for gauging the effectiveness of an ETS and its ideal design components; see for example Dickey, 'Emissions Trading: What Works?' (2009), p. 47.
65 Stein, 'The Legal and Economic Bases for an Emissions Trading Scheme' (2010), p. 192.
66 D. Toke, 'Trading Schemes, Risks, and Costs: The Cases of the European Union Emissions Trading Scheme and the Renewables Obligation', 26 *Environment and Planning C : Government and Policy* 938 (2008), p. 942.
67 M. Betsill, 'International Climate Change Policy: Toward the Multilevel Governance of Global Warming', in *The Global Environment: Institutions, Law and Policy*, 3rd edn, eds R. S. Axelrod, S. D. VanDeveer and D. L. Downie (CQ Press, 2011). For discussion of the Protocol's flexibility mechanisms – joint implementation, the CDM and emissions trading – see Chapter 2.
68 D. Golden, 'The Politics of Carbon Dioxide Emissions Reduction: The Role of Pluralism in Shaping the Climate Change Technology Initiative', 17(2) *UCLA Journal of Environmental Law & Policy* 171 (1999), p. 190.
69 M. Hanneman, 'Cap-and-Trade: A Sufficient or Necessary Condition for Emissions Reduction?', 26(2) *Oxford Review of Economic Policy* 225 (2010), pp. 232–6.
70 Ibid., pp. 243–8.

meet projected commitments. In the case of the EU, pioneering action demonstrated the feasibility of an ETS and advanced the EU's position of global leadership in the field.[71]

The 'global' carbon market: ETS around the world

The case for ETS over other regulatory options was furthered by the adoption of such schemes in key jurisdictions. Moreover, despite the absence of a global ETS, the parties to the Kyoto Protocol continue to reaffirm their commitment to supporting the trading of credits generated under the project-based mechanisms such as the CDM and joint implementation of projects by two or more developed countries working together.[72] This 'global context' has been highly influential for domestic policy choices in Australia, not least because, with uncertainty about the emergence of an internationally consistent approach to carbon trading, transnational linkage of ETS offers the next best opportunity for GHG abatement at least cost.[73] In this setting, the 'global carbon market' for the meantime will most likely consist of a number of individual domestic, regional and voluntary ETS, each covered by its own specific legislation and governance arrangements.

Within this complex array of ETS, much attention has been paid to the specific elements in the design of different schemes. Such questions include how broad the coverage of the scheme should be; how emission permits should be allocated; who should receive compensation and how much; whether liable entities should be able to use permits from earlier or later allocation periods; the availability of offsets; and how to undertake monitoring and compliance (see Box 5.2).[74] ETS design issues are often treated as technical matters (despite their significant environmental and socioeconomic ramifications), but in practice their resolution is an 'immensely complex task' involving significant political considerations.[75]

It is therefore pertinent at this point to examine the major ETS that is in operation: that of the European Union. This scheme is important, not only because of the lessons it offers about design of a climate regulatory system but also because of the influence it has exercised over the adoption of similar regulatory 'solutions' in other parts of the world, including Australia. A standardised approach to ETS design now appears unlikely in jurisdictions beyond the EU,[76] but the extent to which jurisdiction-specific schemes can interlink will be vital.

---

71 J. Scott, 'The Multi-Level Governance of Climate Change', 5(1) *Carbon and Climate Law Review* 25 (2011), p. 28.
72 See Kyoto Protocol, *Decision 3/CMP.7, Emissions trading and the project-based mechanisms,* FCCC/KP/CMP/2011/10/Add.1.
73 Stein, 'The Legal and Economic Bases for an Emissions Trading Scheme' (2010), p. 193. Linkage requires the ability to harmonise the emissions units that are to be traded or to create equivalent exchange values.
74 Durrant, *Legal Responses to Climate Change* (2010), Chapter 9; D. Hodgkinson and R. Garner, *Global Climate Change: Australian Law and Policy* (LexisNexis Butterworths, 2008), pp. 244–58.
75 R. Lyster, 'Chasing down the Climate Change Footprint of the Public and Private Sectors: Forces Converge – Part II', 24 *Environmental and Planning Law Journal* 450 (2007), p. 454.
76 Ibid.

> **BOX 5.2 Design issues for ETS**
>
> - **Coverage**: Which industry sectors should have liabilities under the scheme? Which GHGs should be included? Should liability apply 'upstream' (for instance to fossil fuel producers) or 'downstream' (for instance to transportation companies releasing emissions from fossil fuel combustion)?
> - **Allocation**: Should permits be allocated by way of an auction, at which liable entities bid to purchase permits to cover their emissions; or by way of free allocation ('grandfathering'), whereby permits are allocated on the basis of historical emissions; or by setting benchmarks on the basis of performance or emission intensity standards?
> - **Compensation**: How will any auction revenue be spent? Should liable entities (for instance trade-exposed, emission-intensive industries) or others (for instance low-income households) be entitled to compensation to counter the financial burden consequent upon the introduction of carbon pricing? What form should compensation take (free permits, tax breaks, monetary payments)?
> - **Banking and borrowing**: Should liable entities under an ETS be able to bank permits that are in excess of their actual emissions for use in subsequent accounting periods? Should liable entities be able to borrow from future accounting periods to satisfy a permit shortfall?
> - **Offsets**: Are liable entities able to cancel out (a portion of) their liability through use of offsets (e.g. carbon credits from biosequestration activities, renewable energy certificates, international credits generated under the Kyoto Protocol mechanisms such as the CDM) and if so what, if any, quantitative and qualitative restrictions apply?
> - **Compliance**: How will emission reductions be monitored and verified? What authorities will oversee compliance? What will be the penalty for a failure to meet liabilities under the scheme?

European Union ETS

Europe's emissions trading regime commenced in 2005 as an urgent response to climate change. The EU directive 2003/87/EC that set up the European scheme established it as the largest multinational ETS in the world.[77] It was developed independently of the entry into force of the Kyoto Protocol, but its design was 'Kyoto compatible'. Practical considerations, rather than economic rationales *per se*, were influential in the EU ETS design; for example, the scheme allowed the involvement of industry in order to reduce the cost of abatement.[78] The EU ETS currently has 30 Members, these being all 27 EU member countries, together with Norway, Iceland and Lichtenstein.

Phase 1 (2005–07) was the pilot stage of the ETS; it covered CO_2 emissions from the power sector and some but not all industrial sectors. Since the expansion of the scheme in Phase 2 to additional types of industries, the ETS covers around 40 per cent of EU GHG emissions.[79] Adding new sectors has proven difficult.[80] Nonetheless, from Phase 3, coverage is to be extended to

---

77 *Directive 2003/87/EC of the European Parliament and of the Council of 13 October 2003 establishing a scheme for greenhouse gas emission allowance trading within the Community and amending Directive 96/61EC*, OJ L 275, 25.10.2003; *Directive 2009/29/EC of the European Parliament and of the Council of 23 April 2009 amending Directive 2003/87/EC so as to improve and extend the greenhouse gas emission allowance trading scheme of the Community*, OJ L 140, 5.6.2009, pp. 63–87.
78 Stein, 'The Legal and Economic Bases for an Emissions Trading Scheme' (2010), p. 212.
79 European Commission, 'Emissions Trading System (EU ETS)', <http://ec.europa.eu/clima/policies/ets/index_en.htm>.
80 L. Parker, 'Climate Change and the EU Emissions Trading Scheme (ETS): Looking to 2020', 22 *Current Politics and Economics of Europe* 327 (2011), p. 346.

installations involved in the production of chemicals and aluminium and to cover emissions of nitrous oxide and perfluorocarbons.[81] More contentious has been the inclusion of emissions from aviation from 1 January 2012.[82] There have been challenges to the extension of the EU ETS to cover airline emissions by transnational airlines, including those from the United States[83] and China.[84]

The governance of the EU ETS has grown increasingly centralised,[85] as the EU Commission has sought to strike a balance between securing an effective and integrated regulatory framework for the ETS, and providing for decentralised governance by member states. In Phase 1, member states were allowed significant leeway in implementing the EU ETS directive in their domestic legal systems.[86] Instead of an EU-wide cap, each member country could determine its own cap by submitting a National Allocation Plan (NAP) detailing the number of allowances it intended to allocate and the way it intended to allocate them, for review by the European Commission.[87] As Phase 1 preceded the first Kyoto commitment period, the member states were not bound by international emission reduction obligations, and most NAPs over-allocated allowances.[88]

In addition to the over-allocation of allowances at a national level, which saw a substantial fall in the carbon price, other problematic aspects of the initial ETS design included the free allocation ('grandfathering') of 95 per cent of permits to entities covered by the ETS. The 'price pass-through' by industry to electricity consumers[89] resulted in windfall gains to ETS participants and contributed to the initial ineffectiveness of the ETS.[90] The extent to which the lively trade in carbon emissions during Phase 1 has translated into long-term emission reductions is being evaluated.[91] Other commentators suggest that the initial phase successfully introduced the ETS to industry, and that although the ETS had limited influence in stimulating innovation in the early period, gradual

---

81 European Commission, 'Climate Action – Cap', <http://ec.europa.eu/clima/policies/ets/cap/index_en.htm>.
82 Implemented by *Directive 2008/101/EC of the European Parliament and of the Council of 19 November 2008 amending Directive 2003/87/EC so as to include aviation activities in the scheme for greenhouse gas emission allowance trading within the Community,* OJ L 8, 13.1.2009.
83 The European Court of Justice rejected a challenge to the validity of the changes by American aviation groups: see C-366/10, Judgment of the Court (Grand Chamber) of 21 December 2011, *Air Transport Association of America and Others v Secretary of State for Energy and Climate Change.*
84 China has banned its airlines from participating: see N. Nielsen, 'China Confronts EU on Aviation Tax', *EU Observer* (online), 6 February 2012, <http://euobserver.com/9/115136>. For more on the airlines dispute, see Chapter 2.
85 M. Peeters, 'Legislative Choices and Legal Values: Considerations on the Further Design of the European Greenhouse Gas Emissions Trading Scheme from a Viewpoint of Democratic Accountability', in *Climate Change and European Emissions Trading: Lessons for Theory and Practice,* eds M. Faure and M. Peeters (Edward Elgar Publishing, 2008), p. 36.
86 Ibid.
87 S. Bogojevic, 'The Revised EU ETS Directive: Yet Another Stepping Stone', 11(4) *Environmental Law Review* 279 (2009), p. 281.
88 Peeters, 'Legislative Choices and Legal Values' (2008), p. 30.
89 J. B. Skjaerseth, 'EU Emissions Trading: Legitimacy and Stringency', 20(5) *Environmental Policy and Governance* 295 (2010), p. 303; and Bogojevic, 'The EU ETS Directive Revised' (2009), p. 283.
90 Skjaerseth, 'EU Emissions Trading' (2010), p. 303.
91 K. Anttonen, M. Mehling and K. Upston-Hooper, 'Breathing Life into the Carbon Market: Legal Frameworks of Emissions Trading in Europe', 16(4) *European Environmental Law Review* 96 (2007).

improvements will occur.[92] Analysis of the EU ETS now centres on assessing whether the scheme will effectively drive low-carbon investment, and how the design problems of earlier phases of the scheme can be overcome, with the regime ending its second trading period and substantial changes in place for the third phase.[93]

As the EU ETS has moved beyond the pilot phase, the EU has altered various components of the scheme's design, which has helped to increase its efficacy and viability. In Phase 2 (2008–12) the scheme design was tightened by vesting in the European Commission the power to reject or modify NAPs and by increasing the number of allowances to be allocated by auction. Further amendments to the ETS Directive will see the NAPs replaced from Phase 3 (commencing in 2013) by an EU-wide cap and rules for allowance allocation and auctioning,[94] with full auctioning to occur by 2027.[95] To reduce the heavy reliance on credits generated outside the EU under the Kyoto Protocol's CDM and Joint Implementation mechanisms, the use of the Kyoto mechanism credits will be limited to 50 per cent of the total reduction required under the EU ETS from 2013.[96]

The trajectory of the 2020 EU reduction target has been closely watched. Beginning in 2013, the cap will be lowered annually by 1.74 per cent.[97] The EU is also considering a tighter trajectory of reductions, including an option for moving to a 30 per cent reduction below 1990 levels by 2020.[98] In 2010, emission reductions were already 14 per cent below 1990 levels – partly due to the Global Financial Crisis, but also as a result of climate change policies and higher energy prices.[99] Excess stocks of allowances in many member states due to the GFC may further depress the carbon price in Phase 3.[100] In this situation there is a risk of locking in carbon-intensive investments, although tightening the cap further by increasing the reduction targets will help to avoid such an outcome.

Notwithstanding some early implementation difficulties with the ETS, the EU emission reduction targets remain among the most progressive internationally. The ETS is complemented by a corresponding commitment to reducing energy consumption to 20 per cent below current projected levels by means of energy efficiency regulations,[101] and further initiatives to increase renewable energy uptake by 2020.[102] The European Commission is also exploring the

[92] Ibid., but for Phase 3 see M. Peeters and S. Weishaar, 'Exploring Uncertainties in the EU ETS: "Learning by Doing" Continues Beyond 2012', 3(1) *Carbon and Climate Law Review* 88 (2009).
[93] J. B. Skjaerseth and J. Wettestad, 'Fixing the EU Emissions Trading System? Understanding the post-2012 Changes', 10 *Global Environmental Politics* 101 (2010).
[94] *Directive 2003/87/EC*, Articles 9, 9a and 10, as amended by Directive 2009/29/EC.
[95] *Directive 2003/87/EC*, Article 10a, as amended by Directive 2009/29/EC.
[96] *Directive 2003/87/EC*, Articles 11b(8) and 11b(9).
[97] *Directive 2003/87/EC*, Article 9, as amended by 2009/29/EC to bring it in line with the 20 per cent reduction target.
[98] European Commission, 'Analysis of Options Beyond 20 per cent GHG Emission Reductions: Member State Results', Commission Staff Working Paper, SWD(2012)5 final, Brussels, 1 February 2012.
[99] Ibid., p. 5.   [100] Ibid.
[101] European Commission, 'Europe 2020 Initiative: Energy Efficiency Plan 2011', <http://ec.europa.eu/energy/efficiency/action_plan/action_plan_en.htm>.
[102] *Directive 2009/28/EC of the European Parliament and of the Council of 23 April 2009 on the promotion of the use of energy from renewable sources and amending and subsequently repealing Directives 2001/77/EC and 2003/30/EC*, OJ L 140, 5.6.2009.

possibility of introducing a carbon tax to reduce emissions in the transport sector, which is currently not covered by the ETS.[103]

The EU ETS is an important model that demonstrates the feasibility of introducing a complex, highly technical regime to drive structural innovation in emission-intensive industries. However, it is operating in a fragmented and increasingly uncertain global carbon market based upon a proliferation of various forms of carbon price regulation at both international and national levels. These include regional and state-based schemes operating in the United States, self-standing national schemes such as the New Zealand ETS, and a range of voluntary carbon markets, some of which are linked to regulated international credit mechanisms such as the CDM.

Emissions trading in other jurisdictions

In the area of environmental regulatory reform, Australia has often looked not to Europe but to the United States as a source of inspiration for domestic initiatives. The two countries have a number of important similarities: federal systems of governance, a diverse range of ecosystems with the potential to be severely affected by climate change, and a heavy dependence on fossil fuels that has hindered efforts at regulatory reform. As in Australia, concerns about carbon leakage[104] and industry protectionism have also been prominent in the United States.[105]

Despite recent policy and legislative initiatives in the climate change arena (for example federal energy efficiency and vehicle emission standards), the United States remains a long way from developing a comprehensive ETS like that of the EU, or even a national carbon trading regime similar to Australia's. Nonetheless, the common perception that the United States is 'doing nothing' on climate change is a false one, with many initiatives being taken at a sub-national level, including the development of regional and state-based ETS.[106] Many of the sub-national schemes in the United States had their impetus in the federal government's failure to adopt mandatory targets for GHG emissions. Accordingly, schemes such as the Regional Greenhouse Gas Initiative (RGGI) have the explicit goal of promoting action at a national level, while simultaneously providing a 'demonstration' cap-and-trade model. This activism has not been welcomed by all, with some arguing that regional schemes such as RGGI amount to a usurpation of federal legislative power in the climate change field, with constitutional implications.[107]

---

103 European Commission, 'Revision of the Energy Taxation Directive – Questions and Answers' MEMO/11/238 (Brussels, 13 April 2011), < http://europa.eu/rapid/pressReleasesAction.do?reference=MEMO/11/238>.
104 'Carbon leakage' is a concept largely drawn from economic theory. It occurs where there is an increase in emissions in one jurisdiction as a direct result of emission reduction measures implemented in another jurisdiction. Garnaut describes carbon leakage as 'a loss of competitiveness and relocation of trade-exposed, emissions-intensive industries as a result of carbon penalties applying in some countries but not others': *Garnaut Climate Change Review* (2008), p. 230.
105 E. Bluemel, 'Regional regulatory Initiatives Addressing GHG Leakage in the USA', in *Climate Change and European Emissions Trading: Lessons for Theory and Practice,* eds M. Faure and M. Peeters (Edward Elgar Publishing, 2008).
106 Garnaut, *The Garnaut Review 2011: Australia in the Global Response to Climate Change* (2011), pp. 60–3.
107 See for example a complaint filed against the Governor of New York in the Supreme Court of New York State, County of Albany: <http://cei.org/sites/default/files/RGGI%20complaint.pdf>. The complaint notes

Thus, as in Australia,[108] there remain persistent tensions in the United States between the different levels of government over which one has ultimate responsibility for climate change law and policy.

Regional Greenhouse Gas Initiative

RGGI was the first regional cap-and-trade scheme in the United States, covering the states of the north-east and Mid-Atlantic areas, including Massachusetts and New York. The scheme operates within several transmission and electricity trading regimes. Relatively modest standards seek to contain emissions at 2009 levels across the 2009–14 period and thereafter to reduce carbon emissions by 2.5 per cent annually to achieve a 10 per cent reduction in emissions by 2018.[109] The scheme operates within a system of three-year control periods, at the end of which allowances (one per tonne of CO_2 eq. emissions) must be submitted. The allocation of allowances is at the discretion of the participating states. Most states auction close to all of their allowances,[110] and the scheme is designed to ensure that ultimately 100 per cent of allowances are auctioned. Auction proceeds are invested into consumer programs to improve energy efficiency and accelerate the deployment of renewable energy obligations.[111]

There are several limitations to the RGGI model. The scheme covers only carbon dioxide emissions and its application is restricted to large power generation plants (over 25 MW in capacity), which excludes emissions from smaller power generation sources and from other industry sectors. The use of offsets, while allowed, is restricted to ensure that the wider GHG reduction objectives of the scheme are not undermined. To this end consistency, monitoring and verification, and additionality requirements for offsets apply.[112] Eligible offset projects include those that capture or destroy methane from landfill, reduce emissions of sulphur hexafluoride from electricity transmission and distribution equipment, sequester CO_2 through afforestation, reduce CO_2 emissions through non-electric energy efficiency measures in buildings, and avoid methane emissions through agricultural manure management operations.[113]

Overall, as the RGGI introduces only modest compliance costs, it is expected to bring about some structural change in the power sector without introducing any significant carbon leakage issues.[114] The RGGI scheme was designed in contemplation of national cap-and-trade legislation being on the horizon, but the chances of legislation of this type materialising now seem remote. Despite the

---

that the Governor of New Jersey announced in May 2011 that the state is pulling out of the RGGI scheme due to allegations of its ineffectiveness as a climate change mitigation measure.
108 On the ramifications of Australia's federal governance framework for climate law see Chapter 4.
109 Durrant, *Legal Responses to Climate Change* (2010), p. 101.
110 Close to 90 per cent of allowances were auctioned at quarterly regional auctions in the 2009 and 2010 periods. The clearing price at auction in June 2011 was US$1.89.
111 By June 2011 the scheme had so far generated $886.4 million. Eighty per cent of this has been used to fund renewable energy programs (11 per cent), energy efficiency (52 per cent), direct assistance (14 per cent), and other GHG reduction projects (1 per cent): RGGI Inc, *Investment of Proceeds from RGGI CO_2 Projects*, February 2011, p. 2.
112 On the concept of additionality of offsets see Chapters 6 and 10.
113 'Fact Sheet: RGGI Offsets', 19 August 2010, <http://www.rggi.org/docs/RGGI_Offsets_in_Brief.pdf>.
114 Bluemel, 'Regional Regulatory Initiatives Addressing GHG Leakage in the USA' (2008), p. 228.

lack of federal implementation of an ETS, the RGGI model has stimulated interest in regional ETS, with two further regional schemes expected to commence shortly. These are the Midwestern Accord, covering six American states in the midwest and one Canadian province, and the Western Climate Initiative (WCI) cap-and-trade scheme, covering several western American states and four Canadian provinces. Building upon the RGGI experience, the larger WCI scheme will adopt a more ambitious emission reduction target (15 per cent reduction below 2005 levels by 2020) and will have a broader coverage (encompassing nearly 90 per cent of economy-wide emissions in the region).[115]

Californian ETS

Also to be in effect shortly, though slowed by a court challenge, is a cap-and-trade scheme for the state of California, whose GHG emissions constitute a significant proportion of the world's total.[116] The cap-and-trade scheme is one element of a broader regulatory package designed to implement the *California Global Warming Solutions Act*, AB32, enacted in August 2006. The Act places a cap on the emissions of all GHGs in California, starting in January 2013, and requires that the total GHG emissions from all sources be reduced by January 2020 back to their 1990 levels, a reduction of 25–30 per cent compared to the levels when AB32 was passed. In contrast to other jurisdictions, including Australia, the cap-and-trade scheme is viewed as a supplement to direct regulatory measures, mostly targeting energy efficiency and vehicles.[117]

The Californian ETS is established through regulations promulgated by an independent environmental agency, the Californian Air Resources Board (ARB). The scheme will cover large industrial GHG emitters (producing 25 000 metric tons or more of CO_2 eq. per data year), electricity generators, and certain fuel distributors (starting in the second compliance period) with an estimated 85 per cent of the state's GHG emissions covered.[118] The Californian ETS envisages a substantial initial allocation of free permits to the electricity sector to ease the burden of transition to a carbon price,[119] and to emission-intensive, trade-exposed industries to prevent carbon leakage.[120]

---

[115] Western Climate Initiative, 'Design Summary: Design for the WCI Regional Program', <http://westernclimateinitiative.org/the-wci-cap-and-trade-program/program-design>.
[116] California Environmental Protection Agency, Air Resources Board, *Climate Change AB 32 Scoping Plan* (2008), p. 11.
[117] Ibid., pp. 30–67. Other emission reduction measures include the Light Duty Vehicle Greenhouse Gas Standards, Energy Efficiency, Low Carbon Fuel Standard, Million Roofs Program, and High Speed Rail. It is estimated that these regulatory measures will accomplish about 80 per cent of the required emission reductions.
[118] California Environmental Protection Agency, Air Resources Board, 'California Cap and Trade Program Resolution 11–32', 20 October 2011, p. 5.
[119] Appendix 1 to Board Resolution 10–42, <http://www.arb.ca.gov/regact/2010/capandtrade10/res1042app1.pdf>; California Environmental Protection Agency, Air Resources Board, 'Cap-and-Trade Regulation: July 2011 Discussion Draft 1 Appendix A: Staff Proposal for Allocating Allowances to Electricity Distribution Utilities', p. 5.
[120] California Environmental Protection Agency, Air Resources Board, 'Staff Report: Initial Statement of Reasons', 28 October 2011 (ISOR), Appendix J-12, <http://www.arb.ca.gov/regact/2010/capandtrade10/capisor.pdf>.

By contrast, provision for the use of offsets (mostly in the agricultural and forestry sectors) is quite restricted, as offsets are limited to 8 per cent of the compliance obligation for the 2012–20 period.[121] Eligible offsets are those generated in accordance with protocols set up by the ARB for emission reductions achieved in the forestry, urban forestry and livestock sectors; offsets are also allowed for the destruction of ozone-depleting substances (refrigerants). With regard to international offsets, only those offset credits derived from ARB-approved 'sector-based crediting programs' may be used. The Californian ETS will, at this stage, permit only offsets derived from crediting programs under the REDD+ scheme.[122] As the ARB must approve the relevant sector-based crediting programs to ensure that the credits created are real, additional, quantifiable, permanent, verifiable and enforceable,[123] this move is expected to facilitate the development of sub-national frameworks and protocols in developing countries, which may assist in the development of the REDD+ program globally.[124]

The other key feature of the Californian scheme is the use of cost containment mechanisms. Price volatility will be managed by holding a proportion of allowances under the cap in reserve, for sale at a fixed price should the market price of allowances exceed a certain amount, and a reserve auction price for allowances will serve as a price floor to prevent the value of allowances from dropping below a viable level.

Whereas efforts to introduce a national ETS in the United States have been derailed by interests opposed to action to address climate change, in an interesting twist, the ARB's cap-and-trade implementation plan, adopted in December 2010, has been strongly opposed by environmental justice groups. A coalition of environmental justice groups filed a lawsuit in San Francisco claiming that the plan violates California's *Environmental Quality Act* because the ARB had not conducted an adequate environmental impact analysis for the use of cap-and-trade as opposed to other policy instruments, such as a carbon tax. In May 2011 the San Francisco Superior Court upheld this objection and ordered that California take 'no action' to implement the ETS until the ARB had revisited its analysis.[125] Although the injunction was overturned on appeal, allowing the ARB to continue work on the ETS in the interim, ARB decided to postpone the start date of emitters' compliance obligations from January 2012 to January 2013. The ARB

---

121 17 CCR T. 17, Div. 3, Chap. 1, § 95854. The regulations also provide for fairly stringent qualitative restrictions pertaining to use of set protocols to verify offsets. Nonetheless, concerns remain that reductions from offsets could come to dominate the scheme: see A. C. Culkern, 'Offsets could make up 85% of California's Cap-and-Trade Program', *New York Times*, 8 August 2011, <http://www.nytimes.com/gwire/2011/08/08/08greenwire-offsets-could-make-up-85-of-califs-cap-and-tra-29081.html?pagewanted=all>.
122 17 CCR T. 17, Div. 3, Chap. 1, § 95933. On REDD+, see Chapter 7.
123 17 CCR T. 17, Div. 3, Chap. 1, § 95933.
124 C. Cosslett, 'California Leading the Way Towards REDD+ Carbon Markets', *UN-REDD Programme Newsletter*, No. 16, February 2011.
125 *Association of Irritated Residents, et al. v California Air Resources Board, et al.*, San Francisco Superior Court, Case Number CPF-09–509562, May 20, 2011.

completed the analysis of alternative measures in June 2011 and concluded once again that an ETS was the most efficient and cost-effective means of reducing emissions.[126] The Court accepted the assessment as satisfactory and discharged its ruling in early December 2011, clearing the way for commencement of the Californian cap-and-trade scheme.[127]

New Zealand ETS
While the US situation has been characterised by difficulties in getting an ETS in place at all, New Zealand has had an ETS for some time. New Zealand was an 'early mover' in introducing an ETS, which commenced in 2008.[128] Adoption of the ETS in New Zealand was predicated upon a general political consensus that an ETS should be a fundamental part of the policy mix for addressing climate change. That position has fractured over time, with a lessening of support for the ETS by recent governments. A unique feature of the New Zealand ETS is the absence of a cap: there is no limit on the number of permits that can be allocated. Despite this anomaly and the potentially adverse consequences it may have in deterring other jurisdictions from linking their schemes, the 2011 Review of the ETS merely recommended that the next review panel consider 'potential introduction' of an allocation cap.[129]

The New Zealand scheme, although implemented in stages, does have a relatively broad sectoral coverage in its design, encompassing forestry, stationary energy (including coal mining), transport fuels, electricity production, industrial processes, synthetic gases, waste and agriculture.[130] The reporting obligations and surrender obligations commence at different times, depending on the sector. For example, participants in the agriculture sector will not need to surrender units until the period commencing 1 January 2015.[131] While dispute continues over the entry points for various economic sectors, and over the length of transitional phases for some industries, so far the ETS has survived as a largely economy-wide scheme regulating a wide spectrum of GHG emissions, with links to the international emissions trading market. The ETS remains the principal policy response in New Zealand, although a range of energy efficiency and sustainability measures have also been instituted.[132]

In 2009, amendments were introduced into the New Zealand ETS by the *Climate Change Response (Moderated Emissions Trading) Amendment Act 2009* in order to

---

[126] California Environmental Protection Agency, Air Resources Board, 'Supplement to the AB 32 Scoping Plan Functional Equivalent Document', 13 June 2011.
[127] *Association of Irritated Residents, et al. v California Air Resources Board, et al.*, San Francisco Superior Court, Case Number CPF-09–509562, December 6, 2011.
[128] *Climate Change Response Act 2002* (NZ).
[129] New Zealand Ministry for the Environment, Emissions Trading Scheme Review Panel, *Doing New Zealand's Fair Share: Emissions Trading Scheme Review 2011: Final Report* (2011), p. 43.
[130] *Climate Change Response Act 2002* (NZ), Schedule 3. [131] Ibid.
[132] Government of New Zealand, 'Other Government Policies and Measures', last updated 25 May 2011, <http://www.climatechange.govt.nz/reducing-our-emissions/government-policies.html>.

mirror more closely the permit allocation provisions being proposed at the time in Australia under the Carbon Pollution Reduction Scheme. In particular, the amendments sought to avoid adverse effects on New Zealand industry caused by the introduction of the Australian scheme. The amendments removed the limit on the number of emission units that can be allocated to participants engaging in an eligible activity that passes an emission-intensity or trade exposure test. As the industry compensation arrangements in the new Australian carbon pricing legislation echo those of the CPRS, the arrangements in the New Zealand market are likely to remain in place.

The New Zealand climate change regulatory context is atypical in many ways. While New Zealand committed to emission reductions contained in the Kyoto Protocol, much of the power generation in the country already comes from renewable energy sources, such as wind and geothermal. Accordingly, there has not been the same need for deep structural change as in many other developed countries with economies based heavily on fossil fuels. The New Zealand ETS has thus not met with the entrenched resistance of the energy and power sectors that has been evident in jurisdictions such as the United States and Australia. Indeed, unlike many other Annex I countries, a substantial proportion of GHG emissions in New Zealand is derived from agriculture. It is this sector that has proven difficult to integrate into the ETS framework.[133]

Voluntary carbon markets

In addition to mandatory ETS, a number of voluntary carbon markets have emerged through which individuals, businesses and other organisations purchase carbon credits to offset emissions directly from their activities. They do this voluntarily, rather than for legal compliance purposes.[134] This distinction goes to the heart of the differences between compliance-based ETS and voluntary offset schemes, as there are no mandatory caps and associated sanctions for non-compliance under voluntary schemes.

While the volume of trade in the voluntary carbon markets is relatively small (representing less than 0.3 per cent of the total global carbon market), it is nonetheless increasing.[135] Examples of voluntary carbon markets include the Chicago Climate Exchange,[136] the Japanese voluntary emissions trading

---

[133] Emissions Trading Scheme Review Panel, *Doing New Zealand's Fair Share: Emissions Trading Scheme Review 2011*, p. 46.
[134] L. Moore, 'Voluntary Carbon Offsets: a Legal Perspective', in *Climate Change Law: Comparative, Contractual and Regulatory Considerations*, eds W. Gumley and T. Daya-Winterbottom (Lawbook Company, 2009), p. 159; J. Lin and C. Streck, 'Mobilising Finance for Climate Change Mitigation: Private Sector Involvement in International Carbon Finance Mechanism', 10 *Melbourne Journal of International Law* 70 (2009).
[135] N. Linacre, A. Kossoy and P. Ambrosi, *State and Trends of the Carbon Market 2011*, World Bank, <http://siteresources.worldbank.org/INTCARBONFINANCE/Resources/State_and_Trends_Updated_June_2011.pdf>, p. 54.
[136] Chicago Climate Exchange, 'Fact Sheet', June 2011, <https://www.theice.com/publicdocs/ccx/CCX_Fact_Sheet.pdf>. Although trading operations were wound up at the end of 2010, the Exchange has launched a new Offsets Registry Program.

scheme,[137] and voluntary environmental exchanges operating in China, the principal ones being the China Beijing Environmental Exchange (CBEEX), the Tianjin Climate Exchange and the Shanghai Environment Energy Exchange.[138]

Carbon pricing in Australia

Although the international multilateral process no longer gives a clear direction on regulatory frameworks, and the emerging global carbon market is at best a fragmented one, most commentators still assert that it is necessary to adopt some form of economic instrument as the primary response to climate change at a national level. Issues of carbon leakage and competitive disincentives for 'early movers' have not proved insurmountable barriers to adoption of these strategies.[139] Policy-makers seem wedded to the notion of a primary role for economic instruments in climate regulatory frameworks, if only because so much effort has been expended already on designing rules, methodologies and compliance mechanisms to support such measures.[140] In this context, regardless of what comes out of international climate negotiations, emissions trading is likely to remain a dominant regulatory approach, albeit perhaps not in the top-down fashion initially envisaged by the Kyoto Protocol.

Given these trends, we turn to consider the Australian domestic regulatory context and the measures introduced for GHG emission reduction. We also revisit the role of the federal *National Greenhouse and Energy Reporting Act 2007* (the NGER Act), introduced in the previous chapter, which supplies the reporting infrastructure to support the imposition of emission reduction obligations. Initial attempts to introduce a national ETS in the form of the Carbon Pollution Reduction Scheme were shelved in 2010, but have been reinvigorated through legislative establishment of a carbon pricing mechanism (CPM) by the *Clean Energy Act 2011* (Cth). Of necessity, our analysis of the latter is tentative given the relative lack of experience with implementation of the mechanism.

NGER Act: Reporting by liable entities

An important precursor of the introduction of an ETS in Australia was the enactment of national emission reporting legislation in 2007: the NGER Act. This legislation was implemented by the Australian federal government as a

---

[137] R. S. Jones and B. Yoo (OECD), 'Improving the Policy Framework in Japan to Address Climate Change', OECD Economics Department Working Paper, No. 740, 4 December 2009, p. 8. See also Government of Japan, Ministry of the Environment, Office of Market Mechanisms, 'Japan's Voluntary Emissions Trading Scheme (JVETS)', May 2011, <http://www.env.go.jp/en/earth/ets/jvets1105.pdf>.
[138] Linacre et al., *States and Trends of the Carbon Market 2011*, p. 32.
[139] U. Luterbacher and P. Davis, 'Explaining Unilateral Cooperative Actions: The Case of Greenhouse Gas Regulations', 36(1) *Monash Law Review* 121 (2010), pp. 123–5.
[140] R. Garnaut, *Update Paper 6: Carbon pricing and reducing Australia's emissions, Garnaut Climate Change Review – Update 2011* (2011), <http://www.garnautreview.org.au/update-2011/update-papers/up6-key-points.html>.

baseline emission reporting platform for the potential adoption of an ETS. It relies to some extent on voluntary behaviour, as it requires self-reporting of emissions, although with relatively punitive sanctions imposed for failure to report accurately.

The NGER Act, prior to its amendment by the carbon pricing legislation, applied 'only to constitutional corporations producing greenhouse gases, consuming energy, or producing energy over the thresholds specified in the Act from facilities over which the corporate group has operational control'.[141] Rather confusingly, 'facility' is defined as an activity and should not be understood as being restricted to a physical installation.[142] Entities that hold NGER reporting obligations are required to report scope 1 emissions (direct GHG emissions) and scope 2 emissions (indirect GHG emissions resulting from electricity and energy consumption).[143] Scope 3 emissions, which are indirect emissions resulting from downstream consumption of the corporation's products, are excluded. This is significant, as it excludes coal mines and other fossil fuel producers from liability where their products are exported overseas.[144] Both the CPRS and the new carbon pricing mechanism built on the NGER Act framework for their carbon pricing schemes.

In order to harness the NGER reporting framework and experience for the purposes of the CPM, a number of amendments were made to the NGER Act with effect from 1 July 2012.[145] The amendments extend the reporting obligations beyond constitutional corporations.[146] They also separate the reporting obligations in relation to scope 1 emissions and scope 2 emissions.[147] The reasons for these amendments lie in the way the *Clean Energy Act 2011* defines liable entities by reference to the NGER Act. Under the *Clean Energy Act 2011*, liable entities are persons in operational control of a facility that produces 'covered emissions' with CO_2 equivalence in excess of 25 000 tonnes per year.[148] An individual, trust (a trustee or trust estate), body corporate, body politic (the Commonwealth government or a state or territory government) and a local government are all defined as 'persons' for the purposes of the Act.[149] 'Covered emissions' are scope 1 direct emissions released in Australia, for which there is an accounting methodology prescribed under the NGER Act,[150] subject to certain exclusions.[151] This means that some emitters that

---

[141] In his article canvassing the relationship between the NGER Act and the CPRS Chris McGrath provides a detailed account of these key terms: 'Australia's Draft Climate Laws', 26 *Environmental and Planning Law Journal* 267 (2009), p. 272.
[142] NGER Act s 9; see also *National Greenhouse and Energy Reporting Regulations 2008* (Cth) Div 2.4 regs 2.14–2.23.
[143] *National Greenhouse and Energy Reporting Regulations 2008* (Cth) reg 2.23.
[144] See C. McGrath, 'Regulating Greenhouse Gases from Australian Coal Mines', 25 *Environmental and Planning Law Journal* 240 (2008), pp. 257–9.
[145] *Clean Energy (Consequential Amendments) Act 2011* s 2. At the time of writing the amendments had not yet been incorporated into the NGER Act and as such reference is made to the *Consequential Amendments Act 2011*.
[146] See for example *Clean Energy (Consequential Amendments) Act 2011* ss 308, 340.
[147] *Clean Energy (Consequential Amendments) Act 2011* ss 282, 334, amending NGER Act s 10(1).
[148] *Clean Energy Act 2011* s 20(4).   [149] *Clean Energy Act 2011* s 5.   [150] *Clean Energy Act 2011* s 30.
[151] *Clean Energy Act 2011* ss 30(2)–30(12). These are largely designed to prevent coverage of the CPM extending to agricultural emissions.

previously had no reporting obligations under the NGER Act but qualify as liable entities for the purposes of the CPM are, as a result of the amendments, required to register under the NGER Act[152] and report their scope 1 emissions.[153] Unlike corporations registered under the NGER Act, however, they are not required to report their scope 2 emissions, energy consumption or energy production.[154] Consistently with the exclusion under the NGER Act of reporting obligations for scope 3 emissions, the *Clean Energy Act 2011* expressly specifies that emissions covered by the CPM are only those emissions that are released in Australia.[155]

The carbon price legislative package vests administration responsibilities and powers for the NGER Act in the Clean Energy Regulator, the statutory body responsible for the overall administration of the CPM.[156] The report on scope 1 emissions submitted by liable entities to the Clean Energy Regulator forms the basis for assessing whether they have discharged their CPM obligations, that is, whether they have surrendered a sufficient number of units to cover their emissions for the year.

Carbon Pollution Reduction Scheme

Following the 2008 Garnaut Review and an Australian federal government Green Paper and White Paper policy process, a package of draft federal legislation was unveiled in March 2009.[157] The draft legislation encapsulated actions to reduce GHG emissions to between 5 per cent and 15 per cent below 2000 levels by 2020. The moribund draft legislation for a CPRS was relatively comprehensive, although it did not include agriculture in the first instance, and the forestry sector was only included on an 'opt in' basis.

At the core of this proposed cap-and-trade scheme was its definition of 'liable entities'. A liable entity was defined as an entity with operational control of a facility producing direct emissions of CO_2 eq. of 25 000 tonnes or more per annum, with some variation in emission thresholds for certain facilities such as landfill and waste.[158] In defining liability, the CPRS legislation employed similar concepts to those used under the NGER Act, but like the CPM, imposed liability in a substantially different way by extending liability beyond constitutional corporations and excluding scope 2 emissions. As is the case under the CPM, liability under the CPRS was to be imposed where direct emissions from a single facility exceeded a certain threshold, rather than, as is the case under the NGER Act, for the cumulative emissions of all facilities in the control of a corporate group.[159]

---

152 *Clean Energy (Consequential Amendments) Act 2011* s 352 inserting new s 15A into the NGER Act.
153 *Clean Energy (Consequential Amendments) Act 2011* s 367 inserting new Part 3A into the NGER Act.
154 The reporting obligations for 'registered corporations' are contained in the NGER Act s 19(1).
155 *Clean Energy Act 2011* s 30.
156 *Clean Energy (Consequential Amendments) Act 2011* s 353; *Clean Energy Regulator Act 2011*.
157 For details of the bills see Chapter 4.
158 For a comprehensive discussion of the CPRS and its application see McGrath, 'Australia's Draft Climate Laws' (2009).
159 Ibid., p. 280.

National Scheme Caps under the CPRS were to be set at five-year intervals with the total number of tradable permits, known as Australian Emission Units (AEUs), based on an annual cap. To discharge obligations, designated liable entities were to acquire 'eligible emission units'. At first, the cap was to include both auctioned and free allocations, but it was anticipated that the majority of AEUs ultimately would be sold at auction.[160] In addition to the advance cap-setting provisions, the CPRS provided for regulations to specify gateways: an upper and lower limit within which future caps had to be set.[161] This restriction was designed to provide businesses with certainty about their future obligations.[162]

Despite its fairly comprehensive coverage of emissions, industry sectors, and scope for international links, the scheme contained design weaknesses. Specific concessions in the form of free permits and direct financial assistance were made to emission-intensive businesses, such as aluminium smelters and coal-fired electricity generators. Perhaps most telling of all, the cap-and-trade scheme contained weak mid-term targets for national emission reductions. The Greens party cited the weakness of the scheme's 2020 target as the reason for the party's opposition to the CPRS legislation in the Senate.[163]

National Carbon Pricing Mechanism

The CPRS proved to be highly contentious in the political arena and it stalled in its passage through the Australian federal parliament. The minority Labor government that subsequently assumed office remained committed to pursuing 'a price on carbon', although it was not initially clear how this price was to be implemented. As discussed in the previous chapter, a Multi-Party Climate Change Committee (MPCCC) was formed on 27 September 2010 following the federal election, as part of an agreement between the federal government and the Greens party to explore options for the implementation of a carbon price. Four independent experts advised the panel (Ross Garnaut, Will Steffen, Rod Sims and Patricia Faulkner). Professor Garnaut was also commissioned to undertake an update of his 2008 Review.

The 2011 Garnaut Review proposed a hybrid carbon pricing model, consisting of a fixed-price period and then a transition to a full ETS, which has formed the basis for the government's scheme.[164] This model is designed to produce stability in the early years (2012–15) as industry, business and regulatory institutions become familiar with the carbon pricing mechanism and its operation. On 1 July 2015 the trading component will be introduced, 'allowing emission reductions to take place where they are cheapest'.[165] The legislation giving effect to the CPM was passed in

---

[160] I. Millar and P. Curnow, 'Is Carbon Still Relevant? Pricing Carbon in a Post-CPRS Australia', paper presented at AMPLA Conference, 20–23 October 2010, p. 3.
[161] Carbon Pollution Reduction Scheme Bill 2011 cl 15.
[162] Department of Climate Change and Energy Efficiency, 'Carbon Pollution Reduction Scheme – Design Features', last updated 10 July 2011, <http://climatechange.gov.au/government/reduce/carbon-pricing/cprs-overview.aspx>.
[163] See Chapter 4.   [164] See Garnaut, *Garnaut Review 2011* (2011).
[165] Garnaut, *Update Paper 6: Carbon pricing and reducing Australia's emissions,* Garnaut Cimate Change Review – Update 2011 (2011), p. 17.

the Senate in November 2011 after months of intense negotiations among the members of the MPCCC and a long period of political wrangling between the Government and the Opposition.[166]

In many of its features, the CPM bears close similarity to the CPRS. This is particularly the case in terms of the coverage of the scheme and the industry assistance measures. In other respects, however, the negotiations of the MPCCC produced a markedly different carbon pricing regime. Most notable was the omission of the 5 per cent mid-term target (a sticking point with the Greens) and inclusion instead of a higher long-term 2050 target of 80 per cent in the objects provision of the legislation.[167] Other key differences include the institutional architecture of the scheme, the nature of the cap-setting process, and the governance and review measures.[168]

Coverage of the CPM

The CPM covers 60 per cent of Australia's emissions and imposes obligations on approximately 300 emitters, known as liable entities. These entities are liable to surrender emission allowance units commensurate with their 'covered emissions', that is, those GHGs[169] released into the atmosphere in Australia as a direct result of the operation of the entity's facility.[170] Sectors of the economy that have obligations under the CPM include stationary energy, waste, industrial processes, and extractive operations that result in fugitive emissions.[171] Some parts of the transport sector will be covered, namely domestic aviation, domestic shipping and rail transport. Emissions from cars are expressly excluded,[172] although the government has proposed other measures to address emissions from heavy on-road vehicles.[173] Also excluded are emissions from legacy landfill waste (waste accepted by the facility before 1 July 2012).[174]

While emissions from the agricultural sector constituted 15.5 per cent of Australia's total emissions in 2009,[175] they are specifically excluded from the CPM.[176] These emissions will be partly regulated under a new scheme called the Carbon Farming Initiative (CFI), discussed in Chapter 10. Emissions of other GHGs which are also ozone-depleting substances, namely hydrofluorocarbons, sulphur hexafluorides and perfluorocarbons, will be subject to an 'equivalent

---

166 The Clean Energy legislative package comprised 18 bills, principally the *Clean Energy Act 2011* (Cth).
167 *Clean Energy Act 2011* (Cth) s 3(c).
168 See further L. Caripis, J. Peel, L. Godden and R. Keenan, 'Australia's Carbon Pricing Mechanism', 2 *Climate Law* 583 (2011).
169 'Greenhouse gas' is defined by reference to the NGER Act s 7, and therefore includes carbon dioxide, methane, nitrous oxide, sulphur hexafluoride, hydrofluorocarbons specified in the regulations, and perfluorocarbons specified in the regulations: *Clean Energy Act 2011* s 5.
170 Explanatory Memorandum, Clean Energy Bill 2011, pp. 11 and 33; *Clean Energy Act 2011* s 14.
171 Explanatory Memorandum, Clean Energy Bill 2011, p. 29.
172 *Clean Energy Act 2011* ss 30(1) and 30(2).
173 See Chapter 9 for a discussion of proposed transport measures.
174 *Clean Energy Act 2011* ss 30(9)–30(10).
175 Department of Climate Change and Energy Efficiency, *Australia's National Greenhouse Gas Accounts: State and Territory Greenhouse Gas Inventories 2009* (2011), p. 8.
176 *Clean Energy Act 2011* ss 30(4) and 30(6).

carbon price' imposed under amendments to the *Ozone Protection and Synthetic Greenhouse Gas Management Act 1989*.[177]

Setting the carbon pollution cap

The critical aspect of any cap-and-trade ETS is the cap – the amount of emissions permissible in any given period – and by extension, the limit on the number of units that are to circulate in the market. The CPM introduces a new institutional actor, the independent Climate Change Authority (CCA), to oversee the cap-setting process (see Box 5.3). The CCA is tasked with advising the responsible Minister

---

BOX 5.3 Institutional infrastructure: The Climate Change Authority

A significant design feature of the CPM is its provision for independent bodies that form part of the institutional infrastructure of the scheme. In addition to the Clean Energy Regulator, which has overall responsibility for administration of the CPM, there is the Climate Change Authority (CCA), a statutory body established by the *Climate Change Authority Act 2011*. Largely modelled on the United Kingdom's Committee on Climate Change, the CCA is responsible for conducting a range of reviews, including reviewing and recommending the level of the annual pollution caps and related emission trajectories and carbon budgets, reviewing progress towards achieving reduction targets and carbon budgets, and conducting reviews of the overall CPM. The CPRS did not provide for an independent expert body with these functions.

To provide a coordinated and coherent approach to Australia's climate change policy, the CCA will also be responsible for reviewing other established federal climate change measures, such as the Renewable Energy Target, the NGER Act, and the CFI. The reports containing the CCA's reviews and recommendations must be tabled in the federal parliament, and the government is required to table a response.

In performing its functions, the CCA must have regard to certain principles, including that the carbon pricing measures are environmentally effective (that is, informed by science and having scientific integrity); equitable (which includes considering intergenerational equity when assessing the fairness of the cost burden); in the public interest; and supportive of global efforts to tackle climate change. There is also scope for public participation in the process, with obligations on the CCA to consult with the public when conducting its reviews. Emphasis is also given to the international climate change regime, with the CCA specifically obliged to consider Australia's international obligations and undertakings under international climate change agreements, its medium-term (2020) and long-term (2050) emission reduction targets, and its progress towards meeting these targets when making recommendations on the cap.

The CCA is to be established as a body corporate, consisting of nine members appointed by the Minister. These comprise the Chairperson, the Chief Scientist, and seven other members, each of whom must have 'substantial experience or knowledge and significant standing' in at least one of the following fields: climate science, economics, climate change mitigation, emissions trading, environmental and land resource management, investment and business (s 18). The independence of the CCA is provided for by the limited grounds on which its members may be dismissed, and the requirement that any directions it is given by the Minister must be general in nature and not in relation to the conduct or contents of the CCA's review reports. Furthermore, these directions must be tabled in the federal parliament, to make the process transparent.

CCA members are required to disclose to the Minister any interests they have that may conflict with the performance of their functions. They are also obliged to disclose their interests in matters under consideration by the CCA and to abstain from meetings considering such matters.

---

177 *Ozone Protection and Synthetic Greenhouse Gas (Manufacture Levy) Act 2011*; *Ozone Protection and Synthetic Greenhouse Gas (Import Levy) Act 2011*; Explanatory Memorandum, Clean Energy Bill 2011, para. 1.40.

on a level of the cap that would enable Australia to meet its international obligations and achieve the objects of the Act.[178] The Minister must table the CCA's report in the federal parliament, as well as the government's response to the CCA's recommendations.[179] In this way, the Act provides some measure of transparency to the cap-setting process and assurance that the cap set by the Minister will reflect sound policy. In any event, it is anticipated that the government will generally follow the Authority's recommendations as the politically easier course of action.[180]

As the cap is ultimately set by disallowable regulations, it is conceivable that the federal parliament could reject the regulations by which it is implemented and leave the scheme without a cap. The CPM contains a safeguard in the form of a legislatively enshrined default cap to ensure that such a scenario is not capable of jeopardising the ETS. The level of the default cap is in line with achieving the 5 per cent emission reduction target by 2020.[181]

As was the case under the CPRS, the caps will be set five years in advance to create certainty for liable entities about their future obligations, allowing them to make investment decisions more confidently. Consequently, the cap for the first five years of the ETS, which commences on 1 July 2015, will be set during the fixed charge period.[182] Unlike the CPRS, however, the legislative scheme does not provide for 'gateways' to constrain the level at which the cap can be set by prescribing an upper and lower limit. Despite the submissions of some affected entities calling for amendments to provide for an 'upper bound',[183] the removal of the gateways mechanism better enables future governments to respond to scientific and international diplomatic breakthroughs and developments when setting the cap.

Operation of the Carbon Pricing Mechanism

The key unit under the CPM is the carbon unit, which is designated as a form of personal property.[184] Like the Australian Emission Unit under the CPRS, this unit represents 1 tonne of CO_2 eq.[185] A unit price of A$23 per tonne in the first year of

---

178 *Clean Energy Act 2011* s 289. The objects of the Act are set out in s 3. They are (a) to give effect to Australia's obligations under the UNFCCC and Kyoto Protocol; (b) to support the development of an effective global response to climate change, consistent with Australia's national interest in ensuring that average global temperatures increase by not more than 2 degrees Celsius above pre-industrial levels; (c) to take action, directed towards meeting Australia's long-term target of reducing Australia's net GHG emissions to 80 per cent below 2000 levels by 2050, in 'a flexible and cost-effective way'; (d) to put a price on GHG emissions in a way that encourages investment in clean energy, supports jobs and competitiveness in the economy and 'supports Australia's economic growth while reducing pollution'. The last objective has overtones of the concept of 'ecologically sustainable development' central to environmental law. See Chapter 4.
179 *Clean Energy Act 2011* s 292(2).
180 Frank Jotzo, 'Against the Odds, a Nation Warms to a Policy', *The Age* (Melbourne), 11 July 2011, <http://www.theage.com.au/opinion/contributors/against-the-odds-a-nation-warms-to-a-policy-20110710-1h8w5.html>.
181 *Clean Energy Act 2011* ss 17–18.   **182** *Clean Energy Act 2011* s 16(1).
183 See for example AGL, Submission to the Department of Climate Change and Energy Efficiency on the Clean Energy Legislative Package, <http://www.aglblog.com.au/2011/08/agls-submission-on-the-draft-clean-energy-legislative-package/>, p. 3.
184 *Clean Energy Act 2011* s 103. This has ramifications if any buyback or government acquisition of such units is later desired. See Chapter 4.
185 Explanatory Memorandum, Clean Energy Bill 2011, p. 30.

the fixed charge period (2012–13), increasing in the two subsequent years to A$25.50 in the final year (2014–15), is enshrined in the Act.[186] During the fixed price period, liable entities are required to acquire units at the fixed charge rate and surrender sufficient units to cover their emissions for that year. They will be unable to trade surplus units in the event that they make greater emission reductions than anticipated, but may sell back their excess units to the Clean Energy Regulator, for a discounted price.[187] Once the full transition to an ETS has taken place and units are tradable, units will be auctioned by the Clean Energy Regulator and the price of the units will ultimately be set by the market.[188]

For the first three years of the flexible charge period, cost containment measures are in place in the form of a temporary price floor and price ceiling to ensure that the price of units does not fluctuate wildly.[189] Avoiding violent fluctuations is imperative, to aid investor confidence in low-emission technologies and to ensure that the cornerstone of the ETS, the carbon unit, is not undermined by a price drop, as was experienced in the EU ETS.[190] The literature is divided on the utility of these 'interventions' in the market,[191] but their inclusion in the CPM is temporary and subject to review by the CCA.

Another relevant aspect of the operation of the carbon market established by the scheme is the degree to which banking and borrowing of units is permitted. These features are designed to enhance compliance flexibility for liable entities and thereby reduce the costs of the CPM. It is only under the ETS phase (from 1 July 2015) that unit banking and borrowing is possible. Liable entities may retain or 'bank' their carbon units indefinitely, provided they have met their obligations. This enables them to 'store up' their units for surrender or trading in later years. Conversely, no more than 5 per cent of an entity's total liability may be discharged by surrendering units borrowed from the next year.[192]

Offsets for compliance flexibility

Access to overseas credits and markets will be a critical part of the CPM;[193] however, the scheme is designed to ensure that the domestic market is not flooded by cheap international offsets. Significantly, liable entities cannot surrender international offsets in the initial, fixed-price phase of the scheme. In the flexible phase

---

186 *Clean Energy Act 2011* s 100.   **187** *Clean Energy Act 2011* s 116.
188 *Clean Energy Act 2011* s 111.
189 Specifically, there will be a price floor of A$15, rising by 4 per cent per year and a price ceiling of A$20 above the expected international unit price for 2015–16, which will rise by 5 per cent in real terms each year: Explanatory Memorandum, Clean Energy Bill 2011, pp. 123 and 129.
190 D. Ellerman and P. Joskow (Massachusetts Institute of Technology), 'The European Union's Emissions Trading Scheme in Perspective', Report prepared for Pew Centre on Global Climate Change (USA), May 2008, p. 13.
191 Garnaut, *Garnaut Climate Change Review* (2008), p. 310; F. Jotzo, 'A price floor for Australia's emissions trading scheme?', Commissioned paper for the Multi-Party Committee on Climate Change, 17 May 2011, p. 6; and California Environmental Protection Agency, Air Resources Board, ISOR, Appendix E 13–16, <http://www.arb.ca.gov/regact/2010/capandtrade10/capv3appe.pdf>.
192 *Clean Energy Act* 2011 s 133(6)(b).
193 According to federal Treasury modelling, two-thirds of the abatement needed to reach the 5 per cent bipartisan emission reduction target by 2020 will be sourced from overseas abatement activities; in other words, it will not occur in Australia: *Strong Growth, Low Pollution: Modelling a Carbon Price* (2011), para. [5.2.1].

(ETS), only offsets meeting specified criteria concerning their quality are permitted, and during the first five years of the ETS, entities are allowed to use international units to cover only 50 per cent of their emissions.[194] This is a marked improvement over the CPRS, which would have enabled 100 per cent of a liable entity's liability to be discharged with international credits,[195] meaning that liable entities could have avoided reducing their domestic emissions entirely.

The legislation prohibits the use of a number of specified international units in an attempt to uphold the environmental integrity of the scheme,[196] and includes provision to prohibit additional types of units.[197] Despite the quantitative and qualitative limits, the mechanism permits the importation and use of a substantial number of units generated from schemes such as the CDM. The actual reductions that these units are meant to represent have been questioned,[198] and indeed the issue was a key reason for Garnaut's recommendation that there be a limit on the number of such offsets that could be imported into the scheme.[199] For this reason, the CPM has attracted some criticism.

The situation with regard to domestic offsets is different. The federal government appears to be encouraging the use of these, and consequently, liable entities may use units generated under the CFI – that is, units generated for activities that store or reduce carbon in the land sector in Australia – to discharge their liability in the flexible price phase without restriction.[200] In light of Treasury modelling forecasting a strong reliance on cheaper international units under the CPM,[201] the Durban COP decision to extend the Kyoto Protocol to a second commitment period finishing either at the end of 2017 or 2020, to enable the continued generation of Certified Emission Reduction units under the CDM,[202] was a decision critical to the success of the CPM. Australian officials also used the COP as an opportunity to formalise negotiations with their New Zealand and European Union counterparts by establishing working groups to develop mechanisms for linking their respective domestic carbon markets.[203]

---

194 *Clean Energy Act 2011* s 133(7).
195 Department of Climate Change and Energy Efficiency, 'Carbon Pollution Reduction Scheme: Overview and Design Features', <http://climatechange.gov.au/government/reduce/carbon-pricing/cprs-overview.aspx>.
196 An 'eligible international emissions unit' is defined in s 4 of the *Australian National Registry of Emissions Units Act 2011* (Cth). Certified emissions reductions (CERs) from CDM activities are included, other than temporary or long-term CERs. On the CDM mechanism and types of CERs, see Chapter 6.
197 *Clean Energy Act 2011* s 123.   **198** See Chapter 6.
199 Garnaut, *Garnaut Climate Change Review* (2008), pp. 340–1. The Minister has the power to proscribe the use of certain international units under s 123 of the *Clean Energy Act 2011* (Cth).
200 Explanatory Memorandum, Clean Energy Bill 2011, p. 152. No more than 5 per cent of an entity's liability may be discharged using units generated under the CFI during the fixed price period: *Clean Energy Act 2011* ss 125(7), 128(7)–(9).
201 *Strong Growth, Low Pollution: Modelling a Carbon Price*, para. 5.2.1.
202 Kyoto Protocol, *Decision 1/CPM.7, Outcome of the work of the Ad Hoc Working Group on Further Commitments for Annex I Parties under the Kyoto Protocol at its sixteenth session* (2011), FCCC/KP/CMP/2011/10/Add.1.
203 G. Combet, Minister for Climate Change and Energy Efficiency, 'Australia and New Zealand advance linking of their emissions trading schemes' (Media Release, GC 333/115, December 2011), <http://www.climatechange.gov.au/minister/greg-combet/2011/media-releases/December/mr20111205b.aspx>; and G. Combet, Minister for Climate Change and Energy Efficiency, C. Hedegaard, European Commissioner for Climate Action, 'Australia and Europe strengthen collaboration on carbon markets' (Joint Media Release, GC 334/11, 5 December 2011), <http://www.climatechange.gov.au/minister/greg-combet/2011/media-releases/December/20111205a.aspx>.

Assistance measures

The industry assistance provided under the CPM does not depart significantly from the assistance package developed under the CPRS. The federal government has justified the assistance measures as necessary to protect jobs, competitiveness and energy security.[204] Accordingly, entities engaged in emission-intensive, trade-exposed (EITE) activities, along with electricity generators emitting high levels of pollution, are allocated assistance in the form of free permits, which are largely calculated in the same way as under the CPRS.[205]

The assistance for EITE activities under the 'Jobs and Competitiveness Program' will be progressively wound back but is formulated so as to reduce the emission intensity of operations, rather than their absolute emissions.[206] This means emissions (and assistance) may increase under the program. One major difference from the CPRS is the involvement of the Productivity Commission, which has been given the task of reviewing the assistance measures for EITE activities by 2014–15.[207] Among other things, the Productivity Commission must consider whether adopting Garnaut's 'principled' approach would be more economically efficient than the current basis for unit allocation.[208] The assistance for coal-fired electricity generators, however, is not subject to review. Moreover, the obligations on generators receiving assistance are easily satisfied, and the CPM does not impose an obligation to reduce emissions at all.[209]

The government has also introduced some additional assistance measures, which did not form part of the MPCCC agreement.[210] While the assistance to industry remains on the whole very similar to that under the CPRS, the household assistance measures take a different shape. The federal government has claimed that nine out of ten households will receive some level of assistance through changes to the tax system, namely an increase in the tax-free threshold, adjustment to the marginal tax rates, and an increase in the pension and Family Tax Benefit.[211]

Assessment

The CPM can be regarded as a hybrid scheme that recognises the difficulties in instituting a full-blown ETS at the outset. The proposed short-term, fixed price model reflects the realisation in policy circles that, in the absence of a robust international agreement for carbon trading, it is best to begin to effect a transition to a low-carbon domestic economy by way of these simpler, more workable

---

204 Explanatory Memorandum, Clean Energy Bill 2011, pp. 15–16.
205 *Clean Energy Act 2011* Parts 7 and 8.
206 *Clean Energy Regulations 2011* cl 907(4). Regulations Commentary, para. 171.
207 *Clean Energy Act 2011* Part 7, Div. 5.
208 *Clean Energy Act 2011* ss 156(2)(e) and 156(4). See Garnaut, *Garnaut Climate Change Review* (2008), pp. 344–9.
209 *Clean Energy Act 2011* ss 177–180. See also Caripis et al., 'Australia's Carbon Pricing Mechanism' (2011), p. 601.
210 These include the Steel Transformation Plan, the Coal Sector Jobs Package, and the Coal Mining Abatement Technology Support Package. See Department of Climate Change and Energy Efficiency, *Securing a Clean Energy Future* (2011), Appendix D, p. 133.
211 Ibid., pp. 11 and 113–14.

schemes. This marks a departure from the earlier policy preference for a complex scheme that adhered more strictly to neoclassical economic theory in the development of cap-and-trade design features. It also provides an apt illustration of the constraints of political context, discussed earlier in the chapter, which influence the choice of regulatory instrument and its design.

On the whole, the CPM promises to be an important first step in Australia's climate change mitigation policy. Its shortcomings stem from a desire to placate domestic interests while attempting to achieve at times contradictory international objectives – a challenge arguably faced by all developed countries. Moreover, the difficulty experienced in attempting to implement an ETS within Australia has highlighted the need for a sophisticated, integrated legal and governance regime to accompany the market mechanisms.[212] There is growing recognition that the complexities of climate change are unlikely to be amenable to regulation through any *one* regulatory tool, suggesting that a mix of regulatory tools, or at least coordination between market measures and other regulatory initiatives, may be necessary. Thus, in addition to reducing emissions in sectors covered by an ETS, much can also be done through regulation and standards, taxation arrangements, and resource pricing to improve efficiencies in the use of energy in commercial and residential buildings, motor vehicles, and energy generation. In Australia, this lesson seems to have been learned with the current CPM in the sense that the *Clean Energy Act 2011* forms part of a package of economic instruments, governance and institutional arrangements, and incentive mechanisms, rather than existing as a stand-alone ETS.

Conclusion

Although the international impetus for a global ETS has been weakened by the lack of multilateral agreement about future emission reduction commitments, and the initial justifications for the adoption of economic measures seem less compelling, such instruments continue to be highly influential with respect to the policy and legal choices made within many jurisdictions. The need to implement effective measures at a national or sub-national level seems even more urgent as scientific evidence suggests emissions are reaching record highs.

This chapter has canvassed the underlying theory and policy rationale for the adoption of economic instruments in the climate regulatory sphere, noting their foundation in broader governance trends. It has provided a comparative examination of the design and implementation of key ETS to highlight common features across schemes and also jurisdiction-specific aspects that influence the nature and operation of various instruments. ETS are complex, relatively new forms of regulation and 'teething problems' are to be expected. While putting a price on carbon remains the core of mitigation

---

[212] Durrant, *Legal Responses to Climate Change* (2010), pp. 3 and 102–3.

responses to climate change, there are now calls to implement a wide spectrum of regulatory approaches in order to accomplish the transition to a low-carbon economy. Later chapters address those approaches, along with the challenges of adapting to climate change.

Within Australia, neoclassical economic theory has been an important influence on the adoption of an ETS as the preferred legal and policy position. Theory, however, has been bolstered by serious practical considerations concerning the need to harmonise Australia's emission reduction efforts with those of the global community. The CPRS predicated on efficiency paradigms proved to be difficult to implement and ultimately flawed in some of its design features, despite considerable merit in its comprehensive coverage. Further, it represented the first concerted national approach to climate change mitigation. It is clear that Australia must act decisively, and the recently enacted carbon price mechanism may represent a compromise position that eventually will see Australia taking strong action on climate change mitigation.

6

The regulatory network of the Clean Development Mechanism

Introduction: Offsets under the Kyoto Protocol   *page* 199
A case study in CDM practice and principle   203
Persisting concerns about the CDM's environmental integrity   220
The CDM's performance on sustainable development   222
CDM project distribution and equity of access   224
Administrative review of CDM Executive Board decisions   225
What future for the CDM?   227

Introduction: Offsets under the Kyoto Protocol

The Clean Development Mechanism has been referred to several times already in this book. It is a precocious institution with a serious claim to being the jewel in the crown of the climate change regime. It has also attracted a fair amount of criticism from the wing of environmentalism that does not have faith in market-based solutions to environmental problems.[1] Whatever one thinks of the CDM, it repays close study because of its conceptual richness and innovation and its diversity of application around the world.

Article 12 of the Kyoto Protocol establishes the CDM as a mechanism to enable non-Annex I parties to achieve sustainable development. In the process, the mechanism should help Annex I parties to comply with their emission reduction commitments under the Protocol. This is the order in which the CDM's benefits are presented in Article 12(2): sustainable development for developing countries first; facilitation of developed countries' compliance with emission caps second.

The history of the CDM and the international negotiations from which it resulted has been discussed by several authors.[2] We defer to them for this purpose.

---

[1] For example D. M. Driesen, 'Sustainable Development and Market Liberalism's Shotgun Wedding: Emissions Trading under the Kyoto Protocol', 83 *Indiana Law Journal* 21 (2008); and R. E. Goodin, 'Selling Environmental Indulgences', in *Climate Ethics: Essential Readings*, eds S. M. Gardiner et al. (Oxford University Press, 2010), pp. 231–46.
[2] See S. Mathy, J.-C. Hourcade and C. de Gouvello, 'Clean Development Mechanism: Leverage for Development?', 1 *Climate Policy* 251 (2001); Axel Michaelowa, 'Creating the Foundations for Host Country Participation in the CDM: Experiences and Challenges in CDM Capacity Building', in *Climate Change and Carbon Markets: A Handbook of Emission Reduction Mechanisms*, ed. F. Yamin (Earthscan, 2005), pp. 305–20; J. Ellisa et al., 'CDM: Taking Stock and Looking Forward', 35(1)*Energy Policy* 15 (2007); and the articles

Article 12 of the Protocol contains several interesting features from a legal point of view. For example:

- It creates an Executive Board under the authority of the CMP (the Conference of the Kyoto Protocol state parties) to supervise the mechanism.[3] The Executive Board is effectively the regulator of the international market for Kyoto Protocol offsets. It delegates regulatory functions to other actors, who consequently play quasi-regulatory roles.[4]
- Article 12 provides for private 'operational entities' designated by the CMP to certify emission reductions realised by CDM projects. The Kyoto Protocol differs from the traditional state-centric model of international law when it makes public and private entities subjects of the CDM, establishing international bodies that administer the Protocol mechanisms directly and enter into relationships with private entities participating in these mechanisms.[5] The relationship between treaty-based international institutions (the CMP, the Executive Board) and a private entity incorporated under the domestic law of a state raises unusual legal issues.
- The CDM procedures do not foresee any formal right of review of Executive Board decisions. Neither do they establish formal rights to hearings or an obligation of the Executive Board to substantiate its decisions.[6] The growing economic importance of the CDM has led many to call for the reviewability of Executive Board decisions under international law.

In fact, the CDM is a thicket of transnational and what might be called 'transscalar' (from the private to the international scale) legal relationships. Private or public project developers create the emission reductions; private or public entities certify them; private or public or international organisations or state sovereigns purchase the emission reduction certificates; public and international bodies oversee their accounting and cancellation, and so on. The permutations in the relationships and in the legal systems engaged by the Mechanism are significant.

The Kyoto Protocol does foresee that regulatory development will be necessary to accommodate the unusual features of the CDM. The treaty text provides that '[p]articipation under the clean development mechanism ... may involve private and/or public entities, and is to be subject to whatever guidance may be provided by the executive board of the clean development mechanism'.[7] The treaty leaves the details to be worked out by the Executive Board under the supervision of the CMP.

The Kyoto Protocol's Article 12 calls for a dedicated monitoring, reporting and verification (MRV) system for the CDM. The relevant provision sounds straightforward: the CMP is to 'elaborate modalities and procedures with

---

collected in D. Freestone and C. Streck (eds), *Legal Aspects of Implementing the Kyoto Protocol Mechanisms: Making Kyoto Work* (Oxford University Press, 2005), especially D. Freestone, 'The UN Framework Convention on Climate Change, the Kyoto Protocol, and the Kyoto Mechanisms', pp. 3–24.

3 The supervision function is detailed in Kyoto Protocol, *Decision 3/CMP.1, Modalities and Procedures for a Clean Development Mechanism as Defined in Article 12 of the Kyoto Protocol* (30 March 2006), FCCC/KP/CMP/2005/8/Add.1, paras. 2–4.

4 C. Streck and J. Lin, 'Mobilising Finance for Climate Change Mitigation: Private Sector Involvement in International Carbon Finance Mechanisms', 10(1) *Melbourne Journal of International Law* 70 (2009), p. 73.

5 Ibid., p. 79.   **6** Ibid., p. 88.   **7** Kyoto Protocol, Art. 12(9).

the objective of ensuring transparency, efficiency and accountability through independent auditing and verification of project activities'.[8] Straightforward as it may sound, as a matter of both practice and logic the MRV system for the CDM envisaged by the Protocol's drafters potentially rivals in size and complexity the UNFCCC's system for regulating state reporting of GHG emissions (discussed in Chapter 3). To understand why this is so, we need to consider the logic of the CDM, starting with that of an offset. We will then turn to the practice and complexity of maintaining oversight of CDM projects.

The CDM is a system for the creation of GHG offsets, represented by certificates that have market value. This is a key point about the CDM: because it is an offset system, it does not lead to overall emission reductions. It operates to cancel out 'excess' emissions in countries with emission caps.

In general, to create a GHG offset, all of the following conditions must be met. There must be:

(i) a proposed project, which
(ii) itself would not have been realised but for the expected proceeds from the sale of the offsets ('additionality'), and which
(iii) acts as a sink for, or destroys GHG, or creates a product or service that substitutes itself for (i.e. displaces) an existing or planned and comparatively more GHG-intensive product or service, and
(iv) the quantity of GHGs removed or avoided through the project is reasonably quantifiable.

This is not a complete list of conditions for a GHG offset but captures the main ones. The Article 12 Mechanism is known for the additional condition that the operation of the project must promote sustainable development. It is also known for its restrictions on project types, such as offsets from forestry projects,[9] carbon capture and storage,[10] and nuclear power.[11]

---

[8] Kyoto Protocol, Art. 12(7).

[9] Forestry-based CDM projects have been of narrow scope. In brief, different rules apply to Certified Emission Reductions (i.e. the CDM units) generated from the planting and growing of trees. The CDM Executive Board issues temporary rather than permanent CERs for afforestation and reforestation projects, as a precautionary measure for dealing with forest impermanence. Such offsets have special names under the CDM – *temporary CERs* (tCERs) and *long-term CERs* (lCERs) – to distinguish them from normal CERs. The temporary nature of the forestry CERs means that the Annex I buyer has to repurchase them or exchange them for permanent CERs at the end of a commitment period. See Kyoto Protocol, *Decision 5/CMP.1, Modalities and Procedures for Afforestation and Reforestation Project Activities under the Clean Development Mechanism in the First Commitment Period of the Kyoto Protocol* (30 March 2006), FCCC/KP/CMP/2005/8/Add.1. See also O. Van Vliet, A. Faaij and C. Dieperink, 'Forestry Projects under the Clean Development Mechanism?', 61 *Climatic Change* 123 (2003); and S. Scholz and I. Noble, 'Generation of Sequestration Credits under the CDM', in *Legal Aspects of Implementing the Kyoto Protocol Mechanisms: Making Kyoto Work*, eds David Freestone and Charlotte Streck (Oxford University Press, 2005), pp. 265–80. For the Kyoto Protocol's second commitment period, the total additions to a party's 'assigned amount' resulting from CDM afforestation and reforestation activities are not to exceed *1 per cent* of the base-year emissions of that party, multiplied by the duration of the commitment period in years: Kyoto Protocol, *Decision 2/CMP.7, Land Use, Land-Use Change and Forestry* (2011), para. 19.

[10] CCS projects, until recently excluded from the CDM, were given the green light in December 2011: Kyoto Protocol, *Decision 10/CMP.7, Modalities and Procedures for Carbon Dioxide Capture and Storage in Geological Formations as Clean Development Mechanism Project Activities* (2011).

[11] Nuclear power generation projects have been excluded completely from the CDM. Safety, security, and political sensitivities account for the exclusion. Half-hearted negotiations to lift the CDM's restriction on nuclear energy projects are continuing: see International Institute for Sustainable Development, 'SB 34 and AWG Highlights: Tuesday, 14 June 2011', 12(510) *Earth Negotiations Bulletin* 1 (2011), p. 2.

The listed conditions have strict and less strict formulations. For example, condition (ii) might be represented as tighter than the form in which it is stated above, for not only should it be the case that *that project* would not have been established without the expected funding from the sale of the offsets, but also that no project with a *similar effect* would have been established in the normal course of events.

The CDM's logic is thus by its nature difficult. It shares this difficulty with all offset schemes, but makes its implementation even more difficult by adding conditions and inclining towards strict formulations. Because a lot of money rides on the CDM,[12] attempts to simplify its logic or make its conditions easier to satisfy do not always, as we shall see, proceed from pure motives. We may nonetheless accept the following propositions: there is a trajectory of GHG emissions associated with a business-as-usual projection, and there also exists a different, less emission-intensive trajectory which results from adding the proposed CDM project to the original projection. The offset (or bundle of offsets made up of units of 1 tonne CO_2 eq.) is the difference between the two trajectories. To estimate the size of the offset we must therefore make two predictions about future GHG emissions: a business-as-usual prediction and a project implementation prediction. We must then subtract the emissions under one scenario from the emissions under the other. The simplified formula is:

> Emissions to be released in a given society if we change nothing (the baseline)
> *minus*
> Emissions to be released when the impact of the project is factored in
> *equals*
> Reduction in emissions due to the project.[13]

If the CDM project is truly additional (if it would not have gone ahead anyway regardless of CDM funding), the result of the above equation will be a positive number, greater than zero. This reduction in emissions is parcelled up into a tradable commodity (multiples of a certificate implying a tonne of CO_2 eq. emissions avoided) and sold to an Annex I government, or to an industry based in an Annex I country, as an emission allowance.

Predictions about emission scenarios, whether business-as-usual or project-dependent, obviously become less certain the farther they extend into the future. Thus another condition for the creation of an offset – or perhaps it is implicit in condition (iv) above – is that the two trajectories used to produce the difference in

---

12 Annual investment in registered CDM projects rose from US$40 million in 2004 to US$47 *billion* in 2010 and totalled over US$140 billion as at mid-2011. The average investment per project is approximately US$45 million: Clean Development Mechanism (Kyoto Protocol), *Benefits of the Clean Development Mechanism* (UNFCCC, 2011), p. 6.

13 Cf. 'The baseline for a CDM project activity is the scenario that reasonably represents the anthropogenic emissions by sources of greenhouse gases that would occur in the absence of the proposed project activity' and 'CERs resulting from a CDM project activity during a specified time period shall be calculated ... by subtracting the actual anthropogenic emissions by sources from baseline emissions and adjusting for leakage': Kyoto Protocol, *Decision 3/CMP.1* (30 March 2006), paras. 44 and 59.

future emissions, and so the offset, are not projected too far into the future, because the farther we project them the more likely we are to be wrong about their shape. Our margin of error will increase dramatically as reasonable expectations about policy and economic conditions are reduced to guesswork by time. Hence credible offsets are not to be found outside of short-term projections of a few years at most.

Against this preliminary analysis of the CDM we are better able to appreciate the insistence in the Kyoto Protocol that project-based emission reductions are to deliver 'real, measurable, and long-term benefits related to the mitigation of climate change' and 'are additional to any that would occur in the absence of the certified project activity'.[14] We also come to appreciate the need for a system that assesses, verifies, and monitors CDM projects (the MRV requirement in Article 12). This trans-temporal system would have to be concerned not only with past events and observed emissions (as was the case with the verification of state GHG inventories, discussed in Chapter 3), but also with emission forecasts and policy and economic counterfactuals about the future, and whether they are reasonable.

A case study in CDM practice and principle

To illustrate the basic features of the CDM at work, we will consider an actual CDM project. The name of the project is Efficient Fuel Wood Stoves for Nigeria (Nigeria Stoves). For a general view of the process considered in this case study, see Box 6.1.[15]

BOX 6.1 Simplified CDM project approval procedure

This is a simplified summary of the approval procedure for a CDM offset project, leading to registration of the project by the CDM Executive Board and the issue of Certified Emission Reductions (CERs) for sale by the project owners.

Project proposal

The project's compliance with CDM rules is assessed on the basis of the Project Design Document (PDD). The project developer prepares the PDD, making use of an approved emissions baseline-and-monitoring methodology. Non-CDM finance is usually necessary to cover the up-front costs of project development and initial implementation.

↓

---

[14] Kyoto Protocol, Art. 12(5). 'A CDM project activity is additional if anthropogenic emissions of greenhouse gases by sources are reduced below those that would have occurred in the absence of the registered CDM project activity': Kyoto Protocol, *Decision 3/CMP.1* (30 March 2006), para. 43. On additionality, see A. Michaelowa, 'Determination of Baselines and Additionality for the CDM: A Crucial Element of Credibility of the Climate Regime', in *Climate Change and Carbon Markets: A Handbook of Emission Reduction Mechanisms*, ed. F. Yamin (Earthscan, 2005), pp. 289–303.
[15] See also Kyoto Protocol, *Decision 3/CMP.1* (30 March 2006), and Clean Development Mechanism (Kyoto Protocol), *CDM Methodology Booklet* (UNFCCC, 2010), p. 11. For a diagram of the process, see UNFCCC, 'CDM Project Cycle', <http://cdm.unfccc.int/Projects/diagram.html>.

BOX 6.1 (cont.)

Validation

Validation is the independent assessment of the project's compliance with CDM rules by a Designated Operational Entity (DOE). The DOE is an independent auditor (a consultant from the private sector) approved by the CDM Executive Board. Its main objective is to safeguard against the overstatement of emission reductions.

↓

Application for registration

If the DOE determines that the requirements for a CDM project have been met, the DOE, on behalf of the project developer, requests the Executive Board to register the project.

↓

Registration

Registration by the Executive Board constitutes the formal approval of a CDM project. It is a prerequisite for the subsequent verification/certification of the project and the issue of CERs.

↓

Monitoring (ongoing)

The project developer is responsible for monitoring actual emissions (or, where there are no emissions from the project, the developer must monitor the project output that is designed to *displace* emissions elsewhere), in accordance with the monitoring requirements of the approved methodology (monitoring plan).

↓

Verification and certification (singular or periodic)

After a certain period of operation of the project, another DOE (or the same in some cases) verifies that emission reductions have taken place in the amount claimed in the monitoring plan. The DOE's verification report is followed by *certification,* which is the DOE's assurance to the CDM Executive Board that the emission reductions have been verified. The two documents are usually submitted to the DOE together.

Issue of CERs (once or periodic)

The DOE submits its verification report and certification to the Executive Board with a request for the issue of CERs. In the normal course of events, the Executive Board will issue CERs on the basis of the DOE's submission.

Adaptation Fund tax (2%)

Article 12(8) of the Kyoto Protocol provides that proceeds from CDM projects are to be used 'to assist developing country Parties that are particularly vulnerable to the adverse effects of climate change to meet the costs of adaptation'. On this basis, 2 per cent of CERs issued to a project are redirected to the Protocol's Adaptation Fund.[16]

When the CERs are received by the project developer, they are sold in the compliance markets (for example the EU ETS) or voluntary markets. The proceeds fund the ongoing operation of the project or are used to pay back the investor who covered the project's up-front operating costs.

---

[16] Kyoto Protocol, *Decision 3/CMP.1* (30 March 2006), para. 66(a). Projects in Least Developed Countries are exempt: UNFCCC, *Decision 17/CP.7, Modalities and Procedures for a Clean Development Mechanism, as Defined in Article 12 of the Kyoto Protocol* (2001), FCCC/CP/2001/13/Add.2, para. 15. In June 2011, the share of proceeds from CDM project activities for the Adaptation Fund stood at around US$13 million; see UNFCCC, 'Share of Proceeds from the Clean Development Mechanism Project Activities for the Adaptation Fund', <http://cdm.unfccc.int/Issuance/SOPByProjectsTable.html>.

Healthier living with reduced emissions

For billions of the world's poor who rely on open fires to cook their food,[17] owning an efficient, smokeless stove is primarily an issue of health improvement.[18] In addition to being a health hazard, an open fire or an inefficient home-made stove requires a greater expenditure of individual energy to collect the fuel to start the fire or stoke the stove than would be needed under more efficient arrangements. (In developed countries, turning a knob is the only effort required.) This additional energy must of course come from the consumption of additional food – in parts of the world where food is itself hard to get. Often it is the lot of children to forage for the family's fuel supply.[19] In Nigeria, where wood is widely used for cooking and heating,[20] firewood consumption has led to severe deforestation and desertification.[21] Between 1990 and 2005, the annual removal of fuel wood from Nigerian forests increased from 59.1 million cubic metres to 70.4 million cubic metres, an increase of 19 per cent.[22] (The extent of forest in Nigeria, which of course is affected by additional factors besides the removal of wood for fuel, was reduced from 17.2 million hectares in 1990 to 9.1 million hectares in 2010.[23] At that rate, by 2020 Nigeria will have lost all of its forest.) An efficient stove would mean less individual effort wasted in collecting wood and more wood from non-renewable sources spared. It would also mean fewer GHGs released into the atmosphere when performing the daily task of cooking food.[24] To distribute such a stove to Nigeria's poor is therefore to satisfy the two basic aims of a CDM project: that the project contributes to sustainable development and that it reduces a society's projected business-as-usual emissions.

---

17 Over two billion people use biomass to cook every day: N. MacCarty et al., 'A Laboratory Comparison of the Global Warming Impact of Five Major Types of Biomass Cooking Stoves', 12(2) *Energy for Sustainable Development* 56 (2008), p. 58.
18 The challenge of building a cheap, durable, clean-burning stove for the world's poor is discussed in B. Bilger, 'Hearth Surgery: The Quest for a Stove That Can Save the World', *The New Yorker* (21 and 28 December 2009), p. 84 ('Clean air, according to the EPA, contains less than fifteen micrograms of fine particles per cubic metre. Five times that amount will set off a smoke alarm. Three hundred times as much – roughly what an open fire produces – will slowly kill you': p. 86). Indoor air pollution exposure from wood combustion is linked with acute and chronic eye and respiratory conditions: A. R. Siddiqui et al., 'Eye and Respiratory Symptoms among Women Exposed to Wood Smoke Emitted from Indoor Cooking: A Study from Southern Pakistan', 9(3) *Energy for Sustainable Development* (2005). According to the World Health Organization, exposure to smoke from household use of solid fuels is responsible for the premature deaths of approximately 400 000 women and children in India every year: K. Dutta et al., 'Impact of Improved Biomass Cookstoves on Indoor Air Quality near Pune, India', 11(2) *Energy for Sustainable Development* 19 (2007), p. 19. Black carbon from domestic cooking fires also contributes to loss of the cryosphere in the northern hemisphere: V. Ramanathan and G. Carmichael, 'Global and Regional Climate Changes Due to Black Carbon', 1 *Nature Geoscience* 221 (2008); and UN Environment Programme, *Near-Term Climate Protection and Clean Air Benefits: Actions for Controlling Short-Lived Climate Forcers* (2011). On stove projects in the context of the CDM, see P. Cox et al., *Analysis of Cookstove Change-out Projects Seeking Carbon Credits* (Environmental Sustainability Clinic, University of Minnesota Law School, 2011), p. 1.
19 D. E. Bloom, A. K. M. Zaidi and E. Yeh, 'The Demographic Impact of Biomass Fuel Use', 9(3) *Energy for Sustainable Development* 40 (2005).
20 Federal Republic of Nigeria, *Nigeria's First National Communication under the United Nations Framework Convention on Climate Change* (2003), p. 22.
21 UNFCCC, 'Radio Stories for Africa', <http://cdm.unfccc.int/about/multimedia/stories/index.html>.
22 Food and Agriculture Organization, *Global Forest Resources Assessment 2010: Global Tables* (2010), Table 13.
23 Ibid., Table 3.
24 MacCarty et al., 'Global Warming Impact of Five Types of Biomass Cooking Stoves' (2008); and Federal Republic of Nigeria, *First National Communication* (2003), pp. 39–45.

On 17 May 2011, the CDM Executive Board issued 1867 CERs to the Nigeria Stoves project for emission reductions achieved during its initial operating period, from October 2009 to June 2010.[25] A Certified Emission Reduction (a term for a currency unit, exclusive to the CDM[26]) is an internationally recognised tradable emission allowance. From the point of view of an industrial purchaser, its effect is to cancel out one tonne of CO_2 eq. GHG emissions from the industry on whose behalf the CER is purchased. In the standard situation, as indicated earlier, the industrial buyer (emitter) is operating within an Annex I economy in which emission allowances are scarce. The price of domestically generated allowances is lowered by allowing the significantly cheaper[27] offsets created in non-Annex I countries to be imported, thus increasing the number of allowances in circulation, but thereby also keeping the economy's overall emissions higher than they would otherwise be. In such a context, purchasing CERs enables the emitter to minimise the cost of compliance with government regulations. In another situation the buyer might be a sovereign – that is, an Annex I state party to the Kyoto Protocol seeking to cancel out an excess of national emissions (emissions above the Protocol's cap for the country) through the acquisition of UNFCCC-approved offsets.[28] Restrictions normally apply to the quantity of emissions that an industry or state may offset through the CDM.

Returning to our case study, if all 1867 CERs generated by the Nigeria Stoves project during its initial 8.5-month crediting period were sold in the same month they were issued (May 2011) to buyers in, say, the European Union's ETS at the market price for a CER,[29] they would have collectively fetched around €23 670. Nigeria Stoves is a small project in CDM terms. By May 2011, the Executive Board had registered 3146 projects and issued 624.3 million CERs[30] – an average of 198 433 CERs per project. Over its ten-year lifetime, Nigeria Stoves would perhaps manage to generate around 100 000 CERs: a modest amount. Yet this only goes to show that the CDM is able to accommodate large projects as

---

25 UNFCCC, 'Project: 2711 Efficient Fuel Wood Stoves for Nigeria – Issuance Request', <http://cdm.unfccc.int/Projects/DB/RWTUV1245685309.5/iProcess/RWTUV1284458332.96/view>.
26 The term first appears in Article 12(3) of the Kyoto Protocol. It is defined in Kyoto Protocol, *Decision 3/CMP.1* (30 March 2006), para. 1(b).
27 Annex I states benefit economically by outsourcing their emission reductions to developing countries, where the reductions can often be made at very low cost. It has been estimated that the average abatement cost for CDM projects with a renewable crediting period is US$2 per tonne of CO_2 eq.; for projects with a fixed crediting period (except solar projects, which tend to be much more expensive), the average abatement cost is US$10 per tonne of CO_2 eq.: Clean Development Mechanism (Kyoto Protocol), *Benefits of the Clean Development Mechanism* (2011), p. 6. This is much cheaper than, for example, the European Union Allowance or the Australian Carbon Unit.
28 The effect of CER acquisition by an Annex I party is controlled by Article 3(12) of the Kyoto Protocol. As discussed in Chapter 3, a state may be excluded from using the flexible mechanisms, including the CDM, under certain conditions. The conditions that a state must meet in order to use CERs to offset emissions during a commitment period are listed in Kyoto Protocol, *Decision 3/CMP.1* (30 March 2006), paras. 31–32. Private or public entities may transfer and acquire CERs only if the state party that has authorised them to participate in CDM activities is itself eligible to do so at that time: ibid., para. 33.
29 For the price of the so-called ECX (European Carbon Exchange) CER, see Intercontinental Exchange (ICE), <https://www.theice.com/>.
30 UNFCCC, CDM website, <http://cdm.unfccc.int/>.

well as small ones. For a small project in a poor developing country, €23 670 over 8.5 months could spell the difference between a mere idea and actual stoves in homes.

Another interesting fact about Nigeria Stoves is that it was only the second CDM project to be registered in Nigeria.[31] The fact that Nigeria was hosting only three CDM projects by 2009 and only five by 2011 (of the 3146 projects then registered worldwide) suggests an equity problem in the CDM's implementation in Africa. Indeed, the continent as a whole has never been able to capture more than 2 per cent of CDM projects.[32]

Upholding CDM values under pressure of financial interests

The CDM is created by an international treaty and governed by international law, whereas a particular CDM project like Nigeria Stoves is located within a domestic legal jurisdiction. As a consequence of the regulation at these two scales, a CDM project remains under some degree of international and municipal control throughout its lifetime. Because a resulting CER is always, therefore, the product of an activity regulated at both the domestic and international levels, it differs from other carbon offsets (in particular those commonly traded in the voluntary carbon market), which are at most regulated under the domestic law of the state in which they are created, but are often not subject to any but the most generic state oversight.[33]

The CDM's project registration process is conditional upon host state approval. It is one of the first steps in the process. In January 2009, Nigeria's federal environment ministry, in its role as the Designated National Authority (DNA) under the CDM rules (the state's agent for CDM purposes[34]), gave host state approval to the Nigeria Stoves project.[35] In its letter of approval, the Nigerian government stated that it had examined the project's Project Design Document[36] and was 'convinced' that the project, if implemented, 'will result in greenhouse gas emission reduction and more importantly will result in sustainable forest development in Nigeria. Besides, reduction in domestic emissions will decrease upper respiratory infections thereby leading to improved health conditions.'[37] The letter is brief, as such approval instruments tend to be, and does not explain

---

[31] Atmosfair gGmbH, *CDM Project Design Document for Efficient Fuel Wood Stoves for Nigeria*, CDM website, <http://cdm.unfccc.int/>, p. 12.
[32] Africa Carbon Forum, <http://africacarbonforum.com/2011/english/objective.htm>.
[33] See C. Downie, *Carbon Offsets: Saviour or Cop-Out?*, Research Paper No. 48 (Australia Institute, August 2007); and J. Peel, 'Climate Change Law: The Emergence of a New Legal Discipline', 32 *Melbourne University Law Review* 922 (2008), pp. 943–6.
[34] Kyoto Protocol, *Decision 3/CMP.1* (30 March 2006), para. 29.
[35] Federal Republic of Nigeria, Ministry of Environment, *Request for Letter of Approval for Project 'Efficient Fuel Wood Stoves for Nigeria'* (24 January 2009).
[36] A first version of the project's PDD was completed in October 2008; see Atmosfair gGmbH, *Project Design Document* (8 June 2009), p. 3.
[37] Federal Ministry of Environment (Nigeria), *Request for Letter of Approval for Project 'Efficient Fuel Wood Stoves for Nigeria'* (24 January 2009).

the reasoning by which the government reached its positive conclusions about the project's benefits. There is a boosterish quality to the letter. Indeed, 'sustainable forest development' is an exaggeration: Nigeria Stoves aims to reduce forest damage, but no element of the project is directly aimed at forest management.[38]

As a rule, the government of a developing country has an interest in a CDM project going ahead.[39] The project would bring foreign currency into the country and weaken, however slightly, the causes of environmental degradation, and in this case, ill health. Besides the government, two other parties to the transaction are pushing for approval. The project developer's motivation to get the project registered and under way is at least as strong as that of the host state. This makes two parties with the same interest. From an offset purchaser's point of view, the more CERs generated, the lower their price in the market, and therefore the lower will be the cost of compliance within the applicable framework of emission restrictions. In the context of offset trading, an officially approved CER, offered at a good price, which means a price lower than the price of an emission allowance issued by the Annex I party itself, is essentially what a purchaser is after. As a standardised, uniform commodity when put up for sale, each CER is as good as any other, no matter what its origins are.[40] It is not the role of the buyer to care about whether the particular project that generated the CER actually enjoyed the qualities of additionality and sustainability. The buyer is free to assume that it did. What starts in one part of the world as a combined problem of toxic fume inhalation and deforestation, or in another country as a problem of, say, flooding and underdeveloped agriculture, results in both cases in emission credits of exactly the same kind, and the buyer never need know that one CER comes from a stoves project and another from a dam project.

Our focus is on the motivational dynamic that characterises the CDM. The host state (a non-Annex I party), the vendor/project developer, and the purchaser (a private entity or an Annex I government) all have the same interest in the project going ahead. The combined dynamic has the potential to overpower conditional requirements, such as additionality and sustainability. Who, then, is charged with maintaining the integrity of the Mechanism? The answer is, formally, the CMP (the Kyoto Protocol parties in conference), but in practice it is the CDM's 10-member Executive Board.[41] The peculiar motivational dynamic of the CDM places all of the responsibility for keeping the CDM faithful to its objectives on the shoulders of this Executive Board. It is a lot of pressure on a single point in the system. We would therefore expect the regulatory scheme

---

38 The purpose of approval letters probably has more to do with getting governments to vouch that the initiators and developers of the proposed CDM projects are legitimate entities than with the qualities of the projects themselves with respect to mitigation or sustainability.
39 See L. Schneider, *Is the CDM Fulfilling Its Environmental and Sustainable Development Objectives? An Evaluation of the CDM and Options for Improvement* (Öko-Institut, 2007), pp. 46–7.
40 With the exception of CERs derived from a forestry project (afforestation, reforestation).
41 On the constitution of the CDM Executive Board, see Kyoto Protocol, *Decision 3/CMP.1* (30 March 2006), paras. 7–12.

under the Executive Board's control – the quality control and assurance procedures it must apply to eliminate foul play – to be correspondingly strong.[42]

How does the Nigeria Stoves project demonstrate to the CDM Executive Board that it does, in fact, offset the claimed quantities of emissions, that those reductions are additional (that they would not have occurred in the absence of CDM financing for the project), and that the project contributes to sustainable development? Here, the Project Design Document and the 'methodology' applied by the project developer are critical.

Project development and the test for additionality

The PDD describes the purpose of the stoves project as the distribution in selected parts of Nigeria of up to 12 500 efficient fuel-wood stoves, at subsidised prices, for the purpose of replacing inefficient traditional fireplaces (usually, three stones arranged around an open fire).[43] The new stoves, prefabricated in Germany and assembled in Nigeria, effect complete combustion with no visible smoke, and reduce fuel-wood use by up to 80 per cent. In the areas of Nigeria targeted by the project (only a slice of this vast country constitutes the project domain), household energy needs exceed the available renewable woody biomass, and deforestation had become a major concern. A single new stove could potentially save 2.7 tonnes of CO_2 eq. emissions per year. The PDD calculation is that the project as a whole could, by 2019, prevent more than 300 000 tonnes of CO_2 eq. emissions.[44] This is the project's potential on paper, in the absence of implementation constraints. The year 2019 was made the sunset year because the CDM limits a project's crediting period to ten years, or, for some types of project, to two consecutive periods of seven years each.[45] The Nigeria Stoves crediting period runs from mid-October 2009 to mid-October 2019.[46]

Under the project's rules, a participant (stove user) must enter into a contract agreeing to several conditions.[47] The contract and its enforceability are matters of Nigerian law. The contractual conditions include the participant's affirmation that, up to the date of the stove's purchase, wood had been used as the primary household fuel (as opposed to, say, kerosene). They also include undertakings that the user's traditional fireplace will no longer be used and will be disposed of. This condition is to be checked by the project's administrator when the new smokeless stove is delivered to the user. Another condition is that the user will inform the administrator should the project stove cease to be used, or should it be sold to another person or household, and that the user will cooperate with the

---

[42] On the role of the UNFCCC Secretariat in this context, see M. Netto and K.-U. B. Schmidt, 'CDM Project Cycle and the Role of the UNFCCC Secretariat', in *Legal Aspects of Implementing the Kyoto Protocol Mechanisms: Making Kyoto Work*, eds D. Freestone and C. Streck (Oxford University Press, 2005), pp. 175–90.
[43] Atmosfair gGmbH, *Project Design Document* (8 June 2009), pp. 3, 17.   [44] Ibid., p. 3.
[45] Kyoto Protocol, *Decision 3/CMP.1* (30 March 2006), para. 49.
[46] See <http://cdm.unfccc.int/Projects/DB/RWTUV1245685309.5/view>.
[47] Atmosfair gGmbH, *Project Design Document* (8 June 2009), p. 5.

project administrator in other respects for monitoring purposes.[48] The existence of a written contract between project developer and participant is a notable legal element in itself. The PDD outlines procedures that deal with possibilities such as theft of the stove, relocation of the participating household out of the target region, and so forth. Very soon, the complexity of administering such a project becomes apparent.

The PDD makes four arguments in support of the project's contribution to sustainable development: it will reduce the fuel-wood cost for households, lessen indoor air pollution from smoke and avoid its harmful health consequences, contribute to the recovery of forests, and help, through the preservation of wood resources, to avoid conflict between communities over those resources.[49] The PDD asserts that there is no public funding for the stoves project and that the funds needed to subsidise the stoves to make them affordable, as well as the funds needed to administer the project, are to be recovered from the sale of CERs issued to the project by the CDM Executive Board.

Up to this point, the PDD is rather loose in structure. Some of its arguments are also rather loose (such as the one about alleviating intercommunity strife). What finally provides a credible framework is the requirement that the project developer apply an appropriate, CDM-approved, baseline-and-monitoring methodology to the particular facts of the project.

Private entities develop and revise the methodologies that guide the calculation of GHG emission reductions. The methodologies are validated by private accredited auditors (Designated Operational Entities). A valid CDM methodology must be approved by the Executive Board following a period of exposure for public comment.[50] The methodology then becomes a standard that is freely available for use by any entity that is developing a comparable project activity.[51] A methodology contains general guidance on the following main aspects of a project:

(i) a description of the 'project boundary';
(ii) a procedure to identify the baseline scenario (the GHG emissions in the absence of the project);
(iii) a procedure to demonstrate and assess additionality (why the project would not be implemented without the help of the CDM);
(iv) a procedure to calculate emission reductions caused by the project; and
(v) minimum standards for the monitoring procedure.[52]

Over 180 methodologies had been approved by mid-2011, when Nigeria Stoves received its first disbursement of CERs.[53] The developer of a project for which no

---

[48] In Cox et al., *Cookstove Change-out Projects* (2011), p. 27, the authors state that several cook-stove projects they examined utilise such agreements to assist in project monitoring. Participants in projects such as Nigeria Stoves are informed that they are not only receiving a new stove but are participating in a project that requires their cooperation if it is to be successful.
[49] Atmosfair gGmbH, *Project Design Document* (8 June 2009), pp. 6–7.
[50] Kyoto Protocol, *Decision 3/CMP.1* (30 March 2006), paras. 5(d) and (j).
[51] Streck and Lin, 'Mobilising Finance for Climate Change Mitigation' (2009), p. 75.
[52] Adapted from Clean Development Mechanism (Kyoto Protocol), *CDM Methodology Booklet* (2010), p. 30.
[53] See <http://cdm.unfccc.int/methodologies/index.html>.

existing methodology offers a good fit – an increasingly rare occurrence – must produce a new methodology and submit it to the Executive Board for approval; only when the methodology has been approved may the developer continue with the registration procedure.[54] For Nigeria Stoves, a CDM methodology for small-scale cookstove projects was already in place.[55]

In the course of determining the baseline emissions from open fireplaces used for cooking in the Nigeria Stoves target area, the project developer surveyed 392 households (a statistically sound sample under the CDM methodology) to establish the average weight of fuel wood used per household on a typical day (finding: about 13 kg).[56] Summarising this step in a single sentence does not do justice to the underlying sophistication of the data collection techniques, implemented in a region with no physical addresses, no population census, and few other aids to information-gathering. The same is true of the project's finding that 77 per cent of fuel wood used in the surveyed area was taken from non-renewable forest resources.[57] This is not information easily obtained, and by the same token it is not information easily confirmed. As we have often noted in this book, a key aspect of our response to climate change is that low-lying and rather inconspicuous layer at which emissions, emission reductions, and related factual claims are measured, reported, and verified. Without confidence in the information derived, we can have no confidence that we are managing GHG mitigation, and thus the climate, in accordance with our objectives.

The PDD next attempts to demonstrate that, in the absence of the Nigeria Stoves project, the continued practice of open-fire cooking in the target area is the only realistic and credible prospect in the years ahead. That is, no shift towards efficient wood-burning stoves or some other cooking technology that does not rely on non-renewable biomass is planned or likely to happen. Finding arguments to make such a counterfactual forecast in a 'reasonable'[58] way (which is the applicable test) is to come head to head with the problem of additionality. To meet the criterion of additionality, projects must demonstrate that they could not be implemented in the absence of CDM support because of the existence of one or more of seven implementation barriers: an investment barrier, institutional barrier, technological barrier, local-tradition barrier, common-practice barrier, ecological-condition barrier, or social-condition barrier.[59]

The PDD's first argument in this regard concerns law and order: there is no law in Nigeria that prohibits the removal of fuel wood from forests in general, except in protected areas. This would probably be called an institutional barrier, although the PDD does not attempt to categorise it. Even in the few areas protected by forest

---

54 Kyoto Protocol, *Decision 3/CMP.1* (30 March 2006), para. 38.
55 CDM Executive Board, *Methodology AMS-II.G, Energy Efficiency Measures in Thermal Applications of Non-Renewable Biomass* (Initial adoption 2008).
56 Atmosfair gGmbH, *Project Design Document* (8 June 2009), pp. 15–16.   **57** Ibid., p. 20.
58 TÜV Nord, *Final Validation Report for Efficient Fuel Wood Stoves for Nigeria* (CDM website, 8 September 2009), p. 36; and Kyoto Protocol, *Decision 3/CMP.1* (30 March 2006), para. 44.
59 Clean Development Mechanism (Kyoto Protocol), *Executive Board of the CDM: Thirty-Fifth Meeting Report* (UNFCCC, 19 October 2007), Annex 17.

laws, the PDD maintains, people take firewood without regard to the law. To the extent that there are laws protecting forests in Nigeria, the PDD presents evidence that they are not enforced.[60] This would probably be labelled a local-tradition or common-practice barrier in the CDM's terminology.

If Nigeria's laws *could* be strengthened, observed, and enforced, there might be no need for the Nigeria Stoves project. Fuel wood would become more scarce and expensive, forcing many to change their practices. In reality, as the PDD informs us, even the weak laws in place are not observed or enforced, and there is no indication that they are about to be strengthened. Having noted this deficiency, Nigeria Stoves' aim, in effect, is to carve out a small, internationally supervised space within a weakly governed country, in which to introduce reforms that are beyond the government's capacity.[61] The project will have to defend the borders of this space throughout the project's lifetime in order to maintain the integrity of the emission reduction credits. Nigeria Stoves will bring money and technology into the country, improve the lives of the project's participants, and help Annex I countries to comply with their emission reduction obligations. On top of that, it promises to create a pocket of model 'scientific' governance. Delivery of good governance on the back of the CDM is not explicitly recognised in the Mechanism's rules (or in the literature), yet a successful project will tend to reveal this benefit. Pockets of good governance do have a drawback: they lead to a kind of discrimination. In Nigeria Stoves' case, there are wonderful German stoves for the people on one side of the project boundary, three-stone fires for those on the other. The project boundary of Nigeria Stoves was not decided by popular vote. It is governance with plenty of consultation, certainly, but without democracy.

The PDD's second argument for additionality is that fuel-wood stoves with the same efficiency and lifespan as those used by the project are not available in Nigeria (a technological barrier). The locally available 'improved' cooking stoves reduce fuel-wood consumption by no more than 30 per cent, compared with the 80 per cent reduction achieved by the project's German stoves. If the latter were to be sold to Nigerians unsubsidised, they would each cost US$170 – far more than what the average household in the beneficiary population could afford (daily per capita income in Nigeria was US$2.50 in 2007).[62] This is a social-condition barrier. Another social-condition barrier is that bank loans are not available to the target-area households, and no microcredit system has been established in the area.[63] With the Nigeria Stoves subsidy, each stove would cost the participant around US$80.[64]

---

60 Atmosfair gGmbH, *Project Design Document* (8 June 2009), p. 22.
61 Nigeria has a score of 43.3 out of 100 in the 2010 Ibrahim Index of African Governance. It is ranked 37th across all indicators in the list of 53 countries of Africa. On the 'safety and rule of law' scale, in particular, it is ranked 38th. See Mo Ibrahim Foundation, 'The Ibrahim Index', <http://www.moibrahimfoundation.org/en/section/the-ibrahim-index>.
62 TÜV Nord, *Final Validation Report* (8 September 2009), pp. 26, 30.
63 Atmosfair gGmbH, *Project Design Document* (8 June 2009), p. 23.
64 Cox et al., *Cookstove Change-out Projects* (2011), p. 34. We are not told how much the Nigeria Stoves 'improved' cooking stove with 30 per cent efficiency would cost. Not all permutations need to be investigated to the same extent, it seems.

Such arguments probably succeed in persuading the intended audience, and in particular the Executive Board, that the project would enjoy additionality, at least in the short term. But what about additionality over the term of the project's 10-year crediting period (2009–19)? How confident are we that, say, six years hence the government of Nigeria would not decide to spend heavily on energy efficiency projects, including a subsidised stove program? How confident are we that it would not decide to distribute the locally manufactured stove, which, although only 30 per cent more efficient, is still better than an open fire? Or the government might decide to bypass fuel-wood stoves altogether and distribute kerosene appliances or extend the electricity grid to households in the area targeted by Nigeria Stoves. (Cooking with kerosene or electric appliances is even more efficient, and thus less GHG-intensive, than using the Nigeria Stoves system.) Finally, how confident are we that an international charity would not eventually distribute thousands of stoves for free? Any of these reforms that might have occurred in the absence of Nigeria Stoves are now obviated by the establishment of the project, paid for by the CDM. Obviously, the farther we try to look into the future the less confident we will feel about what we imagine to be there.[65] At the same time, it would be inefficient to limit CDM projects to just two or three years simply because we do not trust our longer-term forecasts. The German stove has an average lifespan of 13 years.[66] A three-year crediting period would incur the same start-up and registration costs, deliver less than a third of the subsidy, and move the stove beyond the budget of many households. Practical considerations such as these would probably incline us to compromise and allow a ten-year crediting period, despite our inability to predict government policy or other potential interventions that far ahead.

How would such a compromise on additionality affect the 'environmental integrity' of the CDM, in the narrow sense of its claim to neutralise excess emissions? An individual CER offsets a tonne of CO_2 eq. gas *already emitted*. In the stoves case, it offsets that tonne by promising to make an emission reduction of one tonne sometime in the course of the project's operating period – a reduction that would not have occurred but for the money paid by the emitter to purchase the CER. The emitted tonne is a hard fact. The reduction by which it is to be offset is a promise that is expected to materialise in the future, as the difference between hypothetical emissions under a business-as-usual scenario and actual emissions in a world that includes the project. Another hard fact is that many Nigerians are better off because of the project. It would be cold-hearted to downplay that fact. Unfortunately, however, environmental integrity does not care about soft landings for Annex I economies or the well-being of households in Nigeria. All it cares about is whether the emitted tonne will be cancelled out by a

---

65 See Barbara Haya, *Measuring Emissions against an Alternative Future: Fundamental Flaws in the Structure of the Kyoto Protocol's Clean Development Mechanism* (Energy and Resources Group Working Paper ERG09-001, University of California, Berkeley, 2009).
66 The stove was tested by the German Materials Testing Institute, which estimated a 13-year lifetime: Atmosfair gGmbH, *Project Design Document* (8 June 2009), p. 38.

truly 'additional' action. This is not something we can ever be sure about in the case of a project that runs through to 2019. Because a CER is created on the basis of policy assumptions extending years into the future, its offsetting power is always less than certain.

The above criticism can be addressed in practice by declining to issue CERs in advance of a project's demonstrated emission reductions. This is the CDM's cautious way: only after reductions have been verified by a Designated Operational Entity are CERs issued. When Nigeria Stoves received its first issue of CERs, it did not receive all CERs up to 2019 in one allocation. Rather, its CERs are being issued in instalments. The project is to receive an allotment of CERs only after the DOE has verified the emission reductions for a given period (in the first instance, it was 8.5 months).

It is thus important to distinguish between the estimated lifetime carbon benefits of a CDM project – which are initially calculated in the PDD at the beginning of the project and are apt to change if the baseline is adjusted in the future – and the verified carbon benefits confirmed by the DOE after each verification period. Since baselines are essentially predictions of a future state of affairs, revisiting them over defined intervals is essential in order to make adjustments for any changes in government policy, socioeconomic forces, and other assumptions.[67] Eventually, when the project has reached the end of its crediting period, a final verified number of lifetime carbon benefits would be calculated. In order to maintain this kind of dynamic baseline, the DOE would have to update the baseline during each verification of the project's emission reductions. This process would certainly improve the accuracy of offsetting.[68]

Nevertheless, the essential criticism is not fully deflected by settling for a piecemeal, retrospective allocation of CERs. The DOE's periodic verifications do not always revisit the project's policy assumptions about the business-as-usual trajectory. As one project report put it, there will be 'data and parameters [that] are determined only once and thus remain fixed throughout the crediting period'.[69] The Nigeria Stoves DOE carries out verifications to check whether the project households have received the stoves and are using them as intended. That is, it checks only the trajectory of actual emissions.

We keep returning to a difficulty that no amount of regulation of offset mechanisms can overcome: The carbon dioxide released from the stack of a power plant can be precisely measured; the carbon dioxide that was *not* released by certain Nigerian households over an 8.5-month period because of changed behaviour as a result of the stoves project can only be estimated. Yet it is the very emissions that were *not* released that are the objects being sold as offsets for released emissions in Annex I countries. Would settling on the most conservative estimate of avoided emissions solve the problem? Certainly it would help; all

---

[67] Nicole R. Virgilio et al., *Reducing Emissions from Deforestation and Degradation (REDD): A Casebook of on-the-Ground Experience* (The Nature Conservancy, 2010), p. 18.
[68] Ibid., p. 19.   [69] TÜV Nord, *Final Validation Report* (8 September 2009), p. 36.

CDM methodologies make obligatory the use of multipliers to ensure that such estimates are on the conservative side.[70] Doubt remains, however, perhaps more so in relation to some projects than others.

Let us recall the contract that the Nigeria Stoves participants must sign. They must agree to use the new stove *for cooking*, and to stop using their traditional cook-fires. Let us assume that all 12 500 households abide by their contractual promise throughout the ten-year lifetime of the project. Has the stoves project really displaced open fires? Not necessarily. Fires in non-electrified Nigerian villages could be used for night-time illumination, warmth, and socialising, in addition to cooking. We do not know from the Nigeria Stoves documentation that they are so used, but the PDD does not say that they are not. If they *are* so used, might we not imagine that, in practice, the project participants use the new stoves only for cooking, while open fires are continued for their other important social functions? To some extent, this possibility is a matter for the project's official monitoring (see below). Yet, is it realistic to expect an impoverished people to completely give up one of their few small comforts for another, when they could continue to enjoy both while faithfully abiding by the letter of their contract to cook using only the German stove? How far will the monitors go in noticing compromises and correcting them? Will an instinctive humanitarianism not incline the monitors to see just what they want to see? No matter how much law and regulation and scientific governance we inject into any strip of territory, we would probably never eliminate doubts about the robustness of the offset when pitted against the hard fact of an Annex I emission.[71]

We return to the CDM approval process. After additionality, there is the problem of 'leakage'. Leakage occurs when a CDM project displaces an unwanted activity, in whole or in part, to areas outside the boundaries of the project.[72] For example, if reforestation of a plot of land used for grazing leads to deforestation of other land for grazing, the reforestation project risks being rendered pointless through leakage. But leakage can also occur within the project boundary itself. A study of stove-related offset projects notes that households may undermine some of the benefits of the program 'by cooking more or by compensating for the loss of space heating from their old stoves by burning more fuel, or neighboring regions may use more wood fuel than previously due to lower costs and greater availability'.[73] Leakage is thus not unrelated to the possible scenario in which stoves displace only one function of traditional fireplaces.

The CDM methodology to which Nigeria Stoves is subject outlines leakage scenarios that all projects proposed under the methodology must address: 'The following potential source of leakage shall be considered: [t]he use/diversion of non-renewable woody biomass saved under the project activity by non-project

---

[70] Kyoto Protocol, *Decision 3/CMP.1* (30 March 2006), para. 45(b).
[71] Kevin Anderson has brilliantly made this point in 'The Inconvenient Truth of Carbon Offsets', 484 *Nature* 7 (5 April 2012).
[72] Kyoto Protocol, *Decision 3/CMP.1* (30 March 2006), para. 51.
[73] Adapted from Cox et al., *Cookstove Change-out Projects* (2011), p. 22.

households/users that previously used renewable energy sources'. Also, '[i]f equipment currently being utilised is transferred from outside the boundary to the project activity, leakage is to be considered'.[74] The latter possibility is not an issue in the context of three-stone fireplaces. In relation to the former point, the PDD argues that renewable energy sources have not gained any significant purchase in Nigeria. From this it is said to follow that only a negligible number of persons outside the project boundary who had been prior users of renewable energy sources would now switch to using the forest biomass saved under the project activity.[75] This argument misses the point that, through the operation of the Nigeria Stoves project, demand for a scarce resource (fuel wood) drops, lowering its price and increasing its availability in areas close to the project boundary. The PDD does not deal convincingly with the problem of leakage.

Another issue to be considered by the project developer is 'project-activity emissions', a broad term that may include emissions from such activities as constructing or manufacturing the new stoves, shipping them to the host country, delivering them to the target population, providing stove maintenance services, and so on. The additional outputs of CO_2 eq. emissions from these related actions could be significant. It is certainly possible that project-activity emissions could, in some years, equal or exceed the baseline emission reductions that the project would create.[76] In the Nigeria Stoves case, the project-activity emissions are said to be zero,[77] presumably in part because the emissions from the manufacturing process are released in Germany (and therefore are captured by that country's national system for GHG emissions), and the transport-related emissions are considered either 'negligible' or are written off as emissions from bunker fuels (shipping emissions on the high seas are not attributed to the emissions budget of any country under present agreements).[78] But the reasons for the project-activity emissions being zero in Nigeria's own territory are not convincingly set out in the Nigeria Stoves documents. We might suspect that the various 'negligible' components (policy uncertainty, participant non-cooperation, leakage, project-activity emissions, etc.) do actually add up to significant uncertainty about the amount of emissions that Nigeria Stoves truly offsets. The project may be transparent *enough*, but it is not fully transparent.

The CDM methodology that regulates Nigeria Stoves requires monitoring of stove performance and usage for the duration of the project.[79] While the methodology sets the monitoring standards that a project must meet, it does not specify how the project is to meet those standards. The monitoring plan for Nigeria Stoves must therefore be specifically developed within the framework of the PDD. It is, in fact, an extensive plan, tied to an annual cycle of spot-checks and

---

[74] CDM Executive Board, *Methodology AMS-II.G* (Initial adoption 2008), p. 5.
[75] Atmosfair gGmbH, *Project Design Document* (8 June 2009), p. 25.
[76] Cox et al., *Cookstove Change-out Projects* (2011), p. 22.
[77] Atmosfair gGmbH, *Project Design Document* (8 June 2009), p. 31.
[78] TÜV Nord, *Final Validation Report* (8 September 2009), p. 35.
[79] The foundation for monitoring is given in Kyoto Protocol, *Decision 3/CMP.1* (30 March 2006), paras. 53–60.

other quality controls.[80] We are again reminded of the demanding administrative component of a CDM project, which requires policing of its integrity not only at registration but also for a decade or more after its establishment. Monitoring of Nigeria Stoves is to consist, among other things, of checking annually that a representative number of households are still using the stoves and checking the efficiency of a representative sample of stoves to ensure that they are still operating at the manufacturer's standard of 80 per cent. Where stoves have to be replaced, monitoring is to ensure that the efficiency of the new stoves is similar to that of the ones being replaced.[81] And so forth, in considerable detail.

Project validation and registration

In June 2009, TÜV Nord, a German company that is a Designated Operational Entity under the CDM,[82] submitted to the CDM Executive Board an application for registration of Nigeria Stoves.[83] The application was accompanied by a validation report, also prepared by TÜV Nord.[84] In accordance with the standard procedure, the project developer had retained the DOE to produce the validation report, and to apply on its behalf for certification.[85]

A DOE may undertake a project's *validation* (that the project conforms to all applicable CDM rules for registration[86]) or *verification* (that it is operating as designed, is reducing or displacing emissions, and is entitled to receive CERs[87]), and with the permission of the Executive Board it may do both for one and the same project (as in the case we are considering).[88] The DOE plays a critical role in CDM governance, for the Executive Board tends to follow the advice of the DOE on matters of registration and issue of CERs.[89] A large chunk of the responsibility for the Mechanism's integrity, which as we saw is carried almost entirely by the Executive Board, is effectively delegated to the DOE – an independent third party.[90]

The DOE takes an active role in preparing a CDM project for registration. The model is not a pass/fail examination, but a process of facilitation. This may well be the most appropriate model in a situation where the overall objective is to get a

---

80 Atmosfair gGmbH, *Project Design Document* (8 June 2009), pp. 32–8. **81** Ibid., p. 25.
82 Designated Operational Entities are accredited by the CDM Executive Board: Kyoto Protocol, *Decision 3/CMP.1* (30 March 2006), paras. 5(f) and 20.
83 TÜV Nord, CDM Project Activity Registration Form (on behalf of the proposed project Efficient Fuel Wood Stoves for Nigeria), <http://cdm.unfccc.int/Projects/DB/RWTUV1245685309.5/view>.
84 TÜV Nord, *Final Validation Report* (8 September 2009).
85 Kyoto Protocol, *Decision 3/CMP.1* (30 March 2006), para. 37. In the Nigeria Stoves case, the project developer was a German carbon offset company, Atmosfair gGmbH, not a Nigerian one. This made the Federal Republic of Germany the 'investor country', in the sense that Atmosfair gGmbH would be providing the funds for the project (which it would then recover from the sale of CERs if the project were successfully registered, etc.). In such a case, the investor country must also issue a project approval as a precondition of registration of the project. Germany did so through a letter dated 19 June 2009 (<http://cdm.unfccc.int/Projects/DB/RWTUV1245685309.5/view>), having seen the PDD and the validation report prepared by TÜV Nord.
86 Ibid., paras. 35 and 40.   **87** Ibid., para. 27.   **88** Ibid.   **89** Ibid., paras. 64–5.
90 'Thus, much of the power to create CERs rests with the DOEs': Streck and Lin, 'Mobilising Finance for Climate Change Mitigation' (2009), p. 83. A DOE is an example of a non-state actor bearing some rights and duties under international law.

large number of GHG mitigation projects under way quickly, in response to an urgent climate problem and in the context of continuing strong emission growth in developed countries and relatively low capacity in developing countries to design or support sophisticated offset projects.

In the course of the validation of Nigeria Stoves, TÜV Nord raised with the project developer 15 so-called Corrective Action Requests, 12 Clarification Requests and one Forward Action Request, all types of facilitative guidance meant to improve regulatory compliance.[91] The DOE conducted its own on-site investigation, invited submissions on the PDD from stakeholders, NGOs and others, held interviews with respondents, reviewed the calculations in the PDD, considered the project's compatibility with Nigerian laws, and so on.[92] It concluded that the project's additionality was sufficiently justified in the PDD, the monitoring plan was transparent and adequate, and the calculation of the project's emission reductions was done in a transparent and conservative manner, so that the estimated emission reductions (300 Mt CO_2 eq. emissions) would 'most likely' be achieved within the project's crediting period of ten years.[93] The sophistication of the validation report is in many respects remarkable and convincing. The deeper questions about the fictitious aspects of GHG offsets, however, remain.

Project verification and the issuance of tradable allowances

Nigeria Stoves was registered as a CDM project by the Executive Board in October 2009.[94] Just over a year later, TÜV Nord submitted its first verification report for the project,[95] along with certification that 1867 CERs were due to the project developer for the initial crediting period, corresponding to the calculated emission reductions in that period.[96] During verification, too, the DOE was facilitative in its approach, raising five Corrective Action Requests, six Clarification Requests, and one Forward Action Request.[97] The verification involved, among other things, a review of the monitoring report produced by the project developer,[98] interviews with personnel of the project developer and its contractors, an on-site assessment, resolution of corrective actions, and so on.[99] About 1700 stoves (of the 12 500 planned for the peak of the project) were in use by the date of the first verification.[100] (Nigeria Stoves got off to a slow start because the first shipment of

---

91 TÜV Nord, *Final Validation Report* (8 September 2009), pp. 2, 14.   **92** Ibid., pp. 9–15.
93 Ibid., p. 2.   **94** See <http://cdm.unfccc.int/Projects/DB/RWTUV1245685309.5/view>.
95 TÜV Nord, *Verification Report (First Operational Period): Efficient Fuel Wood Stoves for Nigeria* (CDM website, 14 December 2010).
96 Ibid.   **97** Ibid., p. 2.
98 Atmosfair gGmbH, *Monitoring Report (First Operating Period)* (CDM website, 14 September 2010).
99 TÜV Nord, *Verification Report* (14 December 2010), p. 11. The regulatory basis for the verification procedure, as well as its facilitative philosophy, is Kyoto Protocol, *Decision 3/CMP.1* (30 March 2006), para. 62.
100 Atmosfair gGmbH, *Monitoring Report* (14 September 2010), pp. 14–15. About 1700 stoves had been distributed in the course of the first operating period. However, only 700 stoves were deemed to have been in use during the whole of the monitoring period. Emission reduction calculations were made on the basis of the 700 stoves.

stoves from Germany was detained for months at Lagos port. The documents do not say why customs officers delayed its clearance.[101] The hold-up exemplifies how an ambitious PDD might not be realised in full. Before the CDM project can set up its own regulated space it must hack through a thicket of regulated and unregulated domestic practices.)

The fact that there were now stoves in people's homes made on-site assessment a more significant component of the procedure than had been the case at the validation stage – although both procedures, overall, seem equally arduous.[102] To give an indication of the difficulties encountered during verification, of the 96 households in randomly selected villages visited by the DOE, several households had sold off their stoves. The stoves that had been disposed of needed to be traced and re-assigned to the households that had acquired them, but this could occur only if they were still within the project boundary. In the limited time available to it, TÜV Nord was unable to locate four of the stoves, which were consequently treated as 'drop-outs' and struck from the project's database, along with their estimated emission reductions.[103] Finally, through extrapolation, the DOE was able to estimate the overall number of stoves in use, the amount of fuel wood consumed per day per stove, the portion of non-renewable biomass in the consumed fuel, etc., leading to an estimate of actual emissions under the project, which when subtracted from the hypothetical business-as-usual emissions for the period, resulted in the amount of avoided GHGs that would be credited to the project as CERs.[104]

As noted earlier, the 1867 CERs were released to Nigeria Stoves on 17 May 2011. Considering that a first version of the Project Design Document had already been produced in October 2008,[105] the stoves project was afoot for around three years before it was in a position to recover costs through the CDM. But while the CDM's project approval cycle can be lengthy, a project is not necessarily held up by it. It is common practice not to apply for CDM registration until after a project is under way. At the time Nigeria Stoves applied for registration, it was already partially operational, with financing supplied by a German carbon offsets developer.[106] This underscores the critical role of investors who are willing to support projects in their early stages. Without start-up funds from private investors and from large, publicly supported international institutions such as the World Bank,[107] CDM projects would be few and far between.[108]

If a project fails to gain CDM registration (by mid-2011, about 200 projects were in that category[109]), all is not lost. It may be able to have its offsets

---

101 Ibid., p. 6. **102** TÜV Nord, *Verification Report* (14 December 2010), p. 16. **103** Ibid., p. 20.
104 Ibid., p. 31. These calculations were made originally in the monitoring report (Atmosfair gGmbH, *Monitoring Report* (14 September 2010), pp. 17–20), and the DOE approved them.
105 Atmosfair gGmbH, *Project Design Document* (8 June 2009), p. 3.
106 Ibid., pp. 4, 22 ('The project activity is financed upfront [from] future CERs').
107 The World Bank Carbon Finance Unit (CFU) uses funds contributed by Annex I governments and companies in Annex I countries to purchase CERs through one of the CFU's carbon funds on behalf of the contributor. For information on the growth in the carbon funds managed by the CFU, the projects funded and the developmental benefits, see <http://www.carbonfinance.org/>.
108 The sources of international finance for mobilising CDM projects are discussed in more detail in Chapter 8, on finance and technology transfer.
109 See the CDM database, <http://cdm.unfccc.int/Projects/projsearch.html>.

accredited under a different (non-treaty) scheme, and sold in the voluntary carbon market.[110] Nonetheless, one of the advantages of CDM registration is that the resulting CERs will be sold at a premium, in recognition of their highly regulated and state-approved pedigree, their integration into the international compliance market, and their presumed integrity.

Persisting concerns about the CDM's environmental integrity

Baselines are not a unique feature of the CDM or of offsets. Indeed, the idea of a 'business-as-usual' trajectory is central to the narrative of GHG mitigation in general. For example, future emission pathways for states or other jurisdictions are usually defined in contrast to a business-as-usual, or 'reference', scenario.[111] But while the business-as-usual line is an essential component in the mapping of possible emission futures, in the context of the CDM the baseline is needed to *create* the offset product: the CER. The greater the divergence between the notional business-as-usual line and the emission trajectory realised through the implementation of the CDM project, the greater the value of the project, because the larger the number of CERs issued. As noted in the context of Nigeria Stoves, the baseline is a counterfactual scenario which cannot be known with certainty; it will always be an estimate with a larger or smaller margin of error. If the baseline is wrongly set (if it has a large margin of error), not only is a CER's value questionable, but the CDM's environmental integrity suffers. The project developer has a clear interest in arguing for the steepest reference trajectory, because the steeper the trajectory the more CERs will be issued for the same amount of effort. The buyer of a CER is concerned about its price, not its integrity, as each CER offsets the same amount of emissions irrespective of origin, and in any case most traders do not know the origins of the CERs traded. Thus we remarked that the CDM requires very strong regulation by the CMP and the Executive Board to maintain its environmental credibility as an offset provider, quite apart from its credibility as a promoter of sustainable development.[112]

---

110 VER (Verified Emission Reduction) credits are one such non-treaty scheme. They were developed as a way for entities not subject to Kyoto Protocol restrictions (individuals, corporations without emissions restrictions, etc., usually based in a country without an economy-wide emissions trading scheme or a GHG tax) to offset their emissions by purchasing emission reduction credits validated through a process comparable to that required for CERs. The Gold Standard (GS) is one organisation that validates and issues VERs. Many projects developed for the CDM are also registered through the Gold Standard. Cox et al. note that some types of CDM projects, including stove projects, co-register with GS for two reasons: 'First, the GS is considered by many to be a more robust certification than that provided by the CDM board. Second, the GS tracks and validates offsets of two greenhouse gases (CH_4 and N_2O) that the CDM does not allow to be included in CER offsets issued to cookstove projects, allowing CER projects to earn a "bonus" of VER credits for their offset of these gases': Cox et al., *Cookstove Change-out Projects* (2011), pp. 4–5.
111 For example UN Environment Programme, *Bridging the Emissions Gap: A UNEP Synthesis Report* (November 2011).
112 The CDM has suffered bad press where the regulation has been weak; see for example Q. Schiermeier, 'Clean-Energy Credits Tarnished', 477 *Nature* 517 (29 September 2011).

Much controversy has surrounded companies receiving CERs for capturing and destroying the powerful greenhouse gas HFC-23, a by-product of the production of the (non-greenhouse) refrigerant gas HCFC-22. By mid-2011, there were 19 such registered projects, based in China, India, South Korea, Mexico, and Argentina, with cumulative emission reductions amounting to a staggering 81.3 million CERs.[113] The group CDM Watch has argued that the way the CDM is structured has meant that the manufacturers have been handed an incentive to increase their production of HCFC-22, because the increase leads to more HFC-23 produced, and thus also to a corresponding abundance of CERs earned for destroying it.[114] Where this has been the case, firms have been making money from producing more greenhouse gas than they would have otherwise, which of course amounts to a perversion of the system.[115] It also means that credits have been issued that do not represent real emission reductions in developing countries, but have nevertheless enabled companies in Annex I countries to increase their emissions. (HFC-23 is a greenhouse gas that is also an ozone-depleting gas, so another argument for excluding it from the CDM is that it should be controlled under the Montreal Protocol.[116])

The CDM Executive Board, aware of the concerns expressed by CDM Watch and others,[117] has introduced safeguards in the applicable project assessment methodology designed to prevent abuse of what is essentially the additionality test. As a consequence of this reform, no new plants may qualify for credits related to HFC-23, and the amount of HFC-23 that does qualify for CERs when destroyed at existing plants is tied to each plant's historical production levels.[118] These precautions were not sufficient for the European Commission, which in 2011 legislated a ban on the use of CERs from HFC-23 projects in the EU ETS, but only as of May 2013 onwards.[119]

---

113 The data may be retrieved from <http://cdm.unfccc.int/Projects/projsearch.html>, using the AM0001 methodology as the search term. (AM0001 is exclusive to HFC-23 reduction.)
114 The group's analysis of data from the 19 CDM-registered HFC-23 projects showed that two plants reduced HFC-23 generation when they were ineligible for crediting, and increased HFC-23 generation once they could again claim credits for its destruction. One plant even ceased HCFC-22 production when it was not allowed to generate further offset credits and resumed operation when again it became eligible. Moreover, the analysis revealed that many plants produce exactly the amount of HCFC-22 and HFC-23 for which they are allowed to claim credits, whereas production was lower or varied from year to year before offset credits were rewarded. See the material at the group's website on HFC-23, <http://www.cdm-watch.org/?page_id=451>.
115 L. Schneider, 'Assessing the Additionality of CDM Projects: Practical Experience and Lessons Learned', 9 *Climate Policy* 242 (2009). Schneider is a former member of the CDM's Methodologies Panel and one of the original designers of the CDM system.
116 S. van Renssen, 'The Greenhouse-Gas Gang', 2 *Nature Climate Change* 143 (March 2012).
117 M. W. Wara and D. G. Victor, 'A Realistic Policy on International Carbon Offsets', Working Paper no. 74 (Program on Energy and Sustainable Development, Stanford University, 18 April 2008), pp. 11–12.
118 There has been a significant tightening of the applicable AM0001 methodology between its original version, dated September 2003, and its current version (5.2). The differences between the two are striking. The current version fixes the baseline with reference to historical output in the period 2000–04 (the period just up to the time when the first version would have begun to effect market distortions). The methodologies may be obtained from <http://cdm.unfccc.int/methodologies/PAmethodologies/approved>.
119 European Commission, *Draft Regulation of 7 June* 2011 *Determining, Pursuant to Directive 2003/87/EC of the European Parliament and of the Council, Certain Restrictions Applicable to the Use of International Credits from Projects Involving Industrial Gases*, <http://ec.europa.eu/clima/documentation/ets/docs/qualityreg_en.pdf>.

The CDM's performance on sustainable development

The CDM is not meant only as an offset scheme, as we have noted. Each CDM project is required not only to reduce emissions but also to create sustainable development benefits, as set out in Article 12(2) of the Kyoto Protocol.[120] The delivery of sustainable development benefits on the back of emission reductions is regarded by many not simply as a requirement of the CDM, but as the very condition of the Mechanism's legitimacy.[121] Had the CDM been proposed as a mere offset service that developing countries were to provide to developed countries for a fee, the state parties to the Kyoto Protocol would almost certainly not have agreed to it. As the CDM's very title suggests, the design feature that accounts for the Mechanism's coming into being is that the projects it sponsors are to promote sustainable development (SD) in poor countries. Without sustainable development benefits, rich countries purchasing CERs would be doing no more than paying poor countries to neutralise the greenhouse emission excesses of rich countries. *With* SD benefits, by contrast, CDM participants (both rich and poor) can claim that the Mechanism is delivering long-lasting, transformative assistance to developing countries – benefits that outlast the life of any CDM project and accelerate the host country's social and economic modernisation.[122] The bargain was that the North would receive the offsets it needed to soften the blow of the Protocol's commitment periods, while the South would accelerate its climate-friendly development using funds and technology transferred from the North for the projects.

The responsibility for determining whether a CDM project contributes to national sustainable development resides with the host country's Designated National Authority (in the Nigeria Stoves project, the DNA was Nigeria's federal Environment Ministry). The DNA states in its letter of approval whether and how, in its judgment, the proposed CDM project will contribute to the country's sustainable development. (At the Durban CMP in December 2011, the prerogative of the host states to define their sustainable development criteria in relation to the CDM was reaffirmed.[123])

The CDM's success in delivering sustainable development is a controversial topic which is difficult to settle satisfactorily, partly due to the rich connotations of 'sustainable development' and the challenge of quantifying and measuring the concept's constituent elements. There is wide agreement that SD has three

---

120 See also Kyoto Protocol, *Decision 3/CMP.1* (30 March 2006), Annex, para. 40(a).
121 M. Kenber, 'The Clean Development Mechanism: A Tool for Promoting Long-Term Climate Protection and Sustainable Development?', in *Climate Change and Carbon Markets: A Handbook of Emission Reduction Mechanisms*, ed. F. Yamin (Earthscan, 2005), pp. 263–88; and E. Meijer and J. Werksman, 'Keeping It Clean: Safeguarding the Environmental Integrity of the Clean Development Mechanism', in *Legal Aspects of Implementing the Kyoto Protocol Mechanisms: Making Kyoto Work*, eds D. Freestone and C. Streck (Oxford University Press, 2005), pp. 191–211.
122 'Modernisation' here means a capacity to increase wealth and well-being while reducing GHG emissions.
123 Kyoto Protocol, *Decision 8/CMP.7, Further Guidance Relating to the Clean Development Mechanism* (2011), para. 5.

mutually reinforcing dimensions: economic development, social development, and environmental protection.[124] However, there exists no universally accepted definition of SD,[125] and no agreed operational definition,[126] especially of the 'social development' dimension.[127]

There have been several studies of the CDM's performance in this respect.[128] The results are mixed. Voigt has written that the CDM Executive Board's certification process performs well on the integrity of project-specific aspects, but wider issues of long-term community benefit and localised environmental aspects tend to be ignored.[129] Studies have argued that the CDM does not contribute to the alleviation of rural poverty to any significant extent.[130] (That measure is important because a poor country's highest developmental priority is likely to be poverty alleviation.) Some of the fault seems to lie with host state DNAs.[131] Schneider finds no evidence that host countries give priority to projects with a high impact on sustainable development over those with little or no such impact: 'This has resulted in a situation in which the CDM project portfolio is mainly determined by the economic attractiveness' of projects.[132]

The most recent CDM study, which is also by far the largest study of the CDM's delivery of sustainability benefits ever undertaken, uses 15 indicators of sustainable development, encompassing most of the criteria used in earlier studies.[133] The indicators include improvement or protection of natural resources, efficient utilisation of natural resources, reduction in noise, odours, dust or pollutants, and the promotion of renewable energy, health and safety. The study was carried out under the direction of CDM Executive Board, and therefore cannot be

---

[124] S. Huq, *Applying Sustainable Development Criteria to CDM Projects: PCF Experience* (Prototype Carbon Fund, 2002).
[125] E. Boyd et al., 'Reforming the CDM for Sustainable Development: Lessons Learned and Policy Futures', 12 (7) *Environmental Science and Policy* 820 (2009).
[126] D. Hales and R. Prescott-Allen, 'Flying Blind: Assessing Progress toward Sustainability', in *Global Environmental Governance: Options and Opportunities*, eds D. C. Esty and M. H. Ivanova (Yale School of Forestry and Environmental Studies, 2002); and C. Voigt, 'Responsibility for the Environmental Integrity of the CDM: Judicial Review of Executive Board Decisions', in *Legal Aspects of Carbon Trading*, eds D. Freestone and C. Streck (Oxford University Press, 2009), p. 277.
[127] Schneider, *Is the CDM Fulfilling Its Environmental and Sustainable Development Objectives?* (2007), p. 46.
[128] K. H. Olsen, 'The Clean Development Mechanism's Contribution to Sustainable Development: A Review of the Literature', 84 *Climatic Change* 59 (2007); C. Sutter and J. C. Parreño, 'Does the Current Clean Development Mechanism (CDM) Deliver Its Sustainable Development Claim? An Analysis of Officially Registered CDM Projects', 84 *Climatic Change* 75 (2007); Boyd et al., 'Reforming the CDM for Sustainable Development' (2009); P. Nussbaumer, 'On the Contribution of Labelled Certified Emission Reductions to Sustainable Development: A Multi-Criteria Evaluation of CDM Projects', 37(1) *Energy Policy* 91 (2009); J. Alexeew et al., 'An Analysis of the Relationship between the Additionality of CDM Projects and Their Contribution to Sustainable Development', 10 *International Environmental Agreements* 233 (2010); and Clean Development Mechanism (Kyoto Protocol), *Benefits of the Clean Development Mechanism* (2011).
[129] C. Voigt, 'The Deadlock of the Clean Development Mechanism: Caught between Sustainability, Environmental Integrity and Economic Efficiency', in *Climate Law and Developing Countries: Legal and Policy Changes for the World Economy*, eds B. J. Richardson et al. (Edward Elgar Publishing, 2009).
[130] Schneider, *Is the CDM Fulfilling Its Environmental and Sustainable Development Objectives?* (2007), p. 46.
[131] D. Disch, 'A Comparative Analysis of the "Development Dividend" of Clean Development Mechanism Projects in Six Host Countries', 2 *Climate and Development* 50 (2010).
[132] Schneider, *Is the CDM Fulfilling Its Environmental and Sustainable Development Objectives?* (2007), pp. 46–7.
[133] Clean Development Mechanism (Kyoto Protocol), *Benefits of the Clean Development Mechanism* (2011), p. 10.

considered independent. It found evidence to suggest that 'CDM projects are indeed making a contribution to sustainable development over and above the mitigation of greenhouse gas emissions in the host country',[134] 'the most prominent being employment creation'.[135] It also noted that 'there is much room for improvement in the approaches used for both the declaration and the assessment of sustainable development of CDM projects'.[136]

If the requirement of additionality implies that the CDM should be governed with a strong hand, the requirement of sustainability leads us to the same conclusion. Here, too, strict controls are necessary, as there is nothing in the carbon market's core seller–buyer relationship that provides an incentive to undertake environmentally sustainable projects.

CDM project distribution and equity of access

China is the country with the largest number of CDM projects: by mid-2011, it was host to more than 1600 projects (more than 50 per cent of the global total). The next largest host country was India, with 777 registered projects.[137] Forty-five other developing countries, 18 of which were in Africa, had only one to nine projects each, and 50 more (28 in Africa) had no projects at all.[138] Repeated efforts have been made to improve the CDM's reach in Africa.[139]

Some commentators have suggested introducing differential values for some CERs; for example, two industrial gas credits (whose placement under the CDM has often been criticised) would be equal to one renewable energy CER or one CER from a Least Developed Country.[140] None of these suggestions has been taken up. It is not even clear that greater equity in the distribution of CDM projects would constitute improved governance of the CDM, as some would object to interference with the decisions of investors in a market mechanism.

On a literal reading of the rules, it would appear that the equitable distribution of CDM projects is not the responsibility of the CDM Executive Board, but rather of the CMP. The Board's role is (merely) to report to the CMP 'on the regional and subregional distribution of CDM project activities with a view to identifying systematic or systemic barriers to their equitable distribution'.[141] It would appear, too, that this is a low reform priority for the CDM, considering the other pressures it is facing and the plausible view that equity of access should be improved

---

134 Ibid., p. 5.   **135** Ibid., p. 19.   **136** Ibid.
137 <http://cdm.unfccc.int/Projects/projsearch.html>.
138 <http://cdm.unfccc.int/CDMMaps/displayDNAsMap>.
139 One example is the Nairobi Framework Partners, consisting of the UN Development Programme, the UN Environment Programme, the International Emissions Trading Association, and the World Bank, as well as the UNFCCC Secretariat. The partnership organised the first Africa Carbon Forum in Senegal in 2008, and there have been another two since. The Forum meetings aim to promote the benefits of CDM projects in the interactive setting of a trade exposition. See <http://africacarbonforum.com/2011/english/objective.htm>.
140 J. C. Nagle, 'Discounting China's CDM Dams', 7(1) *Loyola University Chicago International Law Review* 9 (2009).
141 Kyoto Protocol, *Decision 3/CMP.1* (30 March 2006), para. 5(h).

through capacity-building rather than discriminatory regulation. Nevertheless, in Durban in 2011, the CMP directed the Executive Board to continue its efforts to improve the equitable distribution of CDM project activities.[142]

Administrative review of CDM Executive Board decisions

We have referred to the heavy burden of responsibility (and the heavy workload) carried by the CDM Executive Board. There are a large number of applications for CDM projects (more than 3000 in mid-2011), and large amounts of money riding on them (600 million CERs issued by that date). The risks incurred by project developers and providers of start-up finance are significant. Along the way, a number of applications for project registration have been rejected (around 200 as of mid-2011).[143] In addition to straight-out refusal to register a project and refusal to issue CERs, the Executive Board has the power to recommend the suspension or withdrawal of 'designation' from a Designated Operational Entity, after giving the DOE an opportunity to be heard.[144] Suspension or disqualification of DOEs is not a rare event. Where a review of the DOE's past dealings reveals that excess CERs were issued to a project, or the applicable procedures were not otherwise adhered to, the DOE could be made to purchase and transfer to the Executive Board for cancellation a quantity of CERs equal to the excess issued, as determined by the Executive Board.[145] In effect, the DOE could be made to pay a monetary fine. The Executive Board also controls the approval and review of baseline-and-monitoring methodologies, without which project registration cannot proceed. This list is illustrative of the many actions the Board is entitled to take that may have significant consequences for third parties. But there is no UNFCCC body outside the Executive Board with the power to hear grievances from DOEs or CDM project participants from the private sector. The CDM depends for its existence on the participation of the private sector, but in character it remains state-centric.

In such a context, there is an argument for closer supervision of the decisions of the Executive Board, perhaps through some form of administrative review. Streck and Lin observe:

> The Executive Board is the de facto regulator of the CDM, and in playing this role, it makes decisions that affect the rights and interests of private entities. However, it does so without fulfilling due process requirements, such as giving reasons for a decision and affording parties affected by its decisions the right of appeal. Discontent with this state of affairs has already surfaced, with some project developers threatening legal action against the Executive Board and the UNFCCC Secretariat.[146]

---

[142] Kyoto Protocol, *Decision 8/CMP.7, Further Guidance Relating to the Clean Development Mechanism* (2011), paras. 30–2.
[143] See the CDM database, <http://cdm.unfccc.int/Projects/projsearch.html>.
[144] Kyoto Protocol, *Decision 3/CMP.1* (30 March 2006), para. 21. [145] Ibid., para. 22.
[146] Streck and Lin, 'Mobilising Finance for Climate Change Mitigation' (2009), p. 72.

They continue by noting that the limited legal basis for the influence that the Executive Board has come to have could mire the institution in questions about legitimacy:

> Discomfort about the delegation of authority to distant officials adds to concerns about inadequate checks and balances on the international level to the extent that the lack of democratic foundations for international bodies creates serious legitimacy issues ... Where democratic legitimacy is missing, it is important that legitimacy is enhanced by procedural safeguards that promote a widely accepted method of policymaking. Such procedures often form part of the toolbox of administrative law and premise decision-making on notions of predictability, fairness, transparency, rationality, stability, neutrality and efficiency.[147]

Following such arguments by practitioners and scholars in favour of a mechanism for administrative review, the CMP assigned the matter to the UNFCCC's Subordinate Body for Implementation for consideration.[148] Because there is very little precedent at the international level for such a review arrangement, creating an appeal system for the CDM is a significant legal challenge. The SBI produced a paper in April 2011 collating state views on the matter,[149] later followed by a technical analysis of the various options by the UNFCCC Secretariat.[150] At the time of writing, the Kyoto Protocol parties were still deliberating about the main features of an appeal mechanism.[151] Assuming agreement among the parties is reached, the mechanism would be created through a CMP decision. On the form of the institution, the possibilities being considered range from a new ad hoc panel, to using an existing body, such as the Enforcement Branch of the Compliance Committee, to decide the appeals;[152] on the expertise of the adjudicators, most parties have called for legal or regulatory expertise (potentially opening up new opportunities for climate lawyers); and regarding the scope of the appeals, the parties are undecided on whether it should be limited to Executive Board decisions *rejecting* project registration and requests to issue CERs, or whether it should also cover decisions to *approve* such matters.[153] However, improving oversight of the

---

147 Ibid., p. 77.   **148** On the procedural background to this development, see ibid., pp. 96–7.
149 Subsidiary Body for Implementation (UNFCCC), *Views on Procedures, Mechanisms and Institutional Arrangements for Appeals against the Decisions of the Executive Board of the Clean Development Mechanism* (21 April 2011), FCCC/SBI/2011/MISC.2.
150 Secretariat (UNFCCC), *Procedures, Mechanisms and Institutional Arrangements for Appeals against the Decisions of the Executive Board of the Clean Development Mechanism* (17 May 2011), FCCC/TP/2011/3.
151 By the time of the Durban CMP, the 'parties had not found agreement on the mandate to establish the appeals process. The SBI adopted conclusions (FCCC/SBI/2011/L.30), taking note of the revised draft co-chairs' text and agreeing to resume discussions at SBI 36' (in 2012): International Institute for Sustainable Development, 'Durban Highlights: Saturday, 3 December 2011', 12(529) *Earth Negotiations Bulletin* 1 (2011), pp. 1–2.
152 On the Compliance Committee, see Chapter 3.
153 International Institute for Sustainable Development, 'SB 34 and AWG Highlights: Saturday, 11 June 2011', 12(508) *Earth Negotiations Bulletin* 1 (2011), p. 3. Several parties have taken the position that the focus of the work on the question of appeals, as mandated by the CMP, is on a procedure for appeals only against decisions to reject project registration or requests to issue CERs. One difficulty with this position is that certain CDM projects are registered automatically (a special procedure not discussed here), with a review undertaken only if requested by three members of the Executive Board or a party involved in the proposed project. Some states maintain that in such cases, it might be appropriate to allow appeals against CDM Executive Board decisions to approve such registration requests: International Institute for Sustainable Development, 'SB 34 and AWG Highlights: Tuesday, 14 June 2011' (2011), p. 3.

Executive Board by establishing a quasi-judicial review mechanism could come at an insufferable price: more red tape. Bureaucratic checks and balances can be self-defeating where the problem to be solved is an urgent one. Striking the right balance in this area is critical, but it is also critical to recognise that it is a matter of balance and not a single-minded fight for integrity.

What future for the CDM?

The CDM is a venture of unprecedented size and complexity aimed at producing environmental benefits. It has brought about a whole new network of transnational relationships. CDM projects have helped to build national capacity in developing countries related to several aspects of the effort to control climate change, from the basic level of accounting for GHG emissions to the level of climate-related policy and legal reform. Questions remain about the extent to which CDM reductions are real, measurable and verifiable, as well as additional to any that would occur in the absence of a CDM project. There is evidence that the sustainability benefits of CDM projects have been demoted to a secondary concern. Moreover, there is a disproportionate concentration of CDM projects in a handful of countries – an equity problem that remains unresolved.

In 2010–11, when it seemed almost certain that the Kyoto Protocol would have no second commitment period, there was much thought given to the question of what would happen to the CDM when the 2008–12 commitment period expired.[154] The text of the Protocol, at Article 12(2), does seem to tie the CDM to the existence of country-level emission caps: 'The purpose of the clean development mechanism shall be . . . to assist Parties included in Annex I in achieving compliance with their quantified emission limitation and reduction commitments under Article 3.' Without legally binding emission caps, the CDM's demonstrable benefits would dry up. These include, notably, money raised for the Adaptation Fund[155] and transfer of money and technology to developing countries. The withdrawal of Canada, Japan and Russia from the Protocol's second commitment period[156] is already a significant blow to the Mechanism.

---

[154] For example Secretariat (Kyoto Protocol), *Legal Considerations Relating to a Possible Gap between the First and Subsequent Commitment Periods* (UNFCCC, 20 July 2010), FCCC/KP/AWG/2010/10, paras. 45–9; International Institute for Sustainable Development, 'Summary of the Panama City Climate Change Talks: 1–7 October 2011', 12(521) *Earth Negotiations Bulletin* 1 (2011), p. 14; International Institute for Sustainable Development, 'Durban Highlights: Wednesday, 30 November 2011', 12(526) *Earth Negotiations Bulletin* 1 (2011), p. 1. At the June 2011 CMP intersessional meeting, New Zealand proposed a 'docking mechanism' that would shuttle Kyoto Protocol elements, such as the CDM, to a new comprehensive regime: International Institute for Sustainable Development, 'SB 34 and AWG Highlights: Monday, 13 June 2011', 12(509) *Earth Negotiations Bulletin* 1 (2011), p. 1. New Zealand also noted that even in the absence of a second commitment period, developed-country mitigation actions and associated demand for carbon offsets would continue – especially in countries like New Zealand with an emissions trading scheme.
[155] Britta Horstmann and Achala Chandani Abeysinghe, 'The Adaptation Fund of the Kyoto Protocol: A Model for Financing Adaptation to Climate Change?', 2 (3) *Climate Law* 415 (2011).
[156] Kyoto Protocol, *Decision 1/CMP.7, Outcome of the Work of the Ad Hoc Working Group on Further Commitments for Annex I Parties under the Kyoto Protocol at Its Sixteenth Session* (2011).

(Japan was a major purchaser of CDM offsets, with 103 million CERs in its account.)[157]

If the CDM needs emission caps to give it life, countries with emission caps need the CDM to lower the cost of compliance. The CDM enables the maximisation of emission reduction commitments.[158] The European Union continues to rely heavily on the CDM to meet its targets. This is clear from EU statements about the Union's pledged 2020 target of reducing GHG emissions by 20 per cent below 1990 levels. Up to 4 per cent of that reduction would come from CDM credits; were the European Union to move to a 30 per cent reduction target, the CDM share would rise to 9 per cent.[159] As at 31 December 2010, European Union countries had purchased 286 million CERs (the leading buyer was Germany, with 86 million CERs, followed by Spain and the United Kingdom with 43 and 36 million, respectively).[160]

The CDM is enormously important to the future of Australia's climate change policy. While Australia, to date, has made no use of the CDM[161] because it signed up late to the Kyoto Protocol and its emission reduction policies covering the period to the end of 2012 have been unambitious, Australia's emission reduction pledges for the four decades *following* 2012 (viz. 5 per cent below 2000 levels by 2020[162] and 80 per cent below 2000 levels by 2050[163]) promise a significant departure from the country's business-as-usual emissions. The planned departure is largely to be achieved not through GHG reductions in Australian territory but through international emission allowance purchases, projected to reach 434 million tonnes *per year* of CO_2 eq. in 2050.[164] Much of Australia's future mitigation is thus to be outsourced. The CDM will play a big role in offsetting Australia's territorial emissions.

---

157 Secretariat (UNFCCC), *Annual Compilation and Accounting Report for Annex B Parties under the Kyoto Protocol for 2011* (16 November 2011), FCCC/KP/CMP/2011/8, Table 7.
158 International Institute for Sustainable Development, 'SB 34 and AWG Highlights: Monday, 13 June 2011' (2011), p. 1.
159 International Institute for Sustainable Development, 'Summary of the Bangkok Climate Talks: 3–8 April 2011', 12(499) *Earth Negotiations Bulletin* 1 (2011), p. 3.
160 Secretariat (UNFCCC), *Accounting Report for Annex B Parties, 2011* (2011), Table 7.
161 At the time of writing, Australia had zero CER holdings: ibid. The CDM database contained only four projects involving Australian investors. These projects, all of which were registered between 2008 and 2011, consisted of two electricity projects based in India (both co-generation plants fueled by rice husks), one hydropower project in China (the Yunnan Lixianjiang Shimenkan Hydropower Project), and one Philippines-based project involving the catalytic decomposition of N_2O emissions at a plant manufacturing nitric acid. Macquarie Bank Ltd was the investor in the China project. See the CDM database, <http://cdm.unfccc.int/Projects/projsearch.html>.
162 UNFCCC, 'Appendix I – Quantified Economy-Wide Emissions Targets for 2020', <http://unfccc.int/meetings/copenhagen_dec_2009/items/5264.php>.
163 *Clean Energy Act 2011* (Cth) s 3(c)(i).
164 Department of Treasury, *Strong Growth, Low Pollution: Modelling a Carbon Price* (2011), p. 77. At a market price of around $20 per tonne of CO_2 eq., the annual cost of purchasing emission allowances will be in the order of hundreds of millions of dollars.

7

The emerging scheme for the protection of forests in developing countries (REDD)

Introduction: REDD's place in the international climate regime   *page 229*
Deforestation: Some facts and figures   233
Rescaling the deforestation problem   237
Causes of deforestation and REDD's fractious social context   238
Steps towards the international regulation of REDD   242
REDD funding for the preparatory stage   246
Monitoring, reporting and verification of REDD projects   248
Australia's involvement with REDD   250
Conclusion: Will REDD be effective?   253

Introduction: REDD's place in the international climate regime

Forests have played a relatively minor role in the international climate regime to date. This is not because their value is questioned; on the contrary, it is clear that by sequestering carbon while standing, or releasing carbon dioxide when felled, forests and deforestation have significant effects on climate change.

The reason why forest-based mitigation has been very nearly excluded from the international regime has to do with the sheer practical difficulties involved, at every level, in any global effort to protect or augment the world's forests. Action to overcome these difficulties has intensified in recent years within the frameworks provided by several international conventions focused on environmental protection.[1] In this chapter we focus on efforts now being made, within the

---

[1] Including the World Heritage Convention, the Convention on International Trade in Endangered Species, the Convention on Biological Diversity, and the Convention to Combat Desertification. The Collaborative Partnership on Forests, a consortium of 14 forest-related organisations and secretariats, represents an attempt to bring international coordination to an otherwise fragmented field: see <http://www.fao.org/forestry/iyf2011/69194/en/> for the events organised under the CPF umbrella to commemorate the 2011 International Year of Forests. See also Secretariat (Convention on Biological Diversity), *REDD-Plus and Biodiversity* (Convention on Biological Diversity, 2011), CBD Technical Series No. 59.

229

framework of the UNFCCC, to agree to a scheme for the reduction of emissions from deforestation and forest degradation in developing countries: the scheme known as REDD. While REDD is far from being finalised at the international level, much preparatory work is already under way, including demonstration projects (some sponsored by Australia) in anticipation of its establishment. REDD's peculiar situation is that it is a regime with broad international support but with little international regulation yet in place.[2] Nevertheless, it is sufficiently evolved to justify a separate chapter.

The Kyoto Protocol's Clean Development Mechanism (Chapter 6) permits a small set of forestry activities (afforestation and reforestation projects).[3] The permitted CDM activities include planting trees to act as CO_2 sinks – to create 'forests' from the ground up – but the CDM has no dedicated method to prevent the felling and degradation of forests in the first place. Article 2 of the Kyoto Protocol requires Annex I parties to protect and enhance their sinks and reservoirs for GHGs and to promote sustainable forest management practices. The problem with this focus on Annex I parties is that these states are not the ones primarily responsible for today's deforestation.[4] For Annex I countries overall, activities within the LULUCF sector, which includes forestry, served as a net sink, not a net source.[5] In Australia deforestation fell sharply in the early 1990s and has since been kept at historically low levels.[6] Deforestation is now almost exclusive to developing countries. Because developing countries generally lack

---

[2] Forest degradation refers to the loss of vegetation in forests through timber harvesting, fuel-wood gathering, fire, and other activities that do not result in complete conversion of the forest to other land uses: N. R. Virgilio et al., *Reducing Emissions from Deforestation and Degradation (REDD): A Casebook of On-the-Ground Experience* (The Nature Conservancy, 2010), p. 14. In its classification of 'forest', the IPCC uses a minimum crown cover of 10–30 per cent (first articulated in UNFCCC, *Decision 11/CP.7, Land Use, Land-Use Change, and Forestry* (2001), FCCC/CP/2001/13/Add.1). By this definition, up to 90 per cent of a forest can be cleared before it is considered deforested. As such, forest degradation can lead to substantial carbon emissions, and is often an important precursor to deforestation.
[3] Kyoto Protocol, *Decision 5/CMP.1, Modalities and Procedures for Afforestation and Reforestation Project Activities under the Clean Development Mechanism in the First Commitment Period of the Kyoto Protocol* (30 March 2006), FCCC/KP/CMP/2005/8/Add.1. As also discussed in Chapter 6, the barriers to CDM forestry projects include the difficulty of finding buyers for the relatively low-value temporary credits yielded by forestry projects under CDM.
[4] Russia is the main exception among developed countries: see Forest Europe, UNECE, and Food and Agriculture Organization, *State of Europe's Forests 2011: Status and Trends in Sustainable Forest Management in Europe* (Ministerial Conference on the Protection of Forests in Europe, 2011), p. 20. On the state of forests in developed countries, see also Food and Agriculture Organization, *Global Forest Resources Assessment 2010: Main Report* (2010), pp. xvi–xvii; and C. Potter et al., 'Storage of Carbon in US Forests Predicted from Satellite Data, Ecosystem Modeling, and Inventory Summaries', 90 *Climatic Change* 269 (2008).
[5] Thus, between 1990 and 2007, total aggregate GHG emissions excluding emissions and removals from LULUCF for all Annex I countries decreased by 3.9 per cent; aggregate emissions including those from LULUCF decreased by 5.2 per cent. Annex I countries with economies in transition (EIT) provided the strongest LULUCF sink. In these countries, GHG emissions excluding LULUCF decreased by 37 per cent; with LULUCF they decreased by 42.2 per cent. However, note that in Annex I non-EIT countries, GHG emissions excluding LULUCF increased by 11.2 per cent and GHG emissions including LULUCF increased by 12.8 per cent: Secretariat (UNFCCC), *National Greenhouse Gas Inventory Data for the Period 1990–2007* (21 October 2009), FCCC/SBI/2009/12, p. 1.
[6] Department of the Environment, Sport and Territories, *Climate Change: Australia's [First] National Report under the United Nations Framework Convention on Climate Change* (September 1994), pp. 57–8; and C. McGrath, 'End of Broadscale Clearing in Queensland', 24 *Environmental and Planning Law Journal* 5 (2007).

the capacity to respond to the forces of deforestation effectively on their own, there is little point in a treaty 'directing' them to desist from deforestation. It would in any case go against the spirit of the international climate change regime as we know it, which has so far placed legal burdens only on Annex I parties to the Kyoto Protocol. To reverse deforestation, a solution premised upon the cooperation of all parties to the UNFCCC is needed.

REDD is indeed being developed under the Convention rather than the Kyoto Protocol. There is unfortunately very little already in the Convention on which to build a scheme for forests. Article 4(1)(d) contains only a very general commitment by all parties to the sustainable management, conservation, and enhancement of forests – following which the subject is not taken up again in the text of the UNFCCC, which is after all only a 'framework'. While it would have been technically possible for REDD to be incorporated into the more functional architecture of the Kyoto Protocol,[7] tradition and pragmatism suggest that all important work on climate change mitigation that is still to be carried out at the international level and is not an offshoot of the Protocol should be accommodated under the Convention. This ensures, among other things, that the world's largest economy (the United States) is involved with it and supports it.

In its basic logic, though, REDD owes much to the Clean Development Mechanism (a creature of the Protocol). Assuming that REDD is eventually successfully established, it will, like the CDM, raise money from Annex I investors to purchase emission reductions in developing countries. With REDD, the reductions will be effected primarily by projects to prevent deforestation and degradation, established in developing countries with large forested areas. REDD has the potential to go even further than this, potentially generating credits from projects directed to the conservation and enhancement of forest stocks. This more ambitious form of REDD is known as REDD-plus.[8] (For simplicity, we employ the term REDD to mean both.)

As discussed in the CDM chapter, the generation of emission reductions presupposes proof of two emission trajectories: a counterfactual trajectory which *would have* materialised in the normal course of events (in the absence of the project), and an emission trajectory that factors in the operation of the project. The former will be a prediction if it is projected into the future, or it will be a reverse estimate if it is worked out retrospectively. In either case it will be a hypothesis about what would have happened in the project's absence. If the

---

7 At a UNFCCC intersessional negotiating session in 2011, Papua New Guinea, on behalf of the Coalition of Rainforest Nations, said that the most effective way to implement REDD-plus would be to create a new mechanism under the Kyoto Protocol: International Institute for Sustainable Development, 'SB 34 and AWG Highlights: Tuesday, 7 June 2011', 12(504) *Earth Negotiations Bulletin* 1 (2011), p. 1.
8 The constituent elements of REDD-plus are: (1) reducing emissions from deforestation; (2) reducing emissions from forest degradation; (3) conservation of forest carbon stocks; (4) sustainable management of forests; and (5) enhancement of forest carbon stocks: see UNFCCC, *Decision 1/CP.16, The Cancun Agreements: Outcome of the Work of the Ad Hoc Working Group on Long-Term Cooperative Action under the Convention* (2010), FCCC/CP/2010/7/Add.1, Appendix I, para. 70.

project-influenced emission trajectory is lower than that for the business-as-usual scenario, the project may claim to have effected emission reductions and on that basis receive credits. The CDM/REDD logic is in both cases exactly the same in this respect. Where REDD differs from the CDM is in its exclusive focus on forests. Also, it is theoretically inclined to conceive of a country's forests holistically, as a single entity. The CDM, by contrast, has no necessary holistic outlook, operating through a variety of usually piecemeal, unrelated projects, very few of which (less than 1 per cent[9]) are forestry projects. A further minority of CDM projects benefits forests indirectly. The Nigeria Stoves CDM project (discussed in Chapter 6), in which credits were generated from the distribution of stoves using 80 per cent less fuel wood for the same work as traditional methods, resulted in lower CO_2 emissions while also slowing the rate of deforestation within the project boundary. It was an energy-efficiency project, but in effect it paid people to reduce their demands on forests.

Two other interesting differences emerge from the comparison of REDD and the CDM. The CDM was intended to turn GHG mitigation into a global effort, albeit one paid for by Annex I countries. In fact, the Mechanism has been a runaway success in involving wealthier and more industrialised developing countries, especially China and India, while its penetration of the Least Developed Countries, where industry is weak and dispersed, has been insignificant. REDD promises an important role, finally, for LDCs, which are forest-rich. Another interesting difference between REDD and the CDM is that the latter was created to offset growing industrial emissions in Annex I countries. REDD, by setting out to preserve the earth's great tropical forests, is uniquely tackling a problem of growing GHG emissions in the *non-Annex I* world: it is a developing country cure for a developing country problem.

In the final analysis, REDD-simpliciter would be a dedicated program to pay people to leave forests alone. Under REDD-plus, it would pay people to look after forests and improve them. Most of the money for REDD activity would ultimately come from Annex I governments, although much of the initial investment would probably come from non-government sources, with the intention to create REDD credits of one kind or another, which could be sold at cost or at a profit to Annex I governments.

The legal and regulatory challenges facing REDD are equal to or greater than those of any of the other programs of the international climate change regime. The evolution and roll-out of the REDD program offer unprecedented opportunities for climate lawyers with a bent for development work.[10] We hope to draw out some of the richness of the field, as well as its staggering challenges, in the sections that follow.

---

9 Clean Development Mechanism (Kyoto Protocol), 'Distribution of Registered Project Activities by Scope', <http://cdm.unfccc.int/Statistics/Registration/RegisteredProjByScopePieChart.html>.
10 For sound advice in this respect, see M. Wilder and J. Crittenden, *Bringing the Forest to Market: Structuring Avoided Deforestation Projects* (Baker & McKenzie, 2009).

Deforestation: Some facts and figures

The tropical forests of the Amazon and Congo Basins and South-East Asia (Figure 7.1) contain the bulk of the world's terrestrial biodiversity.[11] Thirty countries in these three regions, accounting for 18 per cent of the world's land area and 15 per cent of the population, incorporate 33 per cent of the world's forests (1.3 billion hectares of forested area in total) and 47 per cent of the global growing carbon stock.[12] The vast majority of REDD activity is likely to be directed towards the preservation of these forests, so it is worth considering their features as a distinct group.

When primary forest is considered (that is, forest consisting of native species where there is no visible indication of human activity and the ecological processes have not been significantly disturbed), the three regions together account for more than 50 per cent of all primary forest worldwide: over 830 million hectares.[13] Of the 30 included countries, ten have Least Developed Country status and most of the rest have a GDP of less than US$10 000 per capita (Brazil, Venezuela, Singapore and Malaysia are exceptions).[14] People in most rainforest countries are thus poor, economies are non-industrialised, and national governments are keen to encourage economic development there – indeed, they are likely to consider economic development to be their primary goal.

Tropical forests are largely publicly owned. In the Congo Basin there is almost no private ownership of forests. There is a different balance in the Amazon Basin

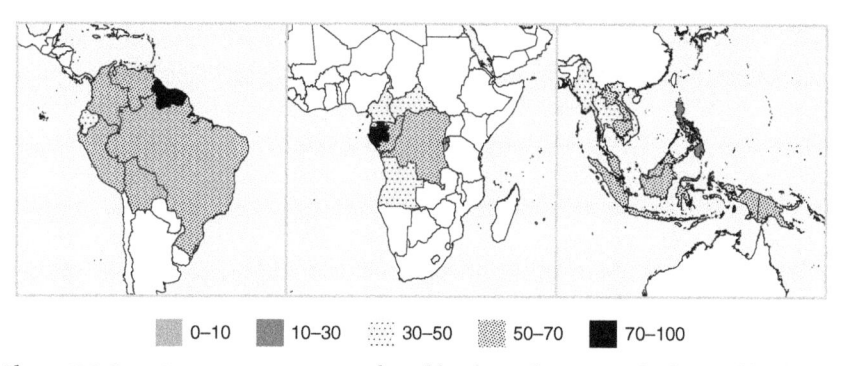

Figure 7.1 Forest area as percentage of total land area by country in the world's three tropical forest regions, 2010
Source: Based on Food and Agriculture Organization and ITTO, *The State of Forests in the Amazon Basin, Congo Basin and Southeast Asia* (2011), Figure 4, p. 14

---

[11] Food and Agriculture Organization and ITTO, *The State of Forests in the Amazon Basin, Congo Basin and Southeast Asia: A Report Prepared for the Summit of the Three Rainforest Basins, Brazzaville, Republic of Congo, 31 May–3 June, 2011* (2011), p. 3. This section also draws on Food and Agriculture Organization, *Forest Assessment 2010* (2010); and J. Blaser et al., *Status of Tropical Forest Management 2011*, ITTO Technical Series No. 38 (International Tropical Timber Organization, 2011).
[12] Food and Agriculture Organization and ITTO, *The State of Forests* (2011), pp. 11, 13, 21.
[13] Ibid., p. 18.   [14] Ibid., p. 11.

and in South-East Asia, where close to 20 per cent of forests are privately owned.[15] Whether publicly or privately owned, forests contribute to local livelihoods. Some governments report 'community management' of some publicly owned forest, which in several cases is quite extensive. For example, in Brazil and the Philippines, 37 and 47 per cent, respectively, of publicly owned forests is reported to be under such community management.[16] There is also an increasing trend of involving private companies in forest management: in Cameroon, the Congo and Indonesia more than 40 per cent of publicly owned forest is managed by private corporations and concessionaires.[17]

The legal and beneficial interest in publicly owned forests is no simple matter, then. This is especially so when the traditional rights of indigenous communities are taken into account. Land tenure is important to REDD's implementation because any agreement to avoid deforestation must take into account people's asserted rights to the forest. These rights will be a factor in who will 'own' the sequestered carbon and be entitled to receive the credits for its upkeep. However, traditional land tenure is often not recognised in legal form in LDCs and other countries, or is arduous to prove. Clearly, this is a huge problem for the implementation of REDD. It is also a good example of imperfections or inequities in domestic law potentially holding up action against climate change at the international level. So far, success stories on land tenure have been isolated and ad hoc.[18]

About 279 million hectares of forest in the three rainforest basins (of the 1.3 billion hectares in total) are managed primarily for the production of wood and non-wood forest products.[19] Another 10 per cent of the area (135 million hectares) is designated for multiple use, which in most cases also includes exploitation of wood and non-wood products.[20] Around 2.3 million people in the combined area are formally employed in logging, wood processing, and the pulp and paper industry. Because much of the employment in logging and wood processing occurs outside the formal sector and official statistics, the figure understates the extent of economic dependence.[21]

Wood removal has been rising for decades in the Amazon and Congo basins, with the yearly amount removed in 2000 being double, in both regions, that for

---

15 Ibid. **16** Ibid. **17** Ibid.
18 For example, to alleviate the threat of deforestation from local agricultural expansion, a project in Bolivia helped indigenous communities living adjacent to a national park gain legal recognition as an indigenous organisation, followed by tenure over ancestral lands bordering the project area: Virgilio et al., *REDD Casebook* (2010), p. 11. In Madagascar, a CDM project to combat forest loss set out to clarify land tenure in the affected area. With approximately 97 per cent of the project area formally owned by the government, the remaining 3 per cent had either been historically held under private use or held under traditional use rights by local residents. With NGO funding, the government of Madagascar established a local registry office near the project site, which enabled the formalisation of previously customary land tenure. Farmers would receive an instrument granting them secure tenure over their lands in exchange for placing a portion of the land under reforestation for the lifetime of the CDM project. These tenure holders then agreed to transfer rights to the carbon sequestered by the trees on their land to the government for the 30-year lifetime of the project: ibid., p. 46.
19 Food and Agriculture Organization and ITTO, *The State of Forests* (2011), p. 25.
20 Ibid., pp. 25, 33.
21 Ibid., p. 28; Food and Agriculture Organization, *Forest Assessment 2010* (2010), p. xxii.

1970.[22] Only in South-East Asia has there been a gradual decline in the amount removed. Formally declared economic activity in the wood processing and pulp and paper industries contributed 2 per cent to GDP in the three rainforest basins combined (more than US$50 billion per year by 2005).[23] Again, however, because there is a lack of data on the subsistence use of forests and on the informal economy, the total contribution of the forestry sector to GDP can be assumed to be much higher.[24]

In these facts we see another fundamental difficulty that REDD faces: information about forests and their uses in tropical countries is generally incomplete or unreliable.

Every year many millions of hectares of forest in the three tropical regions are lost to 'alternative land uses' (mainly conversion of forest to agricultural land) or suffer severe degradation as a result of exploitation of the forest resources. In some developing countries, even with forest protection rules, penalties and enforcement in place, a corrupt political system leads to the destruction of forests at whim. Petherick writes that, often in such cases, publicly owned forests:

> are controlled by just a few civil servants or politicians with discretionary powers – handy conditions for effective bribery. This, and forests' geographical remoteness, helps loggers to get away with declaring less timber than they actually cut and extracting timber from outside allowed areas.[25]

On the positive side, there are signs that the overall *rate* of forest loss has been decreasing in recent times (Figure 7.2).[26] The three rainforest basins reported a net loss of forest area of 5.4 million hectares per year for the period 2000–10 (0.4 per cent annually), down from 7.1 million hectares per year during the previous decade.[27] Most of the reduction in the rate of loss happened in South-East Asia, where the rate has been more than halved in the last 20 years.[28] In absolute terms, 125 million hectares of forest were destroyed in the three rainforest basins over the 20 years up to 2010 (8.5 per cent of all forest in these regions).[29]

Continued deforestation at current rates in Brazil and Indonesia alone would equal (and thus cancel out) four-fifths of the annual reduction targets for Annex I countries under the Kyoto Protocol.[30] Annex I countries would be scaling back their emissions to no more meaningful end than to match the increasing emissions from deforestation in developing countries in the tropics. REDD is being deployed to

---

22 Food and Agriculture Organization and ITTO, *The State of Forests* (2011), p. 28, Figure 19.
23 Ibid., pp. 29–30, Figure 20. **24** Ibid., p.29.
25 A. Petherick, 'A Note of Caution', 2 *Nature Climate Change* 144 (March 2012), p. 145.
26 Food and Agriculture Organization and ITTO, *The State of Forests* (2011), p. 14.
27 Ibid., p. 15, Table 3. **28** Ibid.
29 Compare this figure to 136 million hectares destroyed globally (3.3 per cent of global forest) during the same two decades: ibid.
30 M. Santilli et al., 'Tropical Deforestation and the Kyoto Protocol: An Editorial Essay', 71 *Climatic Change* 267 (2005), p. 268.

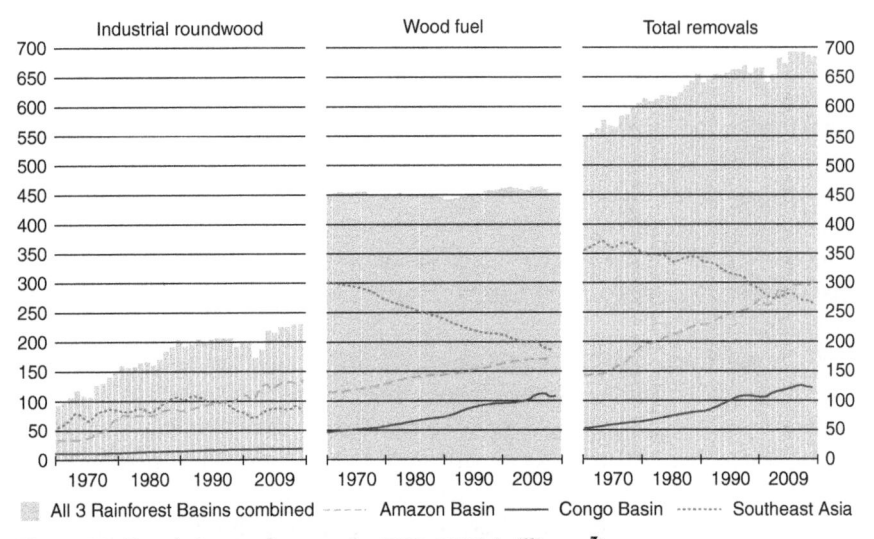

Figure 7.2 Trends in wood removals, 1970–2009 (million m³)
Source: Based on Food and Agriculture Organization and ITTO, *The State of Forests in the Amazon Basin, Congo Basin and Southeast Asia* (2011), Figure 19, p. 28

confront a practice that is not only massive but also very well entrenched, as can be seen from the trend in Figure 7.2.

Another item of positive news is that the area of forest in the three rainforest basins designated primarily for the conservation of biological diversity has grown, with strong growth occurring between 2000 and 2010.[31] At 187 million hectares (14 per cent of the total),[32] it is still a small proportion of the forested area, and much smaller than the area designated for use and exploitation. Another 7 per cent of the total forested area is primarily designated for the protection of soil and water resources.[33] Also increasing is the extent of planted forest. By 2010, a total of 25 million hectares had been planted in the three basins (58 per cent of it in South-East Asia and most of the rest in the Amazon).[34] Forest planting is small compared with the amount of forest that is being destroyed: five times more forest is being destroyed than planted. Also, reforestation restores trees, not ecology.[35] It is bare carbon storage. And it is carbon storage only for as long as it is left standing and not felled for timber. But at least we can point to some encouraging developments, which suggest that REDD's timing is opportune.

If we think of tree planting in terms of the CDM, and avoidance of deforestation in terms of REDD, the urgent establishment of REDD is clearly essential for

---

[31] For example World Bank, 'GEF Grant to Help Brazil Protect an Additional 13.5 Million Hectares in the Amazon', <http://www.worldbank.org/>.
[32] Food and Agriculture Organization and ITTO, *The State of Forests* (2011), p. 26.   [33] Ibid., p. 27.
[34] Ibid., p. 20.
[35] A. D. Barnosky et al., 'Has the Earth's Sixth Mass Extinction Already Arrived?', 471 *Nature* 51 (3 March 2011), p. 51.

narrowing the gap between forest removal and forest replanting. On the basis of the facts considered above we may at least be confident that those 30 countries form a natural target for REDD: If only the scheme could take root in the Amazon and Congo Basins and South-East Asia, these territories of the globe where deforestation is most acute would for the first time be subject to a kind of international regulation.

Rescaling the deforestation problem

The high rate of destruction of the world's forests was noticed and understood as a serious environmental problem long before the same was true of climate change. In spite of this, we have in place two international treaties that try to slow down climate change and none to put an end to deforestation. Efforts towards an international forest convention have been made to that end, but none has succeeded.[36]

Could deforestation be characterised as a truly global problem, like climate change? If we approach this question from the perspective of biodiversity protection or ecosystem services (clean water, prevention of erosion, human amenity and so forth), forest destruction may seem to be a local, national, or at most a transnational (cross-border) environmental problem. But if forests are conceptualised as carbon storage systems, which also actively remove carbon dioxide from the atmosphere, then their preservation and enhancement become strategies in the mitigation of climate change, and deforestation turns into a global issue.

A possible explanation of why there is no international convention on forests is that the state of forests had until recently been thought of as a matter of environmental concern at the national level – to be regulated at that level without any need for international coordination. Now that we are no longer able to think of deforestation as a global–*local* problem (Chapter 1), but only as a global–global one, REDD has rapidly gained traction. Environmental lawyers are better placed now than ever before to protect 'the global forest' as a matter of international concern.[37]

---

[36] See Food and Agriculture Organization and Committee on Forest Development in the Tropics, *Tropical Forest Action Plan* (1985), <http://www.ciesin.columbia.edu/docs/002–162/002–162.html>; UN General Assembly, *Report of the United Nations Conference on Environment and Development, Annex III: Non-Legally Binding Authoritative Statement of Principles for a Global Consensus on the Management, Conservation and Sustainable Development of All Types of Forests* (14 August 1992), A/CONF.151/26 (Vol. III); the Intergovernmental Panel on Forests (1995–97) and the *Intergovernmental Forum on Forests* (1997–2000), <http://www.un.org/esa/forests/ipf_iff.html> (which did not result in any final agreement on forest protection); International Tropical Timber Agreement, opened for signature 27 January 2006 <http://treaties.un.org/doc/source/RecentTexts/XIX_46_english.pdf> (not yet in force); and UN General Assembly, *Non-Legally Binding Instrument on All Types of Forests (Resolution Adopted by the General Assembly)* (31 January 2008), A/RES/62/98.
[37] See W. Boyd, 'Ways of Seeing in Environmental Law: How Deforestation Became an Object of Climate Governance', 37 *Ecology Law Quarterly* 843 (2010).

Causes of deforestation and REDD's fractious social context

Deforestation can be the result of lawlessness, or of laws and policies that are inconsistently enforced or unenforceable in practice or rendered ineffectual by an incompatible set of priorities, such as government-instigated population resettlement in forested zones or the emergence of lucrative international markets in timber or agricultural products. Regulation is necessary to avoid deforestation, but also necessary is the incentive to comply with the regulation and enforce it. Good forest governance has many pillars: policy and law are two; others take the form of institutions, procedures (formal planning and decision-making inscribed in law), practices that are equitable, participatory and transparent, and operational mechanisms for implementation, enforcement and compliance.[38]

With respect to the first two pillars, the majority of the countries in the rainforest basins of the Amazon, Congo and South-East Asia do not *lack* appropriate laws and policies. Of the 30 countries concerned, 26 have a specific forest law (with 10 reporting that their current forest law was enacted or amended after 2000).[39] Fifty-eight per cent of the forested area in the three basins is classified as part of the permanent forest estate, designated by law to remain forever under forest cover.[40] Moreover, 25 of the basin countries, including all of the larger ones, claim to employ a participatory process for the development and implementation of forest-related policies and international commitments. They are not remote laws imposed by fiat.[41]

A less positive picture emerges, though, when other pillars of good governance are considered. For example:

(i) Only 13 per cent of the total forest in the three regions is subject to some kind of management plan. (Experts consider a management plan to be an important instrument for achieving sustainable forest management.[42])

(ii) The area known to be managed sustainably on the basis of accepted criteria for sustainable forest management is only 3.5 per cent of the total.

(iii) Forestry agencies have meagre staffs and budgets to enable the enforcement of forestry laws.[43]

(iv) The extraction of fuel wood, which results in the degradation of forests, is perceived as a traditional practice – a customary right – that is not subject to limitation by laws or their enforcement.[44]

---

38 Food and Agriculture Organization, *Framework for Assessing and Monitoring Forest Governance* (2011), p. 10.
39 Food and Agriculture Organization and ITTO, *The State of Forests* (2011), p. 31.   **40** Ibid., p. 35.
41 Ibid., p. 31.
42 See A. M. Evans and R. Perschel, 'A Review of Forestry Mitigation and Adaptation Strategies in the Northeast US', 96 *Climatic Change* 167 (2009) ('Forest management decisions can increase forests' resilience and ability to adapt to altered precipitation and temperature patterns').
43 Food and Agriculture Organization, *Forest Assessment 2010* (2010), p. xxiii.
44 TÜV Nord, *Final Validation Report for Efficient Fuel Wood Stoves for Nigeria* (CDM website, 8 September 2009), p. 76.

The more we drill down into the causes of deforestation and forest degradation, the more we learn about the difficult environment that the REDD scheme will have to contend with.[45] The point is well illustrated by the situation in the Amazon Basin. The case illustrates the reforms that would be needed, at several levels of governance, to accommodate the REDD mechanism.[46]

The Amazon Basin lost around 3.6 million hectares of forest per year between 2000 and 2010.[47] Eighty per cent of the basin's forest is primary.[48] In absolute terms, the Amazon has lost more primary forest than any other area, worldwide. Most of the Amazon is in Brazil, a country which in recent years has enjoyed a stable and sophisticated democracy, well-developed federal governance structures, and increasing prosperity. Its capacity to host a scheme directed to stopping deforestation is far superior to that of the Democratic Republic of Congo, say, which has suffered from what are perhaps the greatest enemies of REDD and any other aid program: drawn-out civil war and systemic government corruption.[49]

Most deforestation in the Brazilian Amazon has occurred since the 1960s, when the federal government began to subsidise population settlement and economic development in a region encroaching on the forest basin from the south and south-east. By 2001, the human population of the resettlement zone had grown from four million to over 20 million.[50] Trunk roads opened up the forest to a web of smaller access roads. Deforestation was carried out by land grabbers, who claimed land through fraud and violence; loggers, who extracted the most valuable plant species from the forest; colonists and other subsistence farmers, who bought or simply occupied land; and large cattle ranchers with money to invest, who often bought land from the land grabbers, colonists and subsistence farmers. Supporting roles were played by gold miners and migrant labourers, who sometimes became debt slaves to land grabbers, farmers and ranchers.[51] Thus land-clearing became the economic and social norm, and hundreds of thousands of people were directly or indirectly benefiting from it. Moreover, the severe land tenure issues resulting from this long history of annexation and irregular dealings in land overlaid the destruction of the forest with an administrative labyrinth of ill-defined rights.[52]

More recently, Brazil has become one of the world's agro-industrial giants. McAllister shows that the two most important current factors in deforestation are

---

[45] Food and Agriculture Organization and ITTO, *The State of Forests* (2011), pp. 36–9.
[46] This overview draws heavily on L. K. McAllister, 'Sustainable Consumption Governance in the Amazon', 38 *Environmental Law Reporter* 10873 (2008).
[47] Food and Agriculture Organization and ITTO, *The State of Forests* (2011), p. 14.   [48] Ibid., p. 18.
[49] On the DRC's governance problems in the context of REDD, see Norwegian Agency for Development Cooperation, *Real-Time Evaluation of Norway's International Climate and Forest Initiative Contributions to National REDD+ Processes 2007–2010: Country Report: Democratic Republic of Congo* (Norad, March 2011), p. 8.
[50] McAllister, 'Governance in the Amazon' (2008), p. 10874.   [51] Ibid.
[52] T. Chagas, *Case Study: Forest Carbon Rights in Brazil* (REDD Net, 2010); and Blaser et al., *Status of Tropical Forest Management* (2011), pp. 277–8.

cattle ranching and soybean cultivation, both increasingly export-driven.[53] The highs and lows of these two sectors correlate well with patterns of Amazonian deforestation.[54] If ever the causes of deforestation were purely domestic in character, in recent times they are certainly transnational. The years 2002 through 2004, when deforestation rates were increasing, were also the years in which large-scale agriculture in Brazil expanded, as international market prices rose for many agricultural commodities, including soy and beef. Brazil devalued its currency, lowering the price of Brazilian commodities in the international market and fuelling demand for its exports.[55] In 2004, the country became the world's largest beef exporter. Soy followed. From 1999 to 2004 soybean cultivation in the forested areas of the Amazon grew by 15 per cent annually. In 2006, Brazil overtook the United States as the world's largest exporter of soybeans.[56]

After 2004, the market prices of soy and beef declined and the Brazilian currency gained value against the US dollar, slowing the agro-industrial expansion, and according to McAllister, contributing to the decline in Amazonian deforestation rates from 2004 through 2007. Today, another market-driven deforestation cycle might be under way: world demand for biofuels, and thus agricultural land, is expected to put further pressure on the Amazonian forest.[57] Brazil is already the world's second largest producer of sugarcane ethanol (after the United States) and the world's largest exporter; it keeps doubling its production every few years.[58]

As for the nature of Brazil's response to the steady loss of its forest, it is only since around 1999 that federal and state governments began to have the capacity to enforce laws relating to deforestation.[59] It is a threshold that many other developing countries have not crossed yet; hence 'capacity-building' is a phrase frequently reiterated in discussion of REDD. Brazil's federal government has spent about a decade cracking down on illegal logging in the Amazon, and has stated its intention to establish a licensing system for rural Amazonian properties, which would enable documentation of illegal forest clearings. The government's initiatives have been supported by a sophisticated system of detecting and analysing land-clearing through satellite images.[60] By around 2007, police sting

---

[53] McAllister, 'Governance in the Amazon' (2008), pp. 10 875–6.
[54] See Figure 2 in Norwegian Agency for Development Cooperation, *Real-Time Evaluation of Norway's International Climate and Forest Initiative Contributions to National REDD+ Processes 2007–2010: Country Report: Brazil* (Norad, March 2011), p. 22.
[55] Ibid., p. 20. [56] McAllister, 'Governance in the Amazon' (2008), pp. 10 875–6.
[57] Presently, the main areas under sugarcane cultivation are in the south of Brazil, a long way from the Amazon forest: see S. T. Coelho et al., 'Brazilian Sugarcane Ethanol: Lessons Learned', 10(2) *Energy for Sustainable Development* 26 (2006), Fig. 5, p. 31.
[58] Brazil produced 11.5 billion litres of ethanol in 1990–91 and 27.5 billion in 2008–09 (UNICA – Sugarcane Industry Association, 'Ethanol Production – Brazil', <http://english.unica.com.br/dadosCotacao/estatistica/>).
[59] See Blaser et al., *Status of Tropical Forest Management* (2011), pp. 274–88.
[60] See Brazil Ministry of Science and Technology, 'National Institute for Space Research', <http://www.inpe.br/>. In 1999, the environmental agency of the state of Mato Grosso initiated a licensing program for rural properties in which the agency identified land clearings through satellite data and mapped them to specific rural properties to find out whether they were licensed or not (McAllister, 'Governance in the Amazon' (2008), p. 10 877).

operations had resulted in the arrests of over 500 people for environmental crimes (including, notably, more than 100 employees of the national agency responsible for suppressing deforestation), and about 1500 illegal sawmills were closed down, with the fines issued totalling more than US$1 billion.[61] At the same time, however, and inconsistently, the Brazilian government's development programs have called for large infrastructure projects to facilitate industrial agriculture and other economic activities in the Amazon. Projects have included new highways, railroads, gas and power lines, the modification of river channels, and hydroelectric facilities, each of which is itself a direct driver of deforestation.[62] Measures for the alleviation of poverty that reap natural resources often take priority over environmental concerns. When it comes to protection of the Amazonian forest, the Brazilian authorities have steadily improved their methods, but regressions and inconsistencies are still evident.[63]

Brazil's non-governmental sector is not lacking in self-imposed controls. These too must be considered when evaluating the context in which REDD must operate. There is a growing movement in Brazil and countries trading with Brazil for what McAllister refers to as 'sustainable consumption governance'. Brazil's soybean industry implemented a 'soy moratorium'. Its terms oblige the major soybean processors and exporters not to buy soybeans grown on recently deforested land in the Amazon. In March 2008, a study conducted by an independent body to evaluate the effectiveness of the moratorium showed that none of the major areas of deforestation in soy-growing areas of the Amazon had been planted with soy. In the cattle ranching sector, a ranch certification program is emerging that would supply 'rainforest-friendly' beef to export markets. By April 2008, 200 ranchers with operations on over 1.5 million hectares in the Amazonian provinces had signed up to participate, and 100 such properties had been assessed for certification,[64] which requires them to meet standards of agricultural practice such as rotational grazing and the incorporation of trees into pasture land.

---

61 McAllister, 'Governance in the Amazon' (2008), p. 10 876.
62 Ibid., p. 10 877. See also J. Tollefson, 'The Roadless Warrior', 480 *Nature* 22 (1 December 2011).
63 See BBC News (25 May 2011), 'Brazil Eases Rules on Conserving Amazon Rainforest', <http://www.bbc.co.uk/news/world-latin-america-13538578> ('Brazil's Chamber of Deputies has voted to ease restrictions on the amount of land farmers must preserve as forest'); BBC News (7 December 2011), 'Brazilian Senate Eases Amazon Protection Rules', <http://www.bbc.co.uk/news/world-latin-america-16065069>; Editorial, 'Defend the Amazon', 480 *Nature* 413 (22/29 December 2011) ('After five years of stunning success in combating deforestation, the Brazilian authorities had started to ponder how to respond to the growing clamour from landowners and farmers in the region who were being prevented from clearing land to cash in on record prices for commodities such as soya and beef. That sense of a weakening political resolve to protect the rainforest was enough of an incentive for some to begin clearing it again'); and Jeff Tollefson, 'Brazil Set to Cut Forest Protection', 485 *Nature* 19 (3 May 2012).
64 McAllister, 'Governance in the Amazon' (2008), pp. 10 878–9. On the other hand, forest certification has not done as well as ranch certification because most Amazonian timber is used domestically in Brazil. Only about 15 per cent of Amazonian timber is exported. Most of the domestic market for timber does not discriminate between certified and uncertified wood products (ibid., p. 10 880).

These public–private initiatives show that certain market forces (in particular, international consumer interest in sustainable agriculture) can be harnessed to *potentially* reduce deforestation rates. (The cautious language reflects the concern that the soy moratorium could have led to 'leakage', that is, continued deforestation for the planting of non-soybean crops displaced by the expansion of soybean into legitimate agricultural land.) Not all commercial pressures necessarily have negative effects. Moreover, they confirm the existence in Brazil of 'capacity' in both the government and non-government sectors to support a complex regime like REDD. Commercial opportunities rely heavily on voluntary action and on the existence of 'ethical consumers' to bring about change from the bottom up.[65] Change powered by consumer sentiment might be an acceptable policy when the horizons are long, but not when the problem at hand is urgent and where the damage cannot easily be undone.[66] Looking at the evidence positively, though, Brazil seems to have raised itself to a critical threshold, at which REDD, with its financial and technological backing from Annex I countries, could halt deforestation completely within an acceptable time frame. One study estimated that halting Amazonian deforestation would require raising US$7–18 billion.[67]

Steps towards the international regulation of REDD

The development of a REDD mechanism was first endorsed by the UNFCCC parties at their conference in Bali in 2007.[68] At the conference the parties agreed to begin a two-year[69] negotiating process to enable implementation of REDD through long-term cooperative action (LCA), as outlined in the Bali Action Plan.[70] In the 2007 Action Plan, REDD is classified as a mitigation measure for the future. The plan urges parties in the LCA negotiations to consider '[p]olicy approaches and positive incentives on issues relating to reducing emissions from deforestation and forest degradation in developing countries' (basic REDD), as well as conservation, sustainable management of forests, and enhancement of forest carbon stocks (REDD-plus).[71] The phrase 'positive incentives' is the only

---

[65] On the known effectiveness of forest certification schemes, see L. H. Gulbrandsen, 'The Effectiveness of Non-State Governance Schemes: A Comparative Study of Forest Certification in Norway and Sweden', 5 *International Environmental Agreements* 125 (2005).
[66] See Chapter 1.
[67] D. Nepstad et al., 'The End of Deforestation in the Brazilian Amazon', 326 *Science* 1350 (2009).
[68] For an overview of the history of REDD, see F. Bietta, 'From the Hague to Copenhagen: Why It Failed Then and Why It Could Be Different', in *Deforestation and Climate Change: Reducing Carbon Emissions from Deforestation and Forest Degradation*, eds V. Bosetti and R. Lubowski (Edward Elgar Publishing, 2010).
[69] The AWG-LCA's extension to the end of 2011 was authorised in UNFCCC, *Decision 1/CP.16* (2010), VII. The AWG-LCA was given another year's extension at the Durban conference: UNFCCC, *Decision 2/CP.17, Outcome of the Work of the Ad Hoc Working Group on Long-Term Cooperative Action under the Convention* (2011).
[70] UNFCCC, *Decision 1/CP.13, Bali Action Plan* (2007), FCCC/CP/2007/6/Add.1, para. 1.
[71] Ibid., para. 1(b)(iii).

hint in the Action Plan that REDD would require a lot of money to be raised to pay for its ambitious aims.

A second decision at Bali gave parties the green light to proceed with REDD-related actions of their own, on a voluntary basis.[72] The North–South bilateral cooperative actions pursuant to this second decision were meant to lay the groundwork for the scheme in participating developing countries – for example through capacity-building support, baseline estimations of emissions from deforestation, the carrying out of demonstration activities, tentative efforts in monitoring and reporting, and so on – yet 'without prejudice to future decisions of the Conference of the Parties'.[73] There is a pointed urgency in this 2007 decision that seems appropriate to the circumstances of massive forest loss at a time of accelerating climate change.

The latter decision also gave the UNFCCC's Subsidiary Body for Scientific and Technological Advice (SBSTA) the task of commencing a program of technical work on such methodological issues as the assessment of change in forest cover and associated carbon stocks, methods for setting reference emission levels (i.e. baselines, or business-as-usual trajectories), methods for demonstrating reduction of emissions from deforestation and from forest degradation, and so forth.[74] Thus, in a kind of pincer movement against the problem, the interested state parties were to find their own way with respect to specific actions while the SBSTA went about building the technical foundations for a universal, centralised system.

The next landmark decision by the UNFCCC parties on REDD was taken at the Cancun COP in 2010.[75] After reciting the aims of the scheme as set out in the Bali Action Plan, the decision calls on *developing* parties wanting to participate in the scheme to proceed with implementation of the following four elements at nation-state level:

(i) a national strategy and action plan (produced with the monetary and technical support, wherever needed, of developed country parties);
(ii) a 'national forest reference emission level';
(iii) a 'robust and transparent' national system for the monitoring and reporting of REDD activities; and
(iv) an information system on how the several procedural and substantive 'safeguards' itemised in the decision would be addressed and adhered to throughout the implementation of REDD activities.

---

[72] UNFCCC, *Decision 2/CP.13, Reducing Emissions from Deforestation in Developing Countries: Approaches to Stimulate Action* (2007), FCCC/CP/2007/6/Add.1, paras. 3–4.
[73] Ibid., para. 4.   [74] Ibid., para. 7(a).
[75] UNFCCC, *Decision 1/CP.16* (2010), paras. 68–79. It had been preceded by a relatively minor decision in 2009 calling in broad terms on developing parties to identify local causes of deforestation and build up their forest monitoring systems: UNFCCC, *Decision 4/CP.15, Methodological Guidance for Activities Relating to Reducing Emissions from Deforestation and Forest Degradation and the Role of Conservation, Sustainable Management of Forests and Enhancement of Forest Carbon Stocks in Developing Countries* (2009), FCCC/CP/2009/11/Add.1.

Item (ii) is of great practical importance, because it provides for the baseline against which credits will be calculated.[76] A national forest reference emission level (or forest reference carbon-stock level) is not yet possible in most countries with tropical forests; hence the Cancun decision allows, as an interim measure, for the development of *sub-national* forest reference emission levels.[77] Because 'leakage' is a greater problem for REDD than for the CDM, it is preferable to have national approaches to REDD.

The safeguards in item (iv) in the list include ensuring respect for the knowledge and rights of indigenous people, the effective participation of indigenous people and local communities in the scheme, and the imperative that REDD projects are not used for the *conversion* of natural forest (that is, offsetting forest destruction in one part of the country by conservation in another), but instead to provide incentives for the protection and conservation of forests and their ecosystem services.[78] As land tenure issues are central to any scheme that seeks to distribute benefits to people for the purpose of the protection or improvement of land, the decision calls on developing countries to clarify the legal status of forest land destined for REDD projects.[79] (For the legal profession in developing countries, this is, one imagines, welcome news, especially as these new juristic tasks will be among the first REDD tasks to be performed, and therefore are virtually guaranteed access to international funds for their performance.) It also gives the SBSTA a clearer work program than the 2007 decision had managed to do.[80]

In Cancun, the COP also decided that REDD, in its formal UNFCCC-driven roll-out, would be implemented in phases, beginning with the development of national strategies and action plans, progressing through capacity-building by means of demonstration activities, and evolving into broader country-based actions that are fully measured, reported and verified.[81] REDD's implementation, in other words, is to be mainly top-down. (See Box 7.1.) The celebratory mood among delegates on the last day of the Cancun COP had much to do with the progress made at that meeting on REDD.

The Durban COP in 2011 continued the evolution of REDD, settling some technical details about how states are to calculate their emissions from forests and launching a process to explore REDD's funding mechanism. The COP called on parties to submit information on, and justifications for, the development of their forest reference

---

[76] Forest reference baselines are developed by taking into account historical data and adjusting for national circumstances: Subsidiary Body for Scientific and Technical Advice (UNFCCC), *Report on the Expert Meeting on Forest Reference Emission Levels and Forest Reference Levels for Implementation of REDD-Plus Activities* (27 November 2011), FCCC/SBSTA/2011/INF.18, para. 16. One study found that predictions of future forest cover based simply on historical data on deforestation/reforestation activity are 78 per cent accurate, meaning that historical trends are good predictors of future trends (ibid., para. 17). As with the CDM, baselines will have to be adjusted or recalculated over time to take into account changes in management, government policy, and patterns and causes of land-use change: Virgilio et al., *REDD Casebook* (2010), p. 4.
[77] UNFCCC, *Decision 1/CP.16* (2010), Appendix I, para. 71(b).   [78] Ibid., para. 71 and Appendix I.
[79] Ibid., para. 72.   [80] Ibid., para. 75, Appendix II.   [81] Ibid., para. 73.

emission levels.[82] A process for the technical assessment of countries' proposed forest reference emission levels would be established.[83] The COP emphasised that subnational forest reference emission levels would be allowed only as an interim measure, during the transition to full national forest reference emission levels.[84]

BOX 7.1 Governance conditions and challenges for an international REDD credit mechanism

This summary sets out the governance conditions for an international mechanism of credits from the REDD program, as decided at the Cancun COP, and the challenges that such a mechanism may face.[85]

A country will be 'REDD ready' when it is able to demonstrate sufficient capacity in these key areas:
- **Technical:** measurement and monitoring of project activities over time;
- **Institutional:** transparent and accountable government that can enact and enforce laws; land tenure must be clear;
- **Social safeguards:** participation by all stakeholders in REDD activities, including indigenous communities;
- **Economic:** design and implementation of equitable sharing of the benefits of REDD.

It follows that 'REDD readiness' requires:
- substantial in-country consultation to ensure broad participation;
- international financial support to facilitate technical capacity-building, including methodologies to measure and monitor forest degradation; and
- implementation of results-based demonstration/pilot activities to test approaches and methodologies.

Technical implementation challenges faced at all levels of REDD governance, from international to local, include:
- **MRV:** national reference scenarios or baseline-emission measurements that are realistic and comparable across countries (including methods to monitor changes in land use and in carbon stock);
- **Additionality:** capacity to demonstrate that the climate benefits from REDD are additional (i.e. would not have happened anyway);
- **Leakage:** systems to address the risk of emissions shifting elsewhere;
- **Permanence:** managing the risk of 'reversal' of the emission reductions generated.

Some of the main implementation problems encountered to date:
- Policy and regulation are not adequately supportive of sustainable natural resource management.[86]
- Local communities' land tenure rights as well as resource tenure rights are not clear.[87]
- There is conflict between customary and statutory law, leading to disputes over land and resource access.
- Raising private investment may be difficult in the context of uncertainty as to the value of the REDD credits.
- Organised advocacy for the rights of indigenous peoples inhabiting forests is weak or nonexistent.

---

[82] UNFCCC, *Decision 12/CP.17, Guidance on Systems for Providing Information on How Safeguards Are Addressed and Respected and Modalities Relating to Forest Reference Emission Levels and Forest Reference Levels as Referred to in Decision 1/CP.16* (2011), para. 9.
[83] Ibid., para. 15.   [84] Ibid., para. 11.
[85] These are the authors' conclusions based on their experience with REDD projects and the reports of those implementing such projects. See also Virgilio et al., *REDD Casebook* (2010), p. 3.
[86] For example P. T. Hung, *Legal Preparedness for REDD+ in Vietnam: Country Study* (International Development Law Organization, November 2011), pp. 36–41.
[87] For example S. A. Mason-Case, *Legal Preparedness for REDD+ in Zambia: Country Study* (International Development Law Organization, November 2011), pp. 12–22, 35–8.

REDD funding for the preparatory stage

Funding for the early phases of REDD deployment is being sought from bilateral and multilateral sources (that is, from ad hoc partnerships between states as well as from pre-existing intergovernmental organisations such as the Global Environment Facility), while the financing of the later phases has yet to be worked out.[88] This is another way in which REDD is different from the CDM: long before REDD begins to produce international mitigation credits, it will need to be supported financially in an adequate and predictable manner.

Administratively, REDD is a much larger, riskier, and more politically invasive than the CDM. A small project like Nigeria Stoves might plausibly minimise host government contact (in Chapter 6 we noted the minimal role of the DNA in the project approval process) and come to operate inconspicuously within a governance space it has created for itself in Nigeria, but REDD would need the wholesale engagement of a potentially corrupt and inefficient national government. In other words, *national* governance of REDD will need to be strong for the scheme to succeed.[89] In contradistinction to the CDM, REDD is not simply a program created and supported by states, which operates in pockets of a state; it is a program that changes the way a nation-state, as a whole, operates. Norway, which has invested a large amount of its public funds in REDD capacity-building in developing countries, succinctly stated the reason for REDD's holistic approach to state-level coverage and governance: 'A future REDD regime should operate at the national level in order to reduce the risk of within-country leakage.'[90] Similarly, Streck and Lin write that '[t]he advantage of national approaches is that they allow the recipient country to finance holistic forestry management programs that go beyond individual projects. National approaches would also account for the shifting of activities ... that may reduce emissions at one site only to increase them at another.'[91] Forests must be protected as wholes, and for that, the power of the state must be enlisted. The quality of that power and its consistent exercise over time are therefore important matters for REDD.

Streck and Lin argue that substantial public start-up funding is essential in REDD's case – an area that 'markets do not reach' on their own because of the 'enhanced risks and transaction costs'.[92] Public funding means, in essence, Annex I tax revenue. Funding for the establishment of national programs for REDD in

---

[88] UNFCCC, *Decision 1/CP.16* (2010), para. 77. The AWG-LCA has the task of exploring financing options for REDD's full implementation.
[89] C. Streck, 'Reducing Emissions from Deforestation and Forest Degradation: National Implementation of REDD Schemes: An Editorial Comment', 100 *Climatic Change* 389 (2010).
[90] C. Parker et al., *Little REDD Book: A Guide to Governmental and Non-Governmental Proposals for Reducing Emissions from Deforestation and Degradation* (Global Canopy Programme, 2008), p. 45.
[91] C. Streck and J. Lin, 'Mobilising Finance for Climate Change Mitigation: Private Sector Involvement in International Carbon Finance Mechanisms', 10(1) *Melbourne Journal of International Law* 70 (2009), p. 97. See also Virgilio et al., *REDD Casebook* (2010), p. 6.
[92] Streck and Lin, 'Mobilising Finance for Climate Change Mitigation' (2009), p. 95; see also T. Neeff and F. Ascui, 'Lessons from Carbon Markets for Designing an Effective REDD Architecture', 9 *Climate Policy* 306 (2009).

developing countries is slowly being made available, although still in an ad hoc fashion.[93] For example, at a meeting in March 2011, the Policy Board of the UN-REDD Programme (an informal program created by an association of UN organs pursuant to the second Bali decision mentioned above) approved Ecuador's funding request for US$4 million for its full national program. The money is to be contributed by the Food and Agriculture Organization, the UN Development Program and the UN Environment Program, and thus is, in origin, tax revenue from developed countries' assessed contributions to those UN organs.[94] In another example, the United States provided US$4 million to six countries in Central America to assist governments and NGOs with building and harmonising regional capacity for REDD-plus.[95]

What exactly will the money be spent on? Let us consider the objectives of the national REDD program of the Solomon Islands.[96] There the start-up program aims to create 'REDD readiness' through six main areas of work:

(i) supporting broad-based, multi-stakeholder consultations;
(ii) analysing forest resource data;
(iii) developing a REDD-plus 'roadmap';
(iv) awareness raising;
(v) ensuring free, prior and informed consent of indigenous people and other forest-dependent communities; and
(vi) developing capacity to formulate the country's reference emission levels and systems for forest measurement, reporting and verification.[97]

Some of these formulations are vague (see Box 7.1 for more precise formulations of early-stage objectives), and it is not yet clear what criteria will be used to decide the implementation success of a 'national program'.

By the end of 2010, 12 countries in the three rainforest regions that have been the focus of this chapter had made progress in developing their UN-REDD national programs.[98] With a general international agreement about financing the start-up costs of REDD still pending, the work of UN-REDD and other

---

[93] The Green Climate Fund, which is the UNFCCC's new funding mechanism, is still under construction: see Chapter 8.
[94] UN-REDD Programme, *Report of the Sixth Policy Board Meeting* (21–22 March 2011), p. 18.
[95] US Department of State, *Meeting the Fast Start Commitment: US Climate Finance in Fiscal Year 2011* (2011), p. 3.
[96] The Solomon Islands is an interesting case. Its total forest area is approximately 2.2 million hectares, and the country has the highest percentage of forest loss in the South Pacific. The logging industry is the country's single most significant economic sector. It contributes 67 per cent of export earnings, and some 12–13 per cent of total government revenue. As much as 50 per cent of the employed workforce is probably associated directly or indirectly with the forest sector. Officially, annual export earnings in 2007 from this sector were approximately US$110 million. This is indicative of the huge amount of additional annual revenue that will need to be delivered through the North–South pipeline if deforestation is to be brought under control.
[97] Food and Agriculture Organization, UN Development Programme and UN Environment Programme, 'Solomon Islands Now Ready for REDD+ Readiness', *UN-REDD Programme Newsletter* 2 (June 2011), p. 2.
[98] Food and Agriculture Organization, UN Development Programme and UN Environment Programme, *UN-REDD Programme : 2010 Year in Review* (2011), p. 4. In Brazil, REDD-specific legislation is being developed in the federal parliament: Chagas, *Case Study: Forest Carbon Rights in Brazil* (2010). Fiji has finalised a national policy on REDD: Republic of the Fiji Islands, Fiji Forestry Department, 'Fiji REDD-Plus Policy: Reducing Emissions from Deforestation and Forest Degradation in Fiji' (2011).

intergovernmental and non-governmental organisations constitutes an attempt to kick-start implementation so as not to lose time.[99] Once REDD's start-up costs have been met and long-term sources of financing have been decided, though, money should start flowing smoothly into the program: mitigation through REDD is expected to be even cheaper than mitigation through the CDM.[100] Perhaps the most troubling question that still hangs over the program is whether REDD will be financed in the long term at least partly from sales of emission offsets (thus exposing the program to the same criticisms that have bedevilled the CDM's claim to additionality) or solely through non-market-based approaches.[101] At the time of writing, this critical issue, assigned to the AWG-LCA for consideration, had yet to be decided.

Monitoring, reporting and verification of REDD projects

As with the CDM, methodologies for calculating emissions avoided (and, for REDD-plus, emission reductions) will have to be developed for a great range of circumstances. This work has already been set in motion by the NGO sector.[102] As yet, however, there is no UNFCCC body to approve them – no equivalent of the CDM Executive Board. All aspects of the REDD mechanism are thus very much 'under construction'. As indicated earlier, because few developing countries in the tropical regions have the money for regular forest inventories, even basic information on the extent and condition of forests is often outdated or nonexistent. A national approach to REDD would require a predetermined national forest reference emission level and the establishment of a national monitoring system. The implementation of forest carbon inventories is thus emerging as a

---

99 Some developing countries at the UNFCCC negotiations take the position that the early phase of REDD implementation, which includes putting in place forest reference levels, forest accounting, and national strategies, should be fully funded from public and concessional funds. They suggest a REDD window under the Green Climate Fund (see Chapter 8) or establishing a levy on international aviation and maritime transport. They caution against using market mechanisms for REDD, underscoring the need for predictable funding. See International Institute for Sustainable Development, 'SB 34 and AWG Highlights: Saturday, 11 June 2011', 12(508) *Earth Negotiations Bulletin* 1 (2011), p. 3.
100 In 2010, the estimated total value of transactions for forest-based carbon was US$178 million, with the average price per offset around US$5.5 per tonne CO_2 eq.: see D. Diaz, K. Hamilton and E. Johnson, *State of the Forest Carbon Markets 2011: From Canopy to Currency* (Ecosystem Marketplace, September 2011).
101 Chad Carpenter, *Taking Stock of Durban: Review of Key Outcomes and the Road Ahead* (UN Development Programme, 2012), p. 27.
102 For example, at the time of writing, three REDD-related methodologies had been released by the Verified Carbon Standard (VCS) Association (<http://www.v-c-s.org/>) for projects in the voluntary market. They were the 'Methodology for Carbon Accounting in Project Activities that Reduce Emissions from Mosaic Deforestation and Degradation', the 'Methodology for Avoided Mosaic Deforestation of Tropical Forests' and the 'Methodology for Avoided Unplanned Deforestation'. Let us briefly consider the third of these methodologies. It allows projects to calculate avoided emissions by reducing deforestation either on the edge ('frontier') of large cleared areas, such as agricultural zones, or in a patchwork ('mosaic') within standing forests. It was developed through a collaboration between the Brazilian NGO Fundação Amazonas Sustentável and the World Bank's BioCarbon Fund, with financial support from Marriott International, the hotel chain.

7 PROTECTION OF FORESTS IN DEVELOPING COUNTRIES   249

central component of global climate change policy.[103] Information about how forests in developing countries are being managed has been even more difficult to obtain, in many cases.[104] At the Copenhagen conference in 2009, the UNFCCC called on developing country parties to:

> establish ... robust and transparent national forest monitoring systems ... that: (i) Use a combination of remote sensing and ground-based forest carbon inventory approaches for estimating, as appropriate, anthropogenic forest-related greenhouse gas emissions by sources and removals by sinks, forest carbon stocks and forest area changes; (ii) Provide estimates that are transparent, consistent, as far as possible accurate, and that reduce uncertainties.[105]

Action in these important areas is still quite elementary.[106]

Remote sensing technology is available and rapidly improving.[107] It is hoped that satellite readings of forest cover will soon provide much of the required information on a global scale. For example, in May 2011, Brazil's National Institute of Space Research, together with the UN-REDD Programme and the Food and Agriculture Organization, began work to identify and develop start-up activities for establishing REDD information systems. Start-up activities are to include several case studies for the establishment of national satellite forest-monitoring systems, giving countries the opportunity to establish a REDD information system and an autonomous satellite forest-monitoring system.[108] Brazil's involvement in these initial meetings is understandable, as it possesses an unusually sophisticated network of ground stations and satellites. In their readiness process for REDD, other tropical countries, such as those in the Congo Basin, have a long way to go before they can claim a robust and transparent national system for the monitoring and reporting of REDD activities.

REDD explicitly recognises the role of local indigenous communities in monitoring and enforcing forest conservation projects. While remote sensing by satellite can provide important evidence on the level of deforestation over time, it is still not very accurate in assessing change in the carbon content of forests, which requires, among other things, the ability to measure the circumference of trees.[109] As for pinpointing responsibility for ongoing deforestation and forest degradation, this of course is not a job for remote sensing. Adequate

---

103 K. Andersson, T. P. Evans and K. R. Richards, 'National Forest Carbon Inventories: Policy Needs and Assessment Capacity', 93 *Climatic Change* 69 (2009).
104 Food and Agriculture Organization and ITTO, *The State of Forests* (2011), p. 3.
105 UNFCCC, *Decision 4/CP.15* (2009), para. 1.
106 International Institute for Sustainable Development, 'SB 34 and AWG Highlights: Monday, 13 June 2011', 12(509) *Earth Negotiations Bulletin* 1 (2011), p. 1 ('Highlighting information gaps, many countries underscored the importance of measuring, reporting and verifying the provision of financing for REDD+').
107 For Australia's use of this technology, see the third project listed in Table 7.1 below and R. Purdy, *Satellite Monitoring of Environmental Laws: Lessons to Be Learnt from Australia* (UK Economic and Social Research Council, 2010).
108 Food and Agriculture Organization, UN Development Programme and UN Environment Programme, 'INPE and UN-REDD Partnering to Develop National Forest Monitoring Systems', 18 *UN-REDD Programme Newsletter* 3 (May 2011), p. 3.
109 Virgilio et al., *REDD Casebook* (2010), p. 4.

forest monitoring inescapably requires feet on the ground, and those feet have to be attached to people who are in a position to undertake monitoring and measurement of carbon stocks and are motivated to monitor the forest they live in and enforce compliance with the terms of REDD projects.[110] It is estimated that more than 300 million indigenous peoples and members of local communities depend mainly on forests for their livelihoods.[111] While it is understood that these people must be *partners* in REDD, there is still no international consensus on whether REDD should directly compensate project participants (on the model of the CDM), or whether it will be for the state authorities to decide how earnings are shared.[112] If the latter, many countries lack the institutional capacity and legal safeguards to ensure that a centralised REDD-plus regime would equitably allocate incentives to local actors.[113] This is not an MRV problem; it is a benefit-sharing problem. The two are linked, though, because if benefit sharing is not adequately tackled, MRV will suffer.

Australia's involvement with REDD

The foreseeable difficulties in the implementation of REDD are partly alleviated by the attractiveness of the scheme to all sides of politics. No party will oppose a reasonable mechanism to save tropical forests. Because REDD is being developed outside the framework of the Kyoto Protocol, and thus is not associated with compulsory emission caps for developed countries, it can be supported by the political right, which in Australia and the United States (to take the two Annex I states that have always been wary of the Protocol) has preferred voluntary state actions that do not impose restrictions on the economy or lead to new taxes.

Indeed, for the political right, once an emission cap has been ruled out as a measure, a mitigation policy for climate change must, in view of the dearth of robust alternatives, assign a large role to biosequestration. In Australia in 2011, Greg Hunt, the climate change spokesperson for the conservative federal opposition, said that a global rainforest recovery program would be the *single best policy* to reduce global emissions. In an interview, he claimed: 'If you can reduce the emissions by half from the destruction of rainforests by 2020, up to four

---

[110] Subsidiary Body for Scientific and Technical Advice (UNFCCC), *Expert Meeting on Forest Reference Emission Levels* (27 November 2011), para. 46.
[111] Secretariat (Convention on Biological Diversity), *REDD-Plus and Biodiversity* (2011), p. 10.
[112] International Institute for Sustainable Development, 'SB 34 and AWG Highlights: Monday, 13 June 2011' (2011), p. 1 ('On who should be compensated for REDD+, some parties said each country should make the decision at the national level, while others underscored the relevance of ensuring that incentives reach the local communities managing the forests').
[113] Virgilio et al., *REDD Casebook* (2010), p. 6. In 'REDD+ and Indigenous Peoples in Brazil', in *Climate Change, Indigenous Peoples, and the Search for Legal Remedies*, eds R. S. Abate and E. A. Kronk (Edward Elgar Publishing, forthcoming), Andrew Long discusses the key considerations for the design and implementation of REDD+ in a manner that can preserve indigenous peoples' rights while providing for broad environmental, economic and social benefits.

billion tonnes of emissions could be saved. It's about protecting the great rainforests and reducing emissions in a practical way.'[114] In the same interview, he pointed out that Australia's A$200 million International Forest Carbon Initiative (IFCI) was the creation of the former Coalition government (a conservative coalition under Prime Minister John Howard), and noted that the IFCI had been continued by the successor Labor government.[115] From such pronouncements we may conclude that if the left supports REDD, the right supports it even more. This surely augurs well for REDD's future implementation. Or, to put it more accurately: Whatever obstacles REDD may encounter, political ideology probably will not be one of them.

In Australia's fourth national report under the Convention on Biological Diversity, the federal Labor government, which came to power in late 2007, describes the IFCI as supporting international efforts to demonstrate that reduced emissions from deforestation and forest degradation (i.e. REDD) 'can be part of an equitable and effective future global outcome on climate change', and notes that a central element of the Initiative is to take action on REDD through so-called forest carbon partnerships with Indonesia and Papua New Guinea, in particular.[116]

Below, Table 7.1 summarises the IFCI-inspired forest preservation projects funded by Australia in Indonesia, Papua New Guinea and elsewhere in South-East Asia, which were still ongoing at the time of writing and which may be taken to represent Australia's vanguard action on REDD.[117]

Table 7.1 Main forestry projects funded by Australia in developing countries under the informal preparatory framework for REDD

Project	Period	Cost (US$)
Asia–Pacific forestry skills and capacity-building program: The program helps countries in the Asia–Pacific region to increase their capacity to manage forests sustainably. Phase I (2007–09) supported projects in Indonesia, Papua New Guinea, Vietnam, Laos, Cambodia, the Solomon Islands, Fiji, and China in areas such as reduced-impact logging, forest certification, restoration of degraded forests, and research. Phase II focuses on projects that build Indonesia's and PNG's capacity in sustainable management of forests, law enforcement, and regulatory frameworks that support REDD.	2007–12	14.1 million
Australia–Indonesia bilateral package of support on forests and climate: The package provides funding for REDD policy development by Indonesia's Forest Climate Alliance, as well as support for Indonesia's National Carbon Accounting System and the 'Indofire' monitoring system	2007–12	9.2 million

---

114 Australian Associated Press, 'Coalition Urges More Action on Forests, as Rallies Back Pro-Carbon Tax Campaign', *The Australian* (5 June 2011).
115 Ibid.
116 Department of the Environment, Water, Heritage and the Arts, *Australia's Fourth National Report to the United Nations Convention on Biological Diversity* (March 2009), p. 65.
117 From the database of the REDD+ Partnership, <http://reddpluspartnership.org/en/>. On the informal preparatory framework, see UNFCCC, *Decision 2/CP.13* (2007).

Table 7.1 (cont.)

Project	Period	Cost (US$)
Provision of satellite data for South-East Asia to support capacity-building on carbon accounting: As part of Australia's International Forest Carbon Initiative, this project supports implementation of forest carbon accounting systems in developing countries, in particular Indonesia, Cambodia, and Papua New Guinea. Australia has been purchasing, storing and processing satellite data for South-East Asia to enable countries in the region to estimate areas of deforestation and degradation, and in turn, emissions and removals resulting from these activities. The project funds Geoscience Australia to provide and manage Landsat and other remotely derived datasets for South-East Asia. The data are made freely available to the countries concerned.	2008–12	8.7 million
Kalimantan Forests and Climate Partnership: The KFCP is a practical REDD demonstration activity in central Kalimantan, in cooperation with the Indonesian government. Implementation is under way on a 120 000-hectare site. Dedicated REDD-plus facilitators live and work in each of the seven villages in the project area. KFCP seeks to avoid the degradation of peatland. Degradation of peatland through deforestation, drainage, burning, and land-use change is one of the largest sources of GHG emissions in Indonesia. The KFCP is the first large-scale REDD demonstration activity of its kind in Indonesia.[118] *The project has encountered local opposition, illustrative of the ground-level problems in store for REDD.*[119]	2008–12	47 million
Sumatra Forest Carbon Partnership: The partnership is a REDD demonstration activity in Jambi province. It aims to develop a REDD regime for forests on mineral soils. Like the KFCP project (above), *this initiative has been criticised by NGOs.*[120] The problem, for many critics of REDD demonstration projects, is that REDD projects are being established in one part of a country's forest while government deforestation policies continue in other parts. REDD activity of this kind is seen by some NGOs as window-dressing, with REDD reduced to a mere generator of emission reduction credits, rather than a holistic forest protection program.	2010–12 (may extend to 2013)	27.6 million
Papua New Guinea–Australia Forest Carbon Partnership: The partnership aims to reduce GHG emissions from deforestation and forest degradation, improve livelihoods for forest-dependent communities, and promote biodiversity protection. As described by the Australian government, the initial funding includes support for the development and implementation of national climate change policies, capacity-building to enable Papua New Guinea's participation in future international carbon markets, and support for the design of its national forest carbon measurement systems.	2008–13	3 million (initial)

---

118 Secretariat (UNFCCC), *Submissions on Information from Developed Country Parties on the Resources Provided to Fulfil the Commitment Referred to in Decision 1/CP.16, Paragraph 95* (15 August 2011), FCCC/CP/2011/INF.1, pp. 5–6.
119 See C. Lang, 'Kalimantan Forests and Climate Partnership Faces yet More Criticism', <http://www.redd-monitor.org/2011/06/23/kalimantan-forests-and-climate-partnership-faces-yet-more-criticism/>.
120 Friends of the Earth Australia, 'Sumatran Forest Carbon Deal Slammed by Australian and Indonesian Environment Groups', <http://www.foe.org.au/news/2010/sumatran-forest-carbon-deal-slammed-by-australian-and-indonesian-environment-groups>.

Conclusion: Will REDD be effective?

REDD offers an opportunity, in theory, for access by developing countries to additional funding and capacity-building. These resources are urgently needed to support efforts to reduce the rates of deforestation and forest degradation and to conserve and sustainably manage forests for the benefit of current and future generations.[121] Savaresi writes that 'REDD may still present a triple-win solution for climate change, sustainable development, and biodiversity conservation.'[122] Realistically, it is still too early to tell whether the international regime for REDD will succeed in becoming fully established in the forested countries of Africa, South America and South-East Asia, and if it does succeed, what reputation it will earn for environmental integrity. REDD may be able to change some behaviour, but it must compete with other economic factors.

We have noted above that REDD-plus credits could be produced quite cheaply. After the initial start-up, there is little doubt that REDD activities will be cost-effective in comparison to other mitigation options.[123] But what would be the cost of REDD credits when account is taken of all public funds, domestic and international, that will be injected into the administration of the scheme? If the cost proves too high, in comparison to the overheads of piecemeal offset schemes or other emission reduction measures, REDD may never play a major role in international mitigation efforts.[124] A possible response to the prospect of an exorbitant cost per REDD credit is to push for keeping the scheme's administration 'simple'. Calls for greater simplicity have been a feature of the CDM's history. But as with the CDM, the challenge for REDD will be to prevent the interests of producers and investors[125] from undermining the scheme's reputation as a source of truly additional mitigation actions. Simplicity in administration would most likely mean less regulation of the market. There is a risk that while funds would nevertheless continue to flow from North to South for the benefit of forests, our management of the climate change problem would be weakened because of the diversion of funds to unreliable or illusory mitigation credits. Streck and Lin argue that, in order to create an effective REDD mechanism, strong international institutions for quality assurance are needed, even more than for the CDM:

---

121 See W. Boyd, 'Deforestation and Emerging Greenhouse Gas Compliance Regimes: Toward a Global Environmental Law of Forests, Carbon, and Climate Governance', in *Deforestation and Climate Change: Reducing Carbon Emissions from Deforestation and Forest Degradation*, eds V. Bosetti and R. Lubowski (Edward Elgar Publishing, 2010).
122 A. Savaresi, 'Forests, Economics, and Climate Change', 2(3) *Climate Law* 439 (2011), p. 446.
123 E. Corbera, M. Estrada and K. Brown, 'Reducing Greenhouse Gas Emissions from Deforestation and Forest Degradation in Developing Countries: Revisiting the Assumptions', 100 *Climatic Change* 355 (2010).
124 Studies on costs have been carried out on afforestation/reforestation projects; see for example B. J. Strengers, J. G. Van Minnen and B. Eickhout, 'The Role of Carbon Plantations in Mitigating Climate Change: Potentials and Costs', 88 *Climatic Change* 343 (2008).
125 The buyer wants plentiful credits available at the lowest price, whereas the seller wants to produce the largest quantity of credits as cheaply as possible.

[A] governance structure that relies on the delegation of power and control to an international review mechanism should be created to administer the REDD mechanism when it emerges. In this regard, parties to the UNFCCC should contemplate the delegation of certain elements of power to an internationally-established market regulator ... Experience with the CDM should inform the development of better accountability and due process features for the REDD mechanism.[126]

Perhaps above all else, REDD's success is conditional upon a healthy carbon market, just as the CDM's future is:[127] '[M]arket-based approaches only work in the context of a constrained system.'[128] Because no obligatory limits on global emissions have ever been agreed to, and because, after 2012, fewer Annex I countries will have obligatory emission caps (Canada, Japan and Russia will no longer have them), the carbon market could weaken over time, causing the price of credits to fall and investment in carbon reduction projects and grand schemes like REDD to fall with it.[129]

---

[126] Streck and Lin, 'Mobilising Finance for Climate Change Mitigation' (2009), pp. 73, 96.
[127] Bloomberg New Energy Finance, 'EU CO_2 Catches Cold as Durban Talks Approach', <http://www.climatespectator.com.au/commentary/eu-co2-catches-cold-durban-talks-approach>.
[128] International Institute for Sustainable Development, 'SB 34 and AWG Highlights: Monday, 13 June 2011' (2011), p. 1.
[129] As early as 2010 there was evidence that the global carbon market was flagging. See World Bank, *State and Trends of the Carbon Market 2010* (World Bank, 2011), p. 9 ('After five consecutive years of robust growth, the total value of the global carbon market stalled at $142 billion ... Suffering from the lack of post-2012 regulatory clarity, the value of the primary CDM market fell by double digits for the third year in a row, ending lower than it was in 2005').

8

Climate finance, technology transfer and capacity-building for sustainable development

Introduction *page* 255
Green finance and technology for countries in need   256
The existing international regime on finance and technology transfer   259
Role of the Global Environment Facility   263
Breathing life into neglected treaty provisions   268
The new institutions of the Cancun COP   271
Roles and responsibilities of the Cancun institutions   274
Australia's contributions to finance and technology transfer for developing countries   282
The lurking issue of intellectual property rights   284
Intellectual property law and politics in the climate change arena   288
Conclusion   291

Introduction

This chapter discusses the international regulation of the transfer of finance and technology from developed to developing countries for the purposes of climate change mitigation and adaptation, subject to the principle of sustainable development.[1] Much of the transfer in wealth and knowledge that occurs under this heading is aimed at building resident expertise in developing countries (capacity-building) and nudging economic development in the direction of greater sustainability. In the context of climate change, aiding sustainability means helping developing countries cope with the expected climate impacts better than they would have otherwise – that is, with greater 'resilience' and less human suffering – while also helping those countries to *increase their economic growth*.

---

[1] The IPCC defines technology transfer as 'a broad set of processes covering the flows of know-how, experience and equipment for mitigating and adapting to climate change amongst different stakeholders such as governments, private-sector entities, financial institutions, non-governmental organizations (NGOs) and research/education institutions': B. Metz et al., *Methodological and Technological Issues in Technology Transfer: A Special Report of the IPCC Working Group III* (Cambridge University Press, 2000), p. 3.

How is the world to facilitate sustainable economic growth in the least developed of developing countries? How are the large annual revenues pledged to date (US$30 billion in 2010–12, US$100 billion per year by 2020) to be raised and distributed? We shall describe the role of the Global Environment Facility (GEF) in the UNFCCC structure, review the latest initiatives in the international regulation of climate-related finance and technology transfer, examine the role Australia has played in the dissemination of resources for adaptation and mitigation, and discuss the ongoing challenges in this area, in particular the role of intellectual property rights as a facilitator of or obstacle to change.

Green finance and technology for countries in need

Once the climate system has been altered, fixing it will be expensive. The mere effort not to cause even more damage is itself almost unaffordable. At the Copenhagen meeting in December 2009, the UNFCCC parties agreed that Annex I countries would raise money to help poor countries respond to climate change: US$30 billion in the period 2010–12 (the so-called fast-start finance), rising to US$100 billion *per year* by 2020. This has been promised as 'new' money – not simply as development aid taken from existing development accounts and redeployed.[2] Somehow, the wealthier group is to raise these large additional funds and deploy them to assist the adjustment of the less well-off group to changed climatic circumstances. The pledged amounts do not include the cost of turning around the economies of the wealthier countries themselves – Annex I parties commenced this process of internal reform with the coming into force of the Kyoto Protocol – but they give an idea of the huge sums involved.

Raising money internationally, moving it around the world to where it is most needed in an orderly, fair and accountable manner, spending it to procure the desired results of climate change mitigation or adaptation, and conducting measurement, reporting, and verification of the results are four categories of effort that must be meticulously planned, regulated and overseen, on a plane that is above that of domestic law yet engages with it. Fundraising, transfer of funds, project results, and oversight and accountability of the process are only half the picture, because money is not everything in the solution to the climate change problem. The money must be able to unlock ideas and know-how and not trample on human rights or create new threats to society or the environment. New international regulation will be needed, but not everything can be new. Pathways through regulation already in place must be found to facilitate the dissemination of the new information.[3] The regulatory

---

2 UNFCCC, *Decision 2/CP.15, Copenhagen Accord* (2009), FCCC/CP/2009/11/Add.1, para. 8 (reiterated in UNFCCC, *Decision 1/CP.16, The Cancun Agreements: Outcome of the Work of the Ad Hoc Working Group on Long-Term Cooperative Action under the Convention* (2010), FCCC/CP/2010/7/Add.1, paras. 95 and 98).
3 See for example A. Green, 'Climate Change, Regulatory Policy and the WTO: How Constraining Are Trade Rules?', 8 *Journal of International Economic Law* 143 (2005); J. de Cendra de Larragán, 'Can Emissions Trading Schemes Be Coupled with Border-Tax Adjustments? An Analysis vis-à-vis WTO Law', 15(2) *Review of Community and International Environmental Law* 131 (2006); C. Voigt, 'WTO Law and International

thicket to be traversed includes intellectual property (IP) law and domestic and international trade law, both of which can inhibit the free flow of urgently needed technologies. Other inhibiting factors are certain practices that are political or policy-bound rather than legal.

Sustainable growth is a difficult concept to define; rendered narrowly, it means that, as gross domestic product rises, the amount of GHG emissions per unit of GDP is reduced at a steeper rate than it would have been under a business-as-usual scenario (Figure 8.1). Here, as in many areas of climate change regulation,

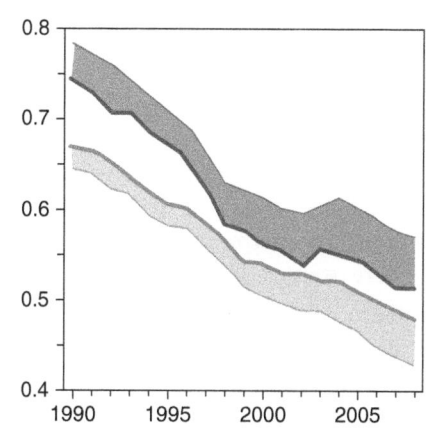

Figure 8.1 Indicators of sustainable growth (defined as progressive reductions in CO_2 emissions per unit of GDP) in developed and developing countries
The vertical axis is denominated in kilograms of CO_2 per US$ of GDP. Caldeira and Davis comment that developing countries have a higher overall carbon intensity of economic activity, implying the availability of relatively cheap GHG abatement opportunities in those countries. In this figure, developed countries (Annex I) are in light grey and developing countries in dark grey. Thick lines represent consumption and thin lines production. The light grey shaded area stands for net imports and the dark grey area for net exports. The figure shows that much inefficient production in developing countries (higher emissions per unit of GDP) is tied to their export industry for Annex I market products. Products for local consumption, by contrast, are relatively 'green'. The sustainable growth profile of Annex I countries benefits significantly from this outsourcing of emissions to non-Annex I countries. Overall, the carbon intensity of both developing countries and developed countries appears to be improving at similar rates: presently, the carbon intensity of economic activity in developing countries is lagging behind that in developed countries by less than a decade. Consideration of a consumption-based perspective, as in this figure, produces less of a difference in carbon intensity of economic activity (the difference between the thick lines) between developed and developing countries than does a production-based perspective. See also G. P. Peters et al., 'Rapid Growth in CO_2 Emissions after the 2008–2009 Global Financial Crisis', 2 *Nature Climate Change* 2 (January 2012).
Source: K. Caldeira and S. J. Davis, 'Accounting for Carbon Dioxide Emissions: A Matter of Time', 108(21) *PNAS* 8533 (24 May 2011), pp. 8533–4.

Emissions Trading: Is There Potential for Conflict?', 1(2) *Carbon and Climate Law Review* 54 (2008); and D. Redmond and K. Kendall, 'Emissions Trading Schemes, Domestic Policy and the WTO', 7 *Macquarie Journal of Business Law* 15 (2010).

counterfactual thinking plays a central role: funds and know-how are to be transferred from rich to poor countries via new, UN-controlled, international programs in order to achieve climate-related gains that would not have been realised in the absence of those programs.

In Chapter 6, on the Clean Development Mechanism, we took a detailed look at an example of finance, technology, and capacity-building, packaged into a project of North–South cooperation in the name of climate change mitigation and sustainable development. That case was 'Nigeria Stoves', in which a UN program (the CDM) used funds raised from the sale of GHG emission allowances to the capped economies of the European Union to enable a sophisticated household stove, manufactured in Germany, to be distributed across a swath of rural Nigeria, replacing traditional cook-fires, which are unhealthy and inefficient as well as destructive of forests.

The stoves project served as a means for the flow of both technology and finance (primarily in the form of a subsidy for each stove) into the impoverished country, and capacity-building aspects included the arrangement whereby the foreign-made stove components were assembled in workshops in Nigeria. People hired locally were trained for this purpose, increasing community knowledge about efficient household energy technology and providing the skills to enable the local workforce to impart that information to others. Plans were in place for the full production of the stove in Nigeria, once a sufficient market for it had been established.[4] The CDM itself may therefore be conceived as a program in finance and technology transfer for sustainable development.[5] While it does not have an explicit mandate for the transfer of technology, studies have shown that it contributes to technology transfer by importing technologies currently not available in host countries.[6] In the context of the international climate change regime, it is probably the most successful conduit to date for these goods.[7]

Why, then, not simply expand the CDM to effect an even greater transfer of finance and technology? One constraint on this pathway is that the CDM is a

---

[4] Atmosfair gGmbH, *CDM Project Design Document for Efficient Fuel Wood Stoves for Nigeria* (CDM website, 8 June 2009), p. 25.
[5] The UNFCCC has a web page on the subject: UNFCCC, 'The CDM and Technology Transfer', <http://cdm.unfccc.int/about/CDM_TT/index.html>.
[6] A substantial proportion of CDM projects transfer technology, whether deliberately or incidentally: 'Overall, 30% of all projects in the pipeline, accounting for 48% of estimated emission reductions, involve technology transfer. The involvement may be as high as 44% of all projects, given that 24% of the PDDs do not specify whether technology transfer occurs and survey results suggest that 60% of these may in fact involve technology transfer': UNFCCC, *The Contribution of the Clean Development Mechanism under the Kyoto Protocol to Technology Transfer* (2010), p. 10. See also H. C. de Coninck, F. Haake and N. H. van der Linden, 'Technology Transfer in the Clean Development Mechanism', 7(5) *Climate Policy* 444 (2008); M. Gechlik, 'Making Transfer of Clean Technology Work: Lessons of the Clean Development Mechanism', 11 *San Diego International Law Journal* 227 (2009); S. Seres, E. Haites and K. Murphy, 'Analysis of Technology Transfer in CDM Projects: An Update', 37(11) *Energy Policy* 4919 (2009); Clean Development Mechanism (Kyoto Protocol), *Benefits of the Clean Development Mechanism* (UNFCCC, 2011); and D. Popp, 'International Technology Transfer, Climate Change, and the Clean Development Mechanism', 5(1) *Review of Environmental Economics and Policy* 131 (2011).
[7] UNFCCC, *The Contribution of the Clean Development Mechanism under the Kyoto Protocol to Technology Transfer* (2010).

creation of the Kyoto Protocol and is technically tied to the existence of commitment periods under the Protocol.[8] A second problem is that the CDM's focus is on mitigation rather than adaptation, and thus its vision is limited. Moreover, it has no design feature to ensure that CDM-related money and know-how are distributed fairly around the world, to address multiple interconnected problems. Its narrow mandate is to produce GHG offsets for sale in compliance markets. Its projects have been concentrated in countries where offsets can be most easily, safely and cheaply produced – not necessarily where finance and technology are needed most. The CDM is driven by project developers, who are often private contractors. It cannot facilitate sector-wide or state-wide approaches.

Above all, the CDM is a market mechanism driven by demand for offsets. Demand is determined by compliance markets, and compliance markets are few and far between. For these reasons, the UNFCCC parties are negotiating a much more ambitious finance-and-technology mechanism than anything that exists to date, and it is to be governed by the Convention rather than the Protocol. We turn, then, to the twenty-year-old text of the UNFCCC.

The existing international regime on finance and technology transfer

The Convention, in keeping with its North/South view of the world, calls on developed countries, and in particular OECD countries (Annex II), to assist developing countries through finance and technology transfer. (See Box 2.2 in Chapter 2.)

There is a significant interdependence between the two goods of finance and technology. Developing countries need finance in order to obtain technology. They need technology not only for its direct applications to climate adaptation and mitigation, but in order to increase their productivity, become wealthier, and be in a position to finance their own growth through technology production and innovation. Clearly, economic or environmental improvement in developing countries requires the presence of both new finance and new technology. And while both, in the context of climate change, must be directed towards mitigation and adaptation, they must also support sustainable development more broadly. In other words, they must have both short-term and long-term benefits for the country.

Article 4(3) of the UNFCCC provides that:

> The developed country Parties ... shall provide new and additional financial resources to meet the agreed full costs incurred by developing country Parties in complying with their obligations under Article 12, paragraph 1 [communication of information relating to implementation]. They shall also provide such financial resources, including for the

---

[8] Kyoto Protocol, Art. 12(2).

> transfer of technology, needed by the developing country Parties to meet the agreed full incremental costs of implementing measures that are covered by paragraph 1 of this Article [i.e. commitment by both developed and developing countries to implement assorted policies and action related to mitigation, adaptation, etc.] and that are agreed between a developing country Party and the international entity or entities referred to in Article 11 [on the financial mechanism] ...

The Convention further provides, in Article 4(4), that the Annex I parties are to assist developing country parties 'that are particularly vulnerable to the adverse effects of climate change in meeting costs of adaptation to those adverse effects' (such as flood, drought, and desertification). Following this, Article 4(5) states:

> The developed country Parties ... shall take all practicable steps to promote, facilitate and finance, as appropriate, the transfer of, or access to, environmentally sound technologies and know-how to other Parties, particularly developing country Parties, to enable them to implement the provisions of the Convention. In this process, the developed country Parties shall support the development and enhancement of endogenous capacities and technologies of developing country Parties ...

The point in the last statement is further developed in Article 4(7) of the Convention:

> The extent to which developing country Parties will effectively implement their commitments under the Convention will depend on the effective implementation by developed country Parties of their commitments under the Convention related to financial resources and transfer of technology and will take fully into account that economic and social development and poverty eradication are the first and overriding priorities of the developing country Parties.

This statement, if not a call for sustainable development in itself,[9] at least emphasises the foremost priority of developing countries – namely, improvement in material well-being and civil society for all citizens. It is also an unambiguously stated quid pro quo, which is key to understanding the kind of deal the Convention is: unless finance and technology are to flow from the highly privileged states to the weak and most vulnerable, implementation of other features of the climate treaty will stall. Nothing meaningful will be done. In the 20 years since the Convention's signing, the North–South flow of finance and technology has been modest, as explained below, and this has been a source of constant friction at international negotiations.[10]

The UNFCCC, in Articles 11 and 21(3), also provides that financial transfers, including funds enabling the transfer of technology, are to be administered by a 'financial mechanism' accountable to the Conference of the Parties. There is no detail in the Convention about how the mechanism would work. The Global Environment

---

9 That call is clearer in the penultimate paragraph of the Convention's preamble. It is discussed in this book in Chapter 2.
10 During the 2011 UNFCCC negotiations, one developing country issued a warning that 'without finance, there would be no mitigation, adaptation – nothing': International Institute for Sustainable Development, 'AWG-LCA 14 and AWG-KP 16 Highlights: Wednesday, 5 October 2011', 12(519) *Earth Negotiations Bulletin* 1 (2011), p. 3.

Facility (GEF), which was already in existence when the UNFCCC was opened for signature, was restructured to play a role in the Convention's financial mechanism. (There is further information on the GEF below.) The financial mechanism of the UNFCCC turned out to be not a discrete institution, but a collection of 'operating entities' with different roles in climate finance (see Box 8.1). Many bilateral climate funds also exist.[11] Funding sources for REDD-related projects, including the UN-REDD Programme, are referred to in Chapter 7.

The term 'environmentally sound technologies', which is used in Article 4(5), quoted above, calls for an explanation. Yamin and Depledge offer this definition:

> Environmentally sound technologies have the potential for significantly improved environmental performance relative to other technologies. Broadly speaking, these technologies protect the environment, are less polluting, use resources in a sustainable manner, recycle more of their wastes and products, and handle all residual wastes in a more environmentally acceptable way than the technologies for which they are substitutes. Furthermore, [they] are not just individual technologies, but total systems which include know-how, procedures, goods and services, and equipment as well as organisational and managerial procedures.[12]

BOX 8.1 Overview of key international financial institutions relating to climate change

Under Article 4 of the UNFCCC, non-Annex I parties are entitled to receive funds from Annex II parties to meet many of their obligations under the Convention. The funds are being managed by several institutions and subordinate funds. They are:

Global Environment Facility: The GEF is a general mechanism for international cooperation in funding projects that protect the global environment and support sustainable development. Within the international climate change regime, it is an 'operating entity' of the financial mechanism of the UNFCCC. It provides financial support for developing countries to meet such treaty commitments as the preparation of national communications. GEF funding also supports national capacity-building,[13] implementation of adaptation activities, including implementation of 'national adaptation programmes of action' (NAPAs), and transfer and implementation of technologies for mitigation.[14]

GEF Trust Funds: The GEF administers three trust funds: the GEF Trust Fund, the Least Developed Countries (LDC) Fund, and the Special Climate Change Fund (SCCF).[15] The

---

[11] See Heinrich Böll Stiftung, 'Climate Funds Update', <http://www.climatefundsupdate.org/listing>.
[12] F. Yamin and J. Depledge, *The International Climate Change Regime: A Guide to Rules, Institutions and Procedures* (Cambridge University Press, 2004), pp. 306–7.
[13] On the UNFCCC's foundational definition of capacity-building, see UNFCCC, *Decision 2/CP.7, Capacity Building in Developing Countries (Non-Annex I Parties)* (2001), FCCC/CP/2001/13/Add.1. Capacity-building has aims such as strengthening relevant domestic institutions at various levels, including focal points and national coordinating bodies and organisations; strengthening national and local networks for the generation, sharing and management of information and knowledge; strengthening communication, education and training, and public awareness of climate change; strengthening integrated approaches and the participation of various stakeholders; and so forth: UNFCCC, *Decision 1/CP.16* (2010), para. 130. For a full discussion of the notion of capacity-building in the UNFCCC context, see Yamin and Depledge, *The International Climate Change Regime* (2004), pp. 315–26.
[14] UNFCCC, *Decision 2/CP.16, Fourth Review of the Financial Mechanism* (2010), FCCC/CP/2010/7/Add.2, para. 3.
[15] Ibid., para. 5.

> **BOX 8.1 (cont.)**
>
> LDC Fund aims to address the needs of LDCs that are especially vulnerable to the impacts of climate change. This includes support for preparing NAPAs. The SCCF was established in 2001 with the objective of implementing long-term measures to help developing countries' economic sectors adapt to the impacts of climate change. The SCCF is used to obtain additional resources from various bilateral and multilateral sources. Its priorities are adaptation, technology transfer, and associated capacity-building activities. The LDC Fund and the SCCF were established under the Convention, and therefore are subject to COP guidance.[16]
>
> **The World Bank**: The role of the World Bank within the international climate change regime is varied and legally complex. The bank's Carbon Finance Unit (CFU)[17] uses money contributed by governments and companies in Annex II countries to purchase project-based GHG emission reductions in developing countries and countries with economies in transition. The emission reductions are purchased through one of the CFU's carbon funds on behalf of the contributor, either from the Kyoto Protocol's Clean Development Mechanism (in the case of developing countries) or Joint Implementation (in the case of economies in transition).
>
> **Other World Bank divisions**: The World Bank operates the Clean Technology Fund and the Strategic Climate Fund, which finance investments in developing countries 'that contribute to lowering a country's greenhouse gas emissions with the objective of achieving transformational change' towards a low-carbon market environment.[18] The bank also has a Renewable Energy Division that funds a variety of programs in developing countries. REDD preparatory activities (Chapter 7) are financed under the bank's Forest Carbon Partnership Facility and Forest Investment Program.
>
> **Adaptation Fund (Kyoto Protocol)**: The Adaptation Fund is a financial instrument under the Kyoto Protocol, and thus is constrained by the Protocol's non-universal membership. It has been established to finance concrete adaptation projects and programs in developing countries. The fund is financed by a share of proceeds from CDM project activities, as well as through voluntary contributions of donor governments. The share of proceeds from the CDM amounts to 2 per cent of CERs issued for CDM project activities in non-LDC countries. The fund's operating body is the Adaptation Fund Board.[19]
>
> **Green Climate Fund (UNFCCC)**: The Green Climate Fund (GCF), reviewed in detail later in this chapter, is a new international institution whose objective is to serve as the UNFCCC's main financial transfer mechanism. Unlike the GEF, the GCF is both a dedicated climate change fund and under the direct authority of the UNFCCC COP, making it in theory much more responsive to the UNFCCC's needs.

On technology transfer in particular, the Convention, at Article 4(1)(h), calls on all parties to '[p]romote and cooperate in the full, open and prompt exchange of relevant scientific, technological, technical, socio-economic and legal information related to the climate system and climate change'. The Convention's Subsidiary Body for Scientific and Technological Advice (SBSTA) was given the task, among others, of advising the COP 'on the ways and means of promoting development and/or transferring' the relevant technologies to non-Annex I countries.[20]

---

[16] Yamin and Depledge, *The International Climate Change Regime* (2004), p. 290.
[17] Carbon Finance Unit, *Carbon Finance for Sustainable Development* (World Bank, 2007).
[18] World Bank, *The Clean Technology Fund* (9 June 2008).
[19] On the Adaptation Fund, see B. Horstmann and A. C. Abeysinghe, 'The Adaptation Fund of the Kyoto Protocol: A Model for Financing Adaptation to Climate Change?', 2(3) *Climate Law* 415 (2011).
[20] UNFCCC, Art. 9(2)(c).

The general legal obligations imposed on states by the UNFCCC were developed to some extent by the Kyoto Protocol. Under Article 10(c) of the Protocol, all parties are to:

> take all practicable steps to promote, facilitate and finance, as appropriate, the transfer of, or access to, environmentally sound technologies, know-how, practices and processes pertinent to climate change, in particular to developing countries, including the formulation of policies and programmes for the effective transfer of environmentally sound technologies that are *publicly owned or in the public domain* and the creation of an *enabling environment for the private sector*, to promote and enhance the transfer of, and access to, environmentally sound technologies.[21]

What is new here is that intellectual property issues are implicitly acknowledged, as well as the need to provide incentives for the involvement of the private sector, for example in the commercialisation of technologies useful to developing countries. It is noteworthy that the constraints of IP interests on the rapid transfer of technology across national borders and into a context of weak governance in some developing countries receive no acknowledgment in the Convention and only a veiled one, above, in the Kyoto Protocol.

The Protocol also imposes the obligation on Annex I parties to provide 'such financial resources, including for the transfer of technology' needed by developing countries to meet the costs of 'advancing' the implementation of existing commitments under the Convention's Article 4 relating to mitigation and adaptation.[22] Thus the Protocol reiterates obligations already articulated in the Convention, while clarifying them or strengthening them to some extent.

Role of the Global Environment Facility

Chapter 1 introduced climate change as a genuinely global problem. It is a problem to which every person contributes, and one that depends for its solution on providing incentives to all people to lessen their contribution to it. At the level of the state, the problem inherent in this situation is that action by states that is not of 'comparable effort' is discouraged. That is, no state will venture ahead (or too far ahead) of other states to lessen its own contribution to the problem, for that would be for itself to accept a cost burden that was to the advantage of all other states and thus essentially a subsidy to them. So either there will be a comparable effort by all states, or there will be no reform at all. To say that a global problem cannot be solved without the cooperation of all (but the poorest of) states is another way of saying that, in the context of a global problem, what any state does is every other state's business.

---

[21] Emphasis added. [22] Kyoto Protocol, Art. 11(2)(b.)

The rationale of the GEF is informed by these considerations. Developed countries are affected by the GHG-polluting activities of developing countries, just as the latter are affected by the GHG emissions of the former. For their part, developing countries depend heavily on financial assistance from the wealthier group to keep their own atmospheric pollution under control. The North–South relationship is an inextricable bond of mutual dependence which climate change, more than any other environmental problem, has brought into plain view. 'You cannot say to China and India, "you have to do something about your cook stoves." Black carbon is the pollution of the poor ... and the rich have to help the poor.'[23] Global environmental problems need global funding to facilitate appropriate responses all around the world.

The GEF was established in 1991[24] to fund environmentally friendly projects in developing countries that benefit the entire world.[25] A response to climate change is only one of several specific goals of the fund,[26] but because measures to reduce emissions of GHGs indisputably benefit the entire world (while generally being unaffordable for developing countries), the funding of projects to mitigate climate change has become a central concern of the GEF. It is a funding process with long horizons, which is appropriate for problems that require long-term solutions.

While the GEF serves as the financial mechanism for the UNFCCC, it has the same function with respect to some other multilateral environmental conventions.[27] As an institution, it is not under the control of the UNFCCC's COP. The GEF's resources are held by the GEF Trust, with the World Bank as trustee. Three smaller climate-related funds were created in 2001 under the GEF's governance structure: the Least Developed Countries Fund, the Special Climate Change Fund, and the Adaptation Fund.[28] All three funds are operated

---

[23] S. van Renssen, 'The Greenhouse-Gas Gang', 2 *Nature Climate Change* 143 (March 2012), p. 143, quoting Frank Raes, head of Climate Risk Management at the European Commission's Joint Research Centre in Italy.
[24] After an initial pilot phase within the World Bank, the GEF was formally established as a separate legal entity in 1994. See *Instrument for the Establishment of the Restructured GEF*, at Global Environment Facility, 'What Is the GEF', <http://www.thegef.org/gef/whatisgef>. On the early history of the GEF, see C. Streck, 'The Global Environment Facility – a Role Model for International Governance?', 1(2) *Global Environmental Politics* 71 (2001), pp. 72–8; and Yamin and Depledge, *The International Climate Change Regime* (2004), pp. 265–6.
[25] Global Environment Facility, 'What Is the GEF', <http://www.thegef.org/gef/whatisgef>; and Streck, 'The Global Environment Facility' (2001), p. 75.
[26] Others include biodiversity, international waters, land degradation, the ozone layer, and persistent organic pollutants.
[27] The other conventions are the Convention on Biological Diversity (1992), the Stockholm Convention on Persistent Organic Pollutants (2001), and the UN Convention to Combat Desertification (2003). States wanted to avoid a proliferation of funds created in concert with a growing number of international environmental conventions: see S. E. Smyth, 'A Practical Guide to Creating a Collective Financing Effort to Save the World: The Global Environment Facility Experience', 22(1) *Georgetown International Environmental Law Review* 29 (2010), p. 83; and Streck, 'The Global Environment Facility' (2001), p. 75.
[28] Smyth, 'A Practical Guide to Creating a Collective Financing Effort to Save the World' (2010), p. 83. As of May 2009, 19 countries, including Australia, had pledged a total of US$236 million to the LDC fund: Department of Climate Change, *Australia's Fifth National Communication on Climate Change: A Report under the United Nations Framework Convention on Climate Change* (2010), p. 132.

by the GEF but remain distinct from the GEF Trust Fund, as they are exclusive to the UNFCCC.

The GEF Trust funds projects overseen primarily by the World Bank, the UN Environment Program, and the UN Development Program (the implementing agencies); over time the group of implementing agencies has expanded. The GEF Council has 32 members, of which half are from developing countries. The arrangement means that GEF policy is set by both contributing and non-contributing participants. The GEF Council is overseen by the GEF Assembly.[29] The GEF Assembly meets every three years and is responsible for strategic guidance. It is made up of all member countries (contributors and recipients).[30] It is worth reiterating that this governance structure is different from, and unrelated to, that of the UNFCCC.

The GEF–World Bank relationship is somewhat complicated. The reason for establishing the GEF as a separate entity from the World Bank (which pre-existed it) was to enhance the involvement of developing countries in the governance of the GEF and the implementation of its projects.[31] However, the equal North–South distribution of GEF Council seats has meant that contributing states have retained control of the allocation of the funding.[32] The World Bank now provides administrative services to the GEF.[33] There is a distinction between the financial management of the fund – the task assigned to the World Bank as trustee – and the task of identifying, appraising, monitoring, and supervising projects to be financed by the GEF Trust.[34] The latter task, initially assigned to three intermediaries (the UNDP, UNEP, and the World Bank itself), was eventually broadened, with more partners added to implement GEF projects.[35]

The GEF lacks an international legal personality but nevertheless displays many characteristics of an independent institution.[36] Streck sees the GEF's legally unconventional nature as an advantage:

---

[29] For the governance structure of the GEF, see *Instrument for the Establishment of the Restructured GEF*, at Global Environment Facility, 'What Is the GEF', <http://www.thegef.org/gef/whatisgef>.
[30] For more on the GEF's governance structure, see Yamin and Depledge, *The International Climate Change Regime* (2004), pp. 296–8.
[31] Streck, 'The Global Environment Facility' (2001), pp. 75–6.
[32] On the GEF's donors and the fund's replenishment history, see Yamin and Depledge, *The International Climate Change Regime* (2004), pp. 266–71.
[33] The GEF Secretariat is housed within the World Bank, and its staff are on World Bank contracts, even though functionally the GEF is independent of the Bank. The GEF Secretariat oversees the GEF's work program, implements the decisions of the Council and the Assembly, and reports to both.
[34] The consequent diminution of the role of the World Bank (compared to its usual powers in relation to trust funds) to that of financial management of the Fund and implementing agency has led to conflict: Smyth, 'A Practical Guide to Creating a Collective Financing Effort to Save the World' (2010), pp. 41, 57, 63.
[35] The GEF partnership now consists of 10 agencies. In addition to the original three, the agencies are the UN Food and Agriculture Organization, the UN Industrial Development Organization, the African Development Bank, the Asian Development Bank, the European Bank for Reconstruction and Development, the Inter-American Development Bank, and the International Fund for Agricultural Development. See Global Environment Facility, 'What Is the GEF', <http://www.thegef.org/gef/whatisgef>.
[36] Streck, 'The Global Environment Facility' (2001), p. 81.

> [T]he GEF offers a model of how modern governance structures should be shaped: on the basis of a minimum of formal agreements and founded more on compromise than legal precision. This openness in structure and regulation fosters a flexible agency with a strong ability to innovate. Constant evaluation and monitoring processes are crucial for this ability.[37]

For almost two decades, the UNFCCC parties have regarded financial support from the GEF as crucial to enable countries 'to integrate climate change into their national development agendas'.[38] However, while developed country donors have provided some 'new and additional'[39] funding to developing countries through the GEF for global environmental benefits, the money has been insufficient to cover the GEF's increasing agenda of UNFCCC matters:[40] 'The Convention and the Protocol do not specify the level of resources to be provided by Annex II parties nor the burden-sharing arrangements among them.'[41] Moreover, as UNFCCC demands have increased, the drawbacks of having to regulate climate change funding through a separate institution such as the GEF have become increasingly apparent to the Convention parties.

Sample GEF projects in the area of technology transfer for climate change adaptation and mitigation are shown in Table 8.1. The *legal/regulatory* subject matter of the first listed project is particularly notable (development of a standardised contract). Generally speaking, all or most such projects have implicit legal/regulatory aspects, just as they promote transfer of finance and technology, broadly conceived. They thus support the growth of climate-related law and legal practice in developing countries.

The first project in the list is also an example of GEF funds deployed to 'leverage' funds from other sources (in this case at a strong 1:9 ratio), transforming what might have been a modest locally funded effort into an internationally supervised effort of global significance.[42] (Public funds can be used to leverage, or unlock, much higher levels of private capital, which would not have been mobilised without the reassurance provided by the public investment. In this example, $9 of private finance is unlocked for every dollar of public finance.)

The Fourth Overall Performance Study of the GEF (2010) was generally positive about the institution, and concluded that GEF support has enabled countries to reduce or avoid GHG emissions and transform markets:

---

37 Ibid., p. 93.   **38** UNFCCC, *Decision 2/CP.16* (2010), para. 1(c).
39 For the meaning of this term and the difficulty in applying it, see Yamin and Depledge, *The International Climate Change Regime* (2004), pp. 276–8.
40 See the criticisms listed in UNFCCC, *Decision 2/CP.16* (2010), para. 1, which summarises the results of the 2009 'Fourth Overall Performance Study of the GEF'.
41 Yamin and Depledge, *The International Climate Change Regime* (2004), p. 267.
42 On the GEF's constrained capacity to leverage funds, see Streck, 'The Global Environment Facility' (2001), pp. 90–1.

GEF climate change funding has supported a solid level of achievement of progress towards intended Global Environmental Benefits, both in reduction and avoidance of greenhouse gas emissions and in sustainable market changes.[43]

Overall, the study estimated that about 65 per cent of sampled GEF climate-related projects showed measurable effects on GHG emissions. It also noted that

Table 8.1 Examples of projects funded by the GEF under the UNFCCC umbrella

Project name and implementing agency	Project description	Cost
Nigeria: Rural Electrification and Renewable Energy Development – World Bank[44]	A project to support the design and implementation of several pilot projects in the expansion of electricity access through grid extension or off-grid generation that include renewable energy options. The pilots provided information for the policy, legal, regulatory and institutional frameworks being developed. The project also supported the implementation of the Nigerian Renewable Energy Master Plan, which develops market models for renewables, including a standard contractual agreement for grid-connected small hydropower and solar PV technologies.	Grant from the GEF Trust Fund: US$1 million; co-financing: US$9 million. Completion date: June 2011.
Technology Needs Assessments for Developing Countries – UNEP[45]	The project will provide targeted financial and technical support that helps developing countries carry out improved Technology Needs Assessments.[46] The intention is that these countries will go beyond identifying technology needs narrowly and will develop national action plans for technologies that reduce GHG emissions, support adaptation to climate change, and are consistent with national development objectives. Financially supported countries have to work towards a national consensus on technologies of high priority, agree on a technology action plan compatible with their nationally appropriate mitigation actions (NAMAs), establish an institutional structure for overseeing implementation, and develop the capacity to revise or adapt the plan as needed.	Total cost US$11 million, of which $8.2 million comes from the GEF's Special Climate Change Fund – Window for Technology Transfer

---

43 Global Environment Facility, *Fourth Overall Performance Study of the GEF: Progress toward Impact* (2010), p. 15.
44 Global Environment Facility, 'Nigeria – Rural Electrification and Renewable Energy Development', <http://gefonline.org/projectDetailsSQL.cfm?projID=2828>.
45 Global Environment Facility, *Report of the GEF to the Fifteenth Session of the Conference of the Parties to the United Nations Framework Convention on Climate Change* (9 October 2009), p. 92.
46 On the meaning of this concept, see J. K. Musango and A. C. Brent, 'A Conceptual Framework for Energy Technology Sustainability Assessment', 15 *Energy for Sustainable Development* 84 (2011).

Table 8.1 (cont.)

Project name and implementing agency	Project description	Cost
Forests of Brazil: Strengthening Public Policies by Using Accurate and Updated Information on Forest Resources – UN Food and Agriculture Organization[47]	Establishment and implementation of a National Forest Monitoring and Assessment System. This is a program activity in the Brazilian Forest Service, which is intended to continue after completion of the project. Launched in 2011, the project aims to improve information on the state and dynamics of Brazil's forest resources and their management, which would in turn improve government decision-making. The project will also allow for more targeted interventions, to address specific threats.	GEF grant of US$8.9 million to be implemented over a five-year period
Enhancing Institutional Capacities on REDD Issues for Sustainable Forest Management in the Congo Basin – World Bank[48]	A project to strengthen the capacities of the Congo Basin countries (Cameroon, Central African Republic, Democratic Republic of Congo, Equatorial Guinea and Gabon) on issues related to REDD and forest carbon stock measurements. The specific focus is on knowledge exchange between the political and technical levels; promotion of participation and representation of stakeholder groups in policy and strategy discussions at the regional level; and the building of capacity for measurement and monitoring of carbon stocks in the Congo Basin forests.	GEF grant of US$13 million

developing countries have used GEF finance to introduce new climate change policies and to develop corresponding environmental legislation and regulatory frameworks.[49]

Breathing life into neglected treaty provisions

For many years, developing countries have been demanding concrete measures to put into effect the UNFCCC/Kyoto Protocol treaty provisions on finance and technology transfer, and in particular for the COP itself to turn on the promised flow of 'adequate and predictable' funding.[50] Whatever its virtues, the GEF is not

---

[47] Global Environment Facility, 'Forests of Brazil: Strengthening Public Policies by Using Accurate and Updated Information on Forest Resources: A Way Forward', <http://www.thegef.org/gef/node/4695>.
[48] World Bank, 'Enhancing Institutional Capacities on REDD Issues for Sustainable Forest Management in the Congo Basin (Project No. P113167)', <http://web.worldbank.org/external/projects>.
[49] Ibid., p. 53.   [50] Kyoto Protocol, Art. 11(2)(b).

a dedicated climate fund and its growing agenda has not been afforded resources proportionately. Developed countries, for their part, have often expressed concern about recipient countries' inability to facilitate and reinforce the benefits of their contributions as the main barrier to finance and technology transfer. The sidelining until recently of non-Annex I adaptation issues (in preference to progress on mitigation by Annex I countries), the difficulty in reaching a common definition of 'technology transfer', and disagreements over the role of IP rights have been recurrent features of these debates.[51]

As a result, the negotiation of finance and technology transfer matters at the COP (and CMP) level has been ongoing. Little progress was made before the Bali COP in 2007. The Bali Action Plan which emerged from that conference emphasised:

> [e]nhanced national/international action on mitigation of climate change, including, inter alia ... Nationally appropriate mitigation actions by developing country Parties in the context of sustainable development, supported and enabled by technology, financing and capacity-building, in a measurable, reportable and verifiable manner.[52]

This was an early indication that monitoring, reporting, and verification (MRV) requirements would be applied to those Nationally Appropriate Mitigation Actions (NAMAs) of developing countries for which the wealthier countries had provided technology and finance. Compared to the original language of the Convention, whose tone conveys a sense of charity, the Bali language suggests that climate aid has conditions: the aid must be disbursed, no doubt, but only if subject to MRV.

Besides NAMAs, the international lexicon includes NAPAs: the National Adaptation Programmes of Action. Under the Convention process, developing countries are required to identify their adaptation activities in NAPAs. International financial and technology support for adaptation may now safely be understood as referring to support for NAPAs. (They are an older and better established instrument than NAMAs, because whereas developing countries have always declared an interest in adaptation, it is only in recent years that they have accepted a responsibility for mitigation.) Thus financial and technological support for both mitigation and adaptation activities is now broadly conditional on the needier countries producing national action plans that include measurable indicators of success.

The Bali Action Plan developed the call for 'enhanced action' in finance and technology transfer in relative detail.[53] Yet although that plan was an improvement on the text of the Convention and the Kyoto Protocol in relation to how technological and financial support for developing countries should be generated, governed, and delivered, as well as on technological cooperation, it was still

---

[51] International Centre for Trade and Sustainable Development, 'The Climate Technology Mechanism: Issues and Challenges', Information Note no. 18 (March 2011), p. 1.
[52] UNFCCC, *Decision 1/CP.13, Bali Action Plan* (2007), FCCC/CP/2007/6/Add.1, paras. 1(b)(i) and (ii).
[53] Ibid., paras. 1(d) and 1(e).

no more than a plan on which subsequent negotiations were to be structured. Progress towards the plan's implementation became evident only in December 2010, at the Cancun COP, in the context of negotiations on the UNFCCC's future.

As discussed in Chapter 2, by late 2009 the international negotiations towards a long-term agreement on climate change, which would update the Convention and the Protocol and perhaps create a one-stream international climate regime, had stalled. The states' adage up until the 2009 Copenhagen COP had been: 'Nothing is agreed [about the way forward] until everything is agreed.' Through 2010 and 2011, when faith in rapid transformative progress on the climate front was all but abandoned, the adage was said to have become: 'Nothing is agreed until *something* is agreed.' The pre-Copenhagen belief that a comprehensive agreement was within reach gave way to the comparatively unambitious aim of making stepwise progress through balanced measures in areas relatively free of disagreement.[54]

'Balance' in the 2010–11 context was often a euphemism for a compromise between developed and developing states, whereby the former would make greater sacrifices, and in particular contribute more money for adaptation measures in the South, in exchange for which non-Annex I countries (excluding LDCs) would accept the imposition of positive, measurable obligations under international law in relation to climate change. Those obligations would range from compulsory regular reporting on emissions and policies, with the possibility of independent review, to legally binding measures on mitigation, such as reduction by an agreed amount of the emission intensity of a developing country's GDP. (Emission intensity of GDP is the amount of GHG emitted for each dollar of GDP. See Figure 8.1. This intensity can fall even as the economy's absolute greenhouse emissions grow. A non-Annex I commitment to reduce emission intensity is thus distinguishable from an Annex I commitment to reduce absolute emissions.)

The 'balance' will not be easily attained. Developing countries have been reluctant to jettison their interpretation of the UNFCCC to the effect that Annex I parties must implement decisive mitigation measures, first, before any member of the non-Annex I group should have to accept binding obligations to act on mitigation or even to report its emissions on a regular schedule and agree to verification of those reports. Nevertheless, beginning at the Copenhagen COP in 2009, developing countries with large and growing economies *partially* gave in to the demand for reporting and verification.[55] This enabled the piecemeal issues of REDD (see Chapter 7) and finance and technology transfer to be advanced one year later at the Cancun COP. It was the first sign of progress in this matter since the Bali Conference. The 'new deal' was further advanced at the Durban COP in 2011.

---

54 International Institute for Sustainable Development, 'AWG-LCA 12 and AWG-KP 14 Highlights: Thursday, 7 October 2010', 12(483) *Earth Negotiations Bulletin* (2010), p. 3.
55 UNFCCC, *Copenhagen Accord* (2009), para. 5.

The new institutions of the Cancun COP

The Cancun agreement under the UNFCCC sets the international agenda on finance and technology transfer through at least 2013. The essential new governance institutions for those processes will most likely be in place by that date.

To start, the Cancun agreement calls on developed country parties to provide developing countries with long-term, new, and additional finance, as well as technology and capacity-building support to implement urgent adaptation actions and plans at all levels of government and across all economic and social sectors and ecosystems.[56] In exchange for the promise of enhanced financial support, many developing countries have agreed to implement nationally appropriate mitigation actions (the NAMAs of the Bali Action Plan), the effect of which would be a deviation from projected emissions (based on a business-as-usual trajectory) through to 2020.[57] In other words, through this agreement, wealthy countries have once again undertaken to contribute money and technology, and the developing world's fastest-growing economies have agreed to use this assistance transparently and accountably to shift their economic development onto lower-emission pathways. The Cancun compact is important because it provides a mechanism for non-Annex I states to go beyond adaptation and join the mitigation effort which the Kyoto Protocol, through its Annex B emission limits, had confined to Annex I countries.

There is a darker side to the story. We have seen that the CDM is essentially a system by which the non-Annex I group is paid by Annex I states to offset the rising GHG emissions of the latter. There is a risk that, in the absence of an ambitious agreement on Annex I emission caps, Annex I states will settle into a pattern of paying other states for mitigation while undertaking only modest reform themselves. This has been a constant complaint by environmentalists.[58] Moreover, it is still far from clear that the promised provision of financial and technological support will result in regular, comprehensive and transparent reporting and verification. Certainly, developing countries' MRV under the Cancun agreement will be limited, at least at the beginning, to those piecemeal actions receiving international support, which means that it will be very difficult to tell whether the *whole* of any developing country's economy has deviated from its business-as-usual trajectory.

Returning now to the terms of the Cancun agreement, as we have noted, developed parties' financial and technological contributions to the South for mitigation measures are henceforth to be guided by developing country NAMAs.[59] NAMAs are intended to go beyond the project-by-project approach of the CDM and deliver more fundamental changes, often on a larger scale and in

---

[56] UNFCCC, *Decision 1/CP.16* (2010), para. 18.   [57] Ibid., para. 48.
[58] For example D. Morris and B. Worthington, *Cap or Trap? How the EU ETS Risks Locking in Carbon Emissions* (Sandbag, September 2010).
[59] Forty-four developing countries put forth NAMAs for inclusion in the Appendices to the 2009 Copenhagen Accord.

the longer term.⁶⁰ NAMAs already in existence in 2010 were compiled into a document by the UNFCCC Secretariat.⁶¹

Botswana's NAMA is illustrative of the elementary state of those first-generation national plans. Botswana declared in its plan that its mitigation actions would include reducing emissions from the use of petrol in the transport sector and from the burning of coal for energy. The shift away from coal would be enabled by the greater use of natural gas, nuclear energy, renewable energy, and biomass. Carbon dioxide emissions from coal would be further reduced through carbon capture and storage. The country would reduce its deforestation rate and plant new forests. It would target energy conservation and efficiency in mass transport systems, buildings, and low-energy appliances. Botswana's NAMA, like those of most other developing countries in the Secretariat's compilation, makes no attempt to quantify the planned mitigation, demonstrate that it would not have taken place in the normal course of events anyway, or for that matter, dispel the strong impression that certain elements of the plan (for instance the use of nuclear energy or carbon capture and storage) are quite unrealistic. For some actions, Botswana said it would seek international support; other actions it would pursue voluntarily. It promised to report on its mitigation efforts in its periodic national communication pursuant to the UNFCCC, while emphasising that it would allow only the internationally supported components of its NAMA to be subject to international MRV.⁶²

One can imagine the difficulty of linking financial and technological transfers to a plan such as Botswana's and quantifying the mitigation results achieved with Annex I financial and technological support. At the very least, Botswana's plan would have to be elaborated at a much improved level of detail and sophistication. Other countries' NAMAs are a hodgepodge of targets, strategies, policies, programs and individual projects, from a target for carbon neutrality by 2020 for the Maldives, to a plan involving grid-enabled electric vehicles for Chile, to a sustainable bio-waste treatment project in Tunisia. What developed countries will be looking to support, however, are concrete, verifiable actions.⁶³

Such, then, was the generally unsatisfactory state of NAMAs in 2010, which at the Cancun conference were promised enhanced financial and technological support from Annex I states.⁶⁴ The conference also decided to set up a registry to record the elements of NAMAs seeking international support and to help match up the finance and technology support that was requested with the support that would be offered.⁶⁵ To this end, developing country parties were

---

60 S. van Renssen, 'Taking Charge of Mitigation', 2 *Nature Climate Change* 71 (February 2012), p. 71.
61 Secretariat (UNFCCC), *Compilation of Information on Nationally Appropriate Mitigation Actions to Be Implemented by Parties Not Included in Annex I to the Convention* (18 March 2011), FCCC/AWGLCA/2011/INF.1.
62 Ibid., paras. 24–9.   63 van Renssen, 'Taking Charge of Mitigation' (2012), p. 71.
64 UNFCCC, *Decision 1/CP.16* (2010), para. 52.
65 Ibid., para. 53. Matching requires a process for directing support from developed countries (especially from international public sources) to implement mitigation and adaptation actions in developing countries. The challenge of matching is how to channel multiple sources of international finance in a strategic way to actions in developing countries so that matching leads to implementation of actions into domestic policy

invited to submit to the UNFCCC Secretariat information on NAMA elements for which they sought support, along with the estimated costs, emission reductions and anticipated time frames for implementation. In turn, developed countries were invited to submit concrete proposals about the money and other resources they could make available.[66] The commencement of the registration process for NAMAs, and for the donor funding available to match those actions requiring international support, was announced at the Durban COP in 2011.[67]

To summarise thus far, as a result of Cancun, internationally supported mitigation actions in developing countries will be measured, reported, and verified. This will be done in accordance with guidelines under the Convention that have yet to be developed, although they are likely to comprise an extension of the MRV system for national GHG inventories and national communications already in place (see Chapter 3). While this may seem to be an almost imperceptible advance in international regulation, it is in its political context a notable reform, as it emphasises developing country responsibility for mitigation and reporting, in addition to adaptation. However, it is important to keep in mind that the UNFCCC has yet to define what could be in a NAMA, what financial support exists for NAMAs, and how the two will be matched up.

The parties in Cancun also agreed in principle that even the *domestically* supported mitigation actions undertaken in developing countries would be subject to some form of MRV. However, this would be done by the concerned developing country itself: there would be no international, independent assessment of actions that are undertaken and paid for by a developing country itself. Guidelines for domestic as opposed to international MRV are to be developed under the Convention.[68] The matter remains highly sensitive, with developing countries seeing it as potentially impinging on their national sovereignty.

The above discussion reveals once more the key governance role of MRV: without it, one country cannot know what another is doing; there can be no coordination, no systematic management of the climate problem, no trust. Without concessions on MRV, the flow of finance and technology from the wealthier to the poorer states would have remained weak and unsystematic. Perhaps the shift in attitude is not surprising, considering that the anticipated expenditure of hundreds of billions of dollars, much of it coming from domestic tax revenue, must eventually call for accountability.

The good intentions, general principles and Cancun regulations discussed in this section and further detailed in the next section are still to be implemented.

frameworks without derailing countries from their development paths. In order for the relevant actions to be most effective, it is important to ensure that different potential sources of finance (domestic and international, public and private) do not 'compete' for the same domestic actions. A matching mechanism might support, say, actions that are not likely to be financed by the carbon market (due to their high transaction cost or low-volume GHG reductions). See generally J. A. Kim, J. Ellis and S. Moarif, *Matching Mitigation Actions with Support: Key Issues for Channelling International Public Finance* (OECD/IEA, 2 December 2009), COM/ENV/EPOC/IEA/SLT(2009)8.

66 UNFCCC, *Decision 1/CP.16* (2010), paras. 54–6.
67 UNFCCC, *Decision 2/CP.17, Outcome of the Work of the Ad Hoc Working Group on Long-Term Cooperative Action under the Convention* (2011), paras. 46–8.
68 UNFCCC, *Decision 1/CP.16* (2010), paras. 61–2.

Years will pass before the new system of finance and technology transfer can be evaluated. The present situation is still very much a work in progress.

Roles and responsibilities of the Cancun institutions

The Cancun conference formalised the existence of two institutions created a year earlier under the controversial Copenhagen Accord.[69] They are the Green Climate Fund and the Technology Mechanism.

'Paradigm shift': The Green Climate Fund

The Copenhagen Accord's promise of new money, elevated at the Cancun COP into a decision of the UNFCCC, means that there is now a formal commitment by developed countries to provide new and additional resources for the period 2010–12 approaching US$30 billion, to be spent on adaptation and mitigation in developing countries.[70] Developed country parties also pledged at Cancun that, in the context of 'meaningful mitigation actions and transparency on implementation' by developing countries, they would raise US$100 billion per year by 2020 to address adaptation and mitigation expenses in the South.[71] A large share of the promised international funding is to flow through the Green Climate Fund.[72] For the first time in the history of the international climate change regime, the North–South financial flow has been quantified, and for the first time the Convention parties have their own institution through which to deliver the funding.

The GCF 'will be accountable to and function under the guidance of the Conference of the Parties'.[73] It will be governed and supervised by a board that will have full responsibility for funding decisions.[74] It will, according to the COP, promote 'the *paradigm shift* towards low-emission and climate-resilient development pathways'.[75]

Soon after the Copenhagen Accord was signed in December 2009, the UN Secretary-General appointed a High-Level Advisory Group on Climate Change Financing to study potential sources of revenue to meet the above commitments on finance. The Advisory Group concluded that the largest chunk of the promised revenue would have to come from pricing GHG emissions globally:

> Based on a carbon price of US$20–US$25 per ton of CO_2 equivalent, auctions of emission allowances and domestic carbon taxes in developed countries with up to

---

69 See UNFCCC, *Copenhagen Accord* (2009), para. 8 (Copenhagen Green Climate Fund) and para. 11 (Technology Mechanism).
70 UNFCCC, *Decision 1/CP.16* (2010), para. 95; UNFCCC, *Decision 3/CP.17, Launching the Green Climate Fund* (2011), Annex, para. 3.
71 UNFCCC, *Decision 1/CP.16* (2010), para. 98.   **72** Ibid., para. 100.
73 UNFCCC, *Decision 3/CP.17* (2011), Annex, para. 4.   **74** Ibid., Annex, para. 5.
75 Ibid., Annex, para. 2, emphasis added.

10 per cent of total revenues allocated for international climate action could potentially mobilize around US$30 billion annually. Without underestimating the difficulties to be resolved, particularly in terms of national sovereignty and incidence on developing countries, approximately US$10 billion annually could be raised from carbon pricing international transportation, assuming no net incidence on developing countries and earmarking between 25 and 50 per cent of total revenues. Up to US$10 billion could be mobilized from other instruments, such as the redeployment of fossil fuel subsidies in developed countries or some form of financial transaction tax, though diverging views will make it difficult to implement this universally.[76]

In the best case, then, the above-listed methods would raise half the required annual amount – about 50 of the 100 billion US$ per year. The case assumes that cap-and-trade or equivalent systems for raising carbon revenue will soon be established in all major industrialised economies. It requires us to imagine that, for example, the United States will have priced its national emissions by the end of this decade. This is a possibility which, for the moment, seems unlikely.

According to the Advisory Group, the other half of the required amount will have to come from several relatively obscure and speculative sources, as well as from the most obvious of sources: Annex I states' general fiscal revenue (new taxes). About the latter source, the Advisory Group wrote:

> Direct budget contributions based on existing public finance sources, such as domestic revenues, could continue to play an important role, as Governments may prefer to increase direct budget contributions before they implement new instruments. The political acceptability of such sources will depend on national circumstances and on the domestic fiscal environment, which has currently put many developed countries under extreme pressure. Nevertheless, the Advisory Group expects that direct budget contributions will play a key role in the long term.[77]

In other words, the sources of finance for the considerable North–South flows promised in Copenhagen and reiterated in Cancun are still only vague and uncertain ideas, which await systematic exploration at the COP level. In relation to the fast-start finance for 2010–12, information submitted by the middle of 2011 by 10 developed country parties which had already made their contributions or budgeted their pledges suggested that most of this funding was to come from public sources.[78] As an example, US fast-start finance in 2011 totalled US$3.1 billion. It consisted of government appropriations worth $1.8 billion

---

[76] M. Zenawi and J. Stoltenberg, *Report of the Secretary-General's High-Level Advisory Group on Climate Change Financing* (United Nations, 5 November 2010), pp. 5–6.
[77] Ibid., p. 6.
[78] The information also indicated that bilateral and multilateral agencies were being used as channels for delivery of the financial support. Most submissions indicated that the resources provided were either new and additional, or that they helped to mobilise new and additional funds from other sources. Regarding access to these resources, most of the 10 developed countries reporting provided examples of concrete mitigation and adaptation projects undertaken in various developing countries, including specific REDD-plus initiatives: Secretariat (UNFCCC), *Submissions on Information from Developed Country Parties on the Resources Provided to Fulfil the Commitment Referred to in Decision 1/CP.16, Paragraph 95* (15 August 2011), FCCC/CP/2011/INF.1.

and $1.3 billion from development-finance and export-credit agencies.[79] The Durban COP at the end of 2011 did not make any progress on clarifying the longer-term sources of funding. It set up a work program to 'analyze options for the mobilization of resources from a wide variety of sources'.[80]

In terms of Australia's contribution to the longer-term fund, Jotzo, Pickering and Wood write that '[b]ased on Australia's wealth and emissions, we find that a fair share for Australia may be around 2.4 per cent [of the US$100 billion per year], or $2.4 billion a year by 2020'.[81] They suggest that most of this sum, if it were raised, would have to be publicly financed, such as through a carbon levy on international transport, reduced tax breaks for fossil-fuel use and production, and increased taxation of Australia's exports of coal and other resources.

As for the governance structures needed to enable the systematic transfer of the finance and technology to the world's most vulnerable, by 2011 these were just coming into life. We will briefly discuss their design and functions.

The COP, in its Cancun decision, designated the Green Climate Fund as an operating entity of the financial mechanism of the Convention under Article 11 of the UNFCCC, just as it had done many years earlier for the Global Environment Facility.[82] The Green Climate Fund is to be governed by a 24-member board, comprising an equal number of members from developing and developed countries. The World Bank is to serve as the interim trustee of the fund.[83] The administrative competence to manage the financial assets of the GCF, as they eventuate, has thus been assigned to the World Bank until a permanent trustee is found.[84]

The UNFCCC parties set up a Transitional Committee to develop the operational features of the Green Climate Fund.[85] The Committee held its first meeting in April 2011.[86] Of necessity, the meeting was occupied with matters relating to the running of the Committee itself. Nevertheless, some preliminary Committee discussions on substance have highlighted future priorities and challenges, and are of interest from a legal point of view:

- Legal and institutional arrangements for establishing the GCF and bringing it into operation, including fiduciary management issues, are high on the design agenda.
- Rules of procedure, functions, and responsibilities of the GCF's board are seen as critical.

---

[79] US Department of State, *Meeting the Fast Start Commitment: US Climate Finance in Fiscal Year 2011* (2011), p. 1.
[80] UNFCCC, *Decision 3/CP.17* (2011), Annex, para. 4.
[81] F. Jotzo, J. Pickering and P. J. Wood, *Fulfilling Australia's International Climate Finance Commitments: Which Sources of Financing Are Promising and How Much Could They Raise?* (Centre for Climate Economics and Policy, Crawford School of Economics and Government, Australian National University, October 2011), CCEP working paper 1115, p. i.
[82] This was reiterated in UNFCCC, *Decision 3/CP.17* (2011), para. 3. [83] Ibid., Annex, para. 26.
[84] Ibid., para. 16. [85] UNFCCC, *Decision 1/CP.16* (2010), paras. 102–12.
[86] Transitional Committee of the Green Climate Fund (UNFCCC), *Co-Chairs' Summary Report on the Initial Meeting of the Transitional Committee for the Design of the Green Climate Fund* (UNFCCC, 12 May 2011), TC-1/6.

8 CLIMATE FINANCE, TECHNOLOGY TRANSFER AND CAPACITY-BUILDING

- The relationship with the trustee (the World Bank) and matters related to fiduciary responsibility for the GCF are identified as issues for resolution.
- Of interest to international lawyers, in particular, will be the eventual relationship between the GCF and other bodies established under the Convention, as well as that between the GCF and states themselves.
- The methods used to manage the projected large scale of the GCF's financial resources will no doubt give rise to new forms of risk, liability, and conflict. The financial resources are to be contributed by a number of sources and distributed to states through a variety of financial instruments and modes of access, including direct access,[87] which must be consistent with the overall objective of a balanced allocation between adaptation and mitigation.[88]
- A process for the administrative review of funding decisions made by the GCF's board has yet to be considered.

Also awaiting design are mechanisms to ensure the periodic independent evaluation of the GCF's performance and its financial accountability, and mechanisms to evaluate the performance of activities supported by the fund, particularly with respect to the requirement that funded actions meet environmental and social safeguards.[89]

As interesting as this new regulatory sphere may prove to be from a legal point of view, we note the observation of GermanWatch (an NGO) that 'an operationalisation of the fund without the clear prospect that it will be filled with money cannot be sold as a big success'.[90] This is not to say, however, that money is everything, at least not in the beginning. Raising international revenue for climate change adaptation and mitigation is surely made more difficult in the absence of a fair and rational system governing decisions about its management. Petherick writes that:

> [t]he challenge of selecting truly effective projects may be dwarfed by that of ensuring the money actually gets to them. This is because the 20 countries that are predicted to suffer most from the impacts of climate change score badly on the most widely used global corruption index ... The average grade given to the ten most climate-vulnerable countries in the world – a list that includes the Democratic Republic of Congo, Haiti and Zimbabwe – is a measly 2.5.[91]

The GCF is meant to supply that governance. Therefore the quality of the Cancun governance structures is likely to be a crucial factor in facilitating the flow of

---

87 The GCF will set up national implementing entities that applicants can approach directly for access to the fund's holdings, rather than going through international organisations.
88 Transitional Committee of the Green Climate Fund (UNFCCC), *Report on the Initial Meeting* (2011), p. 6.
89 Ibid., p. 7.
90 S. Harmeling, *Successful Start for the Design of the Green Climate Fund* (GermanWatch, 2011), p. 6.
91 Where 0 = extremely corrupt and 10 = corruption extremely rare: A. Petherick, 'A Note of Caution', 2 *Nature Climate Change* 144 (March 2012), p. 144.

funds from donors.[92] Regulation introduces transparency and accountability. The GCF must also earn the confidence of donors and recipients by ensuring that the fund operates in accordance with the letter and spirit of its design. It seems that the international regime must move slowly, if it is to move at all, despite the evidence that the window for meaningful action has almost closed.[93]

Technology mechanism

Technology development and transfer to developing country parties[94] are the focus of the second international institution established at the Cancun conference. The Technology Executive Committee, together with the Climate Technology Centre and Network, constitute the UNFCCC's new Technology Mechanism.[95] The Durban arrangements aim to make the Technology Mechanism fully operational in 2012.[96]

The functions of the Technology Executive Committee[97] are quite broad, and it certainly does not (and could not) have powers to effect changes in the area of intellectual property rights. (The Green Climate Fund, by contrast, is intended to enable concrete projects.) The TEC's functions are at the strategic level, and include:

- analysing policy and technical issues related to the development and transfer of technology for mitigation and adaptation;
- recommending actions to promote technology development and transfer so as to accelerate mitigation and adaptation;
- facilitating collaboration between governments, the private sector, non-profit organisations, and academic and research communities on the development and transfer of technology for mitigation and adaptation; and
- supporting the development of technology road maps (action plans) at the national level.[98]

The functions of the Climate Technology Centre and Network are also rather broad. Contrary to what its name may suggest, the Centre will not itself produce any technology. We do not yet know how the CTCN will turn out in practice, or where it will be headquartered, but its intended functions give us a diagnosis of the international regime's current ailments in the region of technology transfer, as seen through the eyes of the UNFCCC parties. The CTCN will:

---

[92] At present, donors must make assessments of trustworthiness case-by-case; for example 'US support prioritizes ... countries *with the political will to implement large-scale efforts* to reduce emissions from deforestation': US Department of State, *Meeting the Fast Start Commitment* (2011), p. 2, emphasis added.
[93] For example UN Environment Programme, *Bridging the Emissions Gap: A UNEP Synthesis Report* (November 2011).
[94] UNFCCC, *Decision 1/CP.16* (2010), IV.B.   [95] Ibid., para. 117.
[96] UNFCCC, *Decision 2/CP.17* (2011), paras. 133–6.
[97] The Committee comprises 20 expert members, elected by the Conference of the Parties and serving in their personal capacity. Nine members are from Annex I parties and the rest from developing states: UNFCCC, *Decision 1/CP.16* (2010), Appendix IV, para. 1.
[98] Ibid., para. 121; see also UNFCCC, *Decision 4/CP.17, Technology Executive Committee: Modalities and Procedures* (2011).

- provide advice and support to developing countries related to the identification of technology needs and the implementation of environmentally sound technologies;
- facilitate training and support for programs to build developing countries' capacity to make appropriate sustainable technology choices and to operate and maintain that technology;
- facilitate the prompt deployment of existing clean technology in developing countries, based on identified needs;
- collaborate with the private sector, government agencies, and research institutions to encourage the development and transfer of existing and emerging environmentally sound technologies, as well as opportunities for 'North–South, South–South and triangular technology cooperation'.[99]

The list continues in a similar vein.[100] In summary, whereas the Technology Executive Committee is expected to operate at the strategic level of international policy development, the CTCN will have a facilitative role at the national level. Its intention to provide advice and support related to the *identification* of technology needs is of particular importance in view of the fact that a range of commercial interests are actively promoting their respective technologies (wind, solar, nuclear, etc.) to developing countries in a context where the latter often do not have sufficient expertise to make informed choices about which technology is best suited to their needs.[101] The CTCN could help developing countries not to be duped into proceeding along pathways of lesser sustainability.

A complicating factor in all of this is that the notion of 'developing country' in reality encompasses middle-income countries with advanced technological capabilities, in addition to the multitude of lesser developed and LDCs. The key terms that have been used in the international climate change negotiations since 1990 (developed/developing, North/South) are not so helpful when we consider that large emerging economies, including China, India, and Brazil, are also technological innovators and producers themselves. Like climate adaptation needs, which tend to be specific to each country, overly broad statements about how to meet the diversity of technological 'needs' in developing countries are not likely to be helpful, because technologies tend to be country- and sector-specific. Hence the emphasis on drawing up and implementing NAPAs and NAMAs, which are meant to be not simply needs assessments but national implementation plans for concrete action.

---

99 UNFCCC, *Decision 1/CP.16* (2010), para. 123. A reference to South–South cooperation is made in two instances in the CTCN's mandate, reflecting the importance of the technological capabilities already acquired by emerging economies such as China, India, and Brazil, from which other developing countries and LDCs can benefit.
100 The terms of reference of the Climate Technology Centre and Network are given in UNFCCC, *Decision 2/CP.17* (2011), Annex VII.
101 International Centre for Trade and Sustainable Development, 'The Climate Technology Mechanism: Issues and Challenges', Information Note No. 18 (March 2011), p. 9.

The necessary means to enable the transfer of funds from the Green Climate Fund to the Technology Mechanism have yet to be designed. More generally, neither the quantity of resources with which the Technology Mechanism will be endowed, nor its possible links with the operational entities of the Convention's financial mechanism (including the GEF and GCF), are clear at this stage. Some of the priorities for the expenditure of the international funds, once they start being raised in earnest, are beginning to take shape in the context of the UNFCCC negotiations. Among these priorities is a need to enhance what the UNFCCC process refers to as the *endogenous* capacities and technologies of developing country parties, as well as:

- cooperative research and demonstration programs;
- deployment of existing 'soft and hard' technologies for adaptation and mitigation;[102]
- climate-change observation systems and related systems of, information management; and
- national systems of technology innovation.[103]

The last point is particularly noteworthy, because the CTCN's general intention to foster partnerships to accelerate innovation and the dissemination of environmentally sustainable technologies *to* developing countries does not necessarily amount to supporting clean energy innovation *in* or *by* those countries. If finally the Technology Mechanism leads to the creation of national or regional technology innovation centres, this would be the first time endogenous technologies and patents are directly encouraged and facilitated on a global scale.[104] This would go some way towards bridging the equity gap between North and South, which, as we have often noted in this book, is a problem inseparable from climate change.

Big UN governance?

We may wonder how many of the objectives reviewed in this section are appropriately carried out by a UN institution. After all, finance was globalised long ago through private initiative, and 'the private sector diffuses technology on a commercial basis every day'.[105] From one point of view, the climate problem is so urgent that government and/or UN intervention in the technology market is necessary. Large-scale dissemination of environmentally sound technology is required, not at the normal market-driven pace, but at an accelerated pace, to

---

[102] Technologies for adaptation can comprise 'hard' technologies, such as drought-resistant seeds, seawalls and irrigation technology, and 'soft' technologies, such as crop rotation patterns, as well as information and knowledge: Y. de Boer, 'Address by UNFCCC Executive Secretary', Forum on Climate Change and Science, Technology, and Innovation, Beijing, China (24 April 2008), p. 3.
[103] UNFCCC, *Decision 1/CP.16* (2010), para. 120.
[104] International Centre for Trade and Sustainable Development, 'The Climate Technology Mechanism' (2011), p. 8.
[105] World Business Council for Sustainable Development, *Enabling Frameworks for Technology Diffusion: A Business Perspective* (WBCSD, 2010), p. 6.

achieve an early and drastic reduction in GHG emissions as well as the necessary adaptation to the adverse effects of climate change.[106]

Yet the call for greater government intervention in the market, whether or not it involves the UN, is sure to rankle a number of politicians, economists, and others – and not only on ideological grounds. Some scepticism might be expected among businesses concerning the effectiveness of international arrangements to encourage the transmission of technology. It is argued that government interference at the international level as much as the national one can be wasteful and may stifle innovation.[107] If governments want environmentally sound technologies to take off commercially, what they should do, from this point of view, is not set up more large UN programs but collectively cap their emissions, thereby pricing GHG pollution globally. With the 'polluter pays' principle fully implemented, the market could be left to do the bulk of the work in discovering and propagating technology in the most efficient way.[108]

Nevertheless, what are we to do in the absence of global pricing of GHGs? There is a broad consensus that as long as no monetary value is put on GHG emissions, through ambitious commitment periods of binding caps for both developed and developing economies, new clean technologies will have a hard time competing in the marketplace.[109] Yet not only are Annex I governments (Canada, Japan, Russia) pulling out of a second Kyoto commitment period, or signing up to it with unambitious targets only; they are also continuing to subsidise the older, GHG-intensive technologies. This is perhaps why the establishment of the Technology Mechanism has been one of the UNFCCC's least contentious projects: it facilitates some remedial action while the more intractable problems continue to be debated. The proof will be in the practice, and the practice lies in the future: the details of the new international technology regime will take years to work out.[110]

---

[106] UNFCCC, *Decision 1/CP.16* (2010), IV.B.
[107] David Brooks, a *New York Times* columnist, contrasting the Republican ideology in US politics with a common, though not uncontentious, view of Democratic ideology, writes: 'Democrats generally seek to concentrate decision-making and cost-control power in the hands of centralized experts ... Republicans at their best are skeptical about top-down decision-making. They are skeptical that centralized experts can accurately predict costs. They are skeptical that centralized experts can predict human behavior accurately enough to socially engineer new programs ... They are also skeptical that planners can control the unintended effects of their decisions. They argue that a decentralized process of trial and error will work better, as long as the underlying incentives are right. [They] believe that the world is too complicated, knowledge is too imperfect. They have much greater faith in the decentralized discovery process of the market': David Brooks, 'Where Wisdom Lives', *The New York Times* (6 June 2011).
[108] Overall, the speed and time frame for the eventual deployment of technologies at a large scale are likely to differ substantially depending on the type of mitigation measure agreed to. Ambitious, binding targets for industrialised countries are most likely to rapidly push technologies into the market. According to Deutsche Bank's Australia-based analyst Tim Jordan: 'If the carbon price isn't locked in to support investment in new lower-carbon baseload generators, then investors will hold off, putting pressure on existing high-carbon plants to meet growing electricity demand' (S. Maher, 'Tony Abbott Tells Firms: Don't Buy Carbon Permits', *The Australian*, 15 October 2011).
[109] This from a former Bush White House advisor: '[A] 60-minute commute and $5 [per gallon] gas will persuade people to do what no bureaucrat would dare command' (David Frum, 'Obama's Doomed Green Jobs Plan: Just Tax Oil and Let Markets Do the Rest', *The Week*, 26 January 2011).
[110] UNFCCC, *Decision 1/CP.16* (2010), paras. 128–9.

Australia's contributions to finance and technology transfer for developing countries

The Australian government's climate change policy has three 'pillars', one of which is to 'help shape a global solution' to the global problem.[111] It is this policy pillar on which Australia bases its contributions to finance and technology transfer. Australia reports that it has provided a total of approximately A$476 million of new and additional resources over five years (2005–09) for programs related to climate change in developing countries. Approximately $91 million of this amount has been paid to the GEF Trust, with about a third of that ($30 million) earmarked for climate change activities.[112] Examples of activities funded from the earmarked contribution to the GEF are shown in Box 8.2, along with climate-related activities funded from other Australian government sources.

As can be seen from the boxed information, Australia's contributions to climate change finance and technology are by no means distributed only through multilateral organisations such as the GEF or the World Bank.[113] Many of Australia's programs for cooperation on technology, capacity-building, mitigation, and adaptation are in fact administered through bilateral partnerships.[114] If an international regime emerges through the Green Climate Fund and the Technology Mechanism – one that is considered trustworthy and efficient by donor states – it is likely that Australia will rely less on bilateral arrangements and more on the UN-led international system to distribute its aid, although presumably the country will continue to target developing countries in its own region as much as possible, even if the support has to pass through a UN fund.

In June 2010, Australia announced that it would contribute A$599 million to the Annex I countries' fast-start finance pledge for the 2010–12 period. As of June 2011, Australia had made budgetary allocations totalling A$437 million; of this amount, A$201 million had been provided to countries, regions and multilateral initiatives.[115] The Pacific region was due to receive up to A$134 million in fast-start finance for adaptation.[116] Australia stated that it would continue to focus on the Asia–Pacific region but would also expand its engagement in Africa (up to A$25 million).[117] However, seeking to

---

111 Department of Climate Change, *Australia's Fifth National Communication* (2010), p. 129.
112 Ibid., pp. 128, 130.
113 Ibid., p. 129. For Australia's financial contributions to multilateral institutions and programs over the past decade that are related to climate change directly or indirectly, see ibid., Table 7.2, p. 131.
114 For definitions of multilateral and bilateral finance, see the table of definitions at the front of the book.
115 Secretariat (UNFCCC), *Compilation of Information on Resources for the Period* 2010–2012 (2011), pp. 5, 8.
116 This includes finance for the following activities: upgrading transport infrastructure in the Solomon Islands to reduce the harm likely to result from extreme weather events and coastal erosion (A$4 million); in Kiribati, supporting improved water security, increased coastal resilience, and government capacity to plan for and adapt to climate change (A$5 million); and facilitating local adaptation action in the Pacific generally by funding community-based adaptation activities through the GEF's Small Grants Program and supporting NGOs to address priority adaptation needs across multiple Pacific communities (A$5.5 million): see ibid., p. 6.
117 Ibid., p. 11.

8 CLIMATE FINANCE, TECHNOLOGY TRANSFER AND CAPACITY-BUILDING

BOX 8.2 Australia's main commitments to international finance and technology transfer since 2008

Technology cooperation: Carbon Capture and Storage

In 2008, Australia established the Global Carbon Capture and Storage Institute and committed $400 million in funding over four years. The Institute plans to deliver fully integrated industrial-scale CCS demonstration projects.[118] It was developed to facilitate the transfer of know-how between governments and other organisations seeking to deploy CCS technology globally.[119] This is not a project that is expected to deliver commercial applications in the near future.[120]

Technology cooperation: Clean Technology Fund

Australia provided $100 million over three years (2009–11) to support the World Bank's Clean Technology Fund, which seeks to promote increased financing for the demonstration, deployment, and transfer of low-carbon programs and projects with a significant potential for long-term GHG emission reductions.[121] (See also Box 8.1 on the CTF.)

Mitigation: Forestry

Australia invested $200 million over five years (2008–12) in the International Forest Carbon Initiative for REDD projects, as discussed in Chapter 7.[122] The country has also provided $11.7 million to the World Bank's Forest Carbon Partnership Facility, which aims to build confidence in REDD investments by establishing early links between key rainforest countries and potential sources of finance.[123]

Mitigation: Capacity-building

Australia's bilateral activities to promote development pathways of reduced GHG intensity include investment in energy-efficient technology and renewable energy. An estimated $15.1 million was allocated to energy efficiency and $5.2 million to renewable energy in 2008–09. Energy programs that have benefited from Australian support include rural electrification and transmission programs in Laos and Cambodia, implemented by the World Bank. These programs supported grid extensions, efficiency improvements in electricity transmission, and off-grid energy systems, such as solar photovoltaic and small-scale hydropower.[124]

Adaptation

Adaptation projects also transfer finance and technology. Through the International Climate Change Adaptation Initiative, Australia invested A$150 million over three years (2009–11) to meet high-priority climate adaptation needs in vulnerable countries in the Asia–Pacific region.[125]

Adaptation: Capacity-building

Between 2008 and 2011, Australia invested $20 million in the Pacific Climate Change Science Program. The program provides decision-makers with better information on the likely impacts of climate change, by tracking climate trends, providing regional climate projections, and improving understanding of ocean processes, ocean acidification, and sea-level rise.[126]

---

118 Department of Climate Change, *Australia's Fifth National Communication* (2010), p. 128.
119 Ibid., p. 141.
120 For example Australian Treasury, *Strong Growth, Low Pollution: Modelling a Carbon Price* (Commonwealth of Australia, 2011), p. 10 ('By the mid 2030s carbon capture and storage is projected to be commercially viable . . .'). See also Chapter 9
121 Department of Climate Change, *Australia's Fifth National Communication* (2010), p. 128; Secretariat (UNFCCC), *Compilation of Information on Resources for the Period* 2010–2012 (2011), p. 7.
122 Department of Climate Change, *Australia's Fifth National Communication* (2010), p. 128.
123 Ibid., pp. 139–40. See also Australia's contributions to forestry projects (REDD) in neighbouring countries: Table 7.1 in Chapter 7.
124 Department of Climate Change, *Australia's Fifth National Communication* (2010), p. 141.
125 Ibid., p. 128.
126 Ibid., pp. 133; Secretariat (UNFCCC), *Compilation of Information on Resources for the Period* 2010–2012 (2011), pp. 6–7.

bring its budget into surplus in the 2012–13 financial year, the Australian government announced in May 2012 that its projected official development assistance would be scaled back to the tune of A$2.9 billion.[127]

An overarching UNFCCC fund would certainly make up for what is presently missing from Australia's (and other countries') actions in the area of finance and technology transfer, namely a systematic approach to international investment: there exists no globally informed practice beyond bilateral and multilateral action, both of which are essentially ad hoc. This reflects the absence up until the Cancun COP of integrated planning for finance and technology transfer at the UNFCCC level. It is only since 2010 that a global approach to the challenge has been agreed to, with steps towards its implementation commencing in 2011.

In Box 8.3 we consider two cases of small-scale bilateral projects funded by Australia, which under the new (Cancun) regime would most likely be handled centrally, through the UNFCCC's NAPA/NAMA support-matching mechanism and the Green Climate Fund.

The lurking issue of intellectual property rights

The Cancun initiative on the Technology Mechanism took place in the shadow of an emerging 'clean energy race' between industrialised countries, on the one hand, and a number of emerging economies such as China, India and Brazil, on the other.[128] The United States, in particular, has become wary of concessions in the technology discussions that might adversely affect its competitiveness in this area. These concerns, particularly regarding China's growing technological capabilities and 'indigenous innovation' policies, cast a shadow over the global negotiations on the transfer of clean energy technologies, and are the pretext for seeking refuge in arguments about the protection of intellectual property rights.

In this last section of the chapter, then, we turn to the question of intellectual property law. The international IP rights system, as well as that of most domestic jurisdictions, makes no distinction between environmentally sound and other technologies. What, if any, IP barriers lie in the way of developing countries' access to the technologies they need to reduce their GHG emissions? Are these legal rights to exploitation of technological innovation truly an obstacle to the transfer of climate technology, or are they, on the contrary, an

---

[127] Australian Government, 'Budget Paper No. 2, Part 2: Expense Measures: Foreign Affairs and Trade', <http://www.budget.gov.au/2012-13/content/bp2/html/bp2_expense-11.htm>. In the government's words, '[t]he Government will continue to grow Australia's aid budget to 0.5 per cent of Gross National Income (GNI) but defer the target date by one year, from 2015–16 to 2016–17. This measure will achieve $2.9 billion in savings over four years while still growing aid spending by 50.0 per cent over the period 2012–13 to 2015–16.' The Budget Paper does not mention any special shielding of climate-related overseas development assistance (ODA), so we may assume that the announced savings will have an impact in this area, too. The government's sudden decision to 'defer' Australia's ODA growth target in order to present a surplus budget to the Australian public and to financial markets is a sign of the unpredictability and vulnerability of the climate finance promised by Annex I countries for the 2013–20 period.
[128] International Centre for Trade and Sustainable Development, 'The Climate Technology Mechanism' (2011), pp. 2 and 3.

> **BOX 8.3 Two case studies in technology transfer projects funded by Australia**
>
> **Case study 1: Pacific Islands Climate Prediction Project**
>
> | | |
> |---|---|
> | *Type of project:* | Adaptation to climate change |
> | *Technology transferred:* | Climate-prediction software and training |
> | *Recipient countries:* | Samoa, Papua New Guinea, Solomon Islands, Vanuatu, Kiribati, Tuvalu, Fiji, Tonga, Niue, and Cook Islands |
> | *Total funding:* | $5.3 million, 2005–09[129] |
>
> The aim of the project was to expand and enhance the use of information that the meteorological services of 10 Pacific Island countries derived from climate-prediction software. The software was based on that employed by the Australian Bureau of Meteorology to produce seasonal climate forecasts for Australia. Pacific Island meteorological services were trained to provide climate information, including predictions, to help decision-making processes within the relevant agencies of participating countries.
>
> The project had four parts: to develop and install climate-prediction software; train personnel in the use of the software and the establishment of climate-prediction services; facilitate links between project participants and those making climate-sensitive decisions; and train the latter in the effective use of prediction information.
>
> Phase 1 of the project focused on building project participants' capacity to deliver generalised seasonal rainfall predictions. Phase 2, based on pilot projects, involved the development of partnerships between project participants and their 'clients' in the state administrations, for the routine provision and use of customised predictions.
>
> Effective use of the seasonal climate-prediction information by key climate-sensitive sectors was fundamental to the success of the project. The Australian government reports that the tailoring of prediction services to the specific needs of users in each country also helped to ensure the optimal use of the predictions.
>
> **Case study 2: Indonesian National Carbon Accounting System**
>
> | | |
> |---|---|
> | *Type of project:* | Climate change mitigation |
> | *Technology transferred:* | Expert systems, databases, and analysis predicated on monitoring and reporting |
> | *Recipient country:* | Indonesia |
> | *Total funding:* | $2 million, ongoing[130] |
>
> The project aims to increase the capacity for forest carbon monitoring and accounting in Indonesia. As part of the International Forest Carbon Initiative, Australia is assisting with the design and implementation of the Indonesian National Carbon Accounting System (INCAS) and the related Forest Resource Information System (FRIS). Both systems aim to help Indonesia monitor and curb GHG emissions from deforestation and forest degradation. INCAS is modelled on Australia's National Carbon Accounting System.
>
> To implement the INCAS and FRIS, Australia is helping Indonesia complete a countrywide analysis of land cover change. Landsat data from various sources have been provided, as well as assistance to Indonesia in how to utilise its own extensive Landsat archive in these new applications. Computer hardware and software required for processing the data have been supplied, as well as training in image processing.
>
> Under this project, Australia is also assisting Indonesia with research and analysis to relate land-use change to biomass and carbon stocks, which will enable estimates of GHG

---

129 Department of Climate Change, *Australia's Fifth National Communication* (2010), p. 142.
130 Ibid., p. 144.

> **BOX 8.3 (cont.)**
>
> emissions from this source over time. Technical support has been provided to collect primary and secondary literature on forest biomass and allometric equations. Further data and literature reviews will be undertaken with a view to determining additional data collection requirements. Because this project builds Indonesia's 'REDD readiness' (see Chapter 7), we have classified it as a mitigation measure.

essential prerequisite for technology transfer and innovation in green technologies?

Three main modes of technology transfer to developing countries are described in the literature:

(i) providing products incorporating the technology;
(ii) licensing the capability to produce such products (to an 'indigenous' firm or a joint venture with the developing country);
(iii) supporting the development of national capability to research and produce the products independently of a licensor.[131]

The primary method of technology transfer to date has been (ii), that is, commercial transfer from the developed world's private sector by means of licensing or foreign direct investment. Participation in this private-sector network is the normal way for a company in the developing world to gain the technology it needs.[132]

Outside the politics and aspirational statements of the UNFCCC negotiations, the widely held position is that IP laws positively contribute to the development and dissemination of new technologies for combating climate change, much as they do in any other innovative technology field: the protection created by such laws encourages innovation, for it provides the means to generate a commercial return on investment in the development of low-carbon technologies. By offering protection against a loss of control of knowledge, the IP regime facilitates the acquisition of new knowledge. It also gives companies the confidence to license their proprietary technologies for use or further development where they are most needed.[133] Indeed, case studies compiled by the International Energy Agency and the UN Environment Program conclude that one of the most significant impediments to the successful transfer of environmentally sound technology is the *lack* of IP laws or IP law enforcement in some developing countries.[134] Such observations

---

[131] J. H. Barton, 'Intellectual Property and Access to Clean Energy Technologies in Developing Countries: An Analysis of Solar Photovoltaic, Biofuel and Wind Technologies', Issue Paper No. 2 (International Centre for Trade and Sustainable Development, December 2007), p. 3.

[132] J. H. Barton, 'New Trends in Technology Transfer: Implications for National and International Policy', Issue Paper No. 18 (International Centre for Trade and Sustainable Development, February 2007), p. x.

[133] World Intellectual Property Organization, 'Climate Change: The Technology Challenge', 4(1) *WIPO Magazine* 2 (February 2008), p. 3. Patent information can also make a valuable contribution. Published patent documents offer a vast and freely accessible source of technological information on which others may build. The European Patent Office, in the context of a joint project with the UN Environment Programme and the International Centre for Trade and Sustainable Development, provides free access to all patent documents related to clean energy technologies worldwide: International Centre for Trade and Sustainable Development, 'The Climate Technology Mechanism' (2011), p. 9.

[134] World Intellectual Property Organization, 'The Technology Challenge' (2008), p. 3.

imply that it is, if anything, the stricter enforcement of existing IP laws, instead of any relaxation of such laws, that is the greatest challenge facing international climate negotiators who want to facilitate the dissemination of environmentally sound technology.

Despite the consensus among experts on this point, there is a persistent concern in political circles that the IP regime has a detrimental effect on the cost of technology acquisition and the rate of its distribution, and thus that the governmental authorities (or the UN) must somehow intervene. This, in turn, produces a reaction from ideological opponents who believe that governments are generally less adept than markets at 'choosing winners', that political pressures often push in unprofitable directions, and that the pace of transfer in the context of inducements that do not interfere with IP rights should be left to the market. The risk in such discussions is that generally correct criticisms of government efforts to support particular technology sectors are overblown into a libertarian orthodoxy rejecting all such efforts, even though, as Barton points out, government interventions have played and continue to play important roles in the economic development of many countries, including those in the Annex I group.[135]

For such reasons, the issue of IP in the international negotiations on technology transfer has been divisive. Until Cancun in 2010, developing countries pressed for the characterisation of IP as a potential barrier to technology transfer. Developed countries resisted such a view, given the essential role they saw IP playing in their own economies in providing incentives for innovation in clean technology. A polarised debate followed the Bali meeting in 2007.[136] Japan, for example, advocated strict protection of intellectual property rights.[137] By contrast, the African Group negotiating bloc supported the establishment of a global pool for technology transfer and IP rights, to give developing countries access to IP-protected technologies.[138] Bolivia, as part of an association of Latin American countries, advocated the use of compulsory licensing to facilitate technology transfer.[139] As a result, during the 2010 negotiations, all the draft decision language on IP remained in disputed (bracketed) text, and ultimately there was no reference to IP in the final text of the Cancun decisions.[140]

Thus one of the oldest and relatively most settled of legal questions became, in the climate change context, mired in politics.[141] While the topic of finance and

---

[135] Barton, 'New Trends in Technology Transfer' (2007), pp. xi–xii.
[136] A. A. Latif, 'Technology Transfer and Intellectual Property: A Post-Copenhagen Assessment', 14(1) *Bridges Monthly* 17 (February 2010), p. 17.
[137] International Institute for Sustainable Development, 'SB 32 and AWG Highlights: Monday, 7 June 2010', 12(468) *Earth Negotiations Bulletin* (2010), p. 1.
[138] Ibid.   [139] Ibid., p. 2.
[140] International Centre for Trade and Sustainable Development, 'The Climate Technology Mechanism' (2011), p. 3.
[141] It also remains rather secretive. The updated program of work of the Expert Group on Technology Transfer (EGTT) for 2010–11 includes an activity to prepare a stock-taking paper on the role of IP in technology transfer. At the 32nd session of the UNFCCC's subsidiary bodies (May–June 2010), the parties agreed that the results of the work of the EGTT on IP should remain an internal working paper of the EGTT: Subsidiary Body for Scientific and Technical Advice (UNFCCC), *Report of the Expert Group on Technology Transfer* (UNFCCC, 24 November 2010), FCCC/SB/2010/INF.4, p. 5.

technology transfer did find a way forward at the Cancun COP, the specific question about how to handle IP protection in the framework of the Technology Mechanism and Green Climate Fund was left behind.

Intellectual property law and politics in the climate change arena

Arguments about IP have often soured the North–South relationship. How does the IP issue, transported into the context of climate change, compare with older debates?

Barton writes that IP protection generally plays a very different role in relation to climate change than it does in other fields. It is instructive to consider Barton's contrast between the renewable energy industry and the pharmaceutical sector. In the latter sector, a patent may have a very substantial impact in the market for the drug because the drug may not have any substitutes. In such a case, the patent holder may be able to charge a price well above production cost. In the case of solar energy, wind power, and biofuels, by contrast, the underlying technologies have long been patent-free. Rather, as Barton notes, what is usually patented in this sector is an improvement to the basic idea. Moreover, these renewable energy technologies all produce the exact same end: energy. This leads to competition between a number of patented renewable energy products, which in turn leads to lower prices and a broader sharing of the benefits of these technologies. Moreover, as Barton notes, not only is there competition among the companies involved in, say, solar PV, or within the renewable energy sector as a whole (PV against wind power), but there is also competition between that sector and traditional (unclean) sources of fuel or electricity (wind power against natural gas).

As a result, because of the number of companies in the renewables sector driving down prices through competition, a developing country entering the field as a producer of a renewable energy product is likely to be able to obtain a licence for a patented product on reasonable terms.[142] A firm in a developing country will still need to license some or all of the technology it needs for a particular renewable energy product, but the licensing of existing technology will often be a cheaper and faster option than the re-engineering of that technology.[143] Thus the issue of IP does not raise issues of affordability, or indeed of life-or-death choices, in the climate change context nearly as often as it does in the context of health and pharmaceuticals.

---

142 Barton, 'Intellectual Property and Access to Clean Energy Technologies' (2007), p. 4.
143 Barton, 'New Trends in Technology Transfer' (2007), pp. 21–2. The available evidence is inconclusive on the benefit of the alternative pathway, namely nationally funded research programs oriented towards helping firms in developing countries gain the technology they need to compete globally. Clearly, there have been major benefits of such research in the *developed* world, but the success of the developing world programs is less clear: Barton, 'Intellectual Property and Access to Clean Energy Technologies' (2007), p. xi.

In addition to the above point about relative affordability, the accessibility of environmentally sound technology is best considered on a case-by-case basis. For example, as Barton has demonstrated, the wind sector is competitive enough that developing countries will be able to build wind farms with equipment from the global market without facing prohibitive IP costs. By contrast, it is much more difficult for them to enter the global market for wind *turbines*, because the existing industrial leaders are hesitant to share their leading technology, out of fear of creating new competitors.[144] Here, too, there are exceptions: China and India have built successful firms producing wind-technology components, including turbines, thus integrating themselves with the global industry as suppliers. It may be assumed that they too, like countries of the developed world, would hesitate to share their edge with other countries in the developing world.[145]

In the international market for GHG offsets under the CDM, IP issues have not loomed large. In the Nigeria Stoves case (Chapter 6), IP did not figure as an issue at all. Indeed, one argument for that project to be given the green light by the CDM Executive Board was that, one day, the hyper-efficient German stove would be fully manufactured in Nigeria, presumably under a very affordable licensing agreement. As a typical small CDM project, Nigeria Stoves suggests that technology transfer is occurring at a steady rate under the CDM without IP constraints.[146] Technology transfer under bilateral aid arrangements is common.[147]

Thus even a brief analysis of the legal obstacles to technology transfer in the climate change field reveals a complex picture, although not one of insurmountable obstacles. The same IP laws that constrain the spread of technology in the case of certain pharmaceuticals could facilitate it, or at least have a neutral role, in the case of renewable energy products (or, in the case of the German stove, energy-efficient products). Other barriers, such as tariffs applied to renewable fuels (e.g. ethanol), are far more prohibitive than any barrier presented by IP,[148] and raise issues of international law that are of a quite different nature. Working in the opposite direction to protectionism and tariffs, free trade has been steadily spreading, and economies of scale now favour production facilities that serve more than one nation.

In sum, restrictions on the transfer of environmentally sound technology may have less to do with IP law itself, or even with business interests – from a

---

[144] Barton, 'Intellectual Property and Access to Clean Energy Technologies' (2007), p. xi.
[145] The old dualist discourse on technology transfer emerged more than 20 years ago, and seems almost irrelevant today, when there has been an enormous change in the skills available to a large portion of the developing world, in particular the middle-income and largest nations, such as China, India, and Brazil.
[146] See Clean Development Mechanism (Kyoto Protocol), *Benefits of the Clean Development Mechanism* (2011) and other studies of the CDM's performance on technology transfer cited earlier in the chapter.
[147] See Boxes 8.2 and 8.3 for examples. In another example, the US Overseas Private Investment Corporation 'committed US$300 million for financing a project [in Kenya] that will double the generating capacity of a geothermal power plant, adding new electricity to the country's grid through the use of environmentally friendly American technology': US Department of State, *Meeting the Fast Start Commitment* (2011), p. 7.
[148] Barton, 'Intellectual Property and Access to Clean Energy Technologies' (2007), p. 14.

business perspective, global technological integration is desirable – than with *political* restrictions on the transfer of technologies, which are motivated by ideas of national interest. Methods to overcome the persistence of the North–South political rhetoric at international negotiations might include the following:

- Internationally agreed guidelines on technology licensing on fair and reasonable terms for developing countries;
- Arrangements for greater use of alternative innovation models (prizes, open innovation, etc.) and collaborative research and development;[149]
- Building of capacity for environmentally sustainable research and innovation in developing countries – which is, as we saw earlier in this chapter, already an aim of the UNFCCC's new Technology Mechanism.[150]

Other ideas under consideration include using money from the new Green Climate Fund to purchase licences, or creating a 'Global Technology IP Rights Pool' for climate change that promotes access for developing countries to IP-protected technologies and associated know-how on non-exclusive terms (along the lines suggested above by the African Group negotiating bloc), with or without the payment of royalties.[151] Developed countries could agree to devote a portion of their research and development funding to the special needs of developing nations. They could seek to ensure that companies in developing countries have an opportunity to participate in such efforts. This could be done as part of the international climate change negotiations, where the commitment to make the technology more readily available would be made in exchange for stronger environmental constraints on developing nations.[152] A more extreme solution would be exclusion of the technology from patentability, or the imposition of compulsory licensing.[153] Interestingly, a 2007 European Parliament report on climate change included a proposal to look into the feasibility of amending the World Trade Organization Agreement on Trade Related Aspects of Intellectual Property Rights (TRIPS) in order to allow for the compulsory licensing of 'environmentally necessary' technologies:

> [The Parliament] asks for swift progress to be made in updating the WTO's definition of environmental goods and services ... but recommends, as a starting point, a specific link to climate change, in order to reach agreement on the removal of tariff

---

149 Yamin and Depledge, *The International Climate Change Regime* (2004), p. 305.
150 For a detailed analysis of current trends in patent policy and administration in key states, including such topics as compulsory and public sector licensing and the development of Climate Innovation Centres, the Eco-Patent Commons, and environmental prizes such as the L-Prize, the H-Prize, and the X-Prize, see M. Rimmer, *Intellectual Property and Climate Change: Inventing Clean Technologies* (Edward Elgar Publishing, 2011).
151 D. Cressey, 'Cancelled Project Spurs Debate over Geoengineering Patents', 485 *Nature* 429 (24 May 2012).
152 Barton, 'Intellectual Property and Access to Clean Energy Technologies' (2007), p. 20.
153 One difficulty with this extreme end of the spectrum is that, even where a technology has been developed in a publicly funded institution, and therefore is government-funded research, in cases where such research is licensed, domestic law might require that domestic manufacturers be favoured: ibid., p. 7.

and non-tariff barriers to 'green' goods and services that prevent or slow the dissemination of low-carbon technologies; [and] recommends launching a study on possible amendments to the WTO Agreement on Trade Related Aspects of Intellectual Property Rights in order to allow for the compulsory licensing of environmentally necessary technologies, within the framework of clear and stringent rules for the protection of intellectual property, and the strict monitoring of their implementation worldwide.[154]

In the final analysis, if states believe in the value of technology transfer as a weapon against climate change, and if they find that it outweighs their other concerns, then the technical, legal, or ideological barriers to its rapid diffusion can be overcome. The Technology Mechanism agreed to in Cancun represents a potentially positive development, particularly in view of the longstanding demand by developing countries for the institutional strengthening of technology transfer under the UNFCCC.[155] Seen in an optimistic light, the modest institutions created by the Convention parties in Cancun may be able to make an important difference through their facilitative and coordinating powers.

Conclusion

Developing nations will need to adapt to climate change, but many must also seek to reduce their own emissions of GHGs while pursuing sustainable development. For these tasks, they will need access to finance and environmentally sound technology. Barriers to *financial transfer* include the basic problem of finding new and additional sources of public and private finance, distributing the money raised fairly and accountably, and ensuring that the results are the best that money can buy. Establishing a framework to facilitate the transfer of environmentally sound technology from developed to developing countries is one of the most challenging tasks that the international community has had to tackle in its efforts to get climate change under control. Barriers to *technology transfer* include those raised by IP rights – or IP politics. Developed countries' concerns about IP protection (and increasingly China's concerns about protecting its own inventions) continue to block progress.

One innovative mechanism already discussed in this book has aimed to break both the financial and the technology barriers: the market for providing carbon

---

154 European Parliament, 'European Parliament Resolution of 29 November 2007 on Trade and Climate Change (2007/2003(Ini))' (2007), para. 9. The TRIPS Agreement includes provisions that allow the exploitation of patented inventions without the consent of the IP owner, such as compulsory licences. TRIPS does not list specific reasons to justify the use of a compulsory licence and leaves the grounds to be determined by national legislation, subject to certain conditions.
155 International Centre for Trade and Sustainable Development, 'The Climate Technology Mechanism' (2011), p. 2; and Latif, 'Technology Transfer and Intellectual Property' (2010), p. 7.

offsets under the CDM creates new finance for adaptation and mitigation and facilitates technology transfer at the same time. However, despite some programs already being operational in finance and technology transfer, the international regime has not yet developed sufficiently to enable finance and technology for adaptation and mitigation to flow predictably, at the required rate, and in a globally coordinated manner.

9

Legal and regulatory frameworks for transition to a low-carbon economy

Introduction *page* 293
Transition to a 'low-carbon' economy   295
Improving energy efficiency: 'Picking the low-hanging fruit'   301
Promoting renewable energy   312
Carbon capture and storage   320
Nuclear power   332
Integration of regulatory measures for technology innovation   335
Conclusion   338

Introduction

In the previous chapter we discussed the importance of capacity-building in developing countries and the establishment of a system for international transfer of technology as components of the international climate change regime. Arrangements for flows of funding, knowledge and technology from developed to developing countries are a manifestation of equity considerations in international climate law, as well as a practical response designed to reduce greenhouse gas emissions in some of the fastest-growing economies. Such technology flows will also assist in preparing vulnerable countries to adapt more successfully to the effects of climate change. Nonetheless, these efforts raise a fundamental preliminary question: namely, are there technologies available that are adequate to achieve international goals of climate change mitigation and adaptation? An associated question is whether legal frameworks exist to deploy such technologies successfully. These questions animate the discussion in this chapter and the following two chapters, which deal respectively with biosequestration and adaptation.[1]

---

[1] In this respect, technologies are taken to extend to 'social technologies': for discussion see R. L. Ison, *Systems Practice: How to Act in a Climate Change World* (Springer, 2010); and R. Garnaut, *Garnaut Climate Change Review* (Cambridge University Press, 2008), p. 424.

In this chapter we examine technologies for climate change mitigation, encompassing energy efficiency improvements, renewable energy, nuclear power, and processes for carbon capture and storage (CCS), all of which primarily target emissions in the energy/power generation sector. Attention is also given to technological improvements that reduce emissions in sectors such as building and construction, and transport, given the significant contribution to overall GHG emissions that they represent in many developed countries, including Australia.[2] This discussion is framed by a review of the relevant scientific and policy literature regarding the technological options for climate change mitigation in the energy sector and related spheres. The chapter considers whether such technologies are adequate to the task of putting the world generally, and Australia in particular, on a pathway that will stabilise emissions, avoid global warming and enable a transition to a low-carbon economy. The emerging consensus seems to be that, at least from a technical perspective, climate change mitigation is feasible using existing technologies, although such measures would need to work in concert with demand management/energy efficiency options. However, a potentially more difficult hurdle is the adequacy of legal and regulatory frameworks for enabling rapid deployment of these technologies, and impediments within those frameworks.

In Australia, introduction of a carbon pricing mechanism (CPM) has added a new layer of complexity to regulatory arrangements for climate change mitigation,[3] with specific ramifications for technology change and innovation.[4] On one view, the CPM will generate a price signal felt throughout the economy, which will drive behavioural change to reduce emissions, especially in the power and industrial sectors, and provide an incentive to adopt low- or even zero carbon technologies. If the CPM is sufficiently robust, then over time, according to the theory underpinning cap-and-trade measures, separate regulatory frameworks to promote the use of particular technologies, such as renewable energy or to drive energy efficiencies may become unnecessary. On another view, an emissions trading scheme such as the CPM by itself is unlikely to achieve the scope, scale and rapidity of technological change required. Therefore transition to a low-carbon economy is best supported by a range of complementary measures, especially where the carbon price signal remains weak. Thus, as we discuss in relation to Australia, the relationship between different measures and technologies is critical – particularly the relationship of various technologies and demand-side measures with the central CPM.

---

[2] Department of Climate Change and Energy Efficiency, *Australia's National Greenhouse Gas Accounts* (Quarterly Update, September Quarter 2011), pp. 5–7.
[3] See Chapter 5.
[4] K. Neuhoff, *Tackling Carbon: How to Price Carbon for Climate Policy*, Version 1.1, 29/9/2008, University of Cambridge, Faculty of Economics, pp. 9–22.

Transition to a 'low-carbon' economy

Increasingly, it is acknowledged that there is a need for 'a radical re-think of our approach to energy, ending our fossil fuel dependence and moving to sustainable solutions before oil scarcity and climate change impact[s] cut off our options'.[5] The International Energy Agency's 'World Energy Outlook'[6] anticipates that the energy mix of 2030 will be vastly different from the current one. Factors precipitating this transition include environmental damage such as the Gulf of Mexico offshore oil spill, energy security, the need for more equitable sources of energy for those segments of the world's population who currently have limited access,[7] and of course climate change. Further, the decade up to 2020 will be critical in efforts to halt or slow global warming trends,[8] but the international law effort is out of step with scientific assessment of climate change risk. Current pledges to cut emissions, such as those agreed through the Copenhagen/Cancun process, even if put into effect collectively, may still result in average warming of 4°C or more.[9]

The costs of mitigation are often seen as a major barrier to decisive action, although a key message from the Stern Review was that the costs of inaction ultimately would outweigh the costs of early intervention.[10] The assumed costs of mitigation depend directly on the assumptions regarding technologies that are or may become available to abate GHG emissions.[11] There will need to be massive investment in new technologies to accompany any transition to a low-carbon economy. Given the urgency of moving away from the trajectory of escalating emissions, there has been considerable interest in how technology can best be deployed in tandem with regulatory efforts to mitigate climate change.

Technological options and their economic feasibility

On one view the challenging task of climate change mitigation is manageable in that technology will 'solve' the problem – it is a 'silver bullet'. While commentators question the extent to which a single technology can offer a comprehensive means of reducing emissions, there is strong agreement that a range of technologies should be adopted to mitigate climate change and encourage adaptation, and to assist in the transition to a low-carbon economy.

---

[5] Ian Dunlop, former CEO Australian Institute of Company Directors, quoted in P. Hearps and M. Wright, *Australian Sustainable Energy: Zero Carbon Australia Stationary Energy Plan* (Melbourne Energy Institute, 2010).
[6] International Energy Agency (IEA), *World Energy Outlook 2011* (2011).
[7] D. Zillman et al., 'Introduction', in *Beyond the Carbon Economy: Energy Law in Transition*, eds Zillman et al. (Oxford University Press, 2008), pp. 6–8.
[8] W. Steffen, *The Critical Decade: Climate Science, Risks and Responses* (Australian Climate Change Commission Secretariat, 2011), pp. 53–5.
[9] See J. Rogelj et al., 'Analysis of the Copenhagen Accord Pledges and its Global Climatic Impact – A Snapshot of Dissonant Ambitions', 5(3) *Environmental Research Letters* 034013 (2010); and M. Meinshausen et al. 'Greenhouse-gas Emission Targets for Limiting Global Warming to 2°C', 458(7242) *Nature* 1158 (2009).
[10] For discussion see Chapter 4.   [11] Garnaut, *Garnaut Climate Change Review* (2008), p. 250.

In a 2004 article published in *Science*, Pacala and Socolow developed the concept of stabilisation wedges as a heuristic device to guide decision-making on emission mitigation technologies.[12] The model seeks to identify the range of technologies available as well as when and how each should be deployed, in effect providing a portfolio of technologies constituting a 'stabilisation wedge'.[13] A 'wedge' is 'an activity reducing the rate of carbon build-up in the atmosphere', over 50 years, from zero to 1.0 gigatonnes of carbon per year.[14] The number of emission-reducing activities, or wedges, required depends on (a) how fast emissions grow and (b) the point at which stabilisation is to occur. The model is based on the amount of reductions necessary to achieve stabilisation of atmospheric carbon at 450–500 ppm.[15] Possible wedge activities include efforts to increase energy efficiency, biosequestration in forests and soils, and decarbonisation of the electricity supply and reductions in emission intensity.[16] Given that emissions have escalated since the article was first published in 2004,[17] an updated version of the model shows that eight wedges would now be needed to stabilise emissions at safe levels (see Figure 9.1).

The authors contend that the low, zero and negative carbon technologies required for the mitigation effort already exist,[18] and they recommend scaling up existing, proven technologies, rather than waiting for a 'technology revolution'.[19] Other analyses contend that meeting the mitigation challenge will require innovation to develop new technologies.[20] Importantly, the wedges concept does not specifically address the question of what policy and legal frameworks might be needed to implement technology choices. However, its identification of different wedges suggests that rather than a single measure, a range of policy and legal measures will be required to effectively reduce emissions.[21]

The stabilisation wedges model is not without difficulties, as it does not take into account the way in which certain policy choices can 'lock in' the utilisation of particular technologies, infrastructure and regulation. For instance, early deployment of existing technologies to reduce emissions, such as the replacement of coal-fired power generation with gas-fired plants, could prevent greater

---

12 The concept has similarities with the scenario-planning and other modelling that has underpinned much of the policy and decision-making built on the findings of climate change science: see Garnaut, *Garnaut Climate Change Review* (2008), pp. 250–2.
13 S. Pacala and R Socolow, 'Stabilization Wedges: Solving the Climate Problem for the Next 50 Years with Current Technologies', 305 *Science* 968 (2004), p. 968.
14 This means each 'wedge' achieves a cumulative total reduction of 25 Gt over 50 years: ibid.
15 However, developments in the scientific research indicate that this concentration will be too high to prevent a global temperature rise of more than 2°C: James Hansen et al., 'A Safe Operating Space for Humanity', *Nature* 461 (2009), pp. 472–5.
16 Pacala and Socolow, 'Stabilization Wedges' (2004), p. 970.
17 Hansen et al., 'A Safe Operating Space for Humanity' (2009), pp. 472–5.
18 Pacala and Socolow, 'Stabilization Wedges' (2004), p. 968.
19 For the economic argument on why increasing scale and early deployment reduces the cost of these mitigation technologies see Ross Garnaut, *Update Paper 7: Low Emissions Technology and the Innovation Challenge*, Garnaut Climate Change Review – Update 2011 (2011), p. 14.
20 Garnaut, *Garnaut Climate Change Review* (2008), p. 423. See also M. Grubb and D. Newberry, 'Pricing Carbon for Electricity Generation: National and International Dimensions', in *Delivering a Low-carbon Electricity Sector: Technologies, Economics and Policy*, eds M. Grubb et al. (Cambridge University Press, 2008), p. 278.
21 Pacala and Socolow, 'Stabilization Wedges' (2004), p. 968.

Stabilization wedges

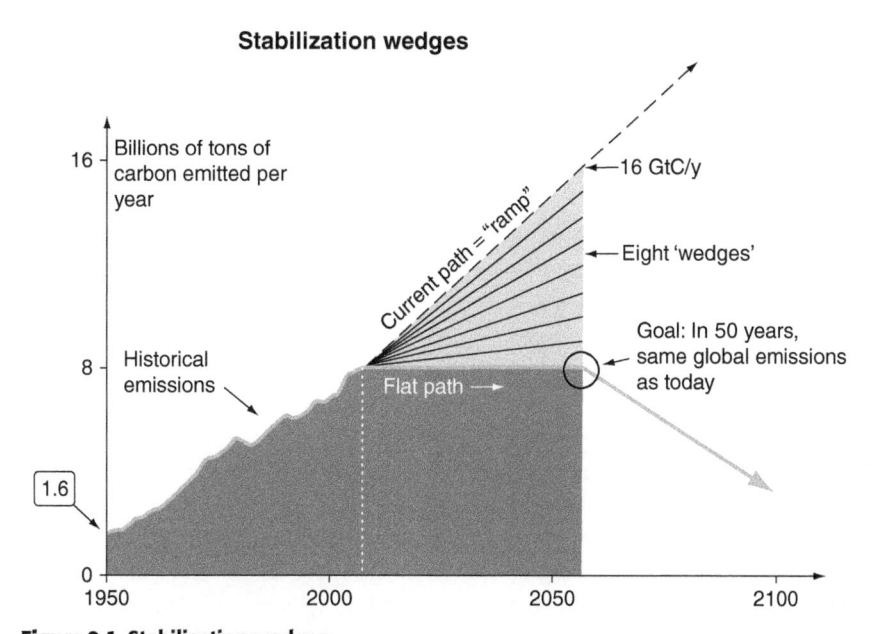

Figure 9.1 Stabilisation wedges
The rate of the 'ramp' is shown in GtC/y (gigatons of carbon per year).
Source: Carbon Mitigation Initiative, 'Stabilization Wedges: Tackling the Climate Problem with Existing Technologies', Presentation Slide No. 5, available at <http://cmi.princeton.edu/wedges/slides.php>.

reductions in emission intensity that may be obtained later as technology advances. Some 'lock-in' is already occurring within Australia as a result of a strong push for a transition from coal to natural gas power generation. This phenomenon is part of the wider problem of path dependency, where factors such as the high economic and social costs of changing the infrastructure lead to inertia and resistance to change. However, with some adjustments to account for the risk of lock-in and to incorporate the need for innovation, the stabilisation wedges concept is a useful tool for considering technology options.

Technological options in the Australian context

The 'wedges' approach has been adopted in the Melbourne Energy Institute's *2020 Zero Carbon Stationary Energy Plan*[22] and the *Low Carbon Growth Plan for Australia* prepared by ClimateWorks, an independent, not-for-profit organisation.[23] These two reports are noteworthy for adding an explicit economic dimension – and costings – to the model. Both reports consider only existing, proven technology,[24]

---
[22] P. Hearps and M. Wright, *Australian Sustainable Energy: Zero Carbon Australia Stationary Energy Plan* (Melbourne Energy Institute, 2010).
[23] ClimateWorks Australia, *Low Carbon Growth Plan for Australia* (2010). See also Institute for Sustainable Futures, University of Sydney, 'Think Small. The Australian Decentralised Energy Roadmap' (Issue 1, December 2011), p. 10.
[24] Hearps and Wright, *Zero Carbon Australia Stationary Energy Plan* (2010), p. 5 and ClimateWorks Australia, *Low Carbon Growth Plan* (2010), pp. 8–9.

given the urgent need to reduce exponentially growing emissions. At the specific policy level, the Australian federal government's thinking on future energy options was articulated in the draft Energy White Paper (December 2011), which canvasses the role of a range of climate mitigation technologies in the nation's future energy mix.

Zero Carbon Australia 2020 Stationary Energy Plan

'Stationary energy emissions' refers to all GHG emissions resulting from the combustion of fuels in stationary equipment to provide energy. These include emissions resulting from electricity generation, from the manufacturing, construction and commercial industries, and from domestic heating. They do not include emissions resulting from transport. The stationary energy sector is the greatest single source of emissions in Australia, accounting for more than 51 per cent of the country's total emissions,[25] and it is the focus of the Zero Carbon Australia plan.

The basic premise is for Australian power generation within the stationary energy sector to move to zero emissions in the space of 10 years. In a comprehensive assessment, the plan considers and weighs the various technology options, provides a time frame for construction of renewable technologies, discusses the infrastructure needed, and provides an outline of the materials, human resources and investment required to realise the plan, including the necessary electricity grid upgrades to ensure reliable supply of electricity from renewable sources.[26]

Technologies advocated in the plan are selected on the basis of their capacity to generate electricity without producing GHG emissions and their ability to be deployed on a large scale within 10 years.[27] These include wind energy, solar photovoltaics (the use of solar cells containing semiconductors that create current upon exposure to light), and particularly, concentrating solar thermal (which uses lenses or mirrors to focus sunlight into a small beam that is then converted to heat to produce electrical power). Technologies such as CCS are rejected as unproven and nuclear energy is discarded principally due to its long implementation time, as Australia has no existing nuclear power capacity. The plan finds that careful siting of electricity generators, coupled with Australia's abundant wind and solar energy resources, make reliable, 24-hour energy supply from renewable energy possible. Achieving transformation to a zero-emission stationary energy sector would require investment of A$370 billion over 10 years, which amounts to 3 per cent of Australia's GDP over that time.[28]

---

[25] Department of Climate Change and Energy Efficiency, 'Stationary Energy Emissions Projections', released 9 February 2011, <http://www.climatechange.gov.au/publications/projections/australias-emissions-projections/stationary-energy.aspx>.
[26] On this point, see further pp. 312–19, below.
[27] Hearps and Wright, *Zero Carbon Australia Stationary Energy Plan* (2010), p. 5.   [28] Ibid., p. xix.

While the Zero Carbon Australia Plan offers an insight into the feasibility of technologies for emission reduction, as well as the required financial and human resource investment, it does not make recommendations regarding the policy and regulatory measures necessary to achieve the plan. Nor does it critically examine the laws and regulatory frameworks that pose obstacles to implementation. As we discuss below, planning laws can be a significant barrier to the adoption of new technology.

Low Carbon Growth Plan

ClimateWorks' *Low Carbon Growth Plan* is the result of an economy-wide analysis of available mitigation options, and identifies 54 opportunities for Australia to reduce its emissions by 25 per cent below 2000 levels in five different sectors (power, forestry, transport, buildings, and industry). For each sector, the report examines opportunities for emission reduction and the tools to overcome potential barriers to their implementation.[29] The resulting 'road map'[30] provides two useful factors to consider when making choices between technology options.[31] The first is the 'risk of lock-in' if the technology is adopted. Risk of lock-in is based on the duration or 'lifespan' of the lost opportunity to reduce emissions (for how long will future emissions be affected by the decision?); lead time (the amount of time required before a technology can be implemented, for example because it requires significant research and development); the size of the potential reduction in emissions; and the cost of remedial measures. For example, a 2011 update of the report found that 5 megatonnes of CO_2 eq. of potential reduction had been forgone due to inaction between 2010 and 2011, at a cost of $5 million per week of delay. The second important factor to consider is 'ease of implementation', that is, the cost of and barriers to implementation. The report modelled the implementation costs from both a societal and an investor perspective to show the difference in the cost if the reduction occurred through public works or was made by the private sector.[32]

The resulting cost curve of opportunities in the energy sector shows that operational improvements to the thermal energy efficiency of coal and gas plants are at negative cost (i.e. they save money); onshore wind comes at a mid-range cost, followed by solar thermal, coal CCS retrofit, tidal energy, and distributed solar PV, which are the most costly under both the investor and societal scenarios.[33] However, based on the 'risk of lock-in' and 'ease of implementation' parameters, the report recommends that certain opportunities be 'implemented now' – namely, increasing gas generation to reduce reliance on coal-fired generation; increasing onshore wind power; investing in solar

---

29 Subsequent updates to the ClimateWorks report have factored in the effects of the CPM and the federal carbon farming legislation: *Low Carbon Growth Plan for Australia: Impact of the Carbon Price Package* (August 2011). See also Chapter 5 and Chapter 10.
30 ClimateWorks Australia, *Low Carbon Growth Plan for Australia – Report Summary* (2011), p. 11.
31 ClimateWorks Australia, *Low Carbon Growth Plan for Australia* (2010), pp. 84–5.
32 Ibid., pp. 9 and 17.   **33** Ibid., p. 39.

thermal with storage; improving thermal operational efficiencies at existing coal plants and reducing transmission and distribution losses; and investing in centralised solar PV.[34]

Australian Government Energy White Paper

The federal government has also assessed national energy resources and technologies in the 2011 draft Energy White Paper, which outlined the projected investment and technology mix for Australia's future energy profile.[35] Significantly, the draft White Paper revealed that substantial financial resources are required in the Australian electricity and gas generation, transmission and distribution sectors between now and 2030.[36] The size of this potential investment raises important issues to be considered in the technology and policy choices Australia will need to make. These considerations now operate against the backdrop of the CPM.[37] In this context, the draft White Paper confirmed what was widely known anecdotally: that 'Australia has some of the world's best renewable energy resources':[38]

- the highest average solar radiation per square metre of any continent in the world;
- some of the world's best onshore wind resources along the southern coast;
- significant potential hot rock geothermal resources;
- large and diverse bioenergy resources (such as agricultural crop wastes, urban garden and food waste, sewage);
- abundant wave energy resources along the western and southern coastlines, and tidal resources.

However, even given the rich diversity of non-fossil fuel energy resources, the draft White Paper emphasises the long-term viability of fossil fuel sources by including in the future energy mix CCS technology for coal and gas-based generation facilities, and expanding gas-fired generation.[39] Indeed, Treasury modelling under a carbon price found that coal plant equipped with CCS and gas could provide over 60 per cent of total generation by 2050.[40] Notably, the draft White Paper is concerned with 'clean energy', not exclusively renewable energy, with 'clean energy' being 'sources of energy, technologies or processes that produce lower or zero greenhouse gas emissions relative to conventional counterparts and that meet appropriate social, environmental, health and safety standards'.[41] Geothermal and large-scale solar energy are also

---

[34] The report also specifies the details of each of these opportunities: ibid., pp. 88–9.
[35] Department of Resources, Energy and Tourism, *Draft Energy White Paper: Strengthening the Foundations for Australia's Energy Future* (2011).
[36] Ibid., p. 197. [37] See Chapter 5.
[38] Department of Resources, Energy and Tourism, *Draft Energy White Paper* (2011), p. 200. [39] Ibid.
[40] Department of Treasury, *Strong Growth, Low Pollution: Modelling a Carbon Price* (2011). This modelling assumes that CCS becomes a viable technology in time. See further pp. 320–32.
[41] Department of Resources, Energy and Tourism, *Draft Energy White Paper* (2011), p. 198.

endorsed.[42] While there are various technology choices to be made and deployed, these options need to work in conjunction with demand-side measures to reduce emissions effectively.

Improving energy efficiency: 'Picking the low-hanging fruit'

It makes good sense, therefore, to introduce energy efficiency measures as part of a suite of technology options to reduce emissions. Energy efficiency can be defined as 'a ratio of function, service or value provided in relation to the energy converted to provide it',[43] or explained in relation to energy intensity, i.e. energy use per unit of activity, such as the amount of fuel consumed per kilometre travelled. Energy efficiency thus constitutes a 'demand-side' measure which, if adopted, reduces the amount of energy required to satisfy social and economic objectives, including national economies and GDP. Demand-side management includes 'strategies' (similar to a stabilisation wedge) which encourage users of power to reduce consumption.[44] Significant emission savings could be made by introducing greater efficiency across all sectors of the Australian economy, from vehicles to residential and commercial buildings. Important gains can also be made in sustainable power use and associated reductions in emission footprints.[45] Energy efficiency incentives may be particularly important for driving technological innovation in the commercial sector of the economy.[46] Similarly, at an international level, the links between sustainable development and greater energy efficiency are belatedly being recognised.[47] However, the UNFCCC and the Kyoto Protocol contain few references to energy efficiency as measures to reduce emissions. Where references do occur in these international instruments, the provisions are of a non-binding nature.[48]

Measures that encourage energy efficiency are often referred to as 'picking the low-hanging fruit' in that they are relatively low-cost compared to other technological options, largely rely on existing or slightly improved processes, and are compatible with instruments such as cap-and-trade schemes and carbon taxes.

---

42 Ibid., p. 200. See also P. Hearps and D. McConnell, 'Renewable Energy Technology Cost Review' (Melbourne Energy Institute Technical Paper Series, May 2011).
43 B. Barton, 'The Law of Energy Efficiency', in *Beyond the Carbon Economy*, eds Zillman et al. (2008), p. 62.
44 Ibid. The International Energy Agency identifies key components of this approach as comprising five main tools: price signals, behavioural change, technology replacement, rationing and market mechanisms: 'Saving Electricity in a Hurry', Energy Efficiency Series, Information Paper, June 2011, p. 18.
45 R. Lyster and A. Bradbrook, *Energy Law and the Environment* (Cambridge University Press, 2006), pp. 10–34.
46 R. Lyster, 'Chasing down the Climate Change Footprint of the Public and Private Sectors: Forces Converge – Part II', 24 *Environmental and Planning Law Journal* 281 (2007).
47 See A. Bradbrook, 'The Development of Renewable Energy Technologies and Energy Efficiency Measures through Public International Law', in *Beyond the Carbon Economy*, eds Zillman et al. (2008), p. 110.
48 Ibid., p. 128.

Nonetheless, there remains substantial inertia in respect of their adoption, and 'legal measures to encourage [energy efficiency] meet a surprising array of difficulties'.[49] More recently, the law has played an important role in introducing incentives to improve efficiencies in many sectors.[50] The *Energy Efficiency Opportunities Act 2006* (Cth) (discussed in Chapter 4) was the first comprehensive move at a national level in Australia.[51]

Laws to stimulate energy efficiency can also 'intervene' to overcome non-price barriers to energy efficiency.[52] Such impediments include imperfect information relating to energy consumption and a lack of knowledge of energy-efficient alternatives. There is also the 'split incentive problem', where the person purchasing the energy-efficient technology is not the same person who benefits from its being energy-efficient. For instance, a landlord may feel no motivation to install energy-efficient lighting, since it is the tenants in the building who will benefit, not the landlord.[53] Other barriers to adoption of efficiency measures are capital and financing.[54] Some commentators suggest there is a wider problem in that national economies are 'locked in' to growth trajectories and development associated with high levels of energy use.[55] Energy efficiency and efforts to limit consumption of energy run counter to these entrenched historical trends.[56]

Federal policy and regulatory context

While there are considerable gains to be made, Australia is a laggard when it comes to energy efficiency.[57] Australia's energy intensity improved by 1.5 per cent between 1990 and 2006, although energy efficiency amounted to just 0.2 per cent of the improvement. In comparison, the IEA found that there was a global average of 1 per cent improvement in energy intensity, and the best performers demonstrated an efficiency improvement of 1.3 to 1.4 per cent.[58] It is interesting that Australia should lag, given that energy efficiency regulation at state level has been in place for some time.[59]

Notwithstanding the relatively poor performance in Australia over recent years, energy efficiency has been a component of intergovernmental

---

49 Barton, 'The Law of Energy Efficiency' (2008), p. 61.
50 N. Durrant, *Legal Responses to Climate Change* (Federation Press, 2010), p. 139.   **51** See Chapter 4.
52 Department of Climate Change and Energy Efficiency, *National Energy Savings Initiative (NESI) – Issues Paper* (2011), p. 3.
53 See Garnaut, *Garnaut Climate Change Review* (2008), p. 581. See also Durrant, *Legal Responses to Climate Change* (2010), p. 149; Australian Housing and Urban Research Institute (AHURI), 'The Environmental Sustainability of Australia's Private Rental Housing Stock', Final Report, No. 159, 2009.
54 There is a role for institutional loan schemes such as climate bonds to provide necessary finance. See for example IEA, 'Energy Efficiency Policy and Carbon Pricing', Energy Efficiency Series, Information Paper, August 2011, pp. 31–2.
55 See for example S. Alexander, 'Earth Jurisprudence and the Ecological Case for Degrowth', in *Exploring Wild Law: The Philosophy of Earth Jurisprudence*, ed. P. Burdon (Wakefield Press, 2011).
56 C. Hamilton, *Growth Fetish* (Allen & Unwin, 2003), p. 182.
57 Institute for Sustainable Futures, 'Think Small' (2011), p. 10.   **58** Ibid.
59 On state legislation see further below.

negotiations under the Ministerial Council for Energy, particularly in terms of the National Framework for Energy Efficiency.[60] The strategy seeks 'to accelerate energy efficiency improvements for households and businesses across all sectors of the economy'.[61] Specific measures include mandatory labelling of products such as white goods to indicate energy efficiency ratings, phase-in of mandatory disclosure of energy efficiency for commercial and residential buildings, and changes to the Building Code Australia. Many of the initiatives in the National Strategy are already in place at the state level (see further below). A federal Task Group on Energy Efficiency[62] recommended new measures at national level, such as a national energy efficiency target requiring energy intensity to be improved by 30 per cent by 2020, and a national energy savings initiative to replace existing and planned state schemes. National energy market reform to 'reduce the barriers to energy efficiency in the Australian energy market' has also been mooted.[63]

National energy saving initiative

Another important Task Group recommendation was consideration of an 'energy efficiency obligation' (also known as a 'white certificate') scheme. This scheme would create incentives for electricity retailers to encourage individual households to save small amounts of energy (for instance, by installing more energy-efficient heating systems).[64] Like the Renewable Energy Target discussed below, electricity retailers would be required to discharge a set annual energy efficiency target or else face a penalty for each unit of the obligation that is not met. The Clean Energy Agreement of 2011 allocated $4 million in funding to develop such a scheme.[65] This initiative is significant, as it recognises that many energy efficiency gains and consequent emission reductions will not be achieved by means of a carbon price alone.

Energy efficiency obligation schemes currently exist in New South Wales, South Australia and Victoria,[66] but jurisdictional differences inhibit their effectiveness.[67] A national scheme could supersede state programs, or alternatively, harmonisation across schemes could occur.[68] Similar policy measures operate in overseas jurisdictions, for instance the Carbon Emissions Reduction Target (UK), the Energy Efficiency Obligation (France), and the White Certificate Scheme (Italy).[69] Should a measure of this kind be introduced in Australia, its interaction

---

[60] Council of Australian Governments (COAG), *National Strategy on Energy Efficiency* (July 2010). All jurisdictions contributed $88.3 million over four years to deliver outcomes under the Strategy.
[61] See COAG, *Communiqué of 2 July 2009*, <http://www.coag.gov.au/coag_meeting_outcomes/2009-07-02/#energy>.
[62] Department of Climate Change and Energy Efficiency, *Report of the Prime Minister's Task Group on Energy Efficiency*, 8 October 2010, p. 3.
[63] Ibid., p. 53.   [64] Ibid., pp. 51–2.
[65] For further details of the MPCCC and the Clean Energy policy package see Chapter 4.
[66] See further Table 9.1.
[67] Department of Climate Change and Energy Efficiency, *Report of the Prime Minister's Task Group on Energy Efficiency* (2010), p. 53.
[68] Department of Climate Change and Energy Efficiency, *NESI Issues Paper* (2011), p. 9.
[69] Ibid., Appendix B. However, these white certificate schemes have had 'teething problems': see Barton, 'The Law of Energy Efficiency' (2008), p. 80.

with the CPM and the Renewable Energy Target would require careful consideration, and design of the actual instrument would be critical.[70] Important design considerations include whether the scheme should adopt a baseline-and-credit or cap-and-trade model; sector coverage; identification of the points of obligation; the treatment of low-income households; and the means of setting targets in respect of peak electricity demand.[71]

Measures targeting energy efficiency in the transport sector
While the foregoing discussion has identified the gains in energy efficiency that can be made in power generation, it is sobering to realise that transport emissions accounted for 14 per cent of Australia's total domestic emissions in 2009. The majority of transport-related emissions derive from road transport, which includes passenger cars, light commercial vehicles, trucks, buses, and motorcycles.[72] Australia has developed an extensive reliance on road transport in past decades. Other transport sectors, such as domestic aviation and shipping, are also major sources of emissions.

The exclusion of particular categories of transportation from the sectors to be covered by the CPM (see Chapter 5) means that energy efficiency objectives are even more important for reducing emissions in the transport sector. The types of fuels that are covered under the CPM are another consideration,[73] with domestic aviation, domestic shipping, rail transport, use of liquid and gaseous fuels for off-road transport, and non-transport use of liquid and gaseous fuels included under the carbon pricing scheme. However, many transport fuels still remain excluded, although the federal government intends to expand the coverage of the carbon price to include heavy on-road vehicles from 1 July 2014.[74] This policy position, however, fails to address the pertinent point made by Bradbrook and Lyster, that 'the crux of the transportation energy problem appears to lie in the road sector, particularly private passenger vehicles'.[75]

Nonetheless, some inroads are being made. In view of the major contribution that road transport makes to GHG emissions, there have been proposals at the federal level to 'consider the introduction of a mandatory light vehicle CO_2 standard, a Commonwealth transport fleet emission target and the development of interoperability standards for electric vehicles'.[76] The adoption of

---

[70] See for example Department of Climate Change and Energy Efficiency, *NESI Issues Paper* (Transport Emissions Projections 2011), p. 21.
[71] Ibid., p. 74.
[72] Transport emissions constituted 14 per cent of Australia's total emissions in 2009: Department of Climate Change and Energy Efficiency, 'Transport Emissions Projections' (2011), <http://www.climatechange.gov.au/publications/projections/australias-emissions-projections/transport-emissions.aspx>.
[73] Department of Climate Change and Energy Efficiency, 'Clean Energy Future: Transport Fuels Fact Sheet' (2011), p. 4.
[74] Ibid., p. 3.
[75] Lyster and Bradbrook, *Energy Law and the Environment* (2006), p. 13. The authors go so far as to describe increasing energy efficiency of motor vehicles as 'perhaps the most important of the various responses which will be required by the Commonwealth government' in reducing GHG emissions.
[76] Department of Climate Change and Energy Efficiency, *Report of the Prime Minister's Task Group on Energy Efficiency* (2010), p. 4.

'averaged' mandatory emission standards for light vehicles by 2015 is also proposed,[77] and this standard would cover all light-duty vehicles, which include passenger, sport utility and light commercial vehicles. There is support for further development of electric vehicles and vehicle fuel efficiency.[78] There has been significant interest in developing alternative fuels in many jurisdictions.[79] Within Australia, the Strategic Framework for Alternative Transport Fuels recommends that 'alternative fuels' (which include natural gas, coal fuel derivatives and LPG) be developed, together with renewable energy and biofuels.[80]

In addition to vehicle and fuel initiatives, there are several federal proposals to modernise and extend urban passenger rail infrastructure to provide genuine alternatives to private car travel. Other expenditure on a national 'smart managed motorways' trial seeks to lower pollution and expand the capacity of existing road networks. After many false starts, there is again renewed interest in implementation of high-speed rail.[81]

To achieve the greatest benefits, the development of energy efficiencies in the transport sector must align with strategic planning. Embedding the consideration of climate change factors in infrastructure planning is critical to reducing emissions from the transport sector.[82] While infrastructure planning and provision are predominantly state and territory matters, there has been commitment through the Council of Australian Governments (COAG) to consider climate change in strategic planning and land use decisions.[83] For example, COAG has agreed to a national objective and criteria for capital city planning, which includes 'address[ing] nationally significant policy issues including [...] climate change mitigation and adaptation'.[84] Furthermore, city plans must be broadly consistent with these criteria. Infrastructure Australia, which advises Australian governments on infrastructure proposals, has the reduction of GHG emissions as one of seven strategic priorities in its assessments.[85]

---

[77] Department of Climate Change and Energy Efficiency, *Securing a Clean Energy Future* (2011), Table 5, p. 127.
[78] Department of Climate Change and Energy Efficiency, 'Clean Energy Future: Transport Fuels Fact Sheet' (2011), p. 3.
[79] See, for comparison, I. Del Guyao, 'Biofuels: EU Law and Policy', in *Beyond the Carbon Economy: Energy Law in Transition*, eds Zillman et al. (2008), p. 265.
[80] Department of Energy, Resources and Tourism, *Strategic Framework for Alternative Transport Fuels* (2011), pp. 5–8.
[81] Australian Government, Department of Infrastructure and Transport, 'High Speed Rail Study', <http://www.infrastructure.gov.au/rail/trains/high_speed/>.
[82] Department of Climate Change and Energy Efficiency, *Report of the Prime Minister's Task Group on Energy Efficiency* (2010), p. 131. Further, see Garnaut, who argues that current funding arrangements result in 'road bias' in Commonwealth funding: *Garnaut Climate Change Review* (2008), pp. 456–7.
[83] See, for example, the COAG Communiqué of 7 December 2009, <http://www.coag.gov.au/coag_meeting_outcomes/2009-12-07/index.cfm#cap_city_strat>, p. 8.
[84] COAG Reform Council, Capital City Strategic Planning Systems, <http://www.coagreformcouncil.gov.au/agenda/cities.cfm>.
[85] Department of Climate Change and Energy Efficiency, *Report of the Prime Minister's Task Group on Energy Efficiency* (2010), p. 131.

Although there are now incentives in place for technological innovation and structural change to promote energy efficiencies in transport and urban planning, just how effective these measures will be in weaning Australians from their dependency on private motor vehicle transport is difficult to judge. An effective stabilisation wedge to reduce emissions in the transport sector will need to combine technology innovation and increasingly prescriptive standards for vehicles with changes in city design. Major behavioural changes in Australian life–work patterns will also be necessary if Australians are to achieve energy efficiency in peak demand power generation and consumption.

Dealing with peak demand

A key issue for energy efficiency regulation remains the acceleration in peak electricity demand that comes with growing affluence and consumption. In this respect, the operation and governing rules of the national electricity market, especially in terms of peak generation load, are an important component of measures designed to increase energy efficiency and to assist in the transition to a low-carbon economy.[86] Under current electricity market rules there are perverse incentives that encourage power generation facilities to address energy issues from the supply side. Typically this means meeting ever-increasing demand – especially peak demand – by expanding and upgrading the power grid and generation capacity, rather than seeking to reduce peak load. Initiatives to assist in 'load spreading' to alleviate the peak load problem could include:[87]

- structuring electricity prices to encourage consumers to shift consumption to off-peak periods;
- installation of 'smart meters'[88] to inform consumers of their consumption patterns and facilitate a shift to greater consumption during off-peak times;
- direct load control by an energy supplier to remotely control certain appliances;
- use of more efficient appliances and equipment;
- distributed generation, where users with on-site generation could provide generation at peak times; and
- the use of smart grids for power distribution.[89]

In many jurisdictions there has been growing interest in so-called smart technologies that facilitate consumer choices concerning energy efficiency. In Denmark, for example, there are trial sites for residential 'smart grid' projects.

---

[86] Garnaut, *Garnaut Climate Change Review* (2008), pp. 445–51.
[87] Department of Climate Change and Energy Efficiency, *NESI Issues Paper* (2011), p. 74.
[88] See for example *National Electricity (South Australia) (Smart Meters) Amendment Act 2009* (SA). Victoria has enacted legislation to enable oversight and regulation of tariff-setting: *Electricity Industry Act 2000* (Vic) Div 6A.
[89] R. Lyster, 'Smart Grids: Opportunities for Climate Change Mitigation and Adaptation', 36(1) *Monash University Law Review* (2010).

BOX 9.1 Smart grids

A distinctly 'technological' approach to energy efficiency is exemplified by the Australian national program promoting smart meters and smart grids. Essentially these measures are designed to reduce peak power demand, and to improve the efficiency and reliability of power distribution. The federal government has recently provided funding for a demonstration project in Newcastle, in the state of New South Wales.[90]

Smart grids use advanced telecommunications and information technology to enhance the energy efficiency of the electricity network, employing meters, sensors and digital controls to control the power load on the network. 'Smart' appliances such as white goods, heaters and air conditioners can be remotely programmed to reduce their use of electricity at peak times. These features reduce the demand on the network but may in some ways infringe upon household privacy. Further, there is no guarantee that having the information will cause consumers to change their behaviour to reduce peak loads.

Efficiency standards for appliances and buildings

As well enhancing energy efficiency in direct power generation, there is significant scope to reduce emissions from the power that is consumed, with increasing attention to energy efficiency standards in buildings and in household electrical appliances (refrigerators, washing machines, dryers, air conditioners, etc).

Energy efficiency and buildings

The energy used in Australian residential and commercial buildings accounts for approximately 20 per cent of Australia's total energy consumption.[91] Accordingly, energy efficiencies in the building sector can result in significant emission reductions. Minimum energy performance standards for new residential dwellings are contained in the Building Code of Australia (BCA).[92] The BCA has also been progressively updated to incorporate minimum energy performance standards for other classes of buildings. These standards now apply to Class 2 and Class 4 buildings (multi-residential buildings) and Classes 3 and 5–9 buildings (commercial and public buildings).[93] More recently, the energy efficiency provisions now require a 6-star energy rating, or equivalent, for new residential buildings, and stricter energy efficiency standards for all new commercial buildings.[94] A major focus of the BCA standards is reducing the amount of energy used by heating and cooling systems, by improving building insulation and increasing the efficiency of water heaters and lighting. The BCA sets in place a plan for improving energy efficiency over time. The Code is enforceable through state and territory legislation, although adoption has been patchy.

---

90 T. Skodvin, 'Smart Grid, Smart City', AusGrid, Australian Department of Resources, Energy and Tourism, <http://www.smartgridsmartcity.com.au>.
91 Australian Bureau of Agricultural and Resource Economics and Science (ABARES), *Energy Update 2011*, p. 5.
92 Australian Building Codes Board (ABCB), 'Energy Efficiency Provisions for Housing', <http://abcb.gov.au/en/major-initiatives/energy-efficiency/residential-housing>.
93 ABCB, 'Energy Efficiency Provisions for Multi-Residential and Commercial Buildings', <http://abcb.gov.au/major-initiatives/energy-efficiency/multi-residential-commercial-and-public-buildings>.
94 ABCB, 'Energy Efficiency', <http://abcb.gov.au/major-initiatives/energy-efficiency>.

Among the legislative measures designed to increase consumers' knowledge about the energy performance of buildings is the *Building Energy Efficiency Disclosure Act 2010* (Cth). The Act requires disclosure to interested buyers and tenants of commercial and government buildings by means of a Building Energy Efficiency Certificate. Certificates are valid for 12 months and record:

- a NABERS (National Australian Built Environment Rating System) energy rating for the building;
- an assessment of tenancy lighting in the area of the building that is being sold or leased; and
- general guidance on how energy efficiency might be improved for owners and tenants.

Similar mandatory disclosure requirements for residential properties are expected to be introduced in Australian federal legislation.[95] Some residential disclosure requirements already exist, with varying degrees of stringency, in state and territory laws.[96] Efforts are under way to develop a Nationwide House Energy Rating Scheme,[97] and to obtain more comprehensive data on the energy efficiency of Australian homes and commercial buildings to inform future regulation.

While there have been some important advances in respect of mandatory disclosure and a range of minimum standards set for buildings, their efficacy at a practical level is inconsistent. Disclosure requirements are pertinent for buildings at the point of sale or when leased, but much housing stock remains in the hands of one owner over long periods, which reduces their effect. Also, it is not clear that energy efficiency is a major factor that will influence the decisions of potential purchasers or tenants. Hence it is important to continue to lift mandatory standards for efficiency in the sector rather than rely on less targeted 'consumer choice' programs. While this prescriptive approach is relatively straightforward for new developments, it is problematic (and often costly) for existing buildings. In the European Union, the Energy Performance Directive mandates a common standard for energy assessment, and requires minimum energy efficiency standards for new buildings but also for existing building stock when there is any major renovation.[98] Similar schemes are contemplated for Australia.

In addition to the public regulation of energy efficiency, private law plays a role in giving effect to mandatory disclosure measures through contract and property documents, such as leases for commercial buildings and contracts relevant to the sale of buildings and land. As Durrant notes, the imposition of standards to meet energy efficiency objectives in 'green leases' has injected a

---

95 Department of Resources, Energy and Tourism, *Draft Energy White Paper* (2011), p. 189.
96 See for example *Civil Law (Sale of Residential Property) Act 2003* (ACT) Part 3; *Building Act 1975* (Qld). See Durrant, *Legal Responses to Climate Change* (2010), p. 142.
97 Nationwide House Energy Rating Scheme, <http://www.nathers.gov.au/>.
98 European Commission, *Directive 2002/91/EC of the European Parliament and of the Council of 16 December 2002 on the Energy Performance of Buildings*.

need for mutual cooperation between landlord and tenant into what was previously considered an arm's length commercial agreement.[99] Standard-setting through legislative terms that are imposed into contracts may overcome some of the difficulties of the 'split incentive' dilemma. However, as Durrant points out, green leases will need to expressly incorporate the specific rights and obligations of the landlord and tenant, mutual environmental performance benchmarks, and cooperative mechanisms for addressing non-compliance and issues in dispute if they are to achieve energy efficiency objectives.[100] The implicit introduction of standards of behaviour into contractual arrangements is not unknown (for example the imposition of obligations on financial institutions with respect to mortgage documents), but exactly how, in practical terms, substantive obligations regarding energy efficiency will be enforced, and landlord–tenant disputes resolved, remain open questions.[101] Whether energy efficiency 'breaches' of green leases will become highly contentious legal issues is a matter for future determination.

Trends toward more sustainable building design and implementation of efficiency standards have been gathering momentum both within Australia[102] and internationally. Climate change adds a stronger impetus to these efforts. To date, Australia has largely relied on a mixture of consumer-driven initiatives such as information disclosure coupled with standard-setting to promote energy efficiency in buildings. The advent of market mechanisms such as cap-and-trade schemes is also possible. Other jurisdictions, notably China, have piloted cap-and-trade or baseline-and-credit schemes for hotels, shopping malls and office buildings as a means of lowering energy intensity.

Energy-efficient appliances

In concert with enhanced energy efficiency standards in the building sector, minimum energy performance standards for electrical appliances are in place in Australia. Pursuant to a cooperative arrangement between the Commonwealth and the states, uniform standards have been set for some appliances, including refrigerators and freezers, hot water systems and air conditioners.[103] Seven categories of electrical appliances are now covered by a mandatory labelling scheme that is designed to provide information about the energy efficiency of different products. The hope is that this rating scheme will stimulate consumer demand and thereby give manufacturers an incentive to produce more energy-efficient goods.[104] The label contains a star rating for the product, in addition to

---

99 Durrant, *Legal Responses to Climate Change* (2010), p. 149. Green leases are mandatory in the context of Australian government office buildings: Department of Climate Change and Energy Efficiency, 'Green Lease Schedules', <http://www.climatechange.gov.au/government/initiatives/eego/green-lease-schedule.aspx>.
100 Ibid.   **101** Ibid., p. 150. These apply to Australian government office building leases.
102 See AHURI, 'The Environmental Sustainability of Australia's Private Rental Housing Stock' (2009).
103 See further Department of Climate Change and Energy Efficiency, 'Overview of Regulatory Requirements – Labelling and MEPS' (2010), <http://www.energyrating.gov.au/programs/e3-program/meps/about/>.
104 Department of Climate Change and Energy Efficiency, 'E3: Equipment Energy Efficiency', <http://www.energyrating.gov.au/programs/e3-program/energy-rating-labelling/about/>.

information on its energy consumption (in kilowatt hours per year). It is estimated that regulation imposing energy efficiency standards and mandatory labelling could reduce Australian household and business energy bills by $5.2 billion by 2020.[105]

The existing mandatory regulations will be expanded to cover products that use other types of energy (e.g. gas), as well as products that do not themselves consume energy but that affect the energy efficiency of certain appliances (e.g. air conditioner ducting). There are also moves to introduce GHG intensity standards or labelling under the proposed Greenhouse and Energy Minimum Standards legislation.[106] Such Minimum Energy Performance Standards at the national level would replace current regulation under state law.[107]

Other initiatives

While much can be achieved through direct regulation, there are other measures at play to increase energy efficiency. In 2010 the federal government established and provided $100 million in funding to Low Carbon Australia, a company given the task of pursuing energy efficiency and carbon-neutral programs by making co-investments to stimulate private sector investment in energy retrofitting projects.[108] Similarly, many measures under the Clean Energy Package are delivered by way of financial and administrative arrangements rather than direct legislative adoption,[109] with the Clean Technology Program providing funding of $1.2 billion over seven years.

State-based energy efficiency schemes

Many federal legislative and incentive schemes in energy efficiency expand upon, or seek to coordinate, Australian state and territory laws that have introduced energy efficiency measures. While state laws cover approximately 65 per cent of the Australian population, many operate differently, with different targets, sectors and underlying objectives, as Table 9.1 indicates.

An example of a state scheme is the New South Wales Energy Savings Scheme.[110] It will run until 1 July 2029 or until replaced by national legislation.

---

105 G. Wilkenfeld and Associates, *Prevention is Cheaper than Cure – Avoiding Carbon Emissions through Energy Efficiency: Projected Impacts of the Equipment Energy Efficiency Program to 2020* (George Wilkenfeld and Associates, 2009).
106 Greenhouse and Energy Minimum Standards Bill 2012 (Cth). See also Department of Climate Change and Energy Efficiency, 'Industry Consultation on the Draft GEMS Bill', <http://www.climatechange.gov.au/media/whats-new/gems-consultation-draft-bill.aspx>.
107 See for example *Energy and Utilities Administration Act 1987* (NSW) and the *Energy and Utilities Administration Regulation 2006* (NSW) regs 4 and 16; *Electricity Regulation 2006* (Qld) s 266 and *Electricity Regulation 2006* (Qld) regs 139–40, 152; *Electrical Products Act 2000* (SA) and the *Electrical Products Regulations 2001* (SA); and *Electricity Safety Act 1998* (Vic) and the *Electricity Safety (Equipment Efficiency) Regulations 1999* (Vic).
108 Low Carbon Australia, 'Energy Efficiency Program' <http://www.lowcarbonaustralia.com.au/page/energy-efficiency-program>.
109 Other initiatives include the Clean Energy Skills Program, energy efficiency information grants, and an increased small business instant asset write-off threshold. See Department of Climate Change and Energy Efficiency, *Securing a Clean Energy Future* (2011), Table 2, pp. 122–4.
110 New South Wales Government, 'Energy Savings Scheme', <http://www.ess.nsw.gov.au/>.

Table 9.1 Australian state energy efficiency schemes

New South Wales	*Electricity Supply Act 1995* Part 9; *Electricity Supply (General) Regulation 2001* Part 9A
	Energy Savings Scheme (ESS): Imposes state-wide energy efficiency improvement targets on energy retailers
	Energy and Utilities Administration Act 1987 (NSW) s 34Q
	Energy Efficiency Reporting Scheme: Prescribed persons must prepare energy savings action plans
Victoria	*Victorian Energy Efficiency Target Act 2007* (Vic)
	Victorian Energy Efficiency Target Scheme Regulations 2008 (Vic)
	Energy Efficiency Target
Queensland	*Clean Energy Act 2008* (Qld)
	Smart Energy Savings Program for businesses with medium to large energy consumption
South Australia	*Electricity Act 1996* (SA)
	Residential Energy Efficiency Scheme: Energy retailers must meet energy efficiency improvement targets as a condition of their licences

The scheme, enacted pursuant to the *Electricity Supply Act 1995* (NSW), places obligations on liable entities (mainly electricity retailers) to obtain Energy Savings Certificates to demonstrate achievement of the Energy Savings Target for that year. The target will range from 0.4 per cent of total electricity sales in 2009 up to 4 per cent of all sales in 2014. The scheme covers the residential, commercial and industrial sectors of the economy, although some activities are excluded such as the purchase of Green Power, activities that are eligible to create renewable energy certificates under the federal Renewable Energy Target at the point of generation, and activities that reduce the scope or quantity of production or service from the use of electricity, such as closing part of a building.[111]

Energy efficiency: the path not (yet) taken

While we have canvassed the main measures in place or soon to be implemented in the energy efficiency sphere in Australia, there remain many potential areas of regulation, market-based mechanisms and incentives that could be adopted. For example, what role might energy efficiency standards play in environmental impact assessment? Is it possible to develop guidelines for development approval authorities as they impose conditions on projects? Do we need an energy efficiency impact 'trigger' under the federal *Environment Protection and Biodiversity Conservation Act 1999*?[112] With many potential legal avenues to enhance energy efficiency, Barton notes, '[e]nergy efficiency law is likely to be detailed and complicated to the point of inelegance, because it addresses multiple barriers and cannot rely on price settings alone. At the same time it is required to work in market systems dominated by price signals.'[113] Although Barton was addressing

---

[111] Energy Savings Scheme Rule of 2009 (NSW), r 5.4.
[112] Lyster and Bradbrook, *Energy Law and the Environment* (2006), pp. 92–3.
[113] Barton, 'The Law of Energy Efficiency' (2008), p. 81.

the international situation, his analysis is highly pertinent to the Australian context given the introduction of the CPM. Yet again this discussion returns us to the question of whether a carbon price signal in itself will be sufficient to drive the necessary technological innovation or whether complementary measures are required. This question has resonated across many policy debates about how best to promote renewable energy uptake.

Promoting renewable energy

Australia's renewable energy resources are some of the best in the world.[114] Legislative measures addressing renewable energy uptake, such as a Renewable Energy Target (RET), were among the first climate laws adopted in Australia.[115] They were designed to overcome the problem that most renewable energy technologies are much more expensive to deploy than conventional fossil fuel-based power sources.[116] Nonetheless, despite the considerable sources of renewable energy in Australia, the question of how to facilitate its uptake continues to vex policy-makers. In the following sections we examine initiatives currently in place at the federal, state and territory levels, alongside barriers to renewable energy deployment.

Renewable energy regulation at the federal level

Federal laws providing incentives for renewable energy have taken a number of forms. Most notably, the Renewable Energy Target, introduced in Chapter 4, seeks to promote renewable energy technologies by creating a market for tradable certificates. However, direct funding through grants and flagship programs also features prominently in the federal government's renewable energy policy. More recently, the government has sought to overcome the financial barriers associated with obtaining private finance through the Clean Energy Finance Corporation (CEFC).

Renewable Energy Target (RET)
The RET (formerly the MRET or Mandatory Renewable Energy Target) was established by the *Renewable Energy (Electricity) Act 2000* (Cth). Under the RET, 20 per cent of Australia's electricity must be generated from renewable energy sources by 2020. Renewable energy is defined in section 17 of the legislation and includes solar energy, wind, ocean waves and tide, geothermal aquifers, wood waste, agricultural waste, bagasse (sugar cane waste), black liquor (a by-product of the paper-making process), and landfill gas. Biomass from native forest was removed

---

[114] Department of Resources, Energy and Tourism, *Draft Energy White Paper* (2011), p. 200.
[115] See Chapter 4.   [116] Durrant, *Legal Responses to Climate Change* (2010), p. 127.

pursuant to the MPCCC Clean Energy agreement.[117] Section 17(2) expressly excludes fossil fuels, and materials and waste products derived from fossil fuels.

Under the scheme, owners of accredited facilities earn renewable energy certificates (RECs) for every 1 megawatt hour (MWh) of electricity generated from renewable sources, which may then be sold to liable entities or third parties. Liable entities are wholesale purchasers of electricity that acquire electricity delivered on a grid with a capacity of 100MW or more – generally electricity retailers.[118] If a liable entity does not present enough certificates to cover its liability, a penalty applies, calculated as a function of the excess.[119] Trading in RECs gives rise to a market, which has a separate existence from the national electricity market, as well as a separate regulator (from July 2012, the Clean Energy Regulator).

In 2010, the RET was split into the Large-scale Renewable Energy Target (LRET) and the Small-scale Renewable Energy Scheme (SRES) (see Box 9.2).[120] This change was necessary because the majority of the RECs were being created from small-scale activities, causing the price of RECs to plummet and undermining the incentive to invest in large-scale renewable energy.[121] The situation was exacerbated by the Solar Credits scheme, which multiplied by up to five the number of RECs that could be created from small-scale activities such as the installation of solar panels or solar hot water heaters. The Solar Credit scheme is now being phased out.[122]

BOX 9.2 Large-scale and small-scale renewable energy schemes

The LRET is the most significant part of the RET for the purposes of Australia's future energy generation profile. Under the LRET, 'liable entities', generally electricity retailers, must buy a certain number of large-scale generation certificates (LGCs) and surrender them to the Regulator on an annual basis. One LGC represents 1 megawatt hour (MWh) of generated renewable energy electricity above the plant's baseline.[123] The number of LGCs a retailer is liable to discharge is calculated using the Renewable Power Percentage (RPP), set annually in regulations. Failure to surrender sufficient LGCs results in the imposition of a shortfall penalty of $65 per MWh, which was increased from $40 by the Rudd federal government.[124] As the LRET is a market mechanism, the price of LGCs depends on supply and demand, and can fluctuate daily. In the past, the price has varied between $10 and $60.[125] The number of LGCs that must be surrendered each year is set according to an annual target, specified in section 40(1A) of the *Renewable Energy (Electricity) Act 2000* (Cth) to achieve the 20 per cent target by 2020.

---

117 *Renewable Energy (Electricity) Amendment Regulations 2011* (Cth).
118 *Renewable Energy (Electricity) Act* 2000 (Cth) ss 31, 32 and 33.
119 *Renewable Energy (Electricity) Act* 2000 (Cth) Part 4.
120 *Renewable Energy (Electricity) Amendment Act 2010* (Cth).
121 Explanatory Memorandum, Renewable Energy (Electricity) Amendment Bill 2010 (Cth), p. 6.
122 Clean Energy Regulator, 'Solar Credits', <http://www.orer.gov.au/Solar-Panels/Solar-Credits/solar-credits>.
123 Those plants that generated electricity for the first time after 1 January 1997 have a baseline of zero.
124 *Renewable Energy (Electricity) Amendment Act 2009* (Cth); *Renewable Energy (Electricity) (Large-scale Generation Shortfall Charge) Act 2000* (Cth) s 6.
125 Clean Energy Regulator, 'Solar Credits'.

> **BOX 9.2 (cont.)**
>
> Under the separate SRES, liable entities, also generally electricity retailers, must buy and surrender small-scale technology certificates (STCs) annually in accordance with a prescribed percentage.[126] One STC is equivalent to 1 MWh of renewable electricity generated by a solar panel, small-scale wind or small-scale hydro system over the course of its lifetime of up to 15 years, or electricity displaced by the installation of a solar water heater or heat pump over the course of its lifetime of up to 10 years. Unlike the LGCs, there is no target and STCs are traded at a fixed price of $40.

Although concerns have been raised as to whether the RET target will be met by 2020,[127] many other voices in the renewable energy sector complain that the 20 per cent by 2020 goal is not ambitious enough to drive renewable energy uptake, particularly expensive technologies such as large-scale solar. A review of the RET in the second half of 2012 created uncertainty about the future of the scheme, which some claim has depressed prices of LGCs. Another emerging problem for renewable energy incentive measures is the question of grid access for new renewable energy generators, which is determined under the rules of the National Electricity Market (discussed below). As long as these broader regulatory structures do not recognise the importance of climate change mitigation, and the role of renewable energy in that regard, isolated measures such as the RET will be ineffective as a means of making renewable energy competitive with conventional coal-fired power sources. Issues of regulatory coordination are also critical to the relationship between the RET and the newly enacted CPM. Serious divergence has arisen in the industry and the policy arena over the necessity for long-term retention of the RET and other complementary measures as the CPM takes effect.

Direct funding and support

In addition to a market-based mechanism, the Australian government has direct funding and other financing initiatives to support research and development, commercialisation and deployment of various renewable energy technologies, such as the Solar Flagships Program.[128] In 2011, as part of the MPCCC Agreement on Clean Energy, legislation was passed to create the Australian Renewable Energy Agency (ARENA), to improve the competitiveness of renewable energy technologies and increase the supply of renewable energy in Australia.[129] ARENA is responsible for coordinating and managing the existing renewable energy programs.[130]

Another element of the Clean Energy Agreement, designed to overcome barriers to renewable energy development in capital markets and to encourage

---

126 For a general overview of the scheme, see Clean Energy Regulator, 'About the Small-scale Renewable Energy Scheme', <http://www.orer.gov.au/About-the-Schemes/sres>.
127 Australian Energy Market Commission (AEMC), *Final Report: Impact of the Enhanced Renewable Energy Target on Energy Markets* (2011), pp. i, 22–23.
128 These are listed in Garnaut, *Update Paper 7: Low Emissions Technology and the Innovation Challenge* (2011), p. 25.
129 *Australian Renewable Energy Agency Act 2011* (Cth) s 3.
130 *Australian Renewable Energy Agency Act 2011* (Cth) s 8.

private investment,[131] is the provision for the establishment of the Clean Energy Finance Corporation (CEFC). The CEFC is intended to provide commercial loans, concessional loans, loan guarantees and equity to facilitate the commercialisation and deployment of renewable energy, energy efficiency, and low-emission technologies.[132] To this end, the government has pledged $10 billion over five years, with half specifically earmarked for renewable energy projects. It remains to be seen how effective the CEFC will be in helping renewable energy and low-carbon projects get off the ground and whether it will play a constructive role in ensuring that the 20 per cent Renewable Energy Target is met.

State-based renewable energy regulation

As in many areas of Australian climate law, federal renewable energy regulation exists alongside disparate state-based schemes.[133] Some previous state schemes, such as the Victorian Renewable Energy Target scheme, have been folded into the national scheme to ensure greater interjurisdictional consistency.[134] However, other schemes, such as Queensland's 15 per cent Gas Scheme, remain in place, and some states, such as South Australia, have adopted renewable energy targets significantly in excess of those of the federal scheme.[135] Similarly, the Australian Capital Territory has renewable energy targets, aiming for 15 per cent of its electricity to come from renewable sources by 2012 and 25 per cent by 2020.[136] In July 2008, a COAG Working Group on Climate Change and Water released a consultation paper exploring the removal of individual state schemes in favour of a single national scheme.[137] Nevertheless, the persistence of state-based renewable energy schemes suggests that a one-size-fits-all approach may not be sufficiently adapted to the local conditions in different states. A preferable avenue may be establishment of a national scheme setting a 'floor' but no 'ceiling' requirement for the adoption of renewable energy.[138]

In addition to renewable energy targets, a number of other measures have been introduced by the states and territories to achieve these goals. The most common and controversial has been solar feed-in tariffs. A feed-in tariff gives renewable technologies an advantage over existing forms of energy generation by providing certainty about the return on investment. The tariff is a guaranteed

---

131 For a discussion of financial barriers, including subsidies to existing emission-intensive technologies, see Grattan Institute, *No Easy Choices: Which Way to Australia's Energy Future?* (2012), pp. 12, 20.
132 Department of Climate Change and Energy Efficiency, *Securing a Clean Energy Future* (2011), p. 121. CCS is excluded from the eligible 'clean energy' projects.
133 Table 4.1 in Chapter 4 provides a list of the relevant legislation.
134 *Victorian Renewable Energy Amendment Act 2009* (Vic).
135 On 2 June 2009, South Australian Premier Mike Rann announced plans to increase the state's renewable energy production target to 33 per cent by 2020: Renewables SA, 'Publications and Reports', <http://www.renewablessa.sa.gov.au/about-us/publications-and-reports>.
136 S. Corbell, ACT Minister for Energy, 'Minister Announces Renewable Energy Targets' (Media Release, 5 May 2011).
137 See COAG, 'Final Report: Jurisdictions' Reviews of Existing Climate Change Mitigation Measures' (19 March 2010).
138 This has parallels with the subsidiarity model operating in the European Union.

rate paid over a set period of time for electricity generated from renewable sources and fed into the electricity grid. Net feed-in tariffs are paid only on the surplus amount of generated electricity. In contrast, a gross feed-in tariff pays the owner for every kilowatt hour produced. The state schemes vary in the type of feed-in tariff adopted, as Table 9.2 shows. The draft federal Energy White Paper is critical of the state-based feed-in tariffs for imposing undue costs on consumers.[139] It recommends harmonisation, and that Australian governments work to ensure that feed-in tariffs do not adversely affect the Small-scale Renewable Energy Scheme.[140]

Table 9.2 Australian state feed-in-tariff laws

Jurisdiction	Legislation	Type of scheme (gross or net)	Tariff rate
New South Wales	Electricity Supply Act 1995 (NSW) s 15A	'Solar Bonus Scheme': gross feed-in tariff for solar power[141]	Set at $0.60 per kWh for connections prior to 27 October 2010; $0.20 per kWh thereafter. No new applications from 28 April 2011.
Victoria	Electricity Industry Act 2000 (Vic) Div 5A	Premium (net) feed-in tariff for solar power[142]	$0.60 per kWh. No new applications from 30 September 2011. Transitional (net) solar feed-in tariff of min $0.25 per kWh for five years, available from 1 January 2012.
		General feed-in tariff (net) for small-scale renewable generation (between 5 and 100 kW capacity)	Established in 2004. Customers receive a 'fair and reasonable price' for excess energy fed into the grid.
Queensland	Electricity Act 1994 (Qld) s 44A	Net tariff for small-scale solar power	$0.44 per kWh fed into the grid.
Western Australia	Electricity Industry (Licence Conditions) Regulations 2005 (WA)	Residential Net Feed-in Tariff Scheme	$0.40 per kWh for connections prior to 30 June 2011; $0.20 per kWh thereafter. No new applications from 1 August 2011 as quota has been reached.[143]
South Australia	Electricity Act 1996 (SA) Division 3AB	Net feed-in tariffs for small-scale solar power	$0.44 per kWh fed into the grid; to be reduced to $0.16 per kWh from 1 October 2011.

---

139 Department of Resources, Energy and Tourism, *Draft Energy White Paper* (2011), p. 212.
140 Ibid., p. 228.
141 The tariff was reduced on the basis that it was becoming too expensive for taxpayers: V. Morello, 'NSW Solar Bonus Scheme in Limbo', *Sydney Morning Herald* (29 April 2011), <http://www.news.smh.com.au/breaking-news-national/>.
142 See Victorian Competition and Efficiency Commission, 'Inquiry into Feed-in Tariffs and Barriers to Distributed Generation', <http://www.vcec.vic.gov.au/CA256EAF001C7B21/pages/vcec-inquiries-current-inquiry-into-feed-in-tariffs—barriers-to-distributed-generation>.
143 Office of Energy, Government of Western Australia, 'Residential Feed-in Tariff: Suspension of Scheme' <http://www.energy.wa.gov.au/2/3654/64/residential.pm>.

Table 9.2 (cont.)

Jurisdiction	Legislation	Type of scheme (gross or net)	Tariff rate
Australian Capital Territory	Electricity Feed-In (Renewable Energy Premium) Act 2008 (ACT)	Net feed-in tariff	No new applications from 14 July 2011. Scheme was closed after the cap was reached – within 24 hours of the scheme commencing.[144]
	Electricity Feed-in (Large-scale Renewable Energy Generation) Act 2011 (ACT)	Large-scale feed-in tariff for large-scale (> 2MW capacity) solar energy facilities[145]	Opened up for a competitive bid from project proponents.

Barriers to renewable energy deployment

Policies for deployment of renewable energy do not exist in a vacuum, so it is necessary to consider the barriers impeding greater uptake of renewable energy generation to understand what kind of legal and policy reform is required. Below we examine two sets of barriers that have their source in Australian legal and regulatory requirements: (1) the National Electricity Market rules for grid access and transmission planning; and (2) planning law barriers.

Grid access and transmission planning

The National Electricity Law (NEL)[146] plays a critical role in determining the viability of renewable energy projects in Australia. The NEL provides rules for network planning regulation, grid access, and augmentation and transmission planning, all of which influence the degree to which renewable energy is likely to receive investment.[147] Getting connected to the electricity grid is a major hurdle. For example, to apply for a grid access permit, the renewable energy generator must pay for an initial grid connection study, which can cost up to A$500 000.[148] Even if successful, the developer must then bear the cost of actually connecting to the grid, including any necessary improvements to transmission lines. The Grattan Institute recommended that reform to network regulation, particularly regarding transmission investment decisions, would better promote renewable energy in Australia.[149]

---

144 Australian Capital Territory Government, Department of Sustainability and Environment, 'Electricity Feed-in Tariff', <http://www.environment.act.gov.au/energy/fit>.
145 Setting the tariff by tender process means that successful bidders receive the tariff they had bid for. Bids will be evaluated for feasibility and cost-effectiveness: Australian Capital Territory Government, Department of Sustainability and Environment, 'Large Scale Renewable Energy Auction', <http://www.environment.act.gov.au/energy/solar_auction>.
146 As contained in the schedule to the *National Electricity (South Australia) Act 1996* (SA) and as incorporated into the legislation of states participating in the National Electricity Market.
147 See A. Kallies, 'The Impact of Electricity Market Design on Access to the Grid and Transmission Planning for Renewable Energy in Australia: Can Overseas Examples Provide Guidance?', 2 *Renewable Energy Law and Policy Review* 147 (2011).
148 Parliament of Victoria, Environment and Natural Resources Committee, *Inquiry into the Approvals Process for Renewable Energy Projects in Victoria* (2010).
149 Grattan Institute, *No Easy Choices* (2012), pp. 11, 21.

Transmission planning is another source of difficulty, as existing transmission infrastructure was created around coal deposits and in many respects is incompatible with the situation where electricity generation comes predominantly from large-scale and distributed renewable energy.[150] Upgrading the grid to accommodate large-scale renewables will involve considerable costs.[151] The regulatory framework, which permits only the 'most efficient' investment decisions in the transmission sector, is problematic here.[152] This market paradigm pervades the regulatory framework as seen in the objectives of the National Electricity Market (NEM), which are exclusively focused on promoting reliable supply to consumers, economic efficiency and 'least cost' solutions, and lack reference to environmental considerations.[153] As Kallies points out, adherence to these principles in the context of the privatised electricity sector is a major barrier to promoting renewable energy generation.[154]

Beyond the regulatory framework, the nature of the NEM, in which all commercial generators compete to sell their electricity to power retailers, is a significant impediment to investment in renewable energy. The ability to generate and sell LGCs is an insufficient incentive to secure investment in new generators. Financiers increasingly require that generators conclude a Power Purchase Agreement with an electricity buyer (retailer) for investor certainty.[155] Indeed, two large-scale solar projects seeking inclusion in the federal government's Solar Flagships program faced a major stumbling block as they were unable to strike the required agreement by the application deadline.[156] Obtaining a Power Purchase Agreement has become increasingly difficult with the rise of vertical integration in the electricity sector.[157]

Planning law barriers

Even if the financial situation is not a barrier, obtaining planning approval may constitute a significant hurdle. National renewable energy goals are implemented through state and territory planning frameworks. There is no requirement that state and territory planning law facilitate national renewable energy policy. Recent changes to the planning framework in

---

150 Kallies, 'The Impact of Electricity Market Design' (2011), p. 148; Victorian Parliamentary Inquiry, *Inquiry into the Approvals Process* (2010), p. 219; and Grattan Institute, *No Easy Choices* (2012), p. 20.
151 See Hearps and Wright, *Zero Carbon Stationary Energy Plan* (2010), Appendix 6.
152 Victorian Parliamentary Inquiry, *Inquiry into the Approvals Process* (2010), p. 227.
153 *National Electricity Law* s 7. See also R. Cantley-Smith, 'A changing legal environment for the national electricity market', in W. Gumley and T. Daya-Winterbottom (eds), *Climate Change Law: Comparative, Contractual and Regulatory Considerations* (Thomson Reuters, 2009); and Lyster and Bradbrook, *Energy Law and the Environment* (2006), from p. 114.
154 Kallies, 'The Impact of Electricity Market Design' (2011), pp. 154, 159.
155 Queensland Parliament, Environment and Resources Committee, *Inquiry into Growing Queensland's Renewable Energy Electricity Sector – Executive Summary* (2011), p. 2.
156 G. Parkinson, 'Solar Flagships May Fly at Half Mast', *Climate Spectator* (5 December 2011), <http://www.climatespectator.com.au/commentary/solar-flagships-may-fly-half-mast>.
157 See D. McConnell, 'Not Dead Yet: Flagship "Collapse" only Part of Australia's Solar Story', *The Conversation* (10 February 2012), <http://www.theconversation.edu.au/not-dead-yet-flagship-collapse-only-part-of-australias-solar-story-5288>.

Victoria and New South Wales in respect of wind farms demonstrate that state governments can thwart national objectives by giving priority to local interests.

In Victoria, amendments to the planning framework have prohibited wind farms in urban growth and tourist zones, effectively creating 'no-go' zones in much of the state, including some areas with the best wind resources.[158] Planning law amendments have imposed a requirement on the proponents of wind farm development to obtain the written consent of owners of all dwellings within two kilometres of the nearest turbine.[159] The Australian Energy Market Commission concluded that these changes 'may increase the resource costs of meeting the LRET, as less economic[al] sites may need to be used, and may reduce the level of future renewable generation in Victoria and affect the achievement of the LRET'.[160]

In New South Wales, despite laws providing a streamlined planning approval process for renewable energy to reduce administrative burden,[161] a similarly strict planning approval process for wind farms has been introduced. A noise assessment regime stricter than any other jurisdiction in Australia, the United States or Europe is now in place.[162] Unlike Victoria, there is scope for the wind farm developer to appeal to the government through a 'gateway' process.[163]

On the other hand, the South Australian government has supported wind energy development, proposing changes to the planning law to require local governments in certain locations with low population density to give preference to the development of wind farms over visual amenity when considering applications for planning approval.[164] The effect of the amendment would be to assign wind farm developments in those locations a status that would remove third party appeal rights and, as a result, engender investor confidence in the viability of the project.[165]

Renewable energy uptake in Australia suffers from a 'left hand/right hand' problem. On the one hand there are major legislative schemes such as the RET and financial incentives in place to promote rapid development and deployment. On the other hand, the detail of regulation in state laws, the National Electricity Market rules and state planning requirements reveals a very patchy level of support. Coordinating all these regulatory frameworks represents a major challenge if renewable technologies are to fulfil their role in climate change mitigation.

---

[158] Victorian Planning Scheme Amendments VC 78 and VC 82.
[159] Victorian Planning Provisions, cls 19.01 and 52.32–3.   [160] AEMC, *Final Report* (2011), p. 6.
[161] *State Environmental Planning Policy (Major Projects) 2005* (NSW); *Environment Planning and Assessment Act 1979* (NSW) Part 3A (large-scale), Parts 4 and 5.
[162] NSW Department of Infrastructure and Planning, *NSW Draft Planning Guidelines: Wind Farms* (December 2011), p. 6.
[163] Ibid., pp. 2–3.
[164] South Australian Government, 'Statewide wind farms amendment', <http://www.sa.gov.au/>.
[165] Garnaut, *Update Paper 7: Low Emissions Technology and the Innovation Challenge* (2011), p. 25.

Carbon capture and storage

Unlike measures promoting renewable energy, regulations in the field of carbon capture and storage are designed to prolong the life of high-emission sources, such as coal, by facilitating the development of technological solutions to deal with GHG emissions from coal-fired power plants and other facilities. The focus here is on geosequestration, typically called carbon capture and storage (CCS). CCS involves the distillation of the carbon dioxide (CO_2) produced by a power plant or other processes, its compression into a liquid-like state, and injection into microscopic pore spaces in stable geological formations (or other 'storage' entities, such as disused petroleum wells) deep underground for long-term storage.[166] Potential sites for CCS include depleted oil and gas fields and deep saline aquifers.[167] CCS can occur in onshore locations within nation-states, in offshore locations within areas of national sovereignty, and in trans-boundary areas, which gives rise to complicated issues regarding jurisdictional cooperation in the regulation of this activity.

The individual stages of the CCS process – capture, transport and injection, and long-term storage – are already undertaken via existing technologies, but there are varying levels of technical and commercial feasibility associated with each component.[168] There are three alternative processes for carbon capture – pre-combustion, post-combustion and oxy-combustion – which differ 'in their current technical maturity cost, commercial applicability and applicability to new and existing plants'.[169] Questions remain about how the stages of the CCS process will work in conjunction to ensure that the sequestration is without risks and can subsist for the immense time periods required. A number of pilot projects around the world have been implemented,[170] although to date there is no large-scale commercial project in operation. Thus carbon capture technologies have been demonstrated only on a small scale and their commercial deployment is predicted to have a lead time of at least eight to ten years.[171]

Therefore, while CCS has received much attention in policy circles,[172] the technology for large-scale capture and long-term storage of CO_2 remains preliminary.[173] The commercial cost of CCS also is a major barrier to its use. Capture

---

[166] House Standing Committee on Science and Innovation, *Between a Rock and a Hard Place: The Science of Geosequestration* (2007), p. 25.
[167] S. Haszeldine, 'Geological Factors in Framing Legislation to Enable and Regulate Storage of Carbon Dioxide Deep in the Ground', in *Carbon Capture and Storage: Emerging Legal and Regulatory Issues*, eds I. Havercroft, R. Macrory and R. B. Stewart (Hart Publishing, 2011), p. 7.
[168] N. Shilling, 'CCS – General Electric's Perspective', in *Carbon Capture and Storage*, eds Havercroft et al. (2011), p. 27.
[169] Ibid.
[170] The most well known is the Sleipner project in Norway. See Durrant, *Legal Responses to Climate Change* (2010), p. 176.
[171] Department of Resources, Energy and Tourism, *Draft Energy White Paper* (2011), p. 226.
[172] Department of Treasury, *Strong Growth, Low Pollution* (2011), Chapter 5, suggests that up to 30 per cent of Australia's electricity needs could be met with CCS in coal and gas plants; see also International Energy Agency, *Energy Technology Perspectives 2010: Scenarios and Strategies to 2050* (2010), p. 75; Department of Resources, Energy and Tourism, *Draft Energy White Paper* (2011), pp. 225–6.
[173] International Energy Agency, *Carbon Capture and Storage Roadmap* (2010), pp. 1, 44.

of carbon emissions often will take place at a significant distance from where it is to be sequestered. Clearly if there are great distances involved in transporting the liquefied CO_2 it will increase costs considerably,[174] although the main cost component in CCS relates to the capture phase.[175] Under current estimates, CCS will not be commercially viable unless the technology is assisted by the introduction of a carbon price (via taxation or an ETS) that is sufficiently high to encourage investment in CCS implementation and operation, or other specifically targeted support measures.

CCS around the globe

Although there are still major issues to be resolved relating to technical and economic aspects of CCS, interest and debate have continued to grow. Some commentators suggest that CCS is now 'one of the core technologies that will be needed to handle the challenge of climate change',[176] while others point to the legal and environmental issues that are yet to be satisfactorily settled.[177] The IPCC encouraged consideration of CCS to address climate change in its 2005 *Special Report on Carbon Dioxide Capture and Storage*.[178] Since that time there has been a surge in legislative and regulatory activity relating to CCS in many jurisdictions worldwide, as well as a proliferation of demonstration projects. In many jurisdictions it became obvious that substantial new laws, both national and transnational, were required to respond to the challenges of the emerging technology.

In the European Union, in the context of a strong commitment to reducing GHG emissions by 20 per cent by 2030, CCS has formed an integral part of projected measures designed to develop sustainable power generation. The EU Commission will require very low emissions from coal power generation by 2020, providing a platform for the deployment of CCS. The Commission initiated several pilot CCS projects, while developing an overarching legal and policy framework for CCS regulation. The EU Directive 2009/31/EC on the geological storage of CO_2 is the outcome of that latter process. The Directive entered into force in June 2009 and forms part of a broader package on climate change and renewable energy.[179] CCS demonstration projects are to form part of the activities covered under the EU emissions trading scheme.[180]

---

[174] Long transportation distances also increase the risk of fugitive emissions and increase the energy required to transport the captured carbon.
[175] For more information on what is involved in this phase, see B. Metz et al. (eds), *Intergovernmental Panel on Climate Change: Special Report on Carbon Dioxide Capture and Storage* (IPCC, 2005), Chapter 3.
[176] Havercroft, Macrory and Stewart, 'Introduction', in *Carbon Capture and Storage*, eds Havercroft et al. (2011), p. 1.
[177] R. Ashcroft, 'Carbon Capture and Storage – A Need for Re-Conceiving Property Interests and Resource Management in the Australian Legal System', *LAWASIA Journal* 70 (2008).
[178] IPCC Special Report, *Carbon Dioxide Capture and Storage: Technical Summary* (2005).
[179] See Chapter 5.
[180] M. Doppelhammer, 'The CCS Directive, its Implementation and the Co-financing of CCS and RES Demonstration projects Under the Emissions Trading System', in *Carbon Capture and Storage*, eds Havercroft et al. (2011), p. 93.

At its heart the EU Directive is designed to address environmental and health risks associated with large-scale deployment of CCS, while at the same time removing legal impediments to its implementation. A number of legal instruments were already in place to deal with environmental risks associated with carbon capture and transport, so the particular focus of the EU Directive was in respect of geological storage. The scope of the Directive is wide, covering the territories of the EU Member States, the EEZ of each nation, and the continental shelf. The Directive also contains detailed provisions for the grant of a storage permit, risk management, and the requirements for closure of a storage site after stabilisation.[181] Issues relating to third-party access and the operation of EU pollution and waste control laws also had to be addressed. The EU Directive provisions were required to be implemented in Member State laws by mid-June 2011. This snapshot of the EU CCS indicates the rapidity with which a comprehensive legal and regulatory regime has been implemented.

By contrast, although there has been strong political support of CCS, there has not been the same development of legal frameworks to support demonstration projects and the technology in the United States and Canada.[182] Commentators from both countries stress that one of the main barriers is that the technology remains uncompetitive, and its long-term viability depends on a carbon price and/or supporting legislation, neither of which appears imminent. CCS projects in the United States thus currently face '[a] complicated web of state and federal property rights issues and perceived public safety concerns'.[183] In addition, CCS projects will be required to obtain a range of approvals under existing legislation. Baugh stresses the need for greater legal certainty and for a defined regulatory structure for determining liability to facilitate CCS in the United States;[184] otherwise large investment in CCS technology is unlikely.

In Canada, geological conditions are favourable to the use of CCS but the national government is reluctant to legislate in the field. Some provincial governments have instigated CCS activities, largely through existing oil and gas regulation, or environmental assessment and permits.[185] One particular legal issue to be addressed at the Canadian provincial level is the 'ownership' of the subsurface where the CO_2 might be stored. Moreover, as Krupa suggests, 'it is clear that Canada lags behind other nations in the development of a comprehensive legal and regulatory framework to address ... liability issues'.[186] While there may be few inherent difficulties in using Canada's existing legal frameworks to utilise CCS, Krupa argues that statutory clarification to address geological storage and liability issues would assist in deployment of the technology. Canada as a nation

---

[181] Ibid., pp. 95–8.
[182] H. Krupa, 'The Legal Framework for Carbon Capture and Storage in Canada', in *Carbon Capture and Storage*, eds Havercroft et al. (2011), p. 40.
[183] L. Baugh, 'US legal and regulatory Challenges of CCS', in *Carbon Capture and Storage*, eds Havercroft et al. (2011), p. 69.
[184] Ibid., p. 79.
[185] Krupa, 'The Legal Framework for Carbon Capture and Storage in Canada', in *Carbon Capture and Storage*, eds Havercroft et al. (2011), p. 45.
[186] Ibid., p. 57.

has many similarities with Australia in terms of economic dependence on fossil fuel extraction, yet while Canada has lagged in terms of legal developments to facilitate CCS, Australia was an 'early mover' in introducing comprehensive statutory regimes at both national and state levels.

CCS in Australia

Given Australia's extensive fossil fuel resources, it is not surprising that CCS has enjoyed broad political support, with its promise of being able to continue to burn coal domestically and to remain a major coal exporter, while minimising accompanying GHG emissions.[187] Thus there are important incentives in Australia for the development of 'clean coal' via CCS technologies. Moreover, CCS offers not only a clean coal possibility, but also potential application in other energy and industrial uses such as steel production.[188] Consequently, the Australian government has been a major proponent of CCS technologies both internationally, through the Global CCS Institute, and domestically, through major statutory regimes at both national and (some) state government levels.

In concert, substantial funds have been set aside by governments to develop clean coal technologies and to support CCS demonstration projects under the National Low Emissions Coal Initiative.[189] A National Carbon Capture and Storage Council was established in 2010 to oversee CCS projects identified for development.[190] The Council includes representatives of the coal industry, oil and gas sectors, coal-fired and gas-fired power generators, the research community, several states, and the Australian government.[191] Also, there has been considerable government activity directed towards locating suitable storage sites and developing infrastructure.[192] There are two major demonstration sites for long-term CO_2 storage: the Otway project, which is currently under way, and the Gorgon LNG project off Australia's north-west coast, which will commence operations in 2015.

While there is significant political support and growing research and development investment in CCS, Durrant argues that it should nonetheless be regarded as a transitional technology as Australia moves towards a low-carbon economy.[193] Other commentators see CCS as integral to the portfolio of measures designed to drive structural change in Australia's energy mix, alongside an ETS,

---

[187] However, as a result of opposition from the Greens, CCS is a notable exclusion from the clean energy projects that will be eligible for funding under the Clean Energy Finance Corporation.
[188] M. Gibbs, 'The Regulation of Geological Storage of Greenhouse Gases in Australia', in *Carbon Capture and Storage*, eds Havercroft et al. (2011), p. 159.
[189] Department of Resources, Energy and Tourism, 'National Low Emissions Coal Initiative', <http://www.ret.gov.au/resources/resources_programs/nleci/Pages/NationalLowEmissionsCoalInitiative.aspx>.
[190] National Low Emissions Coal Council, *National Low Emissions Coal Strategy* (2008), pp. vi–vii.
[191] Department of Resources, Energy and Tourism, 'National Low Emissions Coal Initiative', <http://www.ret.gov.au/resources/resources_programs/nleci/Pages/NationalLowEmissionsCoalInitiative.aspx>.
[192] A Carbon Storage Taskforce was established in July 2008 to develop the National Carbon Mapping and Infrastructure Plan.
[193] Durrant, *Legal Responses to Climate Change* (2010), p. 175.

Renewable Energy Targets, and energy efficiency measures.[194] Despite arguments in favour of CCS, particularly as a transition strategy, the technology has engendered a range of public concerns, principally related to environmental and health risks. Its long-term commercial viability also remains uncertain, although integration of the CCS within the CPM framework may address this issue.

CCS risks and regulatory responses

CCS risks are of two types:[195] global risks including leakage from storage, transportation or distillation (i.e. separation) phases, and localised risks to humans, ecosystems and groundwater. In addition to these two categories there are the legal risks pertaining to long-term liability in respect of the CO_2 storage. There are complex legal and policy questions as to whether private CCS project proponents or the relevant nation-state should bear the potential liability for long-term geological storage of CO_2, as discussed further below. While the regulatory regime that has developed around CCS in Australia deals with a novel technology and unique risks, it has adopted fairly well-known legal measures, often drawing on mineral and petroleum regulation and adopting licensing and permit requirements that are the basis of regulation in the natural resources and environmental spheres. The legal measures regulate exploration of sites, capture, injection, pre-closure storage, and long-term storage. More widely, Durrant identifies the objective of facilitating, promoting and encouraging the storage of GHG substances in geological formations as common to the legislation across the state and federal jurisdictions, but she notes the tension in a regime that seeks to stimulate innovation and investment but also to minimise environmental and health risks.[196]

A specific CCS regulatory framework has developed in several Australian jurisdictions, but a federal or state government authority can also place CCS installation conditions on development approval for specific projects, such as coal or natural gas power generation, under the requisite environmental impact and development approval legislation.

Legislative and regulatory framework

Australia has one of the most well-developed frameworks in the world for CCS regulation, both offshore and onshore. As part of their strong support for the CCS technology, Australian governments contributed to the development of general principles to assist with the roll-out of new statutes. In 2005, guiding principles were developed for CCS technology laws as part of the suite of possible options for emissions reduction. This was driven in part by the health and safety and environmental impact of CCS technology, in addition to a desire to create regulatory certainty for investors. The guiding principles are designed to

---

[194] Gibbs, 'The Regulation of Geological Storage of Greenhouse Gases in Australia', in *Carbon Capture and Storage*, eds Havercroft et al. (2011), p. 159.
[195] B. Metz et al. (eds), *Special Report on Carbon Dioxide Capture and Storage* (IPCC, 2005), p. 34; and Doppelhammer, 'The CCS Directive', in *Carbon Capture and Storage*, eds Havercroft et al. (2011), p. 94.
[196] Durrant, *Legal Responses to Climate Change* (2010), p. 178.

underpin state and federal legislation to achieve a nationally consistent framework for CCS activities in all Australian jurisdictions.[197] Six key areas were designated and broad principles were formulated, as follows:[198]

- *Assessment and approvals processes* should be consistent with national protocols and guidelines.
- *Access and property rights* should be created in respect of surface and subsurface rights.
- *Transportation* should be consistent with national protocols and guidelines.
- *Monitoring and verification* obligations for health, safety and environmental purposes should be imposed.
- *Liability* and *post-closure responsibilities* in respect of health, environmental and financial risks should be provided for.
- *Financial aspects* of the project should be regulated by existing legislative, regulatory and accounting practices.

More general principles such as ecologically sustainable development and occupational health and safety rules were also to apply.[199] These principles are reflected to varying extents in the legislation that has been subsequently enacted in Australian jurisdictions, with Victoria and Queensland implementing more 'stand-alone' statutes. We now turn to consider the Commonwealth CCS legislation.

Offshore Petroleum and Greenhouse Gas Storage Act 2006 (Cth)

While proposed sites for geosequestration in Australia have been identified in both onshore and offshore locations, geosequestration locations in offshore areas mostly fall under the jurisdiction of the federal government. There is a complex offshore regime in coastal Australia known as the offshore constitutional settlement, which creates a mosaic of jurisdictional controls. Nonetheless, the federal government has sovereignty to regulate CCS in most of the offshore locations. Accordingly, the federal government, following a tortured passage of the relevant bill, amended its offshore petroleum legislation in 2008 to provide access and property rights for CCS activities in offshore areas within Commonwealth waters.[200] The federal legislation was based on the 2005 principles,[201] providing, as the Revised Explanatory Memorandum explains, 'a system of

---

[197] Ministerial Council on Mineral and Petroleum Resources, *Regulatory Guiding Principles for Carbon Dioxide Capture and Geological Storage*, 25 November 2005, pp. 6–7.
[198] Ibid., pp. 4–5. [199] Ibid., pp. 11–12.
[200] *Offshore Petroleum Amendment (Greenhouse Gas Storage) Act 2008* (Cth), which amends the *Offshore Petroleum Act 2006* to create the *Offshore Petroleum and Greenhouse Gas Storage Act 2006* (Cth). Victoria also enacted legislation to apply to waters within its jurisdiction: the *Offshore Petroleum and Greenhouse Gas Storage Act 2010* (Vic). The principal federal CCS legislation relies on a supporting array of regulations to manage various risks, including the *Offshore Petroleum and Greenhouse Gas Storage (Greenhouse Gas Injection and Storage) Regulations 2011* (Cth), *Offshore Petroleum and Greenhouse Gas Storage (Environment) Regulations 2009* (Cth), *Offshore Petroleum and Greenhouse Gas Storage (Safety) Regulations 2009* (Cth) and *Offshore Petroleum and Greenhouse Gas Storage (Resource Management and Administration) Regulations 2011* (Cth).
[201] Ministerial Council on Mineral and Petroleum Resources, *Regulatory Guiding Principles* (2005), p. 4.

offshore titles, similar to the offshore petroleum titles'. The amending Act also authorised 'the transportation by pipeline and injection and storage of greenhouse gas substances in deep geological formations under the seabed'. The Explanatory Memorandum to the legislation recognises 'similarities' between petroleum and GHG operations and that each activity can have beneficial and/or detrimental effects on the other. As a consequence, a person must have a permit for geosequestration exploration, as well as injection and holding leases for storing the CO_2. Ten offshore sites have been released for exploration.[202]

In each phase, as outlined in Box 9.3, key issues arise in respect of managing and assessing risk, and these intersect with broader questions about the capacity for third-party review of decisions made under the regulatory regime. One particular issue regarding injection licences, for example, is that it is not mandatory for the Minister to set a condition on the injection licence requiring the licensee to obtain insurance or provide security for short-

---

BOX 9.3 Australian Commonwealth legislative framework for CCS

The *Offshore Petroleum and Greenhouse Gas Storage Act 2006* (Cth) provides the following framework for the various stages of CCS activities:

Exploration: In order to explore in an offshore area for potential storage sites a person must hold a GHG assessment permit (s 289).

Site declaration: The permit holder may apply to the responsible Commonwealth Minister (RCM) for the declaration of a part of the geological formation as 'an identified storage formation' (s 312).

Injection and operations phase: The permit holder is then able to apply for a GHG injection licence over the declared identified storage formation (s 361); operations must commence within five years or the licence will be cancelled (s 360).

Site closure: The licensee must apply for a site-closing certificate once injection operations have ceased (Part I, Div 7). The application must include modelling and analysis of the injected GHG; an assessment of the expected migration pathway and the short- and long-term consequences of such migration; and suggestions as to how the Commonwealth should monitor the injected GHG (s 386).

If satisfied that there are no significant risks of significant adverse effects and the injected GHG is behaving as predicted, the Commonwealth Minister will issue a pre-certificate notice (s 388). The notice will specify a program of monitoring and assessment operations to be undertaken by the Commonwealth as well as an estimate of the total costs involved, which is to be paid by the applicant in advance in the form of a security (s 391). Once the security has been lodged, the Minister will issue a site-closing certificate (s 392).

Site closure assurance period: A period of monitoring and assessment of risks by the Commonwealth then follows.

On a day that is at least 15 years after the site-closing certificate has been issued, the Minister may declare the 'closure assurance period' completed.

Post-closure: Once the closure assurance period is complete, the Commonwealth must indemnify the licence holder against liability for damages incurred post-closure that are attributable to the licence holder's authorised activities (s 400).

Liability transfers to the Commonwealth in those situations where the licensee ceases to exist after a closure assurance period has been declared (s 401).

---

202 Department of Resources, Energy and Tourism, 'Carbon Capture and Storage Acreage Release', <http://www.ret.gov.au>.

term damage.[203] Most of the other pressing questions for potential review of administrative decision-making relate to the long-term storage of CO_2 and the state's assumption of liability in respect of any incidents in the post-closure phase, as demonstrated by the following examples. First, under the legislation, the relevant Commonwealth minister may refuse to issue a pre-certificate notice (required to obtain a site-closing certificate) if not satisfied that the CO_2 is behaving as predicted, or if satisfied that there is significant risk that it will have a significant adverse impact on the conservation or exploitation of natural resources, the geotechnical integrity of a geological formation or structure, the environment, or human health or safety.[204] Secondly, the minister may make a declaration that a 'closure assurance period' is in effect if satisfied that the CO_2 is behaving as predicted and there is no significant risk that it will have a significant adverse impact on any of the aforementioned activities or things.[205]

The issue of who bears the cost of financing long-term monitoring and assessment is addressed, to some degree, by the legislation. As noted in Box 9.3, the Commonwealth requires the CCS operator to finance the monitoring costs incurred by the Commonwealth in the closure assurance period. Similarly, in Victoria the CCS operator must pay for the long-term monitoring costs reasonably incurred by the state,[206] as well as royalties.[207] In Queensland, the relevant minister has the power to require lodgement of security to pay for, among other things, liability incurred by the state because of an act or omission by the CCS operator.[208] In addition, the state's long-term monitoring costs will be funded by financial assurances given under the state's *Environmental Protection Act 1994*.[209]

Aside from the statutory monitoring obligations and related costs, further significant legal issues arise regarding long-term liability. The Commonwealth must indemnify a CCS operator against any common law claims in the post-closure period attributable to authorised acts performed by the CCS operator prior to site closure. This provision was added to the bill by the Senate. It stands in contrast to legislative provisions in Victoria or Queensland, where the state government assumes responsibility for the site and the statutory obligations relating to monitoring and assessment of the injected CO_2, but not the CCS operator's common law liability.[210] CCS operators are liable at common law for damages in actions in negligence for causing harm to, for instance, property or health, or in nuisance for interfering with a person's enjoyment and use of his or

---

203 *Offshore Petroleum and Greenhouse Gas Storage Act 2006* (Cth) ss 364, 372(c).
204 *Offshore Petroleum and Greenhouse Gas Storage Act 2006* (Cth) s 388.
205 *Offshore Petroleum and Greenhouse Gas Storage Act 2006 (Cth)* s 399.
206 *Greenhouse Gas Geological Sequestration Act 2008* (Vic) s 112; *Offshore Petroleum and Greenhouse Gas Storage Act 2010* (Vic) ss 426 and 433.
207 *Greenhouse Gas Geological Sequestration Act 2008* (Vic) s 224; *Offshore Petroleum and Greenhouse Gas Storage Act 2010* (Vic) s 694.
208 *Greenhouse Gas Storage Act 2009* (Qld) s 270.
209 See *Environmental Protection Act 1994* (Qld) s 181(2); Queensland Parliament, *Second Reading*, Legislative Assembly, 3 December 2008, 4064 (Geoff Wilson, Minister for Mines and Energy).
210 *Offshore Petroleum and Greenhouse Gas Storage Act 2010* (Vic), Parliament of Victoria, *Second Reading Speech*, Legislative Assembly, 4 February 2010, 250 (Peter Batchelor, Minister for Energy and Resources).

Table 9.3 Australian state onshore CCS legislation		
State	Principal Act	Commencement
VIC	*Greenhouse Gas Geological Sequestration Act 2008*	30 October 2009
QLD	*Greenhouse Gas Storage Act* 2009	13 February 2009
SA	*Petroleum and Geothermal Act 2000*	1 October 2009
WA	*Barrow Island Act 2003*	20 November 2003

her land. The assumption of this liability by the Commonwealth under the federal legislation indicates that it will be future taxpayers who will bear the long-term liability risk in order to encourage private investment in costly CCS in the short term. The short-term gains need to be weighed against the longer-term costs and risks when assessing the viability of this technology alongside other options that can effect structural change in the energy mix.

Fragmentation in onshore CCS laws

While there is a comprehensive CCS regime in Commonwealth waters, state legislation governing CCS activities at onshore locations reflects a more fragmented approach (see Table 9.3).[211]

It is notable that Western Australia – with vast offshore areas and high levels of fossil fuel extraction – does not have general CCS legislation or regulation in place. In Western Australia, such legislation was to be developed in 2010, but nothing as yet has been introduced to Parliament. The *Barrow Island Act 2003* (WA) is specific to the Gorgon project and was the first statute in Australia to regulate a CCS project.[212] The Gorgon project, one of the largest natural gas projects in Australia, involves natural gas extraction 200 kilometres off the coast near Barrow Island, a nature reserve with high biodiversity. Barrow Island is the site for a plant for processing of LNG, which will be transported via pipeline from the gas field. The raw gas from the field has high concentrations of CO_2 which must be extracted for commercial exploitation of the LNG, and which once extracted will be injected into a saline aquifer off Barrow Island. The project has generated much controversy, and it was assessed and required approval under both Western Australian and federal laws. One condition on the approval of the project was the imposition of CCS technologies for the plant. The Western Australian government entered an agreement with the Gorgon joint venture regarding implementation of the project and there is an indemnification of the state by the joint venture in respect of the disposal and storage of the CO_2, although the exact scope of the ongoing obligations in respect of monitoring or remediation of damage is unclear. Nonetheless, as Campbell notes, the

---

[211] See also Greenhouse Gas Storage Bill 2010 (NSW) and the *Clean Coal Administration Act 2008* (NSW), which establishes the 'Coal Innovation NSW Fund' designed to provide funding for research, development, and demonstration of low-emission coal technologies. Durrant provides a thorough comparison of the relevant state legislation (Durrant, *Legal Responses to Climate Change* (2010), pp. 178–96).

[212] R. Campbell, 'Long-term Liability for Offshore Geo-sequestration', *AMPLA Association Year Book* (2006), p. 522.

assumption of long-term liability for geosequestration by a private group (albeit a group comprising some of the world's major resource companies) can occur where there is a commercial incentive to do so.[213] Such an approach can be contrasted with the stance on long-term liability found in the Commonwealth offshore legislation.

Other state legislative frameworks all cover the CCS stages outlined above, although they differ in their specifications. A notable feature is the extent to which the legislation 'piggybacks' on existing state laws governing petroleum exploration and extraction.[214] While in most cases, sites for CCS will be those previously mined for petroleum, it does not necessarily follow that the best regulatory framework for CCS and the particular environmental issues it raises (such as leakage)[215] is one drawn from the petroleum law field. Indeed, in the context of transport of CO_2, the draft Energy White Paper recommended further work to determine suitability of oil and gas industry pipeline standards for safe application to CCS.[216] A snapshot of the Queensland law illuminates some of these points, as well as providing an overview of the types of permits and licences that might be required in respect of proposed CCS projects (see Box 9.4).

BOX 9.4 Queensland legislative framework for CCS

The Queensland legislative framework for CCS regulation is contained in the *Greenhouse Gas Storage Act 2009* (Qld). The legislation covers the exploration, injection and site closure phases.

Exploration phase

A person must enter a tender process to obtain a *greenhouse gas exploration permit* before commencing exploration for suitable storage sites (Part 2, Div. 2). As part of the application, the person must submit a detailed *work program*, setting out the scope of the intended activities as well as their general cost (s 53). The applicant must satisfy the relevant Minister that he or she has the necessary financial and technical resources and expertise to carry out the exploration (ss 25 and 65).

The applicant *may* inform the Minister of any suitable storage sites identified (s 101), in contrast to the situation in Victoria, where notification is compulsory.[217]

Injection phase

Once a suitable site has been identified and the permit holder wishes to begin injecting greenhouse gases, he or she must apply for a *greenhouse gas injection and storage lease*. Again, this process requires the applicant to submit a *development plan* detailing the nature and extent of the activities to be carried out under the lease (s 139).

Before a lease will be granted, the applicant must obtain all health and environmental approvals (s 40). The Minister must also consider whether there are any overlapping

---

[213] Ibid.
[214] Ministerial Council on Mineral and Petroleum Resources, *Regulatory Guiding Principles for Carbon Dioxide Capture and Geological Storage*, (25 November 2005), p. 14.
[215] Department of Primary Industries, 'A Regulatory Framework for the Long-Term Underground Storage of Carbon Dioxide in Australia' (Discussion Paper, January 2009), p. 11.
[216] Department of Resources, Energy and Tourism, *Draft Energy White Paper* (2011), p. 226.
[217] *Greenhouse Gas Geological Sequestration Act 2008* (Vic) s 56.

> **BOX 9.4 (cont.)**
>
> petroleum interests, and if so, whether the lease would be compatible (ss 196–7, 202, 212). The Minister must not grant approval where the injection and storage activities would have an adverse impact on petroleum resources.
>
> Once granted, the leaseholder has five years to commence injecting GHG substances in accordance with the approved development plan (s 167).
>
> The terms of the lease will specify matters such as (s 141):
> - the site plan and the site's storage capacity;
> - the kind of substance to be injected and its origin;
> - the period and rate of injection;
> - any engineering enhancements; and
> - monitoring of GHG streams and migration (s 145).
>
> **Site closure phase**
>
> At the conclusion of injection activities, the leaseholder must make a **surrender application** (s 176). This application is to detail the current and predicted future **behaviour of injected substances**, their expected **migration pathways** and the short- and long-term consequences of this migration (s 177). The Minister has the power to require the applicant to report on the measures that have been taken to reduce the risks (s 178) and the Minister can approve the application only if he or she is satisfied that the risks have been reduced as much as is reasonably practicable (s 179).
>
> **Long-term liabilities**
>
> On surrender of the lease, any substance injected becomes the property of the state (s 181) and the state assumes responsibility for monitoring and verification of the storage site from this time. As such, it would seem that liability for any harm caused after this time would rest, according to standard common law principles, with the state.[218] The legislation does not provide for Crown indemnity of the leaseholder's common law liability.

While Australia is progressively rolling out its legal framework for CCS, in the process resolving major legal matters as such as long-term liability for state agencies, the looming questions of the commercial viability and long-term prospects for investment in the technology remain. Two developments, one at international law and another in Australian law, are relevant here.

CCS under the Clean Development Mechanism

Internationally, the feasibility of CCS will be enhanced if it is part of the activities recognised under the Clean Development Mechanism and therefore is able to participate in the global emission market. This is primarily relevant to demonstration projects initially, but in the longer term may increase the competitiveness of the technology. Significantly, the parties to the UNFCCC agreed at the 16th COP in Cancun that CCS should be accepted as a project eligible for generating credits under the CDM, subject to the resolution of

---

218 Durrant, *Legal Responses to Climate Change* (2010), p. 195; and Gibbs, 'The Regulation of Geological Storage of Greenhouse Gases in Australia', in *Carbon Capture and Storage*, eds Havercroft et al. (2011), pp. 168–9. See also G. Campbell, 'Carbon Capture and Storage: Legislative Approaches to Liability', 28(3) *Australian Resources and Energy Law Journal* 418 (2009).

issues relating to permanence, monitoring, site selection, environmental impacts, and international law.[219] Australia was one of only 10 countries to make a submission, and reiterated its support for the inclusion of CCS under the CDM.[220] A technical body of the UN developed draft modalities for exploration risk, liability, and transboundary law issues.[221] At the Durban COP, as discussed in Chapter 6, the parties adopted the proposed modalities.

As a consequence, CCS is now a CDM project activity. At the next COP, parties will consider whether to include projects that involve the transport of CO_2 from one country to another as eligible project activities.[222] A country may only host a CCS project for the purposes of the CDM if it obtains the agreement of the UNFCCC Secretariat and enacts domestic legislation to regulate the project.[223] However, the acceptance of the CCS technology under the CDM leaves unanswered many issues relevant to the guiding principles under the UNFCCC, including principles regarding polluter pays, the precautionary principle and equity. In particular, incorporation of the CCS technology under the CDM raises questions of intra- and intergenerational equity: where will such projects be located, and consequently, which nations or entities bear the risk of long-term CO_2 storage?. These matters have generated considerable controversy under Australian law, with the state in most instances (and ultimately the public purse) bearing the risks into the future. Stringent safeguards will be necessary to ensure that nations that have contributed only negligibly to climate change are not placed in the position of having to bear such risks.

CCS under the Carbon Pricing Mechanism

With CCS now covered by the CDM, attention is turning to whether CCS should be included within the ETS in Australia. Although not expressly stated in the *Clean Energy Act 2011* (Cth), it is not intended that emissions from CCS sites will be exempt from the CPM.[224] As provided for in section 10 of the *Clean Energy Act 2011*, the coverage of the CPM extends 'to a matter concerning the exercise of Australia's sovereign rights in the exclusive economic zone or the continental shelf'. According to the relevant Explanatory Memorandum, CCS facilities in these areas 'will be responsible under the general provisions of the

---

219 Kyoto Protocol, *Decision 10/CMP.7, Modalities and Procedures for Carbon Dioxide Capture and Storage in Geological Formations as Clean Development Mechanism Project Activities* (2011), FCCC/KP/CMP/2011/10/Add.2.
220 Subsidiary Body for Scientific and Technological Advice (UNFCCC), *Views on Carbon Dioxide Capture and Storage in Geological Formations as Clean Development Mechanism Project Activities* (26 July 2011), FCCC/SBSTA/2011/MISC.10.
221 Subsidiary Body for Scientific and Technological Advice (UNFCCC), *Draft Modalities and Procedures for Carbon Dioxide Capture and Storage in Geological Formations as Clean Development Mechanism Project Activities* (8 November 2011), FCCC/SBSTA/2011/4.
222 Kyoto Protocol, *Decision 10/CMP.7, Modalities and Procedures for Carbon Dioxide Capture and Storage in Geological Formations as Clean Development Mechanism Project Activities* (2011), FCCC/KP/CMP/2011/10/Add.2.
223 Ibid., p. 16. **224** Explanatory Memorandum, Clean Energy Bill 2011 (Cth), para. 1.32.

bill for any emissions from these facilities'.[225] Interestingly, the industry assistance arrangements under the CPM could encourage the uptake of CCS technology. The proprietors of power stations receiving free units must lodge Clean Energy Investment Plans detailing their plans, if any, to reduce a power station's emission intensity, which could include the installation of CCS technology.[226]

More broadly, an issue for future resolution is whether emission credits or offsets can be generated from storage projects.[227] While most attention to the intersection of an ETS and CCS has been in respect of whether the carbon price signal will stimulate investment in CCS, this brings a different perspective to that discussion. Moreover, if credits can be so generated, what is their status in terms of Kyoto compliance or indeed in terms of later international agreements? Clearly, there are outstanding legal matters regarding CCS as it operates in the national regulatory sphere and in that of emerging international law.

Overall, it is difficult to pinpoint the prospects for CCS precisely. It has potential to contribute to a low-carbon economy by offering a technology that facilitates a transition, working in conjunction with other technology options as part of a technology stabilisation wedge. On the other hand, it also has potential to lock in existing dependence on fossil fuels and to limit the uptake of renewable technologies. Its short-term technical and commercial feasibility remains uncertain, although there is strong support for its rapid deployment in key jurisdictions. The legal and regulatory frameworks for CCS have addressed major public policy questions regarding containment of risk and liability on an intergenerational basis – often in a manner that requires the state to assume long-term responsibilities. Clearly climate change too is a long-term responsibility, and whether CCS can effectively 'work alongside' options such as energy efficiency to achieve major changes needs careful consideration.

Nuclear power

Intriguingly, nuclear power is now often referred to as a clean technology.[228] It is under active consideration in many jurisdictions around the world as a power source that can lessen dependence on fossil fuels and increase energy security.[229] These arguments have seen a modest revival in the nuclear energy sector in recent years, although its share of global energy production is predicted to remain fairly constant.[230] Overshadowing any nuclear 'comeback' are the

---

[225] Explanatory Memorandum, Clean Energy Bill 2011, para. 11.13.   [226] Ibid., para. 6.167.
[227] See Durrant, *Legal Responses to Climate Change* (2010), p. 196.
[228] See for example J. Davies and P. Sullivan, 'Nuclear Power Post-Fukushima: A Framework for an Australian Nuclear Future', 30(2) *Australian Resources and Energy Law Journal* 199 (2011).
[229] D. Zillman, 'The Role of Law in the Future of Nuclear Energy', in *Beyond the Carbon Economy: Energy Law in Transition*, eds Zillman et al. (2008), p. 319.
[230] International Atomic Energy Association (IAEA), *International Status and Prospects of Nuclear Power* (2010), p. 5.

inherent risks. The Fukushima disaster, with graphic images of the disabled Daiichi reactor flashed around the world, has again raised the spectre of the destructive force of nuclear technologies.

In the initial enthusiasm for nuclear energy it was predicted that nuclear energy could provide a cheap and highly reliable power source. Currently, around 15 per cent of electricity generated around the globe is produced by nuclear energy,[231] primarily using uranium as the fuel for the fission reaction. In some countries there is a strong reliance on nuclear energy: France (78 per cent), Japan (pre-Fukushima – 30 per cent), Belgium (54 per cent), United States (20 per cent), and Germany (pre-Fukushima – 28 per cent). Interestingly, Germany after the Fukushima incident made a commitment to rapidly phase out nuclear energy.

The possibility of radiation disasters and concerns about the safe operation of plants and handling of nuclear waste have resonated in the Australian polity. Accordingly, there has been a moratorium on nuclear power generation in Australia for many years. Yet Australia has the world's largest source of uranium and is the third largest producer after Kazakhstan and Canada.[232] Given the diametrically opposed views on nuclear power in Australia, it is unlikely to figure prominently in the 'stabilisation wedges' that Australia deploys for transition to a low-carbon future,[233] and thus it is only briefly considered in this chapter.

Nuclear power in the Australian context

Australia has never had commercially operating nuclear power reactors but has had a small reactor for medical purposes. Currently, construction and operation of nuclear power plants and associated facilities is banned by s 10 of the *Australian Radiation Protection and Nuclear Safety Act 1998* (Cth). A series of reviews over many years has identified issues including the safety of nuclear installation operations, the potential for trade in nuclear materials and equipment, the difficulties of dealing with and transporting radioactive waste, and third-party liability. A difficulty that has beleaguered governments has been public antipathy towards the siting of nuclear facilities and towards waste disposal of even the relatively small amounts of nuclear waste generated. A recent Grattan Institute report observes that more work would need to be done to garner public support for nuclear energy.[234]

By contrast, the federal government's Australian Nuclear Science and Technology Organisation released a report in 2006 claiming that nuclear

---

231 IAEA, *Nuclear Power Worldwide: Status and Outlook* (2007); and M. Schneider, A. Froggat and S. Thomas, 'The World Nuclear Industry Status Report 2010–2011 – Nuclear Power in a Post-Fukushima World – 25 Years after the Chernobyl Accident' (Worldwatch Institute, 2011).
232 Geoscience Australia, 'Uranium Resources', <http://www.ga.gov.au/energy/uranium-thorium/uranium-resources.html>.
233 For an argument that a safe and effective regulatory framework could be adopted in Australia to facilitate nuclear energy, see Davies and Sullivan, 'Nuclear power post-Fukushima' (2011), pp. 211–13.
234 Grattan Institute, *No Easy Choices* (2012), p. 12.

power could be a viable alternative to fossil fuels for generating electricity. A prime ministerial task force undertook a review of uranium mining, processing and the future prospects for nuclear energy in Australia.[235] The Switkowski Review found that nuclear generation was a low-emission technology able to provide baseload power at comparatively low cost in Australia. With a change of federal government in 2007, nuclear power 'went off the agenda', due to the Labor Party's prevailing policy against it. This policy was modified in 2011; however, the draft Energy White Paper suggests the Australian government may be open to the possibility of introducing nuclear power as a back-up source of power in the future.[236]

Legislative and regulatory framework

As Sullivan and Davies summarise,[237] legal issues regarding nuclear technology can be categorised as relating to (1) safety (damage due to radiation), (2) security (misuse of nuclear power and materials) and (3) safeguards (non-proliferation). Despite not having a nuclear energy power generation sector, Australia has a surprisingly detailed and complex framework governing nuclear technology (see Table 9.4).[238] Under the legislative framework, regulatory responsibilities are spread across a number of federal government

Table 9.4 Australian Commonwealth nuclear legislation

South Pacific Nuclear Free Zone Treaty Act 1986	Implements international obligations
Nuclear Non-Proliferation (Safeguards) Act 1987	Implements international obligations
Comprehensive Nuclear Test-Ban Treaty Act 1998	To implement Australia's international obligations under the Comprehensive Nuclear Test Ban Treaty when it comes into force
Australian Nuclear Science and Technology Organisation Act 1987	ANSTO is responsible for the operation of Australia's sole nuclear research reactor
Atomic Energy Act 1953	Establishes Commonwealth control over uranium mining
Australian Radiation Protection and Nuclear Safety Act 1998	Regime for regulation of nuclear facilities including preparation, construction, operation and decommissioning
Commonwealth Radioactive Waste Management Act 2005 – was to be repealed and replaced by the National Radioactive Waste Management Bill 2010	Records Commonwealth government decision to establish a facility for the management of radioactive waste in the NT
Environment Protection and Biodiversity Conservation Act 1999	Environmental Impact Assessment and approval required for all 'nuclear actions'

---

[235] Australian Government, 'Uranium Mining, Processing and Nuclear Energy – Opportunities for Australia: Report to the Prime Minister by the Uranium Mining, Processing and Nuclear Energy Review Taskforce (2006), p. 1.
[236] Department of Resources, Energy and Tourism, *Draft Energy White Paper* (2011), p. 219.
[237] Davies and Sullivan, 'Nuclear Power Post-Fukushima' (2011), p. 211.
[238] OECD, *Nuclear Legislation in OECD Countries: Regulatory and Institutional Framework for Regulatory Activities: Australia* (2008).

departments as well as delegated to various entities, such as the Australian Radiation Protection and Nuclear Safety Agency. Legislation at the state and territory level also exists to govern various aspects of the nuclear fuel life cycle.[239]

The current regulatory framework is not oriented towards facilitating nuclear power generation and use. Supporters claim that nuclear power is a zero-emission energy source, with an advantage over renewable energy technologies in that it provides baseload power.[240] Critics point out that it is not viable due to the high capital costs[241] and the long lead time involved in constructing the plant. Other studies have examined the emissions produced in the construction and decommissioning of nuclear plants, and in dealing with fuel and waste, in comparison to renewable energy sources.[242] While the change of policy indicated by the draft Energy White Paper has left the door ajar for nuclear energy in Australia, the comparatively high costs and long delay involved in its implementation suggest that it will not play a major role in addressing climate change in the foreseeable future.

Integration of regulatory measures for technology innovation

With the move to introduce carbon pricing and emissions trading in the CPM, an important question arises as to the relationship between the various elements of federal climate change regulation and technology choice and deployment – with ramifications also for how state governments configure their respective regulatory frameworks.[243] A neoclassical economics approach to this issue prefers regulation that imposes the smallest compliance costs. Accordingly, some see direct laws for renewable energy promotion and energy efficiency as transitional measures that can be phased out once an ETS is in place, on the assumption that a carbon price will itself lead to sufficient investment in renewable energy and energy-efficient technologies. Garnaut is a vocal proponent of this view,[244] commenting that '[w]ith a carbon price in place, current climate change mitigation policies would not be a cost-effective

---

239 Davies and Sullivan, 'Nuclear Power Post-Fukushima' (2011), p. 214.
240 Ibid., pp. 207–8. This neglects the fact that concentrated solar thermal technologies can provide baseload power: see Hearps and Wright, *Zero Carbon Australia Stationary Energy Plan* (2010).
241 See for example B. McNeil, 'The Costs of Introducing Nuclear Power in Australia', 59 *Journal of Australian Political Economy* 6 (2007); and M. Diesendorf, 'Comparing the Economics of Nuclear and Renewable Sources of Electricity', paper presented at Solar2010, the 48th AuSES Annual Conference (Canberra, 1–3 December 2010).
242 M. Jacobson and M. Delucchi, 'Providing All Global Energy with Wind, Water, and Solar Power, Part I: Technologies, Energy Resources, Quantities and Areas of Infrastructure, and Materials', 39 *Energy Policy* 1154 (2011), p. 1156.
243 See for example the review of the Victorian *Climate Change Act 2010* in light of the introduction of the CPM: Victorian Government, 'Review of the Climate Change Act', <http://www.climatechange.vic.gov.au/home/review-of-climate-change-act>.
244 Garnaut, *Garnaut Climate Change Review* (2008), p. 299.

way to reduce emissions. Most, including the Renewable Energy Target and support for household photovoltaics, should be phased out.'[245]

Others, however, warn against such an approach as too focused on least-cost abatement, which neglects broader environmental goals served by maintaining specific measures for renewable energy uptake,[246] and indeed other technological options. The inclusion of significant financing measures for development and commercialisation of renewable energy in the Clean Energy Agreement suggests that the MPCCC favoured the latter view, although the Agreement is largely silent about the Renewable Energy Target other than that it is to be reviewed by the new Climate Change Authority.

An important consideration highlighted by Garnaut is the cost implications of maintaining policies with differing objectives.[247] He recommends removing policies that seek to target emissions already covered, as these will not result in any further abatement and will only increase costs.[248] In the chapter of the Review entitled 'An Australian Policy Framework', Garnaut follows Nicholas Stern in characterising climate change as a market failure, and thus arguing that the central task of climate change policy should be to correct this failure.[249] Garnaut advocates a market-based solution (namely an ETS) rather than non-market-based regulatory measures. Adopting non-market-based instruments assumes 'that government officials, academics or scientists have a better understanding of consumer preferences and technological opportunities than households and businesses. This is generally unlikely and cannot ever be guaranteed.'[250] Accordingly, state and federal laws and policies designed to support certain technologies or to favour change in certain energy consumption habits (that is, energy efficiency) should be reviewed in light of the ETS to identify 'perverse incentives'.[251] The approach favoured is one that adopts technology-neutral measures that leave the process of innovation and the identification of technological solutions to the market, to ensure that emission reductions are achieved at lowest cost to the community and the government.[252]

This approach retains scope for some limited government intervention where that intervention is targeted to addressing market failures. For example, measures to facilitate the commercialisation of new technologies would be acceptable, as they seek to overcome the barrier to investment stemming from the fact that

---

[245] In this sense, see Garnaut, *Update Paper 7: Low Emissions Technology and the Innovation Challenge* (2011), p. 18.
[246] J. Prest, 'A Dangerous Obsession with Least Cost? Climate Change, Renewable Energy Law and Emissions Trading', in *Climate Change Law: Comparative, Contractual and Regulatory Considerations*, eds Gumley and Daya-Winterbottom (2009).
[247] On this point, see also C. Hepburn and S. Fankhauser, 'Combining Multiple Climate Policy Instruments: How Not to Do It', 3(1) *Climate Change Economics* 209 (2010); and S. Sorrell and J. Sijm, 'Carbon Trading in the Policy Mix', 19(3) *Oxford Review of Economic Policy* 420 (2003).
[248] Garnaut, *Garnaut Climate Change Review* (2008), p. 317; and Sorrell and Sijm, 'Carbon Trading in the Policy Mix' (2003), p. 434.
[249] Garnaut, *Garnaut Climate Change Review* (2008), p. 299.
[250] Ibid., p. 317. The Grattan Institute adopts a similar neoclassical economics approach: *Learning the Hard Way: Australia's Policies to Reduce Emissions* (2011).
[251] Garnaut, *Garnaut Climate Change Review* (2008), p. 318.   [252] Ibid., p. 354.

'private investors are not able to capture for themselves the full social value of their innovations'.²⁵³ There are also factors that may require intervention by governments to facilitate investment in network infrastructure related to electricity transmission, natural gas pipelines, CO_2 pipelines associated with sequestration, and transport infrastructure linked to urban planning.²⁵⁴ The legal rules on third-party access to infrastructure are highly pertinent here. An emerging critical difficulty is the considerable investment required to support sustainable forms of energy production.

Arguably, key technology measures such as the RET and the CPM have different objectives. The CPM is focused on achieving emission reductions throughout the economy at the least cost, while the RET and other renewable support measures are directed towards accelerating the commercialisation of renewable energy technologies. Thus renewable energy laws should not be regarded as a distorting subsidy, but rather as a 'price correction' measure that furthers the polluter-pays principle.²⁵⁵ Another pertinent factor is the level of the actual carbon price required to stimulate investment in alternative technologies and innovation. Reliance on a pricing mechanism to make many technologies surveyed in this chapter competitive with existing fossil fuel technologies would require a carbon price much higher than that envisaged under the CPM. Nevertheless, assessing the interaction of various policy mechanisms is important, as emphasised in a report by the Australian National Audit Office. The report concluded that there is a need for renewable energy and other climate change programs to have clear and measurable objectives, as there are often broad, if not multiple, overriding objectives.²⁵⁶

In other jurisdictions, a similar proliferation of legal and regulatory approaches to addressing climate change and supporting the transition to a low-carbon economy is apparent. For example, despite being part of the EU ETS, the United Kingdom has introduced or is planning to introduce a range of additional measures to enable it to meet its emission reduction goal.²⁵⁷ Significantly, these measures include: a feed-in tariff and an Emissions Performance Standard (EPS) to ensure that no new coal-fired power stations are built without CCS, and also to encourage investment in gas. In California, one of the largest economies in the world, a wide range of measures are in place, apart from an upcoming cap-and-trade scheme.²⁵⁸ Many of these existing measures relate to energy efficiency. Specific statutory instruments include a Low Carbon Fuel Standard, to reduce the carbon intensity of transportation fuels by at least 10 per cent by 2020, and Low Emission Vehicle Standards. As part of the

---

253 Ibid., p. 318.
254 Garnaut, *Update Paper 7* (2011) addresses the intervention measures that Garnaut considers acceptable in the technology innovation realm.
255 Prest, 'A Dangerous Obsession with Least Cost?' (2009), p. 190.
256 Australian National Audit Office, *Administration of Climate Change Programs* (2010).
257 Department of Energy and Climate Change (UK), *Energy Market Reform 2011*.
258 California Environmental Protection Agency, Air Resources Board, 'Climate Change Program', <http://www.arb.ca.gov/cc>.

latter, there are proposals to tighten 'tailpipe' and GHG emission standards for new passenger vehicles and measures designed to encourage purchase of plug-in hybrids and zero-emission vehicles. There are standards for renewable technology use in the power sector,[259] such as the introduction of Net Energy Metering[260] and the California Solar Initiative,[261] which includes $2.167 billion from 2007–17 to install 1940 MW of new solar power.

Conclusion

Developments both in Australia and in other key jurisdictions with a similar legal and regulatory background suggest that a portfolio of regulatory measures to support a variety of technological options for climate change mitigation has found favour. Indeed, in Australia, the introduction of a CPM seems to have stimulated interest in technological options for climate change mitigation beyond carbon pricing, especially renewable energy, measures for achieving greater energy efficiency and – to some extent – CCS. The view from the scientific and technological literature suggests that a range of such technologies will be necessary to reduce GHG emissions within the requisite time frame. As a result, it seems likely that Australia will continue to pursue a combination of measures to facilitate innovation and adoption of technologies to address the imperative of avoiding dangerous climate change. The chapter has highlighted, however, that this policy needs to be underpinned by close attention to regulatory frameworks and the barriers that may arise as a result of a lack of integration between the laws and legal frameworks of different jurisdictions. As we will see in the following chapter, this same challenge also arises in the area of regulation of biosequestration and carbon offsets.

---

[259] California Energy Commission, 'Renewables Portfolio Standards (RPS) Proceeding – Docket # 03-RPS-1078', <http://www.energy.ca.gov/portfolio/>.
[260] Customers who install renewable energy generation are eligible for a credit on their electricity bill for any electricity fed back into the grid: California Public Utilities Commission, 'Net Energy Metering', <http://www.cpuc.ca.gov/PUC/energy/DistGen/netmetering.htm>.
[261] California Energy Commission and California Public Utilities Commission, 'About the California Solar Initiative', <http://www.gosolarcalifornia.org/about/csi.php>.

10

Biosequestration and emission reduction regulation in the Australian land sector

Introduction   *page* 339
Land sector abatement: Concepts and technical requirements   341
Legal issues in biosequestration rights   347
Federal regulation of biosequestration and offsets: The Carbon Farming Initiative   350
State-based regulation of biosequestration and offsets   361
Ensuring integration   370
Conclusion   372

Introduction

The conventional regulatory approach to climate change mitigation, as discussed in Chapter 9, has focused attention on reducing emissions of greenhouse gases from electricity generation and energy use. However, both the international climate change regime and many national schemes recognise the scope for mitigation through biosequestration activities: actions in the land use and natural resources sector that reduce emissions (principally but not exclusively CO_2). There are a number of activities that sequester carbon from the atmosphere in sinks such as forests, which make an important contribution to mitigation.[1] Biosequestration, or carbon sequestration, is the term often given to these activities. On a broad definition, biosequestration extends well beyond simply planting more trees to sequester carbon. It may also include activities that reduce forest loss and the associated carbon emissions,[2] as well as those that increase carbon sequestration rates through agricultural and other land management practices. In addition to the broad spectrum of sequestration activities, other land sector activities may reduce emissions of GHGs such as methane. Another widely used term is 'carbon offsets'. As explained in

---
[1] Kyoto Protocol, Arts. 3.3 and 3.4; see also Chapter 2.
[2] For discussion of Reducing Emissions from Deforestation and Forest Degradation (REDD), see Chapter 7.

Chapter 6, this typically refers to reductions in carbon emissions through sequestration or emission avoidance activities that are used to compensate for emissions generated by carbon-producing activities.[3]

In recent years, climate policy at international and national levels has placed increasing emphasis on the contribution of biosequestration activities and land use changes to reducing emissions.[4] Biosequestration and associated activities may lower the cost of achieving overall emission reductions,[5] and some proponents also argue that abatement in the land sector may be achieved more rapidly than transformations in other sectors.[6] In addition, biosequestration could allow for improvements in other aspects of the environment, such as water quality, soil protection or biodiversity conservation.[7] These improvements are termed 'co-benefits'.[8] Internationally, this renewed interest in the mitigation potential of biosequestration is reflected in the pace of investment and enthusiasm for schemes such as REDD.[9] Nationally, Australia now has a federal legislative regime focused on biosequestration, as well as emission reductions from land-use change activities (the Carbon Farming Initiative or CFI), along with an array of state-based schemes.

This chapter explores the development of land sector emissions abatement measures in Australia, including the nation's longstanding initiatives on carbon offsets together with other emission reduction activities in the land sector such as controlled burning. The chapter focuses particularly on the development of biosequestration regulation at the federal and state levels. Discussion of the relevant legislation is prefaced by an overview of the scientific and technical aspects of biosequestration and emission reduction activities, which form a critical underpinning to legal and regulatory efforts. A key challenge in biosequestration regulation is ensuring regulatory coordination and integration. This involves navigating tensions between legal frameworks and federal–state regimes (regulatory coordination), as well as attention to the relationship between biosequestration, biodiversity conservation, land rehabilitation, water catchment management and associated offset projects.[10]

---

3 See J. Ramseur, 'The Role of Offsets in a Greenhouse Gas Emissions Cap-and-Trade Program: Potential Benefits and Concerns', Congressional Research Service, Report to Congress (RL34436), 4 April 2008.
4 R. Kopp, 'Role of Offsets in Global and Domestic Climate Policy', *Resources for the Future*, Research Brief 10–11 (May 2010); and M. Parry, 'A Property Law Perspective on the Current Australian Carbon Sequestration Laws and the Green Paper Model', 36(1) *Monash Law Review* 321 (2010), pp. 328–9.
5 Wentworth Group of Concerned Scientists, *Optimising Carbon in the Australian Landscape: How to Guide the Terrestrial Carbon Market to Deliver Multiple Economic and Environmental Benefits* (2009).
6 A 2009 report found the technical potential abatement from carbon sequestration to be about twice the total current Australian emissions: CSIRO, *An Analysis of Greenhouse Gas Mitigation and Carbon Biosequestration Opportunities from Rural Land Use* (2009), pp. 12–13. As Garnaut points out, '[t]he realisation of a small percentage of that potential would make a significant difference': *Update Paper 4 – Transforming Rural Land Use*, Garnaut Climate Change Review – Update 2011 (2011), p. 22.
7 United Nations REDD Programme, <http://www.un-redd.org/Home/tabid/565/language/en-US/Default.aspx>; see also Chapter 7.
8 The language of 'co-benefits' refers to projects with both positive environmental outcomes and social and economic benefits: see L. Peskett et al., *Making REDD Work for the Poor*, A Poverty Environment Partnership (PEP) Report, September 2008, p. 5.
9 See Chapter 7 above and L. Godden, A. Kallies, R.J. Keenan and J. Peel, 'Reducing Emissions from Deforestation and Forest Degradation in Developing Countries (REDD): Implementation Issues', 36(1) *Monash Law Review* 139 (2010).
10 See for example Stockholm Environment Institute and Greenhouse Gas Management Institute, *Introduction to Offset Policies*, <http://www.co2offsetresearch.org/policy/index.html>.

Land sector abatement: Concepts and technical requirements

Biosequestration is the most prominent of the land sector abatement measures. The term refers to the process by which atmospheric carbon dioxide is absorbed by vegetation through photosynthesis and subsequently stored as carbon in living or dead biomass. Carbon sequestration sites such as trees, vegetation and soils, and possibly even oceans[11] that remove GHGs from the atmosphere are referred to as 'sinks'. Land use activities such as forestry, agriculture and natural resource management can therefore play an important role in mitigating climate change, either by increasing the rate of and capacity for removal of CO_2 from the atmosphere or by reducing emissions of CO_2.[12]

Carbon offsets have emerged as a significant but not unproblematic tool.[13] In technical terms, a carbon offset is generally defined as a tradable quantum of sequestered GHGs and/or greenhouse emissions that have been avoided.[14] In this sense, a carbon offset 'credit' represents a reduction in carbon emissions or an enhancement of carbon removal from the atmosphere through sinks such as vegetation or soil, relative to a business-as-usual baseline. The concept of carbon offsets, and their inclusion in regulatory frameworks for climate change mitigation, is consistent with wider trends that seek to achieve environmental results by establishing markets for 'ecosystem services': essentially a system of credits and debits to integrate environmental costs into economic decision-making.[15] The 'ecosystem services' concept contains an implicit economic valuation of the 'services' that the environment provides to the human world. Similarly, the recognition of biosequestration activities conceives of activities that sequester carbon as providing a 'service' to the climate and broader environment.

Offset credits can be incorporated into an emissions trading scheme, where they can be used by liable emitters alongside the trade and purchase of emission allowances to meet emission reduction obligations.[16] Outside their use in regulated emissions trading, carbon offset credits can be generated within a range of voluntary schemes. These voluntary schemes allow individuals and

---

[11] For example through the controversial practice of 'ocean iron fertilisation': see C. Bertram, 'Ocean Iron Fertilization in the Context of the Kyoto Protocol and the Post-Kyoto Process', 38(2) *Energy Policy* 1130 (2010); and R. Abate and A. Greenlee, 'Sowing Seeds Uncertain: Ocean Iron Fertilization, Climate Change, and the International Environmental Law Framework', 27(2) *Pace Environmental Law Review* 555 (2010); and W. Rickels, K. Rehdanz and A. Oschlies, 'Economic prospects of ocean iron fertilization in an international carbon market', 34(1) *Resource and Energy Economics* 129 (2012).
[12] UNFCCC, *Land Use, Land-Use Change and Forestry – Fact Sheet*, <http://unfcc.int/methods_and_science/lulucf/items/4122txt.php>.
[13] See Chapter 6.
[14] Other GHGs, such as methane, are also commonly included in offset schemes. See P. Dargusch, S. Harrison and J. Herbohn, 'How Carbon Markets have Influenced Change in the Australian Forest Industries', 73(3) *Australian Forestry* 165 (2010).
[15] See discussion in B. Madsen, N. Carroll and K. Moore Brands, *State of Biodiversity Markets Report: Offset and Compensation Programs Worldwide*, <http://www.ecosystemmarketplace.com/documents/acrobat/sbdmr.pdf>.
[16] S. Fankhauser and C. Hepburn, 'Designing Carbon Markets, Part II: Carbon Markets in Space', 38(8) *Energy Policy* 4381 (2010).

organisations to purchase offsets to achieve carbon neutrality in their activities or reduce their carbon footprint.[17] For example, carbon neutrality programs related to air travel offer a means to offset GHG emissions produced during travel while engaging industry and civil society in climate mitigation efforts.[18] There are also schemes outside the credit-generation offset programs that provide financial incentives and subsidies for landowners to sequester carbon in native vegetation or soils.[19]

Land use activities in Australia under the Kyoto Protocol

Australia has long held that emission reductions in its land sector should be an integral component of its contribution to international efforts to reduce GHG emissions. However, the approach to carbon sequestration within the international climate change regime[20] places some important constraints on the regulatory framework for biosequestration and carbon offsets in Australia, especially efforts that might be undertaken at the federal level. Of particular importance are the types of offset credits that will be recognised in an international context, including the distinction between credits that are Kyoto-compliant and those that are not, and the integrity standards applied to international offsets markets.[21]

Under the Kyoto Protocol, net changes in emissions and removals by sinks resulting from land use, land-use change and forestry activities (LULUCF activities) can be used to meet the parties' obligations to reduce emissions.[22] In Australia, only emissions and removals from the land use activities of reforestation, afforestation and deforestation count towards Australia's target in the first commitment period of the Kyoto Protocol.[23] The Australian government elected not to include additional land use activities, such as forest management, grazing land management and crop land management.[24] Nonetheless, under the Carbon Farming Initiative discussed below, a number of offset projects are possible: these include activities that are Kyoto-compliant but may not be counted towards Australia's 2008–12 Protocol target, as well as activities that are not Kyoto compliant.

Australia's decision to limit LULUCF activities counting towards the 2008–12 Protocol target was based on concerns regarding the accuracy of monitoring and

---

17 Department of Climate Change and Energy Efficiency, *National Carbon Offset Standard – Version 1, November 2009* (2009).
18 K. Levin, B. Cashore and J. Koppell, 'Can Non-State Certification Systems Bolster State-Centered Efforts to Promote Sustainable Development through the Clean Development Mechanism?', 44 *Wake Forest Law Review* 785 (2009).
19 For example the work of non-governmental organisations such as Greening Australia, which have been active in promoting tree plantings as a form of carbon offset: <http://www.greeningaustralia.org.au>.
20 See Chapters 2, 6 and 7.
21 The regulatory framework for the CDM establishes important norms and principles to ensure the integrity of offsets. These standards are of particular importance if there is a desire to sell Australian offset credits in international markets. On the CDM, see Chapter 6.
22 Kyoto Protocol, Art. 3.3.
23 For definitions see Kyoto Protocol, *Decision 16/CMP.1: Land Use, Land-Use Change and Forestry – Annex: Definitions, modalities, rules and guidelines relating to land use, land-use change and forestry activities under the Kyoto Protocol* (2006), UNFCCC/KP/CMP/2005/8/Add.3, p. 5.
24 Durrant, *Legal Responses to Climate Change* (2010), p. 157.

verification of activities, and the fluctuation of carbon stocks in agricultural soil, which can make it very difficult to distinguish natural from human-induced changes. There were further concerns about potential losses of forest carbon stocks in any particular commitment period due to fire or drought.[25] Australia's decision in this instance highlights the technical challenges associated with measurement and verification of carbon sequestration activities. In the ongoing international negotiations over future climate change regulation, experts have urged Australia to propose that the rules should be revised to allow nations to incorporate the benefits of full terrestrial carbon accounting, specifically removing the requirement to account for natural as well as human-induced sources of emissions and sinks in crop lands, grazing land, and forest management practice.[26]

Scope for biosequestration in Australia

In Australia, the capacity of the landscape to sequester carbon is considerable,[27] strengthened by the fact that agricultural and forest land uses are a significant aspect of the nation's economic and social fabric.[28] The land-use change associated with terrestrial carbon sequestration also offers opportunities to achieve multiple public policy benefits in Australia, including adaptation to climate change. Carbon plantings can potentially form part of a broader response to repairing degraded landscapes, improving water quality and soil condition, and conserving biodiversity.[29] They also offer new economic opportunities for landholders and build resilience to the effects of climate change.[30]

While the potential for carbon forestry on currently cleared land in Australia is large, the actual amount that may be utilised for biosequestration will be influenced by the carbon price. At a lower carbon price there is less incentive, for instance, for agricultural producers to invest in biosequestration.[31] Thus, realising even a small proportion of the biosequestration potential in Australia will involve overcoming significant technical, financial, legal and social hurdles. It is currently estimated that only about 65 000 hectares of carbon forestry plantings have been established in Australia.[32] In addition, there are risks associated with the scale of potential land-use change associated with carbon sequestration.

---

25 Ibid.
26 Wentworth Group of Concerned Scientists, *Optimising Carbon in the Australian Landscape* (2009), p. 14.
27 Ibid., pp. 4–5; Garnaut, *Update Paper 4 – Transforming Rural Land Use* (2011), pp. 22–5; and S. Eady et al. (eds), *Analysis of Greenhouse Gas Mitigation and Carbon Biosequestration Opportunities from Rural Land Use* (CSIRO, 2009).
28 Garnaut, *Update Paper 4 – Transforming Rural Land Use* (2011), and Garnaut, *The Garnaut Climate Change Review* (2008), especially Chapter 22.
29 Wentworth Group of Concerned Scientists, *Optimising Carbon in the Australian Landscape* (2009), p. 6; and Garnaut, *Update Paper 4 – Transforming Rural Land Use* (2011), pp. 17–20.
30 Ibid., p. 19.
31 P. Polglase et al., *Opportunities for Carbon Forestry in Australia: Economic Assessment and Constraints to Implementation* (CSIRO, 2011).
32 C. D. Mitchell, R. J. Harper and R. J. Keenan, 'Current Status and Future Prospects for Carbon Forestry in Australia', *Australian Forestry* (forthcoming 2012).

Extensive carbon plantings may compete with agricultural land use, with associated consequences for food and fibre production. The impact of revegetation on water availability within a catchment may be potentially significant,[33] although the planted area would need to be quite large to adversely affect water availability.[34]

In sum, achieving a sufficient scale of carbon plantings, while providing co-benefits and reducing associated risks, requires a sophisticated, integrated regulatory and planning framework. For example, it will be necessary to consider how regulations or incentives for different land use activities under carbon offsets interact with broader land use and resource planning frameworks. Any integrated framework has to build upon a sound and systematic process for ensuring the integrity of the sequestration rights at the heart of the offset system.[35] Legal models that facilitate biosequestration also need to be relatively accessible and easy to implement, so that parties are encouraged to participate in the activity.

Integrity standards for carbon offsets

In the development and implementation of biosequestration schemes and emission reduction activities in the land sector, it is critical to ensure that the credits generated represent genuine abatement. To this end, offset programs have developed key integrity standards and associated compliance regimes[36] to ensure that robust abatement is achieved.

Integrity standards call for accurate measurements and estimates of carbon sequestered or emissions reduced by offset activities that are capable of independent verification (the monitoring and verification requirements).[37] Offset activities must also demonstrate that the reduction in emissions would not have occurred without the offset scheme incentive (the additionality requirement).[38] Furthermore, the activity may also need to demonstrate the capacity for long-term preservation of the carbon sink (the permanence requirement);[39] and that it will prevent material increases in emissions elsewhere that would cancel

---

[33] This is recognised in the Australian National Water Initiative: Council of Australian Governments (COAG), *Intergovernmental Agreement on a National Water Initiative* (2004), cls 55–57. See also P. Polglase and R. Benyon, *The Impacts of Plantations and Native Forests on Water Security: Review and Scientific Assessment of Regional Issues and Research Needs* (Forest and Wood Products Australia, 2008).

[34] There are a number of variables to take into account: R. J. Keenan and A. I. van Dijk, 'Planted Forests and Water', in *Ecosystem Goods and Services from Plantation Forests*, eds J. Bauhus, P. van der Meer and M. Kanninen (Earthscan, London, 2010), pp. 82–4.

[35] Parry, 'A Property Law Perspective' (2010), p. 352.

[36] See Chapter 6, and Durrant, *Legal Responses to Climate Change* (2010), pp. 52–3. Voluntary offset programs have also developed a range of standards and protocols, for instance the National Carbon Offset Standard for voluntary programs in Australia: Department of Climate Change and Energy Efficiency, *National Carbon Offset Standard – Version 1, November 2009* (2009).

[37] Department of Climate Change and Energy Efficiency, *Design of the Carbon Farming Initiative, Consultation Paper* (2010), p. 10. For an associated discussion, see Chapter 3.

[38] Ibid. See also the discussion in Durrant, *Legal Responses to Climate Change* (2010), pp. 52–3 and in Chapter 6.

[39] Department of Climate Change and Energy Efficiency, *Design of the Carbon Farming Initiative, Consultation Paper* (2010). See also Chapter 6 for discussion of these issues in the international context.

out the abatement that would otherwise result from the project (the carbon leakage requirement).[40] These requirements can raise complex scientific, technical, legal and institutional challenges for the design and implementation of a regulatory framework for biosequestration and carbon offsets.

Measurement and verification

Monitoring, reporting and verification of the carbon stocks sequestered through biosequestration activities, together with any changes or subsequent emissions or removal of emissions resulting from these stocks, are critical technical challenges in the implementation of biosequestration regimes. Unless the project is relatively small-scale, the estimation of emissions and removals will require the integration of data obtained through remote sensing technology, as well as accurate and precise ground measurements of forest carbon stocks and subsequent stock changes.[41] While the technical capacity to estimate and monitor sequestration for forest-based abatement activities has increased considerably, substantial technical challenges remain for other land sector activities, such as crop land and grazing management, where the increased carbon storage occurs mainly in soils.[42]

Additionality

Additionality is a critical compliance requirement for the generation of carbon offset credits on a project scale and it is currently subject to considerable debate. For Annex I parties to the Kyoto Protocol, additionality is not relevant to the accounting for absolute emissions in respect of activities contributing to national-level emission targets. However, assessment of additionality has been required for projects implemented under Joint Implementation and the CDM.[43] Establishing that an offsets project or activity would not occur in the course of good farm or forest management, or that a project would not be financially feasible without the additional incentive of carbon credits, is a difficult task and is dependent upon a range of assumptions.[44] Determining additionality on a case-by-case basis can impose a heavy administrative burden and it may dissuade landowners and other parties from participating in projects.

Within a test of additionality, it is often assumed that a baseline of emissions that would have occurred without the offset project can be readily determined. This may be at odds with national or project accounting arrangements that use a historical baseline period, such as the 1990 year baseline under the Kyoto Protocol.

---

[40] Ibid.
[41] For further discussion, see Godden et al., 'Reducing Emissions from Deforestation and Forest Degradation in Developing Countries' (2010), pp. 146–9, and Chapter 7.
[42] See Powlson et al., 'Soil Carbon Sequestration to Mitigate Climate Change: A Critical Re-examination to Identify the True and the False', 62(1) *European Journal of Soil Science* 42 (2011); and F. Garcia-Oliva and O. R. Masera, 'Assessment and Measurement Issues related to Soil Carbon Sequestration in Land Use, Land Use Change and Forestry (LULUCF) Projects under the Kyoto Protocol', 65 *Climatic Change* 347 (2004).
[43] See Chapter 6.
[44] M. Power, 'The Carbon Farming Initiative – Too Little, Too Soon?', 1 *National Environmental Law Review* 57 (2011), p. 62; and Environment Defenders Office Victoria, *The Carbon Farming Initiative – Will it Work for You?* (2011), p. 4.

Carbon offset activities that have been supported by existing government funding arrangements or mandated by regulatory requirements are not generally considered additional.[45] Financial additionality, which requires the economic feasibility of the project to hinge on the income generated by the offset credit, was included in the initial Carbon Farming Initiative design proposals. Garnaut recommended removing the financial element of the additionality test on the grounds that there are often multiple motives for land-use change activities that sequester carbon. Furthermore, a requirement of financial additionality, in particular, involves a highly subjective assessment. For example, activities undertaken with a genuine intent to reduce emissions, such as improving livestock feeding and fertiliser management practices, may also happen to be profitable. In addition, a landholder who may wish to undertake biosequestration activities may also be eligible for subsidies to encourage biodiversity plantings or ameliorate land degradation. It will be difficult to determine whether these are additional activities that would not have been undertaken in the absence of the financial incentive. Garnaut argued that ultimately 'what matters is that the sequestration is new and real'.[46] The CFI, discussed below, embodies Garnaut's recommended approach and no longer includes a financial additionality test. It avoids a project-by-project assessment, instead providing classes of activities on 'positive' (allowable) or 'negative' (definitely not allowable) lists that reflect a general consensus as to what activities are considered 'current' or existing practices, as opposed to 'new' practices.[47]

Permanence

Permanence is another key issue for carbon offsetting arrangements in the land use sector. It is complicated by the fact that carbon sequestration achieved though activities such as forestry and agricultural practices is essentially non-permanent. Abatement can be reversed by both natural and human-induced events, such as land clearing, timber harvesting, bushfire, flooding and natural processes of disease and decay.[48] These events, however, may affect only a small proportion of the sequestered carbon offset pool in any one year or accounting period. Further, sustainable management can both minimise the harm resulting from these events and provide for rapid restoration of the affected area.

Even so, the objective of permanence poses considerable challenges to the design of regulatory frameworks for biosequestration, particularly in striking the right balance between protecting against the risk of reversal of abatement through carbon storage, and preserving land use flexibility in the long term.[49] Potential mechanisms to address risks include setting tighter caps on emissions to allow greater room for

---

45 Garnaut, *Update Paper 4 – Transforming Rural Land Use* (2011), pp. 13–14.   **46** Ibid.
47 Other commentators have proposed the development of more general principles to govern additionality rather than relying on the approach of identifying designated classes: Carbon Trust, *Global Carbon Mechanisms: Emerging Lessons and Implications* (2009), pp. 54–8, 79–81.
48 Durrant, *Legal Responses to Climate Change* (2010), pp. 157–60.
49 K. Cuskelly, 'Legal Frameworks for Regulating Biosequestration in Australia', 28 *Environmental and Planning Law Journal* 348 (2011), pp. 351–2.

error;[50] withholding a proportion of credits issued, to serve as a buffer in the case of reversal;[51] using accounting methods that combine time and mass of carbon stored so that a greater amount of carbon would need to be sequestered temporarily to be equivalent to permanent sequestration;[52] including both removals and emissions from carbon sequestration projects in carbon accounting;[53] and allowing the pooling of credits over larger land areas. Considerations of contractual risk allocation and the response of the insurance industry in covering the risks are also pertinent here. The legal issues that pertain to integrity standards are discussed further below in the analysis of the compliance regime for the federal CFI.

As land sector abatement offset schemes are typically implemented on a project-by-project basis rather than an economy-wide basis, ensuring that carbon sequestered or avoided at one location is not cancelled out by increased emissions or reductions in stored carbon elsewhere is a particularly difficult challenge.[54] For example, increasing native vegetation cover in one location to absorb emissions does not guarantee that under pressure of development, vegetation cover will not be cleared elsewhere. Ensuring alignment between national and project-level accounting for carbon offsets, including penalties or requiring emission permits for reducing forest cover, is thus a critical element of regulatory design.

In practice, it may be difficult to implement these requirements, and so some increases in land sector emissions in particular areas may still occur. In particular, if credits are incorporated into broader emissions trading as an alternative compliance mechanism to surrendering emission permits, it enables liable entities to use credits as a substitute for direct emission reductions. If the credit has been issued for an activity that is not able to meet sound verification procedures, is reversed, or only represents business-as-usual activities, any flaws in the integrity of the credit will be magnified,[55] and may undermine the scheme's broader effectiveness in mitigating climate change.

Legal issues in biosequestration rights

In addition to addressing technical and policy questions of additionality, permanence, and the integrity of biosequestration activities, regulation of such schemes also has to resolve certain fundamental legal issues. In the context of

---

50 R. J. Carpenter, 'Implementation of Biological Sequestration Offsets in a Carbon Reduction Policy: Answers to Key Questions for a Successful Domestic Offset Program', 31 *Energy Law Journal* 157 (2010), pp. 162–4.
51 Ibid., pp. 171–5. This approach is used in the CFI: see p. 360, below.
52 K. Rosenbaum, D. Schoene and A. Mekouar, 'Climate Change and the Forest Sector: Possible National and Subnational Legislation', FAO Forestry Paper 144 (Food and Agriculture Organization, 2004), p. 39. A similar approach is taken under the CDM with its temporary and long-term credits, both of which are of limited duration.
53 This approach was explicitly taken in the proposed Australian Carbon Pollution Reduction Scheme, albeit only for those forestry operators who elected to opt in to the scheme.
54 Power, 'The Carbon Farming Initiative' (2011), pp. 58–9; and Environment Defenders Office Victoria, *The Carbon Farming Initiative* (2011), p. 3. The problem of leakage is also discussed in Chapters 6 and 7.
55 Power, 'The Carbon Farming Initiative' (2011), p. 59; Environment Defenders Office Victoria, *The Carbon Farming Initiative* (2011), p. 3; and L. Chiam, 'Abatements and Offsets: Legal Issues in Reducing Emissions and Developing Offsets Projects', 27(1) *Australian Resources and Energy Law Journal* 105 (2007), pp. 110–11.

biosequestration, one of the most significant issues is the legal nature of 'rights' that pertain to carbon sequestration capacity.

Prior to concerns about climate change, emission reductions and carbon sequestration had no value in a defined economic sense, although they may have had utility in other contexts. With the advent of biosequestration and market-based schemes, the need to assign a value to sequestered carbon and emissions avoided arose as an incentive for participation in such schemes. However, in designing biosequestration schemes to capture this value, it was necessary to resolve threshold questions about whether biosequestration and abatement activities, as a novel form of interest, could be incorporated within legal systems. For many people this issue is encapsulated by the query: Can sequestered carbon be owned? While a simple application of the concept of ownership is misplaced, the inquiry nonetheless points to more specific questions as to how the new forms of value that sequestered carbon represents can be recognised in legal terms. For example, can the carbon be categorised as a proprietary interest or not? A related question is that if the sequestered carbon, or indeed avoided emissions, can be recognised as a legally valuable right, then what is the most appropriate legal model to give effect to that right? Thirdly, can carbon sequestration 'rights' be dealt with at law independently of the legal rights that might exist in relation to the surrounding vegetation and/or land? Finally, how does the carbon sequestration 'right' intersect with the wider legal system, and in particular with land registration and planning laws?

Given the novel legal issues raised by biosequestration and avoided emissions in the land sector, there has been considerable experimentation with different legal models. Furthermore, while voluntary biosequestration offset schemes have been in place for some time in some Australian states, the CFI as a federal scheme for biosequestration and land sector emission avoidance credits only came into effect in 2011. In that sense, we are still very much in a phase of 'learning by doing' when it comes to the legal management of biosequestration and offsetting arrangements.

Another important step to enable incorporation of biosequestration and land sector abatement activities in emissions trading schemes is to confer on offset credits an agreed legal status that will allow them to be traded. In this manner, the credit becomes a fungible interest that can be exchanged between parties.[56] Such a right, as noted, may exist independently of any legal rights held with respect to the vegetation or soil in which the carbon is stored, and independently of the rights of the owner of the land on which vegetation, biotic materials, soil and substratum are physically located. In sum, legal recognition of rights to carbon sequestration provides 'flexibility in the ability to manage forest products, carbon credits, and land over time'.[57]

---

[56] N. Durrant, 'Legal Issues in Carbon Farming: Biosequestration, Carbon Pricing and Carbon Rights,' 2(4) *Climate Law* 515 (2011).
[57] D. Hodgkinson and R. Garner, *Global Climate Change: Australian Law and Policy* (LexisNexis Butterworths, 2008), p. 148.

There now exist various legal models for defining carbon sequestration rights.[58] Indeed, some form of proprietary interest is the usual type of legal right that is adopted,[59] as can be seen in the majority of Australian state statutory regimes for biosequestration (see discussion below).[60] In the federal CFI legislation, offset credits generated under the scheme are designated as personal property.[61] Such 'new generation' property concepts are aligned with the new forms of economic value that carbon sequestration capacity represents.[62]

Specific legislation has been necessary to establish an independent legal right in respect of carbon sequestration, as it is unclear whether such rights in relation to forests and the vegetation that contains sequestered carbon can actually exist at common law. At common law, all things inhering on and in the land are regarded as part of the land: that is, as fixtures. Therefore, at common law, the carbon sequestration capacity would 'attach' to land. Statute has now altered this common law position for biosequestration in Australia,[63] and 'rights' to carbon sequestration are a creature of statute.[64] However, the rules governing such rights often draw upon existing legal rules that have been developed for forestry and land management. This derivation has some difficulties, for instance where real property constructs have been used in biosequestration statutes.[65] As Hepburn contends:

> Framing carbon rights within the confines of a common law servitude, whose origins are derivative of feudal England and the law of the commons, is a retrograde act. The process distorts the core characteristics of the sequestration interest.[66]

The need to create new 'fit for purpose' legal forms, rather than to simply adopt and adapt existing ones, highlights the complexity of creating free-standing carbon sequestration rights in a market-based system.[67] However, even the designation of biosequestration rights as a type of statutory property may not overcome all uncertainties about how such rights will function.[68]

The complexity is even more pronounced given that offset credits are designed to operate as a market mechanism,[69] but must also operate concurrently with the

---

58 Durrant, *Legal Responses to Climate Change* (2010), p. 165.
59 N. Durrant, 'Legal Issues in Biosequestration: Carbon Sinks, Carbon Rights and Carbon Trading', 31(3) *UNSW Law Journal* 907 (2008), p. 914.
60 Ibid., pp. 914–17.   **61** *Carbon Credits (Carbon Farming Initiative) Act 2011* (Cth) s 150.
62 For a discussion of how new property forms evolve, see K. Gray, 'Property in Thin Air', 50(2) *Cambridge Law Journal* 252 (1991).
63 Parry, 'A Property Law Perspective' (2010), p. 332.
64 B. Barton, 'Property Rights Created Under Statute in Common Law Legal Systems', in *Property and the Law in Energy and Natural Resources*, eds A. McHarg, B. Barton, A. Bradbrook and L. Godden (Oxford University Press, 2010).
65 S. Hepburn, 'Carbon Rights as New Property: The Benefits of Statutory Verification', 31(2) *Sydney Law Review* 239 (2009), p. 242.
66 Ibid., p. 245.
67 Ibid., p. 271. Durrant reiterates the call for law reform to ensure 'a more consistent, coherent and environmentally credible approach to the recognition and treatment of biosequestration projects across Australia': Durrant, *Legal Responses to Climate Change* (2010), p. 174.
68 Experience with Australian water law reforms involving the legal separation of interests in land and water suggests that the legal character of such rights may still be unclear in certain contexts. See *ICM Agriculture Pty Ltd v Commonwealth* (2009) 84 ALJR 87.
69 M. Passero, 'The Nature of the Right or Interest Created by a Market for Forest Carbon', 2(3) *Carbon and Climate Law Review* 248 (2008).

many layers of land and resource regulation, such as the Torrens land registration schemes.[70] The complexity becomes acute where land transactions are involved: for example, where a landowner wishes to sell his or her land, but it is subject to carbon sequestration credits held by a third party.

The drafters of the Australian federal CFI legislation had to canvass the complex legal issues discussed above in the course of developing a statutory scheme for biosequestration and the abatement of emissions in the land sector. But the legal position is further complicated due to constitutional divisions of legislative power between the Commonwealth and state governments. The Commonwealth arguably has the relevant heads of legislative power under the Constitution, such as the external affairs power, to enact legislation to give effect to international obligations in relation to emissions trading (see Chapters 4 and 5). In this instance, where the Commonwealth is seeking to regulate biosequestration/avoided emissions, the obligations relate to implementing measures to reduce GHG emissions, such as an offset credit scheme. Thus it is argued that the Commonwealth has the requisite legislative powers in areas such as creating an offset credit scheme. However, under the accepted constitutional division of legislative power in respect of land regulation and natural resource managment, the Commonwealth must rely on state jurisdictions to enact relevant legislation to give effect to the carbon sequestration rights, as the states have traditionally regulated matters relating to land and resources. Accordingly, we first discuss the CFI legislation below, and then the various state regimes.

Some transactional and property-related issues may require further clarification as the CFI and Australia's CPM come into operation more fully.[71] Nonetheless, these statutory instruments have begun to put into effect specific provisions that institute proprietary-style interests in respect of carbon sequestration rights,[72] and provisions designed to facilitate the transactional aspects of the trading scheme.

Federal regulation of biosequestration and offsets: The Carbon Farming Initiative

In 2011, the federal government passed legislation to establish the Carbon Farming Initiative,[73] a statutory biosequestration and land use carbon offsets program with the specific objective of providing incentives for reduction of emissions and sequestration in the land sector. The *Carbon Credits (Carbon Farming Initiative) Act 2011* works in conjunction with several other frameworks, notably detailed regulations that underpin its operation.[74] Essentially, the

---

70 P. O'Connor, 'The Extension of Land Registration Principles to New Property Rights in Environmental Goods', in *Modern Studies in Property Law*, vol. 5, ed. M. Dixon (Hart Publishing, 2009), p. 363.
71 Parry, 'A Property Law Perspective' (2010), pp. 356–8.
72 See for example *Carbon Credits (Carbon Farming Initiative) Act 2011* (Cth) Part 11, Div. 3.
73 *Carbon Credits (Carbon Farming Initiative) Act 2011* (Cth).
74 See for example Australian National Registry of Emissions Units Regulations 2011 and amendments to the NGER Act regulations. On the latter, see Chapter 5.

federal legislation focuses on 'relevant' projects and their regulation, relying on state legislation to be the primary vehicle for the creation of the 'legal right' that forms the basis for the offset credits and in relation to matters regarding the registration of those rights (see further below). The CFI scheme will issue credits for eligible emission avoidance (reduction) or sequestration (removal) projects, and it covers a broad range of potentially eligible activities.

Origins of the CFI

The CFI package is generally consistent with the long-held position of the Australian government with respect to emissions and abatement from the land sector. Rather than subjecting forestry and agricultural activities to mandatory emission reduction obligations under an ETS, policies have focused on establishing markets to *reward* non-compulsory emission avoidance and removal activities in these sectors, at least initially (see Box 10.1).[75]

> **BOX 10.1 Federal biosequestration approaches prior to the CFI**
>
> While the Carbon Pollution Reduction Scheme (CPRS) (the proposed emissions trading scheme that developed to the point of draft legislation[76]) provided some scope for regulating and crediting emission removals achieved by biosequestration, it was limited to forestry projects and these were covered only if the project manager decided to 'opt in' to the scheme. The CPRS legislation itself, rather than a separate piece of legislation, provided for the generation of tradable credits known as Australian Emissions Units (AEUs) for eligible biosequestration projects.[77] The proposed scheme focused on reforestation, rather than on the avoidance of deforestation and degradation, and adopted the Kyoto Protocol definition of reforestation. The agricultural sector as a whole was to be initially excluded from the CPRS for reasons of feasibility and cost.[78]
>
> The greatest difference between the biosequestration provisions of the CPRS and the CFI was that once the operators of forestry projects 'opted in' to the CPRS scheme, they became liable entities under that scheme. Therefore, in the event that sequestration levels dropped, operators would have been required to surrender permits for net emissions. This approach was intended to avoid the administrative and compliance burden associated with meeting the integrity standards of additionality and permanence for the forestry sector.[79]
>
> During this time, the federal government also developed a National Carbon Offset Standard, which, together with the *National Greenhouse and Energy Reporting Act 2007* (NGER Act),[80] established reporting and verification safeguards for the voluntary offset

---

[75] This position differs from the approach taken under the New Zealand ETS, which will include the agricultural sector from 2015, with the point of obligation initially placed with processors rather than individual producers. See *Climate Change Response Act 2002* (NZ); *Climate Change (Agriculture Sector) Regulations 2010* (NZ).
[76] For details of the CPRS draft legislation see Chapter 4.
[77] See generally Carbon Pollution Reduction Scheme Bill 2009 (Cth), Part 10.
[78] Australian Government, *Carbon Pollution Reduction Scheme: Australia's Low Pollution Future, White Paper, Vol. 1* (2008), Chapter 6, particularly pp. 6–44. This initial exclusion was based on practical considerations recognising the difficulty of regulating the thousands of individuals and businesses involved in the agricultural sector.
[79] Department of Climate Change, *Carbon Pollution Reduction Scheme*, Green Paper (2008), p. 127.
[80] See Chapter 5.

> **BOX 10.1 (cont.)**
>
> market.[81] Although the CPRS legislation was never enacted, the Standard was used in the period prior to the introduction of the CFI in 2011 to provide an opportunity for Australian businesses, particularly farmers, to develop recognised offset credits for voluntary carbon markets from a range of land-based activities such as improved forest management, revegetation and the storing of soil carbon. The CFI builds on these earlier federal efforts to regulate standards for the voluntary carbon offset market.

The CFI was introduced prior to the enactment of the CPM and was developed to operate in the absence of a domestic emissions trading scheme if need be. If the CPM had not eventuated, offset credits generated under the CFI might have been traded in the international and domestic voluntary markets or by governments with obligations under the Kyoto Protocol.[82] However, as Garnaut cautions, without explicit links to an ETS in Australia, there would not be sufficient domestic demand for offsets and as such the CFI alone would achieve little in the way of mitigation.[83] In addition, the fragmented approach to covering emissions and reductions from the land sector via a project-based offset scheme in the absence of an economy-wide cap created by an ETS would have the potential merely to shift emissions, and it could not guarantee net emission reductions[84] due to the potential for carbon leakage. The integration of the CFI with the CPM is therefore critical.

Creation and surrender of credits under the CFI scheme

The CFI Act establishes a process for the recognition of eligible offsets, and such projects are assessed in relation to certain rules and standards. Further, the Act enables Australian Carbon Credit Units (ACCUs) to be issued for emission avoidance[85] or sequestration[86] achieved by these projects (see Box 10.2). ACCUs are one of the types of unit that can be used to meet liabilities under the carbon pricing mechanism (see Chapter 5 and below). Farmers, forestry operators and other land managers will not have obligations under the CPM legislation.[87] Instead, they can take advantage of ACCUs created from their offset activities.

---

81 Department of Climate Change and Energy Efficiency, *National Carbon Offset Standard – Version One, November 2009* (2009).
82 Kyoto Protocol-recognised credits for afforestation and revegetation projects can be purchased on the international market by governments with emissions obligations under the Kyoto Protocol, or companies with emission obligations under national ETS, as occurs in the European Union. Non-Kyoto Protocol-recognised credits can only be purchased on the voluntary international offset market.
83 Garnaut, *Update Paper 4 – Transforming Rural Land Use* (2011), p. 15.
84 Power, 'The Carbon Farming Initiative' (2011), pp. 58–9.
85 *Carbon Credits (Carbon Farming Initiative) Act 2011* (Cth) s 53. This includes avoidance projects relating to reducing emissions from agriculture and landfill legacy waste.
86 *Carbon Credits (Carbon Farming Initiative) Act 2011* (Cth) s 54. These are projects to remove CO_2 from the atmosphere by sequestering carbon in (or avoiding emission of GHGs from) living biomass, dead organic matter, or soil.
87 However, Power points out that paying people not to pollute, by rewarding emission reduction activities, is inconsistent with the polluter pays principle: Power, 'The Carbon Farming Initiative' (2011), pp. 60–1.

> **BOX 10.2 Core elements of the CFI**
>
> The Australian Carbon Farming Initiative allows:
> - a *project proponent*[88] who is a *recognised offset entity*[89] carrying out an
> - *eligible offset project*, namely, carbon sequestration and carbon avoidance projects that meet the requirements of the CFI Act,
> - to earn *carbon credits* for storing carbon or avoiding emissions.
>
> For an activity to be an *eligible offsets project* under the CFI, the project must:
> - be within the scope of the CFI legislation;
> - be covered by an approved CFI methodology;
> - be on the 'positive list' of activities deemed to be 'additional'; and
> - not be on the 'negative list' of activities – that is, not have adverse environmental and social effects.
>
> Individual projects must also comply with other scheme requirements, including having the necessary water, planning and environmental approvals from all levels of government.

Third parties can then purchase ACCUs to offset their emission obligations under the CPM.

Offsets projects are categorised under the CFI as either Kyoto offsets projects or non-Kyoto offsets projects, depending on whether the emission removals or avoidance can be used to meet Australia's climate change targets under the Kyoto Protocol or an international agreement that succeeds the Protocol.[90] This distinction is important in terms of the potential markets for resulting credits. Kyoto-compliant ACCUs can be used to meet liabilities under the CPM.[91] In the first three years of the scheme, when there will be a fixed price for emission units, liable parties will be able to meet no more than 5 per cent of their obligations using ACCUs. Following this period, when the fixed price is lifted, there will be no limit on the surrender of ACCUs. Offsets project proponents will also be able to sell CFI credits to international markets. Until 2020, businesses will have to meet at least half of their annual obligations each year by buying Australian carbon units (under the CPM) or CFI credits.[92] Under the ongoing CFI non-Kyoto Carbon Fund, the Australian government will purchase non-Kyoto-compliant CFI credits,[93] which cannot be surrendered under the CPM by liable entities. This fund is

---

[88] *Carbon Credits (Carbon Farming Initiative) Act 2011* (Cth) s 60. 'Project proponents' are expansively defined and include those administering Crown lands and native title holders: *Carbon Credits (Carbon Farming Initiative) Act 2011* (Cth) ss 5, 44(4), 46.
[89] Department of Climate Change and Energy Efficiency, 'CFI Activities – Eligible and Excluded', <http://www.climatechange.gov.au/government/initiatives/carbon-farming-initiative/activities-eligible-excluded.aspx> and 'Carbon Farming Initiative Overview', <http://www.climatechange.gov.au/~/media/government/initiatives/cfi/resources/presentations/CFI_overview_presentation_pdf.pdf>.
[90] *Carbon Credits (Carbon Farming Initiative) Act 2011* (Cth) s 55. Any other projects under the Act are classified as Non-Kyoto Offsets Projects. This would include, for example, storage of soil carbon and forest conservation/cessation of logging in native forests.
[91] Non-Kyoto-compliant ACCUs can also be used under the CPM if the project proponent would have been credited with a Kyoto ACCU if the abatement had occurred before the end of the related accounting period for the first commitment period. See *Clean Energy Act 2011* (Cth) Part 6, Div. 2. Regulations may also prescribe ACCUs that can be used under the CPM: *Clean Energy Act 2011* (Cth) s 5.
[92] Department of Climate Change and Energy Efficiency, Explanatory Memorandum, Clean Energy Bill, pp. 11–12, 33, 92, 94, 119.
[93] Department of Climate Change and Energy Efficiency, *Securing a Clean Energy Future: The Australian Government's Plan* (2011), Table 7, p. 127.

intended as an incentive to undertake land-based action such as storing soil carbon, revegetation and forest conservation measures such as the cessation of logging in native forests.[94] Proponents will also be able to sell non-Kyoto credits on international and domestic voluntary markets.

The CFI and CPM are administered under common governance arrangements, with each Act administered by the Clean Energy Regulator.[95] Additionally, Part 4 of the *Climate Change Authority Act 2011* (Cth) establishes the Land Sector Carbon and Biodiversity Advisory Board to advise the government specifically on land sector initiatives. The Board will report annually to the federal parliament about progress on certain land sector and biodiversity measures.[96] Of particular relevance to the CFI, these include measures to help landholders and regional communities capture the benefits of biosequestration. The Board will also advise the Minister administering the $1 billion Biodiversity Fund on the implementation, coordination of research and key performance indicators for biosequestration measures directed towards protecting, managing or restoring biodiverse ecosystems.[97]

CFI integrity standards

The CFI legislation contains a number of key requirements that correspond to the biosequestration integrity standards discussed earlier. Although innovative legal and regulatory models have been instituted by the legislation to ensure the integrity of credits generated under the CFI, several potential weaknesses remain.

Measurement and verification: The determination of eligible offsets projects

The CFI ensures that offset activities are measurable and verifiable through the criteria applicable to the determination of 'eligible offsets projects'.[98] A central requirement in this regard is that the project must be covered by an approved methodology.[99] A methodology provides detailed rules for implementing and monitoring specific abatement activities and for the calculation of credits.[100] Under Part 9 of the CFI Act, the Minister may make or vary a methodology determination applicable to a specified kind of offsets project.[101] This is contingent on endorsement of the methodology proposal by an independent, expert Domestic Offsets Integrity Committee, and by compliance with certain 'offsets integrity standards'.[102] These standards include a requirement that the emission

---

[94] Ibid. Funding of A$250 million over six years from 2012–13 is available.
[95] See *Clean Energy Regulator Act 2011*.
[96] Part 4, Divisions 2 and 4 provide for the composition of the Board and associated committees. The Board's functions are outlined in s 62 of the Act.
[97] *Climate Change Authority Act 2011* (Cth) s 62.
[98] See generally *Carbon Credits (Carbon Farming Initiative) Act 2011* (Cth) Part 4.
[99] *Carbon Credits (Carbon Farming Initiative) Act 2011* (Cth). See particularly s 27(4)(b) and (c).
[100] *Carbon Credits (Carbon Farming Initiative) Act 2011* (Cth) ss 106(1)–(3).
[101] *Carbon Credits (Carbon Farming Initiative) Act 2011* (Cth), particularly ss 106–7.
[102] *Carbon Credits (Carbon Farming Initiative) Act 2011* (Cth) s 106(4)(b). The Committee may endorse or refuse to endorse the proposal under s 112.

abatement achieved by the project is capable of measurement and verification; that the methodologies are consistent with relevant scientific results published in peer-reviewed scientific literature; and, if relevant, that they are consistent with methods determined under the NGER Act.[103]

Any person can submit a methodology for approval. The federal government has approved methodologies for establishing environmental tree plantings, landfill gas recovery, manure management, and savanna fire management (see Box 10.3).[104] The broad coverage of the scheme includes a number of activities that remain scientifically untested and largely theoretical. It is therefore critical that the safeguards in this area are stringently applied.

BOX 10.3 CFI methodologies: A case study

One of the proposed methodologies to be released for consultation and approved under the CFI Act covers savanna fire management in specified vegetation classes in northern Australia.[105] It is designed to achieve co-benefits of employment, income and maintenance of traditional land management practices for Indigenous communities, who will potentially be involved in offsets projects on Indigenous lands.[106]

The methodology covers controlled fire management across savannas in the fire-prone tropical north of Australia. It will reduce the area that is burnt each year and/or shift the timing of this burning from the late dry season towards the early dry season. These measures will result in a net reduction in fuel consumed, thus generating a corresponding reduction in methane and nitrous oxide emissions released by fire over a given area. The methodology applies only to methane and nitrous oxide emissions because the CO_2 released by fire is taken to be reabsorbed by the landscape in the next growing season.

The methodology contains the measurement of annual emission abatement against a pre-project business-as-usual baseline, determined as the average emissions of the accountable GHGs (methane and nitrous oxide) from savanna burning over a 10-year period (prior to the introduction of strategic fire management in the area).[107] The same process is used to calculate annual emissions in the baseline period and annual emissions in the project period, and hence the reduction in emissions that can be claimed as an offset credit.[108] Following these calculations, there is a process to calculate net emission abatement: the difference between the baseline emissions and the emissions for the project year.[109] To implement this method, proponents will be required to acquire and validate vegetation maps and acquire monthly fire maps.[110]

---

103 *Carbon Credits (Carbon Farming Initiative) Act 2011* (Cth) s 133(1)(b), (d), (h).
104 Department of Climate Change and Energy Efficiency, 'Approved Methodologies', <http://www.climatechange.gov.au/government/initiatives/carbon-farming-initiative/methodology-development/approved-methodologies.aspx>.
105 Department of Climate Change and Energy Efficiency, *Carbon Farming Initiative: Draft Methodology for Savanna Burning* (2011).
106 See discussion of the West Arnhem Land Fire Abatement Project, a pilot savanna burning project that has delivered considerable benefits to local Indigenous people, in P. J. Whitehead et al., 'The Management of Climate Change through Prescribed Savanna Burning: Emerging Contributions of Indigenous People in Northern Australia', 28(5) *Public Administration and Development* 374 (December 2008).
107 A 10-year period is thought to provide a reliable long-term sample of emissions from unmanaged fire in project areas, based on a typical fire return interval for savannas.
108 *Carbon Credits (Carbon Farming Initiative) Act 2011* (Cth) Parts 9.1 and 9.2.
109 *Carbon Credits (Carbon Farming Initiative) Act 2011* (Cth) Part 9.3.
110 *Carbon Credits (Carbon Farming Initiative) Act 2011* (Cth) Part 11.1. Part 11.2 details other reporting and monitoring requirements, with project reports to be submitted in regular reporting periods.

Once a project has been approved as an eligible project, the project proponent has ongoing monitoring and reporting obligations for the purpose of verifying the carbon that the offsets represent. Project proponents must report regularly, and an independent audit must accompany the offsets report.[111] A reporting period must be not less than 12 months, and not longer than five years, and it can be specified (by the proponent) in the offsets report.[112] After the end of a reporting period, the project proponent applies for a certificate of entitlement. The certificate specifies the number of ACCUs generated from the offsets project in respect of the reporting period.[113] Again, the operation of these processes will be critical to ensuring the integrity of resulting offsets. As noted earlier, securing offsets is vital; therefore the considerable administrative and compliance burden created by the statutory rules must be adequately supported by personnel and resources.

Additionality: The 'positive list'

To be approved as an eligible offsets project by the Clean Energy Regulator, the emission abatement must be new and additional.[114] The test for additionality provided by the CFI Act requires that the project is of a kind specified in the regulations, and is not already required to be carried out by, or under, a law of the Commonwealth, state or territory.[115] Before recommending that regulations specify a particular kind of project as additional, the federal Minister must request and have regard to advice from the Domestic Offsets Integrity Committee.[116] The Minister must also have regard to whether the carrying out of a project 'is not common practice' in the relevant industry or kind of environment in which the project is to be carried out.[117]

In essence, the regulations create a 'positive list' by specifying a number of different kinds of offsets projects that are deemed to pass the additionality test.[118] These activities include more conventional reforestation projects, such as the establishment of permanent environmental plantings or permanent mallee plantings after 1 July 2007, as well as the re-establishment of native vegetation from residual seed sources through the exclusion of stock, grazing management, management of feral animals or non-native plant species; the application of biochar to soil; and various methane reduction livestock management practices. For projects on the positive list, no further individual assessment is required, removing any need for case-by-case assessment. This approach streamlines administration and reduces the compliance burden for project proponents. However, there is a clear tension here between ensuring that a project

---

[111] *Carbon Credits (Carbon Farming Initiative) Act 2011* (Cth) Part 6, Division 2.
[112] *Carbon Credits (Carbon Farming Initiative) Act 2011* (Cth) s 76.
[113] *Carbon Credits (Carbon Farming Initiative) Act 2011* (Cth) Part 2, Division 3.
[114] *Carbon Credits (Carbon Farming Initiative) Act 2011* (Cth) ss 27(4)d) and 41.
[115] *Carbon Credits (Carbon Farming Initiative) Act 2011* (Cth) s 41.
[116] *Carbon Credits (Carbon Farming Initiative) Act 2011* (Cth) s 41(2).
[117] *Carbon Credits (Carbon Farming Initiative) Act 2011* (Cth) s 41(3). The provision also includes a catch-all clause allowing the consideration of 'such other matters (if any) as the Minister considers relevant'.
[118] *Carbon Credits (Carbon Farming Initiative) Regulations 2011* (Cth) reg 3.28.

does, on the facts, pass the test of additionality, and that an administratively burdensome component of the scheme is minimised.[119] As discussed, additionality is a difficult concept to regulate effectively. Monitoring of the implementation of the CFI additionality test will be, in practice, most important to ensuring the integrity of projects approved under the CFI Act.

Permanence and enforceability

Several provisions in the CFI Act address permanence and the enforceability of offset credits generated under the scheme. First, to be declared an eligible offsets project, a project proponent must be a 'recognised offsets entity' under Part 4 of the Act.[120] Apart from the proponent being a 'fit and proper person',[121] further relevant requirements are specified in regulations.[122] Project proponents must hold the applicable legal right to the carbon abatement generated through the project activities.[123] In addition, all persons holding an eligible interest in the land to be covered by the offsets project must have consented to the project proponent's application for a declaration that the project is an 'eligible offsets project'.[124] Eligible interests include an estate in fee simple in Torrens Title land and any relevant leasehold interests, as well as interests in Crown land (which will be deemed to be held by the relevant Minister) and in Aboriginal lands held under land rights legislation and deemed native title interests.[125]

The need for the offsets project to accommodate prevailing land laws highlights the manner in which the federal government, due to the constitutional distribution of powers, has to rely on state and territory statutes in many key areas, such as land title and registration, in order to ensure the practical operation of the CFI scheme, as well as the enforceability of offset agreements over an extended period of time. Moreover, a robust and nationally consistent legal framework at a state and territory level for recognising carbon rights associated with biosequestration offset activities is important to the effective implementation of the CFI Act, and particularly to achieving objectives of permanence and enforceability of offset credits generated under the scheme. In the discussion of state-based biosequestration regulation below, we consider the extent to which such goals of uniformity may be constrained by federal governance structures.

---

119 The alternative of a case-by-case assessment, coupled with a simple test of additionality such as that employed by the CDM, could also be a way to balance robust factual assessments with reducing administrative burdens: see L. Schneider, 'Assessing the Additionality of CDM Projects: Practical Experience and Lessons Learned', 9 *Climate Policy* 242 (2009). Yet some argue that the CDM test has been compromised to such an extent in practice that many non-additional projects have been approved: see J. M. Drew and M. E. Drew, 'Establishing Additionality: Fraud Vulnerabilities in the Clean Development Mechanism', 23(3) *Accounting Research Journal* 243 (2010), and the discussion in Chapter 6.
120 *Carbon Credits (Carbon Farming Initiative) Act 2011* (Cth) s 27(4)(f).
121 *Carbon Credits (Carbon Farming Initiative) Act 2011* (Cth) s 64(3)(a).
122 *Carbon Credits (Carbon Farming Initiative) Act 2011* (Cth) s 64(3)(d).
123 *Carbon Credits (Carbon Farming Initiative) Act 2011* (Cth) s 27(4)(h), (i) and (5).
124 *Carbon Credits (Carbon Farming Initiative) Act 2011* (Cth) s 27(4)(k).
125 *Carbon Credits (Carbon Farming Initiative) Act 2011* (Cth) ss 44, 45, 45A.

The 'negative list' and additional safeguards

The requirements for determining an eligible offsets project contain some additional safeguards that are intended to minimise risks and maximise potential co-benefits of offset activities. For example, a project must not involve the clearing or harvesting of native forest or the use of material obtained as a result of such clearing or harvesting.[126] The federal Minister may also declare that certain types of projects are excluded from the CFI scheme – the 'negative list' – if there is a material risk that they will have an adverse impact on water availability, biodiversity conservation, employment, the local community, or access to land for agricultural production.[127] Generally, all regulatory approvals should be obtained for the project as well.[128] These may include, for example, water use licences for plantation projects or planning approvals.

Proponents also have some general obligations to consider relevant regional Natural Resource Management plans. This is a potentially important mechanism in Australia to minimise risks associated with water supply or to promote co-benefits associated with biodiversity conservation. Yet arguably the CFI Act does not go far enough to realise this potential; for example, an application for a declaration of an eligible offsets project must only be accompanied by a statement about whether the project is consistent with the regional natural resource management plan pertaining to the project area.[129] While a project proponent must also notify the Australian Clean Energy Regulator if the project becomes inconsistent with such a plan as a result of a change to the project,[130] there is no positive requirement that a project be consistent with such a plan from the outset, nor is there specific provision for consideration of this factor in making a determination of eligibility under the Act.

The government has proposed the development of a co-benefits index to measure positive biodiversity and community benefits of offsets projects. Project proponents will be able to include details of these benefits on the public register of projects, and this information may allow CFI credits to be sold at a premium.[131] For example, the Aboriginal Carbon Fund (a new financial vehicle to attract investment in carbon projects on Aboriginal lands) has argued for specific recognition of carbon credits generated on Aboriginal land, to allow all of the co-benefits associated with such carbon projects to be fully valued and incorporated into a single tradable instrument.[132]

---

126 *Carbon Credits (Carbon Farming Initiative) Act 2011* (Cth) s 27(4)(j).
127 *Carbon Credits (Carbon Farming Initiative) Act 2011* (Cth) s 27(4)(m) provides that the project must not be an excluded offsets project. Section 56 provides that regulations may be made specifying excluded offsets projects.
128 *Carbon Credits (Carbon Farming Initiative) Act 2011* (Cth) s 28 provides that a declaration of an eligible offsets project may be subject to a condition about obtaining all regulatory approvals.
129 *Carbon Credits (Carbon Farming Initiative) Act 2011* (Cth) s 23(1)(g).
130 *Carbon Credits (Carbon Farming Initiative) Act 2011* (Cth) s 83. This notification requirement provides for civil penalties for non-compliance within the specified time frame.
131 Department of Climate Change and Energy Efficiency, *Design of the Carbon Farming Initiative: Consultation Paper* (2010), p. 17. The Act provides for a publicly available register of offsets projects in Part 12, Division 5.
132 Carbon Shift Advisory Pty Ltd and Aboriginal Carbon Fund, *Design of the Carbon Farming Initiative, Consultation Paper: Submission to the Department of Climate Change and Energy Efficiency* (2011), <http://www.climatechange.gov.au/government/submissions/~/media/submissions/cfi/16-aboriginal-carbon-fund.pdf>.

Nevertheless, there remain critical questions as to the extent to which carbon sequestration can achieve emission reduction objectives as well as co-benefits such as biodiversity protection. Statutory covenants, such as those which operate under section 173 of the *Planning and Environment Act 1987* (Vic), or some variant of 'conservation easements' that are widely used in North American jurisdictions,[133] may provide a more 'fit for purpose' regulatory model for these co-benefit objectives, but their interaction with CFI instruments remains unclear.

Ownership, transfer of credits and compliance

Identifying eligible offsets projects that meet integrity standards such as additionality is only one aspect of the task involved in establishing a robust legal framework for the recognition of biosequestration and other land sector activities in emissions trading. Other critical legal elements concern the ownership and transfer of credits generated from such activities, and mechanisms for ensuring compliance with the legislative requirements.

Under the CFI Act, an ACCU – that is, the credit generated from the eligible offset project activity sequestering or avoiding carbon emissions – is deemed to be personal property.[134] Subject to other conditions being met, the credit will only be awarded to those who hold the exclusive right to obtain the benefit of the sequestered carbon and who have registered that right under a Torrens Title land registration system.[135] The holder of an ACCU is held to be the legal owner of the unit and may, subject to relevant statutory provisions, deal with the unit as its legal owner and give 'good discharges for any consideration for any such dealing'.[136] Interestingly, with respect to the registered credit unit, the CFI legislation provides that the guarantee of 'good title' only extends to those who deal with the registered holder of the unit as purchasers in good faith for value, and without notice of any defect in the title of the registered holder.[137] The legislation also explicitly contemplates the creation of equitable interests in respect of credit purchases and transfers.[138] It contains provisions that deal with transfer and registration procedures for credit units and their transmission.[139] There are also provisions that facilitate the sale of Australian credits to international purchasers.[140]

The CFI Act contains some protections to deal with situations in which credits have been issued following the giving of false or misleading information, where a

---

133 Parry, 'A Property Law Perspective' (2010), pp. 347–8.
134 *Carbon Credits (Carbon Farming Initiative) Act 2011* (Cth) Part 11, Div. 3, s 150.
135 *Carbon Credits (Carbon Farming Initiative) Act 2011* (Cth) s 43. The problems associated with this requirement for the integration of existing state biosequestration regimes are discussed below.
136 *Carbon Credits (Carbon Farming Initiative) Act 2011* (Cth) s 150A(1).
137 *Carbon Credits (Carbon Farming Initiative) Act 2011* (Cth) s 150A(2). This terminology relates to the question of the defeasibility of the interest that is sold, and the language echoes the well-established principles of good faith, purchase for value (consideration), and notice in respect of proprietary transactions.
138 *Carbon Credits (Carbon Farming Initiative) Act 2011* (Cth) s 158.
139 *Carbon Credits (Carbon Farming Initiative) Act 2011* (Cth) ss 151–3.
140 *Carbon Credits (Carbon Farming Initiative) Act 2011* (Cth) ss 154–7.

declaration of a sequestration project as an eligible offsets project has been revoked, or where there has been a complete or partial reversal of sequestration.[141] In these situations, project proponents may be required to relinquish ACCUs. For example, relinquishment may be required in cases where there has been a significant reversal of the removal of CO_2 from the atmosphere through a sequestration project, if the loss of carbon stores is *not* attributable to natural disturbance, to reasonable actions taken to reduce the risk of bushfire, or to conduct engaged in by a third person which is beyond the reasonable control of the proponent.[142] Relinquishment may also be ordered where there has been a significant reversal of sequestration due to natural disturbance or conduct by a third person and the Clean Energy Regulator is not satisfied that the project proponent has, within a reasonable time period, taken reasonable steps to mitigate the effect of the natural disturbance or conduct.[143]

If a relinquishment requirement is not complied with, the CFI Act provides for the imposition of a *carbon maintenance obligation* and the specification of which permitted carbon activities should occur in relation to an area of land.[144] There is no strict requirement that such an obligation be registered on land title; however, the Clean Energy Regulator must take all reasonable steps to ensure that a copy of the declaration is given to the project proponent, to each person holding an eligible interest in the area, and to the relevant land registration official.[145]

The legislation creates civil penalties for contravention of various provisions. For example, a person must not engage in conduct that results or is likely to result in a reduction of the specified level of carbon sequestration in the land area, or in an activity that is not a permitted carbon activity.[146] An injunction may also be available for contravention of a carbon maintenance obligation.[147] Despite these compliance and enforcement sanctions under the legislation, monitoring of the scheme to ensure that 'real' reductions in emissions occur and that the integrity of the credits is retained will remain a complex task.

As an additional protection in this area, the CFI Act introduces a 'risk of reversal buffer' for sequestration projects. This mechanism withholds a proportion of the ACCUs credited for abatement activities as a form of insurance against unintended reversal of the offset through natural disturbance such as bushfire or flood or the wilful conduct of a third party.[148] In such situations, the proponent will not be required to relinquish credits unless he or she has failed to take

---

141 *Carbon Credits (Carbon Farming Initiative) Act 2011* (Cth) Part 7.
142 *Carbon Credits (Carbon Farming Initiative) Act 2011* (Cth) s 90.
143 The proponent is also required to notify the Clean Energy Regulator of such a reversal within 60 days of becoming aware of it: *Carbon Credits (Carbon Farming Initiative) Act 2011* (Cth) s 91.
144 *Carbon Credits (Carbon Farming Initiative) Act 2011* (Cth) Part 8, Div. 2.
145 *Carbon Credits (Carbon Farming Initiative) Act 2011* (Cth) s 97(6). Part 3, Division 5 also provides that the relevant land registration official may make such entries or notations on the land register as he or she thinks appropriate.
146 In addition, an owner or occupier of the land must also take all reasonable steps to ensure that there is no further reduction in carbon sequestration level: *Carbon Credits (Carbon Farming Initiative) Act 2011* (Cth) s 97(9) and (10). Part 21 provides for pecuniary penalties for breaches of these provisions.
147 *Carbon Credits (Carbon Farming Initiative) Act 2011* (Cth) Part 8, Div. 3.
148 *Carbon Credits (Carbon Farming Initiative) Act 2011* (Cth) ss 16–17.

reasonable steps to mitigate the effect of the natural disaster on the offset project.[149] This buffer is set at 5 per cent, unless otherwise provided for by the regulations.[150] A 5 per cent buffer may be insufficient 'insurance', particularly given the likely increase in frequency and intensity of natural disasters under climate change in Australia.[151] A more precautionary approach has been taken in the New South Wales ETS, GGAS. This scheme requires that abatement providers demonstrate that there is at least a 70 per cent probability that net carbon sequestration in any given period exceeds the amount credited under abatement certificates.[152] As Cuskelly argues, when combined with a mandatory and rigorous accounting standard, this rule provides an important 'buffer to ensure that the actual amount of carbon sequestered should be greater than that claimed under offsets'.[153]

What is problematic in the CFI statutory scheme is the relatively short time frames over which carbon sequestration levels should be maintained for sequestration projects.[154] This omission could be addressed via the time frames set for crediting periods. Similarly, Durrant argues that the CFI approach does not adequately provide for the significant permanence risks associated with sequestration projects.[155] The relevant rules under the CDM arguably offer a more appropriate precautionary approach.[156] In contrast, the CFI purports to provide a permanent abatement for each permanent credit issued, according to the approved methodology for that project type. There may, however, be some scope to specify such matters in the methodologies approved under the CFI scheme.

State-based regulation of biosequestration and offsets

A perennial challenge faced in Australian environmental governance is the overlapping jurisdiction of state and federal governments. As canvassed in Chapter 4, this consideration is no less pertinent in the area of climate change regulation, and it has particular significance for schemes relating to biosequestration and offsets given the pre-eminent role played by state law in land use management. Notwithstanding the regulatory arrangements put in place at the federal level in respect of carbon pricing and the incorporation of offset credits under the CFI, a

---

149 *Carbon Credits (Carbon Farming Initiative) Act 2011* (Cth) s 91.
150 *Carbon Credits (Carbon Farming Initiative) Act 2011* (Cth) ss 16(2) and 17(2).
151 Power, 'The Carbon Farming Initiative' (2011), p. 63.
152 *Greenhouse Gas Benchmark Rule (Carbon Sequestration) No. 5 of 2003* (NSW), cl 8.3.
153 Cuskelly, 'Legal Frameworks for Regulating Biosequestration in Australia' (2011), p. 360.
154 For example, the NSW GGAS requires that an abatement provider must demonstrate that it is capable of maintaining the carbon sequestration activity for 100 years in order to be accredited as an abatement provider under the scheme: *Greenhouse Gas Benchmark Rule (Carbon Sequestration) No. 5 of 2003* (NSW), cl 5.
155 Durrant, 'Legal Issues in Carbon Farming' (2011), p. 527.
156 For example, under the CDM, only temporary credits may be created for afforestation and reforestation projects. These temporary credits expire either at the end of the commitment period following the one in which they were issued, or following a maximum specified period of between 20 and 30 years. See Chapter 6.

critical component of the legal framework applicable to biosequestration activities will continue to be the existing state and territory statutory schemes for the creation of carbon sequestration rights, and their coordination and consistency with the federal regime.

Federalism constraints

In Australia's federal system of government, the states retain primary power to make laws regarding land use activities associated with offsets schemes. Under the Australian Constitution, the federal parliament has limited matters over which it exercises exclusive jurisdiction.[157] Section 51 vests in the federal parliament powers to make laws about particular subject matters – powers which have been broadly construed by the High Court.[158] Given that Australia is a party to the UNFCCC and the Kyoto Protocol, giving rise to international obligations, the power to legislate with respect to external affairs (s 51(xxix)) effectively allows the federal government to regulate aspects of biosequestration or offset schemes and climate change responses more broadly.

However, in respect of all the federal legislative powers enumerated in section 51, these are shared with the states, subject to the operation of section 109 of the Constitution in the event of inconsistent laws. Many federal environmental laws are intended to operate concurrently with, or in contemplation of, state legislation. This may mean that both federal and state laws apply in respect of a particular project for biosequestration. For example, the federal CFI relies on state statutory provision for the legal recognition of carbon sequestration rights and provides specifically for the concurrent operation of state and territory laws.[159] Further, depending on the interpretation of relevant environmental impact assessment laws, biosequestration projects may be subject to development assessment and approval requirements at both state and federal levels.[160] Federal and state cultural heritage protection requirements may also be relevant.[161] As such, achieving an appropriate regulatory framework for carbon offsets will require coordination between state and federal legislation.

State-based carbon rights legislation

A critical issue for effective implementation of the CFI throughout the Australian states and territories is the crediting requirements under the CFI. To qualify as an

---

157 *Australian Constitution* s 52 (governing Commonwealth places and the Commonwealth public service), s 90 (dealing with the imposition of customs and excise duties) and s 122 (allowing the Commonwealth parliament to make laws for the territories, such as the Northern Territory and Australian Capital Territory, and with respect to offshore areas within the sovereign jurisdiction of Australia).
158 *Australian Constitution* s 51. See Chapter 4.
159 *Carbon Credits (Carbon Farming Initiative) Act 2011* (Cth) s 294.
160 See *Environmental Protection and Biodiversity Conservation Act 1999* (Cth). State-level environmental impact assessment may also be required.
161 *Environment Protection and Biodiversity Conservation Act 1999* (Cth) ss 12–15C. At state level, cultural heritage protection is also covered by planning legislation.

eligible project proponent and thus be able to receive ACCUs, a person must be the holder of an *applicable carbon sequestration right*.[162] This is an exclusive legal right to the benefit of the sequestered carbon that is registered under a Torrens system of land title registration.[163] Such rights are currently solely under state jurisdiction, and to date, the federal government has sought to rely on state regimes for the creation and recognition of legal rights to carbon.[164] Management of the Torrens Title registration system is also a matter that is the responsibility of the states, not the Commonwealth. Over the years, all Australian states[165] have developed legislation that recognises and regulates forestry rights and carbon sequestration rights (see Box 10.4 for an overview of applicable state schemes), although the rights they create differ in legal character. This statutory recognition of the separate proprietary existence of carbon sequestration rights is innovative in a global context.[166] State statutory schemes separate rights to carbon in vegetation (and in some cases, in soil and other biophysical elements) from other property rights in the land,[167] paving the way for carbon offset trading.[168] An important consideration, therefore, is how these state regimes interact with federal initiatives[169] to support the permanence of carbon offsets.

BOX 10.4 Overview of Australian state biosequestration laws

New South Wales was the first state to introduce statutory recognition of carbon sequestration,[170] and indeed to use such rights as the basis for carbon offsets within a state-based emissions trading scheme, the NSW Greenhouse Gas Abatement Scheme (GGAS).[171] In NSW, a carbon sequestration right is a component of broader forestry rights. The *Conveyancing Act 1919* (NSW), which defines and creates these rights, deems them to be a common law *profit à prendre*.[172] The profit (i.e. the natural takings) from the land is held to be the 'legal, commercial or other benefit (whether present or future) of carbon sequestration by any existing or future tree or forest on the land that is the subject of the carbon sequestration right'.[173] The carbon profit (proprietary interest) may be registered on land title under the *Real Property Act 1900* (NSW); however, this is not compulsory, as the validation of the carbon sequestration interest as a *profit à prendre* is not dependent on registration.[174] To enable the recognition and enforcement through the CFI of offsets from projects already created under the NSW carbon sequestration regime (for example, for use

---

162 *Carbon Credits (Carbon Farming Initiative) Act 2011* (Cth) s 5.
163 *Carbon Credits (Carbon Farming Initiative) Act 2011* (Cth) s 43.
164 Durrant, *Legal Responses to Climate Change* (2010), p. 164.
165 The Northern Territory and Australian Capital Territory do not yet have such legislation.
166 Hepburn, 'Carbon Rights as New Property' (2009), p. 246.
167 See for example *Carbon Rights Legislation Amendment Act 1998* (NSW), amending Part 6, Div. 4 of the *Conveyancing Act 1919* (NSW); *Climate Change Act 2010* (Vic) ss 21–24, replacing the regime under the *Forestry Rights Act 1996* (Vic); *Forest Property Act 2000* (SA) s 3A; *Forestry and Land Title Act 2001* (Qld), inserting Part 6B into the *Forestry Act 1959* (Qld); *Forestry Rights Registration Act 1990* (Tas); and *Carbon Rights Act 2003* (WA). For a comparison of different statutory approaches, see Hepburn, 'Carbon Rights as New Property' (2009). Note that the designation 'proprietary' is used, although it is recognised that this will comprehend a spectrum of varying types of proprietary and quasi-proprietary rights.
168 A. Thompson and R. Campbell-Watt, 'Carbon Rights: Development of the Legal Framework for a Trading Market', 2 *National Environmental Law Review* 31 (2004).
169 The earlier CPRS Bill did not establish the carbon sequestration 'right' but relied on state enactments to provide that such statutory models were compatible with Part 10 of the CPRS Bill.
170 *Conveyancing Act 1919* (NSW) Part 6, Div. 4.   171 See Chapter 4.
172 *Conveyancing Act 1919* (NSW) s 88B.   173 *Conveyancing Act 1919* (NSW) s 88AB(2).
174 *Conveyancing Act 1919* (NSW) ss 87A, 88F, 88EA.

BOX 10.4 (cont.)

in GGAS), the CFI Act imposes CFI permanence obligations,[175] such as replenishment of carbon stocks, that are not currently present in the NSW legal framework.

A substantively similar approach is taken in Tasmania under the *Forestry Rights Registration Act 1990* (Tas).[176] Until the commencement of legislative amendments passed in 2011 (see Box 10.5), Queensland too recognised carbon sequestration rights as a *profit à prendre*, but incorporated them under rights to natural resource products rather than considering them to be a type of forestry right.[177] The agreements to establish natural resource products may be registered on title under the *Land Act 1994* (Qld); however, registration is not compulsory. These agreements can be used to vest the right to all or part of the natural resource product in another person.[178] Transitional provisions under the Queensland legislation will enable the existing *profit à prendre* interests to continue unaffected.[179]

In all three jurisdictions, access and maintenance issues are left to the parties to resolve. In New South Wales, for example, parties *may* enter into a forestry covenant to impose an obligation requiring, among other things, the provision of access to, or the maintenance of trees or forests on, land that is the subject of any carbon sequestration right.[180] In Queensland, the *Forestry Act 1959* (Qld) provides specifically that a registered owner of freehold land may enter into an agreement that may grant him or her the right to enter the land to establish, maintain or harvest natural resource products.[181]

In South Australia,[182] carbon sequestration rights are recognised as a right in the nature of a chose in action.[183] Ownership of the carbon right is tied to ownership of the vegetation until separated by the registration of a Forest Property (Carbon Rights) Agreement under the Act.[184] There are important protections ensuring security of title;[185] however, there exist no specific provisions relating to access and monitoring.

By contrast, in the states of Western Australia, Victoria and now Queensland, carbon rights are treated as a *de novo* statutory interest in land and are not aligned with any common law form of real property. These regimes are potentially more conducive to integration with the CFI, although this may not resolve all potential disputes about how such interests should be interpreted.

The *Carbon Rights Act 2003* (WA) provides that a carbon right in land will be validated where an approved carbon rights form is registered over freehold or Crown land.[186] Registration of carbon rights is dealt with by the *Transfer of Land Act 1893* (WA),[187] and is a prerequisite for recognition of the carbon right as a separate interest in land.[188] As Hepburn notes, however, 'registration does not guarantee the quality or scope of the carbon right. Hence, the quantity of carbon which may be stored on the particular land, and the issue of whether any stored carbon will continue to remain on that land, continue to be unpredictable factors unaltered by the registration process.'[189] In Western Australia, carbon covenants (as distinct from the underlying carbon right) must also be registered. Such a covenant amounts to a contractual agreement regarding the terms, conditions, rights and entitlements relating to the carbon right. The covenant may, for example, be a mechanism

---

175 *Carbon Credits (Carbon Farming Initiative) Act 2011* (Cth) s 22.
176 See *Forestry Rights Registration Act 1990* (Tas) ss 5 and 6.
177 *Forestry Act 1959* (Qld) s 61J(1). A natural resource product is defined to include trees, vegetation and roots, carbon stored in a tree or vegetation and carbon sequestration by a tree or vegetation (Schedule 3).
178 *Forestry Act 1959* (Qld) s 61J(3)(c).   179 *Land Titles Act 1994* (Qld) s 521ZC.
180 *Conveyancing Act 1919* (NSW) s 87A. See also New South Wales Government, Registrar General's Directions, 'Forestry Covenants', <http://rgdirections.lpi.nsw.gov.au/deposited_plans/easements_restrictions/positive_covenants/forestry_covenants>.
181 *Forestry Act 1959* (Qld) ss 61J(3) and 61J(5).
182 The Act provides for Forest Property (Carbon Rights) Agreements which separate the ownership of carbon rights from the ownership of the trees. For a discussion of the South Australian regime, see Hepburn, 'Carbon Rights as New Property' (2009), pp. 252–3.
183 *Forest Property Act 2003* (SA) s 3A(1). The Act was amended by the *Forest Property (Carbon Rights) Amendment Act 2006*, which commenced in July 2007.
184 *Forest Property Act 2003* (SA) s 3A(2).
185 For example, such agreements will bind successors in title to the land and carbon rights: *Forest Property Act 2003* (SA) s 9.
186 *Carbon Rights Act 2003* (WA) ss 5, 6. The coverage of Crown land is notable.
187 *Transfer of Land Act 1893* (WA) Part 4, Division 2A.   188 *Carbon Rights Act 2003* (WA) s 6(1).
189 Hepburn, 'Carbon Rights as New Property' (2009), p. 251.

> **BOX 10.4 (cont.)**
>
> detailing management obligations for maintenance of the forest vegetation to which the sequestration right 'attaches', so as to provide for permanence requirements.[190] The inclusion of this mandatory mechanism in the WA scheme is a clear advantage in the context of ensuring the integrity of carbon offsets in a broader ETS.
>
> In Victoria, a comprehensive regime for carbon sequestration has been introduced, under the *Climate Change Act 2010* (Vic). The legislation is designed to facilitate development of the emerging carbon sequestration industry, bring Victoria's legal framework in line with national approaches, and allow Victorians to easily participate in state and national sequestration efforts.[191] Carbon rights relating to carbon sequestration in forests, vegetation and soils are recognised as an exclusive right to the economic benefits associated with carbon sequestration.[192] The legislation characterises them as an interest in land,[193] which may be registered on title.[194] There is also provision for landholders to enter into a Forestry and Carbon Management Agreement with the owner of the forest carbon right and others, so as to provide for management obligations in relation to carbon sequestration.[195] It is mandatory for an agreement to address certain management obligations, such as the timing and extent of any harvesting of vegetation.[196] An agreement can be recorded on the land register, and the obligations specified in the agreement 'run with the land', binding any person who derives title to an estate or interest in the land from a party to the agreement.[197] Such matters are important, as they relate to the long-term maintenance of carbon stocks. The Victorian regime also incorporates other unique legal models in its detailed provision for carbon sequestration on Crown land.[198]

Evaluating the potential for regulatory coordination between federal and state biosequestration laws is made more difficult by the inconsistencies that exist between state regimes for forestry and carbon sequestration rights. The primary concern is that states have employed significantly different terminology (and arguably inappropriate legal concepts) to describe carbon sequestration rights.[199] As explained in Box 10.4, some states deem carbon rights to constitute recognised common law forms of property, such as a *profit à prendre* or a chose in action. Other states define carbon rights as a new form of interest, characterised by specific statutory provision. While the CFI has broad deeming provisions, which appear to overcome the problem of different state 'carbon sequestration' interests participating in the scheme, reform at a state level to ensure consistency across jurisdictions would help with the transparency of the scheme.

State regimes also rely to varying degrees on private law in areas such as contracts to further define matters associated with carbon rights, such as

---

[190] A key issue in Western Australia is the effect this will have on the Crown's ability to grant mining leases. See Blake Dawson, 'Carbon Farming Initiative: implications for resource companies in Western Australia', Environment Matters, 28 June 2011, <http://www.blakedawson.com/Templates/Publications/x_article_content_page.aspx?id=62743>.
[191] Carbon rights were previously regulated under the *Forestry Rights Act 1996* (Vic), which was repealed in 2010 following the enactment of the *Climate Change Act 2010* (Vic).
[192] *Climate Change Act 2010* (Vic) ss 22, 23, 24.   [193] *Climate Change Act 2010* (Vic) s 27.
[194] *Climate Change Act 2010* (Vic) s 26(6)–(7).   [195] *Climate Change Act 2010* (Vic) ss 27, 28.
[196] *Climate Change Act 2010* (Vic) s 29.
[197] *Climate Change Act 2010* (Vic) ss 32, 33, 34. However, s 28 specifically states that any obligations under such an agreement are not a restrictive covenant.
[198] *Climate Change Act 2010* (Vic) Part 5. See Cuskelly, 'Legal Frameworks for Regulating Biosequestration in Australia' (2011), p. 358 for further discussion.
[199] Hepburn, 'Carbon Rights as New Property' (2009), p. 246; see also Durrant, *Legal Responses to Climate Change* (2010), pp. 165–71.

management obligations and land access requirements. These requirements are typically outlined in agreements, which may need to be registered on title, depending on the jurisdiction. The CFI legislation, as noted, has specific provisions dealing with ownership of carbon credits and the regulation of transactional matters, yet the various states' approaches to the articulation of the carbon sequestration rights and associated management obligations remain important to achieving adequate guarantees of permanence to support the integrity of offset credits. Additionally, most regimes, with the exception of the Victorian and the new Queensland laws, have concentrated on carbon rights associated with forestry, rather than soil carbon or agricultural practices that reduce emissions such as methane. This may require rectification, as offset credits for soil carbon activities are now permitted in the CFI regime, and these activities promise to contribute significantly to abatement.

Overall, state legislation (Table 10.1) reveals a patchwork of approaches to the legal formulations of carbon rights, the extent to which these rights are recorded on land title, the scope of supporting maintenance agreements, and the degree of consistency with the CFI. The interaction of the CFI Act and the state biosequestration regimes exemplifies the major challenge of achieving coordination between regulatory and governance arrangements in a federal system.

Table 10.1 Key provisions of Australian state biosequestration legislation

TAS *Forestry Rights Registration Act 1990*

Section 3

'Carbon sequestration right', in relation to land, means a right conferred on a person (by agreement or otherwise) to the legal, commercial or other benefit (whether present or future) of carbon sequestration by any existing or future tree or forest on the land.

Section 5

(1) A forestry right shall, notwithstanding any rule of law or equity to the contrary, be deemed to be a *profit à prendre* but shall not confer a right of exclusive possession of the land to which it relates.

...

(3) Every forestry right shall, when executed by the parties signing it, have the force and effect of a deed.

NSW *Conveyancing Act 1919*

Section 87A

Forestry right', in relation to land, means ... (b) a carbon sequestration right in respect of the land. 'Carbon sequestration right', in relation to land, means a right conferred on a person by agreement or otherwise to the legal, commercial or other benefit (whether present or future) of carbon sequestration by any existing or future tree or forest on the land after 1990.

Section 88AB

(1) A forestry right shall, for all purposes, be deemed to be a *profit à prendre*.

(2) If a forestry right consists in whole or in part of a carbon sequestration right, the *profit à prendre* deemed to exist by subsection (1) in relation to the carbon sequestration right consists of the following:

  (a) the profit from the land is taken to be the legal, commercial or other benefit (whether present or future) of carbon sequestration by any existing or future tree or forest on the land that is the subject of the carbon sequestration right,

  (b) the right to take something from the land is taken to be the right to the benefit conferred by the carbon sequestration right.

10 BIOSEQUESTRATION AND EMISSION REDUCTION REGULATION 367

Table 10.1 (cont.)

SA *Forest Property Act 2000*
Section 3A
(1) The capacity of forest vegetation to absorb carbon from the atmosphere is a form of property (a carbon right) in the nature of a chose in action.
(2) A carbon right attaches to the forest vegetation to which it relates, and ownership of the right passes with ownership of the forest vegetation unless ownership of the right is separated from ownership of the forest vegetation under a forest property agreement.

VIC *Climate Change Act 2010*
Section 21
In this Act 'forest carbon right' means (a) a carbon sequestration right; or (b) forestry right; or (c) a soil carbon right.
Section 22
In this Act 'carbon sequestration right' means an exclusive right to the economic benefits associated with carbon sequestered by vegetation other than vegetation that has been harvested, lopped or felled.
Section 25
(1) A forest carbon right is an interest in land.
Section 26 Creation and transfer of forest carbon rights
(1) A forest carbon right may be created by the execution of an instrument of transfer of the right by a person who is the registered proprietor of a freehold or leasehold estate in land to which the right applies. [...]

WA *Carbon Rights Act 2003*
Section 5
(1) A person may lodge with the Registrar, for registration, a form for the creation of a carbon right in respect of freehold land or Crown land.
Section 6
(1) When a carbon right form is registered, (a) the carbon right that is the subject of the form is created and becomes a separate interest in the land in respect of which the form is registered; and (b) the proprietor of the carbon right is each person who is registered as a proprietor of that interest.
(2) A carbon right has effect even if it has the same proprietor as the affected land.
(3) [A] carbon right is, in relation to the affected land (a) a hereditament; and (b) an encumbrance.
Section 8
(1) A proprietor of a carbon right has the legal and commercial benefits and risks arising from changes to the atmosphere that are caused by carbon sequestration and carbon release occurring in or on land in respect of which the carbon right is registered.
Section 10
(1) The proprietor of a carbon right may ... enter into a covenant with one or more persons who have an interest in land.
(2) The covenant can be for a right, obligation (which can include a positive covenant) or restriction in relation to land.

QLD *Land Act 1994* s 373R; *Land Title Act 1994* s 97N; *Forestry Act 1959*, s 61K[200]
In this division *carbon abatement interest*, for land, means an interest in the land consisting of the exclusive right to the economic benefits associated with carbon sequestration on the land.
carbon abatement product means all or any of the following –
(a) living biomass; (b) dead organic matter; (c) soil; (d) carbon sequestration by, and carbon stored in, a carbon abatement product mentioned in paragraphs (a) to (c).
carbon sequestration, for living biomass, dead organic matter or soil, includes
(a) the process by which the biomass, matter or soil removes and stores carbon dioxide from the atmosphere; and
(b) the use of the biomass, matter or soil to avoid, reduce or eliminate greenhouse gas emissions.

---

[200] These provisions were introduced by the *Waste Reduction and Recycling Act 2011* (Qld), discussed in Box 10.5.

Interaction of the CFI Act and state biosequestration regimes

As discussed, the CFI Act does not create the rights in sequestered carbon *per se*;[201] rather, the legislation establishes the framework for generating credits (ACCUs) from the carbon sequestered. ACCUs are issued to the project proponent, which the CFI Act defines as the person who is responsible and legally entitled to carry out the project, and who holds the applicable carbon sequestration right.[202] As the applicable carbon sequestration right is something created by state law, it can take a number of forms, as we have seen, from a *profit à prende* to a distinct statutory property right. The CFI Act seeks to take account of this variation.[203] Nevertheless, section 43 provides for a number of fundamental features that the state-created rights must exhibit in order to be 'applicable carbon sequestration rights'.

A carbon sequestration right is admissible in the CFI if it is an exclusive right to obtain the benefit of sequestered carbon. The right may be created in relation to both Torrens system land and state and territory Crown land, so long as it is either a legal interest in land, or, according to state or territory law, an interest in land or a right which 'runs with the land'. Significantly, as far as the state biosequestration regimes are concerned, the rights must be registered under a Torrens system of land title registration. As can be seen from our preceding discussion of the state regimes, this poses some problems. First, with regard to the exclusive character criterion, we have seen that only in the new regimes of Queensland and Victoria is the right to the legal and commercial benefits of the sequestered carbon expressly described as an exclusive right.[204] Second, the registration requirement may prove to be problematic, as registration is not mandatory under state laws. Registration in the applicable land titles registry is possible but not mandatory in New South Wales, Tasmania, Victoria and South Australia.[205] In South Australia, forest property agreements can be registered, but not the carbon rights themselves.[206] Special enforcement provisions apply to registered forest property agreements.[207] Only in Western Australia and the amended Queensland regime (see further Box 10.5) is registration on land title required for the creation of the carbon sequestration right.[208] The other key requirement of applicable carbon sequestration rights is permanence, as ACCUs are only granted for carbon that is sequestered 'permanently'.[209] The degree to which the different state regimes

---

[201] Rather, these rights must be created by state and territory law: Explanatory Memorandum, Carbon Credits (Carbon Farming Initiative) Bill 2011 (Cth), p. 27.
[202] *Carbon Credits (Carbon Farming Initiative) Act 2011* (Cth) s 5.
[203] Explanatory Memorandum, Carbon Credits (Carbon Farming Initiative) Bill 2011 (Cth), p. 28.
[204] *Climate Change Act 2010* (Vic) s 22; *Land Act 1994* (Qld) s 373R.
[205] *Real Property Act 1900* (NSW) s 47; *Forestry Rights Registration Act 1990* (Tas) s 5(2); *Climate Change Act 2010* (Vic) s 26(6); *Forest Property Act 2000* (SA) s 7(1).
[206] *Forest Property Act 2000* (SA) s 7(1). [207] *Forest Property Act 2000* (SA) s 9.
[208] *Carbon Rights Act* 2003 (WA) s 6; *Land Act 1994* (Qld) (new) s 373S.
[209] According to the Explanatory Memorandum, sequestration is considered permanent if it is maintained on a net basis for approximately 100 years: Explanatory Memorandum, Carbon Credits (Carbon Farming Initiative) Bill 2011 (Cth), p. 63.

will achieve long-term compliance with this requirement is for future determination. The Australian government has expressed its intention to work with state and territory governments to 'note the existence on land titles of permanence obligations'.[210] The provisions of the CFI mean that the state biosequestration regimes must create long-term exclusive interests or rights that are registrable and which can burden (i.e. be legally 'enforceable' for) more than one type of tenure. The changes made in Queensland, outlined in Box 10.5, may need to be mirrored in other state schemes to enable effective integration with the CFI.

> **BOX 10.5 Achieving greater integration with the CFI: The Queensland biosequestration regime**
>
> In recognition of the incompatibility of its biosequestration regime with the CFI Act, the Queensland parliament passed legislation designed to bring its regime into line with the CFI.[211] The amendments to the Queensland legislation expand the types of land tenures on which carbon sequestration can occur, and provide for the creation of an exclusive 'cross-tenure long-term right' to carbon sequestration projects, referred to as a *carbon abatement interest*.[212] By requiring registration of the carbon abatement interest, the legislation provides for the longevity of the right, consistent with the CFI principle of permanence. Registration also notifies third parties dealing with the land of the existence of the right which 'attaches' to that land. The new form of right was introduced because the existing *profit à prendre* rights can only be held by a lessee of land granted for agricultural or timber plantation purposes and are to be held as an 'improvement',[213] which is a kind of proprietary interest that does not meet the requirements under the CFI Act.
>
> As the Crown is the statutory owner of the carbon abatement right for native forest timber and vegetation on non-freehold land in Queensland, the amendments extended the biosequestration regime to reserves and unallocated state land under the *Land Act 1914* and to state forests and timber reserves under the *Forestry Act 1959*. The new legislation provides for the Crown's capacity to vest its carbon abatement interest in a landholder.[214] Again, these rights must be registered.[215] Under the CFI Act, Crown lands ministers have an obligation to provide written certification that the state or territory will not deal with the land in a way that is inconsistent with the carbon sequestration right.[216] As such, when deciding whether to vest the interest in another person, the relevant minister in Queensland must consider whether the person is likely to deal with the interest in a way that is inconsistent with the right.[217]
>
> The amendments also extend the types of eligible projects beyond forestry by enabling an interest to be created in respect of dead organic matter and soil.[218] In order to ensure that projects in their jurisdiction have the best chance of being eligible for crediting under the CFI, and to facilitate and benefit from the provisions of the CFI Act, other states may need to consider introducing similar amendments.[219]

---

210 Explanatory Memorandum, Carbon Credits (Carbon Farming Initiative) Bill 2011 (Cth), p. 72. See also *Carbon Credits (Carbon Farming Initiative) Act 2011* (Cth) s 133(1)(f)(i).
211 *Waste Reduction and Recycling Act 2011* (Qld).
212 *Land Act 1994* (Qld) Part 8C. Explanatory Memorandum, Waste Reduction and Recycling Bill 2011 (Qld), p. 5.
213 *Forestry Act 1959* (Qld) 61J(1A).   214 *Forestry Act 1959* (Qld) s 61M.
215 *Forestry Act 1959* (Qld) s 32AA.
216 *Carbon Credits (Carbon Farming Initiative) Act 2011* (Cth) s 27(4)(h).
217 *Forestry Act 1959* (Qld) s 61N.   218 *Land Title Act 1994* (Qld) s 97N.
219 Explanatory Memorandum, Waste Reduction and Recycling Bill 2011 (Qld), p. 29.

Ensuring integration

Offset schemes are frequently promoted as able to generate multiple co-benefits. In addition to providing new income streams for landholders, carbon plantings and other forms of biosequestration such as soil char can potentially form part of a broader response to repairing degraded landscapes, improving water quality and soil condition, conserving biodiversity, and adapting to climate change.[220] Yet depending on the nature, scale and distribution of the offset activities, activities that may well mitigate climate change may nonetheless carry environmental risks. For example, extensive monoculture plantations may sequester carbon, but they have potentially adverse effects on biodiversity, catchment water yield, and the availability of agricultural land.[221]

Promoting co-benefits and minimising associated environmental risks will require a sophisticated integration of land use planning and complementary regulatory measures for other natural resources, such as water and land registration systems, as well as additional incentives to promote participation in offset activities that generate multiple benefits. Now that land sector offsets are to be included in a broader ETS, additional safeguards such as caps on their use may also be warranted.[222]

Land use planning and registration

The location and nature of revegetation offset projects within a catchment is critical to their potential effect on catchment water yield, and their potential contribution to biodiversity corridors and reserve networks. Catchment management planning is widely promoted as the mechanism for achieving integrated natural resource management (NRM). As discussed above, the CFI Act requires proponents to consult relevant regional NRM plans to determine whether their projects are consistent with the applicable plan.[223] Yet, more specific and targeted obligations and resources are required to ensure the achievement of co-benefits and the minimisation of risks associated with offsets in the catchment management arena. Catchment Management Authorities (CMAs) are typically under-resourced. Consequently, their capacity to integrate complex layers of NRM in the context of catchment management can be seriously compromised

---

[220] See discussion in Wentworth Group of Concerned Scientists, *Optimising Carbon in the Australian Landscape* (2009); and Garnaut, *Update Paper 4 – Transforming Rural Land Use* (2011).

[221] For a discussion of the potential impact of plantations on water security, see Polglase and Benyon, *The Impacts of Plantations and Native Forests on Water Security* (2008). See also Department of Climate Change and Energy Efficiency, *Design of the Carbon Farming Initiative: Consultation Paper* (2010), pp. 8–9.

[222] The CPM includes an initial cap on the use of offset credits. During the three-year fixed price period, liable entities can meet no more than 5 per cent of their obligations using ACCUs. However, in the flexible price period there will be no limit on the surrender of ACCUs.

[223] *Carbon Credits (Carbon Farming Initiative) Act 2011* (Cth) ss 23(1)(g) and 83.

in practice.²²⁴ It has also proven very difficult to effectively transfer real power and capacity to regional institutions. As a result, relying on existing institutions such as catchment management authorities to integrate carbon offset schemes with other NRM objectives is problematic. Further, the existing legal framework provides only a limited institutional mandate for the integration of the CFI, as there are many other layers of law and regulation that impinge on biosequestration and offset activities. Moreover, to achieve effective transparency of biosequestration obligations, these rights and obligations should be routinely and uniformly recorded in legal instruments such as land use planning schemes.²²⁵

Furthermore, it may be necessary to ensure that the regulatory regimes for other natural resources potentially affected by offset activities are complementary. The National Water Initiative recognises that activities that may use significant amounts of surface water and groundwater, such as large-scale plantation forestry, may be required to obtain a water access entitlement under relevant state water management legislation.²²⁶ Without a holistic perspective on NRM and land use planning, a regulatory framework based on biosequestration and offset credits may develop into an isolated regime that fails to factor in the repercussions of other matters such as water allocation. On the other hand, the CFI offers the potential for significant investment in rural Australia, which could contribute to long-term gains in productivity and sustainability while achieving climate change mitigation.

Additional incentives for biodiversity plantings

The carbon price incentive for biosequestration activities could be bolstered with additional incentives to encourage biodiversity through co-investment with projects developed under a scheme such as the CFI.²²⁷ This type of multi-benefit planting has driven most international carbon forestry investment to date,²²⁸ although Australian initiatives associated with biodiversity conservation on private land have generally relied on government as the major investor. Programs have employed offsets for land clearing,²²⁹ conservation stewardship payments associated with management agreements and conservation covenants, and auctions for ecosystem services to be provided by landholders.²³⁰ Such

---

224 For a discussion of the potential difficulties of integrated catchment management planning, see D. Farrier, 'Fragmented Law in Fragmented Landscapes: The Slow Evolution of Integrated Natural Resource Management Legislation in NSW', 19 *Environmental and Planning Law Journal* 89 (2002); and D. Farrier, 'Integrated Land and Water Management in New South Wales: Plans, Problems and Possibilities', 5 *Australasian Journal of Natural Resources Law and Policy* 153 (1998).
225 O'Connor, 'The Extension of Land Registration Principles to New Property Rights in Environmental Goods' (2009), p. 363.
226 COAG, *Intergovernmental Agreement on a National Water Initiative* (2004), cls 55–57.
227 Garnaut, *Update Paper 4 – Transforming Rural Land Use* (2011), pp. 17–20.
228 M. Kapambwe and R. Keenan, *Biodiversity Outcomes from Carbon Biosequestration*, Report prepared for the Victorian Department of Sustainability and Environment, 2009.
229 For an overview, see E. Solomon, 'Security for Biodiversity Offsets in New South Wales', 28 *Environmental and Planning Law Journal* 92 (2011).
230 An example is the Bush Tender program in Victoria. See Department of Sustainability and Environment (Victoria), *BushTender: Rethinking Investment*, 2008, p. 1.

schemes could be linked to the CPM, whereby the government could purchase the non-carbon ecosystem services, and a third party would still be able to purchase the carbon sequestration credits. Similar ideas have been promoted by conservation groups.[231] In the United States context, Carpenter proposes rolling over current conservation programs, whose initial purpose may have been habitat conservation, to credit systems under cap-and-trade programs.[232] The introduction of targeted governance arrangements to support land sector and biodiversity initiatives within the CFI package establishes some important institutional capacity to implement some of these suggestions on a trial basis.[233]

Conclusion

The pressing issue of responding to climate change has seen the evolution of new sources of 'value' in practices and activities that sequester carbon and reduce GHG emissions. The legal system has responded by developing novel regulatory models to facilitate their use. In part, the legal system has used familiar property law concepts, but increasingly the existing models of property forged in an earlier era have been found to be inadequate or unsuited to the new tasks.

Accordingly, in Australia there has been the introduction of a completely new statutory system at a national level. It addresses scientific and technical concerns regarding the integrity of biosequestration and land sector offsets to ensure that real gains are made in reducing emissions. At the same time the CFI Act has provided some answers to complex legal questions surrounding the legal character of the sequestered carbon, and/or the avoided emission activities, and how the credits generated are to function in multilevel trading schemes. While there remain significant challenges in effectively coordinating the scheme within a federal governance system, integrating it with other areas of environmental and natural resource management, and ensuring adequate monitoring and compliance, the potential contribution of land-use change to long-term emission reductions is much closer to realisation in Australia.

---

[231] For example, establishing a fund to provide additional funding to projects which improve biodiversity: Environment Defenders Office Victoria, *The Carbon Farming Initiative* (2011), p. 6.
[232] Carpenter, 'Implementation of Biological Sequestration Offsets' (2010), pp. 172–3.
[233] For example the Land Sector Carbon and Biodiversity Advisory Board.

11

Adaptation to climate change through legal frameworks

Introduction *page* 373
Nature of climate change adaptation   374
Coastal adaptation: Sea-level rise   384
Adapting to climatic variability: Water scarcity and increased flood risk   390
Natural disasters: Bushfire risk and adaptive responses   396
The effectiveness of legal frameworks in Australia   401
Regional adaptation: Climate change displacement   401
Conclusion   406

Introduction

Much of the focus in climate law to date has been on mitigation approaches for decreasing greenhouse gas emissions in the atmosphere and minimising their effects. Until recently, adaptation has received much less attention.[1] In general terms, adaptation means action to manage the consequences of a changed climate and reduce human vulnerability to the effects of climate change. There was early concern that a focus on adaptation would distract from efforts to mitigate climate change.[2] Now mitigation and adaptation are recognised as 'interdependent policy strategies'.[3] A sharp demarcation between them is regarded as unhelpful, although the extent to which each is given priority in any given circumstance will vary.[4] Adaptation can take many different forms according to how responses to climate change are conceived and implemented. Law has a pivotal role in identifying risks, and in formulating and implementing adaptation responses.

This chapter considers the manner in which legal frameworks can facilitate adaptation to climate change, given the increasing effects felt around the world. It explores the general nature of adaptation and how this concept has been translated

---
[1] R. Pielke et al., 'Lifting the Taboo on Adaptation', 445 *Nature* 597 (2007), p. 598.
[2] N. Grist, 'Positioning Climate change in Sustainable Development Discourse', 20 *Journal of International Development* 783 (2008).
[3] A. Macintosh, 'A Theoretical Framework for Adaptation Policy', in *Adaptation to Climate Change*, eds T. Bonyhady, A. Macintosh and J. McDonald (Federation Press, 2010), p. 39.
[4] Ibid.

373

into law, before turning to focus on specific case studies of law and adaptation in Australia and the Pacific region.[5] These scenarios deal with coastal impacts and sea-level rise, water governance to account for increased variability, natural disasters, and the displacement of communities. Although grounded in local circumstances, they will confront many communities across the globe.

Nature of climate change adaptation

There has been increased acknowledgment in the scientific community of the 'imperative' of adaptation,[6] given the extent of climate change that is an unavoidable result of existing and likely future levels of GHG emissions.[7] The longevity of GHGs such as CO_2 in the atmosphere means that even if emissions were drastically reduced in coming years, there is likely to be little reduction in the rate of global warming in the following few decades. For instance, the Fourth Assessment of the IPCC in 2007 found that if concentrations of GHGs are maintained at 2000 levels, further warming of about 0.6°C is expected by 2099.[8] Consequent upon such global warming, sea-level rise is also expected to continue for many centuries.[9] Under a low-emission scenario, this is likely to be between 0.19–0.38 m by 2099.[10]

In 2009 climate scientists preparing the 'Copenhagen Diagnosis' warned that if global emission rates continued at present-day levels, just 20 more years of emissions would give a 25 per cent probability of a temperature rise exceeding 2°C. Global sea level is likely to rise at least twice as much as projected in the 2007 IPCC report.[11]

For Australia[12] and the Pacific region,[13] projected warming scenarios foreshadow a spectrum of severe climate change impacts, which raise multiple

---

5 Adaptation challenges are also being addressed in many other parts of the world. For an introduction to the American literature on the topic, see D. H. Cole, 'Climate Change, Adaptation, and Development', 26 *UCLA Journal of Environmental Law and Policy* 1 (2007); D. Farber, 'Climate Adaptation and Federalism: Mapping the Issues', 1 *San Diego Journal of Climate and Energy Law* 259 (2009); and K. A. Miller, 'Climate Change and Water in the West: Complexities, Uncertainties and Strategies for Adaptation', 27 *Journal of Land Resources and Environmental Law* 87 (2007).
6 J. McDonald, 'The Adaptation Imperative: Managing the Legal Risks of Climate Change Impacts', in *Climate Law*, eds T. Bonyhady and P. Christoff (Federation Press, 2007).
7 IPCC, *Climate Change 2007: Impacts, Adaptation and Vulnerability: Contribution of Working Group II to the Fourth Assessment Report of the Intergovernmental Panel on Climate Change* (Cambridge University Press, 2007), Chapter 18.
8 IPCC, *Climate Change 2007 Synthesis Report: Summary for Policy Makers* (IPCC Secretariat, 2007), pp. 7–8.
9 Australian Academy of Science, *The Science of Climate Change: Questions and Answers* (2010), pp. 12–13, <http://www.science.org.au/policy/climatechange2010.html>.
10 IPCC, *Climate Change 2007 Synthesis Report* (2007), pp. 7–8. This is based on the B1 low-emission scenario.
11 I. Allison et al., *The Copenhagen Diagnosis, 2009: Updating the World on the Latest Climate Science*, Executive Summary (UNSW Climate Change Research Centre, 2009). See also I. Allison et al., *The Copenhagen Diagnosis: Updating the World on the Latest Climate Science*, 2nd edn (Elsevier, 2011).
12 Predictions described below are taken from CSIRO, *Climate Change in Australia: Technical Report 2007*, Executive Summary (2007), pp. 10–12. Regional climate change projections in this report are drawn from international climate change research, including from the Fourth Assessment Report of the IPCC and a large body of climate research that has been undertaken for the Australian region in recent years.
13 Predictions for the Pacific region are derived from IPCC, *Climate Change 2007: Impacts, Adaptation and Vulnerability* (2007), 16.1–16.5.

adaptation imperatives (see Box 11.1). The risks of climate change include threats to the quality of life and to property, profound changes to ecosystems, detrimental effects on human health, risks to major infrastructure and primary industries, significant losses of biodiversity, and at a regional scale, the very viability of some small island states.[14]

> **BOX 11.1 Adaptation imperatives in Australia and the Pacific region**
>
> In Australia, the number of hot days is predicted to increase substantially, particularly in the central and north-western regions, portending an increase in heat-related deaths. Reduced rainfall, higher evaporation, and increased frequency and extent of drought are expected for southern Australia. Climate change, when combined with natural climate variability, is predicted to lead to increases in the frequency and intensity of extreme weather events. In southern Australia, bushfires have caused massive loss of life and property in recent years,[15] and it is likely that extreme fire weather will occur more often, with longer, more intense fire seasons. Similarly, flooding in southern Queensland and regional Victoria and in the northern rivers area of New South Wales has had devastating effects on property and infrastructure. This is a precursor to likely increases in heavy rainfall events and associated flooding under climate change. Coastal settlements around Australia face heightened risks from sea-level rise and more frequent storms and flooding. The intensity of tropical cyclones is likely to increase, with the northern and western regions of Australia bearing the brunt of these storms. Significant ecosystem damage is also projected as early as 2020, including mass coral bleaching on the Great Barrier Reef due to rising sea temperatures, and ocean acidification. In addition, the physical climatic and weather changes predicted to result from global warming will have consequential effects on ecosystems, such as biodiversity loss,[16] socioeconomic impacts in areas such as water supply, agriculture, and the provision and maintenance of infrastructure,[17] and effects on human health.[18]
>
> The adaptation challenges faced by many small islands in the Pacific Ocean extend to population displacement and total submergence of the sovereign territory of some states. Other predicted consequences are less acute but still pose long-term adaptation challenges. They include the potential for accelerated coastal erosion; saline intrusion into freshwater sources and increased flooding from the sea; less rainfall coupled with accelerated sea-level rise, compounding the threat to water resources; and the degradation of natural systems such as coral reefs and forests. These challenges are exacerbated by the vulnerability of small islands to climate change due to factors such as a high degree of geographical exposure (the small islands of the Pacific are located in a region already prone to extreme weather events such as tropical cyclones), limited financial and technological capacity to adapt, and more pressing problems in many of the countries involved, such as political instability, rapid population growth, and a limited resource base. Even so, there remains considerable scope for adaptation by communities in these regions, for example in the areas of food security and greater protection against natural disasters.

---

[14] See for example S. Aswani and R. Hamilton, 'Integrating Indigenous Ecological Knowledge and Customary Sea Tenure with Marine and Social Science for Conservation of Bumphead Parrotfish (*Bolbometopon muricatum*) in the Roviana Lagoon, Solomon Islands', 31 *Environmental Conservation* 69 (2004); and J. Barnett and J. Campbell, *Climate Change and Small Island States: Power, Knowledge, and the South Pacific* (Earthscan, 2010). See also the discussion in Chapter 1.
[15] For example, the Black Saturday bushfires in Victoria in February 2009 resulted in over 100 deaths in one day.
[16] R. MacNally et al., 'Biodiversity and Climate Change', Report commissioned by the Garnaut Climate Change Review, Australian Centre for Biodiversity, Monash University, June 2008; and W. Steffen et al., *Australia's Biodiversity and Climate Change* (CSIRO, 2009).
[17] R. Garnaut, *Garnaut Climate Change Review* (Cambridge University Press, 2008), p. 121. For discussion of mitigation and adaptation opportunities in the rural sector see R. Garnaut, *Update Paper 4, Transforming Rural Land Use*, Garnaut Climate Change Review – Update 2011 (2011).
[18] See generally World Health Organization, *Protecting Health from Climate Change: Connecting Science, Policy and People* (2009).

Definitions of adaptation and the role of law

The idea that human and natural systems will have to adapt over time to changing circumstances clearly is not new,[19] nor confined to the effects of climate change.[20] However, climate change introduces a strong impetus for socioecological change. Under this aegis, the concept of adaptation has evolved from primarily a 'response to impacts' to an approach that assesses the capacity of vulnerable groups to adapt, as well as initiating proactive responses that build resilience.[21] Climate change adaptation measures are driven either by modelling potential impacts of climate change on systems to determine an appropriate policy response, or as more pre-emptive and broadly based assessments of vulnerability that are combined with policies for strategic enhancement and development of adaptive capacity to respond to these impacts.[22] The latter model is more suited to the complex and dynamic nature of socioeconomic systems.[23]

Nonetheless, the influence of early systems research remains evident in the prevailing IPCC definition of adaptation as 'the adjustment of natural or human systems in response to actual or expected climatic stimuli or their effects, which moderates harm or exploits beneficial opportunities'.[24] This concept underpins much international and national adaptation governance.[25] Useful to understanding the role of law in adapting to climate change is the typology proposed by the IPCC, summarised in Table 11.1. The diversity of adaptive responses shows that potentially viable measures are not confined to public policy and top-down governance options, but exist along a spectrum of public, community and private actions, and these options are not mutually exclusive.[26] There may also be specific barriers to effective adaptation.

Legal and policy development

Adaptation actions affect a broad range of socioeconomic sectors, which means an effective response will require the coordination of the efforts of a large number of actors, from governments to businesses and individuals. While law

---

19 Barnett and Campbell, *Climate Change and Small Island States* (2010), pp. 1–17. **20** Ibid.
21 J. McDonald, 'Mapping the Legal Landscape of Climate Change Mitigation', in *Adaptation to Climate Change: Law and Policy*, eds Bonyhady, Macintosh and McDonald (2010), p. 2; see also R. L. Ison, *Systems Practice: How to Act in a Climate Change World* (Springer, 2010).
22 See for example P. Tan, 'Adaptation Measures for Water Security in a Changing Climate: Policy, Planning and Law', in *Adaptation to Climate Change: Law and Policy*, eds Bonyhady, Macintosh and McDonald (2010), pp. 137–8.
23 For example Ison, in *Systems Practice* (2010), argues that adopting a linear cause–effect model reveals a fundamental error in framing the problem, as it fails to incorporate the dynamic and multifaceted nature of socio-ecological systems.
24 IPCC, *Climate Change 2007: Impacts, Adaptation and Vulnerability* (2007), 18.1.2.
25 See for example N. Stern, *The Economics of Climate Change : The Stern Review* (Cambridge University Press, 2007) and Garnaut, *Garnaut Climate Change Review* (2008) in Australia.
26 J. B. Ruhl, 'Climate Change Adaptation and the Structural Transformation of Environmental Law', 40 *Environmental Law* 343 (2010), p. 382. In other words, private markets and institutions will adapt by means of individualised and industry-wide strategies and initiatives.

Table 11.1 Types of adaptation

Type	Converse
Anticipatory or proactive adaptation	*Reactive adaptation*
Adaptation before impacts of climate change are observed	Adaptation after impacts of climate change have been observed
Planned adaptation	*Autonomous or spontaneous adaptation*
Resulting from a deliberate policy decision and based on an awareness that conditions have changed or are about to change and that action is required to return to, maintain or achieve a desired state	Adaptation that does not constitute a conscious response to climatic stimuli but is triggered by ecological changes in natural systems or by market or welfare changes in human systems
Public adaptation	*Private adaptation*
Initiated and implemented by governments at all levels and usually directed at collective needs	Initiated and implemented by individuals, households, or private companies and usually in the actor's rational self-interest

Source: Intergovernmental Panel on Climate Change, *Climate Change 2001: Impacts, Adaptation and Vulnerability: Contribution of Working Group II to the Third Assessment Report of the IPCC*, Glossary of Terms (Cambridge University Press, 2001).

and associated governance structures are central to many types of strategic adaptation and planning, these institutions themselves often remain tied to stationary modes of decision-making and retrospective adjustments of damage. If law and policy institutions are to guide more 'proactive' adaptation,[27] then there will need to be a coordinated approach in which legal and policy responses dynamically evolve alongside technological, economic and social adaptation.[28]

In light of the magnitude, complexity and scale of climate change, a number of commentators have attempted to develop a theoretical basis for building law and governance systems that will support adaptation.[29] For example, J. B. Ruhl envisages a structural transformation of environmental law, with the goals of equitably managing the harms and benefits of climate change.[30] Systems of law and governance will be required to respond to environmental alterations as a result of climate change, and will have to manage the direct environmental impacts of human adaptation responses, including, for example, increased pressure on scarce water resources.[31] Ruhl identifies structural trends likely to occur in law, including a shift from 'front-end' decision methods relying on robust predictive capacity to 'back-end' decision methods relying on active adaptive management, and an increased reliance on multi-scalar governance networks.[32]

---

[27] N. Leary et al., 'A Stitch in Time: General Lessons from Specific Cases', in *Climate Change and Adaptation*, eds N. Leary et al. (Earthscan, 2008); J. Birkmann and K. von Teichmann, 'Integrating Disaster Risk Reduction and Climate Change Adaptation: Key Challenges, Scales and Norms', 5 *Sustainability Science* 171 (2010); and Tan, 'Adaptation Measures for Water Security in a Changing Climate' (2010).
[28] Ison, *Systems Practice* (2010), pp. 13 and 260.
[29] Ibid. See also R. K. Craig, '"Stationarity is dead" – Long Live Transformation: Five Principles for Climate Change Adaptation Law', 34 *Harvard Environmental Law Review* 9 (2010).
[30] Ruhl, 'Climate Change Adaptation and the Structural Transformation of Environmental Law' (2010), pp. 375–6.
[31] Ibid., p. 377.
[32] These trends are selected for emphasis from a list of ten structural trends in environmental law: see discussion, ibid., pp. 391–433. 'Multi-scalar' in this context refers to the existence of multiple levels of governance, from the local level (e.g. building of sea walls) to the state and federal level (e.g. water security and food security policies), regionally (e.g. planning for migration associated with climate change) and at a global level (e.g. financing arrangements for adaptation activities in developing countries).

Ruhl's work offers a lens through which to scrutinise legal and governance developments in international and Australian law that seek to adapt to climate change. To date, most legal responses to adaptation in Australia have involved changes to conventional front-end decision methods, for instance through the exercise of planning and development controls to deter maladaptive behaviours.[33] Law can also have a more proactive role in setting measures for dealing with risks and situations of uncertainty through the application of the precautionary principle,[34] particularly as adaptation will often need to occur in situations where, although it is established that there will be broad-scale change, its precise local ramifications may not be clear.[35] Potentially, law can serve another important function in coordinating actions taken in different areas by different actors to build resilience to the effects of climate change.[36] This will necessitate coherent and coordinated governance frameworks to institute a systemic response to adaptation issues, rather than the *ad hoc*, piecemeal approach that has often characterised regulatory efforts to date.

International law

As climate change responses now operate across multiple scales and organisations, regulators at both the international and domestic levels have embraced the need to invest in adaptation. Moreover, more action on adaptation has been initiated as we have come to a better understanding of the time lags between the causes and effects of human activities, due to the extended lifespan of GHG emissions in the atmosphere, and as the potential impacts of climate change have been more precisely identified.

At the international level, however, the legal framework to support adaptation remains rudimentary.[37] While adaptation has been part of the international climate change law and policy landscape since concerns about human-induced climate change were first raised, only minimal references to it are made in the UNFCCC and Kyoto Protocol, as noted in Chapter 2. In the UNFCCC, Article 4(1)(e) requires all parties 'to cooperate in preparing for adaptation to the impacts of climate change' and to develop appropriate and integrated plans in areas such as coastal zone management, water resources, and agriculture, and for the protection and rehabilitation of drought-affected areas. Article 4.4 also places a specific obligation on developed country parties to assist developing country parties that are particularly vulnerable to the adverse effects of climate change in meeting the costs of adaptation.

---

[33] N. Durrant, *Legal Responses to Climate Change* (Federation Press, 2010), p. 250.
[34] See generally J. Peel, *The Precautionary Principle in Practice: Environmental Decision-Making and Scientific Uncertainty* (Federation Press, 2005).
[35] McDonald, 'Mapping the Legal Landscape of Climate Change Mitigation' (2010), p. 3.
[36] See generally J. Ruhl and J. Saltzmann, 'Climate Change, Dead Zones and Massive Problems in the Administrative State: A Guide for Whittling Away', 98 *California Law Review* 59 (2010).
[37] Instead the focus is placed principally on mitigation actions: see Chapter 2.

Likewise, the Kyoto Protocol addresses adaptation only in passing. In the provision made for the CDM, Article 12.8 directs the development of arrangements to ensure that a share of the proceeds from certified project activities is used to help vulnerable developing country parties meet the costs of adaptation. As a consequence, the Adaptation Fund was established, financed from a 2 per cent levy on certified emission reductions issued for CDM project activities.[38]

In international climate change negotiations, developing countries have become increasingly vocal about investment in adaptation. This has taken on an ethical dimension, given that those likely to bear the greatest costs of climate change have made a relatively limited contribution to the problem in terms of historical emissions, and currently have poor capacity to deal with the impacts.[39] Consequently, investment in adaptation has become an essential part of the balanced package of outcomes expected of any international climate agreement. Both the Copenhagen Accord and the objectives of the Cancun and Durban COPs, establishing the Cancun Adaptation Framework and Green Climate Fund respectively, devote significant attention to questions of adaptation financing, including the necessary institutional and technical infrastructure to support developing countries in establishing adaptation policies and actions.[40]

Regional developments

In the Pacific region, Australia has been an active player in policy discussions of adaptation issues, particularly through the Pacific Islands Forum. In a Call to Action in 2009, Forum leaders noted the particular challenges of climate change for Pacific Island states:

> [C]limate change is the great challenge of our time. It threatens not only our livelihoods and living standards, but the very viability of our communities. Though the role of Pacific Island States in the causes of climate change is small, the impact on them is great. Many Pacific people face new challenges in access to water. The security of our communities and the health of populations is placed in greater jeopardy. And some habitats and island states face obliteration.[41]

The Forum has since been actively involved in advocating for increased support from the international community to assist small-island developing states in both

---

38 UNFCCC, *Decision 10/CP.7, Report of the Conference of the Parties on Its Seventh Session, Held at Marrakesh from 29 October to 10 November 2002 – Addendum – Part 2: Action Taken by the Conference of the Parties* (2002), FCCC/CP/2001/13/Add.1. See also Chapters 2 and 6, above.
39 U. Srinivasan, 'Economics of Climate Change: Risk and Responsibility by World Region', 10 *Climate Policy* 298 (2010).
40 See UNFCCC, *Decision 2/CP.17, Outcome of the Work of the Ad Hoc Working Group on Long-Term Cooperative Action under the Convention* (2011), FCCC/CP/2011/9/Add.1, 'Enhanced Action on Adaptation', elaborating the modalities and composition of the Adaptation Committee and considering the activities the Committee is to undertake. See also UNFCCC, *Decision 3/CP.17, Launching the Green Climate Fund* (2011), FCCC/CP/2011/9/Add.1.
41 Pacific Islands Forum, *2009 Forum Leaders' Communiqué, Annex A* (6 August 2009), <http://forum.forumsec.org/pages.cfm/strategic-partnerships-coordination/climate-change>.

mitigation and adaptation efforts, and in coordinating associated development assistance in the region.[42]

National law and policy

Significantly, greater policy and legal development is occurring at national and sub-national levels of governance, suggesting a bottom-up dynamic in this area of climate change regulation. In Australia, it is clear that the issue of adaptation occupies a central place in the policy agenda. In 2007 the Council of Australian Governments agreed on a National Climate Change Adaptation Framework. This framework focuses on addressing knowledge gaps that inhibit effective adaptation, and meeting the needs of business and the community for information on the effects of climate change. The Framework supports the efforts of decision-makers to bring climate change into policy and operational decisions at multiple scales and across many sectors, a position that is reinforced by the more recent Productivity Commission report on barriers to adaptation.[43] The Australian government has also played an important role in developing overarching programs to provide information and funding for state and local initiatives (see Table 11.2).

State governments have likewise been active in developing climate change policies on issues related to adaptation. As part of their general climate change policies, some states and territories include general adaptation plans, which identify sectors at risk.[44] In addition, most jurisdictions have developed more specific action plans, particularly around coastal planning (see Table 11.3). Queensland, for instance, has a comprehensive two-pronged plan for its coastal areas.[45]

Local government roles and responsibilities

A common view among policy-makers has been that while climate change mitigation is primarily a task for national governments and international agreements and processes, responsibility for adaptation policies should fall largely to sub-national and local governments.[46] In some respects, climate change

---

42 Alliance of Small Island States, *Declaration on Climate Change 2009*, <http://forum.forumsec.org/pages.cfm/strategic-partnerships-coordination/climate-change>; and Pacific Islands Forum Secretariat, *Climate Change Issues dominate SIS Leader's Meeting* (Press Release 67/10, 3 August 2010), <http://www.forumsec.org/pages.cfm/newsroom/press-statements/2010/climate-change-issues-dominate-sis-leaders-meeting.html>.
43 Council of Australian Governments, *National Climate Change Adaptation Framework* (2007). Significant investments in targeted adaptation research have also been made by Australian governments. See for example CSIRO, *National Research Flagships: Climate Adaptation* (22 June 2011), <http://www.csiro.au/org/ClimateAdaptationFlagship.html>. See also Australian Government, Productivity Commission, *Draft Report: Barriers to Effective Climate Change Adaptation* (April 2012), <http://www.pc.gov.au/projects/inquiry/climate-change-adaptation/draft>.
44 See for example Australian Capital Territory Government, *Weathering the Change, Draft Action Plan 2, Pathway to a Sustainable and Carbon Neutral ACT 2011–2060*, Options paper for public comment (2011), pp. 32–5; Queensland Government, 'ClimateQ: Toward a Greener Queensland' (2009); and South Australian Government, 'Prospering in a Changing Climate: A Draft Climate Change Adaptation Framework for South Australia', Draft for community consultation (December 2010), <http://tinyurl.com/6vj258f>.
45 J. Bell, 'Planning for climate change and sea level rise – Queensland's new Coastal Plan', 29 *Environmental and Planning Law Journal* 61 (2012).
46 Garnaut, *Garnaut Climate Change Review* (2008), p. 364. For an alternative view, urging more urgent consideration of broader adaptation policies to enhance societal resilience, see Pielke et al., 'Lifting the Taboo on Adaptation' (2007).

Table 11.2 Australian national adaptation policy initiatives

Policy initiative	Content
Adapting to Climate Change in Australia (2010)	Government position paper and vision
Caring for our Coasts	Ongoing assessment of the risks to coastal ecosystems, infrastructure and settlements, and associated actions to be taken
Interactions between Climate Change, Fire Regimes and Biodiversity in Australia (2010)	
National Coastal Risk Assessment (2009)	
Australia's Biodiversity and Climate Change (2009)	Major national vulnerability assessments
Implications of Climate Change for Australia's World Heritage Properties (2009)	
Local Adaptation Pathways Program	Funding to help local government undertake climate change risk assessments and develop action plans in response
Climate Change Impacts and Risk Management	A guide to risk assessment and setting of priorities for business and government
Adaptation Actions for Local Governments (2010)	Report indentifying impact risks and actions that can be implemented by Australian local governments

Table 11.3 Key Australian state adaptation policies

State	Adaptation Policy	Content
WA	State Coastal Planning Policy (2006)	Provides that coastal planning strategies should take into account coastal processes and sea-level change and provides a benchmark of 0.38 m when assessing the potential for erosion on sandy shores
QLD	Queensland Coastal Plan (2012)	Comprises the State Policy for Coastal Management, which provides guidance for maintaining, rehabilitating and protecting coastal land, and the State Planning Policy: Coastal Protection, which applies to land use planning and development decisions
NSW	NSW Sea Level Rise Policy Statement (2009)	NSW Coastal Planning Guideline: Adapting to Sea Level Rise (2010) adopts the benchmarks set out in the NSW Sea Level Rise Policy Statement, which set standards for decision-making by planning authorities
	Priorities for Biodiversity Adaptation to Climate Change (2010)	Information on managing the impacts of climate change on ecosystems and natural resources in NSW
VIC	Future Coasts Program	Filling information gaps and providing guidance for coastal land management and for decision-makers to use when planning for and managing coastal areas
	Victorian Coastal Strategy 2008	A policy of planning for sea-level rise of not less than 0.8 m by 2100
	Sustainable Water Strategies under the Water Act 1989	Regional strategies to plan for long-term water security across Victoria

adaptation is naturally suited to more local levels of governance. In the first instance, the benefits of adaptation measures tend to be quite localised, as in the case of construction of a levee to reduce coastal erosion resulting from sea-level rise. In addition, high levels of variability in the ways in which the effects of climate change are manifested at different times and places suggest that the most appropriate responses are tailored, local ones.[47] Barriers to adaptation also vary between places, including the inability of natural systems to adapt, as well as technological, financial, cognitive, behavioural, social and cultural constraints.[48]

Typically the roles and responsibilities of different levels of government and different sectors in society in relation to adaptation are not clearly defined. However, the impetus of potential liability (see Box 11.2) is likely to give rise to a finer resolution of these roles and responsibilities through the legal system.[49] Much effort has been directed to climate change adaptation at the local level, but in many jurisdictions, Australia included, it has not developed into a purpose-built legal framework that employs discrete regulatory instruments. Instead, adaptation measures have developed utilising policy, incentive and risk assessment models,[50] and/or through existing legal forms, such as planning laws.[51] There has also been greater attention to emergency management of events related to climate change following a spate of natural disasters in Australia. Such local initiatives at times merge with climate change adaptation responses.[52] In the rapidly emerging field of adaptation law, the role of municipal-level regulation and policy is critical, as local governments, particularly in the major capital cities in Australia, have put into effect policy and regulatory initiatives relating to climate change well in advance of national and state laws.[53]

McDonald argues that there are important reasons for implementing legal frameworks for climate change more generally, and her analysis is most relevant to understanding why laws pertaining to local government, designed to facilitate adaptation to climate change, are needed, or alternatively, why amendment of existing laws may be required.[54] First, legal solutions may be necessary where there is a gap between short-term decision-making and the risk of damage that manifests over the long term. Second, local climate laws may provide an enforcement framework for market mechanisms and other incentives. Laws may also be necessary where markets do not adequately protect locally significant places under threat from climate change. Finally, local governments may need to strengthen or complement existing legal frameworks, such as those that pertain to land use planning, or to clarify

---

[47] Garnaut, *Garnaut Climate Change Review* (2008), pp. 597–8.
[48] W. Adger et al., 'Assessment of Adaptation Practices, Options, Constraints and Capacity', in *Climate Change 2007: Impacts, Adaptation and Vulnerability. Contribution of Working Group II to the Fourth Assessment Report of the Intergovernmental Panel on Climate Change*, eds M. Parry et al. (Cambridge University Press, 2007), p. 717.
[49] J. McDonald, 'Paying the Price of Adaptation: Compensation for Climate Change Impacts', in *Adaptation to Climate Change: Law and Policy*, eds Bonyhady, Macintosh and McDonald (2010), pp. 234–5.
[50] H. Füssel, 'Adaptation Planning for Climate Change: Concepts, Assessment Approaches and Key Lessons', 2(2) *Sustainability Science* 265 (2007), cited by McDonald in 'Mapping the Legal Landscape of Climate Change Mitigation' (2010), p. 9.
[51] Leitch et al., 'From Blueprint to Footprint: Climate Change and the Challenge for Planning', in *Adaptation to Climate Change: Law and Policy*, eds Bonyhady, Macintosh and McDonald (2010), p. 64.
[52] McDonald, 'Mapping the Legal Landscape of Climate Change Mitigation' (2010), p. 12.
[53] R. Bell, 'Local Governments Take the Lead in Curbing Greenhouse Gas Emissions', 4(2) *Environmental Practice* 65 (2002); and K. Otto-Zimmermann, 'Local Solutions for Global Challenges', 11(1) *Local Environment* 1 (2006).
[54] McDonald, 'Mapping the Legal Landscape of Climate Change Mitigation' (2010), p. 12.

responsibilities and areas of immunity from liability. In this respect, one of the perennial challenges for local governments is the need to balance the public interest, for example in adaptation, with the economic and social activities of local communities. This dilemma is exemplified by the tensions that surfaced in the sea-level rise cases discussed below. For many local councils, one of the most significant barriers to taking steps to implement adaptation measures is the risk of being sued and/or associated insurance costs.

A two-pronged approach is needed. First, it is desirable to ensure that greenfield developments and new infrastructure are not located in areas vulnerable to climate change. Second, if that is not possible given the coastal location of many of Australia's major cities, municipalities need to tighten regulatory controls, such as building design codes, to reflect predicted events and conditions resulting from climate change.[55] One of the major adaptation challenges will be how to deal with damage and potential loss of life in areas of existing development, and the costs of replacement and repair. Here particularly, the potential liability of local statutory authorities is pertinent (see Box 11.2),[56] although other entities also may be subject to claim.[57] One possible solution lies in the introduction of an indemnity regime funded by the federal or state government to underpin councils' capacity to address the effects of climate change.

> **BOX 11.2 Potential local government liability**
>
> If local governments and planning authorities ignore the need to adapt to climate change, there is a real risk that they may in the long term face civil liability for projects approved without adequate regard for future impacts, including physical harm and socioeconomic losses.[58] Sub-national and local governments may be particularly vulnerable to litigation brought by those affected by climate change,[59] as these organisations will be easier to identify and potentially easier to link to the harm suffered than the entities whose pollution contributed to particular effects.[60] Typically, the legal basis for such claims in common law systems lies in tort law, with a cause of action in either negligence or nuisance. There may also be actions based in administrative law, for example the review of decision-making in planning matters by local councils.[61]

---

55 For example, in response to recommendations of the Victorian Bushfires Royal Commission, the Australian Building Codes Board has published a *Performance Standard for Private Bushfire Shelters* (30 April 2011) and is working with Standards Australia to expedite the review and ongoing development of AS 3959, *Construction of Buildings in Bushfire-prone Areas*, and other bushfire-related standards.
56 McDonald, 'Paying the Price of Adaptation' (2010), pp. 248–9.
57 McDonald identifies potential private tortfeasors: ibid., pp. 242–6. A number of actions against large-scale emitters have been brought in courts in the United States, for instance against oil and insurance companies following Hurricane Katrina: *Comer et al. v Murphy Oil USA, et al.* (5th Circuit, 07–60756), discussed in Durrant, *Legal Responses to Climate Change* (2010), p. 287.
58 J. McDonald, 'A Risky Climate for Decision-Making: The Liability of Development Authorities for Climate Change Impacts', 24 *Environmental and Planning Law Journal* 405 (2007); and P. England, 'Heating Up: Climate Change Law and the Evolving Responsibilities of Local Government', 13 *Local Government Law Journal* 209 (2008).
59 A detailed list of the legal actions already taken against local councils can be found in Baker & McKenzie, *Local Council Risk of Liability in the face of Climate Change – Resolving Uncertainties. A Report for the Australian Local Government Association* (2011), p. 3, <http://www.climatechange.gov.au/~/media/publications/local-govt/alga-report-final-pdf.pdf>.
60 McDonald, 'The Adaptation Imperative' (2007), p. 134.
61 Baker & McKenzie, *Local Council Risk of Liability* (2011), pp. 43–5.

> **BOX 11.2 (cont.)**
>
> There are a range of situations in which local government authorities and other statutory planning institutions may be exposed to negligence and nuisance law claims,[62] and claims in respect of actions or omissions in carrying out various statutory responsibilities.[63] These may include circumstances where authorities are adopting and implementing various standards for strategic planning and development control in respect of climate change impacts such as flood risk, bushfire risk and sea-level rise.[64]

Given these various factors, it is a sensible strategy for local and sub-national governments 'to start incorporating climate change considerations into a wide range of their decisions and activities'.[65] In recent years, local governments have been at the forefront of climate change adaptation law and policy in Australia, as well as in other jurisdictions.[66] In turn, local decision-making with respect to climate change adaptation is generating institutional and organisational change outside the government sector, by development agencies, financiers, insurers, property developers and their professional advisors.[67]

Coastal adaptation: Sea-level rise

Many local governments around Australia have introduced or are in the process of formulating planning measures and development control conditions with a view to adaptation to climate change. While these planning measures are designed to address a range of potential impacts, a common focus given the coastal distribution of much of Australia's population has been sea-level rise.[68] Planning measures concerned with future sea-level rise may limit, quite substantially in some cases, property owners' capacity to develop their land.

Local adaptation measures that restrict development in coastal zones have not gone unchallenged. In Australia this has resulted in a growing number of cases brought before planning and environmental tribunals and courts.[69] These cases have necessitated judicial consideration of the risks of climate change-induced sea-level rise and the capacity of the legal frameworks to respond. Below we

---

62 Durrant, *Legal Responses to Climate Change* (2010), Chapters 18, 20–21.
63 See generally P. McMaster, 'Climate Change – Statutory Duty or Pious Hope?', 20(1) *Environmental Law* 115 (2008).
64 Baker & McKenzie, *Local Council Risk of Liability* (2011), p. 23.
65 England, 'Heating Up' (2008), p. 210.
66 See for example California Natural Resources Agency, *2009 Californian Climate Adaptation Strategy*, <http://www.climatechange.ca.gov/adaptation/index.html>.
67 Durrant, *Legal Responses to Climate Change* (2010), pp. 298–326; and S. Powell, 'An Insurer's Approach to Management of Climate Risks', in *Adaptation to Climate Change: Law and Policy*, eds Bonyhady, Macintosh and McDonald (2010).
68 See generally T. Bonyhady, 'Swimming in the Streets: The Beginnings of Planning for Sea-Level Rise', in *Adaptation to Climate Change: Law and Policy*, eds Bonyhady, Macintosh and McDonald (2010).
69 In addition to the cases considered below, other decisions concerning climate change adaptation include *Charles Howard Pty Ltd v Redland Shire Council* (2007) 159 LGERA 349; *Daikyo (North Queensland) Pty Ltd v Cairns City Council* [2003] QPEC 22; *Mackay Conservation Group Inc v Mackay City Council* [2006] QPELR 209; and *Van Haandel v Bryon Shire Council* [2006] NSWLEC 394. See also B. Preston, 'The Role of the Courts in Relation to Adaptation to Climate Change', in *Adaptation to Climate Change: Law and Policy*, eds Bonyhady, Macintosh and McDonald (2010).

examine seminal cases in this body of jurisprudence: the *Northcape* cases in South Australia, the *Walker* litigation in New South Wales, and the *Gippsland Coastal Board* case in Victoria.

Northcape litigation

An early decision on coastal planning and climate change was the 2007 judgment of the Environment, Resources and Development Court of South Australia (ERDC) in *Northcape Properties Pty Ltd v District Council of Yorke Peninsula*.[70] The case involved an appeal of the Council's decision to refuse consent for subdivision of a large parcel of land near Marion Bay on the Yorke Peninsula. The proposal was covered by a Development Plan under the *Development Act 1993* (SA) dealing with planning of developments near the coast. Objective 11 of the relevant Development Plan sought:

> [t]o encourage development that is located and designed to allow for changes in sea level due to natural subsidence and probable climate change during the first 100 years of the development. This change is to be based on the historic and currently observed rate of sea-level rise for South Australia with an allowance for the nationally agreed most likely predicted additional rise due to global climate change.

One of the supporting 'Principles of Development Control' for the Plan's coastal objectives, concerning the width of any applicable erosion buffer zone for development, also made reference to:

> the effect of a 0.3 metres sea level [rise] over the next 50 years on coastal processes and storms; and the availability of practical measures to protect the development from erosion caused by a further sea level rise of 0.7 metres per 50 years thereafter.

The Council's decision was upheld by the ERDC on the basis, *inter alia*, that the proposal failed 'to make adequate provision for the inland retreat of the foreshore and dunes and associated native vegetation over the next 100 years' in light of the applicable objectives and principles of the Development Plan.[71] This decision was appealed to the South Australian Supreme Court,[72] where the developer argued that the ERDC had misunderstood the expert evidence on the extent of future coastal erosion due to climate change-induced sea-level rise. However, Justice Debelle, delivering the judgment of the Court, found that the ERDC had been correct in its conclusion that, on the basis of the expert evidence, 'in the next 100 years the high-water mark would recede inland by 35–40 metres', inundating the lower-lying lots.[73] The Court confirmed the ERDC's interpretation of the applicable planning provisions, finding that the 'proposal offends so many of the goals and objectives of the Development Plan that development consent must be refused'.[74]

---

70 [2007] SAERDC 50 (19 September 2007).   **71** [2007] SAERDC 50, para. 44.
72 *Northcape Properties Pty Ltd v District Council of Yorke Peninsula* [2008] SASC 57 (4 March 2008).
73 *Northcape Properties Pty Ltd v District Council of Yorke Peninsula* [2008] SASC 57, para. 27.
74 *Northcape Properties Pty Ltd v District Council of Yorke Peninsula* [2008] SASC 57, para. 28.

The decisions in the *Northcape* cases made no explicit mention of climate change. Nonetheless, they signalled that where local planning controls make reference to sea-level rise resulting from climate change, such provisions will be given serious consideration by the courts and duly applied where supported by expert evidence of future coastal erosion.

Walker litigation

Around the same time as the *Northcape* case was being decided by the ERDC, a very similar planning law challenge was under consideration by the New South Wales (NSW) Land and Environment Court in the *Walker* case.[75] This decision has since become renowned for establishing the relevance of the consideration of future climate change risk with respect to development control proposals, specifically in the context of the risk of inundation. The force of Justice Biscoe's initial judgment in the case – which was heavily based on an analysis of the role of principles of ecologically sustainable development (ESD) under former Part 3A of the *Environmental Planning and Assessment Act 1979* (NSW) ('EP&A Act') – was lessened by the subsequent rulings of the NSW Court of Appeal.[76] Nonetheless, the decision prompted legal advisors to recommend that 'proponents and councils make an assumption that there is the potential for greater flooding or inundation than is presently the case (i.e. due to climate change), and that proponents should consider whether any mitigation measures can be designed to alleviate any future flooding impacts'.[77]

The basis of the *Walker* case was a judicial review application sought in respect of a concept plan approval for a residential subdivision and retirement home just south of Sydney. There was strong public opposition to the proposed development, including concerns about the effects of the development on three flood-prone watercourses crossing the site. One of the main grounds for review in the case alleged that the state planning minister, in approving the concept plan, had failed to take into account ESD principles. The 'encouragement' of ESD is one of the objects of the Act.[78] ESD is defined as it is in the *Protection of the Environment Administration Act 1991* (NSW),[79] which elaborates the concept in terms of key principles such as the precautionary principle and the principle of intergenerational equity.[80]

The factual basis for the claim was the absence of any consideration by the Minister or his Department of the potential for the flooding risk on the site to be exacerbated by climate change. The relevant legal issue was whether the

---

[75] *Walker v Minister for Planning* (2007) 157 LGERA 124.
[76] *Minister for Planning v Walker* (2008) 161 LGERA 423.
[77] See A. Whealy and I. Ferguson, ' *Walker v Minister for Planning* [2007] NSWLEC 741 – implications for coastal and flood liable land and major project development', Gadens Lawyers (December 2007), <http://www.gadens.com.au/Publications.aspx?CategoryID=6&navid=0&cid=0>.
[78] *Environmental Planning and Assessment Act 1979* (NSW) s 5(1).
[79] *Environmental Planning and Assessment Act 1979* (NSW) s 4; ESD is defined in the *Protection of the Environment Administration Act 1991* (NSW) s 6(2).
[80] On the ESD issues in local planning, see L. Godden and J. Peel, *Environmental Law: Scientific, Policy and Regulatory Dimensions* (Oxford University Press, 2010), pp. 134–43.

Minister for Planning was obliged to consider ESD principles (and as part of this, climate change-induced flood risk) as an implied mandatory consideration in approving the concept plan.

The judge determined that the ESD principles were an implied mandatory consideration in a decision to approve a concept plan under Part 3A of the EP&A Act.[81] The question that then arose was whether climate change-induced flood risk should have formed part of the Minister's consideration.[82] Justice Biscoe found that climate change-induced flood risk could be described as 'an aspect of the public interest that potentially has a direct bearing on the justice of the decision'.[83] An important issue was the gravity of such flood risk:

> Climate change presents a risk to the survival of the human race and other species. Consequently, it is a deadly serious issue. It has been increasingly under public scrutiny for some years. No doubt that is because of global scientific support for the existence and risks of climate change and its anthropogenic causes. Climate change flood risk is, *prima facie*, a risk that is potentially relevant to a flood-constrained, coastal plain development such as the subject project.[84]

The Land and Environment Court's finding was overturned on appeal to the NSW Court of Appeal, which adopted a narrower construction of the role of ESD principles in decision-making under former Part 3A of the EP&A Act. Despite these findings, the Court of Appeal emphasised that 'the principles of ESD are likely to come to be seen as so plainly an element of the public interest, in relation to most if not all decisions, that failure to consider them will become strong evidence of failure to consider the public interest and/or to act *bona fide* in the exercise of powers granted to the Minister, and thus become capable of avoiding decisions'.[85] The majority also remarked that it was 'somewhat surprising and disturbing' that the Department's report to the Minister did not address ESD principles such as the precautionary principle and the principle of intergenerational equity, and that the Minister did not postpone his decision until he had done so.[86] In subsequent cases, these statements by the Court have provided an avenue for decision-makers to find that ESD principles are a relevant consideration in determining the public interest in the climate change context.[87]

Gippsland Coastal Board case

The case of *Gippsland Coastal Board v South Gippsland Shire Council (No. 2)*[88] was one of the first merits review decisions to consider the relevance of climate change-induced sea-level rise and flooding in an Australian planning context. Together with similar decisions in other Australian jurisdictions, such as

---

81 *Walker v Minister for Planning* (2007) 157 LGERA 124, 192.
82 *Walker v Minister for Planning* (2007) 157 LGERA 124, 191.
83 *Walker v Minister for Planning* (2007) 157 LGERA 124, 192.
84 *Walker v Minister for Planning* (2007) 157 LGERA 124, 191.
85 *Minister for Planning v Walker* (2008) 161 LGERA 423, 454.
86 *Minister for Planning v Walker* (2008) 161 LGERA 423, 455.
87 For example *Aldous v Greater Taree City Council* [2009] NSWLEC 17, para. 40. 88 [2008] VCAT 1545.

the *Northcape* cases discussed above, it has played an influential role in the introduction of adaptation to coastal development planning.[89]

This Victorian case concerned a planning consent for residential development in a low-lying coastal region, which had been issued by the local South Gippsland Shire Council in respect of land in Toora, an area zoned for agricultural and mixed land uses. The grant of permits was opposed by the Gippsland Coastal Board, a regional coastal board under the *Coastal Management Act 1995* (Vic). In its application to the Victorian Civil and Administrative Tribunal (VCAT) for merits review of the approvals, a principal objection raised by the Board was that the proposed dwelling developments were inappropriate in light of projected climate change-induced sea-level rises.

VCAT ultimately refused approvals for the proposed development based on its inconsistency with zoning and planning controls. The Tribunal applied the precautionary principle as a component of ESD to find that development consent should not be granted, in view of likely inundation to the land and proposed dwellings due to sea-level rise. There were no specific provisions in the relevant Victorian legislation – the *Planning and Environment Act 1987* – mandating consideration of the precautionary principle or the potential for sea-level rise, although section 60 of the Act does list extensive matters for consideration by responsible authorities,[90] and the applicable State Planning Policy Framework guides them to balance conflicting interests and objectives in favour of 'sustainable development for the benefit of present and future generations'.[91]

Significantly, the Tribunal noted 'that some level of climate change will result in extreme weather conditions beyond the historical record that planners and others rely on in assessing future potential impacts'.[92] Despite some scientific uncertainty, the Tribunal endorsed a precautionary approach while acknowledging that the 'range of impacts may well be beyond the predictive capability of current assessment techniques'.[93] The Tribunal also emphasised that it was not acceptable to rely upon historical data and previous flood model predictions in assessing future climate change-induced risks.[94]

The precautionary approach adopted in the *Gippsland Coastal Board* case signals an important step in recognising the limits of existing risk assessment methodologies to guide climate change adaptation efforts. It puts into play calls to transcend historical forms of data analysis and associated decision-making.[95] The *Gippsland Coastal Board* case, together with coastal development litigation around the country,[96] also illustrates the potential for the legal framework to incorporate 'principled flexibility' to meet challenges posed by the effects of

---

89 J. Peel and L. Godden, 'Planning for Adaptation to Climate Change: Landmark Cases from Australia', 9(2) *Sustainable Development Law and Policy: Climate Law Reporter* 37 (2009).
90 For example s 60(e): 'any significant effects which the responsible authority considers the use or development may have on the environment or which the responsible authority considers the environment may have on the use or development'.
91 Clauses 10.01 and 10.02.   **92** [2008] VCAT 1545, paras. 40, 45 and 48.
93 [2008] VCAT 1545, para. 42.   **94** [2008] VCAT 1545, para. 42.
95 See for example Craig, 'Stationarity is dead' (2010).
96 For a discussion of the relevant case law, see Preston, 'The Role of the Courts in Relation to Adaptation to Climate Change' (2010).

climate change. In summary, the case law has established principles to guide decision-making on coastal adaptation to sea-level rise. Accordingly, it now forms an accepted part of the planning decision-making framework.

The case law has had important flow-on effects for governments' coastal adaptation policy, as the following case study of developments in Victoria illustrates (see Box 11.3), although government policy has varied in terms of the strictness of controls in the Victorian coastal zone.

> **BOX 11.3 Case study: Victorian coastal policy**
>
> Decisions such as that of the *Gippsland Coastal Board* prompted reconsideration of Victorian government coastal policy, which has evolved substantially since 2008 in conjunction with a large number of cases that have come before VCAT.
> Victorian coastal planning for sea level is based upon a complex of statutory laws and policy documents that guide the exercise of planning and development functions in coastal regions of the state. A key piece of legislation, the *Coastal Management Act 1995*, directs the preparation of the Victorian Coastal Strategy: an overall framework for planning and management of the Victorian coast. The most recent Victorian Coastal Strategy was issued in 2008,[97] and it establishes a general policy requirement to apply the precautionary principle, as well as a more specific requirement to 'plan for sea-level rise of not less than 0.8 metres by 2100, and allow for the combined effects of tides, storm surges, coastal processes and local conditions such as topography and geology when assessing risks and impacts associated with climate change'. The Strategy is given effect within the state planning law framework via its designation as an 'incorporated document' applicable within all planning schemes.
> Decision-making related to planning in Victoria is governed by the *Planning and Environment Act 1987*. Questions of adaptation to climate change become relevant via the operation of section 60(1), which sets out what a responsible authority must consider in deciding planning applications. These matters include the relevant planning scheme (including the Victorian Coastal Strategy), the objectives of planning in Victoria, and 'any significant effects which the responsible authority considers the use or development may have on the environment or which the responsible authority considers the environment may have on the use or development' proposed.[98]
> The *Planning and Environment Act* also sets out the required contents of planning schemes, which include common elements such as an 'overlay' for 'land subject to inundation'. Of primary relevance for climate change adaptation is clause 13.01–1 of the State Planning Policy Framework, which seeks to plan for and manage the potential coastal impacts of climate change, and which was updated to reflect the planning benchmark of a 0.8-metre rise in sea level by 2100. This amendment was supplemented by Ministerial Direction No. 13 on 'Managing Coastal Hazards and the Coastal Impacts of Climate Change', and a General Practice Note titled 'Managing Coastal Hazards and the Coastal Impacts of Climate Change'. The Ministerial Direction sets out various 'requirements to be met' by planning authorities preparing planning scheme amendments that would have the effect of rezoning non-urban land for urban use or development. The requirements take into account the potential risks associated with projected sea-level rise, in conjunction with effects of storm surges, tides, river flooding and coastal erosion. The General Practice Note lists general factors to consider as part of a coastal vulnerability hazard assessment, and specifies that such assessments should be carried out by 'a suitably qualified coastal engineer or coastal processes specialist', but provides little further guidance.
> A stream of cases that came before VCAT from 2009 to 2011 reflect ongoing uncertainty as to how decision-makers are to apply these policy requirements to meet objectives of coastal climate change adaptation.[99] Questions have arisen over who bears the responsibility of

---

[97] The Strategy applies to all Victorian coastal waters, and to all private and coastal Crown land directly influenced by the sea or directly influencing the coastline.
[98] *Planning and Environment Act 1987* (Vic) s 60(1)(e).
[99] E. de Wit and R. Webb, 'Planning for Coastal Climate Change in Victoria', 27 *Environmental and Planning Law Journal* 23 (2010). See also Baker & McKenzie, *Local Council Risk of Liability* (2011), p. 19ff.

> **BOX 11.3 (cont.)**
>
> carrying out coastal hazard vulnerability assessments and their adequacy,[100] whether the risk of future sea-level rise should be borne by purchasers of affected property or managed proactively by the state,[101] and what the ultimate decision should be where climate change impacts are identified.
>
> The case law indicates that VCAT is 'regularly applying the new policies and the requirement for coastal vulnerability assessments in practical terms'[102] in ways that recognise the imperative of climate change adaptation and the need for legal frameworks to respond proactively. Nevertheless, there are a number of difficulties. Chief among them is a governance question: should it fall to individual property owners and developers to produce assessments of coastal vulnerability on an ad hoc, development-by-development basis or should a coordinated government response occur, to give greater planning certainty?

The Victorian case study illustrates the difficult challenges facing governance arrangements more broadly in the area of adaptation planning. These include the need to navigate the different competencies of multiple government agencies, to balance individual freedoms to develop and use property with a view to the broader interests of the state and society, and to ensure resilience in the face of unavoidable climate change. Such themes emerge also in other areas of adaptation planning and management, as the discussion below demonstrates.

Adapting to climatic variability: Water scarcity and increased flood risk

Water resource management is a critical component of climate change adaptation strategy in many jurisdictions. The likely effects of climate change on water resources are considerable and nowhere more so than in Australia, which is naturally a land of climatic extremes: prolonged droughts and flooding rains.[103] In addition, humans rely fundamentally on water and the benefits derived from healthy functioning aquatic ecosystems.[104] Under the conditions of severe drought that prevailed in Australia until the summer of 2010–11, water law and governance systems became relatively adept at managing circumstances of water scarcity. Most jurisdictions have introduced strategic resource assessment, with more detailed strategic planning instruments[105] to support

---

[100] *Myers v South Gippsland Shire Council* [2009] VCAT 1022; and *Myers v South Gippsland Shire Council (No. 2)* [2009] VCAT 2414 (19 November 2009).
[101] For example *Ronchi v Wellington SC* [2009] VCAT 1206.
[102] Gibson, 'Climate Change and Low Lying Areas' (2009).
[103] K. Hennessy, 'Climate Change and Its Projected Effects on Water Resources', in *Water: The Australian Dilemma – Proceedings of the 2003 Invitation Symposium* (Australian Academy of Technological Sciences and Engineering, 2003), p. 175.
[104] R. Letcher and S. Powell, 'The Hydrological Setting', in *Water Policy in Australia: The Impact of Change and Uncertainty*, ed. L. Crase (Resources for the Future, 2008), p. 17.
[105] The exact configuration of the major strategic planning instrument, the Murray–Darling Basin plan, is still to be determined at the time of writing.

adaptation to the prolonged drought and scarcity of water predicted for much of the country under climate change.

More generally, strategic water planning has formed part of the extensive reforms to Australian water law and governance systems that were initiated in 1994.[106] The most recent policy platform, the National Water Initiative of 2004, outlined principles to improve the efficiency and sustainability of water management in Australia.[107] It has driven statutory and institutional reforms at the Australian state level,[108] as well as the introduction of far-reaching Commonwealth water legislation.[109] These reforms have typically emphasised adaptation to water scarcity through the adoption of water resource planning frameworks that set sustainable limits on the extraction of water at a catchment scale.[110]

As Tan argues, 'if we are to build adaptive capacity in the water sector, the first issue to address is over-allocation'.[111] In order to ensure that water systems are able to cope with the predicted stresses of climate change, it will be necessary to right the balance between consumptive and ecological water requirements.[112] Reform of the legal entitlement system for water allocation – for example, the introduction of transferability and the establishment of water markets for temporary and permanent transfer of water[113] – has also provided legal mechanisms to facilitate adaptation to scarcity at the scale of individual entitlement holders and various irrigation industries or areas.[114]

However, severe floods in eastern Australia over 2010–12 are timely reminders that climate change brings variability.[115] Periods of water scarcity alternate with periods of more intense precipitation.[116] Historical parameters for prediction of

---

[106] Key milestones in reform include: Council of Australian Governments, *Communiqué of 25 February 1994 – Attachment: A Water Resources Policy* (1994); Council of Australian Governments, *Intergovernmental Agreement on a National Water Initiative* (2004); and Australian Government, *A National Plan for Water Security* (2007).
[107] Council of Australian Governments, *Intergovernmental Agreement on a National Water Initiative* (2004).
[108] For a discussion of reforms see A. Gardner and K. Bowmer, 'Environmental Water Allocations and their Governance', in *Managing Water for Australia: The Social and Institutional Challenges*, eds Hussey and Dovers (2007).
[109] *Water Act 2007* (Cth).
[110] See further A. Foerster, 'Progress on Environmental Flows in South-Eastern Australia in Light of Climate Change', 39(5) *ELR News and Analysis* 10426 (2009); and A. Gardner, R. Bartlett and J. Gray, *Water Resources Law* (CSIRO Publishing, 2009), pp. 297–347.
[111] Tan, 'Adaptation Measures for Water Security in a Changing Climate' (2010), p. 149.
[112] In developing a model of climate change adaptation law with the goal of promoting the resilience and adaptive capacity of socio-ecological systems, Craig argues that a key principle is to eliminate or reduce non-climate change stresses: Craig, 'Stationarity is Dead' (2010), p. 43.
[113] Council of Australian Governments, *Intergovernmental Agreement on a National Water Initiative*, particularly paras. 23(v), 31, and 58–63.
[114] See O. Sanders, R. Goesch and N. Hughes, *Issues – Insights 10.5: Adapting to Water Scarcity* (Australian Bureau of Agricultural and Resource Economics, 2010).
[115] In Queensland, three-quarters of the state was declared a disaster zone following extensive flooding in late December 2010 and early January 2011. See Queensland Government, *Queensland Floods Commission of Inquiry 2011*, <http://www.floodcommission.qld.gov.au/home>.
[116] See IPCC, *Climate Change 2007: The Physical Science Basis: Contribution of Working Group I to the Fourth Assessment Report of the Intergovernmental Panel on Climate Change*, Summary for Policy Makers (Cambridge University Press, 2007), 11.7.

rainfall patterns no longer serve as reliable indicators of the climatic extremes that may need to be addressed in water resource planning. Yet examination of the available legal mechanisms to adapt to increased flood risk has received comparatively little attention in Australia's national water law and policy reform agendas.

Nature of flood risk: Uncertainty and complexity

Climate change is likely to increase flood risk significantly in Australia, with particularly severe implications for heavily urbanised coastal areas.[117] Densely populated river basins are also a feature of major metropolitan centres in both developed and developing nations. However, high levels of uncertainty remain with respect to localised predictions of extreme events such as floods.[118]

The complexities and uncertainties inherent in climate science in this area mean that law and governance frameworks based on an assumption that climate remains basically constant over the long term will no longer serve as appropriate responses. Rather, as authors such as Ruhl contend, these systems must embrace a transformative and more flexible approach.[119] Water management decisions therefore should no longer proceed on the basis 'that natural systems fluctuate within an unchanging envelope of variability'.[120] New adaptive and more precautionary approaches to managing water are required.

Responsibility for flood risk adaptation

In Australia's federal system of governance, state governments have primary responsibility for water resources law and management, including flood risk mitigation. The federal government plays a significant role in the development of water infrastructure (including flood mitigation works) under various intergovernmental financial arrangements, and for providing financial relief when floods occur. However, the major floodway and associated development controls in urban centres remain principally with state and at times local governments. Given the limited nature of national directives on flood risk management, and that the principal legal responsibilities for flood response lie with local authorities, a regional example of the response to devastating flooding in south-east Queensland offers important insights into Australian adaptation efforts in this area (see Box 11.4).

---

117 CSIRO, *Climate Change in Australia: Technical Report 2007* (2007), Executive Summary, p. 10.
118 IPCC, *Climate Change 2007: Impacts, Adaptation and Vulnerability* (2007), 10.3.
119 This influential hypothesis stems from P. C. D. Milly et al., 'Stationarity is Dead: Whither Water Management?', 319 *Science* 573 (2008). See also S. Westra et al., 'Addressing Climatic Non-Stationarity in the Assessment of Flood Risk', 14 *Australian Journal of Water Resources* 1 (2010) and Craig, 'Stationarity is Dead' (2010).
120 Milly et al., 'Stationarity is Dead' (2010), p. 573.

11 ADAPTATION TO CLIMATE CHANGE THROUGH LEGAL FRAMEWORKS

BOX 11.4 Case study: Queensland flood risk response

Water and land use planning law in Queensland is statute-based, as in other states.[121] The Queensland approach seeks to integrate the planning process across multiple agencies, with explicit provision for adaptive responses to climate change impacts. For example, under the *Sustainable Planning Act 2009* (Qld), the Minister may make state planning policies.[122] One of these planning policies addresses flood risk specifically: *Mitigating the Adverse Impacts of Flood, Bushfire and Landslide 1.0*.[123] This policy stipulates that natural hazard management areas are to be identified and incorporated into planning schemes for the purpose of ensuring that 'certain important types of community infrastructure' remain operational after natural hazard events. The basic standard for flood management is the '1 in 100 years' flood probability datum; however, this may vary with local conditions.

Floods in Brisbane in 2010 clearly tested the provision for infrastructure protection, with many crucial pieces of infrastructure under water and many residential developments inundated, including developments that had been allowed within parts of the metropolitan area that were flood-prone.

An independent Commission of Inquiry investigated the circumstances of these floods.[124] A report makes no direct recommendations to amend the planning scheme to better adapt to increased flood risk. Rather, the recommendations deal with five areas: dam operations; disaster frameworks, preparation and planning; forecasts, warnings and information; emergency response; and essential services. Prior preparation by local councils and groups is emphasised, but only to the extent that it better equips local councils to *respond* to likely or imminent floods (for example by improving warning systems or coordinating essential services).

As in the Queensland example, inquiries following major flood events across Australia[125] have stressed the need to better prepare for extreme flood risk, which is predicted to increase in extent and frequency as a result of climate change. Typically, the reports from such inquiries have emphasised the importance of ensuring that emergency response measures are coordinated and strategically aligned to disaster management plans. The recommendations do adopt a precautionary approach, as prior preparation is emphasised, but they primarily focus on ways of responding to likely or imminent floods. Much less attention, to date, has been given to longer-term strategies such as, for instance, amending the planning processes at planning scheme level to require larger floodway zones.

Nonetheless, there are significant opportunities to introduce a flexible, adaptive approach to extreme flood events in statutory planning frameworks by taking into consideration new levels of flood risk, given climate change. This approach would mean that flood risk standards, such as the '1 in 100 years' probability calculation, which serve as the foundation for decision-making across

---

121 The relevant legislation is the *Water Act 2000* (Qld) and the *Sustainable Planning Act 2009* (Qld). For other states see *Water Management Act 2000* (NSW); *Natural Resources Management Act 2004* (SA); *Water Management Act 1999* (Tas); *Water Act 1989* (Vic); *Water Resources Act 2007* (ACT).
122 *Sustainable Planning Act 2009* (Qld) s 41.
123 *State Planning Policy 1/03*, Department of Local Government and Planning, Queensland Government (14 April 2011), <http://www.dip.qld.gov.au/policies/state-planning-policies.html>.
124 The interim report was released in August 2011. At the time of writing, the final report had just been released: see Queensland Government, *Queensland Floods Commission of Inquiry*, Final Report, March 2012, <http://www.floodcommission.qld.gov.au/__data/assets/pdf_file/0007/11698/QFCI-Final-Report-March-2012.pdf>.
125 Ibid. See also N. Comrie et al., *Review of the 2010–2011 Flood Warnings and Response*, Final Report, 1 December 2011, <http://www.floodsreview.vic.gov.au/about-the-review/terms-of-reference.html>.

much planning law, infrastructure location, building codes, and so forth would need to be actively re-examined in light of how climate change will alter local circumstances. As Powell argues, continuing to rely on the '1 in 100 years' standard means accepting more flood damage, and perhaps greater recovery costs than were considered acceptable when the standard was initially set. The flood event datum, which currently guides planning decisions, effectively marks the point of acceptable failure compared to the cost of building infrastructure with greater capacity to withstand flooding or implementing other adaptation initiatives.[126] This risk assessment focuses on repair and compensation, as opposed to preventing harm. Indeed, the insurance industry has been a major influence in identifying risks and shaping adaptive responses. In this regard, the role of the insurance industry and its risk management paradigms, together with regulatory standards and potential liability, are important factors in determining the capacity for adaptive legal responses to flood risk in Australian cities and regions.[127]

Another important influence will be governance arrangements. As highlighted in relation to planning for coastal sea-level rise,[128] statutory authorities, including local governments, may be open to liability in relation to flood events. These claims could encompass:

- the selection and adoption of standards in planning polices and planning schemes in respect of flood-prone land;
- decisions with respect to applications for development approval of specific projects later affected by flooding; and
- the implementation (or failure to implement) measures designed to mitigate flooding.[129]

More specifically, there is the potential liability of planning authorities to compensation claims related to flood damage, as canvassed by McDonald.[130] Local authorities responsible for the preparation of planning schemes and the determination of individual development applications near floodways may be exposed to litigation for imposing inadequate conditions or failing to impose conditions that address flood risk resulting from climate change.[131] This potential liability should, at the very least, provoke a reassessment of whether existing law adequately responds to future uncertainties regarding flood risk.[132]

---

[126] Powell, 'An Insurer's Approach to Management of Climate Risks' (2010), p. 221; McDonald, "Mapping the Legal Landscape of Climate Change Mitigation' (2010), p. 19.
[127] A report by the Commonwealth Department of Climate Change and Energy Efficiency on 'Climate Change Risks to Coastal Buildings and Infrastructure' (6 June 2011) touches on these matters, although the focus remains on risk assessment.
[128] See Box 11.2.
[129] For more extensive discussion see Durrant, *Legal Responses to Climate Change* (2010), p. 289 and Baker & McKenzie, *Local Council Risk of Liability* (2011), pp. 25–6 and 36–40.
[130] McDonald, 'A Risky Climate for Decision-Making' (2007), and England, 'Heating Up' (2008), p. 217. See also Baker & McKenzie, *Local Council Risk of Liability* (2011), pp. 36–40.
[131] McDonald, 'Paying the Price of Adaptation' (2010), p. 244. See also *Graham Barclay Oysters Pty Ltd v Ryan* (2002) 211 CLR 540.
[132] L. Godden and A. Kung, 'Water Law and Planning Frameworks under Climate Change Variability: Managing Flood Risk', 25(15) *Water Resources Management* 4051 (2011).

In certain instances, there will be statutory immunities in place, particularly where authorities conduct 'works' designed to mitigate the effects of climate change, such as the construction of levee banks for flood emergencies.[133] Nonetheless, clarification of the nature and extent of local governments' statutory responsibilities, especially with respect to adaptation measures, would enhance transparency. Together with an increased flow of information and adequate material resources, such clarification will help authorities institute appropriate defensive measures in response to climate change.[134] Statutory immunities from liability in given circumstances, such as that which operates under section 733(1) of the *Local Government Act 1993* (NSW), should also be actively considered.

Instituting new regulatory approaches

A system that focuses heavily on how humans can *avoid* floods, rather than adapt and strategically plan for them, risks exposing inhabitants to greater flood damage when extreme floods do occur.[135] Floodplain management planning along the lower Danube River in Europe is an example of strategic adaptation: planners have found that restoring floodplains through stronger regulatory controls and allowing greater areas to flood has been beneficial for flood risk management.[136] Similarly, a recent adaptive response in Victoria has been the allocation of compensation payments to buy flood-affected lands from farmers in rural regions to allow more extensive inundation of floodplains.[137] Approaches such as compulsorily acquiring land in established urban areas to extend floodplains, given higher land values, may be controversial.[138]

At the very least, more investigation of anticipatory adaptation approaches to heightened flood risk is warranted. For example, in Victoria, proposed developments in certain coastal and flood-prone areas require coastal vulnerability assessments.[139] This approach could be applied in the area of floodplain management, to enhance current planning practices that guide the delineation of floodways, the location of new developments and the protection of highly vulnerable areas.

Standard regulatory and planning law approaches that rely on the state – essentially planned public adaptation – need not be the sole means of adapting to increased flood risk. Incentive-based tools and community engagement

---

[133] Baker & McKenzie, *Local Council Risk of Liability* (2011), Appendix 2.
[134] Durrant, *Legal Responses to Climate Change* (2010), pp. 289–90.
[135] Godden and Kung, 'Water Law and Planning Frameworks' (2011).
[136] O. Hulea et al., 'Floodplain restoration along the lower Danube: A climate change adaptation case study', 1 *Climate and Development* 212 (2009).
[137] Government of Victoria, Regional Development Victoria, *Assistance Package for Flood-Affected Victorian Irrigators* (27 April 2011), <http://www.rdv.vic.gov.au/news/assistance-package-for-flood-affected-irrigators>.
[138] Macintosh, 'A Theoretical Framework for Adaptation Policy' (2010), pp. 50–5.
[139] de Wit and Webb, 'Planning for Coastal Climate Change in Victoria' (2010).

approaches may complement broader strategic planning.[140] For example, incentives for business and industry to encourage the adoption of water-sensitive urban design, or the use of recycled water, could be created.[141] Similarly, engaging the community in strategic planning exercises on a local scale is one way of disseminating information and making communities aware of climate change impacts and cost-effective responses appropriate to local conditions.[142]

Public concerns have escalated markedly in situations where communities are faced with natural disasters whose scale and frequency are exacerbated by climate change. The following discussion considers Australian adaptation to natural disasters before turning to an example from the Pacific region.

Natural disasters: Bushfire risk and adaptive responses

A prominent part of the Australian national psyche has been stoic fortitude in the face of natural disasters, given the variability that has distinguished Australia's climate and the harshness of much of the physical environment.[143] In addition, Bonyhady suggests that where each disaster is regarded as a 'one-off', future contingency planning is minimal. But as he rightly points out, this form of cognitive dissonance cannot be sustained in light of the increased severity and frequency of natural disasters predicted to accompany climate change.[144] Another explanation for Australia's chequered history of adaptive responses may lie in the fact that, given the extent and complexity of disasters, and with so many people affected,[145] many areas of law and many levels of government, industry, and community are involved in the determination of critical questions regarding responsibility, liability and compensation. Indeed, the capacity of the legal system to unravel those issues is often severely tested.[146]

There is a long list of inquiries, reports, Royal Commissions and similar public investigations that have generated a comprehensive series of recommendations designed to avert the tragedies engendered by natural disasters. For example, the Victorian Bushfire Royal Commission in 2010 stated that '[t]he recommendations we make give priority to protecting human life, and they are designed to reflect the shared responsibility that governments, fire agencies, communities and individuals have for minimising the prospect of a tragedy of this scale ever

---

[140] See generally L. Godden and J. Peel, 'Legal Tools for Environmental Regulation', in *Environmental Law: Scientific Policy and Regulatory Dimensions* (Oxford University Press, 2010), p. 123.
[141] See for example T. Wong 'Water Sensitive Urban Design – The Journey Thus Far', 10(3) *Australian Journal of Water Resources* 213 (2006).
[142] See for example N. Sultana, 'Climate Change Adaptation and Governance in the Coastal District of Bhola in Bangladesh', paper presented at Climate Change Adaptation and Governance Workshop, UNSW, 16–18 November 2010.
[143] T. Bonyhady, 'The Law of Disasters', in *Adaptation to Climate Change*, eds Bonyhady, Macintosh and McDonald (2010), p. 266.
[144] Ibid., p. 267.   [145] D. Farber and J. Chen, *Disasters and the Law: Katrina and Beyond* (Aspen, 2006).
[146] Ibid., p. xix.

happening again'.[147] Yet many of these recommendations appear to fall by the wayside. The pattern of responses to bushfire hazards over time exemplifies such situations, but climate change may motivate a reassessment of these trends, and closer monitoring and long-term enforcement of adaptation measures can be expected.[148]

Strategic planning for bushfire risk

A 2005 report assessing fire risk associated with climate change indicated that '[f]ire risk is influenced by a number of factors – including fuels, terrain, land management, suppression and weather'.[149] The study focused on south-east Australia, an area predicted to be hotter and dryer under climate change. South-east Australia is one of the three most fire-prone areas in the world, along with southern California and southern France. A key report finding was 'that an increase in fire-weather risk is likely at most sites in 2020 and 2050, including the average number of days when the [fire risk] rating is very high or extreme ... For example, Canberra is likely to have more very high or extreme fire danger days by 2050, compared to a present average of 23.1 days.'[150] This prediction of heightened fire risk for the national capital is all the more ominous given the major fires that burnt over 70 per cent of the ACT and cost four lives in January 2003.[151] Bushfires in suburban Sydney in 2002 also caused several deaths and major property damage, and burnt iconic national park sites in the fringing metropolitan region. Similar predictions of heightened fire risk pertain to most major centres in southern Australia.[152]

Fire, though, is an integral part of the Australian continent, and it has been a significant influence on the evolution of Australia's landscape and biodiversity.[153] Similarly, fire risk is not a new phenomenon for Australian society.[154] But again, climate change brings a new urgency to efforts to formulate legal responses. A significant part of the challenge is property losses due to fires, particularly with respect to liability[155] and risk management issues.[156] In the planning law

---

[147] Victorian Government, 2009 Victorian Bushfires Royal Commission, *Final Report Summary* (2010), <http://www.royalcommission.vic.gov.au/finaldocuments/summary/PF/VBRC_Summary_PF.pdf>, p. vii.
[148] See for example *Bushfires Royal Commission Implementation Monitor Act 2011* (Vic).
[149] K. Hennessey et al., *Climate Change Impacts on Fire-Weather in South-East Australia* (CSIRO, 2006), p. 5.
[150] Ibid.   [151] Bonyhady, 'The Law of Disasters' (2010), p. 266.   [152] See Box 11.1.
[153] G. Cary, 'Importance of a Changing Climate for Fire Regimes in Australia', in *Flammable Australia: Fire Regimes and Biodiversity of a Continent*, eds R. Bradstock, J. Williams and A. Gill (Cambridge University Press, 2002), pp. 26–49.
[154] The Black Friday fires in Victoria (1939), the 1967 fires in Tasmania, and the Ash Wednesday fires in Victoria and South Australia (1983) each killed more than 60 people. In 2009 Black Saturday fires killed 173 people in Victoria, the highest number of civilian casualties in Australia outside wartime.
[155] See for example *Thomas v Powercor Australia Ltd (No. 1)* [2010] VSC 489. In December 2011 a class action settlement was approved by the court: *Thomas v Powercor Australia Ltd* [2011] VSC 614. On 9 May 2012 The Victorian Court of Appeal rejected Powercor's appeal of Thomas' right to compensation: see *Powercor Australia Ltd v Thomas* [2012] VSCA 87.
[156] S. Ellis, P. Kanowski and R. Whelan, *National Inquiry on Bushfire Mitigation and Management*, Inquiry report prepared for Council of Australian Governments, 31 March 2004, <http://www.coagbushfireenquiry.gov.au/findings.htm>.

systems, the capacity for strategic adaptation is most evident in development controls, although the question of whether communities should be rebuilt in fire-prone areas is a sensitive one. Other adaptation measures by statutory authorities include land clearance controls and prescribed burning off. These, too, are not free of controversy, or indeed potential liability. Private adaptation by landowners can be encouraged, in part, through the property law system, and forms of adaptation effected by more stringent building design codes are also possible.

Conway and Lim argue that if the Australian community is to embrace living in a bush environment, even a 'green-wedge' suburban bush environment, then adaptation to fire risk, as well as management of it, are essential. Such management includes shared responsibility by various parties, which include planning and development control consent authorities; bushfire risk consultants, especially those advising local government and state authorities; landholders, including the Crown (especially where Crown land includes forested areas); and the general community.[157]

There is also considerable scope for better protection of property in bushfire-prone areas. These protections can be built into regulation of the construction and planning phases of development. Thus bushfire protection measures should be incorporated into subdivision design and housing development, and into the construction and design standards for buildings.[158] Many of these measures are already evident in most jurisdictions,[159] but may need tightening in the face of accelerating fire risk under climate change. More difficult to regulate, but no less critical, is the ongoing maintenance of bushfire protection measures by landholders and the planning for and implementation of hazard reduction activities.[160] Conway and Lim suggest that:

> [m]anagement for bush fire protection flows from the subdivision stage through the building construction phase to the eventual homeowner. If a bush fire protection measure is implemented at any stage, e.g. at subdivision, this needs to be made known to the builder and homeowner.[161]

This signals a general problem for the legal system: measures to address bushfire risk must be 'obvious' and legally enforceable over time. The maintenance of a cleared firebreak imposed at the time of subdivision in a bushfire-prone area is an example: if the firebreak is to be maintained, it would mean that no buildings or development could be constructed on this private land. As Conway and Lim note for New South Wales, the requirement to maintain the firebreak continues as a covenant on the title of the relevant land, but there may be development pressures in the future that act to remove any covenant. Further, as yet there is little research about whether these requirements are actively enforced in the

---

157 A. Conway and L. Lim, 'The Recent Bushfire Crisis in NSW. Where to from Here?', 7 *Local Government Law Journal* 169 (2002), p. 172.
158 Ibid., p. 171.   **159** Durrant, *Legal Responses to Climate Change* (2010), p. 264.
160 Conway and Lim, 'The Recent Bushfire Crisis in NSW' (2002), p. 171.
161 Ibid., p. 171, drawing on the NSW Rural Fire Service document, *Planning for Bushfire Protection* (2001).

longer term. Experience in other environmental and planning law fields with private covenants would suggest that stringent enforcement is unlikely.

By contrast, many private landowners seek actively to clear sites, in tension with native vegetation controls and biodiversity protection under planning laws. Similar controversies exist around the responsibilities of fire authorities and government departments with control over the management of national parks for bushfire fuel load reductions and 'burning off'. These more strategic adaptive measures remain contested, and the planning law and development control systems must 'balance' a range of competing interests.

Disaster strikes: Emergency responses and the legal system

When a bushfire actually strikes, another set of potential risks, responsibilities and liabilities come into play, much of it mediated through the legal system. Thus attention turns to emergency responses and disaster management. Some stories in the media have entertained the possibility of class actions on behalf of bushfire victims.[162] The reality is more constrained. However, in the aftermath of fires in the Australian Capital Territory (ACT) and in Victoria, there have been questions raised about the capacity and effective functioning of the emergency service providers. Much of this critique has crystallised around an alleged failure to warn citizens in danger from fire threat.[163]

Bonyhady provides an in-depth study of the tortuous inquiry process in the ACT following the 2003 fires in that jurisdiction.[164] He charts the problems faced by, first, a relatively narrow governmental inquiry which recommended a reorganisation of emergency services,[165] and then a coronial inquiry where the coroner sought to conduct a relatively wide-ranging investigation into the fire-related deaths. Concurrently there was a civil tort action. The coronial process faced controversial legal challenges from the ACT government and individuals within the government who were connected to emergency services. Its findings about the competence of the emergency services and their state of knowledge were disputed, and ultimately the Supreme Court of the ACT quashed key findings on the state of knowledge about fire risks.

In Victoria, the Bushfire Royal Commission tackled similar controversial and emotive questions, including the competence and actions of the Chief Commissioner of Police, who held overarching statutory responsibility for the coordination of emergency services. Among the recommendations of the Commission was that amendments be made to the *Emergency Management Act 1986* (Vic) to clarify the functions and powers of the relevant Minister and the Chief Commissioner of Police,[166] given the controversy and apparent confusion regarding roles and responsibilities that occurred as the disaster unfolded.

---

162 A 'class action' is more technically a group proceeding: see for example Part 4A of the *Supreme Court Act 1986* (Vic).
163 Bonyhady, 'The Law of Disasters' (2010), pp. 268–9.   **164** Ibid.
165 *Emergencies Act 2004* (ACT).
166 2009 Victorian Bushfires Royal Commission, *Final Report Recommendations* (2009), p. 11.

At a different institutional level, a class action in the Victorian Supreme Court was initiated on behalf of a group of bushfire victims from the devastating Kilmore East fire from 'Black Saturday' 2009.[167] The claims against the state include, *inter alia*, that 'Victoria Police officers breached both the statutory and common law duties owed to [Mrs Mathews] and the group members.' It is also alleged that police officers 'failed to warn residents who were likely to be exposed to the approaching fire or to supervise/coordinate the activities of members of other emergency response organisations ... in relation to the provision of warnings'.[168] At first instance, Justice Forrest held that the claim for breach of statutory duty against the state (i.e. the duty of police officers in respect of the operation of the emergency services statutory functions, including a form of duty to warn) was untenable, but that a claim in negligence was tenable. The claim in negligence is to be heard in early 2013.[169] Furthermore, as McDonald notes, the trend in negligence law has been for the courts to place a relatively restrictive interpretation on the scope of the duty of care held by government authorities.[170] Statutory tort law reforms similarly have narrowed the circumstances in which authorities may be liable in negligence. Whether such an interpretation will extend to the relatively better resourced state governments,[171] and how issues of agency and vicarious liability are resolved, are yet to be determined. What can be drawn from this situation, though, is that the development of law in response to natural disaster risks will be an important component of climate change adaptation.

The scope of potential liability extends much further than statutory authorities and emergency service providers. An alleged cause of a damaging fire on 'Black Saturday' in Victoria was a faulty electricity distribution line. Several power companies and a company responsible for checking the electricity lines were joined as tortfeasors in a class action with the State of Victoria. This jointure highlights the potential liability of companies that provide electricity infrastructure services in a privatised electricity market, where that infrastructure is ageing and potentially unsafe in circumstances of accelerating bushfire risk.[172] The position of 'third party' entities with responsibilities for audit and

---

[167] *Matthews v SPI Electricity; SPI Electricity Pty Ltd v Utility Services Corporation Ltd (No. 2)* [2011] VSC 168 (10 May 2011). A central issue was whether there was a statutory duty created by the *Emergency Management Act 1986* and associated disaster planning.
[168] *Matthews v SPI Electricity and SPI Electricity Pty Ltd v Utility Services Corporation Ltd (No. 2)* [2011] VSC 168, paras. 129–130.
[169] For information see *Matthews v SPI Electricity and SPI Electricity Pty Ltd v Utility Services Corporation Ltd (No. 5)* [2012] VSC 66, <http://www.scvcases.com.au/MyPDF%20Library/%5B2012%5D%20VSC%2066.pdf>.
[170] McDonald, 'Paying the Price of Adaptation' (2010), pp. 248–9.
[171] Arguably one of the public policy reasons for limiting a duty of care for statutory authorities is that such institutions would not have sufficient resources to meet their obligations if charged with extensive duties. See *Graham Barclay Oysters Pty Ltd v Ryan* (2002) 211 CLR 540.
[172] The Victorian Bushfires Royal Commission recommended replacement of ageing network infrastructure. A key recommendation was to replace all single-wire earth return power lines in Victoria with aerial bundled cable, underground cabling or other technology that greatly reduces bushfire risk. See 2009 Victorian Bushfires Royal Commission (2009), Vol. II pp. 151–3, 159.

safety checking of distribution lines is also seen as requiring a more stringent adaptation approach.[173]

The effectiveness of legal frameworks in Australia

Analysis of the diverse case studies on climate change adaptation within Australia has revealed that legal frameworks represent a patchy and at times ad hoc means of responding to climate change. In part this results from the fact that the legal frameworks have not been 'purpose-built' for this function. As in so many areas of law, we find old legal forms, such as causes of action in negligence, being adapted to new purposes. In other fields a more structured and strategic approach is emerging, largely through the adoption of statutory frameworks and associated policy principles to guide decision-making in areas such as planning law. The courts also have a role, with climate change litigation adding a new dimension to governments' and individuals' means of adapting to the effects of climate change. Greater coherence in legal frameworks for adaptation can be expected as Australian society and its institutions gain experience and expertise in this area of governance.

Regional adaptation: Climate change displacement

Although the challenges facing Australia are considerable, this country has significant financial, technological and administrative resources at its disposal that can be deployed to facilitate adaptation to climate change. Many developing countries around the world are not so fortunate, particularly Least Developed Countries in the African and Asian regions and small island states in the Pacific and Indian Oceans.[174] In these regions, the effects of climate change could exacerbate existing resource shortages and/or render some areas uninhabitable, leading to the internal displacement of populations within countries or large-scale migration of populations to surrounding nations. As early as its first report in 1990, the IPCC warned that the gravest effects of climate change may be felt in terms of human migration from areas affected by coastal erosion and flooding, and agricultural disruption.[175] Estimates of the number of people likely to be displaced by climate change range from 50 million to 250 million people by 2050, although these figures are disputed.[176]

Despite the potential scale of the problem, the existing international legal framework for managing it is rudimentary at best. This is not due to a shortage

---

[173] See *Wrongs Act 1958* (Vic) Part IVAA as an example of proportionate liability.
[174] Maplecroft, 'Big Economies of the Future – Bangladesh, India, Philippines, Vietnam and Pakistan – Most at Risk from Climate Change', <http://maplecroft.com/about/news/ccvi.html>.
[175] IPCC, *Climate Change: The IPCC Scientific Assessment* (Cambridge University Press, 1990).
[176] J. McAdam and B. Saul, 'Displacement with Dignity: Climate Change, Migration and Security in Bangladesh', 53 *German Yearbook of International Law* 1 (2010).

of potentially applicable international legal instruments. Rather, the problem arises because existing international laws are not well adapted to the issue of displacement due to climate change. In the following sections, we survey the various international legal regimes that might be applicable and identify the gaps that remain. We then consider the strategies that have been proposed to address these gaps.

Existing international laws

People displaced by climate change are not recognised as a special category under any existing international legal regime. Despite the popular currency of the term 'climate change refugees', refugee law scholars point out that international refugee law is not strictly applicable to the issue of climate change displacement.[177] People displaced by climate change do not come within the narrow definition of 'refugee' under the 1951 Refugee Convention, which is based upon a person having 'a well-founded fear of persecution on account of his or her race, religion, nationality, political opinion or membership of a particular social group'.[178]

The lack of specific international legal provision for 'climate change refugees' raises questions about how climate change displacement should be conceptualised and hence which is the best international regime or set of regimes to manage the problem. From one perspective, human migration in response to climate change may be seen as an environmental problem, with the remedy lying in international laws relating to climate change mitigation, support for adaptation, and state responsibility for harm. From another perspective, though, climate change displacement is a deeply human problem, enlivening the international legal systems governing human rights and the protection of disadvantaged or vulnerable groups such as indigenous peoples or children. Still others argue for climate change displacement to be treated as a matter of security, given the potential for such migration to exacerbate existing conflicts over scarce natural resources or to give rise to new conflicts.[179] This might bring into operation international humanitarian laws, as well as possibly empowering the United Nations Security Council to deal with the question.[180]

Role of international environmental law

As previously mentioned, there is little provision in the current international climate change legal framework for climate change adaptation, and no mention

---

177 E. Burleson, 'Climate Change Displacement to Refuge', 25(19) *Journal of Environmental Law and Litigation* 19 (2010), p. 21; and A. Williams, 'Turning the Tide: Recognizing Climate Change Refugees in International Law', 30(4) *Law and Policy* 502 (2008), pp. 507–10.
178 *Convention Relating to the Status of Refugees*, opened for signature 28 July 1951, 189 UNTS 150 (entered into force 22 April 1954), Art. 1A(2).
179 International Organization for Migration, *Climate Change, Migration and Critical International Security Considerations* (2011).
180 See for example *Climate Change and its Possible Security Implications* (18 May 2009), GA Res 63/281, UN Doc A/63/L.8/Rev.1.

at all of displacement of peoples as a result of climate change. The general requirement on parties to the UNFCCC to cooperate in preparing for adaptation to the effects of climate change may provide a basis for more specific arrangements governing climate change displacement.[181] In addition, adaptation funding provided by developed countries, including technical assistance, may be of use to developing countries that are particularly vulnerable to the adverse effects of climate change. However, no obligation is placed on developed countries or UNFCCC parties more generally to assist or resettle persons displaced by severe climate change effects such as the inundation of entire islands.

Customary rules of international environmental law regarding state responsibility for harm are also unlikely to offer a satisfactory solution. Principle 21 of the Stockholm Declaration on the Human Environment[182] and Principle 2 of the Rio Declaration on Environment and Development[183] impose a requirement of international legal responsibility on states to ensure that activities within their jurisdiction or control do not cause damage to the environment of other states. However, their application to the situation of small island states whose territory is submerged as a result of climate change-induced sea-level rise poses many practical problems.[184] For instance, which states are to be held responsible for the damage, given the multiple contributors to global warming? How can causation of damage be established? If responsibility can be established, what would be an appropriate remedy? Could a remedy be issued on the basis of threatened rather than actual harm? And would an international court such as the International Court of Justice have jurisdiction to determine the claim? These issues place substantial obstacles in the way of a successful claim of international legal responsibility for displacement due to anthropogenic GHG emissions.

Human rights instruments

A more promising avenue may be the international legal framework governing human rights. Potentially applicable human rights instruments include the International Covenant on Civil and Political Rights (ICCPR),[185] the International Covenant on Economic, Social and Cultural Rights (ICESCR),[186]

---

181 United Nations Framework Convention on Climate Change (New York) 9 May 1992, in force 24 March 1994; 1771 UNTS 107, Art. 4(1)(e).
182 *Declaration of the United Nations Conference on the Human Environment*, adopted 1 January 1973, *Report of the United Nations Conference on the Human Environment*, Stockholm, 5–16 June 1972, UN Doc A/CONF.48/14/Rev.1, ch I, reprinted (1972) 11 ILM 1416.
183 *Rio Declaration on Environment and Development*, adopted June 14 1992, *Report of the United Nations Conference on Environment and Development* 3, Rio de Janeiro, June 3–14, 1992, UN Doc. A/Conf. 151/51 Rev. 1, Vol. I, reprinted in (1992) 31 ILM 874.
184 A. Strauss, 'Climate Change Litigation: Opening the Door to the International Court of Justice', in *Adjudicating Climate Change: State, National and International Approaches*, eds W. C. G. Burns and H. M. Osofsky (Cambridge University Press, 2009).
185 International Covenant on Civil and Political Rights, 16 December 1966, 999 UNTS 171 (entered into force 23 March 1976).
186 International Covenant on Economic, Social and Cultural Rights, 16 December 1966, 993 UNTS 3 (entered into force 3 January 1976).

the Convention on the Rights of the Child,[187] the United Nations Declaration on the Rights of Indigenous Peoples,[188] the Torture Convention,[189] and regional human rights treaties such as the European Convention for the Protection of Human Rights and Fundamental Freedoms.[190]

While a specific environmental right is a feature of only a few regional human rights conventions and some national constitutions, there are a number of other human rights that may be relevant, such as the right to life (ICCPR, Article 6), the right to an adequate standard of living, including adequate food, housing and the continuous improvement of living conditions (ICESCR, Article 11), the right to health (ICESCR, Article 12) the right to self-determination (ICCPR, Article 1(1) and ICESCR, Article 1(1)) and the right of ethnic or indigenous minorities within countries to enjoy their own culture (ICCPR, Article 27 and Convention on the Rights of the Child, Article 30). The jurisprudence of bodies such as the international human rights committee, the Inter-American Commission on Human Rights, and the European Court of Human Rights has previously drawn links between environmental harms and the violation of human rights, which might found a basis for a claim respecting rights violation in the context of climate change.[191] However, no international human rights case based on the effects of climate change has yet been successfully litigated: a petition filed by the Inuit indigenous groups of the Arctic region with the Inter-American Commission on Human Rights did not proceed past the admissibility stage.[192]

Nonetheless, interest in the topic is growing. On 28 March 2008, the United Nations Human Rights Council passed its first resolution, noting that 'climate change poses an immediate and far-reaching threat to people and communities around the world'.[193] In March 2009, a further resolution noted that 'climate change-related impacts have a range of implications, both direct and indirect, for the effective enjoyment of human rights'.[194] While this attention at the highest levels of policy-making is welcome, the resolutions do not address the broader question of whether international human rights laws provide an effective

---

[187] Convention on the Rights of the Child, 20 November 1989, 1577 UNTS 3 (entered into force 2 September 1990).
[188] United Nations Declaration on the Rights of Indigenous Peoples, 13 September 2007, A/RES/61/295.
[189] Convention against Torture and Other Cruel, Inhuman or Degrading Treatment or Punishment, 10 December 1984, 1465 UNTS 85 (entered into force 26 June 1987).
[190] European Convention for the Protection of Human Rights and Fundamental Freedoms, opened for signature 4 November 1950, 2123 UNTS 221 (entered into force 3 September 1953).
[191] See for example V. Kolmannskog and F. Myrstad, 'Environmental Displacement in European Asylum Law', 11 *European Journal of Migration and Law* 313 (2009). A broader suggestion that goes beyond the climate context is that of C. Schall, 'Public Interest Litigation Concerning Environmental Matters before Human Rights Courts: A Promising Future Concept?', 20(3) *Journal of Environmental Law* 417 (2008).
[192] Petition to the Inter-American Commission on Human Rights Seeking Relief from Violations resulting from Global Warming caused by Acts and Omissions of the United States (7 December 2005), <http://www.ciel.org/Publications/ICC_Petition_7Dec05.pdf>.
[193] *Human Rights and Climate Change*, UN HRC Res. 7/23, UN HRC, 41st mtg, UN Doc A/HRC/7/78 (28 March 2008), Preamble. In that Resolution, the HRC also requested the OHCHR to study the human rights implications of climate change (para. 1).
[194] UN HRC Res. 10/4, 41st mtg, UN Doc. A/HRC/10/L.11 (31 March 2009).

mechanism for responding to human rights/climate change problems such as displacement.

Promising research work is proceeding,[195] yet it seems that fundamental obstacles persist. Some of these stem from the human rights framework itself, which is based on the principle of holding states responsible for human rights violations occurring within their territory. However, climate change displacement is most likely to affect peoples whose states have played a lesser, even an insubstantial, role in releasing emissions of GHGs. It remains uncertain whether human rights mechanisms are capable of providing an effective remedy for harms that have their origins in actions (or inaction) in the territory of a third state.[196]

Climate change displacement as a security issue

There is also growing attention to the possible security ramifications of climate change. In April 2007, the United Nations Security Council first considered how climate change might affect international peace and security, including an open debate on energy, security and climate.[197] This may pave the way for future Security Council resolutions to address climate change impacts as a threat to international peace and security.[198]

In the South Pacific region, climate change has been cast as a potential security threat. In August 2008, the Niue Declaration on Climate Change was adopted at the 39th Pacific Island Forum, committing members to 'continue to advocate and support the recognition, in all international fora, of the urgent social, economic *and security* threats caused by the adverse impacts of climate change and sea level rise to our territorial integrity and continued existence as viable dynamic communities; and of the potential for climate change to impact on *intranational and international security*'.[199]

An advantage of treating climate change displacement as a security matter is that it may bring into play relatively powerful international legal mechanisms such as the resolution-making powers of the UN Security Council. On the other hand, international humanitarian law pays little attention to the originating causes of conflict, and thus in the climate change context would offer at best an ex post facto incentive to reduce GHG emissions or improve efforts to adapt. In addition, if an international conflict arose or was exacerbated by climate change, enlivening the regimes of international humanitarian law, these laws would offer

---

[195] See for example J. McAdam, *Climate Change, Forced Migration and International Law* (Oxford University Press, 2012).
[196] With respect to extraterritorial application of human rights, see R. Verheyen, *Climate Change Damage and International Law: Prevention Duties and State Responsibility* (Martinus Nijhoff Publishers, 2005); and see discussion in J. McAdam, 'Environmental Migration Governance', Working Paper, University of New South Wales Faculty of Law Research Series, 2009, <http://law.bepress.com/unswwps/flrps09/art1>.
[197] UN Department of Public Information, News and Media Division, Security Council Holds First-ever Debate on Impact of Climate Change on Peace, Security, Hearing over 50 Speakers, UN Doc. SC/9000, 17 April 2007, <http://www.un.org/News/Press/docs/2007/sc9000.doc.htm>.
[198] See discussion in F. Sindico, 'Climate Change: A Security (Council) Issue?', 1 *Climate Change Law Review* 29 (2007).
[199] The Niue Declaration on Climate Change, endorsed at the 39th Pacific Island Forum, Niue, 19–20 August 2008, <http://www.forumsec.org.fj/resources/uploads/attachments/documents/THE%20NIUE%20DECLARATION%20ON%20CLIMATE%20CHANGE.pdf> (emphasis added).

only general protection for affected populations, without providing specific relief for those displaced from their homelands as a result of climate change-related conflicts.[200]

Addressing gaps in the international legal framework

There has been some consideration of ways to address the gaps in the current international legal framework for the protection of peoples displaced by climate change. One area of vigorous debate concerns whether the best way forward is to adapt present laws to better deal with the issue of climate change displacement or the only solution is the creation of a new international convention.[201] Ideas for modifying existing laws include adopting a more expansive notion of a 'refugee' under the Refugee Convention,[202] expanding the principle of non-refoulement under international human rights and international humanitarian law to provide protection for displaced persons in third states whose situation has resulted from climate change, and building on existing protections for internally displaced persons to apply them to situations of climate change displacement.[203]

It appears that neither the incremental nor the 'new treaty' proposals offer an ideal solution. Many legal uncertainties remain over whether expansions of existing legal doctrines are possible and would be effective. With regard to developing a new treaty on the issue of human migration caused by climate change, the slow progress in current international climate change negotiations, as well as the political sensitivity about accepting displaced persons in many developed countries, foreshadow significant hurdles for this proposal. Indeed, some argue that a 'bottom-up' regional or nationally focused approach may be more feasible over the longer term.[204]

Conclusion

As the complexities of how societies can adapt to climate change begin to unfold, it is clear that national legal systems, including that of Australia, will face particular challenges. Science is able to provide general guidance on the nature

---

200 J. McAdam and B. Saul, 'An Insecure Climate for Human Security? Climate-Induced Displacement and International Law', Sydney Centre Working Paper 4, 2009, <http://sydney.edu.au/law/scil/documents/2009/SCILWP4_Final.pdf>.
201 For discussion of the latter proposal see D. Hodgkinson et al., 'Copenhagen, Climate Change "Refugees" and the Need for a Global Agreement', 4(2) *Public Policy* 159 (2009) and B. Docherty and T. Giannini, 'Confronting a Rising Tide: A Proposal for a Convention on Climate Change Refugees', 33 *Harvard Environmental Law Review* 349 (2009); cf. J. McAdam, 'Swimming against the Tide: Why a Climate Change Displacement Treaty is Not the Answer', 23(1) *International Journal of Refugee Law* 2 (2011).
202 See, for example, Republic of the Maldives, Ministry of Environment, Energy and Water, *Report on the First Meeting on Protocol on Environmental Refugees: Recognition of Environmental Refugees in the 1951 Convention and 1967 Protocol Relating to the Status of Refugees* (14–15 August 2006), cited in F. Biermann and I. Boas, 'Protecting Climate Refugees: The Case for a Global Protocol', *Environment* (November–December 2008); cf. Williams, 'Turning the Tide' (2008), pp. 507–10.
203 Williams, 'Turning the Tide' (2008), pp. 510–13.
204 S. Glazebrook, 'Human Rights and the Environment', 40 *Victoria University of Wellington Law Review* 293 (2009).

of climate change and its impacts, and that knowledge is growing more precise, but there remain substantial areas of uncertainty, particularly at local levels.

International law has been important in setting the broad parameters for adaptation. Globally there has also been a progressive move towards earlier assessments of vulnerability to climate change, combined with strategic enhancement and development of adaptive capacity.

While adaptation ideally should be anticipatory,[205] this is a challenge for national legal systems that are, in large measure, predicated on certainty and finality. Significant shifts towards proactive and planned adaptation will be required if nation-states are to achieve 'principled flexibility' in the face of climate change.[206] Further, anticipatory and planned adaptation is perhaps most suited to statutory law-making in fields such as coastal planning for sea-level rise and flood risk reduction. Adjustments in these areas of the legal system, while contested, still may be easier to implement than in other areas of law, such as tort law.[207] The precautionary principle may help guide decision-makers, but there remain barriers to its widespread adoption. More explicit characterisation of the roles, responsibilities and powers of relevant authorities in responding to risks, such as is emerging in the disaster/emergency services arena, would clearly assist.

Overall, current adaptation modes in law are largely structured around 'direct' climate impacts. How more indirect aspects that flow from those direct impacts are to be addressed, such as the apportionment of risks associated with economic loss, is not at all clear. In addition, the role of civil society and more 'bottom-up' autonomous adaptation should not be ignored – for example, localised responses to bushfire risk at the household level, which lie at the intersection of public and private law.[208]

Greater coherence in governance and institutional organisation at a national level may facilitate more effective adaptation, which requires explicit policy and legal guidance. Adaptation is clearly a multi-scalar issue, but in Australia there is limited coordination across multiple levels of government,[209] beyond 'frameworks' such as the national adaptation strategy. Some coordination has occurred, for example in moves to harmonise building standards and codes in relation to bushfire risks, but there are still no national benchmarks for key adaptation issues such as predicted sea-level rise: different standards apply in different states. In this regard, there has been significant policy attention paid to possible barriers to effective adaptation, with the Australian Productivity Commission releasing a draft report for consultation.[210] The report is designed to 'assist COAG [Council of Australian Governments] to advance climate change adaptation

---

[205] M. Prowse and L. Scott, 'Assets and Adaptation: An Emerging Debate', 39(4) *IDS Bulletin* (2008).
[206] McDonald, 'Mapping the Legal Landscape of Climate Change Mitigation' (2010), p. 13.
[207] Common law systems are much more adept at distributing risks and liabilities: see Durrant, *Legal Responses to Climate Change* (2010), p. 4.
[208] McDonald, 'Mapping the Legal Landscape of Climate Change Mitigation' (2010), pp. 22–3.
[209] Durrant, *Legal Responses to Climate Change* (2010), p. 265.
[210] Productivity Commission, *Draft Report: Barriers to Effective Climate Change* (2012).

reforms in Australia by examining the policy frameworks required to facilitate effective adaptation, and the costs and benefits of various adaptation options so as to identify the highest priority reforms'.[211] The draft report identifies a range of barriers to effective adaptation, including market failure, regulatory barriers, governance and institutional barriers, and behavioural barriers. The findings of the Productivity Commission will provide an important platform for identifying how the existing legal and governance frameworks can be better adapted to climate change.

However, in the adaptation field there is as yet no equivalent of the Intergovernmental Agreement on the Environment, which delineates the respective responsibilities of various levels of the Australian political and administrative spheres. Further, the federal government has not taken a decisive lead on adaptation, presenting its role as primarily one of guidance while other actors take the lead in adopting specific measures.[212] While governments may lack the capacity to fine-tune responses, simply improving access to information is insufficient.[213] This is evident in the Pacific regional context, where it is clear that there is a lack of adaptive capacity, if indeed it is at all possible to 'adapt' to loss of sovereign territory. For these communities, adaptation is further hampered by the limitations of the international legal instruments themselves. Such international legal instruments were created in an era that did not contemplate climate change, and therefore they cannot now be readily aligned to address climate change impacts. Moreover, there is a growing lack of coherence in the international framework for climate change law,[214] where the absence of binding international agreements has led to the development of a multi-scalar governance regime. This means that achieving widespread consensus on climate change actions that create discrete legal obligations for nations is increasingly difficult. Thus new treaties that might better address adaptation and displacement due to sea-level rise are unlikely to emerge, at least in the short term.[215]

In summary, the varying fora, specific requirements and approaches to adaptation in different settings mean that adaptation in the legal system, like mitigation, is taking on a multidimensional form, with multiple responses at multiple levels by the various actors. Consequently, one of the most profound challenges for future developments in this area will be how to bring coherence to the proliferating responses. There is growing attention to how best to achieve coherent and effective adaptation at a policy level. There are attempts to identify impediments to adaptation within existing legal and institutional arrangements,[216] and to explore the opportunities that might be presented by climate change while ensuring appropriate measures are in place to safeguard those

---

[211] Ibid., p. iv.   [212] Durrant, *Legal Responses to Climate Change* (2010), p. 251.
[213] Adger et al., 'Assessment of Adaptation Practices, Options, Constraints and Capacity' (2007), p. 1.
[214] For discussion, see J. Peel, L. Godden and R. Keenan, 'Climate Change Law in an Era of Multi-Level Governance', 1 *Journal of Transnational Environmental Law* (forthcoming 2012).
[215] C. Okereke, H. Bulkeley and H. Schroeder, 'Conceptualising Climate Governance Beyond the International Regime', 9 *Global Environmental Politics* 58 (2009).
[216] Productivity Commission, *Draft Report: Barriers to Effective Climate Change* (2012).

people, places and ecosystems at risk.[217] The need for a multi-pronged response reminds us that adaptation will need to be conceived as more than a physical and technical reaction to impacts. It will involve significant institutional transformation and law will figure prominently in developing the pro-active and strategic directions required by such institutional transformations. At the same time, law itself will need to evolve in order to embrace more robust and systemic predictive capacity in areas such as planning law and environmental impact assessment and for more resilient adaptive capacity in its monitoring and compliance. Law will also continue to play a very significant role as the default governance regime that can identify climate change risks – and potential liability – and in providing a means through the courts to test the robustness of decision-making in the face of climate change. There will need to be significant investment in the evolution of our legal system to meet the challenges of adapting to climate change.

---

217 M. Stafford Smith and A. Ash, 'Adaptation: Reducing Risk, Gaining Opportunity', in *Climate Change: Science and Solutions for Australia*, eds H. Cleugh, M. Stafford Smith, M. Battaglia and P. Graham (CSIRO, 2011).

Postscript

The Copenhagen Accord calls for coordinated state action 'to hold the increase in global temperature below 2 degrees Celsius'. In fact, the current emission reduction pledges of the Accord's signatories imply a temperature increase of between 2.5 and 5°C by 2100.[1] Experts estimate the gap between a bearable but still risky 2°C future and the dangerous future that awaits us under the current pledges to be 6–11 Gt of CO_2 eq. emissions per year by 2020 – depending on whether the pledges are followed through in their strong or weak form.[2] To bridge the gap, countries must, starting now, implement increasingly stringent mitigation measures over the next few years, so that by 2020 global emissions are reduced by a further 6–11 Gt CO_2 eq. to around 44 Gt CO_2 eq. for that year.

In its 2011 *Bridging the Emissions Gap* report, UNEP argues that policy-makers have many options for narrowing or closing the emissions gap by 2020. Countries could make their energy systems more efficient than under business-as-usual conditions; they could produce a larger share of their primary energy from renewable energy sources in some combination; they could reduce emissions from the forestry, agriculture and waste sectors through better management strategies and innovative measures such as credit schemes; and they could achieve all of this, and more, with the technologies at hand and at a cost that is not prohibitive.[3] This is not to say that any of these outcomes is inevitable.[4] How quickly renewable energy production grows to meet the world's energy needs, for example, depends heavily on government action to reduce the relative cost of renewable technologies.[5] Change 'will require continued efforts, both "top-down", through international diplomacy, and "bottom-up", through national policy'.[6]

---

[1] UN Environment Programme, *Bridging the Emissions Gap: A UNEP Synthesis Report* (November 2011), p. 16. See also J. Rogelj et al., 'Copenhagen Accord Pledges Are Paltry', 464 *Nature* 1126 (22 April 2010).
[2] UN Environment Programme, *Bridging the Emissions Gap* (November 2011), p. 8. For an overview of the conditionalities attaching to country pledges, see UNFCCC Secretariat, *Quantified Economy-Wide Emission Reduction Targets by Developed Country Parties to the Convention: Assumptions, Conditions, Commonalities and Differences in Approaches and Comparison of the Level of Emission Reduction Efforts* (8 May 2012), FCCC/TP/2012/2, especially pp. 18–20.
[3] Ibid., p. 11. See also S. Pacala and R. Socolow, 'Stabilization Wedges: Solving the Climate Problem for the Next 50 Years with Current Technologies', 305 *Science* 968 (13 August 2004).
[4] K. Johnson, 'Ill Winds Blow for Clean Energy: Cheap, and Abundant, Natural Gas Diminishes Alternative Projects' Appeal', *Wall Street Journal* (9 July 2009). The expectation of low natural gas prices from the huge new shale gas supplies in the United States has caused a number of developers who were making big investments in wind projects to delay or abandon those projects.
[5] International Energy Agency, *World Energy Outlook 2010: Executive Summary* (2010), pp. 9–10.
[6] M. Jacobs, 'Deadline 2015', 481 *Nature* 137 (12 January 2012), p. 138.

As we have sought to illustrate in this book, a wide range of policy measures for the mitigation of GHG emissions have already been adopted and are in use in many different sectors and countries, including Australia. These measures have had some success in reducing emissions, but not, as UNEP warns, to the level required to avoid dangerous warming. Legal frameworks – international and domestic – have in most cases been used to implement the policies. For example, in all Annex I countries, including Australia, energy efficiency improvements through regulation now form a significant part of mitigation policy. Law has a critical role to play in support of mitigation efforts, and a greater range of legal measures remains to be implemented.

While the legal frameworks have matured considerably with respect to their applicability to mitigation of climate change, there has been less progress in the area of adaptation. Mitigation is still perceived as the most urgent policy problem, for the reasons given in the opening paragraph above: the window of opportunity is closing fast.[7] As we approach 2020, adaptation policy and its implementation through the law and other means are likely to evolve quickly. If the state parties to the UNFCCC do not greatly intensify their mitigation effort, despite the urgings of UNEP and others, the adaptation challenge will grow ominously as we prepare to adapt to harsher conditions.

Although generally conceived of as a bottom-up response, climate change adaptation, like mitigation, needs to operate in conjunction with top-down international coordination mechanisms addressed to issues such as capacity-building. Funding for adaptation to date has been ad hoc and often tied to funding for mitigation (as in the case of the adaptation 'tax' applied by the CDM – see Box 6.1 in Chapter 6). With the advent of the UNFCCC's Green Climate Fund and Technology Mechanism, support for the implementation of National Adaptation Programmes of Action may for the first time become predictable and systematic.

In the meantime, countries need to plan and begin to implement processes for adaptation to climate change. Countries with particular vulnerabilities, such as Australia, have already recognised the need for change within established frameworks of planning law, liability, and emergency management regimes.

We have argued that both international and domestic climate law are now established, but that further development is required as the challenges from climate change increase. Domestic law largely takes its lead from the UNFCCC negotiations, which, since Copenhagen, are refining the existing paradigm rather than attempting any radical shift away from it. In fact, since the Durban COP in 2011, any paradigm shift has officially been postponed to 2020. Within the confines of the current space, much interesting legal work remains to be done

---

[7] For example, the United States continues to give priority to mitigation over adaptation: US Department of State, *Meeting the Fast Start Commitment: US Climate Finance in Fiscal Year 2011* (2011), p. 4 ('Our aim is to take a finite but growing core of public money and combine it with smart policies to substantially increase public flows into climate friendly investments in both mitigation, and where possible, adaptation. These resources will be especially important as we ... work towards our collective goal to mobilize $100 billion per year by 2020, in the context of meaningful mitigation actions and transparency on implementation').

in this decade. Perhaps the most complex task of all is to effectively and equitably implement REDD+, so as to reduce emissions from deforestation and forest degradation in developing countries.

At the domestic level, too, each country has much fine-tuning to do, even while international aspirations remain flat. For some nations this will require the introduction of more stringent mitigation laws; for others it will require a continual reassessment of the laws that have been put in place as the knowledge of and experience in climate law increases. In Australia, implementation of the *Clean Energy Act 2011* and associated legislation could easily preoccupy the federal government through 2020 (if the EU ETS experience is any guide). Whether all the regulatory refinement will lead, in time, to a transformation in values – the crossing of a social tipping point after which the fight against climate change becomes an obvious and self-reinforcing priority for all – is probably not something we will know before the end of the decade.

As we endeavour to look ahead into that future, a number of other issues may come to the fore. If the Durban process does not deliver on its promise of an effective, comprehensive, multilateral climate change agreement for 2020 onwards, we may see countries with stronger domestic climate law regimes, such as the European Union, using international trade restrictions to put pressure on other countries to implement stronger, more ambitious climate policies. How the WTO might deal with a dispute over climate-related trade measures remains an open question.[8] Other international tribunals may also become engaged: the Pacific Island state of Palau is currently seeking support in the UN General Assembly for a request to the International Court of Justice for an Advisory Opinion on the responsibilities and obligations of states with respect to reducing harmful levels of GHG emissions.[9]

Again, if current mitigation efforts fail, there may also be a need to consider the more radical technological options, such as large-scale geoengineering.[10] As in many areas, technological efforts in this regard are running far ahead of legal and regulatory discussion, but it is important that we subject all technological options to rigorous assessment to ensure that such measures are effective and legally feasible, and that risks to other aspects of environmental health are not brushed aside. Climate change is thus likely to continue to pose great challenges to our established legal concepts and mechanisms, requiring innovation and transformation in the field of law as much as in other disciplines.

---

[8] For an introduction to the issues see L. Tamiotti et al., *Trade and Climate Change*, WTO-UNEP Report (Geneva, 2009), especially pp. 90–110.
[9] 'Palau Seeks UN World Court Opinion on Damage Caused by Greenhouse Gases', UN News Centre, 22 September 2011, <http://www.un.org/apps/news/story.asp?NewsID=39710&Cr=pacific+island&Cr1=>.
[10] Geoengineering aims 'to intervene in the climate system by deliberately modifying the Earth's energy balance to reduce increases of temperature and eventually stabilise temperature at a lower level than would otherwise be attained': see Royal Society, *Geoengineering the Climate: Science, Governance and Uncertainty* (Royal Society, London, 2009), p. 1, <http://royalsociety.org/policy/publications/2009/geoengineering-climate/>. It embraces a wide range of activities including carbon dioxide removal methods, such as iron ocean fertilisation, and solar radiation management methods, such as cloud seeding.

Bibliography

All material other than UNFCCC/Kyoto Protocol

Abate, R. and Greenlee, A., 'Sowing Seeds Uncertain: Ocean Iron Fertilization, Climate Change, and the International Environmental Law Framework' (2010) 27(2) *Pace Environmental Law Review* 555.

Abbott, C., 'Environmental Command Regulation', in B. Richardson and S. Wood (eds), *Environmental Law for Sustainability* (Hart Publishing, 2006).

ABC Television, 'Climate change drops off the radar in 2010 election', *The 7.30 Report*, 29 July 2010 (online).

ABC Television, 'The 7.30 Report', 27 April 2010 (online).

ABC Television, 'The 7.30 Report', 9 March 2011 (online).

Ackerman B. and Stewart, R., 'Reforming Environmental Law: The Democratic Case for Market Incentives' (1988) 13 *Columbia Journal of Environmental Law* 171.

Adger, W. et al., 'Assessment of Adaptation Practices, Options, Constraints and Capacity', in M. Parry et al. (eds), *Climate Change 2007: Impacts, Adaptation and Vulnerability: Contribution of Working Group II to the Fourth Assessment Report of the Intergovernmental Panel on Climate Change* (Cambridge University Press, 2007).

AGL, *Submission to the Department of Climate Change and Energy Efficiency on the Clean Energy Legislative Package* (online).

Alexander, S., 'Earth Jurisprudence and the Ecological Case for Degrowth', in P. Burdon (ed.), *Exploring Wild Law: The Philosophy of Earth Jurisprudence* (Wakefield Press, 2011).

Alexeew, J. et al., 'An Analysis of the Relationship between the Additionality of CDM Projects and Their Contribution to Sustainable Development' (2010) 10 *International Environmental Agreements* 233.

Alliance of Small Island States, *Declaration on Climate Change* 2009 (online).

Allison I. et al., *The Copenhagen Diagnosis, 2009: Updating the World on the Latest Climate Science*, Executive Summary (UNSW Climate Change Research Centre, 2009).

Allison I. et al., *The Copenhagen Diagnosis: Updating the World on the Latest Climate Science*, 2nd edn (Elsevier, 2011).

Anderson, K., 'The Inconvenient Truth of Carbon Offsets' (2012) 484 *Nature* 7.

Anderson, K. and Bows, A., '"Beyond Dangerous" Climate Change: Emission Scenarios for a New World' (2011) 369 *Philosophical Transactions of the Royal Society A* 20.

Andersson, K., Evans, T. and Richards, K., 'National Forest Carbon Inventories: Policy Needs and Assessment Capacity' (2009) 93 *Climatic Change* 69.

Anttonen, K., Mehling, M. and Upston-Hooper, K., 'Breathing Life into the Carbon Market: Legal Frameworks of Emissions Trading in Europe' (2007) 16(4) *European Environmental Law Review* 96.

Archer, D. and Brovkin, V., 'The Millennial Atmospheric Lifetime of Anthropogenic CO_2' (2008) 90 *Climatic Change* 283.

Arrhenius, S., 'On the Influence of Carbonic Acid in the Air Upon the Temperature of the Ground' (1896) 41 *Philosophical Magazine* 237.

Ashcroft, R., 'Carbon Capture and Storage – A Need for Re-Conceiving Property Interests and Resource Management in the Australian Legal System (2008) *LAWASIA Journal* 70.

Asia–Pacific Partnership on Clean Development and Climate, 'Purposes of the Partnership' (online).

Aswani, S. and Hamilton, R. 'Integrating Indigenous Ecological Knowledge and Customary Sea Tenure with Marine and Social Science for Conservation of Bumphead Parrotfish (*Bolbometopon muricatum*) in the Roviana Lagoon, Solomon Islands' (2004) 31 *Environmental Conservation* 69.

Atmosfair gGmbH, *CDM Project Design Document for Efficient Fuel Wood Stoves for Nigeria*, CDM website (online).

Atmosfair gGmbH, *Monitoring Report* (14 September 2010), CDM website (online).

Australia and Norway, 'Enhanced Action on Mitigation', *Australia–Norway joint submission under the Cancún Agreements* (September 2011), AWG-LCA, AWG-KP included in INF documents FCCC/SB/2011/INF.1 and FCCC/AWGLCA/2011/INF.1 pursuant to paragraphs 36 and 49 of the Cancún Agreements.

Australian Academy of Science, *The Science of Climate Change: Questions and Answers* (Australian Academy of Science, 2010).

Australian Associated Press, 'Coalition Urges More Action on Forests, as Rallies Back Pro-Carbon Tax Campaign', *The Australian*, 5 June 2011 (online).

Australian Building Codes Board (ABCB), 'Energy Efficiency' (online).

Australian Bureau of Agricultural and Resource Economics and Science (ABARES), *Energy Update* 2011.

Australian Bureau of Meteorology and CSIRO, *Climate Change in the Pacific: Scientific Assessment and New Research. Volume 1. Regional Overview* (2011).

Australian Bureau of Statistics, '2006 Census Quickstats' (online).

Australian Bureau of Statistics, 'Population Projections, Australia, 2006 to 2101' (online).

Australian Capital Territory Government, *Weathering the Change, Draft Action Plan 2, Pathway to a Sustainable and Carbon Neutral ACT 2011–2060*, Options paper for public comment (2011).

Australian Capital Territory Government, Department of Sustainability and Environment, 'Electricity Feed-in Tariff' (online).

Australian Capital Territory Government, Department of Sustainability and Environment, 'Large Scale Renewable Energy Action' (online).

Australian Coal Association, 'The Australian Coal Industry – Coal Exports', (online).

Australian Energy Market Commission (AEMC), *Final Report: Impact of the Enhanced Renewable Energy Target on Energy Markets* (2011).

Australian Government, *Carbon Pollution Reduction Scheme: Australia's Low Pollution Future*, White Paper, vol. 1 (2008).

Australian Government, *A National Plan for Water Security* (2007).

Australian Government, Department of Climate Change, *Australia's Fifth National Communication on Climate Change: A Report under the United Nations Framework Convention on Climate Change* (2010).

Australian Government, Department of Climate Change, *Carbon Pollution Reduction Scheme*, Green Paper (2008).

Australian Government, Department of Climate Change, *National Inventory Report* 2007 (2009).

Australian Government, Department of Climate Change and Energy Efficiency, 'Approved Methodologies' (online).

Australian Government, Department of Climate Change and Energy Efficiency, *Australia's National Greenhouse Gas Accounts*, Quarterly Update (September Quarter 2011).

Australian Government, Department of Climate Change and Energy Efficiency, *Australia's National Greenhouse Gas Accounts: State and Territory Greenhouse Gas Inventories 2009* (2011).

Australian Government, Department of Climate Change and Energy Efficiency, *Carbon Farming Initiative: Draft Methodology for Savanna Burning* (2011).
Australian Government, Department of Climate Change and Energy Efficiency, 'Carbon Farming Initiative Overview' (online).
Australian Government, Department of Climate Change and Energy Efficiency, 'Carbon Pollution Reduction Scheme – Design Features' (online).
Australian Government, Department of Climate Change and Energy Efficiency, 'CFI Activities – Eligible and Excluded' (online).
Australian Government, Department of Climate Change and Energy Efficiency, 'Clean Energy Future: Transport Fuels Fact Sheet' (2011).
Australian Government, Department of Climate Change and Energy Efficiency, *Climate Change Risks to Coastal Buildings and Infrastructure* (2011).
Australian Government, Department of Climate Change and Energy Efficiency, 'Comparison of Different Design Options for a Carbon Price', summary table provided for third meeting of the MPCCC on 21 December 2010 (online).
Australian Government, Department of Climate Change and Energy Efficiency, *Design of the Carbon Farming Initiative, Consultation Paper* (2010).
Australian Government, Department of Climate Change and Energy Efficiency, 'E3: Equipment Energy Efficiency' (online).
Australian Government, Department of Climate Change and Energy Efficiency, 'Green Lease Schedules' (online).
Australian Government, Department of Climate Change and Energy Efficiency, 'Greenhouse Friendly' (online).
Australian Government, Department of Climate Change and Energy Efficiency, 'Industry Consultation on the Draft GEMS Bill' (online).
Australian Government, Department of Climate Change and Energy Efficiency, 'Overview of Regulatory Requirements – Labelling and MEPS' (2010) (online).
Australian Government, Department of Climate Change and Energy Efficiency, *National Carbon Offset Standard – Version 1, November 2009* (2009).
Australian Government, Department of Climate Change and Energy Efficiency, *National Energy Savings Initiative (NESI) – Issues Paper* (2011).
Australian Government, Department of Climate Change and Energy Efficiency, *Report of the Prime Minister's Task Group on Energy Efficiency* (8 October 2010).
Australian Government, Department of Climate Change and Energy Efficiency, *Securing a Clean Energy Future: The Australian Government's Plan* (2011).
Australian Government, Department of Climate Change and Energy Efficiency, 'Stationary Energy Emissions Projections', (9 February 2011) (online).
Australian Government, Department of Climate Change and Energy Efficiency, 'Transport Emissions Projections' (2011) (online).
Australian Government, Department of Energy, Resources and Tourism, *Strategic Framework for Alternative Transport Fuels* (2011).
Australian Government, Department of Energy, Water, Heritage and the Arts, 'Generator Efficiency Standards' (online).
Australian Government, Department of Energy, Water, Heritage and the Arts, 'Greenhouse Challenge Plus' (online).
Australian Government, Department of the Environment, Sport and Territories, *Climate Change: Australia's [First] National Report under the United Nations Framework Convention on Climate Change* (September 1994).
Australian Government, Department of the Environment, Water, Heritage and the Arts, *Australia's Fourth National Report to the United Nations Convention on Biological Diversity* (March 2009).
Australian Government, Department of Infrastructure and Transport, 'High Speed Rail Study' (online).
Australian Government, Department of Resources, Energy and Tourism, 'Carbon Capture and Storage Acreage Release' (online).

Australian Government, Department of Resources, Energy and Tourism, *Continuing Opportunities: Energy Efficiency Opportunities (EEO) Program – 2010 Report, A look at results for the Energy Efficiency Opportunities Program 2006–2010, Taken from public reports of assessments undertaken during the period July 2006–June 2010* (2011).

Australian Government, Department of Resources, Energy and Tourism, *Draft Energy White Paper: Strengthening the Foundations for Australia's Energy Future* (2011).

Australian Government, Department of Resources, Energy and Tourism, 'National Low Emissions Coal Initiative' (online).

Australian Government, Department of Treasury, *Strong Growth, Low Pollution: Modelling a Carbon Price* (2011).

Australian Government, Ecologically Sustainable Development Steering Committee, *National Strategy for Ecologically Sustainable Development* (1992).

Australian Government, Energy Task Force, *Securing Australia's Energy Future* (2004).

Australian Government, Geoscience Australia, 'Uranium Resources' (online).

Australian Government, *Legal Architecture for a Post-2012 Outcome: Submission to the AWG-LCA and AWG-KP* (online).

Australian Government, National Emissions Trading Taskforce, *Discussion Paper: Possible Design for a National Greenhouse Gas Emissions Trading Scheme* (August 2006).

Australian Government, National Low Emissions Coal Council, *National Low Emissions Coal Strategy* (2008).

Australian Government, *Nationwide House Energy Rating Scheme* (online).

Australian Government, Productivity Commission, *Carbon Emission Policies in Key Economies: Research Report* (2011).

Australian Government, Productivity Commission, *Draft Report: Barriers to Effective Climate Change Adaptation* (April 2012) (online).

Australian Government, 'Quantified Economy-Wide Emissions Targets for 2020' (2010) (online).

Australian Government, *The National Greenhouse Strategy: Strategic Framework for Advancing Australia's Greenhouse Response* (1998).

Australian Government, 'Uranium Mining, Processing and Nuclear Energy – Opportunities for Australia': Report to the Prime Minister by the Uranium Mining, Processing and Nuclear Energy Review Taskforce (2006).

Australian Greenhouse Office, *National Emissions Trading: Crediting the Carbon, Discussion Paper 3* (1999).

Australian Greenhouse Office, *National Emissions Trading: Designing the Market, Discussion Paper 4* (1999).

Australian Greenhouse Office, *National Emissions Trading: Establishing the Boundaries, Discussion Paper 1* (1999).

Australian Greenhouse Office, *National Emissions Trading: Issuing the Permits, Discussion Paper 2* (1999).

Australian Housing and Urban Research Institute, 'The Environmental Sustainability of Australia's Private Rental Housing Stock', Final Report, No. 159 (2009).

Australian National Audit Office, *Administration of Climate Change Programs* (2010).

Australian Parliament, House Standing Committee on Science and Innovation, *Between a Rock and a Hard Place: The Science of Geosequestration* (2007).

Australian Parliamentary Library Service, 'Carbon Pricing Mechanism – CPRS and Carbon Pricing Mechanism: Comparison of Selected Features' (15 July 2011) (online).

Baker and McKenzie, *Local Council Risk of Liability in the face of Climate Change – Resolving Uncertainties. A Report for the Australian Local Government Association* (2011).

Barnett, J. and Campbell, J., *Climate Change and Small Island States: Power, Knowledge, and the South Pacific* (Earthscan, 2010).

Barnosky, A. D. et al., 'Has the Earth's Sixth Mass Extinction Already Arrived?' (2011) 471 Nature 51.

Barrett, J., 'The Negotiation and Drafting of the Climate Change Convention', in R. Churchill and D. Freestone (eds), *International Law and Global Climate Change* (Graham and Trotman/Martinus Nijhoff, 1991).
Barton, B., 'Property Rights Created Under Statute in Common Law Legal Systems', in A. McHarg, B. Barton, A. Bradbrook and L. Godden (eds), *Property and the Law in Energy and Natural Resources* (Oxford University Press, 2010).
Barton, B., 'The Law of Energy Efficiency', in D. N. Zillman et al. (eds), *Beyond the Carbon Economy: Energy Law in Transition* (Oxford University Press, 2008).
Barton, J., 'Intellectual Property and Access to Clean Energy Technologies in Developing Countries: An Analysis of Solar Photovoltaic, Biofuel and Wind Technologies', International Centre for Trade and Sustainable Development, Issue Paper No. 2, (December 2007).
Barton, J., 'New Trends in Technology Transfer: Implications for National and International Policy', International Centre for Trade and Sustainable Development, Issue Paper No. 18, (February 2007).
Baugh, L., 'US Legal and Regulatory Challenges of CCS', in I. Havercroft, R. Macrory and R. B. Stewart (eds), *Carbon Capture and Storage: Emerging Legal and Regulatory Issues* (Hart Publishing, 2011).
BBC News, 'Brazil Eases Rules on Conserving Amazon Rainforest' (25 May 2011) (online).
BBC News, 'Brazilian Senate Eases Amazon Protection Rules' (7 December 2011) (online).
Bell, J., 'Planning for Climate Change and Sea Level Rise – Queensland's New Coastal Plan' (2012) 29 *Environmental and Planning Law Journal* 61.
Bell, R. 'Local Governments Take the Lead in Curbing Greenhouse Gas Emissions' (2002) 4(2) *Environmental Practice* 65.
Berntsen, T., Fuglestvedt, J. and Stordal, F., 'Reporting and Verification of Emissions and Removals of Greenhouse Gases', in J. Hovi, O. Stokke and G. Ulfstein (eds), *Implementing the Climate Regime: International Compliance* (Earthscan, 2005).
Bertram, C., 'Ocean Iron Fertilization in the Context of the Kyoto Protocol and the Post-Kyoto Process' (2010) 38(2) *Energy Policy* 1130.
Betsill, M., 'International Climate Change Policy: Toward the Multilevel Governance of Global Warming', in R. S. Axelrod, S. D. VanDeveer and D. L. Downie (eds), *The Global Environment: Institutions, Law and Policy*, 3rd edn (CW Press, 2011).
Biermann, F. and Boas, I., 'Protecting Climate Refugees: The Case for a Global Protocol' (2008) 50(6) *Environment* 9.
Bietta, F., 'From the Hague to Copenhagen: Why It Failed Then and Why It Could Be Different', in V. Bosetti and R. Lubowski (eds), *Deforestation and Climate Change: Reducing Carbon Emissions from Deforestation and Forest Degradation* (Edward Elgar Publishing, 2010).
Bilger, B., 'Hearth Surgery: The Quest for a Stove That Can Save the World', *The New Yorker*, 21 and 28 December 2009, p. 84.
Birkmann, J. and von Teichmann, K., 'Integrating Disaster Risk Reduction and Climate Change Adaptation: Key Challenges, Scales and Norms' (2010) 5 *Sustainability Science* 171.
Birnie, P., Boyle, A. and Redgwell, C., *International Law and the Environment*, 3rd edn (Oxford University Press, 2009).
Blake Dawson (law firm), 'Carbon Farming Initiative: Implications for Resource Companies in Western Australia', Environment Matters, 28 June 2011 (online).
Blaser, J., Sarre, A., Poore, D. and Johnson, S., *Status of Tropical Forest Management 2011*, ITTO Technical Series No. 38 (International Tropical Timber Organization, 2011).
Bloom, D., Zaidi, A. and Yeh, E., 'The Demographic Impact of Biomass Fuel Use' (2005) 9(3) *Energy for Sustainable Development* 40.
Bloomberg New Energy Finance, 'EU CO_2 Catches Cold as Durban Talks Approach' (online).

Bluemel, E., 'Regional Regulatory Initiatives Addressing GHG Leakage in the USA', in M. Faure and M. Peeters (eds), *Climate Change and European Emissions Trading: Lessons for Theory and Practice* (Edward Elgar Publishing, 2008).

Bodansky, D., *The Art and Craft of International Environmental Law* (Harvard University Press, 2010).

Boer, B., 'World Heritage Disputes in Australia' (1992) 7 *Journal of Environmental Law and Litigation* 247.

Bogojevic, S., 'The Revised EU ETS Directive: Yet Another Stepping Stone' (2009) 11(4) *Environmental Law Review* 279.

Bonyhady, T., 'Swimming in the Streets: The Beginnings of Planning for Sea-Level Rise', in T. Bonyhady, A. Macintosh and J. MacDonald (eds), *Adaptation to Climate Change: Law and Policy* (Federation Press, 2010).

Bonyhady, T., 'The Law of Disasters', in T. Bonyhady, A. Macintosh and J. McDonald (eds), *Adaptation to Climate Change* (Federation Press, 2010).

Bonyhady, T., 'The New Australian Climate Law', in T. Bonyhady and P. Christoff (eds), *Climate Law in Australia* (Federation Press, 2007).

Bonyhady, T. and Christoff, P., *Climate Law in Australia* (Federation Press, 2007).

Bottomley, S. and Bronitt, S., 'Economics and Government Regulation', in S. Bottomley and S. Bronitt, *Law in Context*, 3rd edn (Federation Press, 2006).

Boyd, E. et al., 'Reforming the CDM for Sustainable Development: Lessons Learned and Policy Futures' (2009) 12(7) *Environmental Science and Policy* 820.

Boyd, W., 'Deforestation and Emerging Greenhouse Gas Compliance Regimes: Toward a Global Environmental Law of Forests, Carbon and Climate Governance', in V. Bosetti and R. Lubowski (eds), *Deforestation and Climate Change: Reducing Carbon Emissions from Deforestation and Forest Degradation* (Edward Elgar Publishing, 2010).

Boyd, W., 'Ways of Seeing in Environmental Law: How Deforestation Became an Object of Climate Governance' (2010) 37 *Ecology Law Quarterly* 843.

Bradbrook, A., 'The Development of Renewable Energy Technologies and Energy Efficiency Measures through Public International Law', in D. N. Zillman et al. (eds), *Beyond the Carbon Economy: Energy Law in Transition* (Oxford University Press, 2008).

Braganza, K., Jones, D. and Plummer, N., *Annual Australian Climate Statement 2010* (Bureau of Meteorology, 2011) (online).

Bravo, G., Kozulj, R. and Landaveri, R., 'Energy Access in Urban and Peri-Urban Buenos Aires' (2008) 12(4) *Energy for Sustainable Development* 56.

Brazil Ministry of Science and Technology, 'National Institute for Space Research' (online).

Breidenich, C. and Bodansky, D., *Measurement, Reporting and Verification in a Post-2012 Climate Agreement* (Pew Center on Global Climate Change, 2009).

Briese, R., 'Climate Change Mitigation Down Under – Legislative Responses in a Federal System' (2010) 13 *Asia Pacific Journal of Environmental Law* 75.

Broder, J., 'Obama shifts to speed oil and gas drilling in the US', *The New York Times*, 14 May 2011.

Brooks, D., 'Where Wisdom Lives', *The New York Times*, 6 June 2011.

Brunnée, J., Doelle, M. and Rajamani, L. (eds), *Promoting Compliance in an Evolving Climate Regime* (Cambridge University Press, 2011).

Bureau of Meteorology, *Annual Australian Climate Statement 2005* (Media Release, 4 January 2006) (online).

Bureau of Meteorology National Climate Centre, *Drought Statement*, 3 July 2008 (online).

Burleson, E., 'Climate Change Displacement to Refuge' (2010) 25(19) *Journal of Environmental Law and Litigation* 19.

Caldeira, K. and Davis, S. J., 'Accounting for Carbon Dioxide Emissions: A Matter of Time' (2011) 108(21) *Proceedings of the National Academy of Sciences of the United States of America* 8533.

Campbell, D., Klaes, M. and Bignell, C., 'After Cancun: The Impossibility Of Carbon Trading' (2010) *University of Queensland Law Journal* 163.

Campbell, G., 'Carbon Capture and Storage: Legislative Approaches to Liability' (2009) 28(3) *Australian Resources and Energy Law Journal* 418.
Campbell, R., 'Long-term Liability for Offshore Geo-sequestration', *AMPLA Yearbook* (2006).
Caney, S., 'Cosmpolitan Justice, Responsibility and Global Climate Change', in S. M. Gardiner et al. (eds), *Climate Ethics: Essential Readings* (Oxford University Press, 2010).
Cantley-Smith, R., 'A Changing Legal Environment for the National Electricity Market', in W. Gumley and T. Daya-Winterbottom (eds), *Climate Change Law: Comparative, Contractual and Regulatory Considerations* (Lawbook Company, 2009).
Carbon Finance Unit, *Carbon Finance for Sustainable Development* (World Bank, 2007).
Carbon Shift Advisory Pty Ltd and Aboriginal Carbon Fund, *Design of the Carbon Farming Initiative, Consultation Paper: Submission to the Department of Climate Change and Energy Efficiency* (2011) (online).
Carbon Trust, *Global Carbon Mechanisms: Emerging Lessons and Implications* (2009).
Caripis, L., Peel, J., Godden, L. and Keenan, R., 'Australia's Carbon Pricing Mechanism' (2011) 2 *Climate Law* 583.
Carpenter, C., *Taking Stock of Durban: Review of Key Outcomes and the Road Ahead* (UN Development Programme, 2012).
Carpenter, R. J., 'Implementation of Biological Sequestration Offsets in a Carbon Reduction Policy: Answers to Key Questions for a Successful Domestic Offset Program' (2010) 31 *Energy Law Journal* 157.
Cary, G., 'Importance of a Changing Climate for Fire Regimes in Australia', in R. Bradstock, J. Williams and A. Gill (eds), *Flammable Australia: Fire Regimes and Biodiversity of a Continent* (Cambridge University Press, 2002).
CDM Watch, 'HFC-23 and N2O Projects' (online).
Chagas, T., *Case Study: Forest Carbon Rights in Brazil* (REDD Net, 2010).
Chalifour, N. J., 'A Feminist Perspective on Carbon Taxes' (2010) 21(2) *Canadian Journal of Women and the Law* 169.
Chiam, L., 'Abatements and Offsets: Legal Issues in Reducing Emissions and Developing Offsets Projects' (2007) 27(1) *Australian Resources and Energy Law Journal* 105.
Chicago Climate Exchange, 'Fact Sheet', June 2011 (online).
Christoff, P. and Eckersley, R., 'Kyoto and the Asia Pacific Partnership on Clean Development and Climate', in T. Bonyhady and P. Christoff (eds), *Climate Law in Australia* (Federation Press, 2007).
Ciais, P. et al., 'Atmospheric Inversions for Estimating CO_2 Fluxes: Methods and Perspectives' (2010) 103 *Climatic Change* 69.
Clean Energy Regulator, 'About the Small-scale Renewable Energy Scheme' (online).
Clean Energy Regulator, 'Solar Credits' (online).
Cleetus, R., 'Finding Common Ground in the Debate between Carbon Tax and Cap-and-Trade Policies' (2011) 67(1) *Bulletin of the Atomic Scientists* 17.
ClimateWorks Australia, *Low Carbon Growth Plan for Australia* (2010).
ClimateWorks Australia, *Low Carbon Growth Plan for Australia: Impact of the Carbon Price Package* (August 2011).
ClimateWorks Australia, *Low Carbon Growth Plan for Australia – Report Summary* (2011).
Coase, R., 'The Problem of Social Cost' (1960) 3 *Journal of Law and Economics* 1.
Coelho, S., Goldemberg, J., Lucon, O. and Guardabassi, P., 'Brazilian Sugarcane Ethanol: Lessons Learned' (2006) 10(2) *Energy for Sustainable Development* 26.
Cohen, J. (2012) 'What Will it Take to Save the Earth?' (2012) 59(7) *New York Review of Books* 47.
Cole, D. H., 'Climate Change, Adaptation and Development' (2007) 26 *UCLA Journal of Environmental Law and Policy* 1.
Collier, P., *The Bottom Billion: Why the Poorest Countries Are Failing and What Can Be Done About It* (Oxford University Press, 2008).

Combet, G., Australian Minister for Climate Change and Energy Efficiency, 'Australia and New Zealand Advance Linking of their Emissions Trading Schemes' (Media Release, GC 333/115, December 2011).

Combet, G., Australian Minister for Climate Change and Energy Efficiency, 'Breakthrough at Durban Climate Change Conference' (Media Release, GC 343/11, 11 December 2011).

Combet, G., Australian Minister for Climate Change and Energy Efficiency and C. Hedegaard, European Commissioner for Climate Action, 'Australia and Europe Strengthen Collaboration on Carbon Markets' (Joint Media Release, GC 334/11, 5 December 2011).

Comrie, N. et al., *Review of the 2010–2011 Flood Warnings and Response, Final Report*, 1 December 2011 (online).

Conway, A. and Lim, L., 'The Recent Bushfire Crisis in NSW. Where to from Here?' (2002) 7 *Local Government Law Journal* 169.

Corbell, S., Australian Capital Territory Minister for Energy, 'Minister Announces Renewable Energy Targets' (Media Release, 5 May 2011).

Corbera, E., Estrada, M. and Brown, K., 'Reducing Greenhouse Gas Emissions from Deforestation and Forest Degradation in Developing Countries: Revisiting the Assumptions' (2010) 100 *Climatic Change* 355.

Cosslett, C., 'California Leading the Way Towards REDD+ Carbon Markets', *UN-REDD Programme Newsletter* 3, No. 16, February 2011.

Council of Australian Governments, *Communiqué of 2 July 2009* (online).

Council of Australian Governments, *Communiqué of 25 February 1994 – Attachment: A Water Resources Policy*.

Council of Australian Governments, *Communiqué of 7 December 2009* (online).

Council of Australian Governments, 'Final Report: Jurisdictions' Reviews of Existing Climate Change Mitigation Measures' (19 March 2010).

Council of Australian Governments, *Intergovernmental Agreement on a National Water Initiative* (2004).

Council of Australian Governments, Inter-Jurisdictional Emissions Trading Working Group, *A National Emissions Trading Scheme: A Report to First Ministers*, 16 December 2004.

Council of Australian Governments, *National Climate Change Adaptation Framework* (2007).

Council of Australian Governments, *National Strategy on Energy Efficiency* (2010).

Council of Australian Governments, 'Reform Council, Capital City Strategic Planning Systems' (online).

Cox, P. et al., *Analysis of Cookstove Change-out Projects Seeking Carbon Credits* (Environmental Sustainability Clinic, University of Minnesota Law School, 2011).

Craig, R. K., '"Stationarity is dead" – Long Live Transformation: Five Principles for Climate Change Adaptation Law' (2010) 34 *Harvard Environmental Law Review* 9.

Crawford, J., 'The Constitution and the Environment' (1991) 13 *Sydney Law Review* 11.

Cressey, D., 'Cancelled Project Spurs Debate over Geoengineering Patents' (2012) 485 *Nature* 429.

CSIRO, *An Analysis of Greenhouse Gas Mitigation and Carbon Biosequestration Opportunities from Rural Land Use* (2009).

CSIRO, *Climate Change in Australia: Technical Report 2007, Executive Summary* (2007).

CSIRO, *National Research Flagships: Climate Adaptation* (22 June 2011) (online).

Culkern, A. C., 'Offsets could make up 85% of California's Cap-and-Trade Program', *The New York Times*, 8 August 2011 (online).

Cuskelly, K., 'Legal Frameworks for Regulating Biosequestration in Australia' (2011) 28 *Environmental and Planning Law Journal* 348.

Czech Republic, *National Greenhouse Gas Inventory Report 2010* (Czech Hydrometeorological Institute, 2010).

Dargusch, P., Harrison, S. and Herbohn, J,. 'How Carbon Markets Have Influenced Change in the Australian Forest Industries' (2010) 73(3) *Australian Forestry* 165.

Davies, J. and Sullivan, P., 'Nuclear Power Post-Fukushima: A Framework for an Australian Nuclear Future' (2011) 30(2) *Australian Resources and Energy Law Journal* 199.
Daviet, F., *From Copenhagen to Cancún: Forests and REDD+*, World Resources Institute (23 November 2010) (online).
Dawson, T. et al., 'Beyond Predictions: Biodiversity Conservation in a Changing Climate' (2011) 332 *Science* 53.
de Boer, Y., 'Address by UNFCCC Executive Secretary', Forum on Climate Change and Science, Technology, and Innovation, Beijing, China (24 April 2008).
de Cendra de Larragán, J., 'Can Emissions Trading Schemes Be Coupled with Border-Tax Adjustments? An Analysis vis-à-vis WTO Law' (2006) 15(2) *Review of Community and International Environmental Law* 131.
de Cendra de Larragán, J., 'Case Note: Republic of Poland v Commission (Case T-183/07, 23 September 2009)' (2010) 1(1) *Climate Law* 199.
de Coninck, H., Haake, F. and van der Linden, N., 'Technology Transfer in the Clean Development Mechanism' (2008) 7(5) *Climate Policy* 444.
de Wit, E. and Webb, R., 'Planning for Coastal Climate Change in Victoria' (2010) 27 *Environmental and Planning Law Journal* 23.
Deane, F., 'A New Legal Avenue for Pricing GHG Emissions? To Trade or to Tax?' (2011) 28 *Environmental and Planning Law Journal* 111.
Del Guayo, I., 'Biofuels: EU Law and Policy', in D. N. Zillman et al. (eds), *Beyond the Carbon Economy: Energy Law in Transition* (Oxford University Press, 2008).
Dernbach, J. and Brown, D., 'The Ethical Responsibility to Reduce Energy Consumption' (2009) 37 *Hofstra Law Review* 985.
Diaz, D., Hamilton, K. and Johnson, E., *State of the Forest Carbon Markets 2011: From Canopy to Currency* (Ecosystem Marketplace, September 2011).
Dickey, S., 'Emissions Trading: What Works?', in W. Gumley and T. Daya-Winterbottom (eds), *Climate Change Law: Comparative, Contractual and Regulatory Considerations* (Lawbook Company, 2009).
Diesendorf, M., 'Comparing the Economics of Nuclear and Renewable Sources of Electricity', paper presented at Solar2010, the 48th AuSES Annual Conference, Canberra, 1–3 December 2010.
Diringer, E., 'Letting Go of Kyoto' (2011) 479 *Nature* 291.
Disch, D., 'A Comparative Analysis of the "Development Dividend" of Clean Development Mechanism Projects in Six Host Countries' (2010) 2 *Climate and Development* 50.
Docherty, B. and Giannini, T., 'Confronting a Rising Tide: A Proposal for a Convention on Climate Change Refugees' (2009) 33 *Harvard Environmental Law Review* 349.
Doelle, M., 'Early Experience with the Kyoto Compliance System: Possible Lessons for MEA Compliance System Design' (2010) 1(2) *Climate Law* 237.
Doppelhammer, M., 'The CCS Directive, its Implementation and the Co-financing of CCS and RES Demonstration Projects Under the Emissions Trading System (NER 300 Process)', in I. Havercroft, R. Macrory and R. B. Stewart (eds), *Carbon Capture and Storage: Emerging Legal and Regulatory Issues* (Hart Publishing, 2011).
Downie, C., 'Carbon Offsets: Saviour or Cop-Out?', Research Paper No. 48, Australia Institute (August 2007).
Drew, J. M. and Drew, M. E., 'Establishing Additionality: Fraud Vulnerabilities in the Clean Development Mechanism' (2010) 23(3) *Accounting Research Journal* 243.
Driesen, D., 'Free Lunch or Cheap Fix?: The Emissions Trading Idea and the Climate Change Convention' (1998) *Boston College Environmental Affairs Law Review* 1.
Driesen, D. M., 'Sustainable Development and Market Liberalism's Shotgun Wedding: Emissions Trading under the Kyoto Protocol' (2008) 83 *Indiana Law Journal* 21.
Duarte, C. et al., 'Abrupt Climate Change in the Arctic' (2012) 2 *Nature Climate Change* 60.
Durant, A. J. et al., 'Economic Value of Improved Quantification in Global Sources and Sinks of Carbon Dioxide' (2011) 369 *Philosophical Transactions of the Royal Society A* 1967.

Durrant, N., 'Legal Issues in Biosequestration: Carbon Sinks, Carbon Rights and Carbon Trading' (2008) 31(3) *UNSW Law Journal* 907.

Durrant, N., 'Legal Issues in Carbon Farming: Bio-sequestration, Carbon Pricing and Carbon Rights' (2011) 2(4) *Climate Law* 515.

Durrant, N., *Legal Responses to Climate Change* (Federation Press, 2010).

Dutta, K. et al., 'Impact of Improved Biomass Cookstoves on Indoor Air Quality near Pune, India' (2007) 11(2) *Energy for Sustainable Development* 19.

Eady, S. et al. (eds), *Analysis of Greenhouse Gas Mitigation and Carbon Biosequestration Opportunities from Rural Land Use* (CSIRO, 2009).

Eckersley, R., 'Kyoto or Copenhagen: From Legally Binding Treaty to DIY Climate Policy', Presentation at *Beyond a Carbon Price: A Framework for Climate Change Regulation in Australia*, Melbourne Law School, 11–12 August 2011.

Editorial, 'Climate Outlook Looking Much the Same, or Even Worse' (2011) 334 *Science* 1616.

Editorial, 'Cool Response to Durban Compromise' (2012) 2 *Nature Climate Change* 59.

Editorial, 'Defend the Amazon' (2011) 480 *Nature* 413.

Editorial, 'Gas and Air' (2012) 482 *Nature* 131.

Editorial, 'The Mask Slips' (2011) 480 *Nature* 292.

Ellerman, D. and Joskow, P. (Massachusetts Institute of Technology), 'The European Union's Emissions Trading Scheme in Perspective', Report prepared for Pew Centre on Global Climate Change (May 2008).

Ellis, J., Moarif, S. and Briner, G., *Core Elements of National Reports* (OECD/IEA, 2 June 2010).

Ellis, S., Kanowski, P. and Whelan, R., *National Inquiry on Bushfire Mitigation and Management*, Inquiry report prepared for Council of Australian Governments (31 March 2004).

Ellisa, J. et al., 'CDM: Taking Stock and Looking Forward' (2007) 35(1) *Energy Policy* 15.

England, P., 'Heating Up: Climate Change Law and the Evolving Responsibilities of Local Government' (2008) 13 *Local Government Law Journal* 209.

Environment Defenders Office Victoria, *The Carbon Farming Initiative – Will it Work for You?* (2011).

Environment Defenders Office Victoria, 'The Carbon Price', Briefing Paper (12 July 2011).

European Commission, 'Analysis of Options Beyond 20% GHG Emission Reductions: Member State Results', Commission Staff Working Paper, SWD (2012) 5 final (Brussels, 1 February 2012).

European Commission, *Directive 2002/91/EC of the European Parliament and of the Council of 16 December 2002 on the Energy Performance of Buildings*, OJ L 1,4.1.2003.

European Commission, *Directive 2009/29/EC of the European Parliament and of the Council of 23 April 2009 amending Directive 2003/87/EC so as to Improve and Extend the Greenhouse Gas Emission Allowance Trading Scheme of the Community*, OJ L 140, 5.6.2009.

European Commission, *Draft Regulation of 7 June 2011 Determining, Pursuant to Directive 2003/87/EC of the European Parliament and of the Council, Certain Restrictions Applicable to the Use of International Credits from Projects Involving Industrial Gases*.

European Commission, 'Emissions Trading System (EU ETS)' (online).

European Commission, 'Europe 2020 Initiative: Energy Efficiency Plan 2011' (online).

European Commission, 'Revision of the Energy Taxation Directive – Questions and Answers', *MEMO/11/238* (Brussels, 13 April 2011).

European Parliament, 'European Parliament Resolution of 29 November 2007 on Trade and Climate Change' (2007/2003(Ini)).

European Union, 'Case C-366/10: Reference for a Preliminary Ruling from High Court of Justice Queen's Bench Division (Administrative Court) (United Kingdom) Made on 22 July 2010 – The Air Transport Association of America, American Airlines, Inc.,

Continental Airlines, Inc., United Airlines, Inc. v The Secretary of State for Energy and Climate Change, 53 *Official Journal of the European Union [C 260]* 9 (25 September 2010).
European Union, 'Directive 2008/101/EC of the European Parliament and of the Council of 19 November 2008 Amending Directive 2003/87/EC So as to Include Aviation Activities in the Scheme of Greenhouse Gas Emissions Allowance Trading within the Community', *Official Journal of the European Union [L 8]* 3 (13 January 2009).
Evans, A. and Perschel, R., 'A Review of Forestry Mitigation and Adaptation Strategies in the Northeast US' (2009) 96 *Climatic Change* 167.
Faaj, O. and Dieperink, C., 'Forestry Projects under the Clean Development Mechanism?' (2003) 61 *Climatic Change* 123.
Fankhauser, S. and Hepburn, C., 'Designing Carbon Markets, Part II: Carbon Markets in Space' (2010) 38(8) *Energy Policy* 4381.
Farber, D., 'Climate Adaptation and Federalism: Mapping the Issues' (2009) 1 *San Diego Journal of Climate and Energy Law* 259.
Farber, D. and Chen, J., *Disasters and the Law: Katrina and Beyond* (Aspen, 2006).
Farrier, D., 'Fragmented Law in Fragmented Landscapes: The Slow Evolution of Integrated Natural Resource Management Legislation in NSW' (2002) 19 *Environmental and Planning Law Journal* 89.
Farrier, D., 'Integrated Land and Water Management in New South Wales: Plans, Problems and Possibilities' (1998) 5 *Australasian Journal of Natural Resources Law and Policy* 153.
Farrier, D., 'The Limits of Judicial Review: Anvil Hill in the Land and Environment Court', in T. Bonyhady and P. Christoff (eds), *Climate Law in Australia* (Federation Press, 2007).
Federal Republic of Nigeria, Ministry of Environment, *Request for Letter of Approval for Project 'Efficient Fuel Wood Stoves for Nigeria'* (24 January 2009).
Federal Republic of Nigeria, *Nigeria's First National Communication under the United Nations Framework Convention on Climate Change* (2003).
Fisher, D. E., 'The Statutory Relevance of Greenhouse Gas Emissions in Environmental Regulation' (2007) 24 *Environmental and Planning Law Journal* 210.
Flannery, T., *The Weather Makers: How Man Is Changing the Climate and What It Means for Life on Earth* (Atlantic Monthly Press, 2005).
Foerster, A., 'Progress on Environmental Flows in South-Eastern Australia in Light of Climate Change' (2009) 39(5) *ELR News and Analysis* 10426.
Food and Agriculture Organization, *Forest Assessment 2010* (2010).
Food and Agriculture Organization, *Framework for Assessing and Monitoring Forest Governance* (2011).
Food and Agriculture Organization, *Global Forest Resources Assessment 2010: Global Tables* (2010).
Food and Agriculture Organization, *Global Forest Resources Assessment 2010: Main Report* (2010).
Food and Agriculture Organization and Committee on Forest Development in the Tropics, *Tropical Forest Action Plan* (1985) (online).
Food and Agriculture Organization and ITTO, *The State of Forests in the Amazon Basin, Congo Basin and Southeast Asia: A Report Prepared for the Summit of the Three Rainforest Basins, Brazzaville, Republic of Congo, 31 May–3 June, 2011* (2011).
Food and Agriculture Organization, UN Development Programme and UN Environment Programme, *UN-REDD Programme: 2010 Year in Review* (2011).
Food and Agriculture Organization, UN Development Programme and UN Environment Programme, 'Soloman Islands Now Ready for REDD+ Readiness', 19 *UN-REDD Programme Newsletter* 2 (June 2011).
Food and Agriculture Organization, UN Development Programme and UN Environment Programme, 'INPE and UN-REDD Partnering to Develop National Forest Monitoring Systems', 18 *UN-REDD Programme Newsletter* 3 (May 2011).

Forest Europe, UNECE and Food and Agriculture Organization, *State of Europe's Forests 2011: Status and Trends in Sustainable Forest Management in Europe* (Ministerial Conference on the Protection of Forests in Europe, 2011).

Fransen, T., 'Enhancing Today's MRV Framework to Meet Tomorrow's Needs: The Role of National Communications and Inventories', World Resources Institute Working Paper (2009).

Freestone, D. and Streck, C. (eds), *Legal Aspects of Implementing the Kyoto Protocol Mechanisms: Making Kyoto Work* (Oxford University Press, 2005).

Friends of the Earth Australia, 'Sumatran Forest Carbon Deal Slammed by Australian and Indonesian Environment Groups' (online).

Frum, D., 'Obama's Doomed Green Jobs Plan: Just Tax Oil and Let Markets Do the Rest', *The Week*, 26 January 2011 (online).

Füssel, H., 'Adaptation Planning for Climate Change: Concepts, Assessment Approaches and Key Lessons' (2007) 2(2) *Sustainability Science* 265.

Garcia-Oliva, F. and Masera, O. R., 'Assessment and Measurement Issues related to Soil Carbon Sequestration in Land Use, Land Use Change and Forestry (LULUCF) Projects under the Kyoto Protocol' (2004) 65 *Climatic Change* 347.

Gardiner, S., 'Ethics and Global Climate Change' (2004) 114 *Ethics* 555.

Gardner, A., Bartlett, R. and Gray, J., *Water Resources Law* (CSIRO Publishing, 2009).

Gardner, A. and Bowmer, K., 'Environmental Water Allocations and their Governance', in K. Hussey and S. Dovers (eds), *Managing Water for Australia: The Social and Institutional Challenges* (CSIRO, 2007).

Garnaut, R., *Garnaut Climate Change Review* (Cambridge University Press, 2008).

Garnaut, R., *The Garnaut Review 2011: Australia in the Global Response to Climate Change* (Cambridge University Press, 2011).

Garnaut, R., *Update Paper 4 – Transforming Rural Land Use*, Garnaut Climate Change Review – Update 2011 (2011).

Garnaut, R., *Update Paper 6: Carbon pricing and reducing Australia's emissions*, Garnaut Climate Change Review – Update 2011 (2011).

Garnaut, R., *Update Paper 7: Low Emissions Technology and the Innovation Challenge*, Garnaut Climate Change Review – Update 2011 (2011).

Gechlik, M., 'Making Transfer of Clean Technology Work: Lessons of the Clean Development Mechanism' (2009) 11 *San Diego International Law Journal* 227.

George Wilkenfeld and Associates, *Prevention is Cheaper than Cure – Avoiding Carbon Emissions through Energy Efficiency: Projected Impacts of the Energy Efficiency Program to 2020* (George Wilkenfeld and Associates, 2009).

Gerrard, Michael (Columbia Law School), *Columbia Law School Climate Law Blog*, available at <http://www.law.columbia.edu/centers/climatechange>.

Ghaleigh, N., '"Six Honest Serving Men": Climate Change Litigation as Legal Mobilization and the Utility of Typologies' (2010) 1 *Climate Law* 31.

Ghaleigh, N. S. and Rossati, D., 'The Spectre of Carbon Border-Adjustment Measures' (2011) 2(1) *Climate Law* 63 (2011).

Gibbs, M. 'The Regulation of Geological Storage of Greenhouse Gases in Australia', in I. Havercroft, R. Macrory and R. B. Stewart (eds), *Carbon Capture and Storage: Emerging Legal and Regulatory Issues* (Hart Publishing, 2011).

Gibson, H., 'Climate Change and Low Lying Areas – Considerations in VCAT', Paper presented at the *Planning and Climate Change Conference*, Monash University, 20 October 2009 (online).

Gilbert, N., 'Dirt Poor' (2012) 483 *Nature* 525.

Gillis, J., 'A Warming Planet Struggles to Feed Itself', *The New York Times*, 4 June 2011, p. 1.

Glazebrook, S., 'Human Rights and the Environment' (2009) 40 *Victoria University of Wellington Law Review* 293.

Global Environment Facility, 'Forests of Brazil: Strengthening Public Policies by Using Accurate and Updated Information on Forest Resources: A Way Forward' (online).

Global Environment Facility, *Fourth Overall Performance Study of the GEF: Progress Toward Impact* (2010).
Global Environment Facility, 'Nigeria – Rural Electrification and Renewable Energy Development' (online).
Global Environment Facility, *Report of the GEF to the Fifteenth Session of the Conference of the Parties to the United Nations Framework Convention on Climate Change* (9 October 2009).
Global Environment Facility, 'What Is the GEF?' (online).
Godden, L., Kallies, A., Keenan R. J. and Peel, J. 'Reducing Emissions from Deforestation and Forest Degradation in Developing Countries (REDD): Implementation Issues' (2010) 36(1) *Monash Law Review* 139.
Godden, L. and Kung, A., 'Water Law and Planning Frameworks under Climate Change Variability: Managing Flood Risk' (2011) 25(15) *Water Resources Management* 4051.
Godden, L. and Peel, J., *Environmental Law: Scientific, Policy and Regulatory Dimensions* (Oxford University Press, 2010).
Golden, D., 'The Politics of Carbon Dioxide Emissions Reduction: The Role of Pluralism in Shaping the Climate Change Technology Initiative' (1999) 17(2) *UCLA Journal of Environmental Law & Policy* 171.
Goodin, R., 'Selling Environmental Indulgences', in S. M. Gardiner et al. (eds), *Climate Ethics: Essential Readings* (Oxford University Press, 2010).
Gore, A., *An Inconvenient Truth: The Planetary Emergency of Global Warming and What We Can Do About It* (Bloomsbury, 2006).
Government of British Columbia (Canada), Ministry of Finance, *Budget and Fiscal Plan 2008/09–2010/11*.
Government of Japan, Ministry of the Environment, Office of Market Mechanisms, 'Japan's Voluntary Emissions Trading Scheme (JVETS)', May 2011 (online).
Government of New Zealand, 'Other Government Policies and Measures', last updated 25 May 2011 (online).
Government of New Zealand, Ministry for the Environment, Emissions Trading Scheme Review Panel, *Doing New Zealand's Fair Share: Emissions Trading Scheme Review 2011: Final Report* (2011).
Grasso, M., 'An Ethics-Based Climate Agreement for the South Pacific Region' (2006) 6 *International Environmental Agreements* 249.
Grattan Institute, *Learning the Hard Way: Australia's Policies to Reduce Emissions* (2011).
Grattan Institute, *No Easy Choices: Which Way to Australia's Energy Future?* (2012).
Grattan, M. and Wroe, D., 'Abbott's Blood Oath to Repeal Carbon Tax', *The Age* (Melbourne), 13 October 2011 (online).
Gray, K., 'Property in Thin Air' (1991) 50(2) *Cambridge Law Journal* 252.
Green, A., 'Climate Change, Regulatory Policy and the WTO: How Constraining Are Trade Rules?' (2005) 8 *Journal of International Economic Law* 143.
Green, F., 'Abbott's Gory Pledge Would Be a Legal Bloodbath', *Crikey*, 13 October 2011 (online).
Grist, N., 'Positioning Climate Change in Sustainable Development Discourse' (2008) 20 *Journal of International Development* 783.
Grubb, M., 'Global Perspective: Implementing Carbon Pricing in a World of Political Resistance and Evolving International Participation' (Melbourne, 14 April 2011) (online).
Grubb, M. and Newberry, D., 'Pricing Carbon For Electricity Generation: National and International Dimensions', in M. Grubb et al. (eds), *Delivering a Low-Carbon Electricity Sector: Technologies, Economics and Policy* (Cambridge University Press, 2008).
Grubb, M. and Yamin, F., 'Climatic Collapse at The Hague: What Happened, Why, and Where Do We Go from Here?' (2001) 77(2) *International Affairs* 261.
Gulbrandsen, L. H., 'The Effectiveness of Non-State Governance Schemes: A Comparative Study of Forest Certification in Norway and Sweden' (2005) 5 *International Environmental Agreements* 125.
Gumley, W. and Daya-Winterbottom, T., *Climate Change Law: Comparative, Contractual and Regulatory Considerations* (Lawbook Company, 2009).

Gunningham, N., 'Environmental Law, Regulation and Governance: Shifting Architectures' (2009) 21 *Journal of Environmental Law* 179.

Gunningham, N., Kagan, R. and Thornton, D., *Shades of Green: Business, Regulation, and Environment* (Stanford University Press, 2008).

Gusti, M. and Jonas, M., 'Terrestrial Full Carbon Account for Russia: Revised Uncertainty Estimates and Their Role in a Bottom-up/Top-Down Accounting Exercise' (2010) 103 *Climatic Change* 159.

Hadley, O. L. and Kirchstetter, T. W., 'Black-Carbon Reduction of Snow Albedo' (2012) 2 *Nature Climate Change* 437.

Haites, E. and Yamin, F., 'Overview of the Kyoto Mechanisms' (2004) 5(1) *International Review for Environmental Strategies* 199.

Hales, D. and Prescott-Allen, R., 'Flying Blind: Assessing Progress toward Sustainability', in D. C. Esty and M. H. Ivanova (eds), *Global Environmental Governance: Options and Opportunities* (Yale School of Forestry and Environmental Studies, 2002).

Hamilton, C., *Growth Fetish* (Allen & Unwin, 2003).

Hamilton, C., *Scorcher: The Dirty Politics of Climate Change* (Black Inc., 2007).

Hamilton, C. and Vellen, L., 'Land-use Change in Australia and the Kyoto Protocol' (1999) 2(2) *Environmental Science and Policy* 145.

Handl, G., 'Transboundary Impacts', in D. Bodansky, J. Brunneé and E. Hey (eds), *The Oxford Handbook of International Environmental Law* (Oxford University Press, 2007).

Hanneman, M., 'Cap-and-Trade: A Sufficient or Necessary Condition for Emissions Reduction?' (2010) 26(2) *Oxford Review of Economic Policy* 225.

Hansen, J. et al., 'A Safe Operating Space for Humanity' 461 (2009) *Nature* 472.

Hardin, G., 'Tragedy of the Commons' (1967) 162 *Science* 1243.

Harmeling, S., *Successful Start for the Design of the Green Climate Fund* (GermanWatch, 2011).

Hartcher, C., 'Green Scheme to Close when Carbon Tax Starts' (Media Release, 5 April 2012) (online).

Harvey, L. D. D., 'An Overview of Climate Change Science in 1977 Marking the Publication of Volume 100 of *Climatic Change*' (2010) 100 *Climatic Change* 15.

Haszeldine, S., 'Geological Factors in Framing Legislation to Enable and Regulate Storage of Carbon Dioxide Deep in the Ground', in I. Havercroft, R. Macrory and R. B. Stewart (eds), *Carbon Capture and Storage: Emerging Legal and Regulatory Issues* (Hart Publishing, 2011).

Havercroft, I., Macrory, R. and Stewart, R. B, 'Introduction', in I. Havercroft, R. Macrory and R. B. Stewart (eds), *Carbon Capture and Storage: Emerging Legal and Regulatory Issues* (Hart Publishing, 2011).

Haya, B., *Measuring Emissions against an Alternative Future: Fundamental Flaws in the Structure of the Kyoto Protocol's Clean Development Mechanism*, Energy and Resources Group Working Paper ERG09–001 (University of California, Berkeley, 2009).

Healey J., (ed.), *Nuclear Power* (Spinney Press, 2006).

Hearps, P. and McConnell, D., 'Renewable Energy Technology Cost Review', Melbourne Energy Institute Technical Paper Series (May 2011).

Hearps, P. and Wright, M., *Australian Sustainable Energy: Zero Carbon Australia Stationary Energy Plan* (Melbourne Energy Institute, 2010).

Heinrich Böll Stiftung, 'Climate Funds Update' (online).

Hennessy, K., 'Climate Change and Its Projected Effects on Water Resources', in *Water: The Australian Dilemma – Proceedings of the 2003 Invitation Symposium* (Australian Academy of Technological Sciences and Engineering, 2003).

Hennessey, K. et al., *Climate Change Impacts on Fire-Weather in South-East Australia* (CSIRO, 2006).

Hepburn, C., 'Regulation by Prices, Quantities or Both: A Review of Instrument Choice' (2006) 22 *Oxford Review of Economic Policy* 226.

Hepburn, C. and Fankhauser, S., 'Combining Multiple Climate Policy Instruments: How Not to Do It' (2010) 3(1) *Climate Change Economics* 209.
Hepburn, S., 'Carbon Rights as New Property: The Benefits of Statutory Verification' (2009) 31(2) *Sydney Law Review* 239.
Hill, T. and Moore, L., 'Australia Ratifies the Kyoto Protocol' (2008) 23(1) *Australian Environment Review* 10.
Hodgkinson, D. et al., 'Copenhagen, Climate Change "Refugees" and the Need for a Global Agreement' (2009) 4(2) *Public Policy* 159.
Hodgkinson, D. and Garner R., *Global Climate Change: Australian Law and Policy* (LexisNexis Butterworths, 2008).
Horstmann, B. and Abeysinghe, A., 'The Adaptation Fund of the Kyoto Protocol: A Model for Financing Adaptation to Climate Change?' (2011) 2(3) *Climate Law* 415.
Hsu, S., 'The Politics and Psychology of Gasoline Taxes: An Empirical Study' (2010) 15(2) *Widener Law Review* 363.
Hulea, O. et al., 'Floodplain Restoration along the Lower Danube: A Climate Change Adaptation Case Study' (2009) 1 *Climate and Development* 212.
Hung, P. T., *Legal Preparedness for REDD+ in Vietnam: Country Study* (International Development Law Organization, November 2011).
Huq, S., *Applying Sustainable Development Criteria to CDM Projects: PCF Experience* (Prototype Carbon Fund, 2002).
Independent Panel Report (chaired by Hon. Grant Tambling), *Renewable Opportunities: A Review of the Operation of the Renewable Energy (Electricity) Act* 2000, Executive Summary.
Institute for Sustainable Futures, University of Sydney, 'Think Small: The Australian Decentralised Energy Roadmap' (Issue 1, December 2011) (online).
Intergovernmental Negotiating Committee, *Report of the Intergovernmental Negotiating Committee for a Framework Convention on Climate Change on the Work of Its First Session, Held at Washington, DC*, from 4 to 14 February 1991 (United Nations, 8 March 1991).
Intergovernmental Panel on Climate Change, *Climate Change 1990: The IPCC Response Strategies. Report Prepared for Intergovernmental Panel on Climate Change by Working Group III* (1990).
Intergovernmental Panel on Climate Change, *Climate Change 2001: Impacts. Adaptation and Vulnerability: Contribution of Working Group II to the Third Assessment Report of the IPCC* (Cambridge University Press, 2001).
Intergovernmental Panel on Climate Change, *Climate Change 2007: The Physical Science Basis: Contribution of Working Group I to the Fourth Assessment Report of the IPCC* (Cambridge University Press, 2007).
Intergovernmental Panel on Climate Change, *Climate Change 2007: The Physical Science Basis: Contribution of Working Group I to the Fourth Assessment Report of the Intergovernmental Panel on Climate Change*, Summary for Policymakers (Cambridge University Press, 2007).
Intergovernmental Panel on Climate Change, *Climate Change 2007: Impacts, Adaptation and Vulnerability: Contribution of Working Group II to the Fourth Assessment Report of the IPCC* (Cambridge University Press, 2007).
Intergovernmental Panel on Climate Change, *Climate Change 2007: Mitigation of Climate Change: Contribution of Working Group III to the Fourth Assessment Report of the IPCC* (Cambridge University Press, 2007).
Intergovernmental Panel on Climate Change, *Climate Change 2007: Synthesis Report* (WMO, UNEP, 2007).
Intergovernmental Panel on Climate Change, *Climate Change: The IPCC Scientific Assessment* (Cambridge University Press, 1990).
Intergovernmental Panel on Climate Change, *First Assessment Report, Vol. 1: Overview and Policymaker Summaries* (World Meteorological Organization, 1990).

Intergovernmental Panel on Climate Change, *Good Practice Guidance for Land Use, Land-Use Change and Forestry* (2003).
Intergovernmental Panel on Climate Change, *Good Practice Guidance and Uncertainty Management in National Greenhouse Gas Inventories* (2000).
Intergovernmental Panel on Climate Change, 'History' (online).
Intergovernmental Panel on Climate Change, *IPCC Guidelines for National Greenhouse Gas Inventories* (2006).
Intergovernmental Panel on Climate Change, *Revised 1996 IPCC Guidelines for National Greenhouse Gas Inventories* (1996).
Intergovernmental Panel on Climate Change, 'Special Report on Emission Scenarios' (2000) (online).
Intergovernmental Panel on Climate Change, Special Report, *Carbon Dioxide Capture and Storage: Technical Summary* (2005).
Intergovernmental Panel on Climate Change, *Working Group I: Scientific Assessment of Climate Change* (World Meteorological Organization, 1990).
Intergovernmental Panel on Climate Change, *Working Group II: Potential Impacts of Climate Change* (World Meteorological Organization, 1990).
Intergovernmental Panel on Climate Change, *Working Group III: Formulation of Response Strategies* (World Meteorological Organization, 1990).
International Atomic Energy Association, *International Status and Prospects of Nuclear Power* (2010).
International Atomic Energy Association, *Nuclear Power Worldwide: Status and Outlook* (2007).
International Centre for Trade and Sustainable Development, 'The Climate Technology Mechanism: Issues and Challenges', Information Note No. 18 (March 2011).
International Energy Agency, *Carbon Capture and Storage Roadmap* (2010).
International Energy Agency, *CO_2 Emissions from Fuel Combustion: Highlights* (2010).
International Energy Agency, 'Energy Efficiency Policy and Carbon Pricing', Energy Efficiency Series, Information Paper (August 2011).
International Energy Agency, *Energy Technology Perspectives 2010: Scenarios and Strategies to 2050* (2010).
International Energy Agency, *Key World Energy Statistics* (2010).
International Energy Agency, 'Prospect of Limiting the Global Increase in Temperature to 2°C Is Getting Bleaker', 30 May 2011 (online).
International Energy Agency, 'Saving Electricity in a Hurry', Energy Efficiency Series, Information Paper (June 2011).
International Energy Agency, *World Energy Outlook* 2009.
International Energy Agency, *World Energy Outlook* 2010.
International Energy Agency, *World Energy Outlook* 2011.
International Institute for Sustainable Development, 'WTO CTE Considers Carbon Border Adjustments and Carbon Footprint Schemes', 7 July 2011 (online).
International Institute for Sustainable Development, 'Summary of the Second Session of the Preparatory Committee for the UN Conference on Sustainable Development: 7–8 March 2011' (11 March 2011) 27(3) *Earth Negotiations Bulletin*.
International Institute for Sustainable Development, 'SB 32 and AWG Highlights: Monday, 7 June 2010' (2010) 12(468) *Earth Negotiations Bulletin*.
International Institute for Sustainable Development, 'UNFCC: SB 32 and AWG Highlights: Wednesday, 9 June 2010' (2010) 12(470) *Earth Negotiations Bulletin*.
International Institute for Sustainable Development, 'AWG-LCA 12 and AWG-KP 14 Highlights: Thursday, 7 October 2010' (2010) 12(483) *Earth Negotiations Bulletin*.
International Institute for Sustainable Development, 'Summary of the Bangkok Climate Talks: 3–8 April 2011' (2011) 12(499) *Earth Negotiations Bulletin*.
International Institute for Sustainable Development, 'SB 34 and AWG Highlights: Tuesday, 7 June 2011' (2011) 12(504) *Earth Negotiations Bulletin*.

International Institute for Sustainable Development, 'UNFCC: SB 32 and AWG Highlights: Thursday, 9 June 2011' (2011) 12(506) *Earth Negotiations Bulletin*.
International Institute for Sustainable Development, 'SB 34 and AWG Highlights: Saturday, 11 June 2011' (2011) 12(508) *Earth Negotiations Bulletin*.
International Institute for Sustainable Development, 'SB 34 and AWG Highlights: Monday, 13 June 2011' (2011) 12(509) *Earth Negotiations Bulletin*.
International Institute for Sustainable Development, 'SB 34 and AWG Highlights: Tuesday, 14 June 2011' (2011) 12(510) *Earth Negotiations Bulletin*.
International Institute for Sustainable Development, 'AWG-LCA 14 and AWG-KP 16 Highlights: Wednesday, 5 October 2011' (2011) 12(519) *Earth Negotiations Bulletin* 1.
International Institute for Sustainable Development, 'Summary of the Panama City Climate Change Talks: 1–7 October 2011' (2011) 12(521) *Earth Negotiations Bulletin*.
International Institute for Sustainable Development, 'Durban Highlights: Monday, 28 November 2011' (2011) 12(524) *Earth Negotiations Bulletin*.
International Institute for Sustainable Development, 'Durban Highlights: Wednesday, 30 November 2011' (2011) 12(526) *Earth Negotiations Bulletin*.
International Institute for Sustainable Development, 'Durban Highlights: Saturday, 3 December 2011' (2011) 12(529) *Earth Negotiations Bulletin*.
International Labour Office, *Growth, Employment and Decent Work in the Least Developed Countries: Report of the International Labour Office for the Fourth Conference on the Least Developed Countries, Istanbul, 9–13 May 2011*, Geneva (2011).
International Organization for Migration, *Climate Change, Migration and Critical International Security Considerations* (2011).
Ison, R. L., *Systems Practice: How to Act in a Climate Change World* (Springer, 2010).
Jacobs, M., 'Deadline 2015' (2012) 481 *Nature* 137.
Jacobson, M. Z. and Delucchi, M. A., 'Providing All Global Energy with Wind, Water, and Solar Power, Part I: Technologies, Energy Resources, Quantities and Areas of Infrastructure, and Materials' (2011) 39 *Energy Policy* 1154.
Johnson, K., 'Ill Winds Blow for Clean Energy: Cheap, and Abundant, Natural Gas Diminishes Alternative Projects' Appeal', *Wall Street Journal*, 9 July 2009 (online).
Jonas, M. et al., 'Benefits of Dealing with Uncertainty in Greenhouse Gas Inventories: Introduction' (2010) 103 *Climatic Change* 3.
Jones, R. S. and Yoo, B., 'Improving the Policy Framework in Japan to Address Climate Change', OECD Economics Department Working Paper, No. 740 (4 December 2009).
Jotzo, F., 'A Price Floor for Australia's Emission Trading Scheme?', Commissioned paper for the Multi-Party Committee on Climate Change (17 May 2011).
Jotzo, F., 'Against the Odds, a Nation Warms to a Policy', *The Age* (Melbourne), 11 July 2011 (online).
Jotzo, F., Pickering, J. and Wood, P., *Fulfilling Australia's International Climate Finance Commitments: Which Sources of Financing Are Promising and How Much Could They Raise?*, Centre for Climate Economics and Policy, Crawford School of Economics and Government, Australian National University, working paper 1115 (October 2011).
Kallies, A., 'The Impact of Electricity Market Design on Access to the Grid and Transmission Planning for Renewable Energy in Australia: Can Overseas Examples Provide Guidance?' (2011) 2 *Renewable Energy Law and Policy Review* 147.
Kapambwe, M. and Keenan, R., *Biodiversity Outcomes from Carbon Biosequestration*, Report prepared for the Victorian Department of Sustainability and Environment (2009).
Karekezi, S. and Kimani, J., 'Have Power Sector Reforms Increased Access to Electricity among the Poor in East Africa?' (2004) 8(4) *Energy for Sustainable Development* 10.
Karekezi, S., Kimani, J. and Onguru, O., 'Energy Access among the Urban Poor in Kenya' (2008) 12(4) *Energy for Sustainable Development* 38.
Karoly, D., 'The Climate Series', *The Monthly: Slow TV Climate Series* (2009) (online).

Kearney, M. et al., 'Early Emergence in a Butterfly Causally Linked to Anthropogenic Warming' (2010) 6(5) *Biology Letters* 674.

Kearney, T., 'Market-based Policies for Demand Side Energy Efficiency: A Comparison of the New South Wales Greenhouse Gas Abatement Scheme and the United Kingdom's Energy Efficiency Commitment' (2006) 23 *Environmental and Planning Law Journal* 113.

Keeling, C. D., 'Rewards and Penalties of Monitoring the Earth' (1998) 23 *Annual Review of Energy and the Environment* 25.

Keenan, R. J. and van Dijk, A. I., 'Planted Forests and Water', in J. Bauhus, P. van der Meer and M. Kanninen (eds), *Ecosystem Goods and Services from Plantation Forests* (Earthscan, 2010).

Kelly, J. and Massola, J., 'Climate Report Reveals Coalition Divisions, as Lib Sceptic Calls It "Offensive"', *The Australian*, 23 May 2011 (online).

Kenber, M., 'The Clean Development Mechanism: A Tool for Promoting Long-Term Climate Protection and Sustainable Development?', in F. Yamin (ed.), *Climate Change and Carbon Markets: A Handbook of Emission Reduction Mechanisms* (Earthscan, 2005).

Keohane, N. O., 'Cap-and-Trade is Preferable to a Carbon Tax', in R. B. Stewart, B. Kingsbury and B. Rudyk (eds), *Climate Finance: Regulatory and Funding Strategies for Climate Change and Global Development* (New York University Press, 2009).

Kim, J. A., Ellis, J. and Moarif, S., *Matching Mitigation Actions with Support: Key Issues for Channelling International Public Finance* (OECD/IEA, 2 December 2009).

Kolbert, E., *Field Notes from a Catastrophe: A Frontline Report on Climate Change* (Bloomsbury, 2007).

Kolbert, E., 'The Island in the Wind', *The New Yorker*, 7 July 2008, p. 68.

Kolmannskog, V. and Myrstad, F., 'Environmental Displacement in European Asylum Law' (2009) 11 *European Journal of Migration and Law* 313.

Kopp, R., 'Role of Offsets in Global and Domestic Climate Policy', *Resources for the Future*, Issue Brief 10–11 (May 2010).

Krey, M. and Santen, H., 'Trying to Catch up with the CDM Executive Board: Regulatory Decision-Making and Its Impact on CDM Performance', in D. Freestone and C. Streck (eds), *Legal Aspects of Carbon Trading* (Oxford University Press, 2009).

Kriegler, E. et al., 'Imprecise Probability Assessment of Tipping Points in the Climate System' (2009) 106(13) *Proceedings of the National Academy of Sciences of the United States of America* 5041.

Krupa, H., 'The Legal Framework for Carbon Capture and Storage in Canada', in I. Havercroft, R. Macrory and R. B. Stewart (eds), *Carbon Capture and Storage: Emerging Legal and Regulatory Issues* (Hart Publishing, 2011).

Kulovesi, K., '"Make Your Own Special Song, Even If Nobody Else Sings Along": International Aviation Emissions and the EU Emissions Trading Scheme' (2011) 2(4) *Climate Law* 535.

Lang, C., 'Kalimantan Forests and Climate Partnership Faces Yet More Criticism' (online).

Latif, A., 'Technology Transfer and Intellectual Property: A Post-Copenhagen Assessment' (2010) 14(1) *Bridges Monthly* 17.

Laurie, V., 'Big Success: Australia's Protected Areas', *Australian Geographic*, 15 July 2011 (online).

Lawrence, P., 'Australian Climate Policy and the Asia Pacific Partnership on Clean Development and Climate: From Howard to Rudd, Continuity or Change?' (2009) 9 *International Environmental Agreements* 281.

Leary, N. et al., 'A Stitch in Time: General Lessons from Specific Cases', in N. Leary et al. (eds), *Climate Change and Adaptation* (Earthscan, 2008).

Leip, A., 'Quantitative Quality Assessment of the Greenhouse Gas Inventory for Agriculture in Europe' (2010) 103 *Climatic Change* 245.

Leitch, N. et al., 'From Blueprint to Footprint: Climate Change and the Challenge for Planning', in T. Bonyhady, A. Macintosh and J. McDonald (eds), *Adaptation to Climate Change: Law and Policy* (Federation Press, 2010).

Lenton, T. et al., 'Tipping Elements in the Earth's Climate System' (2008) 105(6) *Proceedings of the National Academy of Sciences of the United States of America* 1786.
Letcher, R. and Powell, S., 'The Hydrological Setting', in L. Crase (ed.), *Water Policy in Australia: The Impact of Change and Uncertainty* (Resources for the Future, 2008).
Levermann, A. et al., 'Potential Climatic Transitions with Profound Impact on Europe: Review of the Current State of Six "Tipping Elements of the Climate System"' (2012) 110 *Climatic Change* 845.
Levin, K., Cashore, B. and Koppell, J., 'Can Non-State Certification Systems Bolster State-Centered Efforts to Promote Sustainable Development through the Clean Development Mechanism?' (2009) 44 *Wake Forest Law Review* 777.
Linacre, N., Kossoy, A. and Ambrosi, P., *State and Trends of the Carbon Market 2011* (World Bank, 2011) (online).
Liverman, D., 'Conventions of Climate Change: Constructions of Danger and the Dispossession of the Atmosphere' (2009) 35 *Journal of Historical Geography* 279.
Lobell, D. B., Schlenker, W. and Costa-Roberts, J., 'Climate Trends and Global Crop Production since 1980' (5 May 2011) *Sciencexpress* 1.
Long, A., 'REDD+ and Indigenous Peoples in Brazil', in R. S. Abate and E. A. Kronk (eds), *Climate Change, Indigenous Peoples, and the Search for Legal Remedies* (Edward Elgar Publishing, forthcoming).
Louka, E., *International Environmental Law: Fairness, Effectiveness, and World Order* (Cambridge University Press, 2006).
Low Carbon Australia, 'Energy Efficiency Program' (online).
Lowe, I., 'Reaction Time: Climate Change and the Nuclear Option' (2007) 27 *Quarterly Essay* 1.
Luterbacher, U. and Davis, P., 'Explaining Unilateral Cooperative Actions: The Case of Greenhouse Gas Regulations' (2010) 36(1) *Monash Law Review* 121.
Lyster, R., 'Chasing down the Climate Change Footprint of the Public and Private Sectors: Forces Converge – Part II' (2007) 24 *Environmental and Planning Law Journal* 450.
Lyster, R., 'Smart Grids: Opportunities for Climate Change Mitigation and Adaptation' (2010) 36(1) *Monash University Law Review* 173.
Lyster, R. and Bradbrook, A., *Energy Law and the Environment* (Cambridge University Press, 2006).
MacCarty, N. et al., 'A Laboratory Comparison of the Global Warming Impact of Five Major Types of Biomass Cooking Stoves' (2008) 12(2) *Energy for Sustainable Development* 56.
MacGill, I., Outhred, H. and Nolles, K., 'National Emissions Trading for Australia: Key Design Issues and Complementary Policies for Promoting Energy Efficiency, Infrastructure Investment and Innovation' (2004) 11(1) *Australasian Journal of Environmental Management* 78.
Macintosh, A., 'A Theoretical Framework for Adaptation Policy', in T. Bonyhady, A. Macintosh and J. McDonald (eds), *Adaptation to Climate Change* (Federation Press, 2010).
MacNally, R. et al., 'Biodiversity and Climate Change', Report commissioned by the Garnaut Climate Change Review, Australian Centre for Biodiversity, Monash University (June 2008).
Madsen, B., Carroll, N. and Moore Brands, K., *State of Biodiversity Markets Report: Offset and Compensation Programs Worldwide* (online).
Maher, S., 'Carbon Tax Necessary, Julia Gillard Tells Miners', *The Australian*, 1 June 2011 (online).
Maher, S., 'Carbon Tax on Coal Is "Ahead of World"', *The Australian*, 8 June 2011 (online).
Maher, S., 'Tony Abbott Tells Firms: Don't Buy Carbon Permits', *The Australian*, 15 October 2011 (online).
Manney, G. L. et al. 'Unprecedented Arctic Ozone Loss in 2011' (2011) 478 *Nature* 469.
Manning, A. et al., 'Greenhouse Gases in the Earth System: Setting the Agenda to 2030' (2011) 369 *Philosophical Transactions of the Royal Society A* 1885.

Maplecroft, 'Big Economies of the Future – Bangladesh, India, Philippines, Vietnam and Pakistan – Most at Risk from Climate Change' (online).

Markowitz, E. M. and Shariff, A. F., 'Climate Change and Moral Judgement' (2012) 2 *Nature Climate Change* 243.

Mascher, S., 'Australia's National Greenhouse Response: Implications for the Energy Sector' (1997) 16(2) *Australia Mining and Petroleum Law Journal* 126.

Masdar City, United Arab Emirates, 'The Global Centre of Future Energy' (online).

Mason-Case, S. A., *Legal Preparedness for REDD+ in Zambia: Country Study* (International Development Law Organization, November 2011).

Mathy, J.-C., Hourcade, S. and de Gouvello, C., 'Clean Development Mechanism: Leverage for Development?' (2001) 1 *Climate Policy* 251.

McAdam, J., *Climate Change, Forced Migration and International Law* (Oxford University Press, 2012).

McAdam, J., 'Environmental Migration Governance', Working Paper, University of New South Wales Faculty of Law Research Series (2009).

McAdam, J., 'Swimming against the Tide: Why a Climate Change Displacement Treaty is Not the Answer' (2011) 23(1) *International Journal of Refugee Law* 2.

McAdam, J. and Saul, B., 'An Insecure Climate for Human Security? Climate-Induced Displacement and International Law', Working Paper 4, University of Sydney Centre for International Law (2009).

McAdam, J. and Saul, B., 'Displacement with Dignity: Climate Change, Migration and Security in Bangladesh' (2010) 53 *German Yearbook of International Law* 1.

McAllister, L., 'Litigating Climate Change at the Coal Mine', in W. Burns and H. Osofsky (eds), *Adjudicating Climate Change: State, National, and International Approaches* (Cambridge University Press, 2009).

McAllister, L., 'Sustainable Consumption Governance in the Amazon' (2008) 38 *Environmental Law Reporter* 10873.

McConnell, D., 'Not Dead Yet: Flagship "collapse" only Part of Australia's Solar Story', *The Conversation* (10 February 2012) (online).

McDonald, J., 'A Risky Climate for Decision-Making: The Liability of Development Authorities for Climate Change Impacts' (2007) 24 *Environmental and Planning Law Journal* 405.

McDonald, J., 'Mapping the Legal Landscape of Climate Change Mitigation', in T. Bonyhady, A. Macintosh and J. McDonald (eds), *Adaptation to Climate Change: Law and Policy* (Federation Press, 2010).

McDonald, J., 'Paying the Price of Adaptation: Compensation for Climate Change Impacts', in T. Bonyhady, A. Macintosh and J. McDonald (eds), *Adaptation to Climate Change: Law and Policy* (Federation Press, 2010).

McDonald, J., 'The Adaptation Imperative: Managing the Legal Risks of Climate Change Impacts', in T. Bonyhady and P. Christoff (eds), *Climate Law* (Federation Press, 2007).

McGrath, C., 'Australia's Draft Climate Laws' (2009) 26 *Environmental and Planning Law Journal* 267.

McGrath, C., 'End of Broadscale Clearing in Queensland' (2007) 24 *Environmental and Planning Law Journal* 5.

McGrath, C., 'Regulating Greenhouse Gases from Australian Coal Mines' (2008) 25 *Environmental and Planning Law Journal* 240.

McKibben, B., *Eaarth: Making a Life on a Tough New Planet* (Henry Holt, 2010).

McMaster, P., 'Climate Change – Statutory Duty or Pious Hope?' (2008) 20(1) *Environmental Law* 115.

McNeil, B., 'The Costs of Introducing Nuclear Power in Australia' (2007) 59 *Journal of Australian Political Economy* 6.

Meijer, E. and Werksman, J., 'Keeping It Clean: Safeguarding the Environmental Integrity of the Clean Development Mechanism', in D. Freestone and C. Streck (eds), *Legal Aspects of Implementing the Kyoto Protocol Mechanisms: Making Kyoto Work* (Oxford University Press, 2005).

Meinshausen, M. et al., 'Greenhouse-gas Emission Targets for Limiting Global Warming to 2°C' (2009) 458 *Nature* 1158.
Melenberg, B., Vollebergh H. and Dijkgraaf, E., *Grazing the Commons: Global Carbon Emissions Forever?* (Tilburg University, 2011).
Metcalf, G. and Weisbach, D., 'The Design of a Carbon Tax' (2009) 33 *Harvard Environmental Law Review* 499.
Metz, B., et al. (eds), *Intergovernmental Panel on Climate Change: Special Report on Carbon Dioxide Capture and Storage* (IPCC, 2005).
Metz, B. et al., *Methodological and Technological Issues in Technology Transfer: A Special Report of the IPCC Working Group III* (Cambridge University Press, 2000).
Meyer, R., 'Finding the True Value of US Climate Science' (2012) 482 *Nature* 133.
Michaelowa, A., 'Creating the Foundations for Host Country Participation in the CDM: Experiences and Challenges in CDM Capacity Building', in F. Yamin (ed.), *Climate Change and Carbon Markets – A Handbook of Emission Reduction Mechanisms* (Earthscan, 2005).
Michaelowa, A., 'Determination of Baselines and Additionality for the CDM: A Crucial Element of Credibility of the Climate Regime', in F. Yamin (ed.), *Climate Change and Carbon Markets: A Handbook of Emission Reduction Mechanisms* (Earthscan, 2005).
Millar, I. and Curnow, P., 'Is Carbon Still Relevant? Pricing Carbon in a Post-CPRS Australia', paper presented at AMPLA Conference, Perth, 20–23 October 2010.
Miller, K. A., 'Climate Change and Water in the West: Complexities, Uncertainties and Strategies for Adaptation' (2007) 27 *Journal of Land Resources and Environmental Law* 87.
Milly, P. C. D. et al., 'Stationarity is Dead: Whither Water Management?' (2008) 319 *Science* 573.
Milne, J. E., 'Carbon Taxes in the United States: The Context for the Future', in J. Milne (ed.), *The Reality of Carbon Taxes in the 21st Century* (Vermont Law School Environmental Tax Policy Institute, 2008).
Minchin, N., 'Responding to Climate Change: Providing a Policy Framework for a Competitive Australia' (2001) 7 *UNSW Law Journal Forum* 13.
Ministerial Council on Mineral and Petroleum Resources, *Regulatory Guiding Principles for Carbon Dioxide Capture and Geological Storage* (25 November 2005).
Mitchell, C. D., Harper, R. J. and Keenan, R. J., 'Current Status and Future Prospects for Carbon Forestry in Australia', *Australian Forestry* (forthcoming 2012).
Molina, M. et al., 'Reducing Abrupt Climate Change Risk Using the Montreal Protocol and Other Regulatory Actions to Complement Cuts in CO_2 Emissions' (2009) 106(49) *Proceedings of the National Academy of Sciences of the United States of America* 20616.
Moore, L., 'Voluntary Carbon Offsets: a Legal Perspective', in W. Gumley and T. Daya-Winterbottom (eds), *Climate Change Law: Comparative, Contractual and Regulatory Considerations* (Lawbook Company, 2009).
Moran, A., 'Tools of Environmental Policy: Market Instruments versus Command-and-control', in R. Eckersley (ed.), *Markets, the State, and the Environment: Towards Integration* (Macmillan Education Australia, 1995).
Morello, V., 'NSW Solar Bonus Scheme in Limbo', *Sydney Morning Herald*, 29 April 2011 (online).
Morris, D. and Worthington, B., *Cap or Trap? How the EU ETS Risks Locking in Carbon Emissions* (Sandbag, September 2010).
Murphy, K., 'PM to Unveil Details of Carbon Trading Plan', *The Age* (Melbourne), 17 July 2007.
Murray, J. and King, D., 'Oil's Tipping Point Has Passed' (2012) 481 *Nature* 433.
Musango, J. and Brent, A., 'A Conceptual Framework for Energy Technology Sustainability Assessment' (2011) 15 *Energy for Sustainable Development* 84.
Nagle, J., 'Discounting China's CDM Dams' (2009) 7(1) *Loyola University Chicago International Law Review* 9.
NASA Jet Propulsion Laboratory, 'OCO-2: Orbiting Carbon Observatory' (online).

Neeff, T. and Ascui, F., 'Lessons from Carbon Markets for Designing an Effective REDD Architecture' (2009) 9 *Climate Policy* 306.

Nepstad, D. et al., 'The End of Deforestation in the Brazilian Amazon' (2009) 326 *Science* 1350.

Netherlands Environmental Assessment Agency, *National Inventory Report 2010* (2010).

Netto, M. and Schmidt, K.-U. B., 'CDM Project Cycle and the Role of the UNFCCC Secretariat', in D. Freestone and C. Streck (eds), *Legal Aspects of Implementing the Kyoto Protocol Mechanisms: Making Kyoto Work* (Oxford University Press, 2005).

Neuhoff, K., *Tackling Carbon: How to Price Carbon for Climate Policy*, Version 1.1, 29/9/2008, University of Cambridge, Faculty of Economics (online).

Neumayer, E., 'In Defence of Historical Accountability for Greenhouse Gas Emissions' (2000) 33 *Ecological Economics* 185.

New South Wales Government, 'Energy Savings Scheme' (online).

New South Wales Government, 'Greenhouse Gas Reduction Scheme (GGAS)' (online).

New South Wales Government, Department of Infrastructure and Planning, *NSW Draft Planning Guidelines: Wind Farms* (December 2011).

Newell, P. and Paterson, M., *Climate Capitalism: Global Warming and the Transformation of the Global Economy* (Cambridge University Press, 2010).

Nielsen, N., 'China Confronts EU on Aviation Tax', *EU Observer*, 6 February 2012 (online).

Niue Declaration on Climate Change, endorsed at the 39th Pacific Island Forum, Niue, 19–20 August 2008 (online).

Norwegian Agency for Development Cooperation, *Real-Time Evaluation of Norway's International Climate and Forest Initiative: Contributions to a Global REDD+ Regime 2007–2010* (Norad, March 2011).

Norwegian Agency for Development Cooperation, *Real-Time Evaluation of Norway's International Climate and Forest Initiative: Contributions to National REDD+ Processes 2007–2010: Country Report: Brazil* (Norad, March 2011).

Norwegian Agency for Development Cooperation, *Real-Time Evaluation of Norway's International Climate and Forest Initiative: Contributions to National REDD+ Processes 2007–2010: Country Report: Democratic Republic of Congo* (Norad, March 2011).

NSW Rural Fire Service document, *Planning for Bushfire Protection* (2001).

Nussbaumer, P., 'On the Contribution of Labelled Certified Emission Reductions to Sustainable Development: A Multi-Criteria Evaluation of CDM Projects' (2009) 37(1) *Energy Policy* 91.

Oberthür, S. and Lefeber, R., 'Holding Countries to Account: The Kyoto Protocol's Compliance System Revisited after Four Years of Experience' (2010) 1(1) *Climate Law* 133.

O'Connor, P., 'The Extension of Land Registration Principles to New Property Rights in Environmental Goods', in M. Dixon (ed.), *Modern Studies in Property Law*, vol. 5 (Hart Publishing, 2009).

OECD, International Energy Agency, and Eurostat, *Energy Statistics Manual* (2005) (online).

OECD, *Nuclear Legislation in OECD Countries: Regulatory and Institutional Framework for Regulatory Activities: Australia* (2008).

Okereke, C., Bulkeley, H. and Schroeder, H., 'Conceptualising Climate Governance Beyond the International Regime' (2009) 9 *Global Environmental Politics* 58.

Olsen, K. H., 'The Clean Development Mechanism's Contribution to Sustainable Development: A Review of the Literature' (2007) 84 *Climatic Change* 59.

Otto-Zimmermann, K., 'Local Solutions for Global Challenges' (2006) 11(1) *Local Environment* 1.

Oxfam, *Growing a Better Future: Food Justice in a Resource-Constrained World* (2011).

Pacala, S. and Socolow, R., 'Stabilization Wedges: Solving the Climate Problem for the Next 50 Years with Current Technologies' (2004) 305 *Science* 968.

Pacific Islands Forum, 2009 *Forum Leaders' Communiqué, Annex A* (6 August 2009) (online).

Pacific Islands Forum Secretariat, *Climate Change Issues dominate SIS Leader's Meeting* (Press Release 67/10, 3 August 2010) (online).
Parker, C., Mitchell, A., Trivedi, M. and Mardas, N., *Little REDD Book: A Guide to Governmental and Non-Governmental Proposals for Reducing Emissions from Deforestation and Degradation* (Global Canopy Programme, 2008).
Parker, L., 'Climate Change and the EU Emissions Trading Scheme (ETS): Looking to 2020' (2011) 22 *Current Politics and Economics of Europe* 327.
Parkinson, G., 'Solar Flagships May Fly at Half Mast', *Climate Spectator* (5 December 2011) (online).
Parliament of Victoria, Environment and Natural Resources Committee, *Inquiry into the Approvals Process for Renewable Energy Projects in Victoria* (2010).
Parmesan, C. and Yohe, G., 'A Globally Coherent Fingerprint of Climate Change Impacts across Natural Systems' (2003) 421 *Nature* 37.
Parry, M., 'A Property Law Perspective on the Current Australian Carbon Sequestration Laws and the Green Paper Model' (2010) 36(1) *Monash Law Review* 321.
Passero, M., 'The Nature of the Right or Interest Created by a Market for Forest Carbon' (2008) 2(3) *Carbon and Climate Law Review* 248.
Passey, R., MacGill, I. and Outhred, H., 'The NSW Greenhouse Gas Reduction Scheme: An Analysis of the NGAC Registry for the 2003, 2004 and 2005 Compliance Periods', (Centre for Energy and Environmental Markets, 2007).
Pearse, G., *High and Dry: John Howard, Climate Change and the Selling of Australia's Future* (Penguin Books Australia, 2007).
Peel, J., *Climate Change Law: Australian and Overseas Developments* (online).
Peel, J., 'Climate Change Law: The Emergence of a New Legal Discipline' (2008) 32 *Melbourne University Law Review* 922.
Peel, J., 'Ecologically Sustainable Development: More than Mere Lip Service?' (2008) 12(1) *Australasian Journal of Natural Resources Law and Policy* 1.
Peel, J., *The Precautionary Principle in Practice: Environmental Decision-Making and Scientific Uncertainty* (Federation Press, 2005).
Peel, J., 'The Role of Climate Change Litigation in Australia's Response to Global Warming' (2007) 24 *Environmental and Planning Law Journal* 90.
Peel, J. and Godden, L., 'Planning for Adaptation to Climate Change: Landmark Cases from Australia' (2009) 9(2) *Sustainable Development Law and Policy: Climate Law Reporter* 37.
Peel, J. and Godden, L., 'The Environment Protection and Biodiversity Conservation Act 1999 (Cth): Dark Sides of Virtue' (2007) 31 *Melbourne University Law Review* 106.
Peeters, M., 'Legislative Choices and Legal Values: Considerations on the Further Design of the European Greenhouse Gas Emissions Trading Scheme from a Viewpoint of Democratic Accountability', in M. Faure and M. Peeters (eds), *Climate Change and European Emissions Trading: Lessons for Theory and Practice* (Edward Elgar Publishing, 2008).
Peeters, M., 'The EU ETS and the Role of the Courts: Emerging Contours in the Case of Arcelor' (2011) 2(1) *Climate Law* 19.
Peeters, M. and Weishaar, S., 'Exploring Uncertainties in the EU ETS: "Learning by Doing" Continues Beyond 2012' (2009) 3(1) *Carbon and Climate Law Review* 88.
Peskett, L. et al., *Making REDD Work for the Poor*, A Poverty Environment Partnership (PEP) Report (September 2008).
Peters, G. et al., 'Growth in Emission Transfers Via International Trade from 1990 to 2008' (2011) 108(21) *Proceedings of the National Academy of Sciences of the United States of America* 8903.
Peters, G. et al., 'Rapid Growth in CO_2 Emissions after the 2008–2009 Global Financial Crisis' (2012) 2 *Nature Climate Change* 2.
Petherick, A., 'A Note of Caution' (2012) 2 *Nature Climate Change* 144.
Petherick, A., 'Dirty Money' (2012) 2 *Nature Climate Change* 72.
Petherick, A., 'Duty Down Under' (2012) 2 *Nature Climate Change* 20.

Petherick, A. 'Petition to the Inter American Commission on Human Rights Seeking Relief from Violations resulting from Global Warming caused by Acts and Omissions of the United States' (7 December 2005) (online).

Pew Research Center, *Energy Concerns Fall, Deficit Concerns Rise – Public's Priorities for 2010: Economy, Jobs, Terrorism* (25 January 2010).

Pew Research Center, *Increasing Partisan Divide on Energy Policies: Little Change in Opinions About Global Warming* (27 October 2010).

Pew Research Center, *Public's Priorities for 2010* (2010).

Pielke, R., Prins, G., Rayner, S. and Sarewitz, D., 'Lifting the Taboo on Adaptation' (2007) 445 *Nature* 597.

Pizer, W., 'Combining Price and Quantity Controls to Mitigate Climate Change' (2002) 85 *Journal of Public Economics* 409.

Pizer, W., 'Prices vs Quantities Revisited: The Case of Climate Change', Discussion Paper 98–02, Resources for the Future, October 1997.

Polglase, P. and Benyon, R., *The Impacts of Plantations and Native Forests on Water Security: Review and Scientific Assessment of Regional Issues and Research Needs* (Forest and Wood Products Australia, 2008).

Polglase, P. et al., *Opportunities for Carbon Forestry in Australia: Economic Assessment and Constraints to Implementation* (CSIRO, 2011).

Popp, D., 'International Technology Transfer, Climate Change, and the Clean Development Mechanism' (2011) 5(1) *Review of Environmental Economics and Policy* 131.

Potter, C. et al., 'Storage of Carbon in US Forests Predicted from Satellite Data, Ecosystem Modeling, and Inventory Summaries' (2008) 90 *Climatic Change* 269.

Powell, S., 'An Insurer's Approach to Management of Climate Risks', in T. Bonyhady, A. Macintosh and J. McDonald (eds), *Adaptation to Climate Change: Law and Policy* (Federation Press, 2010).

Power, M., 'Emissions Trading in Australia: Markets, Law and Justice under the CPRS' (2010) 27 *Environmental and Planning Law Journal* 131.

Power, M., 'The Carbon Farming Initiative – Too Little, Too Soon?' (2011) 1 *National Environmental Law Review* 57.

Powlson, D. et al., 'Soil Carbon Sequestration to Mitigate Climate Change: A Critical Re-examination to Identify the True and the False' (2011) 62(1) *European Journal of Soil Science* 42.

Prest, J., 'A Dangerous Obsession with Least Cost? Climate Change, Renewable Energy Law and Emissions Trading', in W. Gumley and T. Daya-Winterbottom (eds), *Climate Change Law: Comparative, Contractual and Regulatory Considerations* (Lawbook Company, 2009).

Preston, B., 'Climate Change Litigation (Part 2)' (2011) *Carbon and Climate Law Review* 244.

Preston, B., 'The Influence of Climate Litigation on Governments and the Private Sector' (2011) 2(4) *Climate Law* 485.

Preston, B., 'The Role of the Courts in Relation to Adaptation to Climate Change', in T. Bonyhady, A. Macintosh and J. MacDonald (eds), *Adaptation to Climate Change: Law and Policy* (Federation Press, 2010).

Prime Ministerial Task Group on Emissions Trading, *Report of the Task Group on Emissions Trading* (2007) (online).

Prowse, M. and Scott, L., 'Assets and Adaptation: An Emerging Debate' (2008) 39(4) *IDS Bulletin*.

Purdy, R., *Satellite Monitoring of Environmental Laws: Lessons to Be Learnt from Australia* (UK Economic and Social Research Council, 2010).

Queensland Government, *ClimateQ: Toward a Greener Queensland* (2009).

Queensland Government, *Queensland Floods Commission of Inquiry* 2011 (online).

Queensland Parliament, Environment and Resources Committee, *Inquiry into Growing Queensland's Renewable Energy Electricity Sector* – Executive Summary (2011).

Ramanathan, V. and Carmichael, G., 'Global and Regional Climate Changes Due to Black Carbon' (2008) 1 *Nature Geoscience* 221.

Ramseur, J., 'The Role of Offsets in a Greenhouse Gas Emissions Cap-and-Trade Program: Potential Benefits and Concerns', Congressional Research Service, Report to Congress (4 April 2008).
Rann M., 'Federation Council Agree to Emissions Trading Timeframe' (Media Release, 12 April 2007) (online).
Rayner, S., 'How to Eat an Elephant: A Bottom-Up Approach to Climate Policy' (2010) 10(6) *Climate Policy* 615.
Read, A. and Fisher, D., *The Proudest Day: India's Long Road to Independence* (Norton, 1997).
Redmond, D. and Kendall, K., 'Emissions Trading Schemes, Domestic Policy and the WTO' (2010) 7 *Macquarie Journal of Business Law* 15.
Republic of the Fiji Islands, Fiji Forestry Department, 'Fiji REDD-Plus Policy: Reducing Emissions from Deforestation and Forest Degradation in Fiji' (2011).
Republic of the Maldives, Ministry of Environment, Energy and Water, *Report on the First Meeting on Protocol on Environmental Refugees: Recognition of Environmental Refugees in the 1951 Convention and 1967 Protocol Relating to the Status of Refugees* (14–15 August 2006).
Revelle, R., 'Carbon Dioxide and World Climate' (1982) 247(2) *Scientific American* 35.
Revelle, R. and Suess, H., 'Carbon Dioxide Exchange between Atmosphere and Ocean and the Question of an Increase of Atmospheric CO_2 during the Past Decades' (1957) 9 *Tellus* 18.
RGGI Inc., *Fact Sheet: RGGI Offsets* (19 August 2010) (online).
RGGI Inc., *Investment of Proceeds from RGGI CO_2 Projects* (February 2011).
Rickels, W., Rehdanz, K. and Oschlies, A., 'Economic Prospects of Ocean Iron Fertilization in an International Carbon Market' (2012) 34(1) *Resource and Energy Economics* 129.
Rimmer, M., *Intellectual Property and Climate Change: Inventing Clean Technologies* (Edward Elgar Publishing, 2011).
Rivier, L. et al., 'European CO_2 Fluxes from Atmospheric Inversions Using Regional and Global Transport Models' (2010) 103 *Climatic Change* 93.
Rogelj, J. et al., 'Analysis of the Copenhagen Accord Pledges and its Global Climatic Impact – A Snapshot of Dissonant Ambitions' (2010) 5(3) *Environmental Research Letters* 034013.
Rogelj, J. et al., 'Copenhagen Accord Pledges Are Paltry' (2010) 464 *Nature* 1126.
Rosenbaum, K., Schoene, D. and Mekouar, A., 'Climate Change and the Forest Sector: Possible National and Subnational Legislation', FAO Forestry Paper 144 (Food and Agriculture Organization, 2004).
Royal Society, *Climate Change: A Summary of the Science* (2010) (online).
Royal Society, *Geoengineering the Climate: Science, Governance and Uncertainty* (2009).
Ruhl, J. and Saltzmann, J., 'Climate Change, Dead Zones and Massive Problems in the Administrative State: A Guide for Whittling Away' (2010) 98 *California Law Review* 59.
Ruhl, J. B., 'Climate Change Adaptation and the Structural Transformation of Environmental Law' (2010) 40 *Environmental Law* 343.
Saad, L., 'Water Issues Worry Americans Most, Global Warming Least', *Gallup Politics* (28 March 2011) (online).
Sanders, O., Goesch, R. and Hughes, N., *Issues – Insights 10.5: Adapting to Water Scarcity* (Australian Bureau of Agricultural and Resource Economics, 2010).
Santilli, M. et al. 'Tropical Deforestation and the Kyoto Protocol: An Editorial Essay' (2005) 71 *Climatic Change* 267.
Savage, A., 'Carbon Tax Concerns over Jobs, Power Supply', ABC News (online), 11 July 2011.
Savaresi, A., 'Forests, Economics, and Climate Change' (2011) 2(3) *Climate Law* 439.
Schall, C., 'Public Interest Litigation Concerning Environmental Matters before Human Rights Courts: A Promising Future Concept?' (2008) 20(3) *Journal of Environmental Law* 417.
Schiermeier, Q., 'Clean-Energy Credits Tarnished' (2011) 477 *Nature* 517.

Schiermeier, Q., 'The Great Arctic Oil Race Begins' (2012) 482 *Nature* 13.
Schneider, L., 'Assessing the Additionality of CDM Projects: Practical Experience and Lessons Learned' (2009) 9(3) *Climate Policy* 242.
Schneider, L., *Is the CDM Fulfilling Its Environmental and Sustainable Development Objectives? An Evaluation of the CDM and Options for Improvement* (Öko-Institut, 2007).
Schneider, M., Froggat, A. and Thomas, S., 'The World Nuclear Industry Status Report 2010–2011 – Nuclear Power in a Post-Fukushima World – 25 Years after the Chernobyl Accident' (Worldwatch Institute, 2011).
Scholz, S. and Noble, I., 'Generation of Sequestration Credits under the CDM', in D. Freestone and C. Streck (eds), *Legal Aspects of Implementing the Kyoto Protocol Mechanisms: Making Kyoto Work* (Oxford University Press, 2005).
Schuur, E. and Abbott, B., 'High Risk of Permafrost Thaw' (2011) 480 *Nature* 32.
Scott, J., 'The Multi-Level Governance of Climate Change' (2011) 5(1) *Carbon and Climate Law* Review 25.
Secretariat (Convention on Biological Diversity), *REDD-Plus and Biodiversity*, CBD Technical Series No. 59 (2011).
Seres, S., Haites, E. and Murphy, K., 'Analysis of Technology Transfer in CDM Projects: An Update' (2009) 37(11) *Energy Policy* 4919.
Serreze, M., 'Climate Change: Rethinking the Sea-Ice Tipping Point' (2011) 471 *Nature* 47.
Shakun, J.D. et al., 'Global Warming Preceded by Increasing Carbon Dioxide Concentrations During the Last Deglaciation' (2012) 484 *Nature* 49.
Shilling, N., 'CCS – General Electric's Perspective', in I. Havercroft, R. Macrory and R.B. Stewart (eds), *Carbon Capture and Storage: Emerging Legal and Regulatory Issues* (Hart Publishing, 2011).
Shobe, W. and Burtraw, D., 'Rethinking Environmental Federalism in a Warming World', (forthcoming in 2012) 3 *Climate Change Economics*.
Shue, H., 'Global Environment and International Inequality' (1999) 75 *International Affairs* 531.
Siddiqui, A. et al., 'Eye and Respiratory Symptoms among Women Exposed to Wood Smoke Emitted from Indoor Cooking: A Study from Southern Pakistan' (2005) 9(3) *Energy for Sustainable Development* 58.
Sindico, F., 'Climate Change: A Security (Council) Issue?' (2007) 1 *Carbon and Climate Law Review* 26.
Singer, P., 'One Atmosphere', in S.M. Gardiner et al. (eds), *Climate Ethics: Essential Readings* (Oxford University Press, 2010).
Skjaerseth, J.B., 'EU Emissions Trading: Legitimacy and Stringency' (2010) 20(5) *Environmental Policy and Governance* 295.
Skjaerseth, J.B. and Wettestad, J., *EU Emissions Trading: Initiation, Decision-making and Implementation* (Ashgate Publishing, 2008).
Skjaerseth, J.B. and Wettestad, J., 'Fixing the EU Emissions Trading System? Understanding the post-2012 Changes' (2010) 10 *Global Environmental Politics* 101.
Skodvin, T., 'Smart Grid, Smart City', AusGrid, Australian Government, Department of Resources, Energy and Tourism (online).
Skodvin, T., 'The Asia–Pacific Partnership on Clean Development and Climate: Supplement or Alternative to the Kyoto Protocol?', paper presented at the 48th Annual Convention of the International Studies Association, Chicago, 28 February–3 March 2007 (online).
Smith, K., 'We Are Seven Billion' (2011) 1 *Nature Climate Change* 331.
Smyth, S., 'A Practical Guide to Creating a Collective Financing Effort to Save the World: The Global Environment Facility Experience' (2010) 22(1) *Georgetown International Environmental Law Review* 29.
Solomon, E., 'Security for Biodiversity Offsets in New South Wales' (2011) 28 *Environmental and Planning Law Journal* 92.

Solomon, S. et al., 'Irreversible Climate Change Due to Carbon Dioxide Emissions' (2009) 106(6) *Proceedings of the National Academy of Sciences of the United States of America* 1704.
Sorrell, S. and Sijm, J., 'Carbon Trading in the Policy Mix' (2003) 19(3) *Oxford Review of Economic Policy* 420.
Spash, C., 'The Brave New World of Carbon Trading' (2010) 15(2) *New Political Economy* 169.
Srinivasan, U., 'Economics of Climate Change: Risk and Responsibility by World Region' (2010) 10 *Climate Policy* 298.
Stafford Smith, M. and Ash, A., 'Adaptation: Reducing Risk, Gaining Opportunity', in H. Cleugh, M. Stafford Smith, M. Battaglia and P. Graham (eds), *Climate Change: Science and Solutions for Australia* (CSIRO, 2011).
State of California Environmental Protection Agency, Air Resources Board, 'Assembly Bill 32: Global Warming Solutions Act' (online).
State of California Environmental Protection Agency, Air Resources Board, 'California Cap and Trade Program Resolution 11–32' (20 October 2011) (online).
State of California Environmental Protection Agency, Air Resources Board, 'Cap-and-Trade Regulation: July 2011 Discussion Draft 1 Appendix A: Staff Proposal for Allocating Allowances to Electricity Distribution Utilities' (online).
State of California Environmental Protection Agency, Air Resources Board, 'Climate Change AB 32 Scoping Plan' (2008).
State of California Environmental Protection Agency, Air Resources Board, 'Climate Change Program' (online).
State of California Environmental Protection Agency, Air Resources Board, 'Staff Report: Initial Statement of Reasons', Appendix J-12, 28 October 2011 (online).
State of California, Environmental Protection Agency, Air Resources Board, 'Supplement to the AB 32 Scoping Plan Functional Equivalent Document' (13 June 2011).
State of California, Energy Commission, 'Emissions Performance Standard' (online).
State of California, Energy Commission, 'Renewables Portfolio Standard (RPS) Proceeding – Docket # 03-RPS-1078' (online).
State of California, Energy Commission and California Public Utilities Commission, 'About the California Solar Initiative' (online).
State of California, Natural Resources Agency, *2009 Californian Climate Adaptation Strategy* (online).
State of California, Public Utilities Commission, 'Net Energy Metering' (online).
Steffen, W., *The Critical Decade: Climate Science, Risks and Responses* (Australian Climate Commission Secretariat, 2011).
Steffen, W. et al., *Australia's Biodiversity and Climate Change* (CSIRO, 2009).
Stein, L., 'The Legal and Economic Bases for an Emissions Trading Scheme' (2010) 36(1) *Monash Law Review* 192.
Stern, N., *The Economics of Climate Change: The Stern Review* (Cambridge University Press, 2007).
Stewart, R., 'A New Generation of Environmental Regulation?' (2001) 29 *Capital University Law Review* 21.
Stockholm Environment Institute and Greenhouse Gas Management Institute, *Introduction to Offset Policies* (online).
Strauss, A., 'Climate Change Litigation: Opening the Door to the International Court of Justice', in W. C. G. Burns and H. M. Osofsky (eds), *Adjudicating Climate Change: State, National and International Approaches* (Cambridge University Press, 2009).
Streck, C., 'Joint Implementation: History, Requirements, and Challenges', in D. Freestone and C. Streck (eds), *Legal Aspects of Implementing the Kyoto Protocol Mechanisms: Making Kyoto Work* (Oxford University Press, 2005).
Streck, C., 'Reducing Emissions from Deforestation and Forest Degradation: National Implementation of REDD Schemes: An Editorial Comment' (2010) 100 *Climatic Change* 389.

Streck, C., 'The Global Environment Facility – a Role Model for International Governance?' (2011) 1(2) *Global Environmental Politics* 71.

Streck, C. and Lin, J., 'Mobilising Finance for Climate Change Mitigation: Private Sector Involvement in International Carbon Finance Mechanisms' (2009) 10(1) *Melbourne Journal of International Law* 70.

Strengers, B., Van Minnen, J. and Eickhout, B., 'The Role of Carbon Plantations in Mitigating Climate Change: Potentials and Costs' (2008) 88 *Climatic Change* 343.

Stutchbury, M., 'Carbon Price May Take the Heat Off', *The Australian*, 7 June 2011 (online).

Sullivan, R., 'Greenhouse Challenge Plus: A New Departure or More of the Same?' (2006) 23 *Environmental and Planning Law Journal* 60.

Sullivan, R., *Rethinking Voluntary Approaches in Environmental Policy* (Edward Elgar Publishing, 2005).

Sultana, N., 'Climate Change Adaptation and Governance in the Coastal District of Bhola in Bangladesh', paper presented at *Climate Change Adaptation and Governance Workshop*, UNSW, 16–18 November 2010.

Sunstein, C. R., 'On the Divergent American Reactions to Terrorism and Climate Change' (2007) 107 *Columbia Law Review* 503.

Sutter, C. and Parreño, J. C., 'Does the Current Clean Development Mechanism (CDM) Deliver Its Sustainable Development Claim? An Analysis of Officially Registered CDM Projects' (2007) 84 *Climatic Change* 75.

Symposium, 'Responses to Global Warming: The Law, Economics, and Science of Climate Change' (2007) 155 *University of Pennsylvania Law Review* 1795.

Szerszynski, B., 'On Knowing What to Do: Environmentalism and the Modern Problematic', in S. Lash, B. Szerszynski and B. Wynne (eds), *Risk, Environment and Modernity: Towards a New Ecology* (Sage Publications, 1996).

Tamiotti, L. et al., *Trade and Climate Change*, WTO-UNEP Report, Geneva (2009).

Tan, P., 'Adaptation Measures for Water Security in a Changing Climate: Policy, Planning and Law', in T. Bonyhady, A. Macintosh and J. McDonald (eds), *Adaptation to Climate Change: Law and Policy* (Federation Press, 2010).

The Stockholm Declaration Report of the United Nations Conference on the Human Environment, Stockholm, 5–16 June 1972, UN Doc A/CONF.48/13/Rev.1 (1 January 1973).

Thompson, A. and Campbell-Watt, R., 'Australia and an Emissions Trading Market – Opportunities, Costs and Legal Frameworks' (2005) 24(2) *Australian Resources and Energy Law Journal* 151.

Thompson, A. and Campbell-Watt, R., 'Carbon Rights – Development of the Legal Framework for a Trading Market' (2004) 2 *National Environmental Law Review* 31.

Toke, D., 'Trading Schemes, Risks, and Costs: The Cases of the European Union Emissions Trading Scheme and the Renewables Obligation' (2008) 26 *Environment and Planning C: Government and Policy* 938.

Tollefson, J., 'Brazil Set to Cut Forest Protection' (2012) 485 *Nature* 19.

Tollefson, J., 'Durban Maps Path to Climate Treaty' (2011) 480 *Nature* 299.

Tollefson, J., 'Evolution Advocate Turns to Climate' (2012) 481 *Nature* 248.

Tollefson, J., 'The Roadless Warrior' (2011) 480 *Nature* 22.

Turton, H., *Greenhouse Gas Emissions in Industrialised Countries: Where Does Australia Stand?* (Australia Institute, June 2004).

TÜV Nord, *Certification Report (First Operational Period): Efficient Fuel Wood Stoves for Nigeria* (14 December 2010) (online).

TÜV Nord, *Final Validation Report for Efficient Fuel Wood Stoves for Nigeria* (8 September 2009) (online).

TÜV Nord, *Verification Report (First Operational Period): Efficient Fuel Wood Stoves for Nigeria* (14 December 2010) (online).

UN Department of Economic and Social Affairs Population Division, *World Population Prospects: The 2010 Revision, Volume II: Demographic Profiles* (United Nations, 2011).
UN Development Programme, *Human Development Report 2010 – The Real Wealth of Nations: Pathways to Human Development* (2010).
UN Environment Programme, *Bridging the Emissions Gap: A UNEP Synthesis Report* (November 2011).
UN Environment Programme, *Near-Term Climate Protection and Clean Air Benefits: Actions for Controlling Short-Lived Climate Forcers* (2011).
UN Environment Programme, *Towards a Green Economy: Pathways to Sustainable Development and Poverty Eradication* (2011).
UN General Assembly, *Non-Legally Binding Instrument on All Types of Forests*, Resolution Adopted by the General Assembly (31 January 2008), A/RES/62/98.
UN General Assembly, *Protection of Global Climate for Present and Future Generations of Mankind*, Resolution Adopted by the General Assembly (6 December 1988), A/RES/43/53.
UN General Assembly, *Protection of Global Climate for Present and Future Generations of Mankind*, Resolution Adopted by the General Assembly (21 December 1990), A/RES/45/212.
UN General Assembly, *Report of the United Nations Conference on Environment and Development, Annex III: Non-Legally Binding Authoritative Statement of Principles for a Global Consensus on the Management, Conservation and Sustainable Development of All Types of Forests* (14 August 1992), A/CONF.151/26 (Vol. III).
UN News Centre, 'Palau Seeks UN World Court Opinion on Damage Caused by Greenhouse Gases' (22 September 2011) (online).
UNICA – Sugarcane Industry Association, 'Ethanol Production – Brazil' (online).
United Kingdom, Department of Energy and Climate Change, *Energy Market Reform* (2011).
United Nations, Department of Public Information, News and Media Division, 'Security Council Holds First-ever Debate on Impact of Climate Change on Peace, Security, Hearing over 50 Speakers' (17 April 2007).
United Nations, *World Population Prospects: The 2008 Revision* (online).
US Department of State, *Meeting the Fast Start Commitment: US Climate Finance in Fiscal Year 2011* (2011).
US National Research Council, *Verifying Greenhouse Gas Emissions: Methods to Support International Climate Agreements* (NRC, 2010).
US National Snow and Ice Data Center, 'Artic Sea Ice News and Analysis' (online).
van Renssen, S., 'Taking Charge of Mitigation' (2012) 2 *Nature Climate Change* 71.
van Renssen, S., 'The Final Carbon Frontier' (2012) 2 *Nature Climate Change* 11.
van Renssen, S., 'The Greenhouse-Gas Gang' (2012) 2 *Nature Climate Change* 143.
Van Vliet, O., Faaj, A. and Dieperink, C., 'Forestry Projects under the Clean Development Mechanism?' (2003) 61 *Climatic Change* 123.
Verheyen, R., *Climate Change Damage and International Law: Prevention Duties and State Responsibility* (Martinus Nijhoff Publishers, 2005).
Victoria Planning Panels, Coastal Climate Change Advisory Committee, 'Issues and Options Paper' (February 2010) (online).
Victorian Bushfires Royal Commission 2009, *Final Report and Recommendations* (2010).
Victorian Competition and Efficiency Commission, 'Inquiry into Feed-in Tariffs and Barriers to Distributed Generation' (online).
Victorian Government, Department of Primary Industries, 'A Regulatory Framework for the Long-Term Underground Storage of Carbon Dioxide in Australia', Discussion Paper (January 2009).
Victorian Government, Department of Sustainability and Environment, *BushTender: Rethinking Investment* (2008).

Victorian Government, *Recovering from Floods: 2011 Victorian Floods* (2011) (online).
Victorian Government, Regional Development Victoria, *Assistance Package for Flood-Affected Victorian Irrigators* (27 April 2011) (online).
Virgilio, N., Marshall, S., Zerbock, O. and Holmes, C., *Reducing Emissions from Deforestation and Degradation (REDD): A Casebook of On-the-Ground Experience* (Nature Conservancy, 2010).
Visser, M., 'Birds and Butterflies in Climatic Debt' (2012) 2 *Nature Climate Change* 77.
Voigt, C., 'Responsibility for the Environmental Integrity of the CDM: Judicial Review of Executive Board Decisions', in D. Freestone and C. Streck (eds), *Legal Aspects of Carbon Trading* (Oxford University Press, 2009).
Voigt, C., 'The Deadlock of the Clean Development Mechanism: Caught between Sustainability, Environmental Integrity and Economic Efficiency', in B. J. Richardson et al. (eds), *Climate Law and Developing Countries: Legal and Policy Changes for the World Economy* (Edward Elgar Publishing, 2009).
Voigt, C., 'WTO Law and International Emissions Trading: Is There Potential for Conflict?' (2008) 1(2) *Carbon and Climate Law Review* 54.
Vreuls, H. H. J., 'Uncertainty Analysis of Dutch Greenhouse Gas Emission Data: A First Qualitative and Quantitative (Tier 2) Analysis', paper presented at GHG Uncertainty Workshop, Warsaw, 24–25 September 2004.
Wagner, G. and Zeckhauser, R., 'Climate Policy: Hard Problem, Soft Thinking' (2012) 110 *Climatic Change* 507.
Wara, M. and Victor, G., 'A Realistic Policy on International Carbon Offsets', Working Paper no. 74 (Program on Energy and Sustainable Development, Stanford University, 2008).
Weitzman, M. L., 'Prices v Quantities' (1974) 41(4) *Quantities Review of Economic Studies* 477.
Wentworth Group of Concerned Scientists, *Optimising Carbon in the Australian Landscape: How to Guide the Terrestrial Carbon Market to Deliver Multiple Economic and Environmental Benefits* (2009).
Western Australian Government, Office of Energy, 'Residential Feed-in Tariff: Suspension of Scheme' (online).
Western Climate Initiative, 'Design Summary – Design for the WCI Regional Program' (online).
Westra, S. et al., 'Addressing Climatic Non-stationarity in the Assessment of Flood Risk' (2010) 14 *Australian Journal of Water Resources* 1.
Wewerinke, M. and Doebbler, C., 'Exploring the Legal Basis of a Human Rights Approach to Climate Change' (2010) 10 *Chinese Journal of International Law* 1.
Whealy, A. and Ferguson, I., '*Walker v Minister for Planning* [2007] NSWLEC 741 – implications for Coastal and Flood Liable Land and Major Project Development', Gadens Lawyers (December 2007) (online).
Whitehead, P. J. et al., 'The Management of Climate Change through Prescribed Savanna Burning: Emerging Contributions of Indigenous People in Northern Australia' (2008) 28(5) *Public Administration and Development* 374.
Wilder, M. and Crittenden J., *Bringing the Forest to Market: Structuring Avoided Deforestation Projects* (Baker & McKenzie, 2009).
Wilder, M. and Miller, M., 'Carbon Trading Markets: Legal Considerations', in T. Bonyhady and P. Christoff (eds), *Climate Law in Australia* (Federation Press, 2007).
Williams, A., 'Turning the Tide: Recognizing Climate Change Refugees in International Law' (2008) 30(4) *Law and Policy* 502.
Williams, G., 'Abbott Courts Trouble with Carbon Tax Plans', *Sydney Morning Herald*, 25 October 2011 (online).
Winiwarter, W., 'National Greenhouse Gas Inventories: Understanding Uncertainties vs. Potential for Improving Reliability', paper presented at GHG Uncertainty Workshop, Warsaw (24–25 September 2004).

Winiwarter, W. and Muik, B., 'Statistical Dependence in Input Data of National Greenhouse Gas Inventories: Effects on the Overall Inventory Uncertainty' (2010) 103 *Climatic Change* 19.
Wong, T. 'Water Sensitive Urban Design – The Journey Thus Far' (2006) 10(3) *Australian Journal of Water Resources* 21.
World Bank, 'Enhancing Institutional Capacities on REDD Issues for Sustainable Forest Management in the Congo Basin (Project No. P113167)' (online).
World Bank, 'GEF Grant to Help Brazil Protect an Additional 13.5 Million Hectares in the Amazon' (online).
World Bank, *State and Trends of the Carbon Market 2010* (World Bank, 2011).
World Bank, *The Clean Technology Fund* (9 June 2008).
World Bank, *World Development Report 2010: Development and Climate Change* (2010).
World Business Council for Sustainable Development, *Enabling Frameworks for Technology Diffusion: A Business Perspective* (WBCSD, 2010).
World Health Organization, *Protecting Health from Climate Change: Connecting Science, Policy and People* (2009).
World Intellectual Property Organization, 'Climate Change: The Technology Challenge' (2008) 4(1) *WIPO Magazine* 2.
World Meteorological Organization, '2011: World's 10th Warmest Year, Warmest Year with La Niña event, Lowest Arctic Sea Ice Volume', Press Release No. 935, 29 November 2011.
World Meteorological Organization, 'World Data Centre for Greenhouse Gases' (online).
Wu, P. et al., 'Temporary Acceleration of the Hydrological Cycle in Response to a CO_2 Rampdown' (2010) 37 *Geophysical Research Letters* L12705 1.
Yamin, F. and Depledge, J., *The International Climate Change Regime: A Guide to Rules, Institutions and Procedures* (Cambridge University Press, 2004).
Zahar, A., 'Does Self-Interest Skew State Reporting of Greenhouse Gas Emissions? A Preliminary Analysis Based on the First Verified Emissions Estimates under the Kyoto Protocol' (2010) 1(2) *Climate Law* 313.
Zahar, A., 'Verifying Greenhouse Gas Emissions of Annex I Parties: Methods We Have and Methods We Want' (2010) 1(3) *Climate Law* 409.
Zenawi, M. and Stoltenberg, J., *Report of the Secretary-General's High-Level Advisory Group on Climate Change Financing* (United Nations, 2010).
Zillman, D., 'The Role of Law in the Future of Nuclear Energy', in D. N. Zillman et al. (eds), *Beyond the Carbon Economy: Energy Law in Transition* (Oxford University Press, 2008).
Zillman, D. N. et al., 'Introduction', in D. N. Zillman et al. (eds), *Beyond the Carbon Economy: Energy Law in Transition* (Oxford University Press, 2008).

UNFCCC and Kyoto Protocol material

CDM Executive Board, *Methodology AMS-II.G, Energy Efficiency Measures in Thermal Applications of Non?-Renewable? Biomass* (Initial adoption 2008).
Clean Development Mechanism (Kyoto Protocol), *Benefits of the Clean Development Mechanism* (2011).
Clean Development Mechanism (Kyoto Protocol), *CDM Methodology Booklet* (2010).
Clean Development Mechanism (Kyoto Protocol), 'Distribution of Registered Project Activities by Scope' (online).
Clean Development Mechanism (Kyoto Protocol), *Executive Board of the CDM: Thirty?-Fifth? Meeting Report* (19 October 2007).
Compliance Committee (Kyoto Protocol), *Annual Report of the Compliance Committee to the Conference of the Parties Serving as the Meeting of the Parties to the Kyoto Protocol* (31 October 2008), FCCC/KP/CMP/2008/5.

Compliance Committee (Kyoto Protocol), *Annual Report of the Compliance Committee to the Conference of the Parties Serving as the Meeting of the Parties to the Kyoto Protocol* (2 November 2009), FCCC/KP/CMP/2009/17.

Compliance Committee (Kyoto Protocol), *Annual Report of the Compliance Committee to the Conference of the Parties Serving as the Meeting of the Parties to the Kyoto Protocol* (3 November 2011), FCCC/KP/CMP/2011/5.

Compliance Committee (Kyoto Protocol), *Enforcement Branch Request for Expert Advice: Lithuania* (11 October 2011), CC-2011-3-3/Lithuania/EB.

Compliance Committee (Kyoto Protocol), *Report on the First Meeting* (29 May 2006), CC/1/2006/4.

Expert Review Team (Kyoto Protocol), *Report of the Individual Review of the Annual Submission of Australia Submitted in 2010* (UNFCCC, 2010), FCCC/IRR/2007/AUS.

Expert Review Team (Kyoto Protocol), *Report of the Individual Review of the Annual Submission of the Czech Republic Submitted in 2009* (2010), FCCC/ARR/2009/CZE.

Expert Review Team (Kyoto Protocol), *Report of the Individual Review of the Annual Submission of Iceland Submitted in 2010* (2011), FCCC/ARR/2010/ISL.

Expert Review Team (Kyoto Protocol), *Report of the Individual Review of the Greenhouse Gas Inventories of the Czech Republic Submitted in 2007 and 2008* (2009), FCCC/ARR/2008/CZE.

Expert Review Team (Kyoto Protocol), *Report of the Review of the Initial Report of Australia* (2009), FCCC/IRR/2007/AUS.

Kyoto Protocol, *Decision 3/CMP.1, Modalities and Procedures for a Clean Development Mechanism as Defined in Article 12 of the Kyoto Protocol* (30 March 2006), FCCC/KP/CMP/2005/8/Add.1.

Kyoto Protocol, *Decision 5/CMP.1, Modalities and Procedures for Afforestation and Reforestation Project Activities under the Clean Development Mechanism in the First Commitment Period of the Kyoto Protocol* (30 March 2006), FCCC/KP/CMP/2005/8/Add.1.

Kyoto Protocol, *Decision 12/CMP.1, Guidance Relating to Registry Systems under Article 7, Paragraph 4, of the Kyoto Protocol* (30 March 2006), FCCC/KP/CMP/2005/8/Add.2.

Kyoto Protocol, *Decision 13/CMP.1, Modalities for the Accounting of Assigned Amounts under Article 7, Paragraph 4 of the Kyoto Protocol* (30 March 2006), FCCC/KP/CMP/2005/8/Add.2.

Kyoto Protocol, *Decision 15/CMP.1, Guidelines for the Preparation of the Information Required under Article 7 of the Kyoto Protocol* (30 March 2006), FCCC/KP/CMP/2005/8/Add.2

Kyoto Protocol, *Decision 16/CMP.1, Land Use, Land-Use Change and Forestry – Annex: Definitions, modalities, rules and guidelines relating to land use, land-use change and forestry activities under the Kyoto Protocol* (30 March 2006), FCCC/KP/CMP/2005/8/Add.3.

Kyoto Protocol, *Decision 19/CMP.1, Guidelines for National Systems under Article 5, Paragraph 1 of the Kyoto Protocol* (30 March 2006), FCCC/KP/CMP/2005/8/Add.3.

Kyoto Protocol, *Decision 20/CMP.1, Good Practice Guidance and Adjustments under Article 5, Paragraph 2 of the Kyoto Protocol* (2006), FCCC/KP/CMP/2005/8/Add.3.

Kyoto Protocol, *Decision 22/CMP.1, Guidelines for Review under Article 8 of the Kyoto Protocol* (30 March 2006), FCCC/KP/CMP/2005/8/Add.3.

Kyoto Protocol, *Decision 27/CMP.1, Procedures and Mechanisms Relating to Compliance under the Kyoto Protocol* (30 March 2006), FCCC/KP/CMP/2005/8/Add.3.

Kyoto Protocol, *Decision 1/CMP.7, Outcome of the Work of the Ad Hoc Working Group on Further Commitments for Annex I Parties under the Kyoto Protocol at Its Sixteenth Session* (2011), FCCC/KP/CMP/2011/10/Add.1.

Kyoto Protocol, *Decision 2/CMP.7, Land Use, Land-Use Change and Forestry* (2011).

Kyoto Protocol, *Decision 3/CMP.7, Emissions trading and the project-based mechanisms*, FCCC/KP/CMP/2011/10/Add.1.
Kyoto Protocol, *Decision 4/CMP.7, Greenhouse Gases, Sectors and Source Categories, Common Metrics to Calculate the Carbon Dioxide Equivalence of Anthropogenic Emissions by Sources and Removals by Sinks, and Other Methodological Issues* (2011).
Kyoto Protocol, *Decision 8/CMP.7, Further Guidance Relating to the Clean Development Mechanism* (2011).
Kyoto Protocol, *Decision 10/CMP.7, Modalities and Procedures for Carbon Dioxide Capture and Storage in Geological Formations as Clean Development Mechanism Project Activities* (2011), FCCC/KP/CMP/2011/10/Add.2.
Kyoto Protocol, *Decision 14/CMP.7, Appeal by Croatia against a Final Decision of the Enforcement Branch of the Compliance Committee in Relation to the Implementation of Decision 7/CP.12* (2011).
Kyoto Protocol, *Decision 17/CP.7, Modalities and Procedures for a Clean Development Mechanism, as Defined in Article 12 of the Kyoto Protocol* (2001), FCCC/CP/2001/13/Add.2.
Kyoto Protocol, *Withdrawal by Croatia of Its Appeal against a Final Decision of the Enforcement Branch of the Compliance Committee* (16 August 2011), FCCC/KP/CMP/2011/2.
Secretariat (Kyoto Protocol), *Legal Considerations Relating to a Possible Gap between the First and Subsequent Commitment Periods* (20 July 2010), FCCC/KP/AWG/2010/10.
Secretariat (UNFCCC), *Accounting Report for Annex B Parties* (2011).
Secretariat (UNFCCC), *Annual Compilation and Accounting Report for Annex B Parties under the Kyoto Protocol for 2011* (16 November 2011), FCCC/KP/CMP/2011/8.
Secretariat (UNFCCC), *Applicable Law for the Consideration of Appeals under Decision 27/CMP.1* (15 September 2011).
Secretariat (UNFCCC), *Compilation and Synthesis of Fourth National Communications: Executive Summary* (2007), FCCC/SBI/2007/INF.6.
Secretariat (UNFCCC), *Compilation of Economy-Wide Emission Reduction Targets to Be Implemented by Parties Included in Annex I to the Convention* (7 June 2011), FCCC/SB/2011/INF.1/Rev.1.
Secretariat (UNFCCC), *Compilation of Information on Nationally Appropriate Mitigation Actions to Be Implemented by Parties Not Included in Annex I to the Convention* (18 March 2011), FCCC/AWGLCA/2011/INF.1.
Secretariat (UNFCCC), *Compilation of Information on Resources for the Period 2010–2012* (2011).
Secretariat (UNFCCC), *Handbook for Review of National GHG Inventories* (undated).
Secretariat (UNFCCC), *National Greenhouse Gas Inventory Data for the Period 1990–2007* (21 October 2009), FCCC/SBI/2009/12.
Secretariat (UNFCCC), *National Greenhouse Gas Inventory Data for the Period 1990–2009* (16 November 2011), FCCC/SBI/2011/9.
Secretariat (UNFCCC), *Procedural Requirements and the Scope and Content of Applicable Law for the Consideration of Appeals under Decision 27/CMP.1 and Other Relevant Decisions of the Conference of the Parties Serving as the Meeting of the Parties to the Kyoto Protocol, as Well as the Approach Taken by Other Relevant International Bodies Relating to Denial of Due Process* (15 September 2011), FCCC/TP/2011/6.
Secretariat (UNFCCC), *Procedures, Mechanisms and Institutional Arrangements for Appeals against the Decisions of the Executive Board of the Clean Development Mechanism* (17 May 2011), FCCC/TP/2011/3.
Secretariat (UNFCCC), *Quantified Economy-Wide Emission Reduction Targets by Developed Country Parties to the Convention: Assumptions, Conditions, Commonalities and*

Differences in Approaches and Comparison of the Level of Emission Reduction Efforts (8 May 2012), FCCC/TP/2012/2.

Secretariat (UNFCCC), *Report of the CDM Executive Board No. 35, Annex 17: A/R Methodological Tool, 'Tool for the Demonstration and Assessment of Additionality in Afforestation/Reforestation CDM Project Activities'* (19 October 2007), CDM-EB-35.

Secretariat (UNFCCC), *Sixth Compilation and Synthesis of Initial National Communications from Parties Not Included in Annex I to the Convention; Addendum: Inventories of Anthropogenic Emissions by Sources and Removals by Sinks of Greenhouse Gases* (25 October 2005), FCCC/SBI/2005/18/Add.2.

Secretariat (UNFCCC), *Submissions on Information from Developed Country Parties on the Resources Provided to Fulfil the Commitment Referred to in Decision 1/CP.16, Paragraph 95* (15 August 2011), FCCC/CP/2011/INF.1.

Secretariat (UNFCCC), *Synthesis and Assessment Report on the Greenhouse Gas Inventories Submitted in 2010* (15 July 2010), FCCC/WEB/SAI/2010.

Subsidiary Body for Implementation (UNFCCC), *Views on Procedures, Mechanisms and Institutional Arrangements for Appeals against the Decisions of the Executive Board of the Clean Development Mechanism* (21 April 2011), FCCC/SBI/2011/MISC.2.

Subsidiary Body for Scientific and Techonological Advice (UNFCCC), *Draft Modalities and Procedures for Carbon Dioxide Capture and Storage in Geological Formations as Clean Development Mechanism Project Activities* (8 November 2011), FCCC/SBSTA/2011/4.

Subsidiary Body for Scientific and Technical Advice (UNFCCC), *Expert Meeting on Forest Reference Emission Levels* (27 November 2011).

Subsidiary Body for Scientific and Technical Advice (UNFCCC), *Guidelines for the Preparation of National Communications by Parties Included in Annex I to the Convention, Part I: UNFCCC Reporting Guidelines on Annual Inventories (Following Incorporation of the Provisions of Decision 13/CP.9)* (2004), FCCC/SBSTA/2004/8.

Subsidiary Body for Scientific and Technical Advice (UNFCCC), *Report of the Expert Group on Technology Transfer* (24 November 2010), FCCC/SB/2010/INF.4.

Subsidiary Body for Scientific and Technical Advice (UNFCCC), *Report on the Expert Meeting on Forest Reference Emission Levels and Forest Reference Levels for Implementation of REDD-Plus Activities* (27 November 2011), FCCC/SBSTA/2011/INF.18.

Subsidiary Body for Scientific and Technical Advice (UNFCCC), *Updated UNFCCC Reporting Guidelines on Annual Inventories Following Incorporation of the Provisions of Decision 14/CP.11* (2006), FCCC/SBSTA/2006/9.

Subsidiary Body for Scientific and Technological Advice (UNFCCC), *Views on Carbon Dioxide Capture and Storage in Geological Formations as Clean Development Mechanism Project Activities* (26 July 2011), FCCC/SBSTA/2011/MISC.10.

Transitional Committee of the Green Climate Fund (UNFCCC), *Co-Chairs' Summary Report on the Initial Meeting of the Transitional Committee for the Design of the Green Climate Fund* (12 May 2011), TC-1/6.

UNFCCC, Ad Hoc Working Group on Long-term Cooperative Action under the Convention, *Update of the amalgamation of draft texts in preparation of a comprehensive and balanced outcome to be presented to the Conference of the Parties for adoption at its seventeenth session* (7 December 2011), FCCC/AWGLCA/2011/CRP.38.

UNFCCC, *Conclusions and Recommendations: Sixth Meeting of Inventory Lead Reviewers* (16–17 March 2009) (online).

UNFCCC, Decision 2/CP.1, *Review of First Communications from the Parties Included in Annex I to the Convention* (1995), FCCC/CP/1995/7/Add.1.

UNFCCC, Decision 4/CP.1, *Methodological Issues* (1995), FCCC/CP/1995/7/Add.1.

UNFCCC, Decision 3/CP.5, *Guidelines for the Preparation of National Communications by Parties Included in Annex I to the Convention, Part I: UNFCCC Reporting Guidelines on Annual Inventories* (1999), FCCC/CP/1999/6/Add.1.

UNFCCC, Decision 4/CP.5, *Guidelines for the Preparation of National Communications by Parties Included in Annex I to the Convention, Part II: UNFCCC Reporting Guidelines on National Communications* (1999), FCCC/CP/1999/6/Add.1.
UNFCCC, Decision 6/CP.5, *Guidelines for the Technical Review of Greenhouse Gas Inventories from Parties Included in Annex I to the Convention* (1999), FCCC/CP/1999/6/Add.1.
UNFCCC, Decision 2/CP.7, *Capacity Building in Developing Countries (Non-Annex I Parties)* (2001), FCCC/CP/2001/13/Add.1.
UNFCCC, Decision 10/CP.7, *Report of the Conference of the Parties on Its Seventh Session, Held at Marrakesh from 29 October to 10 November 2002 – Addendum – Part 2: Action Taken by the Conference of the Parties* (21 January 2002), FCCC/CP/2001/13/Add.1.
UNFCCC, Decision 11/CP.7, *Land Use, Land-Use Change, and Forestry* (2001), FCCC/CP/2001/13/Add.1.
UNFCCC, Decision 17/CP.8, *Guidelines for the Preparation of National Communications from Parties Not Included in Annex I to the Convention* (2003), FCCC/CP/2002/7/Add.2.
UNFCCC, Decision 18/CP.8, *Guidelines for the Preparation of National Communications by Parties Included in Annex I to the Convention, Part I: UNFCCC Reporting Guidelines on Annual Inventories* (2002), FCCC/CP/2002/7/Add.2.
UNFCCC, Decision 19/CP.8, *UNFCCC Guidelines for the Technical Review of Greenhouse Gas Inventories from Parties Included in Annex I to the Convention* (2002), FCCC/CP/2002/7/Add.2.
UNFCCC, Decision 1/CP.13, *Bali Action Plan* (2007), FCCC/CP/2007/6/Add.1.
UNFCCC, Decision 2/CP.13, *Reducing Emissions from Deforestation in Developing Countries: Approaches to Stimulate Action* (2007), FCCC/CP/2007/6/Add.1.
UNFCCC, Decision 2/CP.15, *Copenhagen Accord* (2009), FCCC/CP/2009/11/Add.1.
UNFCCC, Decision 4/CP.15, *Methodological Guidance for Activities Relating to Reducing Emissions from Deforestation and Forest Degradation and the Role of Conservation, Sustainable Management of Forests and Enhancement of Forest Carbon Stocks in Developing Countries* (2009), FCCC/CP/2009/11/Add.1.
UNFCCC, Decision 1/CP.16, *The Cancún Agreements: Outcome of the Work of the Ad Hoc Working Group on Long-Term Cooperative Action under the Convention* (2010), FCCC/CP/2010/7/Add.1.
UNFCCC, Decision 2/CP.16, *Fourth Review of the Financial Mechanism* (2010), FCCC/CP/2010/7/Add.2.
UNFCCC, Decision 1/CP.17, *Establishment of an Ad Hoc Working Group on the Durban Platform for Enhanced Action* (2011).
UNFCCC, Decision 2/CP.17, *Outcome of the Work of the Ad Hoc Working Group on Long-Term Cooperative Action under the Convention* (2011), FCCC/CP/2011/9/Add.1.
UNFCCC, Decision 3/CP.17, *Launching the Green Climate Fund* (2011).
UNFCCC, Decision 8/CP.17, *Forum and work programme on the impact of the implementation of response measures* (11 December 2011), FCCC/CP/2011/L.10.
UNFCC, Decision 10/CP.17, *Amendment to Annex I to the Convention* (2011).
UNFCCC, Decision 12/CP.17, *Guidance on Systems for Providing Information on How Safeguards Are Addressed and Respected and Modalities Relating to Forest Reference Emission Levels and Forest Reference Levels as Referred to in Decision 1/CP.16* (2011).
UNFCCC, 'Existing Requirements for Reporting and Review for Annex I Parties under the Convention and the Kyoto Protocol' (online).
UNFCCC, 'Guidelines under Articles 5, 7 and 8: Methodological Issues, Reporting and Review under the Kyoto Protocol' (online).
UNFCCC, 'Initial Reports under Article 7, Paragraph 4, of the Kyoto Protocol and Initial Review Reports' (online).
UNFCCC, *Land Use, Land-Use Change and Forestry – Fact Sheet* (online).
UNFCCC, 'Share of Proceeds from the Clean Development Mechanism Project Activities for the Adaptation Fund' (online).

UNFCCC, 'The CDM and Technology Transfer' (online).
UNFCCC, *The Contribution of the Clean Development Mechanism under the Kyoto Protocol to Technology Transfer* (2010).
UN-REDD Programme, *Report of the Sixth Policy Board Meeting* (21–22 March 2011).
UN Secretary-General, *Kyoto Protocol to the United Nations Framework Convention on Climate Change; Canada: Withdrawal* (United Nations, 16 December 2001), C.N.796.2011.TREATIES-1 (Depositary Notification).

Index

Ad Hoc Working Group on the Durban Platform for Enhanced Action, 90
adaptation to climate change
  Australia and. *See* adaptation to climate change, Australia
  climate change displacement and. *See* displacement
  definition, 367, 376
  international law and, 378–9
  legal and policy development and, 376–8
  nature of, 374–84
  Pacific regional developments and, 379–80
  role of law and, 376
adaptation to climate change, Australia, 380
  bushfire risk and, 396–401
  effectiveness of legal framework, 401
  Gippsland Coastal Board case and, 387–9
  local government roles and responsibilities and, 380–4
  National Climate Change Adaptation Framework, 380
  Northcape litigation and, 385–6
  sea-level rise and, 384–90
  Walker litigation and, 386–7
  water scarcity and flood risk and. *See* water resource management, Australia
anthropogenic greenhouse gas emissions. *See* greenhouse gas emissions
Asia-Pacific Partnership on Clean Development and Climate, 27, 142
Australian climate law, 7
  context of, 16–18
  Copenhagen Accord and, 143
  development of, 139
  Durban Climate Change Conference and, 144
  emissions reporting by liable entities, 187–9
  factors in genesis of, 128–38
  international context of, 139–45
  judicial rulings in, 132–3, 135–8
  Kyoto 'deal' and, 140–1
  lack of support for, 6–7
  liable entity, definition of, 189
  pace of change in, 30
  states and territories, 151–5
Australian climate policy, 9
  Australian Greenhouse Office, 147, 156
  Carbon Farming Initiative. *See* Carbon Farming Initiative
  Carbon Pollution Reduction Scheme, 143, 158, 186, 187, 188, 189–90, 195, 196, 198
  Clean Energy Agreement, 162, 303, 313, 314, 336
  Clean Energy Finance Corporation, 162
  Clean Energy Regulator, 189, 194, 313, 354, 358, 360
  Climate Change Authority, 192–3, 194, 336
  Deeds of Agreement, 148
  development of, 139
  Draft Energy White Paper 2011, 298, 300–1, 316, 329
  early national, 145–7
  energy efficiency and. *See* energy efficiency, Australia
  Garnaut review and, 130–1, 143, 156, 158, 171–2, 189, 190, 195, 196, 336, 346
  Generator Efficiency Standards initiative, 148
  Greenhouse Challenge Plus Program, 147–8
  Greenhouse Challenge Program, 147
  Greenhouse Gas Abatement Program, 148
  Intergovernmental Agreement on the Environment, 145–6
  International Forest Carbon Initiative, 251
  Jobs and Competitiveness Program, 196
  Low Carbon Growth Plan, 300
  Low Emissions Technology and Abatement Fund, 148
  Low Emissions Technology Demonstration Fund, 148
  Multi-Party Climate Change Committee, 160–1, 190, 191, 196
  National Climate Change Adaptation Framework, 380
  National Emissions Trading Taskforce, 156
  National Greenhouse Strategy, 147

449

450 INDEX

Australian climate policy (cont.)
  National Low Emissions Coal Initiative, 323
  National Strategy for Ecologically Sustainable Development, 145
  National Water Initiative, 371
  'no regrets', 147–8
  outside Kyoto framework, 141–5
  renewable energy and. *See* renewable energy, Australia
  Strategic Framework for Alternative Transport Fuels, 305
  sustainability wedges and, 297
  Task Group on Emissions Trading, 157
  Task Group on Energy Efficiency, 303
  Zero Carbon Australia 2020 Stationary Energy Plan 2020, 298–9
aviation and shipping emissions, 88, 179

Bali Action Plan, 242, 243, 270
  finance and technology transfer and, 269–70
biosequestration, 85, 128, 153, 174, 250, 287, 296, 338, 340, 341
  Australia. *See* biosequestration, Australia
  carbon ownership concept and, 348
  carbon sequestration 'rights' and, 348, 349
  'co-benefits', 340, 344, 370
  definition, 333
  risks of, 343–4
biosequestration, Australia, 340
  federalism contraints and, 362
  legal issues in, 347–50
  regulatory coordination and integration and, 340
  scope for, 343–4
  state-based regulation of, 361–6

Cancun Climate Change Conference, 274
  Cancun Adaptation Framework, 379
  Climate Technology Centre and Network, 278–9
  finance and technology transfer and, 271–4
  Green Climate Fund, 274–8, 288, 290, 379, 411
  institutions, roles and responsibilities of, 274–80
  Technology Executive Committee, 278
  Technology Mechanism, 274, 280, 288, 290, 291, 411
carbon capture and storage, 201, 320–1
  Australia. *See* carbon capture and storage, Australia
  Canada, 322–3
  EU, 321–2
  Norway, 15
  USA, 322
carbon capture and storage, Australia, 154
  carbon pricing mechanism and, 331–2
  National Carbon Capture and Storage Council, 323
  Offshore Petroleum and Greenhouse Gas Storage Act 2006 and, 325–6
Carbon Farming Initiative, 191, 195, 340, 342, 346, 347, 348, 350–1
  Aboriginal Carbon Fund, 358
  additionality and, 356–7, 359
  applicable carbon sequestration right and, 363
  Australian Carbon Credit Units, 352–3, 359, 360, 363, 368
  biodiversity planting incentives and, 371–2
  carbon maintenance obligation, 360
  Carbon Offsets Integrity Committee, 356
  catchment management and, 370–1
  certificate of entitlement under, 356
  Clean Energy Regulator and, 354, 358, 360
  compliance under, 359–61
  credits, creation and surrender of, 352–4
  determination of eligible offsets projects under, 354–6
  Domestic Offsets Integrity Committee, 354
  integrity standards, 354–9
  land use planning and registration and, 370–1
  measurement and verification and, 354–6
  native title interests and, 357
  Natural Resource Management plans and, 358, 370
  'negative list' and, 358–9
  non-Kyoto Carbon Fund, 353
  origins of, 351–2
  ownership and transfer of credits and, 359–61
  permanence and enforceability and, 357
  'risk of reversal buffer', 360–1
  state-based carbon rights legislation and, 361–6
  state biosequestration schemes and, 368–72
carbon leakage, 181, 182, 183, 187, 352
carbon offsets, 341
  definition, 333–40
  integrity standards for, 344–7
carbon offsets, Australia, 354
  federalism constraints and, 362
  non-Kyoto compliant, 354
  state-based regulation of, 361–6

carbon offsets schemes, 292
　additionality requirement, 344, 345–6
　Clean Development Mechanism and, 292
　measurement and verification
　　requirement, 345
　monitoring and verification
　　requirements, 344
　permanence requirement, 344, 346–7
carbon offsets schemes, Australia
　Kyoto compliant offsets and, 106, 353
　non-Kyoto compliant offsets and, 353
　see also Carbon Farming Initiative
carbon pricing mechanism, Australia, 138,
　　160–3, 187, 188, 189, 190–7, 294, 312,
　　335, 337, 350
　assessment of, 196–7
　assistance measures, 196
　carbon pollution cap, setting of, 192–3
　Clean Energy Regulator and, 354
　coverage of, 191–2
　energy efficiency schemes and, 304
　offsets for compliance flexibility, 194–5
　operation of, 193–4
carbon sequestration. *See* biosequestration
carbon storage and capture, 324
　Clean Development Mechanism and, 330–1
　risks, 324
carbon storage and capture, Australia, 323–4
　legislative and regulatory framework of,
　　324–30
carbon taxes, 7, 80, 163, 166, 167, 169,
　　170–4, 301
　Australia, 131, 160, 162
　see also emissions trading schemes
Clean Development Mechanism, 4, 20–1, 89,
　　93, 180, 195, 271, 345
　approval process, 215
　Australia and, 228
　carbon capture and storage and, 330–1
　Certified Emission Reduction allowance,
　　206, 207, 208, 214, 220
　comparison to UN-REDD Programme,
　　231–2, 246
　concerns about environmental integrity
　　and, 220–1
　Designated National Authority, 207
　Executive Board, 200, 208, 210, 211, 217,
　　221, 224–7, 248, 290
　finance and technology transfer and, 259
　forestry activities and, 230
　future of, 227–8
　intellectual property issues and, 289
　Kyoto Protocol Art. 12 and, 193–200
　motivational dynamic of, 208–9
　private 'operational entities' and, 200
　project distribution and equity of access
　　and, 224–5
　registration process, 207
　sustainable development and, 222–4, 258
　values of, financial interests and, 207–9
climate change, 2
　adaptation. *See* adaptation to climate
　　change
　Africa, environmental values and, 35–7
　aid and technology transfer and, 61–2
　as global scale problem, 2, 58–9, 168, 263
　as 'global–global' problem, 6–14, 22
　as market failure, 171, 336
　Australia. *See* climate change, Australia
　constraints on first movers, 14–16, 187
　dangerous, 66–7, 165
　displacement and. *See* displacement
　EU response to, 15–16
　mitigation. *See* climate change mitigation
　politics of, 4–5
　popular apathy to, misinformation and, 38–9
　public opinion polls, United States, 34, 132
　science of, 44–51, 129–30
　sensitivity of biological systems and, 48–9
　uncertainties of, UNFCCC and, 57–8
climate change, Australia
　economic costs of inaction on, 130–1
　public opinion on, 131–2
　see also adaptation to climate change,
　　Australia
climate change mitigation, 169
　attitude towards, 411
　carbon pricing and, 170–4
　direct regulation and, 169–70
　finance and, 256–7
　land use activities and, 341
　market-based mechanisms and, 167–9
　regulatory models for, 165–77
climate law
　absence of foundational principle in, 22
　Australia. *See* Australian climate law
　broadening of concept of, 3
　future generations and, 63, 67
　human values and competing interests and,
　　33–5
　integration and regulatory coordination
　　of, 7
　interdisciplinarity and, 30–3
　Massachusetts case and, 133–5
　methodologies for discovering, 18–22
　outlook for, 90–1
　pace of change in, 7
　present generations and, 67
　principles of environmental law and, 22–3
　role of science and economics in, 63–4

452 INDEX

climate law (cont.)
  role of UNFCCC in, 19
  sovereign right of states and, 59–60, 61
  'top-down' and 'bottom-up' nature of, 24–8, 121–8
  weak and non-directive nature of, 3–4, 5
climate system tipping points, 28, 31, 38, 49
Compliance Committee, 9, 26, 106–8, 109–11, 112, 116, 126
  Enforcement Branch, 110–13, 116, 118
  Facilitative Branch, 109, 111, 113, 116, 118
  historical workload of, 113–16

deforestation, 85, 223–31
  as 'global–global' problem, 237
  Brazilian Amazon, 239–42
  causes of, 238–42
  Democratic Republic of Congo, 239
  emission reduction scheme. See UN-REDD Programme
  extent of, 233–7
  rescaling of problem, 237
displacement, 401–6
  as security issue, 405–6
  gaps in legal framework and, 406
  human rights instruments and, 403–5
  international law and, 402–3

Efficient Fuel Wood Stoves for Nigeria project, 203, 205–8, 210, 246, 258, 290
  project development and test for additionality, 209–17
  project validation and registration, 217–18
  project verification and issuance of tradable allowances, 218–20
emission caps, 9, 21, 83–6, 95, 98, 103
  Australia, 190, 193
emission reduction targets, 16, 26–7, 44
  Australia, 6, 23, 26, 143, 148, 151, 228
  non-compliance with, 110, 111, 116
emission scenarios, 71–2, 202
emission-trading privileges, 95
emissions, greenhouse gas. See greenhouse gas emissions
emissions trading schemes, 7, 139, 156, 163, 166, 167, 168, 170–4, 197
  Australia, 17, 30, 71, 130, 131, 155–60, 190, 195, 198, 323, 335, 336
  California, 183–5
  cap-and-trade, 174–7, 181, 192, 197, 275, 301, 304, 309
  carbon offsets and, 341, 348
  EU, 15, 81, 86, 88, 140, 177–81, 184, 194, 337

  New South Wales, 30, 152, 361
  New Zealand, 185–6, 351
  USA, 176, 181–3
  voluntary, 186–7
  see also carbon taxes
energy efficiency
  Australia. See energy efficiency, Australia
  Carbon Emissions Reduction Target scheme (UK), 303
  definition, 301
  Efficiency Obligation scheme (France), 303
  Energy Performance Directive (EU), 308
  green leases, 309
  legal regulation of, 301–2
  nuclear power and. See nuclear power
  'smart grid' projects, 306
  'split incentive' problem and, 302
  White Certificate Scheme (Italy), 303
energy efficiency, Australia, 81
  Building Code of Australia, 307
  Building Energy Efficiency Certificate, 308
  building standards and, 307–9
  Clean Energy Agreement 2011, 303, 314
  Clean Energy Finance Corporation, 312, 315
  Clean Energy Package, 310
  Clean Technology Program, 310
  direct funding and support for, 314–15
  federal policy and regulatory context, 302–12
  Generator Efficiency Standards initiative, 148
  household appliance standards and, 309–10
  households and businesses, 303
  Low Carbon Australia, 310
  National Carbon Capture and Storage Council, 323
  national energy–saving initiative, 303–4
  National Framework for Energy Efficiency, 303
  National Low Emissions Coal Initiative, 323
  Nationwide House Energy Rating Scheme, 308
  New South Wales Energy Savings Scheme, 310–11
  peak demand and, 306
  renewable energy and. See renewable energy, Australia
  Solar Credits scheme, 313
  Solar Flagships Program, 314
  state-based efficiency schemes, 310–11
  statistics, 302
  Strategic Framework for Alternative Transport Fuels, 305

Task Group on Energy Efficiency, 303
transport sector and, 304–6
environmentally sound technologies, 261
ethical consumers, 242
Expert Review Teams, 75, 93, 95, 108–9, 111, 113, 116, 117, 124, 126
  objectivity of, 119
  role of, 103–6
  sovereign states and, 104–5

finance and technology transfer, 292
  Australia's contributions to, 282–4
  intellectual property and, 288
  measurement, reporting and verification and, 273
  modes of, 286–7
forest replantation, 85, 236–7
fossil fuels, dependence on, 39–44

geosequestration. *See* carbon capture and storage
geothermal energy, 42, 82, 150, 186, 300, 312
Global Financial Crisis
  effect on public opinion, 6–7, 132
  impact on emissions, 43, 79
global warming
  2°C limit, 7, 43, 44, 129, 145
  as market failure, 168
  average surface temperature and, 48
  levels, 374
  predictions of, 404
  social cost theory and, 168–9
globally sustainable development, 4, 23–4, 68
  see also sustainable development
green finance and technology, 256–9
greenhouse gas emissions, 45–6
  biosequestration and. *See* biosequestration
  comparability of effort issue and, 81–2
  energy efficiency and. *See* energy efficiency
  fossil fuel consumption and, 39–40
  Global Environment Facility projects and, 267–8
  global monitoring network, 122–4
  historical and current, 56–7
  intellectual property law and. *See* intellectual property law
  international reporting of, 120–4
  land use sector and, 77, 85, 99, 342
  legal and scientific compliance and, 96–7
  limitation of, 76–7
  national inventories of, 74–6
  offsets, conditions for, 193–203
  per capita, 55–6
  regulatory definition of, 165

renewable energy and. *See* renewable energy
stabilisation of, 65–6
stationary energy emissions, 298
transparent reporting of, 125–6

High-Level Advisory Group on Climate Change, 274–5
human rights, 13, 35, 63, 64, 403–5
hydropower, 42

intellectual property law, 284–91

Kyoto Protocol
  'Australia clause', 140–1
  Australian ratification of, 17, 132, 142, 157
  Canadian withdrawal from, 8, 9, 30, 83, 113
  Clean Development Mechanism. *See* Clean Development Mechanism
  commitment periods, 4, 6, 9, 21, 46, 71, 78, 85, 86–7, 90, 103, 121, 144, 222, 227
  Compliance Committee. *See* Compliance Committee
  compliance system, 106, 116–18
  emission allowances and market mechanisms and, 88–9
  emission caps. *See* emissions caps
  Expert Review Teams. *See* Expert Review Teams
  globally sustainable development and, 23–4
  land sector emissions abatement, Australia, and, 342–3
  legal principles and rules of, 4, 83–9
  measurement, reporting and verification and. *See* measurement, reporting and verification, Kyoto Protocol
  offsets under, 193–203
  opposition to, 84
  reporting, review and compliance obligations under, 87–8, 118–20
  review procedures, 102–3

land sector emissions abatement, Australia
  concepts and technical requirements of, 341–2
  Kyoto Protocol and, 343
  Land Carbon and Biodiversity Advisory Board, 354
leakage, 215, 216, 242, 244, 246
low-carbon economy, Australia
  integration of regulatory measures and innovation for, 335–8

low-carbon economy, Australia (cont.)
   technological options and feasibility, 299–300
   technological options for, 297–301
   transition to, 295
   see also energy efficiency, Australia, renewable energy, Australia, carbon capture and storage, Australia, nuclear power, Australia

measurement, reporting and verification, Kyoto Protocol
   Clean Development Mechanism and, 200
   direct measurement versus state reporting and, 96–7
   Marrakech Accords and, 95
   state emission reports, reliability of, 97–100

Nigeria Stoves. See Efficient Fuel Wood Stoves for Nigeria project
Niue Declaration on Climate Change, 405
North-South economic divide, 4, 62–3
North-South finance and technology transfer, 260, 274, 275
nuclear power, 332–3
nuclear power, Australia, 333–5
   Australian Radiation Protection and Nuclear Safety Agency, 335
   legislative and regulatory framework for, 334–5
   Switkowski Report, 334

ozone-depleting substances, 13–14

power generation, Australia
   'risk of lock-in' and 'ease of implementation' parameters, 299–300
   stationary energy sector and, 298

Regional Greenhouse Gas Initiative, USA, 181, 182–3
renewable energy, Australia
   Australian Renewable Energy Agency, 314
   grid access and transmission planning and, 317–18
   Large-scale Renewable Energy Target scheme, 313, 319
   'left hand/right hand' problem of, 319
   Mandatory Renewable Energy Target scheme, 6, 147, 150–1, 312–14
   National Electricity Law, 317
   National Energy Market, 318, 319
   planning law barriers and, 317–19
   Power Purchase Scheme, 318
   promotion of, 312

Queensland Gas Scheme, 315
Renewable Energy Target scheme, 303, 304, 311, 315, 324, 336, 337
Small-scale Renewable Energy Scheme, 313, 316
Solar Flagships program, 318
state regulation and, 315–16
Victorian Renewable Energy scheme, 315
wind power. See wind power

solar energy, 42, 150, 279, 288, 298, 299, 300, 312
stabilisation wedges, 296–7
storylines. See emission scenarios
sustainable consumption governance, 241
sustainable development, 4, 18, 21, 22, 23, 38, 136, 145, 249, 253, 258
   Agenda 21 Programme of Action for Sustainable Development, 145
   Clean Development Mechanism and, 222–4, 258
   principles of, 146
   promotion of, 70
   see also globally sustainable development

transboundary harm principle, 60

Umbrella Group, 176
United Nations Framework Convention on Climate Change
   approved offsets, 206
   background to, 46–54
   commitments and, 74–82
   equity and, 63, 67, 68–9
   extension by Protocols and, 82–3
   finance and technology transfer and, 259–63
   Global Environment Facility, 4, 81, 93, 246, 256, 261, 263–8, 276
   globally sustainable development and, 23, 68, 70
   legal principles and rules of, 4, 54–64
   National Adaptation Programmes of Action, 269
   national communications and, 79–81, 82, 93–4
   national GHG inventories and, 93, 94
   Nationally Appropriate Mitigation Action, 269, 271–3
   objective and principles of, 64–73
   open international economic system and, 68, 70–1
   precautionary principle and, 67–8, 69–70
   reporting, review and compliance obligations under, 87–8, 93–6

review procedures, 102, 103
Subsidiary Body for Scientific and
    Technological Advice, 243, 244, 262
UN-REDD Programme and, 231
see also UN-REDD Programme
UN-REDD Programme, 144, 184, 261, 270
Australian involvement with, 250–1
Cancun decision and, 243–4
capacity building and, 240
comparison to Clean Development
    Mechanism, 231–2, 246
Durban Climate Change Conference and,
    244–5
effectiveness of, 253–4
holistic approach to coverage and
    governance and, 246
incomplete and unrealiable information
    and, 235
international climate regime and, 223–32
international regulation of, steps towards,
    242–5
land tenure and, 234
monitoring, reporting and verification of,
    248–50

Policy Board, 247
preparatory stage funding, 246–8
remote sensing technology and, 249–50
rights of indigenous people and, 244
role of indigenous communities in, 249–50
social context of, 238–42
Solomon Islands, 247

water resource management, Australia,
    390–6
institution of flood regulations, 395–6
National Water Initiative, 391
nature of flood risk and, 392
responsibility for flood risk adaptation,
    392–5
wind power, 20, 42, 150, 186, 279, 288, 289,
    298, 299, 312
Australia, 318–19
New South Wales, 319
South Australia, 319
Victoria, 319, 323
World Bank, 264, 276
relationship with Global Environment
    Facility, 265

For EU product safety concerns, contact us at Calle de José Abascal, 56–1°,
28003 Madrid, Spain or eugpsr@cambridge.org.

www.ingramcontent.com/pod-product-compliance
Ingram Content Group UK Ltd.
Pitfield, Milton Keynes, MK11 3LW, UK
UKHW010856060825
461487UK00012B/1156